Bringing Art into the

Australia Canada Mexico Singapore Spain United Kingdom United States

Elementary Classroom

Joan Bouza Koster
Broome Community College

Education Editor: Dianne Lindsay
Assistant Editor: Tangelique Williams
Editorial Assistant: Keynia Johnson
Marketing Manager: Becky Tollerson
Project Editor: Trudy Brown
Print Buyer: Mary Noel
Permissions Editor: Bob Kauser

Production Service: Penmarin Books
Text Designer: Harry Voigt
Copy Editor: Jean Schiffman
Cover Designer: Stephen Rapley
Cover Printer: Phoenix Color
Compositor: Publishers' Design and Production Services, Inc.
Printer: Phoenix Color

Printed in the United States of America

1 2 3 4 5 6 7 04 03 02 01 00

For permission to use material from this text, contact us by
Web: http://www.thomsonrights.com
Fax: 1-800-730-2215
Phone: 1-800-730-2214

Library of Congress
Cataloging-in-Publication Data
Koster, Joan Bouza.
Bringing art into the elementary classroom / Joan B. Koster.
p. cm.
Includes bibliographical references and index.
ISBN 0-7668-0541-7
1. Art—Study and teaching (Elementary)—United States—Handbooks, manuals, etc. 2.
Art—Study and teaching (Elementary)—Methodology—United States. I. Title.

N362.K688 2000
372.5'044—dc21

00-031489

This book is printed on acid free, recycled paper.

For more information, contact
Wadsworth/Thomson Learning
10 Davis Drive
Belmont, CA 94002-3098
USA
http://www.wadsworth.com

International Headquarters
Thomson Learning
International Division
290 Harbor Drive, 2nd Floor
Stamford, CT 06902-7477
USA

UK/Europe/Middle East/South Africa
Thomson Learning
Berkshire House
168–173 High Holborn
London WC1V 7AA
United Kingdom

Asia
Thomson Learning
60 Albert Street, #15-01
Albert Complex
Singapore 189969

Canada
Nelson Thomson Learning
1120 Birchmount Road
Toronto, Ontario M1K 5G4
Canada

Part-Opening Illustration Credits

Part One, p. 1: "*At the Museum*." Crayon—Heather, grade 2.
Part Two, p. 219: "*My Teacher*." Marker and crayon—Alison, grade 5.
Part Three, p. 419: Stuart Davis, *International Surface No. 1*, 1960. National Museum of American Art, Smithsonian Institution. Gift of S. C. Johnson & Son, Inc.

Contents

Preface

THE PURPOSE OF THIS BOOK

This book is about learning with, through, and about the visual arts. Its purpose is to enable educators to use the powerful graphic communication system of art as a way to reach, teach, and empower our children. There have been many textbooks written about how to teach the visual arts to children. Each of them represents an attempt to put into words the multifaceted process of introducing children to the world of art. The viewpoint and recommendations of each author have grown out of the educational philosophy and research current in the field at that particular time. This text also grows out of the educational climate of its time. It represents an effort to bring the discipline-based approaches of the art educator to the elementary classroom teacher and to introduce the art educator to the literature-based approaches of the contemporary classroom. It attempts to join together these two fields, which have long been artificially separated into "academics" and "specials."

TO WHOM IS THIS BOOK ADDRESSED?

How art is currently taught varies widely. The classroom teacher may be responsible for squeezing an art project here and there into an already full curriculum. There may be a beleaguered art "specialist" delivering art to hundreds of children weekly, perhaps from a traveling cart or—with luck—in an art room. No matter where you are on the spectrum of art program delivery, this text will show you in practical ways how to work together with your fellow teachers to create an environment in which children become artists, as they also become readers and writers.

This book addresses first those who will soon be entering the field of teaching and strives to give them the confidence they need to teach art in a meaningful way. Secondly, it addresses current art specialists and classroom teachers who are ready to work together to change how they teach art to their students.

The companion text, *Growing Artists: Teaching Art to Young Children,* focused on the delivery of art in the more open settings of child care, preschool, kindergarten, and early primary. This text is directed toward those who work within the more constrained curricula of the elementary school in first through sixth grade. It is designed to help classroom teachers and art specialists respond positively to what children do with art materials. Hopefully it will empower these teachers to teach each child the art skills needed to express ideas using the language of art, and it will help dedicated educators no matter what their discipline to become advocates for the integration of art and learning.

THE APPROACH OF THIS BOOK

The viewpoint and recommendations of this book are based on the mind-expanding work of Howard Gardner (1990b, 1991, 1993), the research of Wilson and Wilson (1977), and the current work of many teacher researchers on the relationship between art and literacy (Hubbard, 1989; Olson, 1992; Ernst, 1994; Steward, 1995). It is the thesis of this book that art as we know it is a culturally based symbolic language. New research on how children acquire language skills challenges us to change how we teach the language of art. It is time for educators from a wide range of backgrounds to come together to create a new approach to art education in our schools.

This book emphasizes the integration of all the arts into our children's education with its main focus being the teaching of the visual arts. There are many excellent books that address general arts education. Although many of the approaches to teaching visual art are similar to those in music and dance, and the performing arts form a basic component of many of the art lessons presented in this book, it is difficult to provide sufficient technical information on how to teach the many facets of the visual arts while at the same time providing detailed directions for the effective teaching of drama, music, and dance.

The visual arts cover the broad range of ways people manipulate materials and environment to create aesthetic meaning. Teaching children how to draw, paint, work with clay, and more, as well as how to respond to the artwork of others, requires teachers who feel competent in artistic production and thinking. This book is designed to give teachers that confidence.

ABOUT THE AUTHOR

In writing this book, I bring together my own thirty years of experience, first as an art teacher in a wide variety of educational settings, and then as an elementary classroom teacher. It is a response to the difficulties and exhilaration that I have experienced as I have tried to share the wonder of art creation with my college students. It also draws on the diverse experiences of my colleagues and teammates and, most importantly, the inspiring work and comments of the thousands of children I have taught.

Like most dedicated teachers, I have searched for the best way to meet the diverse needs of my students. I have read widely, incorporating new ideas, techniques, and current research into my own teaching—sometimes successfully, sometimes not. Faced with the challenge of preparing preservice teachers to teach art to children, I find it is not enough to express what I believe teachers should do or tell them what I have experienced. Each of us must first think deeply about the nature of the artistic experience and why it is an important part of our lives and our children's lives. This book presents the current research on learning and children's artistic development in the context of what it looks like in the classroom. It also addresses the immediate need of preservice teachers for clear, practical advice on how to set up effective art programs. It suggests ways to converse meaningfully with children about their art. Most importantly, it provides basic organizational methods and art techniques that will allow children to create art in a safe and orderly environment.

HOW THE TEXT IS ORGANIZED

The Chapter

Each of the three parts of this book addresses an important component in art education. In Part One: Introduction to the Language of Art, the chapters set the stage for teaching elementary art. The first unit looks at the historical and theoretical influences on elementary art education, presents art as a symbolic language that must be taught in schools, and provides a philosophical framework for teaching art. Chapter 2 looks at how children learn and presents ways to integrate art into the elementary curriculum through art lesson design. Chapter 3 focuses on the importance of creativity and provides ways for teachers to nurture the motivation to create in their classrooms. Chapter 4 addresses the influences that affect children's artistic development and the role of drawing in learning. Chapter 5 presents ways to introduce children to looking meaningfully at the artwork of others.

In Part Two: Teaching Art, the chapters address in detail the nuts and bolts of running an art class, talking to students about their art, responding to diversity, and assessing student work. Chapter 6 looks at ways teachers and students communicate with each other and provides methods for guiding student discussions about their artwork. Chapter 7 introduces incorporating cooperative learning strategies and ways to use art to celebrate diversity. Chapter 8 suggests ways to arrange the classroom, select art supplies, and schedule time for art on a daily basis. How to assess the artwork of children is discussed in Chapter 9. Chapter 10 looks beyond the classroom to the resources to be found in the wider community. Finally, Part Three: Producing Art, provides the basic knowledge of art skills, techniques, and design principles that teachers need to make art come alive in their classrooms.

Within each chapter the information is organized into seven parts. Each chapter begins with a brief discussion of what will be covered in the chapter. This is followed by "Setting the Stage," in which basic terms and concepts are defined and discussed. This is followed by the section "Why . . . ?" in which purposes and goals are outlined. In the "Guiding Ideas" section the theme of the chapter is discussed in light of current research and theory, and recommendations are made for incorporating these ideas into classroom practice. How these practices can be organized and used effectively in the classroom are found in the section "In the Classroom." Each chapter ends with a thought-provoking "Conclusion" and a "Teacher Resource" section that lists books and articles that delve deeper into topics discussed in the text. Here also are suggested sources for the special supplies, computer software, videos, art prints, artifacts, and Web sites that relate to the text.

Special Features

This book is designed to be practical—the kind of book kept open on the desk to refer to while teaching. To make it easier to use, much of the information has been summarized or represented in graphic fashion and set off from the body of the text. These sections are marked with special headings or symbols.

Artists at Work. Share in conversations with real children as they work on and talk about their art. These vignettes, based on the author's journal entries and audio recordings, provide a glimpse into the reality of the classroom.

At a Glance. Tables, charts, and graphic organizers help make the material in the text more understandable.

Books to Share. Children's books that relate to art concepts and media are listed here.

Teacher Tip. These are brief, practical ideas that may prove helpful to teachers using an art medium for the first time. They also include safety tips and ways to adapt art activities to make them accessible for all students.

Teaching in Action. Detailed examples of activities and teaching methods flesh out the ideas presented in the text. These are designed to provide ready-to-use activities for preservice teachers and to be adapted and expanded by those currently in the field.

What Do You Think? Open-ended questions challenge readers to apply the ideas of the text to their own experience.

What the Experts Say. Interspersed throughout the text are carefully chosen quotations taken from a wide variety of sources. These have been selected for their power to provoke, to inspire, and to give a feel for the wide range of thought on art and education.

Glossary. This section defines terms used in the body of the text.

References. This section lists books and Web sites that will be useful to classroom teachers. It includes titles on art history, art appreciation, dance, literature, and music and Internet resources on integrated lesson design, museums, art organizations, educational research, and teacher organizations.

Instructor's Manual

If this book is being used as a text for a course preparing college students to teach, activities, worksheets, questions, and teaching resources to complement the text will be found in the accompanying instructor's manual, available by ordering ISBN 0766-805417.

ACKNOWLEDGMENTS

Many people have contributed to the creation of this book. Each has offered me support in a variety of ways. I wish to thank my grade-level teammates Darlene Gumaer, Pat Kollar, and Ann Scalzo for reading and discussing various drafts. Their contributions to my ideas about writing instruction as well as their focus on the practicality and readability of this book for classroom teachers have been invaluable. I want to thank fellow art teachers Dolores Bugaiski, Joyce Cornelius, Peggy Hoffman, Ken Rozek, and Kelly Smith for allowing me to collect artwork and take photographs in their classrooms. Darlene Darrow, my building administrator, provided both support and understanding throughout the writing process. I also want to thank the teachers of the Maine Endwell School District for allowing me to observe their programs and photograph their students.

Writing a book takes many hours of focused attention. My family has shown patience in the face of the innumerable hours I have devoted to this task and provided much needed support throughout the process. I can never thank them enough.

This book is concerned first and foremost with inspiring our children to become confident artists. I want to thank the thousands of children who have taught me how to become a better teacher as we learned to speak the language of art with each other. It is these children, my young writers and artists, who have provided the impetus to write this book.

Lastly, the thoughtful and detailed advice of the following reviewers was invaluable:

William Charland, Grand Valley State University

John N. Dinsmore, University of Nebraska at Kearney

Linda Ganstrom, Fort Hays State University

G. W. Hawkins, Eastern Washington University

Brian T. Jefferson, Georgia State University

Laurel Lampela, Cleveland State University

Gayle Pendergrass, Arkansas State University

Lee A. Ransaw, Morris Brown College

Michael P. Smith, University of North Florida

Part One

Bringing Art into the Elementary Classroom

Chapter 1

Art and Education Philosophy and Goals

Art is humanity's most essential, most universal language. It is not a frill, but a necessary part of civilization.

Ernest L. Boyer (1983)

ARTISTS AT WORK

"What is art?" I asked.

"Art is when you make things."
Carolyn, grade 1

"It's like . . . drawing and painting."
Mark, grade 2

"Art is making stuff . . . you know, painting, drawing . . . that kind of stuff. . . . Any time you make stuff. Like even in math when you make stuff."
Jesse, grade 3

"Imagination . . . it's using your imagination."
Jocelyn, grade 4

"Oh, I don't know. I should know. . . . Having fun, I guess."
Catherine, grade 5

Introduction

ART IN SCHOOL

Visit almost any elementary school and you will see children's artwork displayed in hallways and classrooms. In these colorful collages, paintings, and drawings we can catch a glimpse of how important art education is in the school and what the teachers believe represents a successful art activity. Are the artworks all alike or are they all different? Does each one reflect a variety of ideas about a class experience? Was each child given a pattern to trace and decorate, or do the works reflect growing skill and experience with art media? Are the images and concerns of our society reflected in the children's artwork? From the classroom walls we can determine how art is defined in our elementary schools.

What do we mean by art in education? Why do elementary school children need to learn about art? In this chapter we will discuss the nature of art and examine what children learn through art. We will look at the current research into children's minds to find out how art education fits into a child's intellectual development. We will see how beliefs about how and what children can and should be taught determine what art experiences the children receive. Finally we will review what art education has been in the past, what it is now, and based on current research, suggest what directions it should take in the future.

How we value art is reflected in the hallways of our schools.

Thinking about Children's Art

What role should art play in elementary school children's education? Should our school hallways look like museums? How do you think art is valued in this school?

Setting the Stage

WHAT IS ART?

Before we can teach art, we need to understand what it is. Unfortunately, within our own culture we often have different and conflicting ideas about what is and is not art. These ideas vary depending on our own experiences with art and our own education in art. Because the word *art* is used in so many different and often contradictory ways, we often look to art experts to tell us whether something is really art or not. For many, if a work is exhibited in a museum or pictured in a book about art, then it must be art, even though it may not meet our personal standards. Graffiti, for example, may be considered an eyesore in the subway station but becomes art when shown in an art gallery. We may wonder why a weaving is praised as fine art in one case and denigrated as a handicraft in another. Why is it so hard to define art?

The nature of art, like that of other important human concepts such as love and beauty, is such that it cannot be confined by words. This is because art is not a singular entity or rigid category but a fluid, ever-changing way that human imaginations interact. We can only describe particular aspects of art in an attempt to differentiate it from other human activities and behaviors.

What Do You Think?

A Personal View of Art

Close your eyes and picture a piece of art you have seen in a book, museum, home, or store. As you read through the section "Ways to Think about Art," compare this work to each idea about art. Which ideas seem to describe the work best? Which seem least useful? Which idea or combination of ideas comes closest to what you think art is?

Ways to Think about Art

Although sometimes contradictory, all the following ideas, drawn both from the past and the present, help illuminate the multifaceted nature of art.

Art as behavior. Throughout human history, art has not always been viewed as a separate human endeavor in which only trained artists participate but rather as a daily part of life. In some societies art is so integral to the fabric of the community that the language lacks a special word for it (Ember & Ember, 1996). Ellen Dissanayake argues persuasively that artmaking is not the province of a few but is a normal behavioral and psychological need to make things special. Art is taking ordinary things and making them more than ordinary so that attention is drawn to them. "Regarding art as a behavior—an instance of 'making special,'" she suggests, "shifts the emphasis . . . to the activity itself (the making or doing and appreciating)" (1995, pp. 222–223). Seeing art as a behavior that all people, not just specialists, engage in enlarges and enriches our understanding of art and makes it inclusive rather than exclusive, a vital part of being human.

Art as culture. Across cultures the nature of the works produced varies tremendously. Visual images and forms have been used to communicate ideas, ask and answer questions, stir emotions, provide comfort, and spur memory. People have used a variety of tools and materials to tell stories and record their history. Images and symbols are intimately involved in the religious, political, and ceremonial aspects of most societies. Carefully chosen and arranged patterns, colors, and textures decorate the mundane utensils of daily life and enhance the spaces where people live, work, and play. Monuments and special signs mark important events or the graves of loved ones. Such works communicate what is important within the culture.

Cultural traditions and beliefs also influence what the resulting artwork looks like and how it is valued. An object will be deemed art if it fits a cultural category identified with an acceptable artistic purpose. Tradition, religion, politics, or current taste may dictate what subjects and purposes are acceptable for artistic pursuits. Only certain types of art tools and materials may be available or allowed. What is rejected as art in one time and place may be valued in another. Van Gogh's paintings, for example, were disparaged in his own time but are now acclaimed. As such, artworks become the embodiment of cultural fashions and beliefs. "Artistic activities are always in part, cultural, involving shared and learned patterns of behavior, belief, and feeling" (Ember & Ember, 1996, p. 332).

Today we can look at the art of the past and of other cultures as a document to be "read." It provides a way to understand other people's lives.

Art as conscious creation. Because it produces a physical object, art is often defined in terms of its composition or appearance. Works of art can be compared to objects both natural and human-made. For example, what is the difference between a smoothly carved sculpture and a well-weathered piece of driftwood? It has been argued that to be art an object must be the product of human thought, imagination, and workmanship rather than being accidental or found in nature.

But if the difference between a natural object and a work of art is the intercedence of a human mind and hand, then how can artworks be differentiated from other human-made works? One way is to distinguish between their purposes. Utilitarian objects simply make life more hygienic and physically comfortable. Art objects make it more beautiful and interesting. People can wrap themselves in plain cloth or wear elaborately patterned and styled garments. The difference between the two can be seen as art.

Art as craft. "Art when really understood is the province of every human being. It is simply a question of doing things, anything, well," wrote the American artist Robert Henri (Mogelon, 1969, p. 160). The Latin word *ars,* from which *art* derives, originally meant finely or skillfully crafted. Many people feel that in order for something to be valued as art, it should demonstrate a high level of technical skill, its materials carefully chosen to fulfill the final product's intended purpose. If something is art, it is because it is well crafted and suited to its purpose.

Art as form. We can describe and evaluate the physical form of art based on how its visual, tactile, and spatial elements are arranged into an organized whole or composition. The universal elements of line, shape, value, color, texture, space, and form can be found in nature as well as in art forms of all types and can provide a framework for analyzing diverse works. "Form . . . rises above geographical boundaries, and makes works of various cultures meaningful to each other despite the fact that they may be largely alien in other respects" (Ocvirk et al., 1968, p. 4).

This approach focuses on the selection and placement of these basic universal forms into compositions, and there is no limitation to the way artists can visually and spatially combine variations of these elements to create works of art. The artist communicates feelings and ideas by manipulating these elements in ways that are meaningful for the intended audience.

Art as creative product. In our culture we value art that uses visual or spatial art elements and symbols in a way that is uniquely different from any other work ever created. This focus on individual creativity is of especial interest because many other cultures value tradition more highly than individuality and judge works on how closely they match previous works, not on how different they are. "Establishment art in modern Western culture is unique," writes Marvin Harris, "in emphasizing structural or formal creativity" (1980, p. 471).

Art as aesthetic experience. Art is often defined by the aesthetic reaction it causes in the viewer. "When we speak of attending to something from an aesthetic point of view," writes Peter Lamarque, "we mean attending to those features of its design or appearance, . . . its sensuous qualities, which can be isolated from other more utilitarian aspects like its physical composition, the function it fulfills, its ownership, its monetary value, the practical benefits that can be derived from it" (1999, p. 5).

An aesthetic reaction gives the viewer pleasure apart from any other meaning the work may hold. It is a feeling of awe, of marveling as opposed to questioning, analyzing, or understanding. An aesthetic reaction is the sudden drawing in of breath when seeing, for the first time, something deemed beautiful or surprising. It is lazily running one's eyes over the surface of a work, absorbing the nuances of curve and angle without thinking about its meaning. "Why try to understand art?" the artist Pablo Picasso asked. "Why not try to understand the song of a bird? Why does one love the night, flowers, everything around one, without trying to understand them?" (Goldwater & Treves, 1945, p. 421).

Art as self-expression. We express ourselves when we give vent to our deepest feelings, emotions, and thoughts. Creating art is one way for individuals to do this. Art has often been described as a window into the artist's soul. "[A]rt is not just a series of pretty objects; it is rather a way we have of articulating our interior life," says Michael Parsons (1987, p. 13). The artist has been seen as the instrument of making the emotions of the subconscious visible. The noted illustrator and artist N. C. Wyeth believed that if the artist felt deeply enough, the emotions felt for an object would "bypass the brain, travel down the arm, and in some magical way, flow into the blank surface" (Merryman, 1991, p. 59).

The practice of art therapy is built upon this belief that art is a reflection of the subconscious. A patient may be asked to create art freely or in response to suggestions, which a trained therapist then carefully analyzes.

Art as historical construct. How people view art has varied throughout history. At different times objects have been recognized as art based on the general preferences of the period. For example, in Western culture what has been acclaimed art has often depended on the philosophical beliefs of the time. In medieval times art was in the service of religion, and cathedrals, sculptures, and paintings were created to glorify God. Renaissance artists created art that celebrated an ideal but human-centered existence; they portrayed the actual world as accurately as they could using new techniques such as perspective.

In the eighteenth century many ideas came together to form the basic concepts underlying how we in modern Western society view art. During this period of rapid industrialization and the celebration of individualism, people began to believe that the sole purpose of art was to provide an aesthetic experience. Fine art was seen as something

Books to Share

Reading a book about being an artist is a good way to start a discussion about art. Share the following books and questions with students to start them thinking about what art means to them:

Picture Books

Collins, P. L. (1992). *I Am an Artist.* Brookfield, CT: Millbrook Press.
An artist responds aesthetically to beautiful things.
Question to ask: Do you think a person has to make something to be an artist?

Florian, D. (1993). *The Painter.* New York: Greenwillow.
A painter tells what he thinks and feels as he paints.
Question to ask: Do all artists think about the same things when they make a piece of art?

Freeman, D. (1959). *Norman the Doorman.* New York: Viking.
A little mouse living in a museum decides to become an artist.
Question to ask: Do people need to win a prize to know they are artists?

Lionni, L. (1995). *Matthew's Dream.* Emeryville, CA: Children's Book Press.
A visit to an art museum inspires a young mouse to become an artist.
Question to ask: Why might some parents not want their child to become an artist?

Novels

Paulsen, G. (1991). *The Monument.* New York: Dell.
An artist inspires a young girl to become an artist while teaching her town a new way to see art.
Question to ask: How do artists communicate with their audience?

created solely to be looked at. Works that served some useful purpose or were purely decorative were relegated to the less valued status of handicraft or applied arts.

Based on these categories, architecture, design, and all the crafts from jewelry making to pottery were by their practical function separated from the higher arts of drawing, painting, and sculpture. This has led to conflicting views of many artworks. For example, a weaving intended to be worn as a garment would not be considered fine art, because fine art, by definition, does not include utilitarian objects. Conversely, the same weaving hung on the wall solely to be looked at is no longer functional and may now be ranked as fine art.

Some argue that this artificial division of art into high and low categories ignores the fact that all works have many layers of function depending on context. Even a work created solely to be admired can become a commodity if sold or a decoration if hung to enhance a room. Functional works, on the other hand, can also elicit aesthetic response.

At a Glance 1.1

Ways to Think about Art

Each of the following viewpoints has been proposed as a way to differentiate art from other human activities and illuminate certain aspects of art.

- *Behavioral:* Art represents a biological need to mark events and objects and make them special in some way.
- *Conceptual:* The artist's idea is more important than the actual construction or display of an artwork.
- *Contextual:* Art is the result of the interaction between the creator and the social, cultural, and physical environment.
- *Expressive:* Art is the expression of human feelings and emotions.
- *Formal:* Art is an organized arrangement of visual and tactile elements that create a significant form.
- *Mimesis:* Art is an imitation of nature or reality.
- *Relative:* Art is what is defined as art at this time and in this place. It is linked to what came before it and what will follow it.
- *Symbolic:* Art contains universal or culturally meaningful symbols. It is a language without words.

Art as commodity. The idea that artworks are one-of-kind objects that can be ranked in aesthetic value against other artworks, given a monetary value, and then bought and sold as an investment is a peculiarly Western concept, not a universal one. When art is viewed this way, it becomes necessary to define criteria that will differentiate true or fine art from the mundane and less-valued utilitarian.

However, setting standards is difficult. Not only are personal aesthetic responses to artwork impossible to stratify but also, in an attempt to demonstrate their individual creativity, artists purposely challenge and break established rules. Because it is so hard to rank the aesthetic quality of artworks, critics, historians, dealers, and museum curators, who are considered art experts, rather than the public or the artists themselves, often become the main interpreters of what constitutes fine art. What these experts say and write about a work determines how it is revered and its value in the art market. These experts often denigrate the opinion of lay people, considering popular art forms such as cartooning and folk art inferior compared to works that are less accessible and comprehensible to the untrained viewer.

Art as play. George Szekely believes that "[h]aving fun is the prime motivation for making art" (1991, p. 9). The physical activity of creating art, such as pushing and pulling clay, making broad strokes

The Sargent Family, 1800.
National Gallery of Art. Gift of Edgar William and Bernice Chrysler Garbisch.

From the Museum

The Sargent Family was painted in the early eighteenth century by an unknown American artist. Why do you think the artist made this painting? What does the picture tell you about family life in early America? Do you think that it is a historical document or a work of art? Which definition(s) of art do you think might best fit this particular work?

of color, and cutting and tearing paper, can excite the senses and produce feelings of pleasure. Anthropologist Alexander Alland (1977, p. 39) includes play, alongside aesthetic response, form, and communication, as one of the four main elements he defines as part of all art. The artist playfully explores materials and ideas, trying out possible combinations, rejecting some, selecting others, and deriving pleasure from finishing a work. "There is satisfaction in such experiences that make from the useless, the useful; from the ugly and discarded, the beautiful and purposeful" (Sunderlin & Gray, 1967, p. 1).

Art as symbol system. One of the difficulties in looking at art from all these different viewpoints is that it is easy to lose sight of what all art has in common. Whether it expresses an emotion, conveys a religious belief, or performs a function, a work of art transforms human experience into culturally understandable visual symbols that communicate meaning. Art can be viewed as a visual, wordless, symbolic system—in other words, a language. The limitations of the printed word to explain art must be accepted as the inability of one symbolic system to replace another.

Why . . . ?

WHY IS ART A LANGUAGE?

Artists strive to make works that skillfully communicate with their audience and that follow artistic rules that their community understands. In this way art resembles oral and written language. Both are meaningful symbol systems used to communicate human experiences, feelings, and beliefs. Over and over writers have used the metaphor of art as language. "[T]he arts are the language of a whole range of human experience . . ." (Silberman, 1973, p. 743). "[C]rayons and paint are indeed 'another language'" (Cohen & Gainer, 1995, p. xi). "Through the language of the arts we can help integrate our splintered world" (Edwards, 1979, p. 15). "Art is a universal visual language" (Linderman, 1989, p. 5). The artist Eric Gill perhaps put it most eloquently: "What is a work of art? A word made flesh. . . . A word, that which emanates from the mind. Made flesh; a thing, a thing seen, a thing known, the immeasurable translated into terms of the measurable" (Goldwater & Treves, 1945, p. 457).

There are many ways to compare art and language. Paul Bohannan (1992, pp. 197–200) identifies the following characteristics of language, which can also be applied to art:

- *Both are pervasive.* All human beings have language and cultural art forms.
- *Both are built from basic units.* Language is based on a system of sounds called *phonemes.* These are the smallest bits of sound that have meaning for speakers of a particular language. Although humans are born with the ability to make all sounds, every language selects only a few, usually less than fifty.

  Art is also based on basic elements such as line, shape, and color. Toddlers around the world create similar scribbles and marks reflective of the way little fingers, wrists, hands, and arms can move. Their eyes see the same range of colors. It does not take long, however, for children's art to reflect the native culture using those lines, shapes, and colors most meaningful to the child's community.

- *Both have a syntax or grammar.* Sounds alone do not make a language. Random marks do not make art. Syntax is the set of rules that make the sounds of a language understandable. Art also follows a set of culturally determined rules that make it meaningful. Drawing objects smaller and higher up on a piece of paper, for example, is one way artists in our culture indicate distance on a flat surface.
- *Both are culturally specific.* Just as there are many differences in human languages, there are worldwide differences in art forms that can make them unintelligible to people of other times and cultures. Although it is possible to respond to the way form and space have been manipulated in a particular artwork, just as we can hear the melodic sounds of a poem in an unfamiliar language, the deeper meaning is clear only to members of the community in which it was created. Any interpretation or translation by those outside the time and place of creation will be influenced by their own cultural heritage. "Today we see the art of the past as nobody saw it before," writes John Berger. "We actually perceive it in a different way" (1977, p. 16). We can appreciate prehistoric paintings on cave walls for their skill and expressiveness, and they may give us clues to the life and thought of their time, but they leave us wondering about why they were painted deep in caves and what they meant to the artists who created them.
- *Both change over time.* Elizabethan English is not the same as twenty-first-century English. Shakespeare's plays, although written in the language of his day, sound antiquated to our ears. Art in the past often had a different original purpose than it does for us today. Rembrandt's masterpieces, for example, were designed to perpetuate the status of the wealthy burghers of Holland. Today his paintings are revered as a high point in our artistic heritage.
- *Both are learned symbol systems.* The same human capacity for symbol creation is found in both language and art (Harris, 1995). Both use symbols to communicate ideas. These symbols are highly complex, requiring the audience to provide context and linkages. Without education these would be meaningless. It is through interaction with others in our own culture that we learn the complex meanings and relationships embodied in the cultural symbols. Language is learned only in social communities. Children raised in isolation do not learn to speak (Miller, 1979). Artistic activities also require shared and learned patterns of behavior, belief, and feeling. Children in Western culture, for example, learn to hold paintbrushes differently from children in Asian cultures.

"My First Sleep Over."
Crayon—Ryan, grade 2.

My First Sleep Over
by Ryan

When I was 5 years old I met someone named Seth. We soon became best friends. Since we were best friends we had a sleep over at my house. We had a lot of fun. We went to my room. We laughed so hard my mom could hear us. We shared almost all my toys and played at least 10 songs. Then my mom told us to go to bed.

Thinking about Children's Art

Each form of communication conveys information differently. What are the similarities and differences between art and writing? In this illustrated story by a second grader what different pieces of information do we learn from the written words and the drawn symbols? How does having both pictures and words increase our understanding of the child's experience?

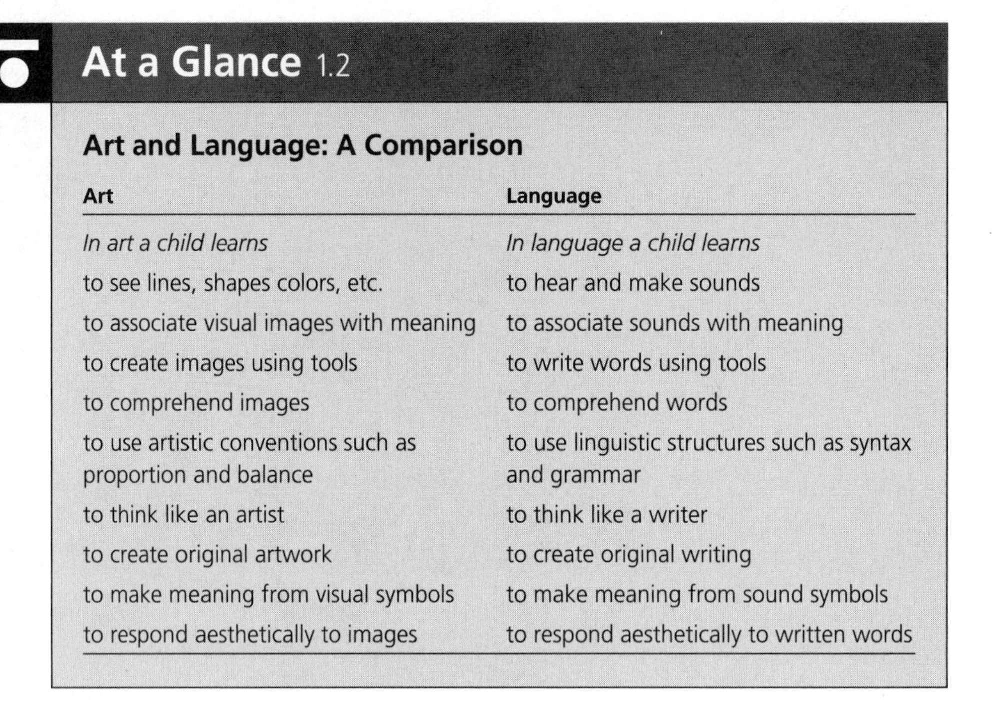

At a Glance 1.2

Art and Language: A Comparison

Art	Language
In art a child learns	*In language a child learns*
to see lines, shapes colors, etc.	to hear and make sounds
to associate visual images with meaning	to associate sounds with meaning
to create images using tools	to write words using tools
to comprehend images	to comprehend words
to use artistic conventions such as proportion and balance	to use linguistic structures such as syntax and grammar
to think like an artist	to think like a writer
to create original artwork	to create original writing
to make meaning from visual symbols	to make meaning from sound symbols
to respond aesthetically to images	to respond aesthetically to written words

Guiding Ideas

THE ROLE OF ART IN SCHOOL

If art is defined as a language, then its role in education becomes clear; it provides another way that children can learn and express themselves. Children learn both languages from early childhood. Children as young as two can identify pictures as representations (Winner, 1982). Two- and three-year-olds can distinguish between writing and drawing (Steward, 1995). Both of these cultural symbol systems, although still rudimentary, are already set in place to be used for learning. By the time children arrive at elementary school, not only can they speak and understand, but they can also create meaningful drawings, paintings, and sculptures. Most importantly, they can translate information from one symbol system to the other. The language of art can be used in all the ways that oral and written language can:

- *To teach.* Art can be used to present new concepts. Artworks can show children images that words alone can describe only superficially.
- *To provide practice.* Children can create artworks that use the concepts being taught. For example, after learning that stories have beginnings and endings, students can draw pictures that show something starting and ending.
- *To record.* Art provides graphic images that students can use to record and remember what happened in science experiments, on field trips, in stories read, and more.

What the Experts Say

Thoughts on Art

[A] principal use of art consists in its helping the human mind to cope with the complex image of the world in which it finds itself.
Rudolph Arnheim (1991, p. 28)

Art and education are two of the most noble achievements of humankind. They have both led individuals to sublime heights of achievement and revealed the infinite potential of *Homo sapiens*.
Peter Smith (1996, p. 1)

The arts constitute one of the important forms of representation through which humans share what they have thought, felt, or believed.
Elliot Eisner (1988, p. 4)

- *To respond.* The language of art is responsive. Students can create visual symbols to represent what they understood and felt, such as graphically showing the feelings of different characters in books they have read.
- To *assess.* Teachers can use paintings, drawings, sculptures, and other art forms to analyze how well the student learned. A detailed painting of life in pioneer days or the life cycle of a butterfly can graphically show what the student knows about the subject.

These kinds of activities are found in many classrooms. Perhaps because there are more similarities in the appearance of early writing and art, they are more likely to occur in the earliest school years. As the child progresses through the elementary grades, the language of art is used less and less. Daily activities focus on developing skill and competence in oral and written language so it can be used for more advanced learning in the higher grades. The language of art is relegated to a small percentage of a child's day. Children are rarely given the same kind of intensive, systematic instruction in art as they are in reading and writing. As children mature, they are asked less and less often to use art to learn or to respond artistically across the curriculum. A language not used is soon forgotten. Fluency disappears, and one struggles to say the simplest phrases. When older children do use the language of art, they are often unhappy with the results. They do not have the skills needed to express the complex ideas required at their level of thinking.

What the Experts Say

Art and Achievement

Children who participated in the Arts Infusion Program—a sequential curriculum-based approach to arts in education—showed improved academic performance on the Stanford Achievement Test.
Greater Augusta Arts Council (1995)

Elementary children who participated in related drawing activities showed consistently better quality writing than did control groups.
Blaine H. Moore and Helen Caldwell (1993)

Students who participated in the SPECTRA arts program, Hamilton, Ohio, made significant gains in vocabulary, reading and math compared to a control group.
Richard L. Luftig (1994)

HISTORICAL INFLUENCES ON ART EDUCATION

If art is such a powerful and useful language, why does it get pushed to the sidelines of elementary education? As we have seen, one factor has been the Western view that to be art a work must be unique and recognized by art experts. Art, as confusingly defined by the contemporary art world, seems far removed from the daily task of teaching young children reading, writing, and math skills. Another factor is the way art has been taught in different historical periods. Practices from the past continue to influence how art is taught in elementary classrooms today.

Apprenticeship

For thousands of years most artists learned their craft from someone who was considered expert in that skill. The master-apprentice relationship was seen as the natural way to learn the techniques of the artist. The apprentice watched the master at work and carried out small tasks. As the apprentices' skill grew, the masters gave them a more important role in the production of the workshop.

At no time were all children expected to experience and master all the art forms. Apprentices learned only the craft of their master. Potters taught pottery. Stone carvers taught sculpture techniques. This led to a highly efficient system for producing skilled craftspeople, which still operates in many traditional societies today and can be found even in some specialized occupations in our own, such as internships for physicians and student-teaching for future educators.

Influence on art education. The apprentice-master model has been very influential in art education practices. From this model arises the belief that only an expert can teach art and that learning art requires mastery of a great many skills not needed by most people. In addition, since in many cases skills were passed from parent to offspring, it often appeared that talent ran in families—all of which caused the job of teaching and making art seem to be the province of a few well-trained, gifted specialists rather than the task of classroom teachers and their students.

But an industrialized, technological society needs a different model for art education. Our culture is a highly visual one. We are surrounded by artworks that try to convince us to buy certain products and believe certain ideas. Students need to be taught to read and to comprehend the messages in the visual images that surround them and then make wise decisions. Because our society values creativity and individuality, we also have many opportunities to make artistic choices of our own, from choosing the cut and style of our clothing to deciding if we will visit an art museum. Students need to learn how to appreciate art and to understand how being knowledgeable in art can enrich their lives.

This does not mean that we should lose sight of the importance of the apprentice-master model as a way of teaching art. After all, it has been effectively used for thousands of years to produce many highly skilled artists. Howard Gardner has pointed out that the strength of this way of teaching is that "the learning is contextualized—that is, the reasons for the various procedures being taught are generally evident, because the master is in the process of producing goods or services for which there is an explicit demand and evident use" (1991, p. 122). In the same way, art education, to be successful, needs to be contextualized in our schools. Students will more readily learn the skills of art if it is not a separate entity taught once a week and divorced from classroom learning but is an integral part of the curriculum and an important way for students to learn. In order to do this, the teacher must fill the role of master, guiding student apprentices on the journey to fluency in the language of art.

Formal Art Instruction

Horace Mann, as part of his initiative for public schooling in Massachusetts, wanted drawing included in the curriculum. He believed that encouraging students to use their hands would make school less oppressive for working-class students. Under his influence formal instruction in drawing was mandated in the Massachusetts public schools by 1870 (Smith, 1996). This was the official start of art education in American schools.

However, the rigid and formalized drawing program put in place was founded on the German and English industrial model and on the belief that imitation, practice, and drill were the way to teach drawing and design. This instituted rigid, step-by-step methods of teaching art to young students. It also separated what students were being taught from what artists, such as the Impressionists in France, were doing and established art education as a program separated from the heritage of art.

Influence on art education. The influence of this program has been far ranging because it supplied teachers with a ready formula for teaching art. It continues today in the practice, under the guise of teaching children how to follow directions, of giving students patterns to cut out and assemble so that all the artworks resemble a teacher-made model. Despite art educators' constant criticism of it, and the many alternatives available, the practice continues in the mistaken belief that this helps students practice art skills and learn to follow instructions.

Art Education as Refinement

For a variety of historical and social reasons knowledge and appreciation of certain kinds of art have come to be considered the mark of a cultured, educated person. Throughout much of history, whether in the castles of Europe or the palaces of Chinese emperors, the wealthy and powerful have been the major patrons of certain art forms. It is the wealthy leisure class who has had time to appreciate the "finer" things in life, including art. Upwardly mobile middle-class families sought to emulate them by encouraging their children to appreciate art. Private finishing schools for young women taught drawing and painting. Well-to-do English and American families sent their children to the continent to see classic and Renaissance works firsthand. Being educated about art came to be associated with wealth, refinement, and fine character.

With the arrival of public education, attempts were made to inculcate these same higher levels of taste and character in the children of the working class. Noticing that teachers put magazine clippings on classroom walls as decoration, Oscar W. Neale began selling reproductions of famous artworks, selected with the additional purpose of teaching moral virtues. These became widely popular, and lessons were marketed, which introduced children to masterpieces usually from the Renaissance and the eighteenth-century European Romantic period. From the subjects of the works or based on the artists' lives, students received lessons on developing moral character and appreciating art (Chapman, 1978).

Influence on art education. Today learning about art must go beyond simply exposing students to the works of the great Western masters with a few examples from other cultures thrown in. The artworks displayed and discussed must represent the diversity and commonalities of our students and allow the many voices of our world to speak. Looking at art provides the context in which students and teachers can address issues of gender, age, class, ethnicity, and culture as symbolized in art (Efland et al., 1996).

Laissez-Faire Free Expression

At the beginning of the century child art was widely regarded as an imperfect imitation of realistic adult art. Early psychologists, however, came to see children's art as solely an expression of inner feelings, and this combined with the self-expressive emphasis of the Expressionist movement in art led to untrained children's artwork becoming widely admired and often compared to the work of adult artists (Smith, 1996). Children's artwork was seen as something that developed naturally from the need for self-expression and release of emotions. In America, Viktor Lowenfeld (1947) was an influential advocate for the importance of not interfering with or directing children as they created art. Young artists, according to Lowenfeld, progressed through a series of unalterable stages of art creation. Teachers were warned against interfering with this natural progression and imposing "their own color schemes, proportions, and manner of painting upon children" (Lowenfeld & Brittain, 1975).

Advocates promoted free expression in children's art through the use of large paper, fat brushes, bright paint, and paper collages. The noted educator Marion Richardson, for example, emphasized that tools should be child-sized (Silberman, 1973). Teachers trained during this period feared they would inhibit the artistic development of their students if they gave drawing lessons or provided examples or models. Educators discouraged and disparaged copying from models and tracing and emphasized creating one-of-a-kind products. Emphasis on creativity often meant that teachers were afraid to apply structure: "[A]rt was not so much taught, than caught" (Eisner, 1983, p. 12).

Influence on art education. The fear of stifling self-expression and creativity continues to inhibit many teachers from teaching art. As a result, it is easy to understand why art education often becomes simply putting some art supplies on a table with minimal instruction.

Art on the Cheap

Growing out of the exigencies of the Depression and World War II, money for art supplies—always limited—became more so. Art in schools at mid-century came to rely on found materials, the discarded junk of a growing consumer economy.

Elementary school art took on a character of its own. Cut paper and collage became favored school art activities because they required only inexpensive and free materials. Books and teachers' magazines carried articles on art activities that used cheap supplies, such as cardboard tubes, paper plates, and margarine containers. Students, given egg cartons, newspapers, and other discards and no instruction in art skills, created throw-away art that was not highly valued by parents and did not resemble the work of fine artists. This created the impression that art education was simply a matter of playing around with discards and therefore did not require a high level of financial support or teacher training.

Influence on art education. Many teachers continue to look for low-cost ways to include art in their classroom. Certainly found art activities and collage deserve a role in school art programs. However, they cannot be the mainstay of elementary art. If art is to be taken seriously in the school curriculum and properly funded, students also need high-quality art supplies and careful instruction in how to use them, as well as how to look at and talk about art.

Art as a Product

Because art produces a very visible, tangible product, people often view it as a subject whose main purpose is to make decorations for the school hallways and to establish good public relations for the school. Art teachers are judged by how elaborate their showcases are. Classroom teachers give children patterns and preprinted pictures to color so the display outside their classroom will look attractive.

Influence on art education. The decorative arts are not highly valued in our society. Decoration is a frill we can live without when under pressure. Using art mainly for this purpose relegates it to the sidelines of an educational system regularly under attack from all quarters to produce more literate, mathematically and scientifically competent citizens.

Rather than seeing art as a way to fill up empty hallways, teachers and administrators need to discover that carefully displayed student art can not only present and celebrate the learning going on in the classroom but can also educate parents and community members about the substance of education.

CURRENT DIRECTIONS IN ART EDUCATION

In the last twenty years educators have made a renewed effort to change the product-oriented, laissez-faire approaches of art education in the elementary school. One of the most influential initiatives launched by the Getty Center for Education in the Arts in the mid-1980s, proposed that art education be discipline based. Art education, they advocated, should be based on the four disciplines of art: art history, art criticism, aesthetics, and art production (Clark et al., 1987).

"Flying Bird."
Tempera—Michael, grade 1.

Thinking about Children's Art

Working alone at the easel this young child has created a dynamic picture of a bird without instruction or direction from the teacher. The provision of an easel in a painting corner at the primary grades grew out of the free expression movement in art education. Do you think that an easel or painting area where children can work independently on artwork of their choice still belongs in the elementary classroom?

Discipline-Based Art Education

Discipline-based art education (DBAE) advocates that in addition to creating art, students also need to look at, describe, and evaluate the artwork of others. The belief is that an art program based solely on hands-on art projects does not give students a picture of the place of art in society nor does it prepare them to appreciate, understand, and judge the artwork of others or the visual images in the world around them. The Getty curriculum proposal called for regular art instruction that would foster in students knowledge about art and enable them to understand its production and develop appreciation for the aesthetic, cultural, and historical characteristics of art as a basis for making judgments about it.

Discipline-based art education presents art as a subject to be studied in the same way that literature or math is studied. Too often the public perceives art only as the actual production of a work. This is equivalent to considering writing as the whole of language arts instruction (see At a Glance 1.3).

In the last decade of the twentieth century an evolving DBAE philosophy found more and more acceptance among leading art

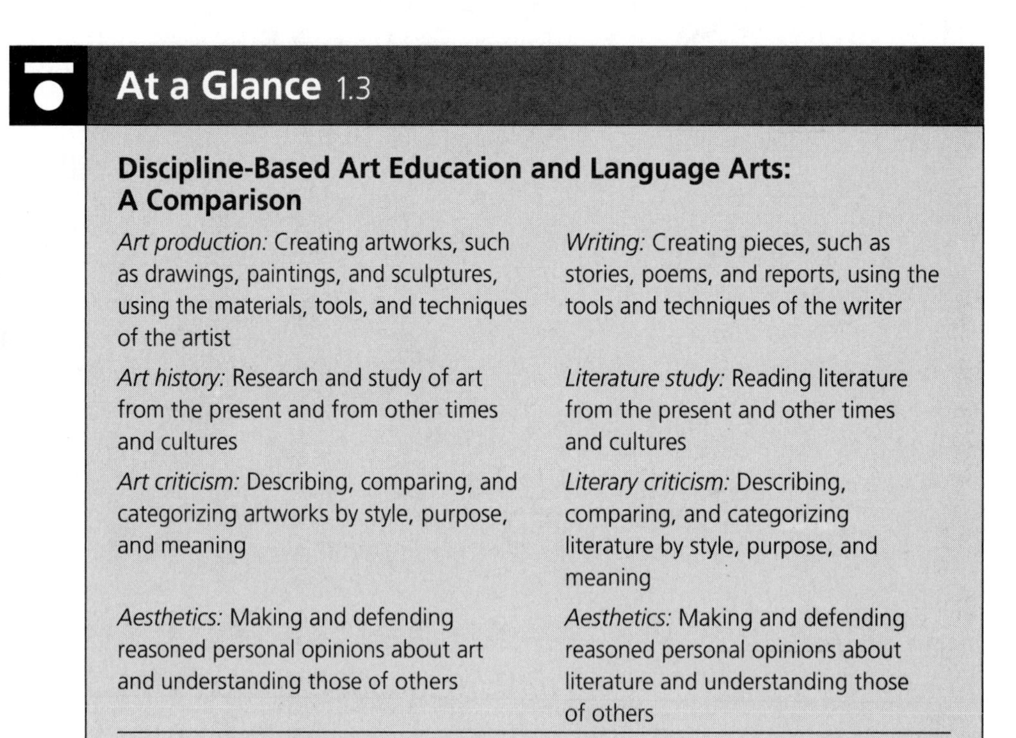
At a Glance 1.3

Discipline-Based Art Education and Language Arts: A Comparison

Art	Language Arts
Art production: Creating artworks, such as drawings, paintings, and sculptures, using the materials, tools, and techniques of the artist	*Writing:* Creating pieces, such as stories, poems, and reports, using the tools and techniques of the writer
Art history: Research and study of art from the present and from other times and cultures	*Literature study:* Reading literature from the present and other times and cultures
Art criticism: Describing, comparing, and categorizing artworks by style, purpose, and meaning	*Literary criticism:* Describing, comparing, and categorizing literature by style, purpose, and meaning
Aesthetics: Making and defending reasoned personal opinions about art and understanding those of others	*Aesthetics:* Making and defending reasoned personal opinions about literature and understanding those of others

educators. It is the guiding principle of most art education textbooks on the market today. The four disciplines clearly represent the way that art functions in our society and provide a framework upon which to build curriculum.

National Standards for the Visual Arts

The National Standards for the Visual Arts (1997) for students in kindergarten through eighth grade provide general goals for teaching art. These are the skills that all students need in order to use the language of art successfully. At the same time, these goals are difficult to achieve without integration of art into the classroom curriculum. Standard 6, in particular, recognizes the importance of relating art to the student's total education.

In the Classroom

APPLYING THE STANDARDS

In the last decade art education has been revitalized by new standards-based curricula that intertwine art and the content of language arts, math, social studies, and science. State education departments and local school districts have each reworked and applied these standards to art curriculum (Peeno, 1995). Programs such as Arts PROPEL, SPECTRA+, Image Making within the Writing Process (Olshansky, 1993), and LTRTRA: Learning to Read through the Arts (Office of Educational Research, 1993) demonstrate that art can be integrated fully into the mainstream of teaching. But how does a classroom teacher incorporate art into plans for an already full day? The goal of this book is to present a wealth of methods and ideas that will enable teachers to weave the language of art into the everyday fabric of the classroom. At a Glance 1.4 provides an overview of suggested teaching structures as they relate to the standards and tells where in this book to find detailed information on applying the structure.

A Language Approach to Art in Education

Discipline-based art education has had a positive influence on art education. Most art education curricula now recommend the inclusion of the study of artworks by others and the increased use of discussion and writing about art. Integrated approaches to teaching have demonstrated the improved academic performance of students who learn through the vehicle of art. The National Standards have provided the direction. Change at the classroom level, however, has been slow. Many classroom teachers feel just as unprepared to discuss artworks as they do to teach art skills. It is the goal of this book to demonstrate practical ways to do both. By borrowing language-teaching methods and format, teachers will be better prepared to use the language of art in all its forms with their students.

Language arts education underwent changes and faced challenges of its own in the 1990s. A literature-based approach to teaching reading and writing has given classroom teachers many positive teaching strategies that engage students in more meaningful reading and writing. To varying degrees, in many classrooms teachers have replaced lockstep basals and worksheets with journal writing, silent reading, mini-lessons, writing workshop, and other activities that immerse students in language acquisition. The components of effective language arts education, summarized by Reggie Routman (1991, pp. 9–10), are as follows:

- *Observation:* Children observe competent adults reading and writing.
- *Participation:* Children participate in reading and writing in collaboration with a competent adult or peer who explains what to do.
- *Practice:* Children receive independent skills practice with self-correction and self-direction. A competent adult stays nearby to help if needed.
- *Performance:* On a daily basis children share with an audience what they learned or accomplished.

At a Glance 1.4

Applying the Standards*

Standard 1: Understand and be able to apply media, techniques, and processes

When children are knowledgeable and skilled in the use of the tools and materials of art, they can express more complex ideas. We do not expect children to discover how to read and write complex thoughts without instruction. Neither should we expect children to learn art skills on their own.

In the Classroom

To meet this standard:

- Have students apply what they know about art media and techniques in cross-curriculum projects and thematic teaching (Chapter 2).
- Nurture the creative process (Chapter 3).
- Introduce art concepts, media, and techniques when students are ready to learn them (Chapter 4).
- Model artistic thinking and process (Chapters 6, 11).
- Use guided discovery, behavior management, and environment design to establish safe working conditions, and provide time for exploration and practice with different media during an independent writing/art workshop time (Chapter 8).
- Introduce students to a wide range of safe, quality art media, and demonstrate techniques for working with these materials (Chapters 8, 11–13).

Standard 2: Use knowledge of the structures and functions of art

We expect students to understand the basic grammar and vocabulary of our language, to be able to write in complete, meaningful sentences, and to be able to manipulate these to create writing that tells stories, persuades, or is poetic. In the same way students must learn the vocabulary of art and explore how this vocabulary is composed in different artworks, and then use what they have learned to create and understand art that serves different purposes.

In the Classroom

To meet this standard:

- Develop a rich vocabulary of art terms to describe both the appearance and meaning of artworks by comparing and contrasting artworks that have different forms and functions (Chapter 5).
- Introduce the elements of art and the principles of design and find examples in the environment, in their own art, and that of others (Chapter 12).
- Examine how art is used in contemporary life (Chapter 13).

Standard 3: Choose and evaluate a range of subject matter, symbols, and ideas

We expect children to read, recognize, understand, and write different genres of literature. Poems, stories, letters, and essays each have their own forms, purposes, and meanings. Art also takes different communicative forms. Paintings, posters, illustrations, diagrams, models, and murals use different expressive features and organizational principles to communicate ideas.

In the Classroom

To meet this standard:

- Describe, identify, compare, and contrast subject matter, symbols, and ideas as found in art from across time and place (Chapter 5).
- Plan discussions, mini-lessons, and cooperative group structures during which students look at and talk about their own art and that of others (Chapters 6–8).

- Provide the contexts in which students must produce art forms with specific purposes, such as creating a poster that attracts attention, an illustration that reflects the meaning of a story, and a painting that captures the joy of a fall day (Chapters 11–13).

Standard 4: Understand the visual arts in relation to history and culture
Learning about the history of art helps children understand the evolving nature of the artistic process and why the art that is familiar to them looks the way it does. It introduces them to the art of the world and communicates the values and lifestyles of the people who created it. Children need to learn to "read" art from other cultures and civilizations just as they learn to read historical documents.

In the Classroom
To meet this standard:

- Teach art in concert with social studies and literature studies and through thematic units (Chapter 2).
- Provide opportunities for students to research the lives of artists and the role of art in different cultures (Chapter 5).
- Incorporate works by artists of all ages, genders, cultures, and beliefs into lessons in all subject areas (Chapter 7).

Standard 5: Reflect upon and assess the characteristics and merits of their work and the work of others
What makes something good? Why do we like it? The critical analysis of literature is an integral part of language arts instruction. We want children to select good books to read. We want them to write well. In the same way we want children to be able look at artworks and explain why they respond to them in certain ways.

In the Classroom
To meet this standard:

- Provide opportunities for students to share their feelings and ideas about art in many different ways (Chapter 5).
- Use alternative assessment tools such as projects and portfolios (Chapter 9).
- Foster an atmosphere in which diverse ideas and opinions are welcomed and valued (Chapter 7).
- Teach students to use evaluative tools such as revision, conferencing, and self-assessment (Chapters 6, 8, 9).
- Present and display art in ways that attract attention and discussion (Chapter 10).

Standard 6: Make connections between visual arts and other disciplines
Howard Gardner's theory of multiple intelligences and the research on how children learn provide justification for teaching children concepts through the use of all the possible ways of presenting knowledge. Art spans all the domains of knowing and provides a way to bring them together. It does not belong on the sidelines of education. Like reading and writing, art belongs in every classroom, every day.

In the Classroom
To meet this standard:

- Teach art in concert with the other arts, and institute thematic teaching and cross-curriculum projects (Chapter 2).
- Present lessons that use multiple approaches to capture attention, apply knowledge, and evaluate students (Chapter 3).

*Content Standards (material printed in bold type) excerpted from the *National Standards for Arts Education,* published by Music Educators National Conference (MENC). The complete National Standards can be found at http://artsedge.kennedy-center.org/forms/k-4-stand.html or obtained from Music Educators National Conference, 1806 Robert Fulton Drive, Reston, VA 20191.

"Friends."
Watercolor—Stephanie, grade 6.

Thinking about Children's Art

After reading the book *Wind in the Willows* (Grahame, 1980, NY: Holt) this student created a painting that expressed her idea of friendship. How well should students be able to communicate ideas and feelings through art by the time they complete elementary school? How do the National Standards help us challenge children to think more deeply about their art and the art of others?

These practices mirror those of art education. Children learning the language of art must observe art being created and discussed by competent adults. They need to participate in creating and discussing art in collaboration with teachers and peers. They must have time for the independent practice of art skills. There must be many opportunities for young artists to share their artwork and ideas about art. These four components will provide the underlying threads that weave throughout the methods and teaching structures presented in the following chapters.

Art in Education

Karen Hamblin (1995) warns against putting too much reliance on justifying art education solely on the basis of its benefits for learning in other subject areas. It is important to remember that art is a vital human activity. In a powerful education program that approaches art as a distinct and important language, art does much more than just service other parts of the curriculum.

Art goes beyond content and allows students to build bridges between verbal and nonverbal ways of interacting with the world. It develops critical thinking skills. "In the arts, there is no rule to 'prove' the correctness of an answer," Eisner points out. "[C]hildren must rely on that most exquisite of human intellectual abilities—judgment" (1983, p. 7). Creating and looking at art is personally fulfilling. It is an essential part of life. Experiencing art to the fullest, in its broadest definition, is important to the overall development of our students as human beings and as members of our culture.

Conclusion

THE ROLE OF ART IN EDUCATION

As the expressive and symbolic aspects of human behavior, language and art are twin offspring of culture. Because they are both communication systems and because language is often used in art, just as art is often used to carry a linguistic message, it is easy to think of art as a form of language.
Alexander Alland (1980, p. 479)

It is the thesis of this book that viewing art as a language is one key to effective art education. Our culture emphasizes linguistically based thinking and learning. Much research and practice has gone into developing effective teaching strategies for language instruction. By understanding that art is also a language, teachers can apply to art education many of the same techniques used to teach children spoken and written language skills. They can use art in the same ways they use language. Teachers can also derive confidence from the fact that as members of our culture not only do they already possess many language skills but they also have a native understanding of cultural art forms. Most importantly, seeing art as a language will encourage teachers to use it as another way that students can express what they have learned.

Art provides students with a powerful visual and symbolic communication tool. Like spoken and written language, art skills must be taught in order for students to perform at the highest levels. We do not expect children to teach themselves how to read and write. We are not afraid to make them practice forming letters properly and editing their work for grammatical errors. Nor do we avoid teaching students to read and write purposely as well as for their own enjoyment. Our goal is to produce students who speak, read, and write at a level that will allow them to function successfully in our society. It should also be our goal to produce students who are capable of using the language of art with equal facility. The language of art is not just another way to communicate, a way that we can choose to ignore. It is an integral part of the way we learn.

Art education in our schools must no longer be relegated to Friday afternoons or a weekly forty-minute art period. We must move beyond the rows of cut-out pumpkins on the wall and the box of "junk" in the art corner. Viewing art as a symbolic language equal in power to the spoken and written word can provide a theoretical basis for designing meaningful art education programs that permeate school curriculum. Understanding art as a means of communication elevates it from a purely decorative and subsidiary role in the classroom.

Art, like language, can be used to express inner feelings, but that is not all it can do. Art and language both document what a child has learned or thought about, but in very different ways. Creating art is a cognitive process that draws on and embraces all the different intellectual domains of the mind. Art, taught meaningfully, develops both mind and body. Art must stand beside language and be an equally important communications tool in the education of our children. The language of art is integral to the learning process and vital in producing students who will become adults capable of understanding, valuing, and using art in their lives.

Teacher Resources

REFERENCES

Alland, A. (1977). *The artistic animal: An inquiry into the biological roots of art.* New York: Doubleday.

Alland, A. (1980). *To be human*. New York: John Wiley.

Arnheim, R. (1991). *Thoughts on art education.* Los Angeles: Getty Center for the Arts.

Berger, J. (1977). *Ways of seeing.* New York: Penguin Books.

Bohannan, P. (1992). *We, the alien.* Prospect Heights, IL: Waveland Press.

Boyer, E. L. (1983). *High school: A report on secondary education in America*. New York: Harper & Row.

Chapman, L. (1978). *Approaches to art in education.* Orlando: Harcourt Brace.

Clark, G. A., Day, M. D., and Greer, W. D. (1987). Discipline-based art education: Becoming students of art. *Journal of Aesthetic Education, 21*(2), 129–193.

Cohen, E. P., & Gainer, R. (1995). *Art: Another language for learning.* Portsmouth, NH: Heinemann.

Dissanayake, E. (1995). *Homo aestheticus: Where art comes from and why.* Seattle: University of Washington Press.

Edwards, B. (1979). *Drawing on the right side of the brain.* Los Angeles: Tarcher.

Efland, A., Stuhr, P., & Freedman, K. (1996). *Postmodern art education.* Reston, VA: National Art Association.

Eisner, E. (1983). *Beyond creating.* Los Angeles: Getty Center for the Arts.

Eisner, E. (1988). *The role of discipline-based art education in American schools.* Los Angeles: Getty Center for the Arts.

Ember, C., & Ember, M. (1996). *Cultural anthropology.* Englewood Cliffs, NJ: Prentice-Hall.

Gardner, H. (1991). *The unschooled mind.* New York: Basic Books.

Goldwater, R., & Treves, M. (1945). *Artists on art.* New York: Random House.

Greater Augusta Arts Council and Aiken County School District (1995). *Arts infusion correspondence.* National Endowment for the Humanities. http://www.aspin.asu.edu/%7Erescomp/contents.html 7.10.99.

Hamblin, K. A. (1993). Theories and research that support art instruction for instrumental outcomes. *Theory into Practice, 32*(4), 191–198.

Harris, M. (1980). *Culture, people, nature.* New York: HarperCollins.

Harris, M. (1995). *Cultural anthropology.* New York: HarperCollins.

Lamarque, P. (1999). The aesthetic and the universe. *Journal of Aesthetic Education, 33*(2), 1–17.

Linderman, M. G. (1989). *Art in the elementary school.* Dubuque, IA: W. C. Brown.

Lowenfeld, V. (1947). *Creative and mental growth.* New York: Macmillan.

Lowenfeld, V., & Brittain, W. (1975). *Creative and mental growth.* New York: Macmillan.

Luftig, R. (1994). *The schooled mind: Do arts make a difference? An empirical evaluation of the Hamilton Fairfield SPECTRA+ Program 1992–1993.* Hamilton, OH: Fitton Center for Creative Arts.

Merryman, R. (1991). *First impressions: Andrew Wyeth.* New York: Abrams.

Miller, E. (1979). *Introduction to cultural anthropology.* Englewood Cliffs, NJ: Prentice-Hall.

Mogelon, A. (1969). *One hundred ways to have fun with an alligator.* Blauvet, NY: Art Education.

Moore, B. H., & Caldwell, H. (1993). Drama and drawing for narrative writing in the primary grades. *Journal of Educational Research, 8*(2), 100–110.

Ocvirk, O., Bone, R., Stinson, R., & Wigg, P. (1968). *Art fundamentals.* Dubuque, IA: W. C. Brown.

Office of Educational Research. (1993). *Learning to read through the arts.* New York: New York City Board of Education.

Olshansky, B. (1995). Picture this: An arts-based literacy program. *Educational Leadership, 53*(1) 44–47.

Parsons, M. (1987). *How we understand art.* New York: Cambridge University Press.

Peeno, L. (1995). *Adaptations of the National Arts Standards.* Reston, VA: National Art Education Association.

Routman, R. (1991). *Invitations: Changing as teachers and learners.* Portsmouth, NH: Heinemann.

Silberman, C. (1973). *The open classroom reader.* New York: Random House.

Smith, P. (1996). *History of American art education: Learning about art in American schools.* Westport, CT: Greenwood Press.

Steward, E. P. (1995). *Beginning writers in the zone of proximal development.* Hillsdale, NJ: Erlbaum.

Sunderlin, S., & Gray, N. (1967). *Bits and pieces: Imaginative uses for children's learning.* Washington, DC: Association for Childhood Education International.

Szekely, G. (1991). *Play to art.* Portsmouth, NH: Heinemann.

Winner, E. (1982). *Invented worlds: The psychology of the arts.* Cambridge, MA: Harvard University Press.

RESOURCES

Organizations

Americans for the Arts
1 East 53rd Street
New York, NY 10022
212-223-2787

Association for the Advancement of Arts Education
655 Eden Park Drive, Suite 730
Cincinnati, OH 45202

Getty Center for Education in the Arts
1875 Century Park East, No. 2300
Los Angeles, CA 90067
213-277-9188

Kennedy Centers and Schools: Partners in Education
Washington, DC 20566

National Art Education Association
1916 Association Drive
Reston, VA 22091-1590

National Endowment for the Arts
Washington, DC 20506

Videos

Arts for life. (1990). The Getty Center for Education in the Arts. 15 min.

Teaching in and through the arts. (1995). The Getty Center for Education in the Arts. 25 min.

The arts and children: A success story. Goals 2000 Arts Education Partnership. 15 min.

Web Sites

Americans for the Arts
artsusa.org

Arts Edge
artsedge.Kennedy-center.org

Arts over America—National Assembly of States Arts Agencies (links to state arts councils)
nasaa-arts.org

Center for Arts in the Basic Curriculum
newhorizons.org

Getty Institute ArtEdNet
artsednet.getty.edu

National Art Association Web Page
naea-reston.org

National Endowment for the Arts
arts.endow.gov

Chapter 2

Art and Learning
Connections and Themes

Integration of the curriculum is an excellent way to increase richness and contribute meaningfulness.

Renate Numela Caine and Geoffrey Caine (1991, p. 119)

ARTISTS AT WORK

In the Integrated Classroom

In this third-grade classroom, two girls are sitting on the rug reading aloud animal stories they have written. At the computers several children are busy typing up research reports on animals. On the floor by the sink several others are painting a mural of the animals they are studying. In a corner the teacher and a small group of children are having an animated discussion about the painting *Peaceable Kingdom* by Edward Hicks, trying to decide which animals Hicks had actually seen and which ones he copied from other people's drawings and descriptions.

"Come see my paintings," a girl says to a visitor. "See, here's my rabbit. I'm doing a project on rabbits. See, I painted him curled up in his burrow. You can see inside, like it's been cut open, but he doesn't know it. I saw that in a book my teacher read us. Then I painted him running around looking for food. He's afraid of the owl in the tree because rabbits are the owl's prey. I used lots of dark colors because it's night. I wrote a poem about it. I just love workshop time. Come, come hear my rabbit poem!"

Introduction

INTEGRATING ART

In our culture we expend great energy on the mastery of linguistic skills and much less on the mastery of artistic ones. Children's cognitive functioning is assessed mainly through intelligence and achievement tests, which focus on linguistic skills. The most common teaching style is highly verbal in format. Instead of seeing art as a complementary symbol system that can be used for recording, responding, and assessing knowledge in the same way that written and spoken language can, art is not systematically taught.

As we saw in Chapter 1, the language of art is too powerful to ignore or allow to languish on the sidelines of our children's education. It must be integrated into the mainstream of teaching. There are many different levels of art integration ranging from using art as a time filler, such as when teachers tell students who have finished their writing assignment to make a drawing to go with it, to focusing an entire unit of study around a carefully selected artwork. In this chapter we will examine the most effective ways to integrate art into daily instruction based on what we know about how the brain functions and in light of Howard Gardner's multiple intelligences theory. Then we will see how classroom teachers can improve learning in all areas by teaching with, through, and about art every day.

"Rabbits in Their Burrow."
Crayon and marker—Laurel, grade 3.

Thinking about Children's Art

How has this third grader represented in her drawing what she has learned about animal habitats? In what way has she shown that rabbits live in burrows?

Setting the Stage

WHAT IS INTEGRATED LEARNING?

"Let the main ideas which are introduced into a child's education be few and important, and let them be thrown into every combination possible," wrote Alfred North Whitehead (1929, p. 2). From the work of Whitehead and John Dewey (1958) to the current trends in thematic teaching, the interconnection of all learning has been a recurring theme in education. Integration of subject matter and concepts is not a new idea but one that has occupied curriculum designers throughout this century. Tried in many different forms, integrated learning curricula have been presented as interdisciplinary learning, integrated unit design, thematic teaching, the project approach, literature-based instruction, and whole language. New thinking about intelligence and how the brain processes information has given further support to the integration of art and all learning in the classroom.

Brain-Based Learning

The brain is designed for learning. Infants are born ready to make sense of the world in which they find themselves. From the beginning the brain absorbs sensory and spatial information. During childhood the connections multiply like the spreading branches of a tree so that by adulthood the connections in the brain number over one hundred trillion (Johnson, 1991). "Our propensity to be active learners and interpreters of our experience—our drive to understand—is a powerful one," says Bruer (1994, p. 277).

Effective teaching strategies activate the brain to learn. Using the language of art is a powerful way to accomplish this:

Use art to stimulate the brain. Because the brain is survival oriented, it is attracted to changes in the environment. Each experience is embedded in a context of events and sensations, which are received on both conscious and unconscious levels. Familiar situations are registered automatically with minimal processing and leave a feeling of comfort or, if too bland, boredom. Lack of stimulation can actually affect how children's brains develop (Caine & Caine, 1991). Unusual events, on the other hand, inspire curiosity and excitement.

Wake up students' brains by incorporating art in the classroom. Hang intriguing artwork on the walls, display sensory-rich materials and objects, and incorporate hands-on art activities into passive, monotonous lessons to make students more alert and ready to learn. "[E]nthusiastic involvement," the Caines remind us, "is essential to most learning" (1991, p. 57).

Use art to create a conducive learning environment. The brain never has the chance to focus on just one bit of information at a time.

What Do You Think?

How important is art in your life? Can you remember an occasion when art made you think about something in a new way? Do you think it is important for children to think artistically every day?

It is constantly monitoring body functions, emotional state, and a wealth of sensory input. All this information is processed and interconnected to all our experiences. Physical well-being, biological drives, and emotions also play an important role in how we learn (Goleman, 1995). These states will affect how we can teach students and what they will remember. Stress and threat can flood the brain with harmful chemicals that reduce students' capacity to learn complex concepts. Exercise, relaxation, and curiosity promote optimal brain functioning (Hart, 1983).

A classroom environment that allows for physical movement, that is stress free, and that excites the imagination will activate the learning process in young brains. Kneading clay, swirling a paintbrush, and rubbing a print provide opportunities for purposeful physical movement and relaxation. Exploring art materials can be a pleasurable experience that has the potential to tap into brain chemicals such as dopamine, which is associated with pleasure, and endorphin, which heightens attention. Learning centered around themes or ideas that elicit deep feelings can also invoke the emotions and activate learning.

Use art to activate long-term memory. There are three different kinds of memory: *short-term,* or working, memory, plus two types of long-term memory: *taxon* and *spatial.* Short-term information is held in the brain for a few seconds, just long enough for us to notice and step over a bump in the sidewalk or brush our hair out of our eyes.

Taxon memory is built up by rehearsal and repetition; we use it to remember street addresses, phone numbers, and how to drive. Once set, these memories are difficult to change, but lack of use often causes them to fade. This kind of memory is illustrated by the difficulty of trying to remember a new phone number. The memories in the taxon system are highly organized and habit-like and include skills such as spelling and multiplication tables.

The spatial memory, on the other hand, is relational, quick, open ended, and flexible. It is more like a map. Long-term memories are formed almost instantly when our brain places them on a map of interconnected memories. For example, if a new store opens in the neighborhood, in only one visit you can register its location, appearance, and products sold because the store fits into your memory's map of the neighborhood.

All three memory systems are essential for learning. Short-term memory controls immediate response, taxon memory allows us to develop skills, and spatial memory is for concepts. When all are activated, learning is at its peak. However, only a small amount of information can be held in short-term memory, and embedding information in the taxon memory takes time and repeated practice, and such information is often lost when not used regularly. It is the fast and flexible spatial memory that teachers must activate if they wish students to retain concepts and understandings learned in school throughout their lives.

Activating spatial memory means replacing worksheets and teacher talk with complex activities that expose students to subject matter in many different ways. Art, in concert with all the ways of knowing, can be incorporated as another way to record data and express ideas. In school this kind of memory is activated through hands-on experience and sensory input such as in illustrating stories, making masks, and performing in a drama, looking at or creating art, and drawing sketches of science observations.

Use art and language together. Long-term memory constantly forms and reforms interconnections with incoming data, and every piece of information influences every other piece. "[T]he content of brain activity," writes Steven Pinker, "lies in the patterns of connections and patterns of activity among the neurons. Minute differences in the details of the connections may cause similar-looking brain patches to implement very different programs" (1997, p. 25). Throughout life, knowledge develops through the creation of relationships and patterns. "The brain," write the Caines, "is both artist and scientist, attempting to discern and understand patterns as they occur and giving expression to unique and creative patterns of its own" (1991, p. 81). The ideal teaching process, therefore, is to present lessons in a way that allows the brain to create meaningful networks of relationships that form patterns.

One way to enhance learning patterns is by combining visual and verbal learning. Research has shown that verbal information and visual/spatial information are stored in different ways by the brain and when used in combination form a potent memory aid. Children, for example, learn to read concrete words that can be visualized, such as *duck* and *tree,* quicker and remember them longer than abstract words, such as *legal* or *sensible.* Foreign-language students learn words that they hear, say, and act out better than those they only write or hear the teacher say (Neisser, 1982). Students who take notes by

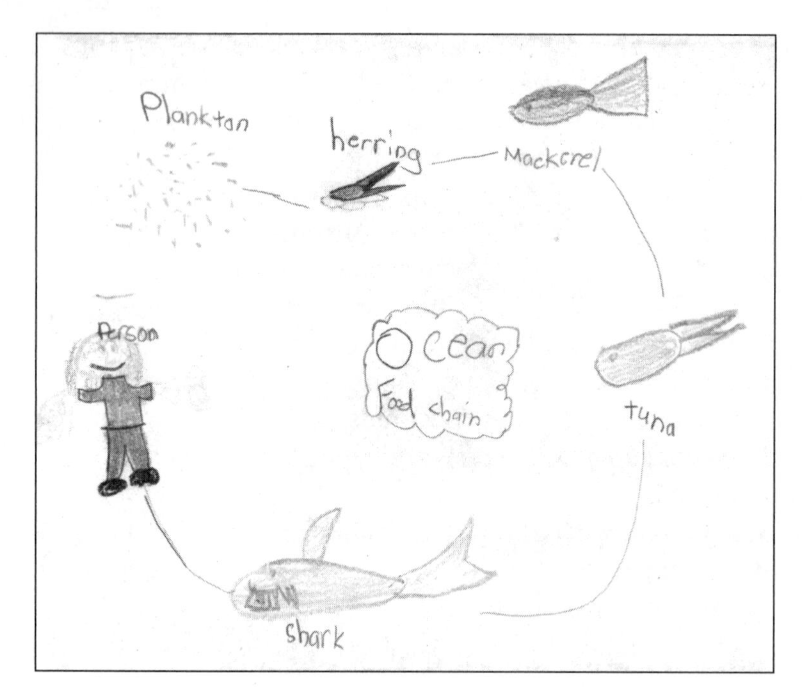

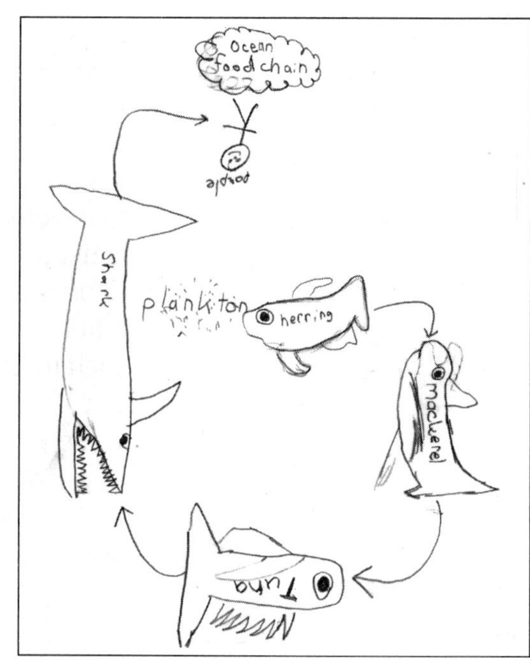

"Ocean Food Chains."
Crayon and pencil—Kate, grade 2 (*left*).
Pencil—Ryan, grade 2 (*right*).

Thinking about Children's Art

As part of a thematic unit focused on life in the oceans, children were asked to create a picture of an ocean food chain. How has creating these diagrams helped them to think more deeply about the concept? What artistic decisions did they make in designing their pictures?

drawing and using graphic symbols in conjunction with writing will remember that information better. The addition of color, texture, and dimension flesh out concepts.

Use art to build on personal experience. Nothing is learned in isolation; past experiences combine with current learning to form new and unique understandings for that individual (Frazee & Rudnitski, 1995). Nelson (in Perkins & Salomon, 1989), for example, found that during museum visits, when mothers pointed out previous, related personal experiences to their children at each display, those children remembered much more about the visit than others whose parent only discussed factual information. The mothers had in fact helped their children build their own personal connections.

Too often there is such a rush to cover new material or provide exciting new experiences that children have no time to build the mental connections that will establish the new learning in long-term memory. We should never assume that if we cover a topic, the child has learned it. Previously learned information must be integrated into every lesson. Children are not passive participants in the learning process. They must be involved in rich, experience-based conversation with the teacher for learning to be successful. It becomes the teacher's job to design instruction that will allow children to connect their past learning with the new. The effective teacher recognizes that no one method of teaching will reach every student every time. Art also offers an alternative way to reach students who do not always respond to the traditional verbal-mathematical approach.

The Theory of Multiple Intelligences

The theory of multiple intelligences also provides strong support for art integration. Howard Gardner (1983, 1991, 1993) has challenged our view of the pre-eminence of verbal skill as the dominant method of teaching and learning. His theory of multiple intelligences provides a more complex view of how people think and learn. Gardner's intelligences, divided into eight domains, represent the biological and psychological potentials within each individual. These eight domains are based on research in human development, work with the breakdown in cognitive skills following brain injury, and a wide variety of psychological tests. Gardner defines these intelligences as being universal to humankind, involving "the ability to solve problems or fashion products that are of consequence in a particular cultural setting or community" (1991, p. 14). By identifying distinct but interlocking intellectual capacities or intelligences, Gardner has reminded us of the breadth of human potential and the many ways that children learn (see At a Glance 2.1).

Implications of Multiple Intelligences Theory

Seeing intelligence as a broad spectrum of abilities rather than only as verbal and mathematical ability enriches our understanding of human potential. As Gardner points out, what is seen as intelligent behavior will vary with the situation in which one finds oneself. Having all the abilities of a rocket scientist will not help a person survive in the middle of the rain forest, even though the Yanomami do so every day. Accepting the idea that intelligence is multidimensional allows teachers to honor the special abilities of every child. David Lazear (1994) summarizes this broadened view of intelligence as follows:

- *Intelligence is not fixed.* Environmental, social, and cultural factors influence the development of skill in the different domains. A child born in a culture that has no written language does not learn how to write and thus will never be a great writer. However, that does not mean the potential was not there. If later that child learns a written language, becoming a successful writer is a possibility. Gardner believes that there may be some upper genetic limit to potential but that it is rarely ever reached because of cultural or experiential limitations (1993, p. 47).
- *Intelligence can be enhanced.* Because there is a neurological base to intelligence, skill in any domain of learning can be improved

At a Glance 2.1

Gardner's Multiple Intelligences

- *Linguistic Intelligence.* The ability to manipulate the symbols of language. Strength in this intelligence is manifested in the work of writers, poets, orators, editors, and politicians.
- *Logical-Mathematical Intelligence.* The ability to manipulate numerical patterns and concepts. Strength in this intelligence is manifested in the work of engineers, scientists, lawyers, and mathematicians.
- *Visual-Spatial Intelligence.* The ability to visualize the configuration of objects in space. Strength in this intelligence is manifested in the work of architects, painters, navigators, map makers, chess players, and sculptors.
- *Musical Intelligence.* The ability to manipulate rhythm and sound. Strength in this intelligence is manifested in the work of singers, instrumentalists, and composers.
- *Bodily-Kinesthetic Intelligence.* The ability to use the body to solve problems or to make things. Strength in this intelligence is manifested in the work of athletes, truck drivers, dancers, surgeons, artists, and mechanics.
- *Interpersonal Intelligence.* The ability to understand and work with others. Strength in this intelligence is manifested in the work of teachers, ministers, nurses, and managers.
- *Intrapersonal Intelligence.* The ability to understand oneself. Strength in this intelligence is manifested in the work of philosophers, mystics, and counselors.
- *Naturalist Intelligence.* The ability to sense and make use of important distinctions in the natural world such as identifying flora and fauna and being sensitive to animal behavior. Strength in this intelligence is manifested in environmentalists, botanists, conservationists, herbalists, and farmers.

through experience and practice. Research shows that learning actually physically changes the brain. Nutrition, aging, even exercise have been shown to affect brain function. The brains of rats raised in enriched environments are larger and contain more cells than those of rats from impoverished environments (Bower, 1999).

- *Intelligence is a multidimensional phenomenon.* There is not one way of knowing but many, and each person has unique strengths and preferences. "[E]ducators," writes Howard Gardner, "need to take into account the differences among minds and, as far as possible, fashion an education that can reach the infinite variety of students" (1999, p. 186).

Is There an Artistic Intelligence?

Although one might assume there is an artistic intelligence, Gardner (1993) believes that all the intelligences he has identified can be used for either artistic or nonartistic purposes. How an intelligence is used seems to depend upon a combination of individual choice and cultural factors. The linguistic intelligence, for example, can be used to write a grocery list or to compose a poem. The spatial intelligence can produce a sculpture or a map. For this reason the language of art should be especially valued, because it can be a way to communicate ideas from so many intellectual domains. In turn the creation of visual art often requires abilities that draw on several of the intelligences. To produce a painting artists must draw not only on the perceptual skills of the visual-spatial domain but also on the bodily-kinesthetic domain for the physical skills needed to control the tools, and on the logical-mathematical domain in order to sequence and create patterns in the artwork. Art crosses and links the intelligences in ways that should give it a preeminent role in our educational system.

Why . . . ?

WHY INTEGRATE LEARNING?

Integrated learning builds on the brain's propensity to find connections and thereby facilitates student learning for the following reasons:

- *Content connects.* Subject matter from across disciplines is presented in a connected way. An artwork, for example, may illustrate an event under discussion in social studies. Exploring Navajo rug weaving techniques may not only develop weaving skills but also help students better understand the significance of weaving in the story *Annie and the Old One* by Miska Miles (1972, New York: Little Brown).
- *Different tasks tap multiple intelligences.* It is difficult to isolate and assess just one intelligence, because in actual learning activities several domains are activated. For example, to illustrate a story students must use the linguistic intelligence to read it, the spatial intelligence to visualize the illustration, and the kinesthetic intelligence to manipulate the pencil. In addition the student may draw on the intrapersonal intelligence to discover personally meaningful visual symbols and the interpersonal intelligence as they share their ideas with others.
- *Multiple approaches activate the senses.* Each discipline has its own skills and format. When we integrate studies, we must present information in many different ways. Second graders studying ants may observe ants on the playground, graph the number of ants seen, read stories about ants, use magnifiers to identify the body parts of ants, sing about ants, draw pictures of ants, and write ant poems. These activities activate the senses physically, visually, auditorially, spatially, verbally, and mathematically (see At a Glance 2.2).

At a Glance 2.2

Learning Activities Grouped by Multiple Intelligences

In designing lessons make sure to include activities that incorporate as many of the different intelligences as possible. This does not mean that every activity must include them all but that in the context of the school day you should tap into all the eight intelligences in some way.

Verbal/Linguistic Activities

- Tell
- Read
- Retell
- Write
- Explore sound-symbol-word connections
- Do word analysis
- Build vocabulary

Logical/Mathematical Activities

- Manipulate numbers and symbols
- Calculate
- Measure
- Sort and group
- Sequence
- Compare and contrast
- Find and make patterns
- Chart, list, and outline
- Make and use graphic organizers
- Solve problems using information and logic

Intrapersonal Activities

- Care for oneself and one's belongings
- Respond personally to stimuli
- Express thoughts and feelings
- Record thoughts and feelings
- Control and analyze thoughts, feelings, and actions
- Evaluate and praise oneself

Interpersonal Activities

- Share
- Work in cooperative groups
- Give and receive feedback
- Interview and question others
- Practice conflict management skills
- Identify similarities and differences in others
- Create and follow rules

Visual/Spatial Activities

- Find and identify visual and spatial elements in nature and art
- Visualize ideas and thoughts
- Create two- and three-dimensional artworks (draw, paint, sculpt, etc.)
- Solve visual and spatial problems
- Design maps, graphs, and models

Musical/Rhythmic Activities

- Listen to sounds, rhythms, and songs
- Create sound, rhythms, rhymes, and musical pieces
- Use and identify musical and rhythmic elements
- Clap, chant, and sing
- Play musical instruments

Bodily/Kinesthetic Activities	
Use all the senses	Mime
Exercise the entire body	Dramatize
Play sports and games	Use tools in art, instruments in music, pen in writing, etc.
Move and dance	
Naturalistic Activities	
Observe natural objects and events	Group, classify, and identify natural objects
Collect natural objects	

Guiding Ideas

LEARNING WITH, THROUGH, AND ABOUT ART

The evidence for integrating art into daily instruction is compelling. It seems an ideal vehicle through which students can build relationships and connect what they are learning. The potential for art to motivate and excite learners and to make learning come alive is limited only by the teacher's imagination and will. Teachers can incorporate art into daily instruction by carefully selecting artworks, art media, and art techniques that correlate with and enhance what students are learning in other subject areas. With thoughtful planning, teachers can teach their students how to think as artists.

Researchers have identified three ways to use art in integrated teaching (Dobbs, 1997; Goldberg, 1997):

1. *Learning with art.* Art can be a vehicle for studying other subjects. For example, a fourth-grade math class studying the characteristics of geometric shapes and the calculation of perimeter and area might begin by identifying shapes in a reproduction of an artwork such as Piet Mondrian's *Diamond Painting in Red, Yellow and Blue* and then follow up by determining the perimeter and area of some of the shapes.
2. *Learning through art.* Students can use art to express what they are thinking about and what they have learned. The fourth-grade geometry class mentioned in item 1 is in the middle of a thematic unit called "Structures for Living." Students could record what they are learning about geometry in their journals in the form of labeled diagrams. Teachers could then challenge them to apply this information as they study the shelters that animals and people construct for protection from the environment. Then, after studying the architecture of Frank Lloyd Wright, they could develop plans for a dream house to fit a particular environment, for which they calculate perimeter and living areas.

What the Experts Say

Integrating Learning

Children are not ready to encounter the world in the form of an endless succession of isolated entities; as their fantasizing and myth-making activities suggest, they seek a comprehensive vision of reality.
Edmund Burke Feldman (1981, p. 85)

There is very little worth teaching that cannot be told through the arts or that can be adequately conveyed without the arts. The arts can be the prime vehicle for general education or can be integrated with other fields so as to be pervasive. It is difficult to identify among our several arbitrary categories of knowledge a better medium for general liberal education at all levels than the arts.
Jerome J. Hausman (1980, p. 15)

We live within a separate subject, discipline-oriented conception of education. . . . Possibilities for multiple intelligences force us to face a crossroads.
Craig Kridel (1990, p. 86)

3. *Learning about art.* Learning *with* and *through* art depends on knowing *about* the media, methods, processes, and concepts of the discipline of art as well as developing skill in talking about, responding to, analyzing, and creating art. Lessons must allow students to explore, practice, and apply the content of art. The fourth-grade geometry students looking at Mondrian's painting will be better able to describe what they see if they have had many opportunities to look at various artworks and develop a vocabulary of art. They will be less frustrated and more satisfied with their dream-house constructions if they have had many experiences using the chosen art materials and know how to apply design principles.

Learning with Art

There are many ways teachers can relate artistic learning to their particular subject matter. No matter what the subject matter, the language of art can enhance presentation and instruction. Integrating art into daily lessons broadens the range of responses students must make. It may seem easier to give students worksheets with photocopied maps, graphs, or diagrams. Requiring students to draw their own may be more time-consuming; the results may not be as uniform, and students may need instruction in how to proceed in the beginning. The end result, however, will help them remember more and think more deeply about what the teacher wants them to learn.

Ways to teach with art in any classroom. At the primary level the majority of students spend most of their time with one teacher.

Piet Mondrian. Tableau No. IV: Lozenge Composition with Red, Gray, Blue, Yellow, and Black, *1924/25.* National Gallery of Art. Gift of Herbert and Nannette Rothschild.

From the Museum

Piet Mondrian (Dutch, 1872–1944) based many of his artworks on straight lines and primary colors arranged in perfect balance. He wanted to create an objective style of art which would reflect the order found in the universe. How does this approach to art relate to mathematical thinking? How could you build connections between Mondrian's work and the mathematical concepts children need to learn?

Their classroom teacher becomes one of the most important role models in their lives. Children who are fortunate enough to have a teacher who values art and makes a place for it in the classroom on a daily basis will learn far more about what it means to be an artist and to think artistically than they would from an occasional art lesson. At the same time, by fostering the transformation of learning from one symbol system to another, the teacher provides the students with a deeper, more complete level of understanding.

At the upper elementary levels students often work with a core of teachers who teach specialized subject areas, such as science, math, social studies, and language arts. Applying the language of art in all these disciplines is essential for the development of artistic confidence and the ability to express and understand complex ideas.

There are many ways to incorporate art into the self-contained classroom and into teaching concepts in other disciplines, such as the following:

- *Interweave artworks into lessons.* Exhibit and discuss examples of artwork to illustrate concepts in the field.
- *Use visual tools.* Use graphic organizers, webs, and maps to visually represent the relationship between ideas.
- *Record ideas graphically.* Student notebooks, classwork, and tests can be set up so that notes and ideas are recorded both in words and in graphic symbols.
- *Create an aesthetic learning environment.* Classrooms can offer an aesthetically pleasing environment that provides subject-related sensory stimulation and features displays of related artworks.

Integrating art into specific subjects. There are also many ways to relate art to particular subject matter. A few examples are provided here, with many more offered throughout this book:

- *Math:* Art, for example, can effectively illustrate math concepts. Instead of coloring worksheets showing six objects, first graders can draw their own six objects. Third graders can use pictures as well as words and numbers to explain how they solved a multiplication problem. Middle-level students can write illustrated math stories that show their understanding of a concept. The Math/Art Project (MAP) integrated geometric math concepts and art approaches, which resulted in better achievement on district math tests especially for female and African-American students (East Carolina University, 1997).
- *Science:* In science class students can draw diagrams and pictures as well as write descriptions in response to scientific observations and demonstrations, bringing the power of art and language to the understanding of scientific concepts. Keeping a nature sketchbook can help students see the detail in the design and structure of the

"UFOs." Laura, grade 5.

Thinking about Children's Art

This fifth-grade student's science project combines many different approaches to learning. As part of the project she has built an electromagnet, written a report about the search for extraterrestrials, and created a visual display. How has art been used to enhance and communicate about her work? What kind of lesson planning is needed to enable children to use art in this way?

natural world. Making three-dimensional models can help students visualize many scientific concepts.

- *Social studies:* Since the days of progressive education, art has always played a role in the teaching of social studies. Constructing dioramas, maps, and models all help children learn more about the history and cultures they are studying. Cultures of the past speak to students through their arts. For example, grinding pigments and mixing their own paints enables students to better appreciate Paleolithic cave art. Digging and preparing clay introduces the discoveries of the Neolithic era. Students at all levels will gain greater understanding of historical concepts by creating illustrated timelines and maps and using color, drawings, and visual webs in their note taking.
- *Language arts:* Nowhere in the curriculum is the relationship between two disciplines closer than in language arts and art. From the primary grades, where the picture precedes the writing of a story, to the middle-school years, where the writing elicits the illustration, art is an integral part of language arts activities. Art is most effectively integrated into language arts when students participate in a combined writing/art workshop (see Chapter 8). But even when taught separately art is an important part of language instruction.

Teaching in Action

Drawing on the Story

Phyllis Whitin (1996) describes how the realization that feelings and themes could be expressed as colors, shapes, and symbols transformed how she taught literature. She found the following benefits to having students draw as well as write responses to literature they had read:

- Sketching gave visual form to ideas that were impossible to describe in writing. Drawing and writing each have their own unique perspectives.
- Students having difficulty writing can use sketches as a "tool for seeing the whole" (p. 13).
- Discussing sketches and students' choices of symbols and colors helped expand the whole group's experience of their reading.

Introducing Whitin's "Sketch to Stretch" method:

- Read aloud a short story or chapter from a book that evokes a strong reaction associated with it.
- Introduce colors, shapes, and symbols as tools to represent ideas. For example, if the story is sad, ask what color shows sadness. Have students suggest other colors. Emphasize that there are many possible choices; the important thing is to have a reason for one's choice.
- Continue by having students suggest shapes and symbols for a single idea, such as a turned-down mouth or a cracked glass.
- Have students make a sketch reflecting their ideas and feelings about the story.
- Share the sketches in small groups and then with the class, drawing out insights into the meaning of the story.

At all levels students need opportunities to study the illustrations in books and discuss the relationship between the word on the page and the artist's visual conception. Students need to use their art skills to illustrate their original stories and poems and to design sets for dramatic productions and skits. Students can also dissect and analyze the persuasive combination of art and writing found in posters and advertisements.

Learning through Art

Learning through art means challenging students to reveal what they are learning through artistic expression. Lessons that incorporate learning through art ask students to respond to the subject under discussion using the language of art. Art becomes an integral way that students make sense of what they experience and allows them to apply their understandings through artistic forms.

Learning through art means that educators see art as a valuable way to explore experiences, communicate ideas, and evaluate what

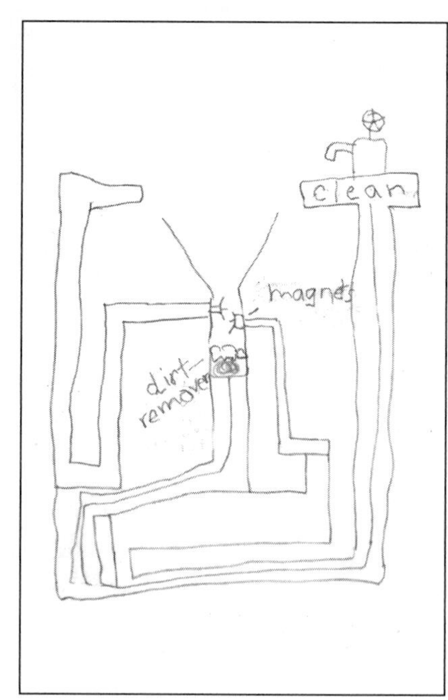

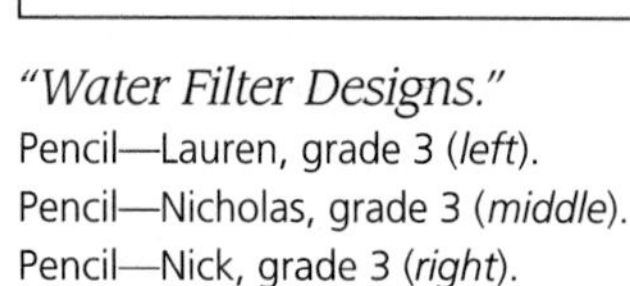
"Water Filter Designs."
Pencil—Lauren, grade 3 (*left*).
Pencil—Nicholas, grade 3 (*middle*).
Pencil—Nick, grade 3 (*right*).

Thinking about Children's Art

As part of a thematic unit focused on water and following a science experiment in which students worked in groups to build water filters from funnels, cotton, gravel, and other materials, students were asked to draw their own design for a water filter in their journals. What drawing challenges does this assignment present to them? What have the students learned about filtering water? How has this drawing assignment prepared them for an upcoming field trip to a sewage treatment plant?

knowledge the students are acquiring. Although teachers can do this on a small scale by incorporating into a math or social studies lesson a "related" art activity, as in the example cited in "Drawing a Story," there is a tendency for them to allow the art part of the lesson to become a tag on, less valued than the main focus of the lesson. An even more effective way to incorporate art as a communication medium on an equal basis with the other domains of learning is to unify the concepts and information to be taught using a thematic or project approach.

Thematic teaching. In designing thematic instruction, teachers select a major theme around which they build all instruction. This approach allows them to seamlessly integrate art into ongoing or state-specified studies in social studies, language arts, mathematics, and the sciences and draws on all the multiple intelligences. Because it will be the main focus of student learning for a significant length of instructional time, it is important that the theme selected be relevant to the students'

Teacher Tip

Choosing a Theme

The following questions will help in selecting a broad-based, meaningful theme that encompasses all the disciplines of learning:

- Does the theme address basic questions about our interrelatedness with the world?
- Will it inspire and challenge the students?
- Does it match the students' interests, abilities, and skills?
- Will it allow students to do "real" research? (That is, can they do direct observation, interview experts, read firsthand sources, conduct actual experiments, etc.?)
- Does it allow students to use the practices of the different disciplines to reach an understanding? (That is, can they look at the question as a scientist, a poet, a historian, a musician, a social scientist, an artist, etc.?)

lives and experiences. Appropriate themes according to the Caines should "invoke emotions, provide a personal challenge, and stir the imagination" (1991, p. 112). When teachers select themes thoughtfully, art fits in smoothly.

The theme should be an overarching, general question or metaphor that ties subjects together in deep and meaningful ways. For example, a second-grade thematic unit "Life is a Celebration" can incorporate the study of personal traditions, family customs, ethnic art forms, individual self-fulfillment, and cultural rituals in a way that a unit focusing just on the topic of "Holidays around the World" could not. In making their selection teachers need to ask themselves if the theme selected will be broad enough to include the concepts to be taught but still relevant to the students' lives beyond the classroom. At a Glance 2.3 provides examples of themes that can be expanded into rich, meaningful units.

During the thematic study teachers select and incorporate skills and information from all subject areas that relate to the theme and that allow students to develop an integrated view of the topics and concepts (see At a Glance 2.4). Visual artworks and art media to be studied during thematic teaching are selected on the basis of how they relate to and enhance the theme.

In thematic teaching art should be an important vehicle of communication. Students must record what they are learning so they can share it. Making sketches during the experiences, drawing plans, and creating visuals to show to the class can all be important ways art links together parts of a thematic unit.

At a Glance 2.3

Some Themes for Integrated Teaching: Questions and Metaphors

A world of dreams
Above and below
Across a continent
Art of persuasion
At the crossroads
Becoming a writer
Building and breaking
Building character
Can we make a better world?
Causes and effects
Deep down underground
Exploring new worlds
Facing fear
From farm to market
From friend to friend
From hand to hand: helping others
Hanging in balance
How do living things survive?
Images from the past
In the footprints of the dinosaurs
Inventing change
It's a mystery
Looking closely
Life is a celebration
Living in peace
Mapping the way
Making memories
Masks and mysteries
Messages from the past
Microscopic views
Playing with form
Sending messages
Seeing with artist's eyes
Taking command: Who is a leader?
Taking flight
Taking risks
Taking sides
Tracking time
Through the lens
Visions of our world
Water for life
Water world
We are all connected
We are what we eat
What is a family?
What makes a hero?
What does the future hold for us?
What is the relationship between animals and people?
What is the relationship between plants and people?
What's out there in space?
Where in the world are we?
Who am I?
Who is an American?
Window into the past
Worlds of the imagination

Project-based learning. Project-based learning is another way that art can be integrated into the curriculum. Unlike a thematic unit, this approach begins at the ground level with a topic that is familiar and important in the lives of the students. From this, learning then expands across disciplines as students build a foundation of skills, knowledge, and concepts (Katz & Chard, 1991). For example, a second-grade class might begin by talking about what they ate for breakfast. This can expand into how the different foods they eat are grown and delivered to their breakfast table, which introduces students to farming, transportation, and distribution systems. A fifth-grade class might begin by talking about their experiences with lakes and ponds. This can develop into a detailed study of why the pond

At a Glance 2.4

Building a Thematic Unit

Theme: A broad question that connects the topics to our interrelationship with the world.
Example: What is the role of trees and their products in our lives?

Topics: Discrete subjects that relate to the everyday experiences of the students.
Example: Trees in our neighborhood; wood products in the classroom.

Concepts: Patterns, causes and effects, and other relationships derived from facts, information, and skill application.
Example: Concepts about trees such as oxygen and water cycles, importance of forest products, deforestation.

Facts and Information: Verifiable knowledge gained from a variety of sources such as books, observations, experiments, and experience.
Example: Kinds of trees, growth patterns, lumber industry and statistics, reforestation projects, wood and uses of in buildings, furniture, paper making, everyday objects, and sculpture.

Skills: Processes and techniques for acquiring and applying information.
Example: Dating trees using tree ring analysis, classifying trees by leaf structures, conserving wood through architectural planning.

Teaching in Action

Sample Fifth-Grade Thematic Plan

Art Connection
Topic: Wood and Paper
Concepts: Role of wood and paper in artwork; importance of recycling paper
Facts and Information: History of paper making, kinds of paper and wood, featured artists: Romare Bearden, Marisol, Pablo Picasso
Skills: Making and using recycled paper and wood to create original artworks such as paper collages and wood sculptures

Movement and Dance Connection
Topic: Dances of the lumber camps
Concepts: Role of dance in world of work
Facts and Information: Life in a lumber camp
Skills: Identifying dance patterns and using them to create original dances

Music Connection
Topic: Songs of the lumber camps
Concepts: Use of song to express concerns and joys about work
Facts and Information: European roots of traditional Canadian and American work songs
Skills: Identifying melody patterns and using them to compose original work songs

Significant Thematic Question
What is the interrelationship between trees and people?

Literary Connections
Topic: Trees in literature
Concept: Role of descriptive language and personification in creating mood and meaning
Facts and Information: Tree names and terminology, poetry, and stories about trees
Skills: Identifying adjectives and descriptive phrases, writing poetry and stories

Scientific Connections
Topic: Life cycle and classification of trees
Concept: Role of trees in water and oxygen cycles, and habitat creation
Facts and Information: Classification system, transpiration, animal habitats
Skills: Identifying trees by leaf and form, measuring tree ring growth, calculating transpiration.

Mathematical Connections
Topic: Statistics
Concept: Statistical relationships
Facts and Information: Kinds of graphs and statistical analyses
Skills: Reading and constructing graphs

Historical and Social Connections
Topic: Our forest resources—uses and abuses
Concept: Patterns of use directly affect forest growth
Facts and Information: Location and uses of forest regions of the world, history of paper industry
Skills: Reading for information, mapping, analyzing causes and effects

"Rainforest." Crayon—Heather, Kate, Johnny, and Philip, grade 2.

Thinking about Children's Art

As part of a thematic study of Living on the Earth, second graders worked in cooperative groups to show the animals that live in the earth's different biomes. This group created a picture of the rainforest with its great diversity of life. Each student read books about the rainforest and wrote down the names of animals found there. Then they each contributed some animals to the picture. How have they combined words and visual images? What might be a good follow-up activity?

near their school is polluted and how this affects local wildlife, in the process of which students discover the water cycle and the importance of water for life.

Sylvia Chard (1999) suggests that the best project topics are those about which everyone in the group, teacher included, can share a story or personal experience. For example, most children can tell stories about their shoes, hats, house, pets, or going shopping.

- *Building bridges:* The first week focuses on memories and draws students in by tapping into what they already know. Initial whole-group discussions allow for the teacher and students to share a story or experience that relates to the topic. The students then draw pictures about the topic from memory and brainstorm related words and questions. During this time the teacher assesses what the students seem to already know and what misunderstandings and questions they have.
- *Fieldwork:* This is followed by what Chard calls *fieldwork,* during which students are immersed in real-life, topic-related experiences. Depending on the topic, these experiences can take many forms: a walk in the community, participation in an ethnic festival, a trip to a museum or botanical garden, or a visit from circus performers. Each experience uses all of the approaches to learning. Students studying shoes might visit a shoe store, interview the salespeople, make drawings of the store, map the location of the shoes, and write reports about their trip. Each day they might draw pictures of their own shoes from direct observation and create graphs of the kinds of shoes they and their classmates wear.
- *Small group work:* During the study teachers elicit from the students questions about things that interested them or that they wondered about. Based on these interests and questions teachers bring in related materials and activities to explore. As students and teachers interact during these explorations, topics of specific interest will emerge. Groups or individuals may become interested in one facet of the experience or another. These students develop in-depth investigative projects, which are then shared with the whole class.
- *Including art:* In the project approach art is seen as an important way for students to record information and explore ideas. Children record their memories through drawings. In fieldwork they capture their observations in sketchbooks and journals. Teachers choose artworks to be studied based on the students' interests and explorations. For example, if the students are researching and sketching the birds that visit the class bird feeder, then teachers could introduce the art and life story of John Audubon.

Learning about Art

It is not enough, however, to expect that students will use art meaningfully and creatively to express what they are learning without direct instruction in those concepts and skills that apply uniquely to art. Integrating art requires that students also learn about art: its history, principles, vocabulary, techniques, and methods. Although students benefit greatly from looking at and talking about a particular artwork, the experience becomes even more meaningful when they have the

Art and the project approach "Memory drawing: My favorite tree."
Marker—Laurel, grade 3 (*left*).
"Observation drawing: Trees in the park."
Charcoal—Laurel, grade 3 (*right*).

Thinking about Children's Art

As part of a project on trees, third graders were asked to draw a picture of their favorite tree from memory. Then they went to the park and made sketches directly. Compare this student's memory drawing with the observational drawing. What differences do you see? What has this student learned about the structure of trees? Why is it important for children to draw both from memory and from actual experience?

opportunity to physically explore the ideas, media, and techniques of the artist. It is one thing to say that an artist has painted a picture of a flower and quite another to compare the artwork to one's own experiences of manipulating a paintbrush, mixing colors, and making design decisions. Therefore it is important to accompany the presentation of a featured artwork with related hands-on art production.

Based on his theory and his observations of how art has traditionally been taught, Howard Gardner has suggested the following guidelines for teaching about art (1993, pp. 141–153):

Making art is essential at the elementary level. At ages ten or less, essentially the elementary years, making art should be central to the study of art. Hands-on approaches and direct experience solving artistic problems are essential for coming to understand artistic thinking. Every classroom should be equipped with high-quality, beautifully organized art supplies, and sufficient time should be provided for students to work on artistic projects. Chapter 8 provides information on how to select, arrange, and manage art production in the classroom.

Teaching in Action

Sample Second-Grade Project: Trees

Week 1: Building Bridges from Memories

- *Discussion:* Do you have a favorite tree or a story about a tree to tell us?
- *Journal:* Write about a special tree.
- *Art:* Draw a picture of a special tree.
- *Drama/Movement:* Act out your experience with a tree.

Week 2: Fieldwork

- *Field trips:* Walk in the woods, visit lumber yard.
- *Observation:* Drawings and writing about trees in "Tree Journals," sketches of woods and lumber yard.
- *Math:* Count and graph wood products in the classroom and at home. Explore how wood is measured and sold in lumber yards.
- *Research:* Where do wood products (furniture, paper, pencils, etc.) come from?
- *Interview:* Invite people who work with wood to visit the class—a carpenter, wood sculptor, handmade-paper artist, collage artist, furniture salesperson, lumber mill worker.
- *Art:* Explore wood and paper by making sculptures and collages.
- *Literature:* Read stories, poems, and nonfiction works that provide information on trees.

Weeks 3 and 4: Small Group Projects

Students break into small groups based on their interests and investigate a particular facet of the topic. For example, one group might identify and map the trees that grow around the school, another might make a leaf collection book, a third might build a model of a lumberyard, and so on. During this time the teacher works closely with each group helping it formulate questions, find resources, and record its progress by taking notes and photographs. At regular intervals the groups share what they are doing with the whole class.

Week 5: Sharing

The unit culminates with a student-planned celebratory event that allows students to share what they have learned with each other and with their families. Art plays an important role as they design and prepare signs, posters, handouts, and room displays that explain their projects and document the process of learning (see Chapter 10). The teacher allows time for the students to summarize the major concepts they have discovered. For example, to culminate this tree project the students become a forest of talking trees. Students, dressed in tree costumes, take the role of a tree and share what they learned about the importance of trees. Some recite original stories and poems, sing songs, present skits, show their artwork, or take visitors on a tour of the displays. After the event the class meets as a group and writes a class book that explains why trees are important for life.

Children should study their own work first. Aesthetic activities—looking at, talking about, and analyzing art—should grow out of the children's own artwork and the problems they are trying to solve and slowly lead into the study of the artworks of others that they can relate to their own artistic experiences. Teachers should expect children to share their artwork with each other in a variety of ways, including with a small group, with the whole class, and in conferences with the teacher; these activities should precede and set the tone for the presentation of the featured artwork. Chapter 3 presents ways to create and share art from the very first day of school. During these sharing times teachers model and help students practice ways to look at and talk about art. Chapter 6 delves deeply into the language and structures of sharing and responding to students' art.

There should be a purpose to making art. Rather than a single art lesson, artistic learning should be organized around meaningful projects carried out over a period of time that allow for discussion and reflection. The integrative approaches presented in this chapter provide models of ways to make the creation of art an integral part of learning and thereby significant.

Art lessons should build on what students already know. Because artistic development requires continuing exposure to core concepts and recurrent problems, an art curriculum should spiral, returning to the same artistic ideas on a slightly more advanced level each year, rather than being designed sequentially. At a Glance 2.5 shows one possible continuum of art concepts and skills that might be found over the elementary grades. Students' experiences with art vary widely, however. It is the daily interaction between students and teachers that determines the level, sequence, and delivery format of the lessons presented. Educators must constantly ask, What have these students learned so far and what should they learn next? Based on this ongoing assessment they can then develop art lessons that will be personally meaningful for the students.

Individual schools and school districts can develop their own, more customized baseline grade-level charts by surveying each teacher in the school or district and establishing what is currently being taught. This way the schools and districts can discover the overlaps and discontinuities and address them so that a stronger, more focused art program results.

Art activities should be used to assess artistic growth. Assessments should be authentic and reflect the particular intelligences and developmental growth areas involved. At a Glance 2.6 provides one way to look at artistic learning. Teacher should assess art skill and knowledge through the language of art.

At a Glance 2.5

Sample Continuum of Art Skills

By the End of First Grade

Concepts

Sensory understanding
- Identify and sort materials using senses

Spatial understanding
- Know objects can be viewed from different sides

Art structures
- Recognize lines
- Name and identify the basic colors
- Recognize their light/dark variations
- Identify the basic geometric shapes

Art history
- Know art is created by different people to tell stories, express feelings and ideas

Art response
- Find the lines, colors, and shapes in an artwork
- Can express how an artwork makes them feel
- Can create visual images in response to an artwork

Creative problem solving
- Can solve a problem using past experience

Production
- Can use basic art media to express an idea or feeling

Skills (*Note:* These are just four of many possible media)

Drawing
- Can make a variety of lines by varying pressure or application methods
- Can draw basic shapes
- Can combine different shapes and lines to express an idea

Paper
- Can cut basic shapes without pre-drawn lines
- Can cut two shapes from a folded paper
- Can fold paper into halves and quarters
- Can accordion fold
- Apply proper amount of glue

Painting
- Can mix light and dark colors using black and white
- Can paint different lines using brush

Modeling
- Can roll clay into ropes using palms
- Can form spheres and cylinders
- Can join two pieces securely

By the End of Second Grade

Concepts

Sensory understanding
- Know the five senses and how to use them safely to explore the environment

Spatial understanding
- Know own position in relation to objects in environment
- Know that changing one's position does not change a work's physical structure but does change the sensory experience

Art structures
- Recognize and describe variations in lines, shapes, colors
- Identify textures and patterns
- Can name the basic three-dimensional forms
- Can differentiate two- and three-dimensional objects and artworks

Art history
- Know art has been made by different people from different places for different purposes
- Identify art that tells stories, expresses ideas and feelings, changes the environment, and is useful

Skills

Drawing
- Can draw a sequence of related drawings
- Uses overlap and position on paper to show depth
- Can draw simple figures in action

Paper
- Can cut complex shapes by moving paper or changing scissors direction
- Can fold paper multiple times and cut out symmetrical and duplicate shapes
- Can make simple three-dimensional forms from paper

Paint
- Can mix secondary colors
- Choose proper size brush for purpose
- Know many ways to apply paint with a brush

Modeling
- Can make cubes, cones, and rectangular forms
- Can combine forms to express an idea
- Can smooth surface to finish piece

By the End of Second Grade (cont.)

Concepts	Skills
Art response ■ Talk and write about artwork in terms of subject matter, color, line, shape, pattern, texture use, emotional response, and craftsmanship ■ Can compare two works on the basis of one or two elements ■ Can listen to and restate the opinion of another *Creative problem solving* ■ Can think of more than one way to solve a problem; know and accept that others may think of different ways *Production* ■ Choose a combination of line, color, shape, pattern, and texture that will reflect a special feeling or express a particular idea	

By the End of Third Grade

Concepts	Skills
Sensory understanding ■ Know that what they perceive is the result of careful observation using their senses *Spatial understanding* ■ Can conceptualize changes in viewpoint; identify top view, side view, inside, outside, worm's eye view, near, far, cross-section *Art structures* ■ Identify the elements used in an artwork and describe how they are arranged ■ Identify symmetrically balanced composition *Art history* ■ Know that artists at different times and places have used a variety of media and techniques for different purposes ■ Use art elements to describe art from other places *Art response* ■ Write and talk about the relationship of ideas with subject, media, and techniques chosen by the artist ■ Can compare artworks based on the way ideas are expressed ■ Can support an opinion with an example *Creative problem solving* ■ Can brainstorm many ideas to solve a problem, then select one that will lead to a successful solution *Production* ■ Can create works that express the same idea using different media and techniques	*Drawing* ■ Select line quality to match purpose ■ Combine overlap and placement to create depth ■ Draw combinations of figures to express ideas ■ Draw plans for work in other media *Paper* ■ Can cut a wide range of materials ■ Glue diverse forms and materials together securely ■ Know basic folding techniques ■ Have a repertoire of decorative paper techniques *Painting* ■ Mix a variety of colors by controlling the proportions added ■ Manipulate brush effectively to match purpose ■ Paint foreground and background ■ Create textural effects and patterns *Modeling* ■ Form a pinch pot with even thickness of sides ■ Use tools to create textures ■ Smooth away joint so it does not show

(continues)

At a Glance 2.5 continued

By the End of Fourth Grade

Concepts

Sensory understanding
- Know that observation skills can be intensified through concentration and exercise

Spatial understanding
- Know that two- and three-dimensional objects change appearance depending on point of view and that this effect can be exaggerated for aesthetic purposes

Art structures
- Know that colors vary in value and intensity and understand and use the color wheel; identify balanced compositions
- Recognize the symbolic use of the art element

Art history
- Can compare and contrast artworks from several different cultural groups including their own
- Explain differences in artwork based on the artist's purpose as reflected in the use of media and techniques

Art response
- Write and discuss how the use of art elements, media, and technique relate to the artist's purpose and the idea expressed
- Describe an artwork using art vocabulary
- Can restate another's opinion and compare it to their own

Creative problem solving
- When presented with a problem with specific limitations, can generate diverse solutions and then successfully create within the limitations

Production
- Create artworks independently using the artistic process
- Choose media, technique, and design to relate to intended purpose and meaning

Skills

Drawing
- Use changes in value and color to increase depth
- Use line quality to add meaning to work
- Plan relationship among figures
- Use foreground, background, overlap, and size differences to show depth
- Use contour drawing and gesture drawing techniques to record observations and ideas

Paper
- Can cut complex, detailed shapes
- Can create varied two- and three-dimensional effects that enhance ideas
- Use color, overlap, size, texture, and position to create contrasts

Painting
- Control a range of tints, shades, and neutrals
- Use color wheel to mix tertiary colors and create color schemes
- Can make colors dull using complements
- Choose paint application methods that relate to purpose
- Paint background first when appropriate
- Effectively combine paint with other media when appropriate
- Use and care for brushes appropriately

Modeling
- Can produce even thickness slabs
- Can use slabs to construct forms
- Consider design of all sides of work
- Know many surface treatments and joining methods

By the End of Fifth Grade

Concepts

Sensory understanding
- Know that visual perception is affected by many factors, such as background affects colors seen, odor intensifies reality of images, color of light affects perception of color, etc.
- Know the illusion of texture can be created on smooth surfaces and visual clues and experience tell one how it feels

Skills

Drawing
- Use positive and negative space to enhance quality of drawing
- Use proportion and position to create depth
- Use balance and variety in compositions
- Create textural effects
- Create drawings in preparation for major works

By the End of Fifth Grade (cont.)

Concepts

Spatial understanding

- Know the viewer's position affects the appearance of an object's shape and size and that three-dimensional objects can be represented on a two-dimensional surface using this quality

Art structures

- Identify balance and variety in designing compositions
- Identify positive and negative space in two- and three-dimensional work

Art history

- Can identify and categorize subjects, styles, and purposes of artists in their own culture and others

Art response

- Can explain in written, oral, or graphic form the meaning and purpose of an artwork with reference to the arrangement of visual elements and style
- Can evaluate an artwork based on how well its design and style reflect its purpose
- Can give several art-related reasons for an opinion

Creative problem solving

- When presented with a criteria-based problem and a choice of materials and techniques, can set own limits and successfully solve the problem

Production

- Produce meaningful artworks that reflect thoughtful selections of style, technique, and materials

Skills

Paper

- Know a variety of ways to create particular papers for specific effects
- Can score and fold paper
- Can make handmade paper

Painting

- Can mix colors as needed
- Use relationship between colors to create visual effects
- Use appropriate techniques for tempera and watercolor work

Modeling

- Can roll even thickness coils
- Can join coils to create forms
- Can make close-fitting lids and place handles for effective use
- Constantly turn work and check proportion
- Know several finishing techniques

By the End of Sixth Grade

Concepts

Sensory understanding

- Can discriminate and analyze what is perceived based on previous experience and can differentiate between real and illusionary images

Spatial understanding

- Understand cultural differences in the perception and representation of depth and space

Art structures

- Understand and identify unity in artistic compositions

Art history

- Can trace the development of a style or art movement with reference to the artist's life and historical and cultural events

Skills

Drawing

- Draw three-dimensional geometric forms
- Draw proportional figures
- Use shading to reflect a single light source
- Use simple one-point perspective
- Can draw the same subject in several styles

Paper

- Create shading and dimensional effects in paper collages
- Independently design and construct three-dimensional forms from paper
- Have a repertoire of ways to fasten paper together
- Independently make handmade paper when needed to enhance an idea

(continues)

At a Glance 2.5 continued

By the End of Sixth Grade (cont.)

Concepts

Art response
- In written, oral, and graphic form compare and contrast artworks in terms of stylistic, technical, historical, and cultural differences
- Can evaluate an artwork based on how well its design and style reflect its purpose or message
- Can evaluate different opinions about an artwork or art situation and then take and defend a position

Creative problem solving
- Experiment in an orderly way to test the effectiveness of possible solutions to a problem and then choose the most appropriate solution

Production
- Create meaningful artworks for a wide range of purposes that reflect understanding of design, media, technique, and style

Skills

Painting
- Can mix colors as needed when using acrylic paint
- Know several different ways to use acrylic paint
- Choose brushes and application methods that best match intended style

Modeling
- Work clay to proper consistency
- Can combine coil and slab constructed forms

At a Glance 2.6

Correlating Developmental Growth and Multiple Intelligences–Based Skills

Developmental Growth Areas	Multiple Intelligences–Based Skills
Cognitive: Students should be able to . . . Know, remember, and recognize information Understand, explain and compare, and contrast information	Verbal/linguistic: To accomplish this students will . . . Tell, read, retell, write, do word analysis, build vocabulary
Logical/mathematical Create and acquire meaning from symbols Evaluate the merits of ideas or organizers	Logical/mathematical Manipulate numbers and symbols Use information to solve a problem Group, sort, find, and use patterns Identify causes and reach conclusions Put things in sequence Combine information in new ways Chart, list, and outline Make and use graphic solution based on information Solve problems using logic
Affective: Students should be able to . . . Be self-aware Be curious	Intrapersonal skills: To accomplish this students will . . . Evaluate and praise themselves Express their thoughts and feelings

Developmental Growth Areas	Multiple Intelligences–Based Skills
Be self-reflective Be self-confident Think independently Be personally responsible	Respond personally to stimuli Record their thoughts and feelings Control and analyze their thoughts, feelings, and actions Take care of themselves and their belongings
Social: Students should be able to . . Bond with others Communicate ideas and feelings to others Cooperate and collaborate with others Compromise and mediate Empathize and accept differences Be responsible to the group	Interpersonal skills: To accomplish this students will . . . Share Work in cooperative groups Give and receive feedback, question and interview others Practice conflict management skills Identify similarities and differences in others Create and follow rules
Visual perception: Students should be able to . . . Recognize and respond to visual and spatial elements Understand and use visual elements Understand and use spatial relationships Solve visual and spatial problems	Visual/spatial skills: To accomplish this students will . . . Find and identify visual and spatial elements in nature and art Create two- and three-dimensional artworks (draw, paint, sculpt, etc.) Visualize ideas and thoughts Design maps, graphs, and models
Auditory perception: Students should be able to . . . Identify and respond to sounds, music, and rhythms Understand and use musical and rhythmic elements Solve rhythmic and musical problems	Musical/rhythmic: To accomplish this students will . . . Listen to sounds, rhythms, and songs Clap, chant, and sing songs Play musical instruments Create rhymes, rhythms, and musical pieces
Physical: Students should be able to . . . Develop fine and gross muscle control Perform coordinated body movements Coordinate hand and eye movements Recognize and respond to sensory information Solve physical problems	Bodily/kinesthetic skills: To accomplish this students will . . . Exercise and play sports and games Move, dance, mime, dramatize Use tools in art, instruments in music, pen in writing, etc. Participate in sensory and kinesthetic activities Create new ways of moving and using tools

In the Classroom

TEACHING ART

The building blocks of effective teaching are the daily lessons and activities that enable students to grow as learners and future members of our society. As we have seen, these lessons become more meaningful when they activate the brain and match the different ways that students learn. Interdisciplinary lessons, thematic teaching, and the project approach provide several possible frameworks for meaningful art instruction.

How do these frameworks look in the everyday ebb and flow of the elementary classroom? This section sets out a broad vision for art instruction that provides opportunities for students to look at, talk about, write about, and create art. The broad strokes of this outline will be filled in with specific details in the following chapters.

The Embedded Art Unit

Within every interdisciplinary study, every theme unit, and every project approach topic, teachers should include lessons that teach the skills and concepts of the artist. These lessons form an *embedded art unit,* which consists of the following:

- The artworks to be studied
- The art skills to be introduced and mastered
- The activities that may be done
- The overlapping concepts from other subject areas
- The art assessments to be used

Initiating the art unit. A carefully selected artwork should provide the unifying focus for the entire art unit, just as a well-written piece of literature is chosen as the focus of a literature study. By studying this artwork students will learn how and why it was made and respond to and analyze the social, cultural, and artistic forces that shaped the artist who made it. The artwork will provide direction in teaching about art media and techniques and, in general, serve as the "text" for learning about art. The artwork should be selected based on the following criteria:

- It relates to the students' experience in some way.
- It relates to the grade-level curricula in other subjects.
- It incorporates a meaningful theme or underlying concept upon which to build further study.

Teachers then build all instruction in the unit from the historical, social, and physical nature of the selected artwork. For some artworks the study of one discipline may play a more important role than that of another. For example, a study of William Johnson's *Going to Church* could tie into an intensive historical study of the African-American experience. Victor Vasarely's *Orion MC*, on the other hand, can be closely related to the scientific study of the eye, optical illusions, and the physics of color and light. In selecting an artwork it is helpful to create a web showing relevant concepts and skills that can be elicited from the artwork. At a Glance 2.7 provides an example of this kind of web. We will discuss other criteria for selecting artwork in more detail in Chapter 5.

Although the number of artworks selected for study by each grade level will vary depending on the complexity of the work and how it relates to the rest of the curriculum, eight to ten should prove sufficient for most school year programs. The goal is to allow in-depth study of each work. Introducing a new artwork every week does not allow sufficient time for students to become familiar with the work, to learn that looking at a visual image is a complex activity, and to discover the multiple layers of meaning. This does not mean, however, that related artworks or artworks studied previously cannot be displayed and compared to the work under consideration, just as in a literature study, books and stories are compared to the featured work.

Presenting an initiating work. The presentation of the artwork selected for study should begin with great fanfare. If possible take students to see the actual artwork. More likely this will not be possible and you will need to use a reproduction instead. A large poster-sized print, slide, video, or CD-ROM image projected on a large projection screen can all be used to familiarize the students with the work.

Introduce the work with a minimum of comment. Instead ask probing questions, such as the following:

- Have you ever seen anything like this before?
- How does it make you feel?
- Who do you think made it, and when?
- How do you think it was made? What catches your eye first?
- What are some words you would use to describe how this feels?
- How would a scientist, poet, or mathematician describe this work?

Playing thematically related music helps create a relaxing and pleasant beginning to the study as the students complete the initial assessment activity, responding to the work in writing and through art. Make sure the artwork is prominently displayed at the student's eye level for the duration of the study. Allow space near the work to add supplementary artworks and related materials such as charts and webs over time. If possible, provide students with color reproductions to put in their journals. (See "Teacher Resources" in Chapter 5 for sources of postcards and other small reproductions.)

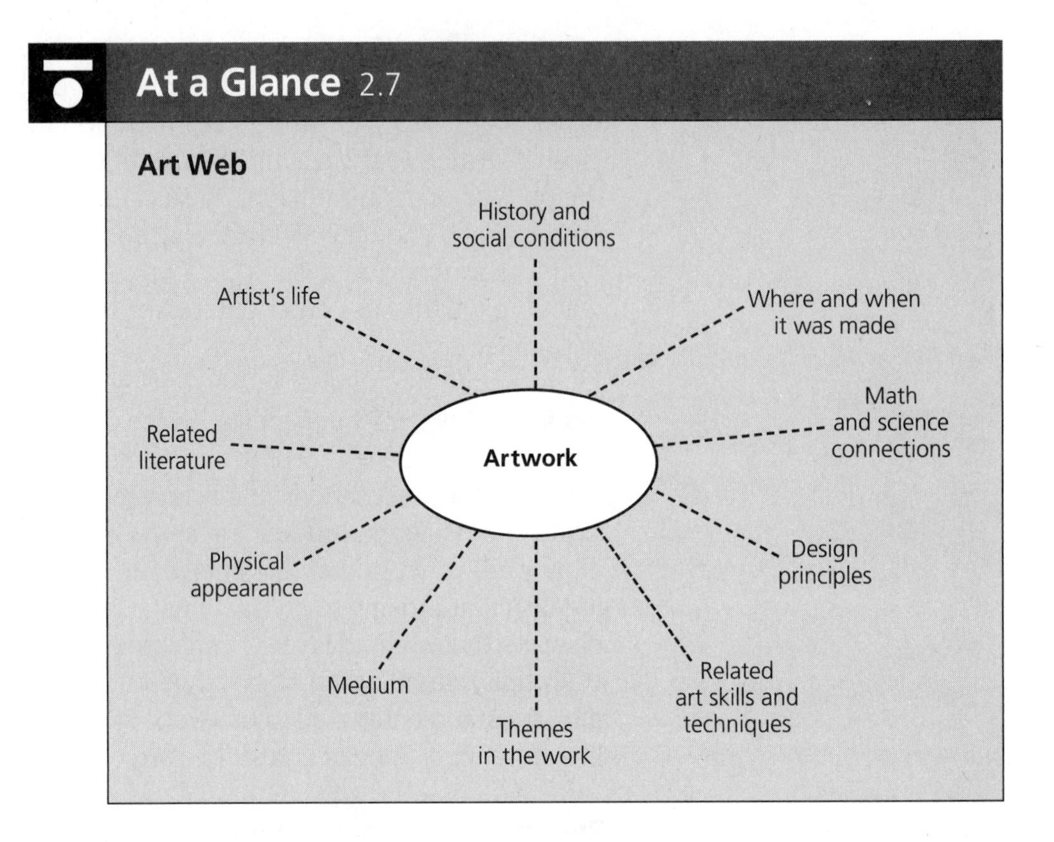

The initial assessment. After presenting the artwork, teachers should closely follow it with the initial assessment. This is the time when students show how the artwork has affected them and also indicate what they already know about it.

The preliminary assessment can be as simple as having students write about the work in their journals and then draw a picture that reflects their view of the artwork. Teachers can also design a variety of more formal assessments. A format that is used with every work can provide cross-unit comparisons. A response sheet that is specific to an individual artwork can provide more complete information on that particular work.

Following the initial assessment teachers need time to go over the results. They should review what the students wrote and drew, and they should think about what the students seem to know. The students' responses may also provide information on what particularly interests them about the work or questions that they have. Based on this information teachers can decide the following:

- What topics, concepts, and skills need to be covered and who will be responsible for covering each of these areas
- What format of instruction will be used
- What field trips, guest visits, videos, and other extension experiences will be offered and who will arrange them

At a Glance 2.8

Art Unit Overview

Initiating Art Experiences

- Presentation of a significant artwork or piece of literature, music, or dance
  1. Students look at and discuss initial reaction to artwork.
  2. Teachers gather relevant unit materials.
- Initial assessment
  1. Students draw and write about the artwork.
  2. Teachers assess what is known and plan instruction.
- Extension experiences: Field trips, guests, happenings

Cross-Discipline Connections

- Teachers present connected lessons in a variety of subject areas.
- Students discover the artwork's connection to related historical, cultural, literary, scientific, and mathematical learning.
- Students experience related arts units in dance, music, and drama.

Artistic Knowledge and Skill Development

- Students receive instruction in related art skills and concepts.
- Students practice and apply what they have learned by creating their own artworks and by making responsive comments about the artwork and related works.

Final Assessment

- Students respond and analyze the artwork based on what they have learned.
- Students complete criteria-based assignments and create responsive artworks that require them to use the skills and knowledge they have learned.
- Students, peers, and teachers evaluate individual growth.
- Teachers review student portfolios.

- What materials, resources, related literature, and art media will be needed and who will obtain them
- What the students will be expected to do
- What the final criteria-based assessment will be and how, where, and when will it be administered

After analyzing the initial responses, teachers select, from the art-related materials they have collected, the information and activities that will be most beneficial to the students. This allows the art unit to be custom designed for that particular student body.

Even though the same artwork may be used every year, the actual student activities will vary to reflect what they already know or have learned. This makes the curriculum more responsive to student needs and past experiences. It allows the curriculum to grow and change with the students. If, for example, the initial assessment shows that students do not recognize the use of perspective in the composition, then this can become a focal point of instruction.

Teaching in Action

A Sample Embedded Art Unit

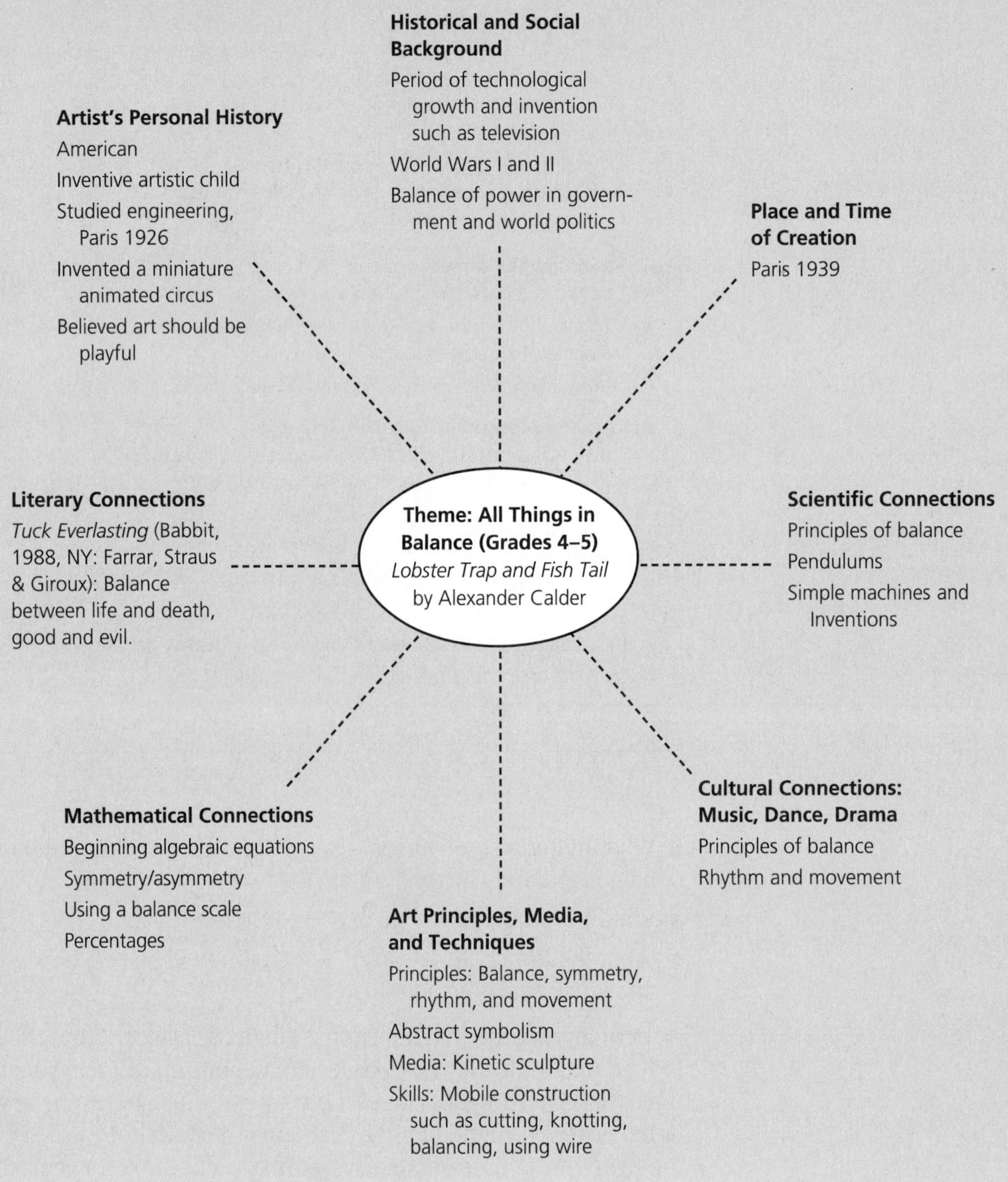

Historical and Social Background
Period of technological growth and invention such as television
World Wars I and II
Balance of power in government and world politics

Artist's Personal History
American
Inventive artistic child
Studied engineering, Paris 1926
Invented a miniature animated circus
Believed art should be playful

Place and Time of Creation
Paris 1939

Theme: All Things in Balance (Grades 4–5)
Lobster Trap and Fish Tail by Alexander Calder

Literary Connections
Tuck Everlasting (Babbit, 1988, NY: Farrar, Straus & Giroux): Balance between life and death, good and evil.

Scientific Connections
Principles of balance
Pendulums
Simple machines and Inventions

Mathematical Connections
Beginning algebraic equations
Symmetry/asymmetry
Using a balance scale
Percentages

Cultural Connections: Music, Dance, Drama
Principles of balance
Rhythm and movement

Art Principles, Media, and Techniques
Principles: Balance, symmetry, rhythm, and movement
Abstract symbolism
Media: Kinetic sculpture
Skills: Mobile construction such as cutting, knotting, balancing, using wire

Teaching in Action

Sample Preliminary Art Assessment

The preliminary art assessment can provide information to be used in planning an art unit. It also provides a starting point from which students can compare what they have learned at the end of the unit.

1. What is the first thing you notice about this work?
2. How do you think it was made?
3. What can you say about the artist?
4. When do you think it was made?
5. How would you describe this work to someone who has never seen it?
6. In the space below draw a picture that reflects how you feel about this artwork.

On the other hand, if their responses show they already understand this concept, then this topic might only be touched on lightly during instruction.

Extension experiences. Following the introduction of the artwork and the initial assessment, students need to share experiences that heighten their interest in the work. Field trips, guests, and other participatory special events will increase the students' involvement in the artwork and may provide opportunities to build curriculum connections. For example, if a piece of Pueblo Indian pottery is the featured artwork, a visit to a local clay deposit will not only introduce students to clay but can also be used to begin a study of erosion. During these experiences students should have opportunities to observe knowledgeable adults and peers discussing and creating art. Chapter 10 provides many ways to expand student art experiences.

Cross-Discipline Connections

Rather than being isolated on the edge of a child's total instruction, art instruction must be tied into the mainstream of teaching and must be closely related to what students are learning in the other subjects.

Howard Gardner's theory of multiple intelligences emphasizes the different ways that each individual processes information and provides direction for teachers who want to reach all of their students. Thinking about lessons in terms of the eight multiple intelligences is one way to build interconnected lessons that reach across subject divisions and provide information in richly integrated ways. Using a web based on the multiple intelligences is a helpful way to interconnect art and learning (At a Glance 2.9).

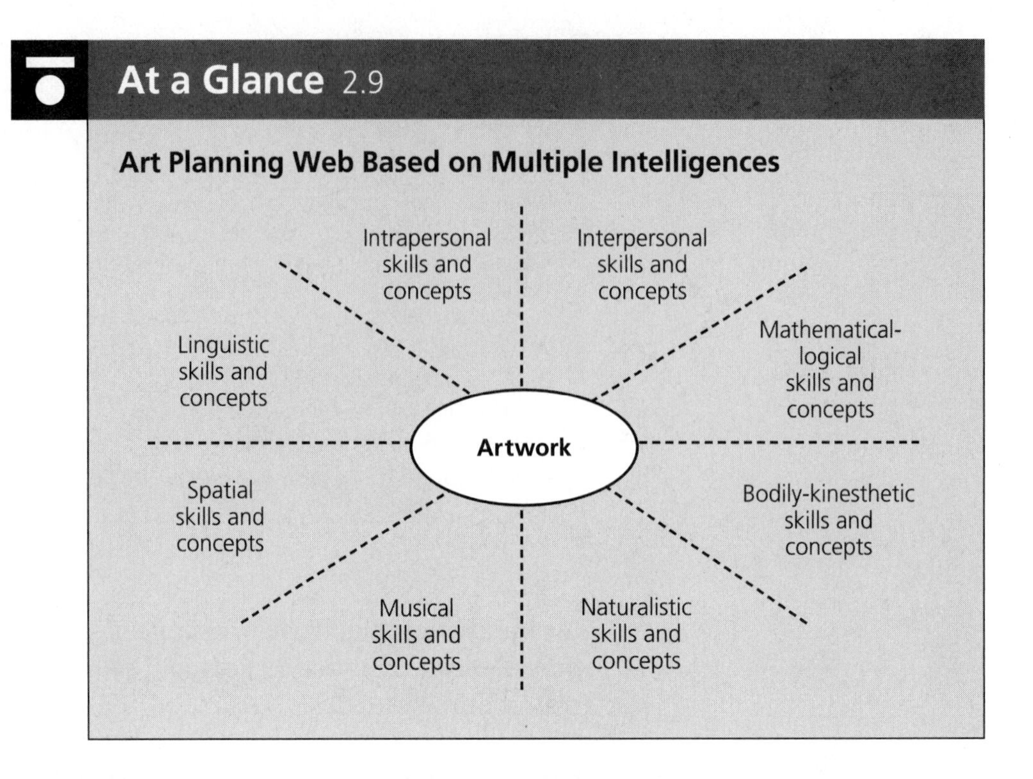

Related arts immersion. In his introduction to the Symposium on Integrated Arts Education, Tom Anderson emphasized the importance of teaching all the arts: "Each art takes a different form and through its different means gives different insight. Together, the arts provide the holistic quality of understanding, the many points of view necessary for social wholeness and cultural health" (1995, p. 10). Although this text focuses on the visual arts, music, dance, and drama are equally important in developing students' understanding. Multiple-intelligences planning is one way to include all the arts into daily instruction. In conjunction with disciplinary studies students should also study related artworks and artists and learn about and perform related music, dance, and drama. Similar music, dance, and dramatic units that focus on the same theme or topic should accompany the embedded art units.

Artistic Knowledge and Skill Development

The art unit must also consider what art concepts, skills, and techniques will be introduced and practiced. Teachers should not assume that students are already competent using the tools and concepts of the artist. It is important to provide direct instruction, opportunities for practice, and ways for students to measure their progress. When lessons are well planned and take into account the way students learn best, new concepts and skills are leaned quickly and less re-teaching is needed. Effective teaching strategies must be incorporated into every lesson. Whether delivered to the whole class or a small group, a successful art lesson should contain the following components:

- Introduction to the lesson
- Statement of lesson's purpose
- Presentation
- Student response
- Summarizing activity
- Closure
- Assessment

The introduction. The beginning of whole group and small group instruction should capture students' attention, build connections with past learning, and introduce the topic of the lesson. Also called a warm-up, motivation, or anticipatory set, the introduction is an essential component of every lesson. Well-planned introductions are brief but intriguing. They draw the students into the lesson and connect what they know to what they will learn. Introductory activities should draw on all the multiple ways of learning and regularly feature movement, singing, and cooperative activities as well as talking, reading, and looking.

If teachers pay attention to the preparation of eye-catching instructional materials, they will be rewarded with increased interest on the part of the students. In an age of television-jaded children, instructors need to create an exciting learning environment that is a pleasant, welcoming place for students. Using an overhead projector, showing a video or slides, displaying large reproductions of artwork, creating large, brightly colored vocabulary cards and charts, or projecting computer or laser disk images on a large-screen TV will all help capture the students' attention. (Chapter 3 will further explore creative ways to begin instruction.)

The statement of purpose. Students need to know why they are participating in the lesson. Are they going to learn a new skill, study a new style of art, or review something they have done before? Teachers cannot assume that students will figure this out on their own. Once they capture student attention with the introduction, teachers can summarize previous learning and present the focus or objectives of the lesson, all in a simple statement. For example, following the transition, a teacher might say, "Yesterday the whole class looked at Monet's series of paintings of Rouen cathedral. Today we will experiment applying paint in different ways to see if we can figure out how Monet used the paint to create the impression of sunlight and shadow we noticed yesterday."

If the lesson to be taught is a logical follow-up to the previous one, another approach is to ask students to explain what they learned in the previous lesson and then predict what they might learn next. If the first lesson, for example, dealt with building a mold for handmade paper, students might predict that the day's lesson would address how to use the mold. Teachers can also show students the materials that they will use or the artwork they will discuss to help in their predictions. This method allows students to learn to make connections on their own and also helps the teacher to assess how well the students understand the purpose of the previous lessons.

The presentation. The presentation of a lesson can take many forms depending on what is being taught. Keep the students' attention by doing more than simply standing in front of them and telling them what to do or what they should know. Teachers can present factual information through the use of videos, graphic organizers, movement activities, and games. For example, use a video to illustrate the development of Chinese art, create a partially completed web for students to fill in based on reading or research, distribute cards with color names and have students form them into a color wheel, or play a game of concentration matching styles of art with associated artists. Art techniques can be demonstrated in interactive ways, such as by having students make suggestions as to what to do next or by inviting selected students to act out the method as it is explained. Develop thinking skills by asking questions that require students to apply and synthesize information. (Chapter 6 presents many ways to demonstrate and question effectively.)

Student response. A lesson in which a teacher merely shows or tells something is not complete. Students must have an opportunity to put what they are learning into practice. Every lesson plan must carefully consider how to facilitate the immediate participation of every student. The following instructional formats have been shown to increase student learning. We will discuss each in more detail in following chapters.

- *Discussion:* Students take turns expressing their ideas and opinions as part of a small group or with the whole class (Chapter 6).
- *Questioning:* Students respond to teacher- or student-initiated questions (Chapter 6).
- *Partnering/peer conferencing:* Students share ideas and responses with another student (Chapter 6).
- *Role play and modeling:* Students practice expected behaviors (Chapter 6).
- *Cooperative learning:* Students work in groups to gain or share knowledge and ideas (Chapter 7).

- *Independent work time:* Students use the concept or skill in a project of their own design (Chapter 8).

Summarizing activity. The lesson must have a definite end or closure. Allow sufficient time for the group to come together as a whole to briefly summarize the lesson. This activity should review the material in a way that will help students remember what they learned. Sometimes the point of the lesson can be embedded in a catchy phrase, a clever song, a hand or body motion, a rhyme, or a visual image. Other concepts may be better summarized through a story, a poem, or a simple, well-phrased statement. At times teachers can ask students to create their own summarizing statement to share orally or to be written in their journals.

Closure. Following the closure of the lesson students need to make a transition into the next activity. A good exit transition refocuses students on what they will be doing next. Students behave better and are ready for the following lesson more quickly when they are clearly told what the teacher will expect of them. If students are making the transition from a whole group lesson to independent workshop time, the closure can be as simple as having each student explain his or her plans before leaving to get supplies. Ringing a bell can signal that it is time to stop work and begin to clean up. If teachers use the same closure regularly, students become accustomed to it and will be ready to respond quickly and then move with ease to the next activity.

Assessing the art lesson. Assessment is a constant process. During the lesson teachers must monitor student responses and questions. That is why it is important to include opportunities for as many students as possible to respond in some way during the lesson. Watching what students do and listening to what students say as they work provides immediate feedback on what they are learning.

As misunderstandings, confusions, or exciting ideas become apparent, it is important for the teacher to make constant adjustments. A lesson plan is there as a guide, but teaching is an interactive process between student and teacher. The actual lesson delivered will never perfectly match the one written on paper.

Following the lesson teachers need to closely observe and question the students to determine if they are correctly using the skill, technique, or concept taught. Teachers can examine artworks, review journals, and hold conferences; these activities will help them decide if and when reteaching is needed.

Transferring Knowledge

Even though instruction may be carefully integrated, educators must remember that skills and concepts that have been learned in one context may not automatically carry over into different contexts. Children need to be taught how to transfer their knowledge. David Perkins (1991) emphasizes the need to review with students what they already know and connect their past experience to the new context whether it is across disciplines or in learning a new artistic skill. The same semantic memory that helps a child skillfully weld a paintbrush will interfere with the child learning to make prints. The printing context is very similar to painting with a brush: There is paint and an object to dip in it, but the physical motions of press and lift are very different. Teachers need to ask their students what part of the process is similar to others they have done, what elements are different. How, for example, is printmaking like painting? How is it different?

The same is true when presenting interdisciplinary material. Teachers need to elicit from students what they have experienced or learned in other contexts to help them connect it with the new learning. This means that teachers must be aware of what is being taught in other subject areas, which makes collegial collaboration even more important. A discussion of Monet's *Water Lilies,* for example, will be far more meaningful if the teacher and students can relate the painting to the pond study done in science class. Educators need to move away from teaching as if everything were a brand new or discrete concept or skill and instead take the time to help students build the cross-connections of real learning.

Final Art Unit Assessment

The purpose of the final assessment tasks is to allow students, teachers, and parents to see how artistic growth has taken place.

Student response and analysis. Students revisit the featured artwork, bringing the new meanings they have absorbed and created during the unit study. This provides the students the opportunity to apply critical thinking skills and to make the connections between disciplines that are essential to meaningful learning. The final assessment process is multifaceted, involving a variety of tasks.

- Criteria-based activities can be used to assess knowledge and skill levels. Completed responsive artworks can be shared and discussed.
- Collaborative culminating projects and writing provide a comparative assessment.
- Student self-evaluations and peer evaluations allow students to monitor their own progress.
- Teachers also need to evaluate the entire curriculum and record student learning for the next year's teachers. As we see in Chapter 9, a portfolio system can help make all this possible.

At a Glance 2.10

Sample Primary Lesson Plan

Lesson: Mixing Colors

This lesson can be embedded in an interdisciplinary unit on the senses, in a thematic unit, "Eyes on the World," or in a project approach unit, "Rainbows." It can also correlate with a science unit on color and with learning to write color words.

Who? Student Composition

This lesson is appropriate for first or second grade of about twenty-five students who have already been instructed on how to use tempera paint appropriately and who are experienced at cleaning their paint brushes.

When? Time Frame

40 minutes.

Why? Objectives

By the end of this lesson the students will be able to

- Cognitively: Name the color combinations that produce green, orange, and purple.
- Affectively: Have confidence that they can successfully mix two colors to make a third.
- Perceptually: Identify the colors that result from mixing two primaries together.
- Physically: Use a brush to effectively mix two colors together.
- Socially: Share paint without mixing the base colors together.

Where?

- Introduction and presentation: Students sitting in a circle
- Student response: At desks
- Summary activity: In group on rug

What?

Materials needed by teacher:

- *Mouse Paint* (Walsh, 1995. San Diego, CA: Harcourt Brace)
- Chart paper and markers
- Individual serving of red, yellow, and blue tempera paint, a water jar, and a brush

Materials needed by students:

- Serving of red, yellow, and blue tempera paint
- Paintbrushes
- Water jars
- Newspaper
- White paper 9″ by 12″

How? Lesson Organization

- Warm-up: Say, "When I call out a color, touch something on your clothing or in the room that is that color." Call out the three primary colors. Ask, "Why do you think I chose those three colors?" Go around circle and have children respond.
- Introduction: Say, "Today we will read a story about colors. Listen and see if you can discover what is special about red, yellow, and blue." Read *Mouse Paint* to the class. When done, ask, "What did you learn about mixing colors?"

(continues)

At a Glance 2.10 continued

- Statement of purpose: "Today we will try mixing our own colors just like the mice did."
- Presentation: Ask, "What colors did the mice use to make orange? List response on chart paper. (Write the color name using that color marker.) Repeat for the other two colors. Say, "Let's try one of these combinations." Ask, "Which one should we try?" Ask, "Who remembers how we should mix our paint so our colors stay bright and clean?" (Have students come up and demonstrate how to place the paint on the newspaper, clean the brush, then take a second color, and how to get fresh water when needed.) Demonstrate: Mix together the combination chosen modeling the method just shown by the children. Have a child come up and paint the resulting color next to the color name on the chart.
- Student response: Say, "Now you are going to work at the tables with a partner to mix all three colors." (Lesson extension: "When you are done with our color-mixing experiment, you can make a painting using the leftover paint, work on your artwork from last time, or experiment mixing other colors from these paints.") "Now, look for someone wearing the same color as you. Raise your hand when you find a match. I will call on you and if you match the person you name, you are to go together to get a paint tray, two brushes, and a piece of paper." When all are working, move around the room and ask students to describe what they are doing and the results they are getting, notice those mixing their colors effectively, and provide further instruction to those having difficulty. Compliment group on working well.
- Summary activity: As students finish their paint-mixing samples, collect the samples and tack them to the bulletin board to dry. When all are done with their samples, have students clean up and then call group to meeting zone with their journals and a box of crayons. Say, "Look at our wall of colors!" Ask, "What happened when you mixed the paints? Did you get the same results as the mice? Is our chart correct? How did it look when you were mixing the colors? Are all of our oranges, greens, and purples exactly alike? Why might they be different?" Have pairs come up and explain how they mixed their color samples. (If time is limited, have each student turn to the child sitting next to him or her and explain how the colors mixed.)
- Closure: Say, "I saw many of you using these colors in your paintings. Now when I give you the three colors red, yellow, and blue, you know I am really giving you six colors . . . hmmm . . . or are there more colors possible? Next time we paint, you can experiment some more." Say, "In your journals write down how to make these different oranges, greens, and blues so you will remember these special combinations. Use our chart to help. If you have time, draw a picture showing how you mixed the colors. When you are done writing in your journal, please put it away and then get ready to line up at the door."

Assessing the Lesson

Were the students successful in mixing the colors? Could they name the combinations? Did they record these accurately in their journals? Which students had difficulty? In what do they need further instruction? When students paint on their own during later workshops, do they mix these colors purposefully?

At a Glance 2.11

Sample Intermediate Lesson Plan

Lesson Plan: Personal Style and the Art of Vincent Van Gogh

This lesson could be integrated into a study of style in music and literature. It could correlate with a discussion of style in literature and European lifestyles and art movements of the 1800s, or it could be part of a thematic unit, "Seeing with an Artist's Eyes."

Who? Students

This lesson is appropriate for upper elementary students who have had many painting experiences, have studied the artwork of several painters, can work in cooperative groups, and understand and use the artistic process.

When? Time Frame

This lesson requires a forty-minute, two-part presentation, several hours of workshop time, and a forty-minute summary activity.

Why? Objectives

By the end of this lesson the students will have

- Cognitively: Defined the word style and differentiated between the styles of several artists.
- Affectively: Responded emotionally to the qualities of style in an artwork and understand that others may respond differently.
- Perceptually: Found visual differences among different styles of art.
- Physically: Effectively used art materials and stylistic techniques to express a personal feeling.
- Socially: Worked with others to reach agreement on identifying styles in artworks.

Where?

- Presentation: Whole group (Note: If the lesson will be presented to an entire grade level, the introduction could be presented to the whole group in an auditorium setting)
- Student response: At desks, tables, easels, art centers
- Summary activity: Class gathered in a group for sharing

What?

Materials needed by teacher:

- Series of slides showing the works of Vincent Van Gogh correlated with the song "Vincent" by Don McLean (*American Pie* album)
- Chart paper and markers
- Large reproductions of artworks by other artists studied who have distinctive styles—suggested are Rembrandt, Picasso, Cezanne, Pollock, Warhol. Make sure some of these share similar subjects with Van Gogh's
- Reproductions of several works by Van Gogh
- Art cards showing works by Van Gogh and others
- Handouts: Biography of Vincent Van Gogh, lyrics to "Vincent"

(continues)

At a Glance 2.11 continued

- Chart listing the steps of the artistic process posted in work area
- Art games about style
- Books about Vincent Van Gogh

Materials needed by students:

- Choice of art supplies

How? Lesson Organization

- Warm-up: Show slides and play tape of "Vincent." Ask, "Which of Van Gogh's paintings did you like best?" Go around circle and get responses, or if group is large, have them write their responses in their journals.
- Statement of purpose: Vincent Van Gogh is one of the world's most well-known and beloved artists. In this lesson we will explore how an artist's personal style communicates his or her thoughts and feelings in different ways to different people.
- Presentation, part 1: Show a reproduction of one of Van Gogh's works. Say, "Study this reproduction of a painting by Van Gogh. Take five minutes to describe the artwork in your journals and record what it makes you think about and feel. If you have time, briefly sketch the painting." Hang up the other works while they are writing. When all have written something in their journals, redirect their attention to the new works. Discuss: "Here are some artworks we have seen before. How are Van Gogh's works different from or similar to these?" List the students' comments on the chart paper. From the discussion develop a simple definition of the word *style,* such as "style is the way someone chooses to do something." If necessary differentiate it from subject matter using the reproductions as examples. Have students give examples of different hairstyles, clothing styles, writing styles, learning styles, etc. Talk about how styles change, the role fads play, and what happens when someone or something is "out of style." Say, "Write a definition of style in your own words in your journals. If you have time, draw two quick sketches reflecting different styles." Have students volunteer to read some of their definitions. Ask, "How can we describe the style of Van Gogh's works?" List their ideas on a separate piece of chart paper. Ask, "How distinctive is Van Gogh's style?"
- Student response, part 1: Say, "Now you are going to work in cooperative groups to find out how distinctive it is. Each group will be given a set of twelve art cards showing artwork by many artists. As quickly as you can, separate the art into that done by Van Gogh and that done by others. You will have two minutes to do this." At the end of two minutes have one student in each group bring up the Van Gogh cards and tack them to bulletin board. Have whole group come to an agreement that all the works are Van Gogh's. Adjust and discuss as needed.
- Presentation, part 2: Ask, "Why do you think Van Gogh's style is so unique?" Give a brief retelling of Van Gogh's life or read *Camille and the Sunflowers* (Anholt, 1994, Hauppauge, NY: Barron's), emphasizing his deep desire to be an artist and his rejection by the art teachers and art world of his time. Talk about what was happening in European art at this time. Point out that his paintings now sell for millions of dollars whereas when he first painted them, they were relatively worthless. Ask, "How did Van Gogh show what he experienced and

how he felt through his paintings? Why do people like his style of art today?" List the responses on the chart paper.

- Student response, part 2: Ask, "Have you ever tried to show how you were feeling in a piece of art? During workshop time think about a piece of artwork that you might make that shows how you feel about something. Ask yourself what art media would work best? What style would you use or invent? Explore different possibilities by making many sketches in your journal. Then select one to develop into a work of art using the artistic process." (If necessary, refer students to the steps of the process.) During workshop time work individually and in small groups with students to help them develop their ideas. Give mini-lessons on using line quality, color combinations, textural effects, and brush strokes to show emotions. (Lesson extensions: Let students do more than one piece of art. Make a class mural on the theme of feelings. Provide art games that require students to identify different styles of art. Display books about the work of Van Gogh.)
- Summary activity: Have students share their artwork with the group. Ask students to respond to the works on an emotional level. How do they feel looking at the work? Discuss why students might have different reactions to the same work. Then do this criteria-based assignment: Pass out the lyrics to "Vincent." Say, "Read the lyrics to this song and using what you know about Van Gogh's life and his style of art and reflecting on what you experienced making this artwork, explain what the song means to you.
- Closure: Say, "This lesson gave you the opportunity to discover ways style can be used to communicate your feelings. In your journal record what you learned about yourself from studying Van Gogh's work and in creating this piece of art."

Assessing the Lesson

Assess student understanding by reading their criteria-based assignment. Look for references to Van Gogh's life, a discussion of style and its use to express oneself, and an understanding of how style changes. Assess delivery of lesson by asking yourself, was there ample time for students to complete the different parts of the lesson, were all students engaged in creating an artwork, did the reproductions selected make style clear to the students?

Conclusion

LEARNING IN CONCERT

At the deepest levels of cultural understanding and communication, the most effective teaching and learning must encompass and utilize a variety of interconnected symbol or notational systems. In other words, it must be holistic. This is central to the relationship between culture and the teaching of the arts.
Michael Sikes (1995, p. 29)

In the classroom each student's search for meaning must be channeled and focused to best match personal needs with the objectives of the curriculum. Learning experiences can be either positive or negative, welcomed or dismissed, exciting or boring depending on how they are designed.

A framework for art education that integrates art across the disciplines must create linkages, not battle lines. No one subject is more important than any other. An integrated curriculum recognizes that all divisions in learning are artificial. What are considered distinct disciplines now may not have been in the past and may not be in the future. Teachers need to come together to plan what to teach. Focusing on a significant artwork is one way that learning can become unified.

How the embedded art unit will function in each school will vary. With careful planning the unit can include information and concepts that are already being taught. It can be tied to thematic teaching units, projects, and interdisciplinary lessons. It can utilize the existing skills and knowledge of every one of the students' teachers. It is worth the effort. When the language of art is an integral part of instruction, students experience deeper, more meaningful learning in all areas.

Learning with, through, and about art are each important in their own right, and there will be many times when one approach will best fit a particular teaching situation. However, combining all three in a single lesson is even more powerful. When art is truly integrated into teaching, there is no dividing line between the subjects. Like a well-planned concert, one piece flows into the other to form a uniform whole. Students study and make artworks because they are integral to the concept being taught. Art skills are taught naturally because they are needed. The goal should not be to provide our students with art education but rather to immerse them in a powerful art in education curriculum.

Teacher Resources

REFERENCES

Anderson, T. (1995). Rediscovering the connection between the arts: Introduction to the Symposium on Interdisciplinary Arts Education. *Arts Education Policy Review, 96*(4), 10–12.

Bower, B. (1999) Learning to make, keep adult neurons. *Science News, 155,* 170.

Bruer, J. T. (1994). Classroom problems, school culture and cognitive research. In K. McGilly (Ed.), *Classroom lessons: Integrating cognitive theory and classroom practice.* (pp. 273–290). Cambridge, MA: MIT.

Caine, R. N., & Caine, G. (1991). *Making connections.* Alexandria, VA: Association for Supervision and Curriculum Development.

Chard, S. C. (1999). *The project approach: A practical guide for teachers. Volumes 1 & 2.* New York: Scholastic.

Dewey, J. (1958). *Art as experience.* New York: Capricorn.

Dobbs, S. M. (1997). *Learning in and through art.* Los Angeles: Getty Center for Education in the Arts.

East Carolina University School of Art & Pitt County Schools, North Carolina (1997). *Study of art contributes to learning in mathematics.* Reported at National Art Education Association's 50th Anniversary Convention, March 1997, New Orleans.

Feldman, E. B. (1981). *Varieties of visual experience.* Englewood Cliffs, NJ: Prentice-Hall.

Frazee, B., & Rudnitski, R. (1995). *Integrated teaching methods.* Albany, NY: Delmar.

Gardner, H. (1983). *Frames of mind.* New York: Basic Books.

Gardner, H. (1991). *The unschooled mind.* New York: Basic Books.

Gardner, H. (1993). *Multiple intelligences.* New York: Basic Books.

Gardner, H. (1999). *The Disciplined Mind.* New York: Simon & Schuster.

Goldberg, M. R. (1997). *Art and learning: An integrated approach to teaching and learning in multicultural and multilingual settings.* White Plains, NY: Longman.

Goleman, D. (1995). *Emotional intelligence: Why it can matter more than IQ.* New York: Bantam Books.

Hart, L. (1983). *Human brain, human learning.* White Plains, NY: Longman.

Hausman, J. J. (Ed.) (1980). *Arts and the schools.* New York: McGraw-Hill.

Johnson, G. (1991). *In the palaces of memory: Explorations of thinking.* Albuquerque, NM: University of New Mexico Press.

Katz, L. G., & Chard, S. C. (1991). *Engaging children's minds: The project approach.* Norwood, NJ: Ablex.

Kridel, C. (1990). Implications for general education. In W. J. Moody (Ed.), *Artistic intelligences: Implications for education.* (pp. 85–91). New York: Teachers College Press.

Lazear, D. (1994). *Multiple intelligences approaches to assessment.* Tucson, AZ: Zephyr.

Neisser, U. (1982). *Memory observed: Remembering in natural contexts.* New York: W. H. Freeman.

Perkins, C. N., & Salomon, G. (1989). Are cognitive skills context bound? *Educational Researcher, 18*(1), 16–25.

Pinker, S. (1997). *How the mind works.* New York: Norton.

Sikes, M. (1995). From metaphoric landscapes to social reform: A case for holistic curricula. *Arts Education Review, 96*(4), 26–31.

Whitehead, A. N. (1929). *The aims of education.* New York: Macmillan.

Whitin, P. (1996). *Sketching stories, stretching minds.* Portsmouth, NH: Heinemann.

Practical Guides

For ideas for integrating art and other subjects try:

Anderson, W., & Lawrence, J. (1991). *Integrating music into the classroom.* Belmont, CA: Wadsworth.

Armstrong, T. (1994). *Multiple intelligences in the classroom.* Alexandria, VA: Association for Supervision and Curriculum Development.

Brady, M. (1997). *Dancing hearts: Creative arts with books kids love.* Golden, CO: Fulcrum.

Edwards, C. (Ed.) (1993). *Hundred languages of children.* Norwood, NJ: Ablex.

Heirstein, J. (1995). *Art activities from award winning picture books.* Carthage, IL: Teaching & Learning.

Hendrick, J. (Ed.) (1996). *First steps toward teaching the Reggio Way.* Upper Saddle River, NJ: Merrill.

Kohl, M. A., & Potter, J. (1993). *Science arts: Discovering science through art experiences.* Bellingham, WA: Bright Ring.

McConnell, S. (1993). Talking drawings: A strategy for assisting learners. *Journal of Reading, 36*(4), 260–269.

Miller, E. D. (1998). *Read it. Draw it. Solve it.* Palo Alto: CA: Dale Seymour.

Nelson, K. (1998). *Developing students' multiple intelligences.* New York: Scholastic.

Williams, D. (1995). *Teaching mathematics through children's art.* Portsmouth, NH: Heinemann.

Videos

Arts for life. J. P. Getty Trust, Los Angeles.

Jacobs, P. (Ed.) (1986). *Interdisciplinary curriculum: Design and implementation.* Association for Supervision and Curriculum Development, Alexandria, VA.

The arts and children. Goals 2000 Arts Education Partnership.

The arts: Tools for teaching. John F. Kennedy Center for the Performing Arts, Washington, DC.

The role of art in general education. Getty Center for Education in the Arts, Los Angeles.

Web Sites

Project approach discussion group
listservepostoffice.cso.uiuc.edu

Chapter 3

Creative Development
Motivation and Imagination

Creativity isn't an exploration of how we are alike.
It celebrates how we are different and special.

Sydney Gurwewitz Clemens (1991, p. 5)

ARTISTS AT WORK

Creative Thinking at the Scrap Box

Marcello: Look! I found a duck. This paper looks just like a duck. Here's the head, see, and a tail.

Corrine: Hey, it does! I'm looking for some bright colors.

Marcello: Now I need something for it to swim in.

Corrine: How about this piece of blue? It's long. You could put it on the bottom of your paper for a lake.

Marcello: Hmm. No, y'know, I want a round piece like a pond. Let's see . . .

Corrine: Oops, where did that yellow piece I saw before go? I just thought of using it for a flower.

Marcello: Can a pond be green? Here's a green piece just the right size.

Corrine: Sometimes there are green ponds. Like remember when we went to the pond to study the bugs and there was that green slimy stuff in it?

Marcello: Oh, right. Algae or something. I'm all set then. What did you find? Anything good?

Corrine: Yep. Look at this gold piece. I'm going to make a crown out of it.

Marcello: Let's go. I'm gonna create a masterpiece!

Corrine: Me too!

Introduction

CREATIVITY IN SCHOOL

In our schools art and creativity have long been paired. For example, teachers often set aside "creative" arts activities as a time when children are supposed to express their creativity. Creativity, however, is like art. It is not an isolated manifestation of behavior that can be separated from the rest of a student's learning; rather it is an integral part of all subject areas. Like art, it spans all Gardner's intelligences. Students can write an original story or copy someone else's. They can compose a piece of music or sing a song from a book. They can design an innovative experiment in science or follow the procedures on a worksheet. Creativity is the process through which we make special and unique meaning from our experiences and knowledge.

Our beliefs about the nature of creativity are embedded in the educational decisions we make and the lessons we choose to teach. Many teachers are not quite sure what the creative process is or know how to nurture it. Some fear the unpredictable results of allowing students to be "creative." As we will see in this chapter, creativity is not total freedom, although it requires fluid thinking. It is not a lesson to be taught but a way of processing and applying information and solving problems that must be carefully nurtured both in the art program and throughout the entire school curriculum.

Setting the Stage

WHAT IS CREATIVITY?

"Even to begin to encompass creativity," writes Howard Gardner, "one must take into account a huge number of factors and their multifarious interactions" (1995, p. 27). As with art, there is no one accepted definition of creativity. A wide range of researchers and theorists have generally looked at creativity from one of three different perspectives: Some have looked at the *characteristics* of people deemed highly creative; others have looked at their *creative products;* still others have concentrated on their *processes* for creating those products or solving problems.

Characteristics of Creative People

Because creativity seems to mysteriously well up from inside us, many researchers have looked into the subconscious to find the roots of creativity. Early psychoanalysts, such as Sigmund Freud, believed that both creation and fantasy arose as the result of unfilled wishes and represented a return to the state of childhood play. Producing creative work was a healthy way to express one's unconscious needs and desires. Others have felt that creativity was the result of the interaction between the conscious and unconscious as when the creator

What Do You Think?

Which of the following art activities would you consider creative? As you read this section, think about how different researchers might view these examples:

Thinking of twenty different ways two paintings are similar.

Figuring out a way to support an unbalanced sculpture upright.

Copying a painting by Raphael using fluorescent colors.

Painting a picture that is acclaimed as the most original work of the century.

was in a dreamlike state between sleep and wakefulness (Kubie, 1958). Carl Jung (1972) believed that creating was a way to dip into a human collective unconscious that transcended time and culture.

Another approach has been to look at the life histories of artists, writers, inventors, and others who have produced highly original work or startling changes in everyday life. Freud, for example, looked at the life and work of Leonardo da Vinci (1989). Howard Gardner (1985) examined the creative efforts of a range of notable people, such as Picasso, Einstein, and Martha Graham. Alice Miller (1990) has studied the relationship between creativity and repressed childhood traumas in artists such as Picasso.

From these and other studies Alane Starko (1995, p. 68) has summarized the childhood characteristics of successful creators. She cautions, however, that these descriptors are the result of focused study on often small samples of people with very specialized careers and from a range of time periods, and that it is easy to "think of a creative exception to every item listed" (see At a Glance 3.1). Although teachers cannot affect the birth order or early home life of their students, they can mirror the environmental conditions of these eminent creators by providing a stimulating classroom where diverse ideas are encountered, exploration is encouraged, and supportive role models are provided.

Other researchers have compared those they consider creative with those deemed less so. Some researchers have characterized creative people, for example, as more spontaneous and expressive and less inhibited than average people, open to experience and approaching tasks playfully. Such characteristics have been attributed to a variety of factors. Maslow (1968), for example, believed that everyone is born with creative potential but those who are the most mentally healthy are the most free to create. Others have postulated that creativity is due to the way an individual interacts with the environment (Rogers, 1962).

At a Glance 3.1

Characteristics of Eminent Creators
Based on Starko (1995, pp. 67–69)

- Firstborn
- Childhood difficulties or early trauma
- Stimulating, often unconventional home environment
- Exposed to a wide range of ideas
- Early successes
- Enjoyed learning, either in or out of school
- Hobbies and collections
- Supportive role models, mentors, or parents
- Freedom to explore

Researchers have suggested that the following traits have a strong relationship to creative functioning:

Intelligence. Some researchers feel that a threshold of intelligence is necessary for major creative contributions, although they have not found a relationship between superior intelligence as measured by IQ tests when compared to the creativity tests they have devised (Barron, 1969; Roe, 1952; Getzels & Jackson, 1962). Interestingly some researchers have found that individual accomplishments often seem to be related more to hard work and self-discipline than innate ability (Bloom, 1985; Walburg, 1969), nor have they found a correlation between age and creativity, and the age of peak creativity seems to vary widely (Amabile, 1996).

Divergent thinking. Guilford (1986) has created a model of intelligence that includes divergent thinking—the ability to generate many different solutions to a problem—as one of the basic processes. Many other researchers have used his definition to identify creative individuals. Divergent thinking is characterized by the following

- *Fluency*: Generating many ideas or solutions
- *Flexibility:* Seeing things from different perspectives
- *Originality:* Producing unique ideas
- *Elaboration:* Improving ideas by adding on or expanding them

Independence in thought. MacKinnon (1961, 1978) found that architects, writers, and scientists identified as highly creative in their field were self-motivated, curious, and willing to learn. They were not always easy to get along with, but they were open to new ideas, could see new possibilities within themselves, and were able to see things from a variety of perspectives.

Self-evaluative. Those identified as creators also had a high tolerance for anxiety when they did not understand something, and they were always learning. Independent people are comfortable taking risks and evaluating their results against their own personal standards. As Alane Starko says, "New ideas are seldom accepted. . . . Unless people are able to set their own standards for evaluation, they can make little progress in independent thinking" (Starko, 1995, p. 72).

Synthetic. Creative individuals can combine often discrepant knowledge or objects to create something new. They can see relationships between things that are unlike. Vygotsky (1978) saw the beginnings of creativity in the child's ability to substitute one item for another during imaginative play. For example, a child pretending to be a space explorer may imagine that the bed is a spaceship and the light on the ceiling is the moon. Vygotsky did not see symbolic play as equivalent to adult creativity but rather as an early stage of creative development. He believed that adults, who have more complex skills and knowledge, can think more abstractly and therefore can consciously direct their efforts toward the creation of art or the discovery of scientific concepts.

Logical and skilled. Weisburg (1986) found that when people were given a task that required them to use a familiar object in a new way, they didn't just suddenly discover the solution. First they tried more common methods. Weisburg believes that creativity is not a specialized event but rather a series of ordinary cognitive processes that sometimes lead to a unique solution. Since every person brings a personal set of skills and knowledge to a task, there is always the chance that a new idea or object will emerge. Margaret Boden has compared this process to that of the well-programmed computer, which given enough knowledge and skill can through trial and error create something new (Boden, 1990).

Taking this idea further, Howard Gardner (1995) argues that people are not creative in some general way. No one can be expected to be highly creative in every discipline. Rather, each person is creative in particular domains of knowledge. This is because successful ideas are more likely to occur if the person has a firm base of experience and knowledge upon which to build. A professional artist would, for example, be expected to be highly creative in art rather than in physics.

Characteristics of Creative Works

There are two types of creative works. First there are the ideas, inventions, and concepts that change everyone's lives: the electric light bulb,

Teaching in Action

Nurturing Creative Traits through Art

Researchers have identified many cognitive and affective characteristics that seem to be correlated with creative behavior. As teachers we need to think about ways to nurture and reward those mental traits that lead to more creative functioning. Here are some suggestions to get started:

Fluency

Encourage students to generate many ideas before settling on a course of action.

Examples

- Draw several sketches for a poster or painting.
- Brainstorm varied color combinations for a weaving.
- Arrange collage papers in several different ways before gluing them down.

Flexibility

Create situations in which students have to look at things from a new perspective.

Examples

- Study artworks that have similar subjects but are different styles or from different cultures.
- Encourage students to on occasion turn their artwork upside down or look at it reflected in a mirror to gain a different perspective.
- Have students re-create an artwork or book illustration in a different style, color combination, or art medium.

Originality

Reward original ideas and thinking with more than a "that's nice."

Examples

- Say, "I've never thought of it that way. I see you are really thinking."
- Set aside a table or wall for displaying original work done independently at home or school. Title it something like "Inventor's Corner" or "Wild Ideas."
- Publish a class newsletter or newspaper and include write-ups about original ideas or thinking demonstrated by the class.

Elaboration

Provide opportunities for students to expand or build on their ideas.

Examples

- Encourage students to take an initial artwork and redo it in a different medium. For example, a student could make a clay sculpture based on a painting.
- Suggest that students create a series or set based on an initial idea, such as instead of one painting of a sunset, make five, each showing the sun lower in the sky, or instead of a single mug, make a matching place setting.
- Have students enlarge or create a miniature of one of their artworks.

Independent Thought

Create an environment in which it is safe for students to take risks.

Examples

- Model questioning and wondering about ideas for which you do not know the answer, such as, "I wonder why this artist attached these pieces on to the sculpture."

- Have students create their own self-evaluations (see Chapter 9 for guidance).
- Do not grade work that is preliminary or for the student's personal use, such as sketches, notes, drafts, and journals.

Synthesis

Set up situations and problems that require students to apply what they know in new combinations.

Examples

- After studying two very different styles of art, have students combine them to create a composite style.
- Have students combine two or more different art media in one work.
- Have students select two very different subjects or topics and combine them into a unified work or presentation.

Logic

Make students aware of times when they are thinking logically.

Examples

- Say, "I see you used trial and error to solve that problem. First you did. . . . Then you did . . ."
- Say, "Tell me some of the things you tried (or: thought about) before you reached this conclusion."
- Ask, "Should this step follow that one?"

the telephone, the plays of Shakespeare, the theories of Einstein, the art of Picasso. Margaret Boden calls these *H-creative* ideas because they must be viewed in *historical* perspective to be appreciated (Boden, 1990, p. 51). The culture we live in determines which among the many millions of creative ideas that people have daily will be considered H-creative. In fact, many H-creative ideas, which are often extremely unusual and challenge the status quo, are rejected or ignored when they first appear and only become accepted over time. " [N]othing is or is not creative in and of itself," says Howard Gardner. "Creativity is a communal or cultural judgment" (1995, p. 56).

Boden calls the second kind of creative production *personal* or *P-creativity.* P-creative ideas and works are those that are new for the person who produced them. Everyone is P-creative in different ways throughout their lives. Teresa Amabile describes this process as the ability to break out of the familiar and to see in new directions (Amabile, 1996). As such we are all constantly producing creative products: a new recipe from the leftovers in the refrigerator, a faster way to get to work when the road is under construction, or a new strategy for teaching subtraction with regrouping. Children also produce creative products. "[C]hildren's minds develop not just by learning new facts," states Boden, "but also by coming to have ideas which they simply could not have had before" (1990, p. 57). The products of personal creativity may not be earth shattering, but they are often

At a Glance 3.2

Children's Creative Art Products

1. Solving a problem

   Examples:

   - Figuring out how to attach a bent twig to a piece of paper
   - Discovering the right amount of red and yellow to make the perfect orange sunset
   - Balancing the cardboard shapes on a mobile

2. Developing a theory or concept

   Examples:

   - Describing a unique way two paintings are similar
   - Discovering how two modeling compounds are similar and different and then applying workable techniques from one to the other
   - Explaining why they think Van Gogh's painting of sunflowers is more creative than a copy of it

3. Creating an original product

   Examples:

   - Arranging paper shapes into a one-of-a-kind composition
   - Drawing an illustration for a story or poem
   - Designing a poster to persuade people not to litter

4. Giving a unique performance

   Examples:

   - Creating a script, costumes, and masks for a dramatization of "The Three Little Pigs"
   - Creating a movement that reflects the pattern they see in a painting
   - Pretending they are a particular artist and explaining why that artist painted in a certain style

innovative and useful. This is the creativity we talk about when we talk about nurturing creativity in children.

The Creative Process

Perhaps the most interesting part of creativity, and the part of most import to teaching, is the creative process. What mental processes and skills does an individual need to arrive at a creative outcome? This process has been described in different ways by researchers such as Theresa Amabile (1996), Michael Csikszentmihalyi (1990), and David Perkins (1981), but most seem to agree that it begins with finding a highly motivating problem, immersing oneself in study or research directed toward solving it, developing and using needed

"Village."
Cut paper—Amy Jo, grade 5 (*left*).
"Landscape."
Cut paper—Carrie, grade 5 (*right*).

Thinking about Children's Art

In these two collages each student has chosen to cut out different shapes and arrange them in different ways. Is it possible to pick the one that shows the most creativity or are they each creative in different ways?

skills and knowledge to gain insight into possible solutions, and finally producing the solution or product.

When students combine different paper shapes in new ways to make a picture, or teachers design an original method for teaching a basic concept, they use the creative process. This process can be seen as skills, actions, and mental states that combine to produce an original action or product. Being aware of the creative process allows teachers to understand better how to nurture creativity in the classroom. The process can be divided into seven basic components:

- Motivation
- Problem finding
- Knowledge
- Skill
- Immersion
- Incubation and insight
- Production

The creative process in action. Imagine a small child trying to build a clay horse. She wants her horse to look like it is running, something she has never done before. This is her motivating problem. She has never seen a real horse, but has seen pictures in books and on TV and knows that horses have four legs that bend. This is her knowledge. She makes four thin clay cylinders for legs, lays the body on its side, attaches them, and bends them into what she thinks approximates running. This is her skill. She stands up her creation only to see the delicate and uneven legs collapse. She sighs and remakes the legs thicker. Again the weight of the body collapses the bent legs. Ignoring what is going on around her she tries other arrangements for the legs but none work. This is immersion. Deep in thought, she pushes back from the table and stares off into space. This is incubation. Suddenly she has an idea. This is insight. She begins working furiously. This is production. When she is finished, she proudly shows her running horse leaping over a sturdy fence, which helps support the body and allows the legs to run free (see At a Glance 3.3).

Motivation. Motivation is the drive to accomplish a goal. Extrinsic motivation comes from outside, as when one is told to do something in order to avoid receiving a punishment or in the hope of receiving a reward. Intrinsic motivation, on the other hand, comes from inside the individual, as when one passionately pursues a goal solely for inner satisfaction. Therese Amabile (1996) has found that people are most creative when they feel motivated by inner drives such as curiosity, challenge, and enjoyment.

The sensory and kinesthetic aspects of handling art materials and the process of absorbing the visual aspects of color, texture, and form attract and activate children's curiosity and motivation to explore. Teachers can use this powerful aspect of art to excite students about learning.

Problem finding. Motivation alone is not enough. There must also be a problem to explore. Finding such a problem provides the "why" for creative processing. Research by Getzels (1982) found that the ability of college art students to find a unique problem for a still-life correlated positively with future success as artists up to twenty years later. Problems vary in their potential for creative processing, and teachers need to consider carefully what kinds of problems students need in order to develop their creativity.

Knowledge. We must provide our students with knowledge about the world. In order to invent something new an individual needs to know what already exists. Children cannot combine paper shapes into fanciful dogs if they have never seen a dog. Teachers cannot design innovative lessons if they do not know the concepts to be taught.

Knowledge is essential for creativity to flourish. A successful art program introduces students to the art of the world. They should know what has been done and who has done it and understand the factors that surround the work. They should acquire a vocabulary of art terms and understand the elements of art and the principles of design. Rather than limiting students' creativity, this kind of knowledge

At a Glance 3.3

The Creative Process

Motivation: One's inner drive to create

Problem finding: The impetus to start

Knowledge: What one has learned and understood

Skill: The experience one has had with the materials, techniques, and concepts

Immersion: The process of thinking deeply about ideas

Incubation and insight: Thinking about, trying out, and revising one's ideas

Production: The tangible expression of the creative process

allows students to make choices and to combine elements and ideas in innovative ways.

Knowledge they acquire in other parts of the curriculum will also affect students' creativity in art. Studying the human skeleton and how it moves in science classes, for example, gives students knowledge that will help them draw people in action. Learning about historical events in social studies will make artwork from that period more understandable so students can create more thoughtful responses. Writing about personal experiences in language arts will provide a reservoir of ideas from which to create personally meaningful artwork.

Skill. Creative processing requires a reservoir of skills. Everyone has experienced the frustration of imagining a wonderful solution to a problem but being unable to carry it out because of a lack of skill. Students need to be able to read and write, calculate, and research in order to produce creative works in all fields.

To create and respond to works of art students must have a wide range of skills. In the art program this means allowing ample time for exploration so students can try out a new medium before they are expected to use it in a finished piece. Students need many opportunities to practice using the vocabulary of art to talk and to write about artwork before they are expected to create original responses.

The art program should allow students to master the subject. Too often art programs are built on the premise that children need to try every art form once every year or look at a new artwork every week. As a result students never develop skill or confidence in any one area of the widely diverse field of visual arts. In language arts instruction students are slowly introduced to different genres and writing skills over the course of the school program. Students may spend weeks reading and analyzing one piece of literature. Which students will be the most competent in weaving: the ones who did one simple weaving activity for forty minutes each year, or the ones who spent three months not only learning the process of weaving using different looms and yarns but also studying the cultural and historical context of the craft?

Immersion. In order to create, students must be able to immerse themselves in their work. Students cannot be expected to reach high levels of creativity when they are assigned a topic and an art medium, allowed a few minutes to think about it, and then expected to make an art project in the twenty or so remaining minutes. Yet this describes much of what happens in art lessons in many classrooms. Rather students must delve deeply into ideas and topics, have opportunities throughout the day to think about these concepts, and be given time to represent these ideas visually using the artistic process. The elementary curriculum must be organized so that art is an integral part of what the student is studying across all the disciplines. Integration of the curriculum will also bring the creative and artistic process to the other subjects.

Incubation and insight. When students have knowledge and skills and are motivated to use them, they are ready to tackle creative pursuits. The incubation stage of the creative process is the playground of the artist. Here is where the artist tries out ideas, explores possible solutions, and makes decisions about the artwork. Students need to learn how artists think in the context of reflecting and analyzing their own artistic ideas. Incubation and insight is the trying and testing of ideas. It is planning and reorganizing, drafting and revising, refining and redoing, concentrating and sharing the possible ways to approach and solve a problem. This is the heart of creativity. It is where knowledge, skill, and ideas come together and begin to take form. (Chapter 11 addresses this artistic process.)

Production. The production of the work should be the culmination of thoughtful reflection on the original idea, done with the most skill and knowledge that students at that level can obtain. This is the high moment of creativity when knowledge, skill, and meaning-making come together. It is also a very important part in teaching students to appreciate the art of others. It is only when the hands-on production follows planning, revision, and sharing that students begin to understand how an artist tries out ideas, discarding some, elaborating others, and incorporating knowledge—all for the purpose of creating meaning.

If a teacher expects students to produce an attractive finished artwork, which meets the teacher's criteria, in the twenty minutes

Books to Share

Creativity

The following picture books celebrate a diversity of creative ideas and problem solving:

Burke-Weiner, K. (1992). *The Maybe Garden.* New York: Beyond Words.
A boy plants a garden of fantastic colors and shapes while his mother plants a real one.

Dobrin, A. (1975). *Josephine's Imagination.* New York: Scholastic.
A Haitian girl uses her imagination to create a doll from one of her mother's broken brooms.

Druscher, H. (1985). *Simon's Book.* New York: Lothrop, Lee & Shepard.
A sleeping boy's incomplete drawing of a monster cavorts with the pen and ink to create a completed storybook.

Gestein, M. (1984). *The Room.* New York: Harper & Row.
Detailed drawings show how successive inhabitants of an apartment decorate it in different ways.

Hoban, R. (1989). *Monsters.* New York: Scholastic.
John loves to draw monsters, which are viewed in different ways by his parents, his art teacher, and his doctor in this surprise-ending book illustrated by Quentin Blake.

Keats, E. J. (1966). *Jennie's Hat.* New York: Harper & Row.
Delightful collages show a young girl creatively "improving" her new hat.

Pinkwater, D. M. (1977). *The Big Orange Splot.* New York: Scholastic.
Much to the initial distress of his neighbors a man paints his home in exuberant colors and patterns.

Schotter, R. (1996). *Dreamland.* New York: Orchard.
A boy's fantastic machine drawings become real when his uncle opens an amusement park.

Steptoe, J. (1997). *Creativity.* New York: Houghton Mifflin.
Charles, an African-American student, creates some ingenious ways to help himself and his new Hispanic friend learn to appreciate their differences and similarities.

Williams, K. L. (1990). *Galimoto.* New York: Lothrop, Lee & Shepard.
Using discarded materials, an African boy builds a toy car.

following the presentation of a lesson, those students will not understand the point of creating art. Those who cannot produce within such constraints come to believe they are not capable in art. Instead of appreciating the thought and reflection behind art creation, students subjected to this kind of art instruction will always believe that artworks are instantly and magically created by gifted artists. It is only through experiencing the creative and artistic process that students truly come to understand and appreciate their own art and the art of others.

Why . . . ?

WHY NURTURE CREATIVITY?

Adherence to tradition and conformity have been the standard for acceptable behavior in many places and at many times. In our society today, however, being innovative is highly valued. We want to hear new songs, wear the latest fashions, and see the most recent movies. Our everyday lives are complex, requiring many creative solutions to daily problems. We are faced with constant technological change in the workplace—change that demands workers who are flexible and creative at solving problems. Ever-increasing amounts of knowledge force us to create new approaches in all fields. Innovative teachers, for example, are finding creative ways to increase the learning of their students by using computers and the Internet in their classrooms.

There is no way to know what particular knowledge or skills our students will require as adults. We need to teach them the right attitude for dealing innovatively with change. "Our experience of creativity in childhood shapes much of what we do in adulthood, from work to family life," write Goleman, Kaufman, and Ray in *The Creative Spirit.* "The vitality—indeed the very survival—of our society depends on nurturing adventuresome young people capable of innovative problem solving" (1992, p. 58). Nurturing the creative process in our students is the best way we can prepare them for the future.

When students spend most of their time solving problems that have only one correct answer, they come to rely on outside sources for the answer. They do not learn to think through the problem for themselves and are ill prepared to deal with the complexities that make up real-world problems. They become fearful of making mistakes and learn only in response to acquiring a grade. For many students this kind of teaching is deadly. They give up on school and school learning and turn their creativity to disruption and avoidance strategies.

Using the creative process allows all students to become risk takers, hone their skills and knowledge, and practice higher thinking skills.

Becoming risk takers. Being comfortable taking risks is essential for growth as an individual. The infant who is not allowed to explore by touching suffers sensory deprivation and does not develop normally. Children who are fearful do not learn. Classrooms that encourage creative behaviors are open to questioning, trying, and failure. Welcoming creativity into the classroom also welcomes diversity. There is not always a right answer or only one way to reach a solution. Students learn to accept diverse ideas and solutions to problems. They become confident that they can figure out the solution instead of waiting for the teacher's answer.

"Future world."
Pencil—Scott, grade 4.

Thinking about Children's Art

Asking students to draw their idea of what a city of the future might look like provides an open-ended way for them to combine what they have learned about the basic needs of a community with their own creative solutions.

Honing skills and knowledge. The most creative problems are those that motivate students to use the skills and knowledge they already have and to seek more if needed. Formulaic problems require only a good memory and skill in following a pattern in order to find the correct solution. To use long division, for example, the student needs to know place value, the division tables, and the steps of the process. There is no mystery to the process, no need to explore or learn more.

To solve an open-ended problem of how to make wings for an original cardboard bird sculpture flap up and down, however, the student has no model to follow. Instead the student must apply what he or she has learned about simple machines and the way glue and cardboard interact, while testing a variety of possible solutions, some of which may fail and some of which may work. The student may

What the Experts Say

Art and Creativity

The idea that an artist should be original is a cultural idea—in some societies the ability to replicate a traditional pattern is more valued than originality.
Carol and Melvin Ember (1996, p. 552)

To be creative, a work of art or a scientific theory has to be understood in a specific relation to what preceded it.
Margaret Boden (1990, p. 60)

Since the arts are open-ended and generate individual responses with no single right answer, they encourage participation and interaction. Everyone can contribute and discover a voice or medium for their thoughts, reactions and ideas.
Nancy Cecil and Paula Lauritzen (1995, p. 4)

When you, or your children, become dependent on someone else's idea of what the final product should resemble, the freedom of self-expression becomes lost, and the product is no longer a reflection of your own creative efforts.
Linda C. Edwards (1990, p. 65)

also need to go look at toys and machines to see how others have designed flapping parts.

Practicing higher thinking skills. Creative problems ask students to go beyond passive ways of thinking. They ask students to apply what they know to unfamiliar situations, order their ideas and make connections, and then put it all back together to form a new whole, a whole that must then be evaluated for its success. This process is not always neat and tidy, but it is essential. Creativity requires that all the thinking skills work in concert. Knowledge and comprehension allow application to follow. Analysis and synthesis occur tempered by evaluation. (See At a Glance 3.4.)

Guiding Ideas

CONSTRUCTING KNOWLEDGE

Perhaps the most creative thing children do is construct their own meaning of the world. Cognitive-field learning theorists see learning as the result of the interaction of individuals with their psychological environment or life space (Lewin, 1951). This life space consists of a person's goals, fears, needs, and abilities as they appear at the present moment and those parts of the environment of which the person is perceptually aware (see At a Glance 3.5). Perception is the process by which a person reaches out to the life space environment, encounters a part of it, creates a relationship with it, acts on the relationship, and then makes meaning from the entire process. Learning takes place

At a Glance 3.4

Taxonomy of Thinking Skills

Based on Bloom (1956)

Knowledge: Remember, define, or identify information.

Key tasks: Learn vocabulary, specific facts, accepted conventions, basic concepts, and sequences.

> ***Example:*** Naming the three primary colors.

Comprehension: Describe, compare, or contrast information.

Key tasks: Translate from one symbol system to another, summarizing, seeing consequences.

> ***Example:*** Making a picture that shows what happened in the story.

Application: Use what they have learned to solve a problem.

Key tasks: Take action based on knowledge and experience.

> ***Example:*** Using the primary colors to mix all the colors needed for a landscape.

Analysis: Consider available information, identify causes and effects, and then reach a conclusion or make a generalization.

Key tasks: Recognize the form and pattern as a means of understanding meaning.

> ***Example:*** Deciding that a work is in a particular style based on the way the paint was applied and the colors were used.

Synthesis: Apply what they know and can do to a new situation.

Key tasks: Create something unique by arranging ideas or elements to form a whole that was not present before, to produce a work of art, a plan, or a hypothesis.

> ***Example:*** Making an illustration that shows what might have happened if the story had a different ending.

Evaluation: Judge the relative value of an idea, solution, or product.

Key tasks: Form an opinion and provide supporting facts.

> ***Example:*** Determine if the colors in an artwork effectively create the mood of tranquillity.

when new concepts based on these experiences are acquired or old ones are changed.

Learners, therefore, are constructors of their own knowledge. In order to learn, children must take an active role, must do or observe something in the life space environment and then create new, exploratory understandings from what they see happening. This constant interaction with the life space causes learning to take place (Bigge & Shermis, 1999).

If we perceive students as creative participants in their own learning and understand that each student's life space is different

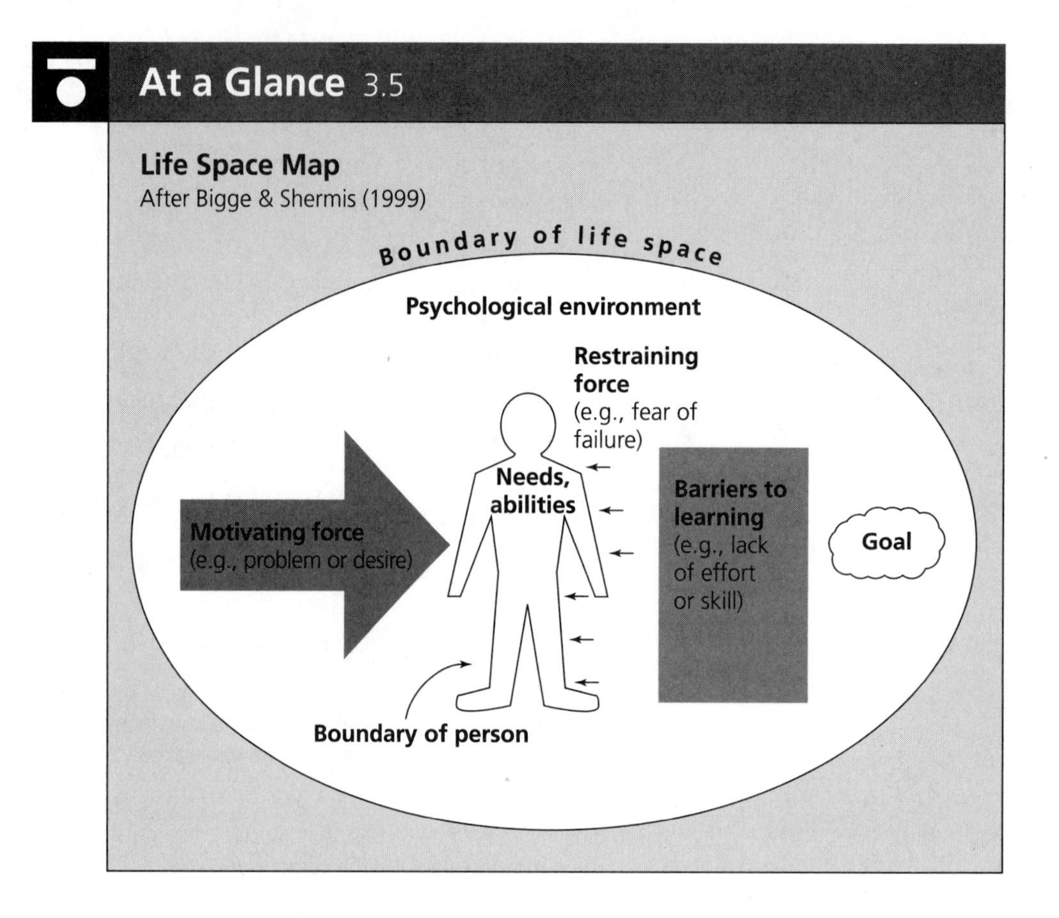

from another, and therefore each student constructs his or her own unique understandings, then we must approach teaching in a way that engages each student in the learning process on a personal level. At the same time we need to draw our diverse students together so that the group learning experience becomes part of each individual's life space.

Effective teaching based on this approach to learning is built on the concepts of the common experience, matching task and student, exploratory learning, and problem raising and solving.

The common experience. First there must be an intersection of the student's life space with the teacher's and with that of the other students'. Activities must be designed to draw every student toward the same goal. This requires the teacher to see through each student's eyes and visualize how an activity will appeal to that student. Teachers must become experts at reaching into their students' life spaces. What games do my first graders like to play? What stories do my third graders like to read? What TV shows or singers are popular with my fifth graders? What is it about colonial times, the moon, mammals, or any other required teaching content that relates to each of my students' current life spaces? The answers to these questions will provide the links that tie everyone's learning together. Every object or activity must have an allure that attracts student attention, draws that object or activity into their personal life space, and motivates them to choose to participate.

Matching the task and the student. When individuals pursue personal goals or work at avoiding adverse situations, they are acting purposefully—choosing those things that will take them toward their goal or away from peril. There is always the risk that they may fail due to lack of ability, effort, task difficulty, or luck. These are barriers that prevent a student from reaching a desired goal. Teachers must carefully craft learning situations to match abilities and reward effort, and recognize the role of chance by celebrating lucky occurrences and accepting unexpected reverses.

Focus on exploratory learning. Understanding is constructed from experience, and children acquire experience through exploring with their senses. It is not enough for children to watch or listen. Children of all ages learn best when information is presented in multisensory ways. Research shows that when students can use several senses, they are more likely to remember (Berliner & Casanova, 1996). In order to discover patterns and relationships students need to look and listen, touch and move, smell and taste.

Through exploration each child actively participates in the learning process, using sensory information, trial and error, and past learning to solve problems that lead to new understandings. As children handle materials, explore causes and effects, and try out new ideas, they construct their own concept of how the world works (Case, 1991).

Carefully planned multisensory experiences and hands-on activities allow children to develop deeper cognitive understandings of the particular concepts that they are studying. Teachers can foster learning by providing thoughtfully selected materials to manipulate and by designing open-ended activities that stimulate children to explore new relationships. For example, teachers could challenge children to discover their own ways of applying paint using objects other than a paintbrush. In doing so, students will explore the relationship between their body movement and the shape, size, and flexibility of the objects.

Problem raising and problem solving. An ideal way to get a group of students working toward the same goal is to create a problematic situation that makes them curious, uncomfortable, or excited. The problem must be compelling—students must want to investigate its solution, but the problem must not be so difficult that there is a high chance of failure or frustration. When activated, problem solving calls on students to gather evidence, formulate possible ways to solve the problem, try them out, and produce the best solutions.

Exploratory Understanding and the Creative Process

Embracing the cognitive-field theory of learning means accepting that what students learn is directly related to how they acquire the learning. Rather than being told information or required to memorize facts, students need to learn how to solve problems and develop higher-level thinking skills, which can then be used to solve problems of all kinds (Bigge & Shermis, 1999). This is a creative activity, and in solving these kinds of problems, students put the creative process into action and come up with solutions that are original to them.

In the Classroom

INVITATION TO CREATE

Teachers must invite students to become immersed in the creative process as a way of forming concepts. They need to reach into their students' life spaces by providing stimulating experiences that excite them to play with ideas. Teachers should challenge students to find questions to answer and problems to solve, which will start them on a course of independent thinking, risk taking, and discovering of possibilities that will last them all their lives. Although art is the focus of the following strategies, the same approaches can be applied across the disciplines.

When students enter our classrooms, they bring with them all their previous experiences. Each student has different beliefs, needs, goals, and interests. It is the teacher's task to discover what these are as well as what the students already know about art and what they believe about themselves as artists. It is only when teachers have this knowledge that they can connect their life spaces to the students' and make plans for teaching these particular students at this particular moment in their lives.

Activating Knowledge

The initial interactions between students and teachers should be ones of discovery. The start of a school year or the beginning of a semester is not the time to teach something new but to assess where to begin. This is not a new idea: Generations of teachers have begun the year by asking students to write and draw about themselves or what they did on their summer vacations. "[T]he beginning of instruction," writes John Dewey, "shall be made with the experience the learners already have" (1958, p. 54). There are many wonderful ways that teachers can begin this discovery process and set the creative process in motion.

Community circle. From the very first, community circle can be a regular feature of the students' day. Community circle brings the whole class together to share in an intimate way. It is a place to greet each

"A Day at the Beach."
Cut paper—Matt, grade 2.

Thinking about Children's Art

Children's art can give us information about what they know and how they solve problems. What can you tell about this second grader from his artwork? What problems did he have to solve in recreating his experience at the beach?

other at the beginning of the day or a lesson. Sitting in a circle on the floor or in chairs arranged in a circle, the whole class can respond to a warm-up activity or share experiences by answering a related open-ended question or giving a personal response. Have students respond to questions that help them get to know one another better. What did they do over vacation? What is their favorite book (movie, music, food, animal, artwork, art material, etc.)? Community circle allows students to share what is important in their lives and to develop ideas and responses to experiences that can then be expressed both in their writing and their art.

During this personal sharing it is helpful to pass a special object, such as a stuffed animal in the lower grades or a feather or beautiful stone in the upper grades, to each speaker in turn. This helps the group focus on the one who is speaking. Rhythmic and movement activities can also provide focus. Students can clap a rhythm or move their hands or arms in a special way between each student's comment.

It is important for students to know that they are expected to participate. This is the time to acknowledge everyone's contribution to

Teaching in Action

Activating Prior Knowledge

Activating prior knowledge is the act of tapping into the backgrounds, attitudes, and abilities that students bring to the art lesson. The goal is to get students thinking about related ideas or events in their own lives or from previous lessons. The following questions demonstrate how to relate lesson content to students' lives at different grade levels:

Grade	Lesson Content	Activating Question
First	Identifying geometric shapes in an artwork	Can you think of something that you use everyday that has a similar shape?
Third	Making clay pots	Think of your dishes at home. What sizes, shapes, and colors are they? What kinds of designs are on them?
Fifth	Studying Moore's *Reclining Mother and Child*	How is Moore's work similar to or different from other sculptures we have studied?

the group. You may allow students to pass the first time around the circle, but they must respond when asked a second time. As students learn that all responses are welcomed, this will become less of a problem.

Personal art. Questions about what makes each student unique can lead into art activities that allow them to visually share information about themselves. For the first few days, for example, plan several art activities, such as drawing a self-portrait or making a picture of their homes or a collage that reflects things they like to do. These activities should be designed to utilize skills and materials that are already familiar to the students and, at the same time, provide personal information about each student. They can do artwork in student journals, in a booklet about themselves, or on squares of paper that can be hung together to form a class quilt. Take time to have students orally share about their lives using the artworks as starting points.

Group art. The beginning of the year is an ideal time for cooperative art activities. Cooperative teams can work on posters illustrating a class rule or make signs for the different centers or activity areas in the room. These kinds of activities help students get to know each other and emphasize the positive ways students can interact. Chapter 7 provides many ideas for group activities and details how to manage them effectively.

Teaching in Action

Brainstorming

1. Propose a question, problem, or topic to the group. Ask them to think silently of an idea or word related to it.
2. Select one person to be the recorder. This can be the teacher in the primary grades and a student in the upper grades. This person will record the group's ideas on a large sheet of chart paper or a blackboard.
3. Have students share their ideas as the recorder writes them on the chart.
4. Establish and enforce the following rules:
   - There is no discussion or criticism of ideas during brainstorming.
   - All ideas are accepted and written.
   - Silly and far-out ideas are welcome.
   - The more ideas the better.
   - "Hitchhiking"—building on or combining ideas—is welcome. No one owns the ideas. Teamwork is encouraged.
5. When everyone's ideas are exhausted, ask students to study the list. Do they see any similarities or ideas that go together? Code these ideas with a matching color or symbol.

Shared experiences. Students may also share some broad cultural experiences such as shopping, sports, and watching television. It is the teacher's task to find out what students have in common through reading their journal entries, in discussions, and by overhearing their conversations. These shared experiences can then become the basis of highly motivating warm-up activities. For example, having students name their favorite sports team and then creating a display of team logos can be an effective draw into a lesson on the use of symbols in art, literature, and math.

Expanding experiences. Teachers can also expose their class to new experiences that tie their students together through a bond of shared knowledge. Reading a book or poem aloud to the class, studying the work of a well-known artist, investigating a problem, going on a field trip, inviting visitors to the classroom, or hosting a special event expands the experience of the students and introduces into their life space knowledge beyond what they otherwise might have experienced on their own.

Brainstorming. Brainstorming is one of the best ways to effectively share and build on the creative ideas of a group. This strategy can be used in many ways. Primary students can brainstorm a list of subjects for their artwork. Intermediate students can brainstorm different ways to apply paint. The lists generated through brainstorming can

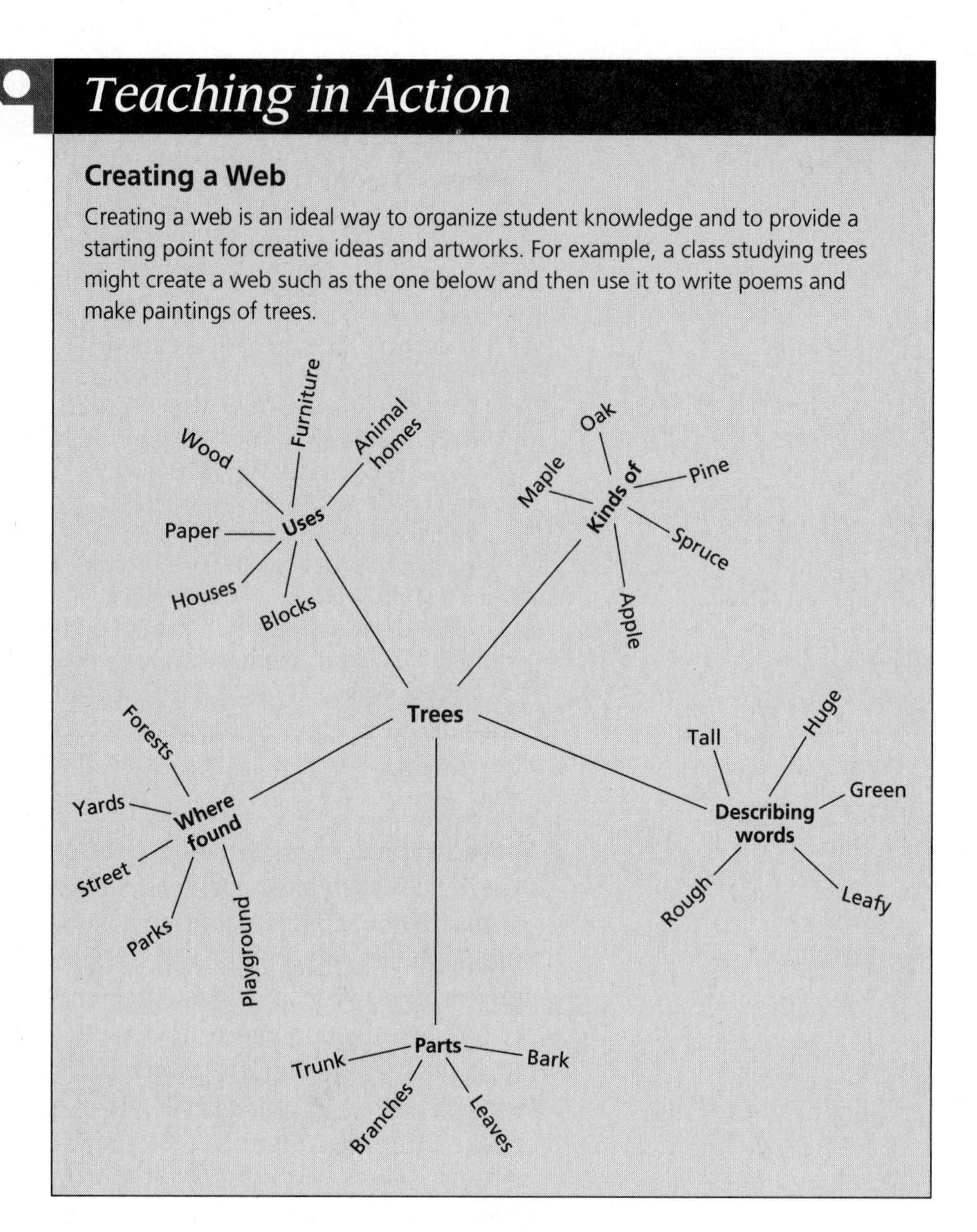

be converted into charts and webs, to be posted or copied and distributed for student use.

Charting and webbing. Charting or webbing can follow brainstorming or can be used as a separate strategy. These methods provide a way of recognizing the knowledge or ideas of a group and showing that you value them. You can use this knowledge to build understanding of related concepts.

Create a class chart by listing one or more headings at the top of the paper and having students suggest words or ideas to go under each heading. The simplest webbing technique is to write the word or concept in the center of a large paper and then have students provide words or ideas that are related to it. As a student gives an

Teaching in Action

Art Warm-Up Ideas

Warm-ups are short, intense activities that get the whole class focusing on the same idea and thinking creatively. They are an ideal way to bring art into the classroom. They can be used as part of a community circle time, to introduce an art lesson or a lesson in any subject, between lessons, while waiting in line, and any other time to capture students' attention.

- Ask an open-ended question about art and have each student answer it in turn.
- Create a visual pattern by calling out a name and tossing a ball of yarn to that student. That student then calls a name, holds on to the yarn, and tosses the ball to a chosen student until all students hold an attached piece of unwound yarn. Try this with students in a circle or with two lines facing each other. If students are careful, they can place their piece of yarn on the floor and everyone can step back and marvel at the pattern.
- Create a "Who, Me?" box. Have students write personal favorites for such things as pets, colors, sports, foods, artwork, art materials, etc. on a slip of paper and put it in the box. Draw one a day and read one item off the slip. Have all students who share the same favorite stand. Often there are quite a few. Continue reading, having students sit down when there is no longer a match until only the originator of the slip is left standing. Give this student a special greeting, such as a high five, or a special assignment for the day, such as passing out papers. This activity helps students discover that they share both similarities and differences with others in the class.
- Draw or paint an imaginary picture in the air without talking. When done, pass the invisible crayon (pen, pencil, brush, etc.) to the next student in the circle or line and invite him or her to draw.
- Display an unusual object related to the lesson.
- Display an artwork and have each student invent and perform a movement inspired by it.
- Display an artwork and make one-word or one-sentence responses to it.
- Display and respond to a thought-provoking quote from an artist or about art.
- Display art materials in an unusual way; for example, make "brush people" by dressing brushes in doll clothes, "serve" art by arranging art supplies to look like table place settings, pull recycled art supplies (tubes, cardboard, newspaper, cans, etc.) out of a recycle bin.
- Dress in clothing, hat, or costume related to the lesson topic or subject of an artwork.
- Find lesson-related elements on students' clothing.
- Lead a chant that uses an art vocabulary word.
- Mime an art activity.
- Perform a magic trick, such as pulling a paintbrush out of your sleeve.
- Read a short book or section from a book.
- Recite a poem.
- Pass a special item around the circle. Each student must make a statement about it.

(continues)

Teaching in Action continued

- Play an art guessing game, such as Twenty Questions, about an artist or artwork.
- Play an audiotape with music or sounds related to an artwork.
- Put several topic- or artwork-related items in a bag. Pull them out one by one and ask students to comment on objects or figure out what they have in common with the topic or work.
- Sing a related song.
- Show a brief video or a few selections from a laser disc or CD-ROM.
- Take a brief walk somewhere related to the lesson.
- Tell an art riddle or joke.
- Tell a true personal story.
- Toss a ball around the circle. The student with the ball must make a statement or answer a question about an art topic.
- Wear a lesson-related piece of jewelry and discuss it.
- Whisper a secret art-related message and have students pass it around the circle.

Note: These warm-up ideas are just a beginning. More warm-up ideas will be found throughout the text. But the range of possible warm-ups is limited only by one's imagination.

idea, discuss where it would be best to place it in relation to the other ideas already written on the paper. Special charts such as Venn diagrams and graphs work well for information that has shared characteristics. Cooperative teams and individual students can also create charts and webs.

Warm-ups. Instruction, in order to be effective, needs to build upon the shared experiences of the students. The art warm-up provides an ideal structure with which to relate what will be taught across the disciplines to the students' experiences. Some basic human experiences are shared by all students; feelings, family, friendship, and the wonder of nature can provide entry points into many activities. For example, having students bring in and describe a natural object such as a stone, leaf, or piece of bark from a place they have visited can be an ideal warm-up for a lesson on landscape painting. Exploring the contents of pockets, book bags, or the desk can be the start of a self-portrait, still life, or mural about school.

Kinesthetics. Kinesthetics awareness is sensing the motions and sensations of our bodies and perceiving our position in space. It is different from our other senses in that it includes input from all the sense organs and internal organs. Children learn with their whole bodies. Activities that require movement are more engaging and more likely to be remembered. Kinesthetic activities that combine art and movement make wonderful beginnings and endings to lessons of all kinds. "There is a muscular element to expressing and remembering as well as to making art," write Herman and Hollingswood (1992, p. 9). These kinds of activities ask students to become aware of their kinesthetic responses as they create and look at art. Heighten kinesthetic awareness in the following ways:

- Have students imagine they are drawing with an invisible crayon. Encourage them to move their whole body as they draw a life-sized picture of some familiar object such as a car or dog.
- Call out or use a drum or music to announce different speeds and motions as students draw, paint, or model with nonhardening clay.
- When looking at artwork, students can take the position of people or objects in the work. Ask, "How would your body feel if you were this person, this tree, this building, this large, green shape?"
- Have students move their bodies to express the movement they perceive in an artwork, or invite them to move.

Sensory experiences. Sensory stimulation activities, such as listening to rain on the roof or touching the surface of a carved gourd, are powerful experiences that can be used to reach into the life spaces

Books to Share

Sensory Perception

Read these books to heighten children's perception of their environment.

Emberly, E. (1992). *Go Away Big Green Monster.* New York: Little, Brown.
As the pages turn, openings in each page form pictures that end up as part of a "monster."

Jenkins, B. (1995). *Looking Down.* New York: Houghton Mifflin.
Starting with a view of earth, each collage illustration moves closer and closer, ending with a close-up of a ladybug.

Jonas, A. (1987). *Reflections.* New York: Greenwillow.
Turned upside down, the pictures in this book turn into completely different ones.

Lionni, L. (1975). *On My Beach There Are Many Pebbles.* New York: Mulberry Books.
Beautiful pencil drawings of both real and amazing pebbles heighten sensory awareness of the tactile quality of pebbles.

O'Neil, M. (1969). *Fingers Are Always Bringing Me News.* Garden City, NY: Doubleday.
Each poem describes a different person's fingers and what they touch and feel.

Showers, P. (1991). *The Listening Walk.* New York: HarperCollins.
A child taking a walk hears different sounds.

Young, E. (1991). *Seven Blind Mice.* New York: Philomel.
Blind mice use their senses to explore an elephant.

Ziebel, H. (1989). *Look Closer!* New York: Clarion.
Close-ups of common objects are followed by full views.

Starfish.

Thinking about Children's Art

How will looking closely at a starfish and experiencing its texture help a child be more creative in art? How could this sensory experience be expanded into a lesson on ocean life?

not just of young children but also of students at all levels. Sensory experiences are not something that can be put out on a table along with the paint and paper. Instead daily interactions with students should be full of statements, questions, and happenings that share the teacher's wonder and valuing of the sensory qualities of objects and the environment.

These kinds of experiences must be brought into focus by sensual words that draw students into daily sensory experiences. Point out the fuzziness of a child's sweater, the gleam of light on the polished tile floor, and the damp smell after the rain. Expand every lesson no matter what the subject by describing the sensory qualities of the materials and objects being used: the grainy texture of the paper, the stickiness of the glue, the sweet odor of tempera paint, the way the light highlights the shape of the textbook. Doing so will not only help students absorb sensory information but will also awaken their interest in what they are doing.

Nurturing the Motivation to Create

We cannot make a student want to solve problems or create something unique, but we can provide an environment in which the motivation to learn will grow out of the children's own natural curiosity. Intrinsic motivation comes from inside a person. It is the inner drive to create. Activating prior knowledge and drawing on sensory experiences is the beginning. We also need to maintain a classroom atmosphere that welcomes creativity by providing the following:

Choice. Allow students to choose from a range of materials, activities, and ideas that they can use in many ways. Creative assignments are open-ended. This means that the students have the opportunity to make many decisions about how to organize their work. Pre-drawn pictures, cut out patterns, and lockstep directions restrict the artistic choices students can make about their work. A box of colored and patterned paper scraps, on the other hand, allows the students to choose the size, color, and shapes of paper they wish to use.

Time. Provide students ample time to explore, think, and create. They are not pressured to finish in a limited amount of time. "If intrinsic motivation is one key to a child's creativity, the crucial element in cultivating it is time: open-ended time for the child to savor and explore a particular activity or material to make it her own" (Goleman, Kaufman & Ray, 1991, p. 65).

Stimulation. Make sure something new is continually happening in the room. Display new artworks and interesting natural and human-made objects; introduce new materials and discuss new ideas. Combine familiar items with artworks and artistic concepts drawn from a wide range of times, places, and cultures.

Teaching in Action

Sensory Experiences

Visual

- *New view.* Display an object in an unusual position, such as upside down or sideways. Try drawing it the way it appears and in the right position.
- *Viewfinders.* Provide students with cardboard tubes or cardboard pieces with openings cut into the center. Use these viewfinders to examine sections of objects and artworks more closely.
- *Colored viewfinders.* Put colored cellophane over the viewfinders and study the way the color changes what one sees.
- *Lighting effects.* Darken room and shine a strong light (a filmstrip projector works well) on familiar objects from unusual angles. Change the color of the light using cellophane or colored light bulbs.
- *Look center.* Put out magnifying glasses, plastic mirrors, fly-eye viewers, textured plastics, prisms, holographic papers, Fresnel and other lenses, and other visually interesting topic-related objects. Encourage students to visit this spot and explore sketching what they see and writing descriptions in their journals.

Touch

- *Touch bag/box.* Prepare a touch bag or box containing a variety of tactilely interesting objects, such as smooth stone, rough bark, aluminum foil ball, and so on. (*Note:* Be sure objects do not have sharp edges.) Invite students to reach inside, touch one object, and describe what they feel. Extend this activity by inviting students to draw a creature or machine that has that same texture.
- *Texture scavenger hunt.* Give students a list of textures, such as rough, smooth, wet, bumpy, and have them find an example of each in the classroom or, better yet, outside on the playground or school grounds.
- *Touch center.* Display topic-related objects with unusual textures in a special location. Change the objects often and invite students to bring in objects they find. Encourage students to visit this spot and explore sketching the objects and writing descriptions in their journals. Be inventive in looking for items for the center. From the kitchen try cereals, dry beans and grains, ice cubes, foils and wraps, utensils, fruits and vegetables. From nature select rocks, fossils, sanitized bones (soaked in bleach), moss-covered bark, wood, leaves, flowers, gravel, and sand.

Smell

- *Atmospheric.* Pay attention to odors in the classroom. Make sure it is always clean and fresh smelling. Check for allergies and then use an air freshener, potpourri, or soap that leaves a pleasant odor. Open windows in fair weather. Bring children's attention to the smells of the different art supplies: the waxy odor of crayons, the earthy smell of clay.
- *Scent art supplies.* Try changing the scent of paints or homemade modeling doughs by adding safe scents such as those found in different shampoos, dish detergents, potpourri, and scented oils. Also try strong-smelling spices: cinnamon, allspice, nutmeg, cumin, coriander, thyme, marjoram, cloves, savory, and mint.
- *Scent center.* Soak a cotton ball in a liquid scent, or glue dry-scented material such as spices or potpourri to a piece of paper. Place inside a lidded plastic container such as a margarine, yogurt, or icing container, and tape the lid closed.

(continues)

Teaching in Action continued

Poke several small holes in the top. Invite students to smell the scent and then imagine and draw and write about a place or person of which it reminds them.

Sound

- *Mystery sounds.* Tape record a variety of unusual sounds or purchase a tape of sound effects. Play one sound and have students imagine what it might be. Invite them to write and draw their ideas.
- *Sound sculpture.* Explore the different sounds that result from gently tapping objects of different materials together, such as a pencil tapping a piece of paper, or a metal rod tapping a ceramic bowl. Invite students to invent a sound sculpture based on this exploration.
- *Sound studio.* Set up a tape recorder, microphone, and earphones in a corner of the room. Encourage students to create a tape of oral commentary, music, or sound effects to accompany one of their artworks.
- *Listening center.* Set up a tape recorder and earphones and provide tapes of music in a variety of styles from different cultures. Students can listen to music of their choice while drawing and writing.

Taste

- *Taste testers.* Provide many opportunities for students to sample foods with which they may be unfamiliar. Young children are often afraid to try new tastes. Emphasize the sensory qualities of the experience and the importance of taking risks to learn new things. Give only tiny samples and do not force students to try. Have students write and draw about the experience.
- *Taking a taste.* Study still lifes by different artists that feature foods. Have students describe or write about the tastes that they see using as many adjectives as they can.
- *Taste in a box.* Have students study the way different foods are packaged. How do the advertising images on the box tell you about the tastes inside?

Flexibility. Be willing to change direction and follow up on interesting ideas and student interests.

Encouragement. Value individual differences and unique ideas and encourage risk taking and experimentation. "Individuals who ultimately make creative breakthroughs," writes Gardner, "tend from their earliest days to be explorers, innovators, tinkerers. Never content to follow the pack . . ." (Gardner, 1995, p. 52).

Comfort and respect. Welcome failures and mistakes as part of the learning process. Make students feel secure in being able to express their ideas openly and encourage them to try something new. Accept and discuss differing opinions. Do not allow insults and ridicule.

Enjoyment. Many have emphasized the similarity between creative processing and play. Stephen Nachmanovitch, for example, says,

Open-ended lesson design: Still-life arrangements

"Basket of Fruit." Watercolor and crayon—Garrett, grade 3 (*top*).

"Picnic Basket." Watercolor and crayon—Ashley, grade 3 (*bottom*).

Thinking about Children's Art

Following a lesson on the importance of fruit in nutrition, children were asked to paint a picture of a still-life arrangement of fruit. Instead of drawing the classroom in the background, the teacher encouraged the students to imagine their fruit baskets were in a special place. How did this encourage the children to use the creative process?

Teaching in Action

Designing Lessons that Allow the Creative Process to Flourish

The creative process flourishes in lessons that are open-ended and allow many choices. Small changes in wording can make a difference in a student's creativity.

1. Provide a starting point and perhaps a direction for the assignment, but do not dictate the end result.
   - *Open-ended:* "Now that we have an understanding of how perspective can make things look far away, use this understanding to create three different drawings that show depth."
   - *Restrictive:* "Draw a house, a tree, and a road in perspective."
2. Design lessons that challenge the student's problem-solving abilities.
   - *Open-ended:* "Starting with just the three primary colors, see how many other colors you can make."
   - *Restrictive:* "Using the primary colors, mix orange, green, and violet."
3. Draw on student knowledge and challenge them to use it in new ways based on what they already know and have explored.
   - *Open-ended:* "Based on our study of Greek temples, design a contemporary home, store, or office that combines these elements in a new way."
   - *Restrictive:* "Based on our study of Greek temples, build a model of one of the famous temples."

"Creative work is play. It is free speculation using the materials of one's chosen form" (in Cameron, 1992, p. 77). Set aside ample time for students to have fun, to laugh and play together as they work. Emphasize the enjoyable aspects of the work. Do not divide activities into work and play or tell students, "You may do art when you finish your work."

Recognition. In an environment open to the creative process creative ideas, actions, and works are cherished, honored, and displayed. They are judged by the artist, by the teacher, and by peers as representing a unique and meaningful artistic statement. Recognition does not mean giving prizes and awards. Extrinsic motivation or outside coercion, such as tests, grades, punishments, and rewards (for example, stickers or happy faces), have been shown to reduce inner motivation and decrease creative functioning (Amabile, 1996). Rather, recognition means celebrating everyone's creativity by welcoming diverse ideas and providing activities that immerse students in the creative process.

Finding Problems

When students know that their ideas and experiences are welcomed in the classroom, they are ready to attack problems creatively. Finding a motivating problem or question to investigate is the impetus that puts the creative process in motion. There are many different kinds of problems that children face in school. Not all of them result in creative processing.

Formulaic problems. Many problems have a known form, a known method of solution, and a solution known to others if not to the student. Most problems teachers give students in school are of this type, such as multiplying two multidigit numbers or writing a paragraph with a topic sentence and three supporting statements based on information from the textbook. This type of problem relies on memory and sequencing for successful solution. Creative processing is not required by such problems, and the unfortunate student who does try to solve them in a unique way is usually reprimanded to follow directions.

The Caines characterize what is learned in solving these types of problems as "route" learning and compare it to following a set of directions to reach a particular destination (1994). Because a route is quick and convenient to teach and results in easily tested skills and knowledge, it is a common method of teaching. However, as anyone who has tried to follow someone else's directions to a particular address knows, it is easy to make a mistake and once lost hard to find one's way back. If, instead, one spends time exploring an area, going up and down the streets and developing a mental map of the region, not only will one have the fun of discovering new places but also one will acquire a great deal more information, allowing for the creation of many other possible routes. Learning to solve formula-type problems should be only one part of our students' education. In order to think creatively students must have ample time to explore and create their own mental maps of learning.

Teacher Tip

Creating a Classroom Climate that Nurtures Creativity

Not this:	But this:
Competition	Cooperation
Exclusion	Acceptance
Coercion	Invitation to join in
Criticism	Approval
Time constraints	Flexible scheduling
Rewards	Recognition
Work	Play
Failure	Learning experience
Single-mindedness	Diversity of ideas

At a Glance 3.6

Finding Problems to Solve

Formulaic Problem

- Has a required form or set of steps
- Has a best way to be solved
- Has one right or best answer

Examples:

Solving an addition or subtraction problem

Spelling a word correctly

Building a model from preprinted pieces that are to be cut out and attached together

Criteria-Based Problem

- Is teacher-created
- Has specified limitations
- Requires the use of specific skills and knowledge
- Allows choice within the criteria
- Has a range of correct answers

Examples:

Having students build a sculpture from toothpicks that is between 6 and 10 inches tall

Assigning students to draw a figure made up of at least ten rectangles and then calculate the outside perimeter of the total design

Emergent Problem

- Is discovered
- Creates the need to obtain and use skill and knowledge
- May or may not have a solution

Examples:

Trying to figure out why the tree outside the classroom is dying

Figuring out why an artist's style changed

Discovering a way to attach an unusually shaped object to a collage

Because unique art is highly valued in our society, creative processing is considered an essential part of art production. For this reason formulaic art problems are especially inappropriate and should be avoided. This kind of art problem asks students to follow set directions or use a pattern to arrive at a product that is highly similar to a provided model. Examples of this kind of activity, commonly found in elementary school, include tracing a pumpkin-shaped pattern, cutting it out, and then gluing on eyes, nose, and mouth, or having students cut out preprinted worksheets of story-

Teaching in Action

Criteria-Based Art Problems

Criteria-based art problems are the most common way of initiating artistic, creative problem solving in school. This is because the teacher can control to a large extent the materials and methods to be used and can use this format to get students to apply skills and knowledge. Teachers must take care, however, that the criteria are not so restrictive as to dampen student motivation and that the problem is truly opened ended with many possible acceptable solutions. In designing criteria-based problems ask these questions:

Will all students have or be able to obtain sufficient knowledge and skill to come up with a solution?

Lack of skill and knowledge results in frustration more often than in creative behavior. For example, imagine being expected to design an original weaving when you have never woven before. How creative would you be?

Will this problem draw on the interests of the students and get them excited?

The best problems are either based on students' lives or on studies that interest them. Designing a poster advertising their favorite music group or musician will be intrinsically more motivating than making a poster for an assigned type of music. Teachers will detect lack of interest and resultant lack of creative processing in a problem when students spend little time on their projects, do mediocre work, settle on the easiest solution, or copy each other.

Will all solutions be welcomed and valued?

When designing a criteria-based problem try to imagine the most extreme solutions possible. Although no one can predict how students' creative minds will work, imagining the ultimate response may help to refine the criteria at the start and prevent discouragement later on.

book characters, coloring them, and then gluing them on to craft sticks or a paper bag to make a puppet. Both these activities use art supplies and skills but are formulaic and do not elicit the creative process nor any higher-level thinking skills.

Open-ended, criteria-based problems. In these types of problems teachers give students a problem that has a set of criteria or parameters within which they must work but for which there is more than one acceptable solution. Examples of this kind of problem include those that give specific guidelines, such as create a design using only three colors, and those that require the use of a specific method, such as draw a design composed of a variety of contiguous rectangles having a total area of eight inches. If the problem is one that is inherently motivating to the students and is truly open-ended in allowing sufficient student choice, then this kind of problem may elicit creative processing.

Criteria-based problems can be designed to be very challenging for students to solve, but teachers should not rely upon them as the only avenue for creativity. The reason is that in most of these cases the teacher is the one who has selected the problem. Students have not had the opportunity to problem-find for themselves. The teacher has ownership of the problem, the range of choices, and what is the acceptable limits for the solution.

Emergent problems. This is the kind of problem that surfaces or emerges in the process of thinking, investigating, or working. Motivation is usually very high to solve this kind of problem because it has grown out of something already interesting or important to the student and often stands in the way of reaching the desired goal. Emergent problems can arise during a discussion, while doing research, or while creating an artwork. Teachers need to be on the lookout for emergent problems in the classroom and seize on them when they occur. Look for students arguing over the meaning of a painting, struggling to mix just the right color paint, or discovering contradictory facts about an artist's life in two different sources. These kinds of problems, especially if the teacher furthers interest by providing needed resources and skills, almost always involve creative processing. Teachers can also set up situations that are likely to give birth to emergent problems for students to discover on their own. Thematic studies, integrated units, and projects of all kinds are often beset with problems that must be solved.

Conclusion

DISCOVERING MEANING

If, in early life, children have the opportunity to discover much about their world and to do so in an exploring way, they will accumulate an invaluable "capital of creativity" on which they can draw in later life.
Howard Gardner (1995, p. 51)

It is not enough to produce students who have a basic understanding of what art is. The art program, as well as the whole school curriculum, must be designed to foster creative growth in its students. Nurturing the creative process requires careful attention to the learning environment and how we expect students to learn. Schools have always imparted knowledge and skills. But in order to motivate our students to think creatively, we must provide much more.

- We must provide our students with choices, not restrictions.
- We must immerse our students in studies that penetrate their life spaces and are built on their perceptions, experiences, and existing knowledge.
- We must provide ample time for students to explore materials and ideas and to develop exploratory understandings based on relationships and patterns they discover.

- We must welcome and value unique ideas and innovative approaches.
- We must provide open-ended, criteria-based problems rather than formulaic ones and set up situations that allow emergent problems to arise and be discovered so that students are motivated to solve problems using the creative process

This is a lot to accomplish in the limited confines of the typical school day. Can it be done? In the following chapters we will see that there are many ways to inspire learning that use the language of art and allow creativity to thrive in our classrooms. The goal of the creative process is not the resulting piece of work, although many people think it is. Rather, it is the production of a way of solving a problem or expressing an idea. There is never just one solution to an artistic problem, any more than there is only one way to write a poem or compose a piece of music. There are infinitesimal ways to utilize and combine elements meaningfully. Each student's work represents a particular combination of knowledge and skill and reflects that student's thoughts and ideas at that place and that moment in time. The same student given the same materials at another time and place will produce a different solution. This is what makes teaching so exciting. When we allow the creative process to flourish, every moment in the classroom is a wonderful surprise.

Teacher Resources

REFERENCES

Amabile, T. M. (1996). *Creativity in context.* New York: Westview.

Barron, E. (1969). *Creative person and creative process.* New York: Holt, Rinehart and Winston.

Berliner, D., & Casanova, L. (1996). *Putting research to work in your school.* Arlington Heights, IL: Skylight.

Bigge, M. L., & Shermis, S. S. (1999). *Learning theories for teachers.* White Plains, NY: Longman.

Bloom, B. S. (Ed.) (1956). *Taxonomy of educational objectives: Handbook 1: Cognitive domain.* New York: David McKay.

Bloom, B. S. (1985). *Developing talent in young people.* New York: Ballantine.

Boden, M. A. (1990). *The creative mind.* New York: Basic Books.

Caine, G., & Caine, R. (1994). *Making connections.* Menlo Park, CA: Addison-Wesley.

Cameron, J. (1992). *The artist's way: A spiritual path to higher creativity.* New York: G. P. Putnam's Sons.

Case, R. (1991). *The mind's staircase.* Hillsdale, NJ: Erlbaum.

Cecil, N. L., & Lauritzen, P. (1995). *Literacy and the arts for the integrated classroom.* White Plains, NY: Longman.

Clemens, S. G. (1991). Art in the classroom: Making every day special. *Young Children, 46*(1), 4–11.

Csikszentmihalyi, M. (1990). *Flow: The psychology of optimal experience.* New York: HarperCollins.

Dewey, J. (1958). *Experience and education.* New York: Kappa Delta Pi.

Edwards, L. C. (1990). *Affective development and the arts.* New York: Macmillan.

Ember, C., & Ember, M. (1996). *Cultural anthropology.* Upper Saddle River, NJ: Prentice-Hall.

Freud, S. (1989). *DaVinci and a memory of his childhood.* New York: Norton.

Gardner, H. (1985). *Frames of mind.* New York: Basic Books.

Gardner, H. (1995). *Creating minds.* New York: Basic Books.

Getzels, J. W. (1982). The problem of the problem. In R. Hogarth (Ed.), *New directions for methodology of social and behavior science: Question framing.* San Francisco: Jossey-Bass.

Getzels, J. W., & Jackson, P. W. (1962). *Creativity and intelligence.* New York: Wiley.

Goleman, D., Kaufman, P., & Ray, M. (1992). *The creative spirit.* New York: Dutton.

Guilford, J. P. (1986). *Creative talents: Their nature, use and development.* Buffalo, NY: Bearly Ltd.

Herman, G. N., & Hollingsworth, P. (1992). *Kinetic kaleidoscope.* Tucson, AZ: Zephyr.

Jung, C. G. (1972). *The spirit in man, art and literature.* Princeton, NJ: Princeton University Press.

Kubie, L. S. (1958). *Neurotic distortion of the creative process.* Lawrence, KS: University of Kansas Press.

Lewin, K. (1951). *Field theory in social science.* New York: Harper & Row.

MacKinnon, D. W. (1961). Creativity in architects. In D. W. MacKinnon (Ed.), *The creative person* (pp. 291–520). Berkeley, CA: Institute of Personality Assessment Research.

MacKinnon, D. W. (1978). *In search of human effectiveness.* Buffalo, NY: Creative Educational Foundation.

Maslow, A. H. (1968). *Toward a psychology of being.* Princeton, NJ: Van Nostrand.

Miller, A. (1990). *The untouched key: Tracing childhood trauma in creativity and destructiveness.* Garden City, NY: Doubleday.

Perkins, D. N. (1981). *The mind's best work.* Cambridge, MA: Harvard University Press.

Roe, A. (1952). *The making of a scientist.* New York: Dodd, Mead.

Rogers, C. R. (1962). Toward a theory of creativity. In S. J. Parnes & H. F. Harding (Eds.) *A source book for creative thinking.* New York: Scribner's.

Starko, A. J. (1995). *Creativity in the classroom: Schools of curious delight.* White Plains, NY: Longman.

Vygotsky, L. S. (1978). *Mind in society.* Cambridge, MA: Harvard University Press.

Walburg, H. J. (1969). *A portrait of the artist as a young man.* Exceptional Children: 56(1), 5–11.

Weisburg, R. W. (1993). *Creativity: Beyond the myth of genius.* New York: W. H. Freeman.

Practical Guides

Benzwie, T. (1988). *A moving experience: Dance for the lovers of children and the child within.* Tucson, AZ: Zephyr.

McKim, R. H. (1980). *Experiences in visual thinking.* Belmont, CA: Wadsworth.

National Dance Association. (1990). *Guide to creative dance for the young child.* Reston, VA: National Dance Association.

Stein, M. I. (1984). *Making the point: Anecdotes, poems & illustrations for the creative process.* Amagansett, NY: Mews.

Whitkin, K. (1978). *To move, to learn.* New York: Schoken.

Video

Creative beginnings. Ambrose Video Publishing, Inc., New York.

Creative movement: A step towards intelligence. Kulture, West Long Branch, NJ.

Creativity: A way of learning. NEA Distribution Center, Saw Mill Road, West Haven, CT.

Chapter 4

Artistic Development Growth and Potential

Every child reinvents language, walking, love.
Art is rediscovered in a child's initial scrawl . . .

David Goleman, Paul Kaufman, and Michael Ray
(1992, p. 57)

ARTISTS AT WORK

In a first-grade class

Look! I just made a picture of my family. See, here's my brother and my dad. I gave him a funny hat. And my mom—she's wearing her red dress like she did on Sunday when we went to the movies.

In a third-grade class

This map shows the way I come to school. See, here—this L-shape is the school. I tried to show it from the sky like a plane would see it. This is my bus. I drew it here at my house and here where we turn by the railroad bridge and now it's at the school and we're all getting off.

In a fifth-grade class

I'm trying to draw this car just right. I want it to look real—you know, like what it looks like. But it's hard. Oh, this isn't right. . . . [Erases furiously]

Introduction

THE ART CHILDREN

Art begins with the infant making marks. Whether the child draws with a brilliantly colored crayon or by moving a finger through wet sand, these first marks reflect the child's earliest cognitive and physical interaction with the visual and spatial elements of art.

But the infant is not the child. The child is not the adolescent. The adolescent is not an adult. Neither is the art of the young child the same as that of a mature artist. The infant grips the crayon tightly in the fist and scribbles wildly. The adult gracefully tucks the pencil between thumb and forefinger and delicately shades the picture. What is the difference? Do children really create art? Can their work be compared to the work of adult artists?

Before we can begin teaching children the language of art, we need to understand how children develop artistic skills and attitudes. We need to understand why the artworks produced by children vary from child to child and from age to age and use this information to select and design appropriate art activities for children at different grade levels.

How does working with art tools and concepts help children grow? This unit begins by presenting the major interpretations of child art that have shaped art education in this century. It explores how art helps children develop into competent individuals and looks at the factors that influence individual artistic development. Based on this work, we explore ways to develop children's visual graphic symbols. This unit ends by looking at ways to frame drawing instruction in the classroom in light of children's artistic development.

Setting the Stage

WHAT IS CHILD ART?

Over the last hundred years psychological and educational researchers have tried to describe and explain why children create the art they do. Their diverse interpretations of the meaning of child art have influenced art education in our schools, and many of the educational practices they suggest can be found in the kinds of art programs that we offer to our students.

What children do with artist's materials is as challenging to explain as art itself. Child art, like art by adults, is an open concept that is continually being redefined in light of changing societal needs and values. Child art, for example, can be compared to adult art or seen as a distinctly different form with its own purposes. It can be analyzed as a symbol system or a physical object. As Brent Wilson points out, interpretations of child art often tell us as much about the researchers' cultural assumptions and beliefs as they do about the actual artwork (Wilson, 1997).

What Do You Think?

Do you remember creating art as a child? What kind of art did you do? Was it enjoyable or frustrating? What do you think you learned from participating in art experiences?

Child Art Forms Are Universal

The most researched and discussed artwork has been that of children under five. Their early mark and shape making have been a subject of discussion for many researchers (Di Leo, 1970; Gardner, 1980; Winner, 1982). The scribbling and early symbol development of the youngest children, infants to age five, so similar to the pictographs of early humans, attracted early researchers as they attempted to explain why children's artwork looks the way it does. Rhoda Kellogg (1969, 1979), for example, collected thousands of drawings done by young children in the United States and other countries and looked for patterns. She found that children under two began with uncontrolled scribbles, followed by increasing control over direction and placement. Between the ages of three and four, children began to draw shapes and could remember and repeat these shapes in their drawings. Between the ages of three and four, more complex symbols developed, especially those of humanlike figures.

Kellogg, influenced by the work of Carl Jung, saw these early drawings as universal symbols born of the human unconscious. Child art, in her view and the view of others, appeared to pass through stages similar to the history of artistic expression beginning with the handprints and markings of early humans (Fein, 1993).

Based on this view, Kellogg and others advocated that child art not be evaluated by adults and that children be left alone to create their art. This strongly influenced art education for young children especially at the preschool and kindergarten levels. That influence appears in the practice of setting out materials at the art table and allowing the children to play freely without adult interference or instruction. Presenting adult artwork is avoided because the theory holds that it may interfere with the child's natural tendencies.

Child Art Is the Product of the Unconscious

At the beginning of the century Sigmund Freud and other psychoanalysts began to see artwork as one way of discovering a person's inner feelings. In this view every piece of art grows out of the subconscious. Strict adherents of this belief hold that direction, evaluation, and correction of children's artwork is not only unnecessary but can even be damaging to the child's psyche. Rather, children's artwork is

Books to Share

Art Development

Reading about the childhood of diverse people who became artists helps students understand that no one is born a famous artist and helps them put their own work in perspective.

Picture Books

Everett, G. (1991). *Li'l Sis and Uncle Willie.* New York: Hyperion.
The art of African-American artist William H. Johnson tells the story of his life.

Lepschy, I. (1992). *Pablo Picasso.* Hauppauge, NY: Baron's.
This brief book explores the difficulties of being a creative child.

Winter, J. (1998). *My Name Is Georgia.* New York: Harcourt Brace.
The author emphasizes O'Keeffe's perseverance as a woman pursuing an artistic career.

Books for Intermediate Readers

Croll, C. (1996). *Redoute: The Man Who Painted Flowers.* New York: Philomel.
A village boy, Pierre-Joseph Redoute, grows up to be "painter of flowers" to the French court.

Greenfield, H. (1990). *First Impressions: Marc Chagall.* New York: Abrams.
This book describes the childhood and adult life of Chagall in detail, with particular emphasis on his years as a struggling art student (this is one in a series).

Moore, R. (1993). *Native Artists of Africa* and *Native Artists of North America.* Santa Fe, NM: John Muir.
Interviews with contemporary African artists in the first book and Native Americans in the second reveal how they learned their art and why they became artists.

to be viewed as a window into the child's soul. The teacher is warned not to indicate in any way to a child that a piece of artwork may not be acceptable. Everything is to be praised and cherished.

The influence of this theory is found in self-expressive art activities in which individual expressive aspects are encouraged and emphasized and the resulting work viewed as a personal statement that may or may not be comprehensible to others. The practice of art therapy is reflected in this idea. Art therapists, trained in psychotherapy, provide opportunities for patients to freely create art and then use this artwork to draw out the patient's inner feelings or to mediate and heal (Rubin, 1984).

Child Art Represents What the Child Sees

Others eminent in the field of art have postulated that children draw things the way they see them. Rudolf Arnheim (1969) conducted many experiments to determine how children and adults perceive objects and space. Arnheim proposed that perception is a form of cognition. Sensory input is converted by the brain into a generalized concept of

Age 1 to 2

Age 2 to 3

Age 3 to 4

Age 4 to 5

Age 5 to 6

Children's figure drawings.
Marker—ages 1 to 6.

Thinking about Children's Art

What elements seem similar in these pictures and which seem different? These samples show that not only does child art change as children grow, but that there is also great variation in how children approach drawing the human figure within age groups as well. What implications does this have for teaching?

the physical object. The child's experience of a pet poodle, for example, is converted into a simplified image applicable to all dogs. What the child draws represents this generalized mind picture. These mental images become the basis for intellectually understanding one's spatial position in relation to other objects, or what Arnheim calls "visual thinking." "Early artwork," according to Arnheim, "is one of the most powerful means available to the human mind for orienting itself in the environment" (1989, p. 17).

Perceptualists believe that most people generally see and remember in the gestalts or simple stereotypes that they draw, such as lollipop trees and stick figure people (McFee & Degge, 1980). Artists, on the other hand, see more deeply. They function in a perceptual mode. They are able to sense more detail and spatial qualities in their surroundings and then express this in their art.

Perceptualists see the purpose of art education as helping children expand their stereotypic graphic images and enabling them to function in the perceptual mode of the artist by enlarging their personal mental images. Children need to be taught how to "see like artists" by participating in rich visual, sensory, and spatial activities. Art activities such as finding and touching lines on the floor or looking at details of an object through cardboard viewfinders grew out of this idea.

Child Art Shows the Child's Growth

Maturational stages are based on the belief that children pass through ordered patterns of behavior at different ages. Based on this predictable sequence of growth, stages are isolated that describe the expected behavior of the typical child at a given age. Within an age group the majority of children should, by definition, be functioning at that given stage.

Biological maturation. These developmental stages reflect to some extent the biological maturation of the growing child. Infants begin with limited wrist and finger coordination. Young scribblers grasp the marker in their fist and move their whole arm as they draw. During the early childhood years hands and wrists become more flexible and under the child's control. Visual motor coordination also improves rapidly during this period. These developments are reflected in the carefully placed shapes of the child's early symbols.

By the time children enter the primary grades, they have already passed many biological milestones that affect the art they can produce. They have established a dominant hand and can hold a drawing tool between the thumb and fingers in a fairly mature grip. Children now have control over what kind of line they will draw. They can move the fingers and thumb in opposition as when using a scissors, allowing them to cut with increasing skill. They have made rapid improvement in visual motor coordination, the ability to integrate the

At a Glance 4.1

Motor Development

Based on Gallahue (1989, pp. 24–41)

Characteristic	Age	Development
Visual acuity: Ability to distinguish detail	5–7	Rapid development
	7–8	Plateau
	9–10	Rapid development
	10+	Mature
Visual motor coordination: Ability to integrate eyes and hands in tracking and grasping an object	3–7	Rapid development
	7–9	Slight improvement
	10–12	Mature
Figure-ground differentiation: Ability to separate an object from a background	3–4	Slow improvement
	4–6	Rapid improvement
	7–8	Slight improvement
	8–12	Mature
Depth perception: Ability to judge distance relative to oneself	3–4	Frequent errors
	5–6	Few errors
	7–11	Rapid improvement
	12+	Mature

eyes and hands in order to track objects and motions. They can now plan and control the appearance of their artwork.

During the elementary years the child continues to mature biologically. Between the ages of five and seven children improve rapidly in visual acuity—the ability to see distant objects—reaching maturity by the ages of eleven and twelve. Figure-ground differentiation—the ability to separate an object from the background—follows a similar pattern. Children also slowly improve in depth perception—the ability to judge distance relative to themselves. During this period children concurrently improve in their ability to represent distance and proportion in their art. Although biological maturation is not a lockstep process, and individual differences will be apparent, most children by the time they complete the intermediate years demonstrate mature levels in all these areas, just as their artwork may also reflect a more mature vision of the world.

Stages of art development. In the last hundred years many researchers have tried to create an orderly sequence of drawing levels that reflect the artistic maturation of children. In American art education some of the most influential work in this area was that of Viktor Lowenfeld (1947). Lowenfeld created stages of art development that built on the work of earlier researchers. His model reflected what was seen as an ever increasing tendency toward more detail and realism as children mature (see At a Glance 4.2).

At a Glance 4.2

Stages of Artistic Development
Based on Lowenfeld and Brittain, 1987

Age	Stage	Characteristics
2–4	Scribbling	Random lines and shapes
4–7	Preschematic	First representational symbols
7–9	Schematic	Combines symbols to represent concepts
9–12	Gang stage (dawning realism)	Increased detail, use of overlap and awareness of audience
12–14	Pseudonaturalistic	Shading, proportion, and perspective appear
14+	Artistic decision	Some continue to pursue naturalistic drawing; others abandon art

Maturation models and cognitive development. Many researchers have attempted to unite the basically descriptive categories of the maturational art model with corresponding cognitive development. Sonja Dennis (1992), for example, found that increased detail in children's artwork corresponded with increasing working memory capacity in children ages five to ten. Theodore Zernick (1992) relates artistic developmental stages to Piaget's view of cognitive development, pointing out, for example, that the development of spatial overlapping in the dawning realism stage fits Piaget's definition of a new order of cognitive development (Piaget, 1959).

Child Art Represents What the Child Knows

We know that as children learn to speak, they begin to use language to increase what they know. They repeat words, sentences, and stories. They use these to make statements and ask questions. Soon they become readers, absorbing the ideas of others from the written page. They learn to write, struggling to put their knowledge of the structure of language into an understandable form that others can read. Children also learn the language of art in the same way. They repeat lines and shapes and forms. They put these together to create representations of what they think things are. They read the visual images around them. They learn to combine visual, spatial, and textural elements to communicate their ideas to others. But the language of art is not the same as the language of words. Rather, they are two different ways of learning about, responding to, and communicating about our world.

Perceptual learning. Children's first experiences in life are through the senses. Learning is the process of making sense of the sights, smells, sounds, tastes, and textures of our world. In learning spoken language, a young child sees an object and hears a word. The next time the child sees that object, he or she says that word. But the child does not live in a purely verbal world. The child has learned more than just a sound-object relationship.

In the same sensory experience the child has noticed the visual and spatial qualities of the object: its shape, size, color, texture, and form. Rudolf Arnheim (1969, 1989, 1997) has focused on the role of vision in forming cognitive understanding. His experiments show that vision is more than a biological process. It is a complex act of cognition that he calls *visual thinking.* Sensory information is processed as detailed specific events and at the same time generalized into standard images that contain the essential information of the original. In seeing the object, the child classes it with other objects previously experienced. Is it red and round like an apple? Tall and shiny like a glass vase? It is from these memories that early art comes. This process allows children to create an understandable conception of the world from the often confusing sensory input they experience. When children create an image in an artwork, they are using those generalized properties they have formed from their sensory experiences.

Social learning. Children are not alone in this process of learning. As they interact with the world around them, they are surrounded by parents and siblings, relatives and friends, neighbors and teachers. Lev Vygotsky (1978) describes the process of learning language as occurring through social interactions. Adults and older children provide models for children to observe and imitate. What do they say? How do they expect the child to respond? What do they tell the child to do? From this constant interaction with adults and peers children absorb the social context of what is happening around them and associate the words they hear and the images and objects they see with many layers of social meaning.

Cultural learning. In the same context children also learn how objects and images are viewed by their culture. Because children will have different experiences as they grow, each child's learning will be unique in many ways. From the community around them children learn the culturally shared meaning that envelops each object and image. What do people do with that object or image? Do they hold it carefully or casually? Do they give it to the child or take it away? Is it something to play with, to eat, to worship, or to avoid? Because we live in a multicultural society, many children learn meaning in the context of their particular ethnic, religious, and racial heritage. Is it ordinary or beautiful? Is it used for ceremonial occasions or for everyday? Certain objects may have significant meaning for particular children.

"A great ball game."
Marker—Joe, John, and Marcelo, grade 3.

Thinking about Children's Art

The boys who drew this picture share a common cultural interest in the game of baseball. How meaningful would this work be to someone who had no knowledge of the game? What cultural symbols have the children used in their drawing?

Children, however, are also products of the wider culture. Children growing up in the same community, attending the same school, and watching the same TV shows will have similar sensory and social experiences. These children may share common ideas about the artistic qualities of objects and events in their lives. As they go through the educational system, they will be exposed to those art objects that have historical and social significance as determined by the teachers and administrators of the schools they attend. They will also be confronted with the different aesthetic beliefs of other cultures and times as they study history and read literary selections. Through art education they will assimilate our cultural translation of these varied aesthetics.

Development of Symbols

From this often conflicting mixture of cultural and educational experiences children learn the linguistic and aesthetic qualities of objects and images and how they are valued. All this learning becomes the basis for the development of generalized symbols, which play a major role in the development of thought. Using linguistic symbols, children name and categorize objects. They learn which objects and events go with others to create often repeated sequences, such as using a spoon and bowl to eat cereal. They can talk and communicate about these

What the Experts Say

Views of Artistic Development

Developmental stages are inadequate as a basis for determining art behavior. Past experience, environment and many other variables do not follow an age pattern.
June McFee (1961, p. 32)

A child's artistic ability is a function of what he has learned.
Elliot Eisner (1972, p. 105)

Art is not the privilege of a few gifted people. We are only beginning to understand the particular conditions needed for talent to come to fruition. . . .
Rudolph Arnheim (1997, p. 11)

objects and events. They can pretend to eat imaginary cereal with an imaginary spoon.

Howard Gardner (1991) sees symbolic thought in the young child as developing first through language. At certain points or "crests" of development linguistic understanding overflows into other symbol systems such as visual art. Toddlers name their scribbles. Two-year-olds make engine sounds as they draw a dump truck. Three-year-olds tell simple stories to accompany drawings that show spatial relationships—a roof on a house, a head on a body. Four-year-olds represent the number of things in their art—two eyes on a face, five fingers on a hand (see At a Glance 4.3). Between the ages of five and seven children become able to use one symbol system to represent another. Gardner calls this "second-order" symbolization. Children can now write letters to represent a spoken word and draw a picture to illustrate a story they have heard. It is at this point that most children enter school, where for the next twelve years they will be immersed in a highly organized learning system designed to lead to mastery of our linguistic notational system—reading and writing.

Cognitive theorists such as Dale Harris (1963) and Howard Gardner (1991) see children's art as a visual expression of what they know. The child's art is dependent on the child's level of cognitive understanding. For example, Gardner sees the drawing of accurate numbers of eyes, legs, and ears in a picture as being reflective of an understanding of numerical relationships. In the cognitive interpretation what the child knows is reflected in the detail and organization of the artwork. Higher cognitive function or understanding is indicated by more elaborate and complex art production.

Based on this theory, artwork can be used to assess what children at different ages understand and to analyze their cognitive development. The Goodenough Draw-A-Man test (1926), in which children are asked to draw a picture of a person and the child's intellectual ability

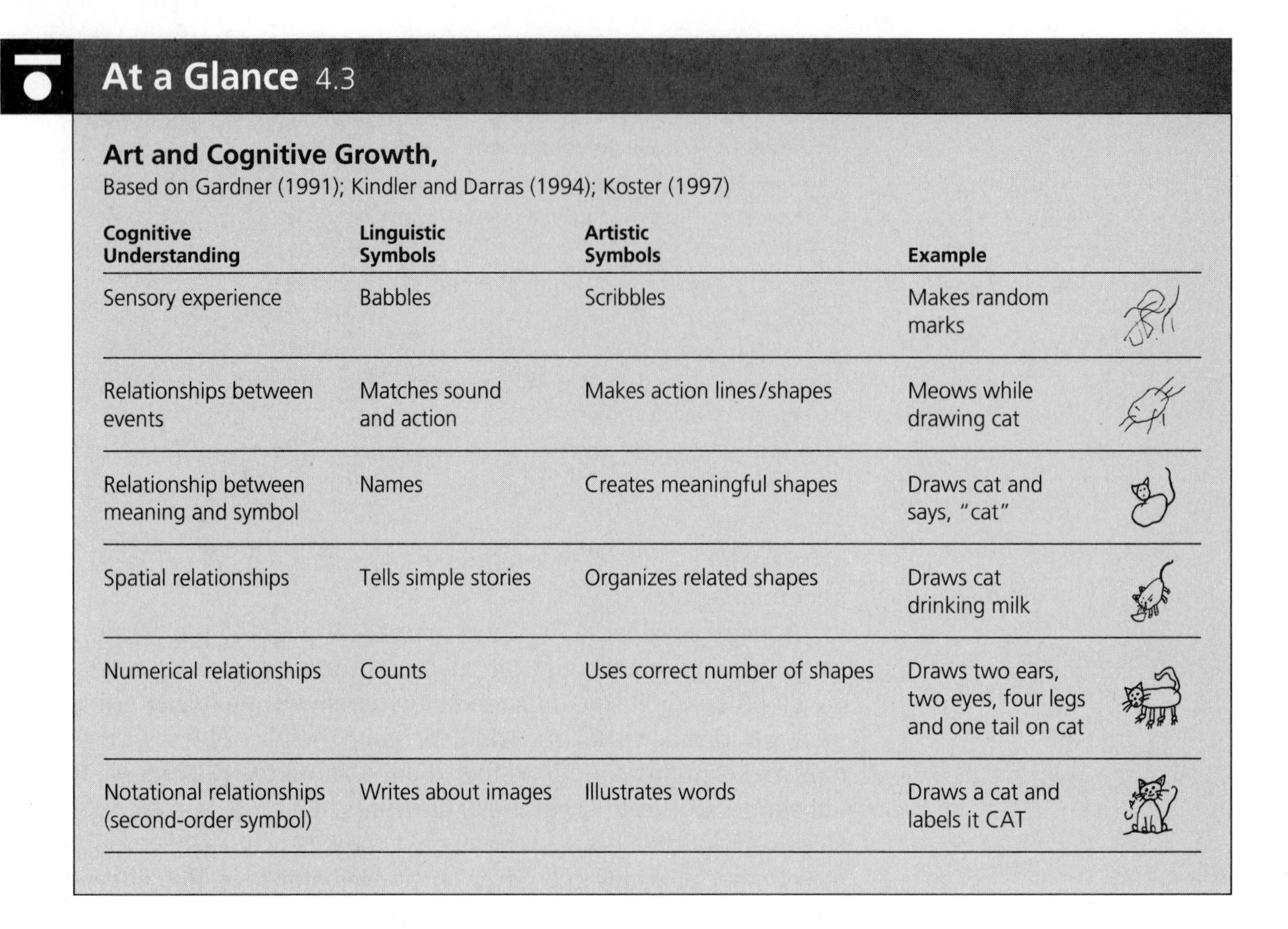

At a Glance 4.3

Art and Cognitive Growth,
Based on Gardner (1991); Kindler and Darras (1994); Koster (1997)

Cognitive Understanding	Linguistic Symbols	Artistic Symbols	Example
Sensory experience	Babbles	Scribbles	Makes random marks
Relationships between events	Matches sound and action	Makes action lines/shapes	Meows while drawing cat
Relationship between meaning and symbol	Names	Creates meaningful shapes	Draws cat and says, "cat"
Spatial relationships	Tells simple stories	Organizes related shapes	Draws cat drinking milk
Numerical relationships	Counts	Uses correct number of shapes	Draws two ears, two eyes, four legs and one tail on cat
Notational relationships (second-order symbol)	Writes about images	Illustrates words	Draws a cat and labels it CAT

is then assessed based on how many details are included in the drawing, is an example of this theory in practice. Another commonly found example is having students draw a picture following an experience and then using it to assess what they remembered or learned.

The U-Curve of Artistic Development

Researchers at Harvard Project Zero have focused on the arts as cognitive processes with the goal of gaining recognition for the arts as important domains of learning. To compare children and adult artists researchers applied the same criteria to both child art and the art of professional artists (Goodman; Carothers & Gardner; and Winner et al.; in Davis, 1997). They found that based on expressive qualities such as balance, line, and repleteness, drawings by children under five ranked closer to adult art than did the work of elementary school children ages five to eleven. The elementary school children, however, were better able to recognize these expressive qualities in the art of others. The researchers hypothesized that it is just this awareness that may be seen as "intruding on the child's freedom to produce 'flavorful'

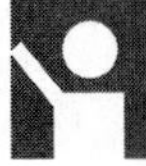

Teaching in Action

Sharing One's History

Children benefit from seeing that adults were also once children who created art like theirs. They learn that people create images in many different ways over their lifetime. If you have artwork from your childhood, take time to share it with your students, or share the book *Heidi's Horse* by Sylvia Fein (1976), which shows how one girl progressed from her preschool scribbles to elegant horse sketches as an adolescent.

Other Ways to Share Artistic Development

- Ask students to bring in their artwork and a photograph from when they were younger and create a bulletin board of their work then and now.
- Buddy intermediate students with primary students and have students share artwork with each other.
- Start portfolios of artwork that are passed from grade to grade.

drawings. Experienced expectations of perception may translate into constraints on production" (Davis, 1997, p. 51).

These results produce a U-curve model of artistic development, which begins at the top with the drawings of young children whose works are recognizable and clear without stereotypes and which often combine reality mixed with fantasy and unique solutions to visual problems such as X-ray and multiple viewpoints (Hubbard, 1989). At the bottom of the trough of the U-model are drawings by eight-to-eleven-year-olds that reflect cultural stereotypes and rigid viewpoints. This has been called the "literal stage" by Ives and Gardner (1984) because it marks the period when children are becoming fluent in the symbolic system of language. Most students' drawings then remained at the literal stage unless they chose to pursue drawing as adolescents (see At a Glance 4.4).

These results give a different picture of development from the linear models proposed by others, such as Lowenfeld and Kellogg. In the U-shaped model of cognitive development early abilities appear, disappear, and then reappear. Most individuals in our culture stop drawing during adolescence, and only the artistically persistent ascend to the other high point of the U. Since children begin school at the high point of drawing development, blame for this decline in artistic expression has been placed on the lack of continued artistic training and the de-emphasis on drawing skill during the elementary school years. These researchers strongly recommend teaching drawing as regularly as the other cognitive symbol systems of language and math (Davis, 1997).

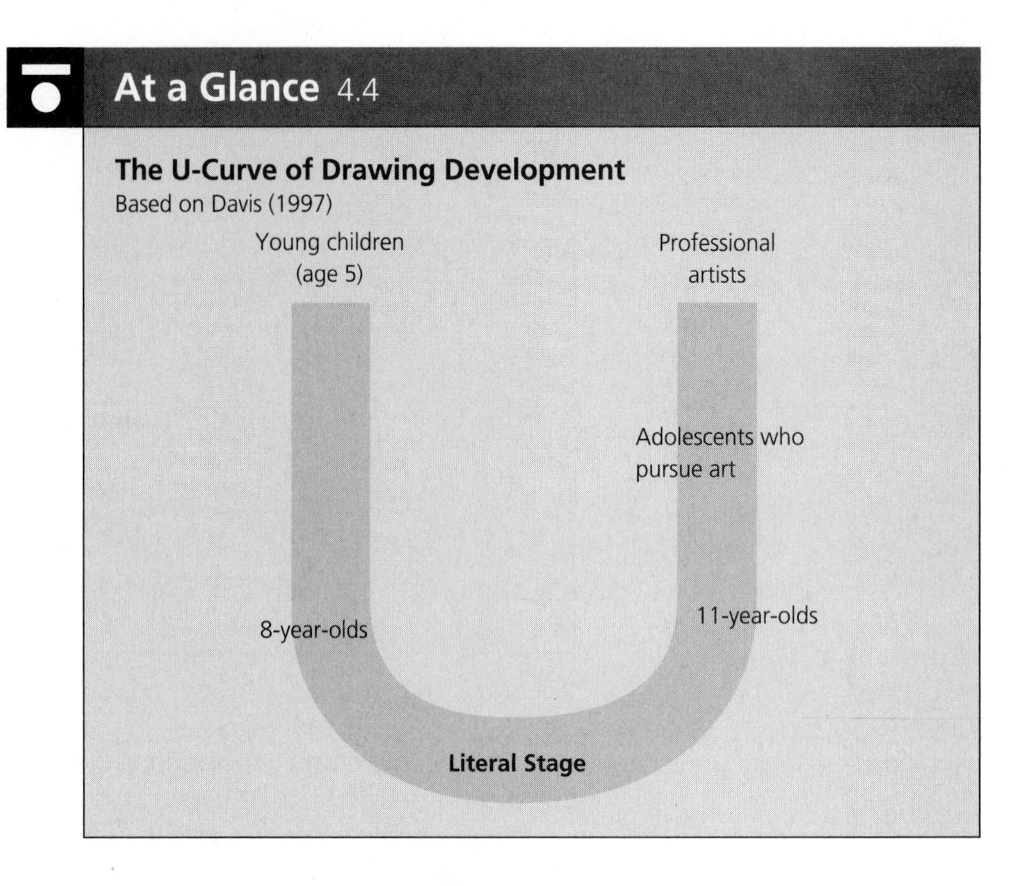

Why . . . ?

WHY TEACH ART TO CHILREN?

Regardless of how child art is viewed, it is vital to include the teaching of art in elementary school. Participating in art pursuits helps students develop their potential in every developmental growth area.

- Cognitively: Well-designed art activities allow students to apply and synthesize knowledge, solve problems, and make their own decisions.
- Physically: Using a wide range of materials and tools in purposeful ways develops students' ability to control large and small muscles and improves hand-eye coordination.
- Creatively: Open-ended art activities are intrinsically motivating with no one correct answer. Art inspires students to question, wonder, and explore to discover unique combinations and solutions.
- Perceptually: Through art, students learn to use their senses more acutely as they develop understanding about the nature of objects, actions, and events that make up their environment.
- Socially and Emotionally: Art provides many opportunities for students to work with others to reach a common goal. It also provides a forum for learning to respect and cherish the unique contributions of other perspectives as well as our own.

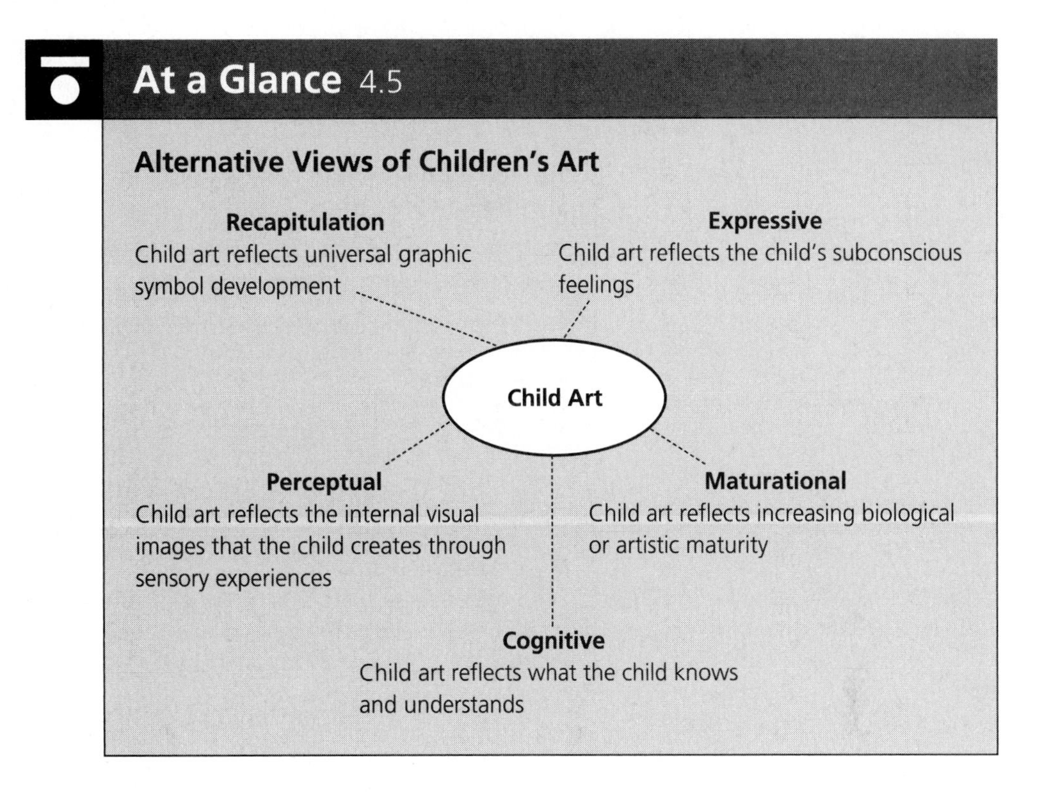

At a Glance 4.5
Alternative Views of Children's Art
Recapitulation
Child art reflects universal graphic symbol development
Expressive
Child art reflects the child's subconscious feelings
Child Art
Perceptual
Child art reflects the internal visual images that the child creates through sensory experiences
Maturational
Child art reflects increasing biological or artistic maturity
Cognitive
Child art reflects what the child knows and understands

INFLUENCES ON CHILDREN'S ART

Guiding Ideas

The developmental model has had great influence on art education over the last fifty years. In a developmental stage theory such as Lowenfeld's it is expected that every child will pass through each period of development with an ever-increasing tendency toward more maturity and realism. Such a linear view of development is attractive to educators.

Having an idea of what kind of art behavior to expect at a certain age or grade level can be beneficial in that it may help a teacher select those art activities that a child can do successfully. But it can also be harmful in that it limits the teacher's view of what the child can potentially do or understand. A teacher of five-year-olds, for example, would not mention the use of perspective, assuming, based on Lowenfeld's model, such young children will not be developmentally ready for the concept until they are twelve to fourteen years old. In addition, because stages of development are seen as a function of maturity and not education, the quality and the nature of instruction become less important than providing simple opportunities to create art.

Stage theories of development may also cause teachers to misread their students' artistic potential. They might perceive children who continue to use simple stereotypical images past the age of eleven as slow or untalented in art, stuck forever in the trough of the U. They might also view those who draw realistically at a young age as artistically advanced or gifted.

What the Experts Say

Research on Drawing across Cultures by Elementary School Children

- *Africa:* In cultures with no tradition of realistic art children did not use linear perspective in their drawings (Wangboje, 1970).
- *Bali:* Drawings by Bali children are influenced by traditional shadow puppets and can be easily differentiated from those by American children of the same age (Belo, 1955).
- *China:* Children's drawings are from the point of view of a small rise above the scene, similar to adult Chinese landscapes (Goodnow, 1977).
- *Honduras:* Children who have little access to pencils draw higher-quality pictures using fingers in sand (Bernbaum in Ives & Gardner, 1984).
- *Israel:* Children draw right to left as opposed to American children, who draw left to right, reflecting the direction of their respective written languages (Lieblich, Ninio, & Kugelmass in Ives & Gardner, 1984).

In fact, while models of artistic development can provide some direction for educators, it is important to see each student's art as a result of a unique combination of factors.

Cultural Influences on Art Development

To be valid, stages of artistic development must be universal; that is, they must appear in the development of children regardless of culture or art instruction. Cross-cultural research, however, has consistently found that although all children begin by making marks and scribbles that reflect the physical immaturity of the toddler, cultural stylistic images, adult models, and instruction quickly influence the drawings children produce. By the age of three or four most children already show the influence of their culture in their work.

For example, when the adult art of a culture was not realistic, children did not demonstrate the expected realistic stages of development in their drawings (Alland, 1983). Wayne Dennis (1966) found that children raised in cultures with rich visual images and surrounded by many drawings of people scored higher on the Goodenough Draw-A-Man test. Howard Gardner goes so far as to state, "By the time a child has reached the age of seven or so, his development has become completely intertwined with the values and goals of the culture" (1991, p. 109).

These and many other studies show that the role of cultural images cannot be ignored and that the ideal drawing progression from simplistic schema to detailed realism is a cultural construct reflective of a Western view of art. This has led to the increasing call for teachers to

"Boom box." Pencil—Laurie, grade 4.

Thinking about Children's Art

The influence of cartoons and coloring books can be found in many children's drawings. What symbols has this child borrowed from cartoons in creating her drawing of a dog listening to a radio?

expose children to a wider variety of multicultural artwork and to acknowledge and recognize the influences of children's native culture on their art production.

Social Influences on Art Development

Adults and peers also play an important role in the development of children's artwork. Researchers have found that preschoolers make more complex body parts on drawings requested by an adult than on ones they drew independently. They also tended to produce more rigid figures showing little action or experimentation than they did on ones they drew spontaneously. "For adult consumption and 'good' drawings," writes Jacqueline Goodnow, "it appears 7-year-olds add detail and fall back on tried and true formulae, avoiding novel and risky procedures . . . ." (Goodnow et al., 1986, p. 501).

The research of Brent and Marjorie Wilson (1977) found that older students' artwork was most influenced by drawings they had seen and those done by themselves. The Wilsons proposed that a drawing was not a representation of the actual object but a sign or symbol for it. The children learned these symbols from observing the way adults and peers made drawings and from drawing they saw going on around them. Skill in drawing develops from copying other drawings. "Without models," say the Wilsons, "there would be little or no visual sign making by children" (1977, p. 395).

The Wilsons' research has had a major influence on art education in recent years. Studying adult artworks, direct teaching of drawing skills, and the copying of adult works—long disparaged by Lowenfeld and several generations of art teachers—have now reappeared in many art programs, especially at the upper levels.

Multimedia View of Artistic Development

Anna Kindler and Bernard Darras (1997) offer a more dynamic view of child art, which has the potential of accommodating a broad definition of child art, rather than just looking at drawing skill or attempts at realism, and which recognizes that there is more than one way to grow in art. They believe that artistic development is influenced by how art behavior is regulated by the social, cultural, and educational environment of the child artist. In their model of development those art behaviors that are rewarded and encouraged will be developed, while those that are ignored or punished will diminish. The resulting artwork is therefore a mix of development and societal influences. They divide artistic development into three segments, which are interwoven into unique combinations throughout each individual's life.

Development of pictorial imagery. The first segment is the development of pictorial imagery, which usually takes place in the early childhood years. It begins with the child's realization that physical actions can create marks, followed by a period in which the child begins to control the nature and relationship of these marks. These marks are drawn not only in visual combination with each other but with sounds and actions as well. The child, for example, may draw a line while humming like an engine to represent a train. These same marks also become associated with changeable socially shared meanings. The child may verbally call a circle a face in one picture and a swimming pool in another. Pictorial imagery develops when control over the media is sufficient for the child to create symbols that can be "read" by others without a running verbal commentary, even though children will continue to verbalize about these more concrete images.

Although there is a progression toward pictorial imagery, it is important not to view these as linear stages. Kindler and Darras point out that children who can make pictorial images continue to scribble and create kinesthetic action pictures as well (1997). They retain through life these methods of interacting with art materials. Even adults often scribble and practice shape making in their doodles or when exploring a new material.

Initial imagery. The second strand is the development of initial imagery. These are pictorial images that are socially and culturally acceptable and understandable. The images are generic rather than specific; for example, a tree is represented by a stick and a ball rather than being shown as having a tapering trunk and many individual branches. For most students these images are developed and solidified by the middle years of elementary school and are sufficient for the limited purposes to which they will use art unless challenged by the art program. This can be compared to acquiring sufficient reading skill to read the comics but not a science text. They will progress further in image creation only if their teacher shows them the need to acquire higher-level art skills in order to communicate more complex ideas. For example, the stick and ball tree suffices for a greeting card made in a casual Friday art period but will not work in a science notebook, where the student is expected to capture the nuances of a specific tree being observed over time.

Imagery choice. The third strand consists of the range of possible imagery that individuals, under the influence of social and cultural needs or restrictions, may or may not choose to pursue. These images are divided into two major types: generic and individualized:

Generic images: These are generalized, simplified images that hold social and cultural meaning. This family of imagery contains pictograms and symbols and often bears a close relationship to the initial imagery or writing of a culture. Examples include the pictographs of

Generic images: Skin diagram.
Marker and colored pencil—Lori, grade 5.

Thinking about Children's Art

Simplified symbols are the basis of many complex graphic images. In this page from a fifth grader's science notebook a variety of symbols have been used in drawing a cross-section of human skin. What are some of the ways the student has shown the differences between skin layers. How would lessons on texture and pattern help students create more understandable diagrams?

early humans, the hieroglyphics of ancient Egypt, and the symbolic shapes sewn into the cloth *molas* of the Kuna Indians of Panama. These images try to compress information into a visual symbol that represents a rule or pattern. Other examples include abstract geometric models, logos, cartoons, clip art, and scientific diagrams.

Individualized images: These are specific images in which the focus is on what makes the image unique. It includes both subjectless, self-expressive creations and detailed copies of reality. The abstract artwork of the Expressionist painters as well as the art of the Renaissance, photography, cinematography, and virtual reality are all examples of uniquely individualized images.

Initial imagery: Houses, trees, and cars. Marker—grade 1.

Thinking about Children's Art

These examples done by first graders show that they have already learned the culturally accepted pictorial images for commonly drawn objects. Even so they are not all exactly the same. What factors account for the variation in their drawings? Which classroom activities promote the acquisition of these types of images? Which ones help children acquire more complex imagery?

Individualized images: "Landscape."
Pastels—Sherry, grade 6.

Thinking about Children's Art

After reading the book *Bridge to Terabitha* (Paterson, 1987, NY: Harper Trophy), this student produced her own unique vision of the bridge. How has the student used perspective and shading to add complexity to her image?

Recommendations for Teachers

Seeing child art as a multifaceted process that has many possible visual imagery outcomes encourages teachers to broaden the role of art in the classroom.

Primary. During the period of initial imagery development, from kindergarten, first and second grades, and well into the third grade, children need activities that recognize the social and cultural nature of image development and allow the intermixing of language and gesture.

Example activities for developing initial imagery include the following:

- Sharing their artwork and orally describing it or telling a story about it
- Comparing the images in their artwork in terms of artistic elements and choices
- Looking at and discussing changes in artwork they have done over time
- Looking at and describing artworks from many different cultures
- Exploring different ways they can move their hands, arms, and bodies when drawing, painting, and using modeling materials

Intermediate. Starting in second grade and proceeding through the intermediate years students need activities that allow them to develop a range of imagery including both generic and individualized images.

Example activities for developing generic imagery include the following:

- Studying and designing logos and symbols
- Drawing cartoons
- Making scientific diagrams, charts, and graphs
- Inventing lettering styles

Example activities for developing individualized imagery include the following:

- Looking at and discussing artworks that represent different styles and approaches to similar subjects and ideas
- Drawing and sculpting from observation
- Introducing methods of representing space on a flat surface
- Exploring photography and videography

A Question of Talent

In any group of students there will always be some who seem to draw better than others. Often there is the class artist whose drawings are admired by fellow classmates or one who is regularly asked by the teacher to illustrate the class book or newsletter. Are these students naturally more gifted in art than others?

Before we identify a child as talented in art, we must first decide on what criteria to base this assessment. Is drawing the best measure of a student's art ability? Being able to draw realistically has long been viewed as the mark of the fine artist in our culture. This emphasis on realistic drawing skill to the exclusion of other art skills is the result of several factors. In part it reflects the influence of European art history and the high valuing of the seminal work of realistic artists such as Rembrandt and da Vinci. The work of these artists has been held up to the general public as the epitome of art creation.

Also researchers who have studied child art have overwhelmingly looked at drawings, not collages or clay works or puppets. Lowenfeld's model, in particular, emphasized the relationship between realistic drawing and art ability. Based on this view of art development, tests for artistic talent, such as Clark's Drawing Abilities test, rely heavily on the students' ability to use perspective and proportion in their drawings (Clark & Zimmerman, 1994).

Another unfortunate outcome of viewing realistic drawing as the naturally unfolding result of maturation or the recapitulation of human development is the resulting lack of instruction in drawing. Many teachers, particularly at the elementary level, are afraid to instruct children in drawing. When a student can draw well, then it must be because of a "natural" talent. As many art instructors have long known, however, drawing realistically is not a gift but is based on a set of techniques that can be taught (Nicolaides, 1941; Edwards, 1979). Given proper instruction, adequate practice, and sufficient motivation, most students can learn to draw realistically.

Perhaps the most important factor, however, is that in our educational system we value linguistic learning above all others. Of all the art forms drawing is closest to language. Drawing in our culture uses the same tools and the same hand position as writing. The preschoolers' scribbles contain the forms and motions of the beginning of writing. Primary school children draw their stories before they write them. Children in our culture are given more opportunities to draw than to do any other art form. It is not unexpected to find that in preliterate cultures drawing is often not present, and skill in pottery or basketry is more highly valued.

Judging students' art abilities solely on the realistic quality of their drawing is short sighted and limiting. As Kindler and Darras show, there are many different kinds of images, and art encompasses many media and skills as well. Drawing is only one facet of art creation. Certainly the ability to capture one's thoughts easily in a graphic form is an important one. Having this level of drawing skill expands one's ability to communicate effectively, and drawing instruction should have a major place in the art program. But being able to select compatible colors, position objects within a space, or create three-dimensional forms is also important.

In our culture there are many careers, ranging from editing to industrial design, that require high levels of designing skill and the ability to work with shapes, patterns, colors, and textures but that do not require realistic drawing skills. The rapidly expanding use of technology in these fields, such as manipulating images in a computer graphics program, increases the need for a wide range of art skills.

"Teddy Bear."
Crayon and cut paper—Ellen, grade 1.

Thinking about Children's Art

Looking at her favorite teddy bear a child has produced two images—one drawn and one constructed of cut paper shapes. What different skills did the child need to create each image? If only one or the other image was shown, how would you judge this child's artistic ability?

Individual Differences in Artistic Development

Looking across the broad spectrum of art skills, we often find individual variation in the artwork students produce. Some students will excel in some art forms but not in others. The child who draws realistically may not be able to make an equally realistic three-dimensional carving. Individual differences will be found in every class and at every level.

Factors affecting art production. There are many reasons why children's art displays such variation. Each child is a unique individual. Personal history, emotional state, experience with the art medium, social context, and fine motor control will all affect a child's artwork. Even from day to day a child's approach to art production will vary significantly.

- *Experience:* A child experimenting with a new form of drawing an object may produce work that looks less detailed and controlled than when drawing an often repeated image. Inexperience with an art medium or lack of sufficient time to explore the medium before being expected to use it to create an artwork can also negatively affect the appearance of a child's art.

- *Motivation:* Motivation plays an extremely important role in how effectively a child uses art materials. Some children from as early as three or four derive intense pleasure from creating art. These children willingly spend hours drawing, painting, cutting, or working with clay. If these children find themselves in homes where art materials are readily available and their art production encouraged, they are well on the way to success in art. Skill develops from practice, and the more a child uses art materials, the higher will be the level of work produced.
- *Role models:* Having role models is also important. If the child has older siblings or adults who spend time doing art on their own and with the child, the resulting art will be more skillful as well. Attending a preschool or kindergarten that provides opportunities for the child not only to explore art media but also to develop art skill through guidance and practice and to use art in responsive activities will increase the child's ability to use the artistic process (Koster, 1997).
- *Visual images:* Being surrounded by a wide variety of art forms provides children with models of cultural aesthetic forms. The Wilsons suggest that these models are important because they provide examples that children can duplicate far more easily than they can either invent on their own or draw from real life (1977).

Hindrances to developing art abilities. Sometimes a child's artwork seems less competent than expected: first graders who scribble while their peers draw neat houses. Third graders whose clay pots sag and crack. Fifth graders who pour paint on their papers while their classmates carefully paint geometric designs. Low-level art production can have many causes; teachers can address most of them through proper art instruction.

The following are some possible causes and cures:

- *Limited art background:* A child who has limited access to art activities, graphic images, and role models may enter school with a limited repertoire of art skills. These students benefit from integrated art programs that provide many opportunities to look at and to create art.
- *Lack of experience:* Even experienced artists need to explore and play with a material before beginning a serious work. Students confronting an art material or technique for the first time often return to an early stage of representation or may produce artwork that looks less controlled (Smith, 1979). When introducing a new medium or method, no matter what the grade level, always allow time for exploration.

- *Emotional state:* Students who have experienced a major trauma often use art materials as a safe way to release emotion. An angry student may slap and pound a piece of clay. Children who have survived a house fire or a tornado may draw pictures of houses and then scribble violently over them as they relive the experience. Students in these situations are not concerned with producing a finished artwork, and their work should not be judged against any standards.
- *Poor fine motor control:* Even with previous experience many primary and intermediate students have not yet developed sufficient fine motor control to use art materials skillfully. For these students cutting, pasting, painting, and drawing are difficult. They squeeze too much glue out of the bottle and blob paint across their papers. If these students are prejudged as artistically untalented, they lose any motivation to try and may stop producing art entirely. On the other hand, if these students are encouraged and given instruction designed to increase their art skills, they retain their motivation to create art. By eleven or twelve, if they have retained interest in art due to effective art teaching, many of these students will discover they have developed the fine motor skills needed to produce successful artworks.
- *Lack of confidence:* Many students have suffered an experience that has convinced them they lack artistic talent, for example, an unthinking comment by a teacher or parent or ridicule by peer. Many individuals report a "crystallizing experience," either positive or negative, which made them decide they had ability in one domain or another (Armstrong, 1994, p. 22). These students need an art program that allows them to experience success. Using the artistic process as described in Chapter 11 is especially helpful as it provides a structure in which they receive support from their peers and teacher throughout the creation of their work of art.
- *Lack of initiative:* Some students may have experienced a limiting art program that consisted of dutifully following directions or putting together precut pieces. These students may feel lost in an art program that expects them to respond to artworks and to initiate art projects on their own. Unsure of what the teacher expects, they may be content to do the bare minimum or to copy someone else's idea. These students benefit from guided discovery lessons that allow them to explore materials and procedures in a structured, open-ended format.
- *Labeling:* Labeling a person gifted or exceptional in art can be beneficial. Students whose art skills are so recognized are likely to aspire to an art career. But unfortunately by selecting some students as talented, it communicates to the rest that they are not. It is important to remember that just because a child struggles with art media,

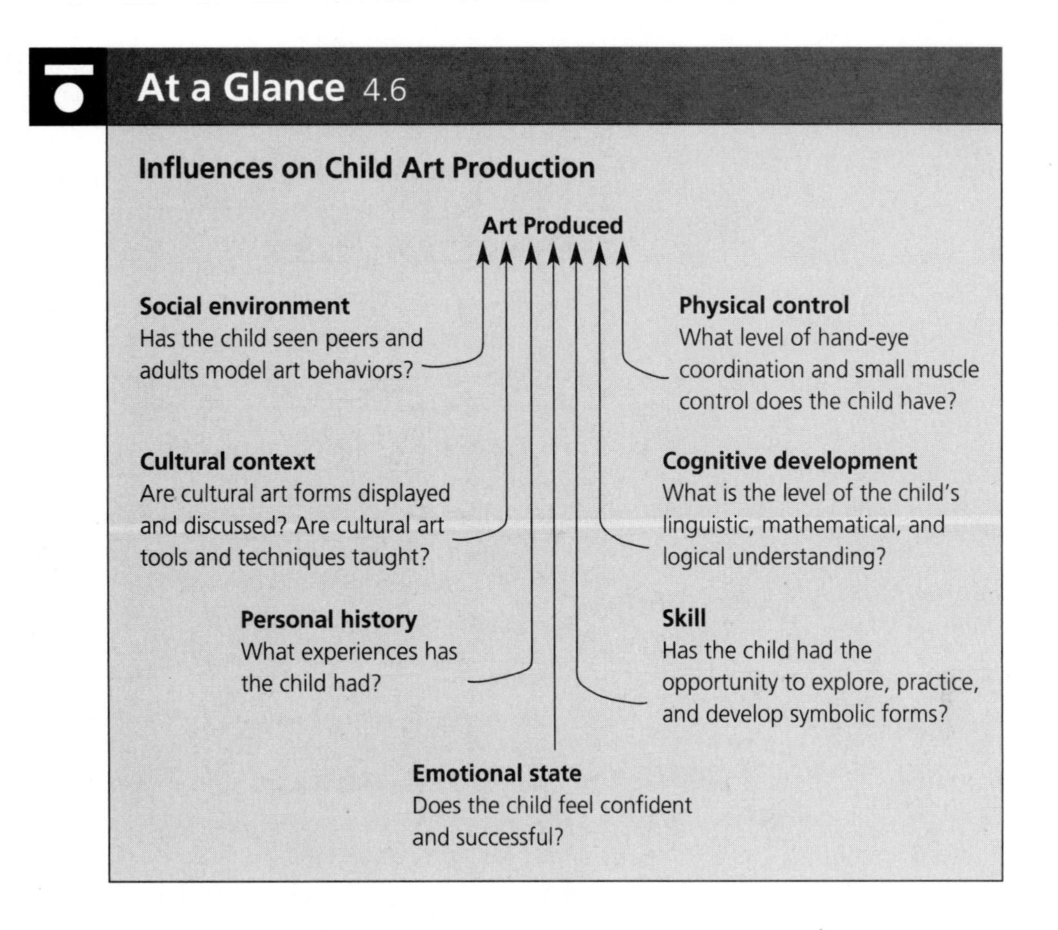

that does not predetermine that child's artistic future. Howard Gardner (1983) points out that art abilities take a very long time to develop, perhaps because they span the intelligences and require a rich store of mental images. Unlike music and mathematics, early precocity in art is uncommon, and most artists do not reach their full flowering until late in life. Some people who have done little artwork most of their lives have been able to successfully take up art in their later years.

At a Glance 4.6
Influences on Child Art Production
Art Produced
Social environment
Has the child seen peers and adults model art behaviors?
Physical control
What level of hand-eye coordination and small muscle control does the child have?
Cultural context
Are cultural art forms displayed and discussed? Are cultural art tools and techniques taught?
Cognitive development
What is the level of the child's linguistic, mathematical, and logical understanding?
Personal history
What experiences has the child had?
Skill
Has the child had the opportunity to explore, practice, and develop symbolic forms?
Emotional state
Does the child feel confident and successful?

In the Classroom

DRAWING AND LEARNING

Although other art forms may be missing from a school's curriculum, drawing is found in every classroom. From the very first day of school teachers ask students to draw: perhaps their summer vacation, a self-portrait, or a name tag for their desks. Using drawing, primary children write their first stories. Through drawing, intermediate students represent, for example, how the Aztecs built their pyramids. In labeled diagrams science students record the structure of a plant cell.

All these activities require students to use a variety of drawing skills and make drawing instruction essential. Students who lack

At a Glance 4.7

Tendencies in Children's Initial Image Drawings

In designing instruction in drawing it is important to understand how children draw. Most children by the time they enter elementary school have made hundreds of drawings. Most were done without instruction and reflect a certain tendency to simplify when representing objects. Brent and Marjorie Wilson and Al Hurwitz (1987) identify several graphic tendencies commonly found in untrained artists' drawings. These drawing approaches are found in the artwork of people of all ages and are what give both children's art and folk art their characteristic appearance.

- *Avoidance of overlap:* Objects are frequently placed so that they do not cover or hide one another.
- *Most common view:* Objects appear in the way they are most often seen or from their most important side. For example, houses and faces are most often shown from the front, animals from the side.
- *Repetition of successful configurations:* Students use and reuse, in a variety of often imaginative contexts, those subjects they feel they have mastered. The same house may reappear as a supermarket and then as a birdhouse. When drawing new subject matter, students also frequently repeat the shapes of objects that satisfy them. A student who can draw a horse's head, for example, will draw a similar head shape for a deer or a cow.
- *Tendency toward balance:* Drawn objects are often centered on a paper or, if placed to one side, balanced by another image.
- *Embellishment:* Novice artists tend to deal with complexity in form by adding more decoration to simple figures rather than by changing their basic form. A house becomes a mansion by adding many doors and windows. Decoration may also be used to fill in empty spaces.
- *Size:* More important objects are shown larger or out of proportion to the rest. A student will draw a person taller than the adjacent house or with the head bigger than the body. In drawings of faces the eyes are often placed at the top of the head oval rather than at the midpoint.
- *Transparency:* Objects that are inside or behind another object are drawn inside the boundaries of the other. For example, the student draws a car with a whole person visible inside the car, as if the doors were transparent. These kinds of solutions have been termed "X-ray drawings."
- *Mixed viewpoints:* A top view of one object is combined with a side view of another. In drawing a still-life, for example, the student draws the side view of a bowl on the top view of a table.

drawing skills or feel incompetent lose an important way of learning. It is vital that all teachers provide their students with the skills needed to use drawing as a way of acquiring knowledge and making meaning out of their learning experiences. Drawing is a tool that will help them discover insights and relationships that may not have been apparent from words alone.

Variations in drawing development: Fruit bowls and trees. Bowls of fruit on tables.
Pencil—grade 3 (*top*).

Trees with fences around them.
Pencil—grade 3 (*bottom*).

Thinking about Children's Art

These images, drawn from memory, represent the work of a heterogeneously grouped third grade. The class was asked to draw a bowl of fruit on a table and a tree with a fence around it. Can you find examples of some of the common tendencies in children's drawings, such as x-ray views and mixed viewpoints? What factors might explain the wide variation in the ability to represent three-dimensional objects in a drawing? Should all these students receive the same drawing instruction?

Drawing Instruction

As students learn more about the world, they increasingly desire or need to add more complexity to their artwork. They also want to make their art look "right" by making their drawing better match what they see and by incorporating elements of the cultural style they see around them. Some natural tendencies, such as simplification, balance, and embellishment are helpful in this process. Others, such as mixed proportion, are in conflict.

Drawing instruction needs to build on the tendency to simplify, to create balance, and to embellish. These are key skills in all drawing styles using both generic and individualized images. Instruction can also make use of the ability of students to imagine and draw from different viewpoints.

On the other hand, students need many experiences of drawing objects from different sides and angles so that they build up a repertoire of alternative images, such as a profile and three-quarter view of the face. Instruction in the concepts of overlap, relative size, perspective, and proportion will help students more closely approximate the style of realism so highly valued in our culture.

Drawing well often seems like a magical skill. "To many people," writes Betty Edwards, "the process of drawing seems mysterious and somehow beyond human understanding" (1979, p. 2). How then does one go about teaching children how to draw? This question has challenged art educators for a long time.

In many ways teaching drawing is like teaching reading. Reading can also seem like a magical skill to those who cannot read. Skilled readers can often no more explain how they learned to read well than can those skilled in drawing explain why they can render a perfect likeness. It just seems to happen.

Because reading is a highly valued skill, much research has been done to find the most effective teaching methods. Effective drawing instruction parallels reading instruction in some surprising ways. For example, the following practices have been shown to correlate with the successful acquisition of reading skills. They also provide direction for teaching drawing.

Exposure. Early exposure to books and written print have been shown to correlate with ease in learning to read (Purcell-Gates et al., 1995). The Wilsons and Hurwitz found that children in Egypt who had little exposure to drawing or drawn images exhibited an impoverished drawing style (1987). It is important to expose students to a wide range of drawing styles from both the past and the present that illustrate how artists represent many subjects. Students need to see the drawings of Rembrandt and the soup cans of Andy Warhol, the giant flowers of Georgia O'Keeffe and the wall paintings of ancient Egypt.

Teaching in Action

Negotiated Drawing

An effective way to model the process of drawing is to have students participate in making the drawing decisions. Maureen Cox (1997) calls this "negotiated drawing" and outlines the following steps of this process:

1. Choose any topic.
2. Provide real objects to look at.
3. Have children sit on a rug in front of the teacher.
4. Begin by saying, "Can you help me draw a ______? [name the selected object]. It will be my hand that does the drawing but your eyes and brain that tell me what to do."
5. Ask a series of questions that relate to drawing the object. After each question solicit responses from the students and then discuss and act on their ideas. Begin by asking what should be drawn first. What shape should it be? Where should it be placed?
6. On occasion make a purposeful mistake that will elicit correction from the students. This demonstrates to students that drawing is not a photographic process but a constant interaction between what the eyes see and what looks right on the paper. For example, if drawing a person, begin by drawing the head at the bottom of the paper and let students explain why it needs to be higher up on the paper.
7. If students have trouble describing a shape, invite them to draw it in the air. Use analogies and compare the shape to one with which they are familiar. If students get too specific in their directions, suggest that try that idea in their own drawings.

Note: Cox emphasizes that it is not important to finish the drawing. In fact, this can be overwhelming to novice artists and also require too much focused attention from the group. Concentrate on drawing the part that will give students some new strategies or approaches to drawing. When that part is drawn, transition into a student practice session by telling a story about the object that will inspire their imaginations. Leaving the objects in view allows the students sufficient time to apply the ideas demonstrated in their own drawings.

Modeling. Seeing effective reading strategies modeled by an expert—either a teacher or a peer—improves reading (Palinscar & Brown, 1984). Teachers would not put first graders in a room of books and then expect them to teach themselves to read. Nor should they give children pencil and paper and expect them to draw well. Teachers must model strategies that help students through the process. Maureen Cox's negotiated drawing method is one approach that can be used at all levels (1997).

Application. Researchers have shown that applying background knowledge to make predictions before reading, testing the predictions while reading, and analyzing them at the completion of reading are effective ways to increase comprehension (Hunt & Joseph, 1990). Students must have many opportunities to look at drawings done by adults and peers and think about how the artist drew them. They need to try drawing the picture themselves to test their ideas and then analyze the structure of the drawing based on their experience.

Technical knowledge. Instruction in the use of drawing materials, and in the techniques and methods of rendering and showing depth, mirror instruction in the structure and meaning of the written word, such as grammar, phonics, and vocabulary.

Beginning to Draw

Although some drawing activities may begin on the first day of school, careful introduction of drawing as an important mode of communication sets the stage for full incorporation of drawing into the learning process. Rather than describing specific lessons, the following section investigates ways to incorporate drawing instruction into every student's day.

Drawing, like reading, requires early and intimate exposure. Drawing instruction begins not when the student first picks up a pencil but the moment the student sees someone else drawing or sees drawings displayed around the environment. The Wilsons and Hurwitz (1987) find that learning to draw requires children to acquire a culturally specific vocabulary of shapes and images, which are borrowed either from adults or peers and from graphic images in the environment.

If this vocabulary is lacking, students will develop a limited and predictable drawing style. If the adult and peer models are not present or are hesitant about their skills, students may reject drawing as a needed skill. If students feel they cannot draw in the style recognized by their culture, they may abandon drawing altogether as adults.

This is why it is not sufficient for students to draw only in an occasional art class. Students must be immersed in drawing every day. They need to see drawings by peers and adults on the walls of the classroom and in the hallways. They need to talk about and analyze drawings. Teachers need to use drawing as part of their instruction. A student does not learn to read after a lesson or two; neither will students learn to draw well if instruction is relegated to an occasional lesson.

Developing Visual Graphic Symbols

All students begin by drawing the visual images about which they feel confident. For elementary school children these will come from their repertoire of initial imagery. As students are challenged by drawing to learn tasks and try to record special experiences and ideas, they will refine or develop symbols to suit particular purposes. The fourth grader closely observing a spider in science class draws the three body parts in proportion, where previously a simple circle and eight lines would have sufficed.

Ways to encourage students to develop a repertoire of rich symbols:

- Surround students with visual images and natural objects of all kinds.
- Provide many opportunities for students to observe objects and living things and then sketch them.
- Collect a wide variety of drawings of a particular object, such as a house or a butterfly, and then have students compare and contrast them.
- Look at artwork from many cultures and discuss how symbols for similar objects are represented.

Whole to Part

For most students drawing instruction should focus on helping them see the proportions and relationships between parts. At all levels teachers can show a student photographs and drawings of the chosen subject and ask questions that help them see size and placement differences. Is the horse's head smaller or larger than its body? Is the neck wider than its leg? Are the back legs even with the front legs? Does the back curve or is it straight? Sometimes using a drawing material, such as a crayon or piece of chalk, on its side helps a student lay in a framework for a subject.

Starting at the intermediate level, teachers can demonstrate how to look at a graphic model and then use simple guidelines or sketch lines to establish proportional relationships and to plan its placement in the picture frame.

Part to Whole

Many teachers and how-to-draw books try to help children by presenting drawing as a series of steps breaking down an image into basic shapes or forms. This approach is appealing because it provides simplified forms that fit cultural stereotypes of objects. Mona Brookes (1986), Ed Emberly (1997), and Mark Kestler (1998) in particular have enjoyed great popularity among the general public with their instructional books.

Many of these drawing programs are based on cartoon-like techniques, presented as drawing formulas. Mona Brookes, for example, reduces all drawn images to five basic circular shapes and three sets of basic lines: curved, straight, and angled. Mark Kestler approaches drawing three-dimensional forms in perspective by carefully positioning dots and then joining them. Not surprisingly using their formulas results in drawings that strongly reflect the style of the authors.

Does this method of teaching drawing work? Certainly some children who follow a teacher's step-by-step drawing, whether in a book or in an instructional situation, do produce a drawing that is more mature looking than what they would produce uninstructed. In the same way children who are asked to copy a Raphael will produce a higher level of composition than they could on their own. In both cases they are following a graphic model.

Turning a complex three-dimensional form into an arrangement of geometric shapes, however, may or may not make it easier to draw. For many young children and novice artists, visualizing the complex form of a horse's head as a rectangle, for example, requires a high degree of abstraction. These students are often more interested in trying to capture the contour of the subject and get frustrated when told to draw it as a rectangle. It is interesting to note that many students who use drawing books on their own do not follow the step-by-step instructions but rather copy the finished illustrations, just as they might copy a famous artwork or pictures from the comics.

For some upper-level students these drawing books help meet the need for easy-to-copy graphic images. They appeal to the student who is highly motivated to draw a particular subject realistically, such as horses or cars, or who is interested in cartooning. It is worthwhile to offer such students these books as long as they are supplemented with an ample supply of artwork reproductions that expand the student's exposure to other approaches to drawing.

In the classroom. For teachers instructing children in how to draw, it may be helpful to point out that seeing basic similarities in shape is one strategy that artists use to help them draw a form more accurately. At the primary level start with examples that are very close, such as a rectangle for a table top and a circle for a ball. At intermediate levels demonstrate how a few lightly drawn shapes and lines can help position a subject and form the underpinnings for a contour drawing of an animal or person.

Making Connections across the Curriculum

Expecting students to learn to draw through an occasional lesson is unrealistic. The Wilsons and Hurwitz (1987) recommend daily drawing instruction divided among observational, memory, imaginative, verbal to visual, and experimental approaches. This instruction can be combined with work in many disciplines.

- *Journals:* Encourage students to draw as well as write in their journals. Show examples of journals kept by both peers and adults. Offer the journals of Leonardo da Vinci (1975) as a model. Use journals for observational and memory drawings. Reading-response journals provide a perfect place for drawing from words.

Approaches to drawing: Dragons.
Marker and crayon—grade 1.

Thinking about Children's Art

Compare and contrast these sketches of dragons done by students in a first grade class. How have they used contours and geometric shapes? What difficulties do they seem to have had making these drawings? How have they used details to clarify their imagery?

- *Notes:* Help students devise graphic organizers and symbols that will make their note taking more efficient and utilize visual as well as verbal skills. Using organizers requires drawing from memory and using verbal to visual prompts.
- *Illustration:* Have students illustrate concepts and ideas from literature they are reading. Story maps, character studies, and reading responses can all include a drawing component. Students can draw directly from the words, create drawings derived from the techniques and styles of those in the books, or draw upon their own imaginations.
- *Diagrams:* Provide several sample drawings showing how a specific item might be diagrammed, such as a plant cell. Discuss the use of symbol, line type, color, and shading to make the diagram more

Books to Share

Drawing

Inspire students to draw with these books:

Brenner, B. (1999). *The Boy Who Loved to Draw: Benjamin West.* New York: Houghton Mifflin.
Harding, W. (1994). *Alvin's Famous No-Horse.* Austin, TX: Holt, Rinehart and Winston.
Hest, A. (1996). *Jamaica Louise James.* Cambridge, MA: Candlewick.
Johnson, C. (1955). *Harold and the Purple Crayon.* New York: Harper & Row.
McClintock, B. (1996). *The Fantastic Drawings of Danielle.* New York: Houghton Mifflin.

The following picture books are excellent introductions to the relationship of size and distance and to point of view at all levels:

Banyai, I. (1995). *Zoom.* New York: Viking Penguin.
Banyai, I. (1998). *Re-Zoom.* New York: Viking Penguin.
Hutchins, P. (1997). *Shrinking Mouse.* New York: Greenwillow.
Lacoe, A. (1995). *One, Two and Three: What does each one see?* Millbrook, CT: Millbrook.
Rotner, S., & Olivo, R. (1997). *Close Closer Closest.* New York: Atheneum.

This book presents perspective in a light-hearted way that appeals to all children:

Johnson, C. (1960). *A Picture for Harold's Room.* New York: Harper & Row.

These books for student use present different approaches to drawing:

Berenstain, B. & J. (1996). *Berenstain Bears DRAW-IT!* New York: Random House.
Emberly, E. (1997). *Ed Emberly's Big Green Drawing Book.* New York: Little, Brown.
Kestler, M. (1998). *Drawing in 3-D.* New York: Simon & Schuster.
McGill, O. (1995). *Chalk Talks! The Magical Art of Drawing with Chalk.* Millbrook, CT: Millbrook.
Vaughnan-Jackson, G. (1990). *Sketching and Drawing for Children.* New York: Berkley.

useful. Give examples of effective ways to label it. Have students redraw diagrams from memory to help them remember the information better while developing memory drawing skills.

- *Maps:* As an alternative to preprinted maps consider having students draw their own. One method is to allow students to study a map and then challenge them to redraw it without looking. This technique helps students develop a better sense of geographical locations and features (Brown & Cambourne, 1987).
- *Explore relationships:* Students can use drawings to show concepts and relationships that they may not be able to express in written form. Ruth Hubbard found that first-grade students combined words, drawings, and symbols taken from cartoons to show change and

Teacher Tip

Demonstrating Drawing

Although most drawing methods can be demonstrated on a blackboard, using a large sheet of white paper or an overhead projector is more effective. The white drawing on the blackboard is a negative of what the students will be doing and does not allow demonstration of shading techniques. Drawing in black on white more closely mirrors the students' situation. An overhead projector is particularly helpful for demonstrating drawing as the teacher can more easily avoid obstructing the students' view.

Students also enjoy drawing on overhead transparencies. Teachers can invite them to share drawing discoveries with the class or to work on group drawings to be projected as part of a presentation in one of the subject areas.

motion as they made daily observations of a rotting pumpkin (Hubbard, 1989). Janet Olsen (1992) found that intertwining drawing and reading produced deeper understanding of the written text.

- *Make sense of information:* Ask students to apply what they are learning through a drawing. Students studying simple machines can draw a machine that does a simple task and is made of at least three simple machines. Drawing the machine in addition to writing a description of it forces the student to develop graphic images to delineate the spatial relationships among the parts.
- *Study:* Converting information into another form of representation has been shown to strengthen memory. Students who draw the signing of the Declaration of Independence and then label all the important participants will remember this event better than those who try to memorize a list of names.

The Relationship between Drawing and Writing

Many researchers have documented the connection between writing and drawing. Rhoda Kellogg (1973), for example, noted that the strokes for every letter appeared in the scribbles and shapes of the toddler. Lev Vygotsky (1978) felt that gesture, dramatic play, drawing, and writing all represented different moments in a unified process of acquiring written language. The first critical moment is when the child realizes that certain scribbles and shapes can have meaning related to known objects. The second critical moment is when the child discovers that other symbols and shapes can stand for sounds that have meaning and that represent known objects. These two moments highlight the difference between art and written language. Because it precedes directly from sensory input, art is considered a first-order representation, while writing, which requires two mental operations, is considered a second-order representation (Vygotsky, 1978).

Teaching in Action

Using Art to Expand Writing

Making a drawing first or during writing can help students:

- Discover ideas for writing.
- Write more descriptively about character and setting.
- Expand writing that is too brief.
- Solve troublesome parts of a story.
- Organize the sequence of action.
- Become more confident writers if they are learning disabled.

Sample Activities

- *Discovering ideas:* Have students draw a picture. Next to the picture have them jot down a list of words inspired by the picture. From the words develop an idea for a piece of writing.
- *Developing characters:* Brainstorm different kinds and characteristics of people. Then have students fill a large sheet of paper with drawings of as many different kinds of people as they can. Select one or more characters from the drawings to use in a story. Have students draw those characters moving in different ways and sketch close-ups of the face showing different emotions. Draw scenes showing the characters interacting in different ways. Finally show the characters involved in a sequence of actions that create a story line. As students write their stories, encourage them to refer to their sketches and make more if needed.
- *Developing setting:* Have students look at paintings that show a particular place and list the general characteristics that make the scene distinctive: sky features, buildings, types of vegetation, textures and colors. Note how the paintings show season and time of day. Have students draw a picture showing the setting of a story they are thinking of writing. Encourage them to use the list they just created in developing the features of their setting.
- *Developing plot:* Build on the students' familiarity with the comic strip format by having students fold paper into equal boxes. They can use four, eight, or sixteen depending on the complexity of their story. In the first box they should write the title of the story. In the following boxes they should write a brief statement of action and then draw a picture that adds more detail. They can use word balloons to show bits of conversation. Students may fold more paper if they need additional boxes. Then have them write based on their cartoons. If developing paragraphing skills, encourage them to write a paragraph for each box they have drawn.

Awareness that writing and drawing are different occurs very early. Children as young as two can identify drawing from writing (Gardner, 1980; Harste, Woodbridge, & Burke, 1984). Scribbles that children call "writing" often reflect the written culture of their language. Four-year-olds in Arabic cultures produce curlicues and dots; American children make wavy lines that go left to right (Steward, 1995). Child-made marks may also be influenced by the initial letter of the child's name. A child whose name begins with N will draw linear marks. A child whose name starts with C will make curves.

"Climate Wheel."
Marker and pencil—Luis, grade 5.

Thinking about Children's Art

In this assignment students were challenged to design a visible symbol for the word climate. How has this student combined generalized images into a complex representation of the word's meaning? In what way does this kind of assignment develop both drawing and vocabulary skills?

As children reach school age, they will often draw pictures accompanied by scribbled writing. They use the pictures to provide the detail and context that their limited writing skills cannot. In the primary grades writing and drawing continue to complement each other. Early writers draw a picture and then write a simple sentence to describe it.

As children become more skilled writers, the relationship between writing and drawing reverses. The illustration is created after the writing. Ruth Hubbard (1989), for example, observed that primary children would draw maps, pictures, and diagrams to expand the meaning of their simple sentences. As students gain competence in writing, the need for a supplementary drawing becomes less necessary, leading to

Teacher Tip

Pictures to Words

Because we live in a highly linguistic culture, many students respond well to language-inspired drawing activities, and such activities should play an important role in drawing instruction. It is important to remember, however, that not all students can move with facility from words to images. In fact, for some students moving from images to words may be a better approach.

Janet Olsen (1992) recommends the visual narrative approach for students who are having difficulty with writing, particularly those with learning disabilities. In this approach students use drawing as an avenue into written expression. Some suggested approaches include the following:

- *From picture to words:* Students draw a detailed picture of a character, event, or sequence of events. They then write, using their drawing as a prompt. This approach helps students include more descriptive detail in their writing.
- *Drawing over writing hurdles:* Students who are in the act of writing often reach a point where they cannot think of what to say or how to express an idea. Teachers can encourage them to insert a quick drawing at that spot instead of stopping their writing. This allows the young writer to maintain the flow of writing rather than experiencing the frustration of getting stuck. Later they can return to the drawing and with help, if necessary, convert it into words.
- *Expanding the story:* Many struggling writers feel that they have expressed all their ideas in just a few short sentences. To help them add to their writing, have them write each sentence on a sheet of paper and then draw a detailed illustration of it. Next to the illustration they should then write a list of descriptive words. Using these pictures and words they can then return to their writing and expand their ideas.
- *Sentence building:* Some students have difficulty constructing sentences that are descriptive. This activity works particularly well with detailed observation assignments such as in science. Have the students select a colored pencil and draw one thing that they observe. Then using the same colored pencil write a sentence about it. Next select a different color, add another part to the drawing, and rewrite the sentence in the new color to include the new piece. Continue until the sentence becomes too awkward.
- *Talking drawings:* Have students draw a picture of something that relates to the topic of study. For example, if the class is studying trees, have each student draw a tree. Around the drawing have students write facts and ideas about the topic. Encourage them to use arrows to point out features in the drawing that are mentioned in the captions. Students can also imagine the drawing is talking about itself and create comic book–style word-bubble captions.

an abandonment of illustration, often at the same time they move from picture books to more sparsely illustrated chapter books.

For many students even at the intermediate level, however, creating a picture continues to help expand their writing. This is particularly true of those who are visual learners. Janet Olson (1992) found that students could use drawing in many ways to improve their writing.

At a Glance 4.8

Drawing and Writing Development
Based on Cox, 1997; Krampen, 1991

Phase	Description	Age
Early Writing	Writing scribbles resemble the first letter of child's name—curved for curved letters such as C, zigzag for linear letters such as N.	2–3
Letter Drawing	Growing interest in copying. Letter forms are incomplete, reversed, or mirrored. Writing may be directionless or float.	3–4
Formal Writing	Direct copying influences marks made in drawings, tendency to draw left to right in direction of writing although mistakes in writing direction still occur frequently.	4–6

Conclusion

BECOMING ARTISTS

Normally, when children are set a topic they have difficulty not because they lack imagination but because they have difficulty in drawing the objects.
Maureen Cox (1997, p. 101)

There is no question that as children grow, their artwork changes. Anyone who has observed an individual child's art over a period of years knows that over time scribbles become shapes, shapes become objects, and objects become parts of pictures that reflect the child's experiences and knowledge. Child art serves many functions. Art can provide emotional release. Children who have experienced traumatic events often scribble over their drawings. Aggressive feelings can be released through bashing a piece of clay. Art shows what the children are thinking. A detailed drawing of a place visited on vacation records what the child remembered from the trip. The influence of visual culture found in the cartoon-like images that regularly appear in children's art cannot be ignored.

We can view children's art in many ways:

- As the recapitulation of human artistic development
- As the product of the unconscious
- As visual thinking
- As the beginning of writing
- As a reflection of cognitive processing
- As a sequence of stages from scribble to realistic drawing
- As a reflection of their culture

- As the imitation of the art behavior of peers and adults
- As a multimedia approach to image creation

All these ideas about why children's art is the way it is are based on careful observation of children and their art. Each one offers a different insight into this fascinating process. Teachers need to blend these different views into a more multifaceted picture of child art. We can view the creation of visual images as the combination of perceptual, emotional, social, cultural, and physical growth with individual differences in attitude and experience. By understanding the wide variety of factors that influence children's art, we will be better prepared to respond to children's art behaviors and to instruct them in the language of art. We must be aware of the importance of cultural influences and role models in the teaching of art. We must adjust our teaching to meet the needs of learners at different levels of experience and schooling. But art is most effectively taught when it is viewed, as is language, as the acquisition of skills, techniques, and concepts. Our students become artists, as they become writers, when they can skillfully handle the tools of the domain to express ideas in a way meaningful to our culture.

Teacher Resources

REFERENCES

Alland, A. (1983). *Playing with form: Children draw in six cultures.* New York: Columbia University Press.

Armstrong, T. (1994). *Multiple intelligences in the classroom.* Alexandria, VA: Association for Supervision and Development of Curriculum.

Arnheim, R. (1969). *Visual thinking.* Berkeley, CA: University of California Press

Arnheim, R. (1989). *Thoughts on art education.* Los Angeles, CA: Getty Center for Education in the Arts.

Arnheim, R. (1997). A look at a century of growth. In A. Kindler (Ed.), *Child development in art* (pp. 9–16). Reston, VA: National Art Education Association.

Belo, J. (1955). Balinese children's drawings. In M. Mead and M. Wolffenstein (Eds.), *Childhood in contemporary cultures.* Chicago: Chicago University Press.

Brookes, M. (1986). *Drawing with children.* Los Angeles: Tarcher.

Brown, H., & Cambourne, B. (1987). *Read and retell.* Portsmouth, NH: Heinemann.

Clark, Z., & Zimmerman, E. (1994). What do we know about artistically talented students and their teachers? *Journal of Art and Design, 13*(3), 275–286.

Cox, M. (1997). *Drawings of people by the under-5's.* Bristol, PA: Falmer.

da Vinci, L. (1975). *The notebooks of Leonardo da Vinci.* Garden City, NY: Dover.

Davis, J. (1997). The "U" and the wheel of "C": Development and devaluation of graphic symbolization and the cognitive approach at Harvard Project Zero. In A. Kindler (Ed.), *Child development in art* (pp. 45–58). Reston, VA: National Art Education Association.

Dennis, S. (1992). Stage and structure in the development of children's spatial relations. In R. Case (Ed.), *The mind's staircase* (pp. 229–246). Hillsdale, NJ: Erlbaum.

Dennis, W. (1966). Goodenough scores, art experience and modernization. *Journal of Social Psychology, 68*, 213–215.

Di Leo, J. H. (1970). *Young children and their drawings.* New York: Brunner/Mazel.

Edwards, B. (1979). *Drawing on the right side of the brain.* Los Angeles: Tarcher.

Eisner, E. (1972). *Educating artistic vision.* New York: Macmillan.

Emberly, E. (1997). *Ed Emberly's big green drawing book.* New York: Little, Brown.

Fein, S. (1976). *Heidi's horse.* Pleasant Hill, CA: Exelrod.

Fein, S. (1993). *First drawings: Genesis of visual thinking.* Pleasant Hill, CA: Exelrod.

Gallahue, D. (1989). *Motor development: Infants, children, adolescents.* Dubuque, IA: Benchmark.

Gardner, H. (1980). *Artful scribbles.* New York: Basic Books.

Gardner, H. (1983). *Frames of mind.* New York: Basic Books.

Gardner, H. (1991). *The unschooled mind.* New York: Basic Books.

Goleman, D., Kaufman, P., and Ray, M. (1992). *The creative spirit.* New York: Dutton.

Goodenough, F. L. (1926). *Children's drawings as measures of intellectual maturity.* New York: Harcourt Brace.

Goodnow, J. (1977). *Children's drawing.* Cambridge, MA: Harvard University Press.

Goodnow, J., Wilkins, P., & Dawes, L. (1986). Acquiring cultural forms: Cognitive aspects of socialization illustrated by children's drawings and judgments of drawings. *International Journal of Behavior, 9*(4), 485–505.

Harris, D. (1963). *The concept of development: Children's drawings as measures of intellectual maturity.* New York: Harcourt Brace.

Harste, J. C., Woodward, V. A., & Burke, C. L. (1984). *Language stories and literacy lessons.* New Haven, CT: Yale University Press.

Hubbard, J., & Joseph, D. (1990). Using prediction to improve reading comprehension of low-achieving readers. *Journal of Clinical Reading, 3*(2). 14–17.

Hubbard, R. S. (1989). *Authors of pictures, draughtsmen of words.* Portsmouth, NH: Heinemann.

Ives, S. W., & Gardner, H. (1984). Cultural influences on children's drawings: A developmental perspective. In R. W. Ott and A. Hurwitz (Eds.), *Art in education: An international perspective* (pp. 16–30). University Park, PA: Pennsylvania State University Press.

Kellogg, R. (1969). *Analyzing children's art.* Palo Alto, CA: National Press Books.

Kellogg, R. (1973). Stages of development in preschool art. In H. P. Hoffman (Ed.), *Child art: The beginnings of self-affirmation.* Berkeley, CA: Diablo Press.

Kellogg, R. (1979). *Children's drawings/children's minds.* New York: Avon.

Kestler, M. (1998). *Drawing in 3-D.* New York: Simon & Schuster.

Kindler, A. M. (1997). *Child development in art.* Reston, VA: National Art Education Association.

Kindler, A. M., & Darras, B. (1997). Map of artistic development. In A. Kindler (Ed.), *Child development in art* (pp. 17–44). Reston, VA: National Art Education Association.

Koster, J. (1997). *Growing artists: Teaching art to young children.* Albany, NY: Delmar.

Krampen, M. (1991). *Children's drawings: Icononic coding of the environment.* London: Plenum.

Lowenfeld, V. (1947). *Creative and mental growth.* New York: Macmillan.

Lowenfeld, V., & Brittain, W. L. (1987). *Creative and mental growth.* New York: Macmillan.

McFee, J. K. (1961). *Preparation for art.* Belmont, CA: Wadsworth.

McFee, J. K., & Degge, R. M. (1980). *Art, culture and environment: A catalyst for teaching.* Dubuque, IA: Kendall/Hunt.

Nicolaides, K. (1941). *The natural way to draw.* Boston: Houghton Mifflin.

Olson, J. L. (1992). *Envisioning writing.* Portsmouth, NH: Heinemann.

Palinscar, A. S., & Brown, A. L. (1984). Reciprocal teaching of comprehension-fostering and comprehension monitoring activities. *Cognition and Instruction, 1*(2), 117–175.

Piaget, J. (1959). *The child's conception of the world* (J. Tomlinson and A. Tomlinson, Trans.). Savage, MD: Rowman & Littlefield. (Original work published 1929.)

Purcell-Gates, V., McIntyre, E., & Freepon, P. A. (1995). Learning written storybook language in the classroom. *American Education Research Journal, 32*(3), 659–685.

Rubin, J. A. (1984). *Child art therapy.* New York: Van Nostrand Reinhold.

Smith, N. R. (1979). How a picture means. *New Directions in Child Development, 3*, 59–72.

Steward, E. P. (1995). *Beginning writers in the zone of proximal development.* Hillsdale, NJ: Erlbaum.

Vygotsky, L. (1978). *Art, mind and society.* Cambridge, MA: Harvard University Press.

Wangboje, S. I. (1970). Some issues on art education in Africa: The Nigerian experience. In B. J. Davis (Ed.), *Education through art.* Washington, D.C.: National Art Education Association.

Wilson, B. (1997). Child art, multiple interpretations, and conflicts of interest. In A. Kindler (Ed.), *Child development in art* (pp. 81–94). Reston, VA: National Art Education Association.

Wilson, B., Hurwitz, A., & Wilson, M. (1987). *Teaching drawing from art.* Worcester, MA: Davis.

Wilson, B. & M. (1977). An iconoclastic view of the imagery sources in the drawings of young people. *Art Education, 30* (1), 5–11.

Winner, E. (1982). *Invented worlds: The psychology of the arts.* Cambridge, MA: Harvard University Press.

Zernick, T. (1992). Some considerations of Piaget's cognitive structuralist theory and children's artistic development. In G. W. Hardiman (Ed.), *Foundations for curriculum development and evaluation in art education* (pp. 111–124). Champaign, IL: Stipes.

Practical Guides

Allen, K. E., & Marotz, L. R. (1994). *Developmental profiles.* Albany, NY: Delmar.

Coles, R. (1992). *Their eyes meeting the world.* New York: Houghton Mifflin.

Hart, K. (1988). *I can draw: Ideas for teachers.* Portsmouth, NH: Heinemann.

Kaupelis, R. (1989). *Learning to draw: A creative approach to expressive drawing.* New York: Watson-Guptill.

Videos

Drawing. Creative Young Child Series GPN.

Something to crow about: Basic drawing. Available from Crystal Productions, Glenview, IL.

CD-ROMs

You can draw. Available from Crystal Productions, Glenview, IL.

Chapter 5

Aesthetic Development
History and Culture

When students are asked to think about the nature of art . . . they are moved to probe the conceptual structure through which they understand the world.

Marilyn Stewart (1995, p. 79)

ARTISTS AT WORK

Looking at ***Woman Seated Beside a Vase of Flowers*** by Edgar Degas

Katherine: I see a woman looking off somewhere. She seems tired or something.

Joe: Yeah . . . I see that too. Maybe worried. I don't know what all those flowers are for.

Teacher: Describe the flowers for us, Joe.

Joe: There's all sizes and colors. I've never seen a real bunch of flowers with all those colors. I don't know all the different kinds. I see some daisies.

Brian: I think the artist just wanted to paint some flowers and stuck the woman in later. Like she's not important. It's unbalanced.

Teacher: Do you always try to balance your pictures?

Francis: I usually think about it when I make sketches, but then I forget when I actually paint.

Tracie: Sometimes I go back and add something in.

Teacher: Is this picture balanced?

Charlene: Not really . . . like there's this empty space in that corner. But that's all right. The picture is interesting to look at.

Teacher: Do you mean it's okay if a picture isn't perfectly balanced?

Charlene: Uh huh. It makes you look over to the woman . . . so you wonder about her.

Teacher: Do you think Degas planned to have the woman off to the side like this so we would wonder about her?

Francis: Yeah.

Joe: Well, maybe the vase was just a little off and he added her later.

Kevin: You know, it's hard to tell. See that white flower? It looks like he painted it over her later. Like he wanted it to look like she was in the picture from the beginning. But I do wonder what she's looking at. It would be boring without the lady—just a bunch of flowers.

Teacher: In your journals I want you to write down the ideas you just shared about this painting. Does a picture have to be balanced? Is it important to know why the artist did something, or is it just enough to see the final result? Then if you have time, make some quick sketches of it. No details. Try moving the vase and lady around. What happens if she is on the other side? What if the bouquet were smaller? What if she were looking at the flowers?

RESPONDING TO ART

Introduction

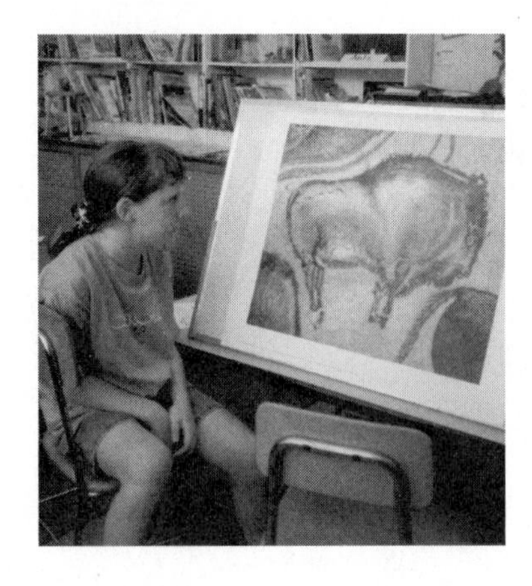

Understanding artworks is an integral part of art education. Our students live in a highly visual world. Learning to comprehend and analyze the visual images—the art—of one's culture is as vital a need as is learning to read its texts. Students need to be able to understand the different uses of art, become aware of how visual images can affect them personally, and develop skill in analyzing and evaluating these images.

Can children understand artworks done by adults and by people from other cultures? What do children need to know in order to respond thoughtfully to artworks? In this chapter we will examine the research on aesthetic development in children, establish a basis for selecting and presenting artworks to study in the context of cultural diversity and inclusive teaching, and investigate exciting activities that bring the art of the world into the classroom while developing both artistic and language arts skills.

Setting the Stage

WHAT IS AESTHETIC DEVELOPMENT?

When we see a visual image, we react in one of many ways. We can see it as simply another object in our environment, or we can respond to its physical appearance or to how it affects us emotionally. We may "read" the image to determine its message or study its history and purpose. We may judge some images more important, informative, or beautiful. How we approach and understand works of art—our "aesthetic response"—is a function of our ability to perceive many qualities and meanings in the piece. How does this response develop?

The Aesthetic Response

On the most basic level an aesthetic response is a reaction to something that is beautiful or awe-inspiring. The adjective *aesthetic* describes the response of the observer to a work of art, an object, or an event. An aesthetic response is the immediate feeling one gets, unmediated by fact, analysis, or judgment, when viewing or hearing something considered overwhelmingly beautiful or surprising. It is focused attention.

Aesthetic responses can be elicited by the beauty found in both nature and art. We can become overwhelmed by the beauty of nature while standing in an orchard where we can smell the fresh-cut grass, feel the cool breeze on our skin, taste a fresh-picked apple, see the sunlight flickering through the leaves. In the same way when we look at a painting, we absorb the color of the paint, the texture of the canvas, the way light casts shadows and highlights, as well as the ambiance of the room in which it hangs.

What Do You Think?

Imagine the most beautiful thing in the world. How do you know it is beautiful? Did someone teach you to recognize its beauty? Does everyone see beauty in the same way? As you read this chapter, think about how you would teach a child to see beauty.

An aesthetic response involves both a physical and mental sensation. We feel moved, carried away, or deeply touched. We may shiver, draw in breath, laugh, sigh, or have goose bumps. Time seems to stop and all other thoughts and worries disappear for the moment. In the process, knowing and feeling are inextricably linked. We are filled with a sense of wonder. We may also respond emotionally as the experience ignites memory, as it affirms or denies one's deepest values, or as it creates expectations for further experiences. For most people an aesthetic response is the first response to a piece of art. Whether this response is positive or negative will depend on how stimulating, meaningful, or familiar the artwork is to the viewer.

A Sense of Beauty

Researchers have wondered why people, and children in particular, respond to artwork the way they do. How does the aesthetic response develop? An aesthetic response begins with sensory perception. Researchers have hypothesized that we are biologically attracted to objects or events in our environment that are unusual or extraordinary. "Life, after all," suggests Ellen Dissanayake, "depends on reacting (or being ready to react) to changes in habitual existence" (1995, p. 50). Infants and toddlers are sensory gluttons who explore features in their environment that catch their eye, move in unique ways, or are tactilely provoking. Similarly the act of looking at an artwork stimulates the senses in a multitude of ways. Because it is different from the surrounding environment, it attracts our eyes. As we move, its appearance changes. It has a tactile surface that invites us to touch even when there are "Do Not Touch" signs, and the subject matter may elicit thoughts of sounds, tastes, and past memories. This is the initial aesthetic reaction.

Many people define such an aesthetic experience as the perception of beauty, but beauty has different meanings to different people. A work that appears beautiful to one viewer may disgust another. Cultural and educational experiences determine how an individual will classify a particular sensory experience. We are not born knowing what is beautiful. How we personally define beauty is the result of our

"A Woman Seated beside a Vase of Flowers."
Oil—Edgar Degas, 1865. The Metropolitan Museum of Art, H. O. Havemeyer Collection. Bequest of Mrs. H. O. Havemeyer, 1929.

From the Art Museum

Edgar Degas (French, 1834–1917) influenced by Japanese prints and early photography often created compositions that appear as if seen in a quick glance. How does understanding some of the factors that influence artists make their work more meaningful to us? Would having students take photographs of each other playing on the playground be a good way to introduce to the work of Degas and the other Impressionists?

uniquely personal backgrounds. Children's first aesthetic models are their parents, siblings, relatives, and friends, who express their own views to the young child: "Look at the beautiful sunset!" "Isn't this sculpture fantastic!" "Look at the way the sunlight is shining on the wall."

Children also acquire aesthetic beliefs from what they see and become accustomed to in their environment. Things that are familiar and comforting become loved and cherished, such as the soft feel of the worn, handmade quilt on the bed or the taste and texture of creamy chocolate pudding. If the child is a member of a particular cultural group, certain objects and artworks that embody that community's deeply held beliefs or traditions will be considered beautiful, such as the stained glass windows in a church or an embroidered, appliquéd folk garment.

What Do Children See When They Look at Art?

Children's responses to never-before-seen works of art therefore will arise partly from these kinds of initial sensory experiences, and from the resulting beliefs they develop, as well as from their mental ability to understand the nature and purpose of art. Research has shown that children tend to look at artworks differently from adolescents and adults. Like their drawings, children's aesthetic responses seem to be related to age, experience, and cultural influences. Young children, for example, do not recognize that art is a unique product of humankind. Rebecca Nye, Glyn Thomas, and Elizabeth Robinson (1995) found that three- and four-year-olds confused the actual object with its picture and could not always tell the difference between a photograph and a painting. Howard Gardner and Ellen Winner (1976) found that young children ages four to seven believed that all works were equally good and that art was easy to do. They thought that everyone, even animals, could create art and that a picture was finished when the paper was full.

Children of different ages also have distinct preferences for certain styles and subject matter, which seem to reflect their own experiences of artmaking. Younger children prefer bright colors and abstract works that resemble their own artistic efforts. School-age children prefer more representational work. By age ten students feel that art should be a precise rendering of reality and that there are expert-derived criteria for judging the quality of artworks. Nine- to eleven-year-olds seem to be very literal in their interpretations of works, looking for and valuing meticulous detail. Adolescents, on the other hand, take a relativistic position and hold that people often have different opinions about art that are equally valid. In forming their own opinions, they show the effect of schooling by referring to elements in the work itself and using artistic vocabulary and art history references (Davis & Gardner, 1993; Gardner & Winner, 1976; Parsons, 1987).

Children's Theories about Art and Beauty

Before seven many children have difficulty understanding that their "reading" of a picture will be different from someone else's. To understand this concept the child must learn to "differentiate between the properties of a picture and the role of the picture as a vehicle for the beliefs and desires of the producer (artist) and the user (beholder)" (Freeman, 1995, p. 42). Based on this, Norman Freeman has proposed that at about the age of seven children acquire a theory about the nature of art in which they see pictures as vehicles of communication between the artist and the viewer about either a real or imaginary state of affairs. At about the age of nine studies seem to indicate that many children move away from the idea that a picture looks like what it represents to

Making choices.

Thinking about Children's Art

Using self-stick notes on which they have drawn their portraits, first graders make a graph of their favorite book illustrators. Does this activity match the aesthetic development of children at this level? How will it increase the ability of these children to make aesthetic decisions?

an interpretative theory in which a picture is judged to show the artist's vision of the world (Feinberg, 1987; Tauton, 1980).

Other studies have shown that children also change in the way they judge beauty. Seven-year-old children believe that ugly subjects make a worse picture than pretty ones, whereas eleven-year-olds argued that whether or not a picture was beautiful depended on the skill and effort of the artist. The younger children also thought that a happy artist would paint happy pictures and a sad one sad pictures and how the viewers felt at the time would affect their feelings about the picture. But the older children believed that the artist controlled the picture's effect and it did not matter how the viewers were feeling at the time they looked at it (Freeman & Sanger, 1993; Freeman & Brown, 1993).

From this research Freeman proposes that the development of these aesthetic theories shows that children are attempting to acquire a more complex understanding of the artistic experience. However, Michael Parsons has suggested that this can only happen effectively if students' thinking about art is challenged by looking at diverse artworks and participating in activities that elicit thinking about the works (Parsons, 1987). Based on his research on children's reactions to artworks, Parsons has created a developmental model of aesthetic response to art (see At a Glance 5.1). Only with education in seeing and understanding art will students reach the highest levels of aesthetic development. "It is helpful to children to talk about paintings," says Parsons. "[I]t may get them to think about what they have not understood" (1987, p. 33).

Aesthetic Development: A Model for Teaching

Like reading a text, there are different levels of responding to an artwork. These range from the initial I do/don't like it response (Parsons' Level 1) to questions of aesthetic philosophy (Parsons' Level 5). As the research shows, aesthetic development requires thoughtfully designed activities that build on children's natural aesthetic responses while challenging them to defend and expand their understanding.

Analyzing an artwork can be compared to the process of studying a piece of literature. Without a relevant vocabulary and a grounding in historical and social influences, most people can do no more than respond on the most basic level to a work of literature or of art. "Development of perception in the aesthetic realm, as in any other complex field of human endeavor, requires careful, intelligent curriculum planning," emphasizes Bennett Reimer. "Without it an arts program will only be fun and games. To the degree that a program promotes deeper artistic discernment it ensures both immediate satisfaction and long term growth" (1980, p. 121). It is the teacher's task to provide instruction and activities that allow students to develop a vocabulary of art while interacting with the work on all the following levels:

At a Glance 5.1

Levels of Aesthetic Development

After Parsons (1987)

Level 1, Favoritism

- Reacts to obvious stimuli
- Demonstrates a strong attraction to color
- Rarely finds fault with a work
- Likes knowing what the subject is
- Freely associates memories with work
- Has little awareness of the point of view of others

Level 2, Beauty and Realism

- Prefers representational art
- Admires skill, patience, and care
- Judges work on its realism, beauty, and technical skill
- Can separate the subject from the idea or feelings of the work
- Acknowledges that others may have a different point of view

Level 3, Expressiveness

- Looks at art for the experience it produces
- Judges work on its emotional effect
- Appreciates creativity, originality, and depth of feeling
- Does not believe art can be judged objectively
- Sees beauty, realism, and skill as relevant to value of work

Level 4, Style and Form

- Sees art as a social, not individual accomplishment
- Is aware that artworks exist within a cultural tradition
- Believes that meaning comes from the audience and that public needs can determine the artist's choices
- Finds medium, form, and style significant

Level 5, Autonomy

- Values art for its ability to raise philosophical and social questions
- Sees art as transcending culture
- Understands that tradition is a social construct
- Sees meaning as never finished, always open to reinterpretation by the audience

- *Affective response:* Students become aware of how and why they and others respond in a certain way to a communicative experience, whether it is a good story or an exotic work of art. By focusing their attention on this awareness, they can deepen their personal response to art and become better able to express it in words.

What the Experts Say

Responding to Art

What distinguishes beauty in nature from beauty in art (or nature from art in general) is that the latter has had some form imposed on it by its human creator.
Ellen Dissanayake (1995, p. 29)

[T]he capacity, variable among peoples as it is among individuals, to perceive meaning in pictures (or poems, melodies, buildings, plots, drama, statues) is, like all other human capacities, a product of collective experience.
Clifford Geertz (1976, p. 14)

We should help students develop better theories of art so that they can make better sense of their experience of art and can experience art differently.
Michael Parsons (1994, p. 43)

No one places books in front of two-year-olds and expects them to understand the written text. Reading words, everyone agrees, is a skill that must be learned. But pictures are another matter. It is commonly believed that pictures are not read at all, rather, they are seen, and seeing entails immediate understanding.
Ellen Winner (1982, p. 112)

Consistent exposure to high quality art trains the eye to become aesthetically perceptive and sophisticated. Eventually, this exposure may even minimize the negative effect of unattractive and meaningless images on our aesthetic sensitivities.
Joan J. Honigman & Navaz Peshotan Bhavnagri (1998, p. 206)

- *Comprehension:* Students use past knowledge and skills to describe the experience. In both reading and art appreciation this involves instruction in vocabulary and structure and the methods needed to clearly communicate to others.
- *Evaluation:* Students apply their knowledge and use critical skills to compare literature or artwork to previously studied pieces or to important ideas and standards in order to evaluate the quality and significance of the work for themselves and others.
- *History:* Students place the work in the context of other works with reference to the social, historical, and cultural aspects that surround the work. This involves looking at the work as representing a certain time, place, and people, as well as analyzing its influence upon its own milieu and on that of others.
- *Philosophy:* Based on the comprehension, evaluation, and contextual analysis of the work, the student asks and attempts to answer questions that have broad implications for the field of art, such as the following:

  What is art?
  Must all art be beautiful?
  Who is an artist?
  Does art have meaning beyond the culture that made it?

Stars
High in the sky
Like tiny light bulbs
For the night.

"Stars."
Tempera—Melissa, grade 2.

I float into space.
I see many stars.
They are like night lights
To light my way to the moon.

"Night Lights."
Tempera—Neal, grade 2.

Thinking about Children's Art

As part of a unit on space students looked at and shared their feelings about Vincent Van Gogh's painting *Starry Night* during circle time. Later these two students created these artworks at the easel in the painting center and then wrote poems about them during writing workshop. How has this activity helped these students interweave art and writing to communicate their ideas?

At a Glance 5.2

Artistic Roles

An individual can interact with art in any of the following ways. It should be our goal as teachers to enable students to move seamlessly from one role to another.

Artist: Can create an object that is accepted as art.

Art critic: Can look at his or her own art or the work of others and analyze and interpret it to others.

Art historian: Can relate an artwork to the social and cultural context of his or her own time or that of others.

Aesthetician: Can express his or her own philosophical viewpoint about the nature and value of art and can analyze and react to the views of others.

Why . . . ?

WHY SHOULD CHILDREN STUDY ARTWORKS?

Just as reading and writing are closely intertwined, so are talking about and creating art. One process is not more important than the other. Looking at culturally acclaimed artworks is essential for the creation of art. Students cannot be expected to rely only on sensory input or peer- and teacher-created models for ideas and examples, any more than they can be expected to write well without ever reading well-written published books. They need to have many opportunities to talk about how other artists have manipulated art media and creatively solved artistic problems.

Alternatively the creation of art is essential for an understanding of the art of others. Telling students that they are looking at a painting has little meaning if they have never painted. They have no understanding of the skills needed, the problems faced, or the effectiveness of the artist's technique. Because of the interdependence of the one on the other, the presentation and analysis of artworks must always be totally integrated into the whole art instruction of the student.

But aesthetic development is important not just in terms of artistic growth. It is also vital for the cognitive and emotional development of our children.

- *Activate learning.* Aesthetic experiences incorporated into daily classroom activities activate sensory pathways and make learning more exciting and memorable.
- *Build intrapersonal vocabulary and understanding.* Learning to describe aesthetic reactions to art helps children acquire a vocabulary that allows them to express their inner feelings more effectively.

Books to Share

The Aesthetic Experience

In the following books authors share aesthetic experiences with nature, art, and literature:

Bouchard, D. (1994). *The Elders Are Watching.* Golden, CO: Fulcrum.
An ecological message is interwoven with artwork by Northwest Coast Native American artist Roy Henry Vickers.

Dewey, A. (1995). *Sky.* New York: Green Tiger.
Different views of an ever-changing sky are captured in soft, subtle pastel drawings.

Howe, J. (1987). *I Wish I Were a Butterfly.* New York: Harcourt Brace.
A cricket, believing he is ugly, wishes he were a butterfly.

Locker, T. (1995). *Sky Tree.* New York: HarperCollins.
The seasons are shown through changes in paintings of a tree silhouetted against the sky.

Philip, N. (Ed.) (1995). *Songs Are Sung.* New York: Orchard.
Inuit poems are illustrated with bold textured paintings.

- *Develop comprehension of visual images.* Acquiring a vocabulary to talk about and analyze artistic elements and principles of design enables students to better understand how visual images in our media-saturated culture are created, discover their messages, and evaluate them more critically.
- *Foster understanding of others.* Learning to see the world from the viewpoint of the artist or from another observer is a major milestone in mental development. It reflects the understanding that all people do not see the world in the same way.
- *Mobilize higher thinking processes.* Looking at artworks is a multilayered process that unites sensory experience with cognitive processes. Students need to compare and contrast, make inferences and interpretations, analyze and evaluate based upon sensory input.

ARTWORKS FOR LEARNING

Guiding Ideas

Bringing the world's great art into the school expands the possibilities for motivating and inspiring students and provides many learning opportunities. Artworks should be integrated into the school day in many ways.

In the Classroom

Displaying art in the classroom helps students become familiar with the works while creating an appealing environment. Artworks that are being studied and related artworks should be displayed at student height. Locate the works where students will see them on a regular basis. Art that is part of a theme unit or lesson is best displayed in the group meeting area, where it can easily become the focus of discussion. Consider creating a small "gallery" where you can display related art and works that have already been studied. Label works with title, artist, and a brief statement of origin.

Actual pieces of folk art and crafts can be used as they were intended. Provide a variety of baskets and pottery pieces to hold supplies such as paper clips and scrap paper. Store drawing pencils in a pierced-work tin container.

In the Hallways

Quality reproductions of artworks and original works, if available, that have been studied or are related to student studies should also be displayed in the hallways or other public places of the school. Honoring these works shows their importance beyond the classroom lesson. It allows students who have moved on to other grades to revisit and remember old friends. This does not mean that students' artworks are displaced. Rather student work should be intermingled with these works.

Selecting Artworks to Study

Artworks to be studied in such depth need to be selected carefully. For many students these will be their first and perhaps only encounter with the world of art. Through these experiences they will form and broaden their personal definition of art. This provides the perfect opportunity to introduce them to works that come from many times and cultures and that will challenge and excite their vision.

In order to do this, select artwork based on the following guidelines:

- *Quality.* Artworks should represent the best of their type. They should be well crafted, original in design, and recognized by others as notable. Look for works that are in museums, are described in articles or books, or are sold in art galleries or at juried fairs.
- *Variety of media and techniques.* There should be a wide range of works representing many media and technical approaches. Painting reproductions are most readily available and frequently overused. Too often students are left with the impression that painting is the only important art form. Make sure that sculpture, prints, collages, crafts, and unconventional art forms are equally represented. If, for example, four works are studied in a theme unit, each should represent a different art form.
- *Variety of styles, cultures, and artists.* Artworks have been created for many different purposes by people all over the world. Expand

students' artistic vision by presenting works that enrich and challenge their definition of art. Look to the past, but also look to the present. Select contemporary works created by artists of different racial and ethnic groups as well as the traditional works of early civilizations. Make sure to include women artists and artists of different ages.

- *Meaningful.* Works to be studied must be meaningful in some way to the students viewing them. Many works appeal to basic human interests. Faces, for example, are fascinating to children. Even infants will look longer at a face image than any other. Food, home, family, and everyday activities can also draw students, particularly primary children, into a work and provide a basis for discussion. Works that relate to topics being studied across the curriculum draw their meaning from context. Alexander Calder's mobile *Fish Tail and Lobster Trap* will have a deeper meaning for students studying the ocean than for those involved in a desert study.
- *Representative.* It is important to include works that represent the cultural backgrounds of all the students. Strive for balance by selecting works that let all students know that their ethnic heritage and beliefs are valued. Artworks should not come from just one art tradition or represent the work of one racial, ethnic, or gender group. Nor should the art of one group be superficially presented in the context of a holiday, such as hanging up pictures of Native American art only at Thanksgiving. Teachers must guard against selecting only works they like or that are familiar. Embracing diversity creates an accepting environment where differences are celebrated and our students' vision is broadened.

Sources of Artwork

Artworks to be studied should represent the best examples available.

Original artworks. Original artworks, of course, should always be the first choice. Students need to see the brush strokes, catch the light reflecting off the surface textures, and have the opportunity to walk all around a monumental sculpture. Trips to museums, galleries, and art shows and visits by professional artists must be an integral part of every art program.

Fine art reproductions. It is also important, however, for students to have close contact with artworks daily. They need to see the work they are studying day after day. It should inhabit their classroom and their mind. It should become as familiar and comfortable as an old friend. It should be accompanied by other old friends that have been examined earlier and by related artworks that can be compared to it.

Teacher Tip

Artworks selected for in-depth study should have many linkages. Use this selection checklist to determine if an artwork is appropriate for study.

Check each box that applies to the artwork under consideration. Select works that meet all or most of the criteria.

- ☐ It is from a museum collection, is published in a book or article, was purchased at a juried fair, or is a technically well-done example of ethnic folk art.
- ☐ It is in a medium that is familiar to the students.
- ☐ It is a different medium from that studied in the two previous units.
- ☐ It can be used to introduce students to new techniques, media, or art concepts.
- ☐ It comes from the cultural tradition of some of the students in the class.
- ☐ It is from a different cultural tradition than that of the two previous artworks studied.
- ☐ The artist who created this work is of a different gender, ethnicity, or racial group than that of the last two artists studied.
- ☐ It has a subject with which the students can identify or that will intrigue them.
- ☐ It relates to the literature being taught.
- ☐ It relates to the science being taught.
- ☐ It relates to the social studies being taught.
- ☐ It relates to the music being taught.
- ☐ It relates to the dance being taught.
- ☐ Other artworks can be compared or contrasted with it.
- ☐ It will challenge students' ideas about art.

- *Posters:* Fine art reproductions make it possible for every classroom to display a masterpiece. Works from many times, places, and cultures are available at reasonable cost and in a variety of sizes (see "Resources" at the end of this chapter). Purchase poster-sized prints for classroom discussion and display.
- *Book-sized:* Medium-sized prints are perfect for small study groups and a classroom art file. These often appear on calendars and in magazines.
- *Mini-prints.* Postcard-sized prints are for sale at museums and from suppliers. Even smaller prints can be clipped from catalogs and magazines. Use these in student journals and for sorting activities and art games.

Art artifacts. Every culture produces works that embody tradition. Such works represent the ethnic heritage and lifestyle of the people. They are intended for daily or ritual use and are often made with great skill and reverence. Very often they are unsigned, and yet they retain the mark of the artist. They are not uniform or mass produced. They have unique forms and colors.

Many crafts fit this category. Because they are intended to be used, they are durably constructed and relatively inexpensive. They provide an opportunity for students to handle and use an artwork. Every classroom can have a beautiful handmade basket or piece of pottery for students to examine and learn to love.

When selecting an artifact, look for those that reflect the hand of the artist and the community in which it was made. It should be of high technical quality and represent a traditional art form of the artist's culture. Its materials should come from the locality where it was made (see At a Glance 5.3).

These kinds of artifacts, such as quilts, baskets, and pottery, can often be brought in and shared by students and teachers. Also craft fairs and charitable organizations sell such works and provide information on the creators and on how the money will be used to help them.

Using Mini-Prints

Small, postcard-sized prints can be purchased or constructed from pictures of art clipped from magazines and catalogs and glued on tag board. These provide an ideal tool for sorting activities and games of all kinds.

Sorting sets. Make up sorting sets, mix them up, and place them in attractive folders, baskets, or boxes. In each set include from four to twelve pairs of prints that match in some way. Create an "Art Smart" center where students can challenge themselves to match the pairs. Suggested sorting sets ranked from easiest to most difficult include the following

- Sets of duplicate pictures
- Sets containing prints with matching cards bearing a related color, shape, or symbol
- Sets that are predominantly the same color, subject, style, etc.
- Sets that illustrate different art forms or styles
- Sets that illustrate art from different cultures
- Sets that illustrate the work of different artists
- Sets of similar subjects represented by art from different times and cultures

Mini-print games. Offer art games along with other games at free choice time. Many commercial games are available (see "Resources" at the end of this chapter). The following traditional games can be easily made using art mini-prints:

At a Glance 5.3

Multicultural Artifacts

- Banners
- Baskets
- Batik
- Beads
- Beadwork
- Calligraphy
- Clay figurines
- Cloth, hand-painted, hand-dyed, or hand-printed
- Dolls, handmade
- Eggs, hand-decorated
- Embroidery
- Ethnic clothing
- Furniture, handmade
- Glassware, hand-blown or formed
- Gourds, carved
- Jewelry, one-of-a-kind
- Lacquerware
- Metalwork
- Paper, hand-cast
- Paper cutouts
- Papier-mâché
- Persian carpets
- Pierced paper
- Pottery, handmade
- Puppets
- Quilts
- Sand painting
- Scrimshaw
- Tapestries
- Tinware
- Weavings
- Wrought iron
- Yarn paintings

- *Concentration:* Place pairs of cards face down. The more pairs used, the harder the game. Turn over two cards at a time. If it's a match, player keeps cards. The winner is the one with the most pairs. Advanced variation: Match print with artist's name, style, culture, etc.
- *Art Connoisseur.* In this twist on Old Maid, make up matching pairs of cards as described for Concentration. On one card write "Art Connoisseur." Play according to the rules of Old Maid, except that the winner is the one left holding the Connoisseur card.
- *Art Bingo.* Make up bingo boards on which are written artists' names, styles, media, cultures, etc. The caller holds up a mini-print and the players cover the word that describes it.
- *Go Fish:* Place a deck of cards face down. Starting with five cards, each student tries to make up the most pairs of cards. On each turn they draw a card from the next player, lay down any pairs in their hand, and take fresh cards from the deck as needed.

Connecting with Curriculum

The study of artworks can be integrated into the existing curriculum through the use of curriculum connections. For example, as part of a fifth-grade social studies unit on Africa, the teacher might display

Pencil—Tracy, grade 5.

Pencil—Sarah, grade 5.

Pencil—Mia, grade 5.

Pencil—Andrew, grade 5.

Journal sketches of a pre-Inca polychrome pot from Pachacamac (Lima, Peru).

Thinking about Children's Art

Sketching in their journals a work of art, such as this pre-Incan Peruvian pot, helps students look more closely at the artwork. It also helps the teacher discover what students find important in the work. What features did all four students include in their artwork?

masks from Africa and talk about how masks are made and used in African culture. Doing so can enrich student learning by providing visual and aesthetic connections to the material being studied. However, take care to avoid simplistic or stereotyped coverage of the art form. Presentation of the works must be accompanied by meaningful discussion and study about the contributions of artists to the cultural and ethnic identity of their people.

For example, the study of African masks could include discussion about the role of masks in the different cultures of Africa and consider the question, Is it all right for Westerners to hang African masks in museums even though they are not considered art by their makers and are usually discarded after use?

This kind of study requires teachers to learn as much about the artwork as they do about the other unit materials they must teach and to make sure that curriculum connections are

- *Relevant.* Artworks should relate directly to the content being studied. If students are discussing contemporary life, then the artwork should reflect the contemporary experience of the people, not just famous works from their past.
- *Real.* The students need to interact with real artworks either through museum visits, traveling art exhibits, visiting artists, or, if that is not possible, through full-sized, high-quality photographic reproductions of the art. Reliance on commercial materials that may provide a brief synopsis about the art and reproducible line drawings for students to color, or miniature reproductions in textbooks, shortchanges student learning. Such commercial materials simplify the visual

experience of the artwork, removing the differentiating complexity of elements such as color and texture, and replaces it with stereotypes that diminish the possibility of aesthetic response and hinder appreciation rather than develop it.

- *In depth.* Casually mentioning that the Pueblos make pottery or the Navajo weave rugs does not constitute a curriculum connection. Students need time to examine the artworks closely, to read books or view videos about artists from that culture, to explore in a hands-on way the media and materials of the culture, and to discuss what they have learned.

Expanding Artistic Vision

Selecting artworks to be displayed and studied is just one part of educating the artistic vision of our students. We need to pay equally careful attention to all the other visual images that surround them at school. It is hard to raise the level of artistic response when students see poorly done commercial cartoon cutouts on the bulletin boards and stereotypical line drawings on their worksheets. We need to select these images based on the same criteria. Look for high-quality bulletin board images that relate to the total environment. Beautiful photographs and posters are available from many sources, or consider using student artwork instead of commercial items.

Analyze the artwork on worksheets closely. Do the images add to the meaning of the sheet? Do they represent quality drawing? Do they expand students' vision of art? White-out unacceptable drawings. Substitute reproductions of the artwork being studied by the class. This is an excellent way, for example, to unify worksheets being used in a thematic study. Art specialists can assist classroom teachers in designing quality graphics for the students' instructional materials.

Going Further

Displaying beautiful artworks is just the beginning, however. Although students will develop some familiarity with these works as they walk past them in the hall or glance at them during a lesson, their aesthetic response will be at a "favorites" level. Without further study and discussion the works will remain disconnected from their history and culture and eventually be viewed as little more than interesting decoration.

In the Classroom

LEARNING TO LOOK

The experience of looking closely at artworks belongs in every elementary classroom. Primary students who are developing an understanding of the nature of art need many opportunities to interact with artworks. Intermediate students who are discovering that art can speak differently to each viewer and who are coming to have initial theories about art need time to think and analyze artworks. All students need to explore the wondrous works of art that speak to us of human culture. These kinds of experiences do not have to be separate from everyday learning. Rather they can provide the basis for developing oral language skills, writing skills, and conceptual organizational thinking skills.

Primary children, and children of any age who have had little experience with viewing art, are at an initial stage of aesthetic development and benefit most from activities that help them develop vocabulary and make them comfortable looking at and responding to a variety of art. Intermediate students need activities that challenge their initial reactions, push them to defend opinions, and provide them with tools for seeing artworks more deeply. This is the basis for the primary and intermediate activities suggested in the following section. At a Glance 5.4 further details aesthetic response activities by grade level.

Engaging the Viewer

All the following techniques can be used to capture the initial attention of students in preparation for an in-depth study of an artwork:

- *Be enthusiastic.* Use a voice that is full of energy and enthusiasm.
- *Engage the senses.* Play related background, or "looking" music," change the lighting, spray a scent.
- *Be playful.* Use a puppet or stuffed animal "art expert" to talk to the children about the work.
- *Tell a story.* Share a story that creates wonderment and mystery. Marianne Saccardi (1997) has written well-researched and finely crafted stories about art from around the world that can be used at all grade levels and that provide a model for teachers' own creations.
- *Awaken curiosity.* Cover up the print with a sheet of paper in which is cut a small opening that allows a tantalizing part of the picture to peek through.
- *Read a book.* Many wonderful children's books tell about artists' lives.
- *Play a game.* Play a version of "I see a color" in which one child names a detail in the artwork and others try to find it. Giving each child a cardboard "looking" tube makes the game even more challenging and fun.

The Affective Response

By the time children enter elementary school, they have already been exposed to thousands of images on TV, in movies, and more and more commonly on the computer screen. They have also been surrounded

At a Glance 5.4

Suggested Sequence of Aesthetic Response Skills

Level	Affective	Descriptive	Critical	Historical	Philosophical
Primary/Novice: Grades 1 and 2 or those new to studying art	Can describe feelings orally ■ Uses similes ■ Uses metaphors Can state the feelings of a peer. Can write a simple 1 or 2 sentence response. Can mentally picture the work.	Can describe the subject of an artwork. Can name the elements of art and identify them in an artwork. Can read and write words for colors, art elements, and the basic art media and tools they have used. Can describe the appearance of an artwork using the taught vocabulary.	Can sort works by subject, media, art elements, and basic stylistic features. Applies basic subject classifications, such as landscape, still life, and portrait. Applies basic style classifications, such as realistic and non-realistic. Can identify the purpose of selected art works. Can identify balanced and unbalanced works.	Can identify artists and places where art has been made. Can give examples of art from different places. Applies knowledge of cultural differences by sorting selected art by culture.	Can compare artworks to familiar objects. Can make simple statements about their artistic beliefs.

Level	Affective	Descriptive	Critical	Historical	Philosophical
Intermediate: Grades 3, 4, 5	Can describe feelings orally and in writing using simile, metaphor, and analogy. Can list the factors that affect one's feelings about an artwork. Can write 1 or more paragraphs in response. Can mentally manipulate an artwork, i.e., imagine it from different views and in different forms.	Can describe how art elements, subject matter, and media are used in combination in an artwork. Can identify and apply the principles of design. Can describe the composition of an artwork. Has an increased reading and writing vocabulary of art terms and can use these words in written responses.	Can classify works in many different ways, including by major stylistic or cultural groupings. Can evaluate if an artwork fits a certain category. Can evaluate which artworks meet specified criteria. Can compare artworks to each other and to works of literature, music, and dance. Can identify symbolism, themes, and multiple functions in selected artworks.	Can place selected artworks on maps and timelines. Can explain how social, historical, and religious events have influenced art. Can list factors that influence the creation of art. Can use reference materials to research and write about selected artworks. Can discuss art in relation to the artist's life story.	Can justify beliefs about art with data-based supportive statements. Can use knowledge of art to offer opinions about hypothetical situations.

Level	Affective	Descriptive	Critical	Historical	Philosophical
Advanced: Grade 6	Can write highly descriptive personal responses to art works that show a rich vocabulary, awareness of sensory qualities. Can explain the reactions of others to an artwork. Can write a well-organized essay. Can make sketches that reflect mental manipulation of artworks.	Can write or orally describe an artwork in terms of its subject, theme, and compositional design. Has a broad knowledge of art vocabulary, definitions, and concepts. Knows how to find information on art when needed.	Can design criteria on which to classify and evaluate artworks. Can defend one's evaluation of artworks with reference to supporting documentation. Can analyze the use of symbols and themes as a function of meaning.	Has a broad knowledge of the art forms created over time throughout the world. Can provide alternative views of an artwork based on its historical, social, and cultural context. Can write a research-based in-depth comparative analysis of artworks representing a particular period of time.	Can defend one's theory against that of others. Can apply theories about art to hypothetical situations. Can apply one's theory to solve a research or artistic problem.

in their homes by the colors, textures, forms, and possibly artworks that reflect the taste of their parents. Children from different ethnic and religious groups may also have experienced folk and religious art forms. It is not surprising that students react differently to the same artwork. Learning that different class members react in different ways is an important first step toward developing intergroup respect.

Sharing the affective response. Before the student can look at an artwork in depth, teachers must acknowledge the students' first reactions. If they do not, the student whose initial reaction is unfavorable will often stop paying attention. The student who reacts deeply, on the other hand, needs time to recover and will be annoyed if the work is instantly discussed critically. By allowing students time to share their feelings, we engage their attention while recognizing the importance of their personal responses. This motivates the students to look closer. As they hear others share different reactions to the same work, they begin to analyze the work more thoroughly in order to defend or readjust their initial thoughts.

Encouraging sharing. When asked to share their response to a work, most children are at a loss for words. It is not often that they are asked to share sensory and emotional feelings. It is the teacher's job to move them beyond the brief "I like it," It's okay," or "It's awful" statements to a deeper understanding of what they are feeling. Teachers need to teach students how to put this feeling into words and then let them practice sharing it with others. This will also allow them to develop

Teaching in Action

Developing Affective Skills

The following strategies can be used in any combination and with any grade level to help students become aware of and then better express what they are feeling. Teachers will also benefit from practicing these skills along with their students.

Practice using similes, analogies, and metaphors.
Examples:
- The tree in this painting is like a giant hand. (simile)
- The tree in this painting bends over the lake in the same way a mother bends over her child. (analogy)
- The tree holds the sun in its branches. (metaphor)

Set up activities that enable students to practice showing sensitivity to the feelings of others.
Examples:
- Students can listen to a partner share a feeling and then repeat it back to the partner for corroboration
- Try having students pick partners and then predict how they will respond to a selected artwork. Compare the prediction to the actual response.
- Brainstorm a list of factors that influence what art people prefer.

Extend the experience beyond just looking and telling.
Examples:
- Look at the work in a new way. Take a new point of view: Look up or down at the work. Use viewfinders—holes cut in a paper, a camera, or a magnifying glass.
- Translate the experience into another symbol system. Write a poem or journal response. Compose a song. Create a dance. Perform a tableau.
- Use other senses. Smell and eat the kind of fruit in a still-life. Listen to forest sounds when viewing a forest scene. Touch the surface of the artwork (if possible). Assume the facial expression and pose of a person in an artwork and think about how it feels.

Help students develop stronger mental images.
Examples:
- Teach relaxation techniques.
- Direct students to look at the work, close their eyes, and try to see it mentally. Practice until students can sketch the work without looking.
- Encourage students to imagine what happened before or after the scene in the picture. Describe what the artwork would look like if it extended in different directions. What would happen if it were shrunk or enlarged or the colors were changed?

fluency of expression as they gain skill in comprehending, analyzing, and evaluating artworks.

There are many ways to allow students to share what they feel when they look at an artwork. Teachers should give students the opportunity to use different forms of response. Address the different strengths of each student by creating a climate that welcomes a range of reaction. Inspired by an artwork, students can write in journals, draw a picture, invent a dance, hum a melody, create a dramatic soliloquy, or associate a taste or smell. Many of these affective response activities are highly motivating to students and make perfect introductions to more formal lessons.

Description

Describing and making meaning of an artwork requires the same skills that reading a book does. Students need to know the basic elements and structures found in a work—the words, sentences, and grammar of art. From these they can build a linguistic description of the appearance of the work.

Artworks can be described in many ways. Students often begin by focusing on subject matter. For example, a student looking at Jasper Johns's *Three Flags* might say, "I see three red, white, and blue American flags—a small one, a middle-sized one, and a large one." Initial responses will reflect inexperience with looking at art. With instruction and practice students' vocabulary, and their understanding of art elements, design principles, and art techniques, can expand, resulting in more meaningful descriptions and understanding (see At a Glance 5.5 and Chapter 12).

Developing vocabulary. Teachers need to model the use of art vocabulary whenever they work with students creating or talking about art. This helps students acquire the words they need in order to communicate more effectively about art. Students should not only hear the words but also use them. Provide plenty of opportunities for all students to speak, read, and write relevant art words. Have students give a brief oral description of an artwork using a specified term. Write words and definitions in journals and on charts. Use art words in math word problems and grammar exercises. Include them in spelling assignments and vocabulary study.

Writing descriptions. Help students develop their writing skills in conjunction with describing art. After looking at an artwork, create a class list of descriptive words and phrases. At the primary level these may consist of subject, color, and shape words. Upper levels may include design characteristics and stylistic terms. Then have students write a description of the work using these terms.

Art Criticism

Only after they describe an artwork can students analyze it. Analysis requires them to look at artworks and make decisions based on the relationships among the work's component parts or on qualities

At a Glance 5.5

Adjectives for Describing Art

Elements of Art

Line	Texture	Color/Value	Shape/Form	Space	Principles of Design	Style
controlled	bumpy	analogous	closed	deep	all-over	avant-garde
cross-hatched	damp	bold	circular	flat	asymmetrical	abstract
crossed	flat	bright	dimensional	negative	balanced	classic
curved	furry	brilliant	distorted	open	complex	conservative
dashed	hard	calm	flat	positive	contrasting	controlled
diagonal	jagged	clear	free-form	shallow	emphasized	dynamic
dotted	leathery	complementary	geometric		focal	emotional
freehand	prickly	cool	heavy		formal	expressive
horizontal	raised	dark	light		harmonious	fantasy
jagged	rough	day-glo	linear		patterned	historical
narrow	sharp	deep	massive		random	imaginary
sketchy	shiny	dirty	mirror		repeated	imitative
smooth	simulated	dull	nebulous		rhythmic	literary
spiral	smooth	exciting	open		simple	metaphoric
stippled	soft	fluorescent	organic		symmetric	mimetic
straight	sticky	grayed	rectangular		unified	naive
swirled	tacky	hot	rotated		various	narrative
thick	velvety	light	spatial			natural
thin	visual	medium	squared			nonobjective
vertical	wet	mixed	symmetrical			optical
wide		muted	three-dimensional			photographic
zigzag		natural	transformed			poetic
		neutral	two-dimensional			primitive
		pale	triangular			realistic
		pastel				romantic
		primary				simplistic
		saturated				spiritual
		secondary				surrealistic
		subdued				traditional
		subtle				
		tertiary				
		warm				

identified in a group of works. An individual work, for example, could be examined for the way texture is used in relation to the subject of the piece. A group of works found to share certain characteristics could be judged as belonging to a particular style. Works can also be evaluated against specific standards, such as in judging the technical quality of a print by checking the border for inappropriate fingerprints. At a Glance 5.6 provides a model for critically viewing an artwork. Not every teacher and student behavior listed needs to be in every art study, but the more that are included, the more in depth will be the analysis.

Teaching in Action

Vocabulary Builders

Have fun building students' art vocabulary while playing these games:

Primary

Art Tag. Write the names of the art elements and any other art words in use on index cards. Choose one student to be It. The student draws a card and reads the word. Each student must touch an example of that word, e.g., if the word is *circle,* the student could touch a button on a shirt. The student who is It must help any student who cannot find something to touch. Then a new It is selected and the next card drawn.

Intermediate

Art Bingo. Select twenty-five or more vocabulary words and make up a card that illustrates each one. Use small reproductions or drawings. Write the word on the back. Make up blank bingo sheets. In the blank spaces have students write their choice of fifteen of the words. Shuffle the cards and then hold them picture side up. Students cover the box containing the same word. Depending on the time available, play to cover a row or the whole card. Give out mini-print* magnets as prizes.

*Mini-print magnets: Cut small illustrations of artworks from catalogs. Glue onto tag board and laminate. To the back attach a piece of magnetic tape.

Comparing artworks. Begin by having students perform simple comparisons. Selected works can be sorted into groups that feature similar art media or elements. Have them identify the varying use of design principles in different styles. Using prior knowledge and subject matter categories, students can identify recognizable features of the work and then infer themes and meaning. At a Glance 5.7 provides examples of questions that elicit different levels of response.

Students need to be able to return to familiar works in order to refresh memories and discover new relationships. Keep artworks that have been studied previously in an accessible location so students can refer back to them as needed. One way to do this is to give students small reproductions, such as postcards, to glue in their journals. Older students can also make sketches and write descriptions to help them remember. Large prints can be stored in a portfolio or hung one on top of another on a bulletin board. Postcards and small prints allow students to physically sort the works by characteristics. Venn diagrams provide an excellent format for students to do this (see At a Glance 5.8).

There are many bases for comparison. Primary students can begin by sorting works into categories by one criterion based on visual appearance such as subject matter or color. With practice students will move on to two, three, or even more criteria. Upper-level students

At a Glance 5.6

A Model for Studying an Artwork

Before Viewing Artwork

Teacher Behavior	*Student Behavior*
Explains objectives	Mentally prepares to look
Pre-teaches needed vocabulary and concepts	Becomes aware of vocabulary and concepts
Asks questions to focus student attention	Makes predictions about artwork; asks own questions
Provides organizers	Takes notes, sketches, visualizes
Shares background information	Recalls prior experiences and knowledge
Suggests a learning strategy	

Learner Outcomes

1. Establishes a purpose for looking
2. Becomes motivated to look
3. Activates prior knowledge
4. Has initial ideas about meaning

During Viewing the Artwork

Artwork Characteristics	*Student Behavior*
Vocabulary	Uses vocabulary
Art elements	Confirms or rejects predictions
Structure	Searches for links to prior knowledge
Composition	Searches for information to answer questions
Presentation	Seeks to identify important vs. unimportant information
Context	Pays attention to new features
	Visualizes meaning

Learner Outcomes

1. Engages in viewing and thinking
2. Generates understanding
3. Becomes aware of gaps in knowledge
4. Refines beliefs and feelings about work

After Viewing the Work

Teacher Behaviors	*Student Behaviors*
Discusses elements and composition using the vocabulary	Links new vocabulary and concepts to prior knowledge
Evaluates predictions	Confirms and rejects predictions
Monitors comprehension—fills in gaps, corrects, clarifies	Identifies important information

After Viewing the Work (cont.)

Teacher Behaviors	*Student Behaviors*
Discusses artist's purpose and context of creation	Analyzes artist's purpose and context of creation
Focuses on higher-order questioning strategies	Infers, applies, reasons, tries to defend answers

Learner Outcomes

1. Increases knowledge of concepts and facts
2. Gains knowledge of artwork's structure, artist's purpose and the context of creation
3. Increases comprehension
4. Constructs in-depth meaning

Written Response to Artwork

Teacher Behaviors	*Student Behaviors*
Guides students to organize materials for response	Plans structure for response
Establishes criteria for response	Discusses ideas
Guides students to summarize and provide support for opinion	Writes response using writing process
Monitors progress	Self-evaluates
Holds conferences	Peer conferences
Shares completed responses	Shares completed response

Learner Outcomes

1. Increases in-depth processing
2. Increases comprehension
3. Increases retention of experience
4. Increases ability to apply vocabulary and concepts
5. Increases writing skills
6. Increases skill in looking at and analyzing artworks

Teacher Tip

Inviting Comparisons

Create a large wall chart or have students create a chart in their journals with the following headings:

Title, Artist, Culture, Medium, Size, Style, Subject, Theme, Description

For each artwork studied have the students fill in the required information. Over time the chart will become a ready reference for comparing artworks in discussion and written responses.

At a Glance 5.7

Sample Questions Inviting Different Levels of Response

Descriptive	Critical	Historical	Philosophical
What colors do you see?	How do these colors affect the mood?	What colors are commonly used in works by this artist?	Should color be a factor in judging a work's effectiveness?
What is the subject?	What does the subject symbolize?	What does this picture tell us about life at this time?	Does all art reflect life?
What art medium was used?	Compare this artist with several others who used the same medium.	Why was this art medium popular at this time?	Does the medium used limit one's artistic choices?
Can you list the different shapes you see?	How would changing the colors of the shapes affect this work?	What influences from other cultures do you find in this work?	Would this piece have the same meaning for people in another culture? Does art have a universal meaning?
Is this piece symmetrical?	What is the importance of the three groupings of figures?	How was the artist inspired by the folk tales of her time?	What is the difference between folk art and fine art? Is fine art more important?

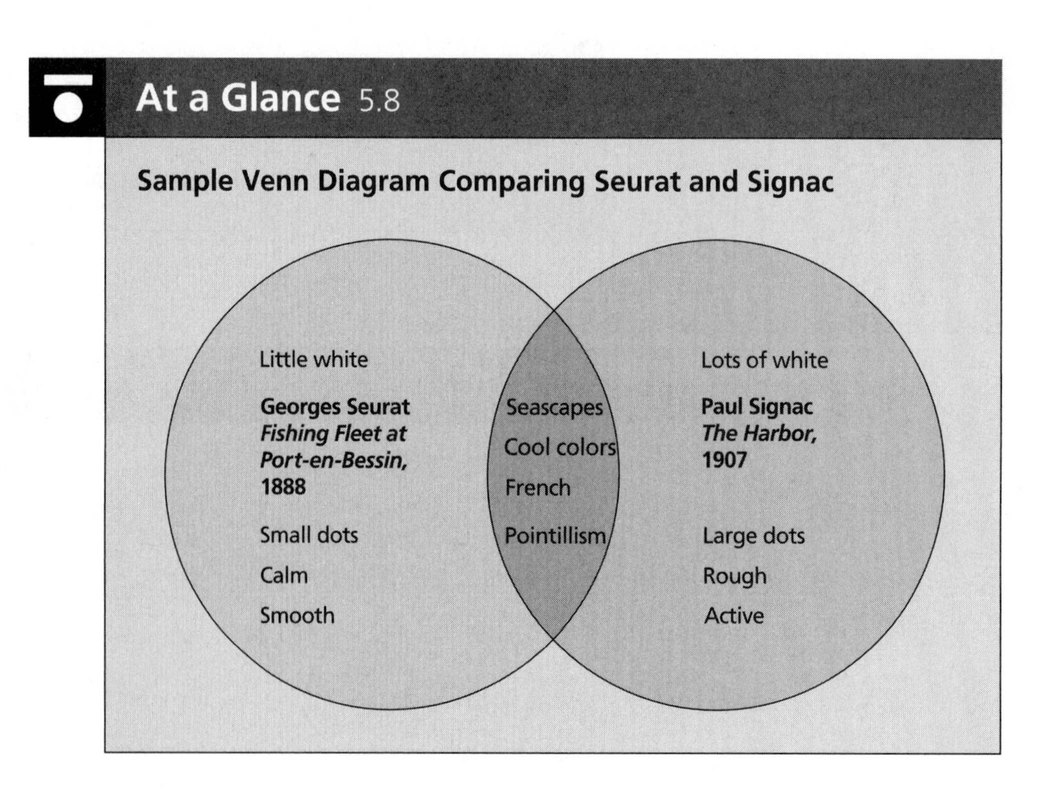

A fourth grader looks for similarities and differences in three artworks. How does this activity help the student become more visually aware? What preparation might help the student be successful at this task?

can add more complex categories such as cultural or historical factors or thematic ideas.

Classifying artworks. Following sorting it is natural to want to name the groupings. Now is the time to teach children about style and the different stylistic trends that have been identified in art (see At a Glance 5.9). The concept of style should be introduced in the primary grades. Provide examples of works by artists with easily recognized styles, such as Rembrandt, Van Gogh, and Klee, for the children to sort and discuss. Display works that feature the same subject but in different styles, such as flower still-lifes by Latour, Matisse, and Van Gogh. Students can try borrowing or inventing different styles for their own artwork.

As students become proficient in recognizing the major styles of drawing and painting, expand to other media including sculpture and folk art. Also introduce works from other times and cultures. Study the stylistic differences in African, Indian, Chinese, and Japanese art. Have upper graders look for stylistic change reflecting invasions and political turmoil in the art of the Egyptians, Greeks, and Romans. With students create a list of factors that might affect an artist's style, and use the ideas generated to analyze a variety of artworks.

Identifying purpose. Art has been created for many reasons. Artworks can be useful, decorative, or illustrative. They can have a religious or political message. Provide opportunities for students to look at works that have differing purposes. Compare and contrast works that have similar messages or uses. How are pieces of literature and art that have similar purposes, such as a fairy tale and a narrative artwork, alike? Study works that have more than one purpose or that have served in different ways over time, such as a clay bowl once used to eat from and now displayed in a museum. Relate a work's

At a Glance 5.9

Style of Art

The following is a brief overview of some common stylistic groupings of art. *Note:* Artists often span several stylistic groups. Artists have been placed here based on their most representative works.

Emotionalism

Art that appeals to the emotions and the imagination.

Examples:

- *Abstract Expressionism:* Art that conveys emotions through the kinesthetic way paint or other materials are applied. Artists: Willem De Kooning, Helen Frankenthaler, Grace Hartigan, Hans Hoffman, Jackson Pollock, Wassily Kandinsky, Franz Kline, Robert Motherwell, Frank Stella
- *Art Nouveau:* Art characterized by complex, flowing, sensuous designs, often with a sexual or decadent connotation. Artists: Gustav Klimt
- *Baroque:* Art of this period (1590–1750) appeals to the emotions. Compositions feature dramatic contrasts and swirling brilliant colors. Artists: Bernini, Caravaggio, Rembrandt, Peter Paul Rubens, Velazquez
- *Expressionism:* Artwork that uses color, distortion, and disturbing images to evoke emotional reaction. Artists: Max Beckman, Arthur Boyd, Otto Dix, James Ensor, Helen Frankenthaler, George Grosz, Wassily Kandinsky, Franz Kline, Kathe Kollwitz, Oskar Kokoschka, Edvard Munch, Emil Nolde, Georgia O'Keefe, José Clemente Orozco, Jackson Pollock
- *Fauvism:* Art that focuses on the use of vivid, pure color and simplified forms to capture images of reality. Artists: Pierre Bonnard, André Derain, Raoul Dufy, Franz Marc, Albert Marquet, Henri Matisse, Georges Rouault, Edward Vuillard, Maurice de Vlaminck
- *Naivism:* Art that uses simple or primitive techniques often associated with folk art methods. Artists: Henri Rousseau, Grandma Moses
- *Neo-Impressionism:* This category was invented to describe the work of several important artists whose work derived from Impressionism but contained personal statements. Artists: Paul Gaughin, Odilon Redon, Georges Seurat, Vincent Van Gogh
- *Photorealism:* Extremely detailed artworks, based on real subjects, that try to capture raw, intense feelings by showing unusual subjects, poses, or combinations of objects. Artists: Francis Bacon, Chuck Close, Richard Estes, Lucian Freud, Frida Kahlo, Malcolm Morely, Paula Rego, Gerhard Richter, Andrew Wyeth
- *Romanticism:* Art that tries to make everything look more beautiful and emotional than reality. Artists: Albert Bierstadt, George Caleb Bingham, William Blake, Rosa Bonheur, Frederick Church, Thomas Cole, John Constable, John Singleton Copley, Camille Corot, Eugène Delacroix, Francisco Goya, Edwin Landseer, Odilon Redon, John Martin, Francois Millet, Paul Nash, John M. W. Turner, Benjamin West
- *Surrealism:* Art that attempts to represent the dreams and fantasies of the unconscious mind. Artists: André Breton, François Boucher, Louise Bourgeois, Carlo Carra, Marc Chagall, Giorgio de Chirico, Salvador Dali, Paul Delvaux, Max Ernst, Alberto Giacometti, Paul Klee, René Magritte, André Masson, Roberto Matta, Joan Miró, Paul Nash, David Siqueiros, Yves Tanguay

At a Glance 5.9 continued

- *Pointillism:* Art that uses small dots of different colors that the eye blends together. Artists: Georges Seurat, Paul Signac

Imitationalism
Art that tries to represent the world as it appears to human eyes.

Examples:

- *Realism:* Art that focuses on representing figures and objects as they appear to the human eye. Artists: John Audubon, Gustav Courbet,Thomas Eakins, Winslow Homer, Edouard Manet, Andrew Wyeth
- *Renaissance:* The artists of the fourteenth and fifteenth centuries developed the system of perspective and shading still used to represent three-dimensional objects on a flat surface. Artists: Sandro Botticelli, Pieter Bruegel, Michelangelo Buonarotti, Albrecht Durer, Piero della Francesca, Hans Holbein, Masaccio, Andrea Mantegna, Titian, Raphael, Andrea del Verrocchio, Leonardo da Vinci

Symbolic
Art that stands for a particular idea or concept.

Examples:

- *Baroque:* Technically accurate art that depicted direct, understandable themes based on classical and religious ideas, often with a focus on controlled lighting effects. Artists: Merisi da Caravaggio, Jean-Baptiste Chardin, Artemisia Gentileschi, Frans Hals, Judith Lester, Rembrandt van Rijn, Peter Paul Rubens, Georges de la Tour, Diègo Velazquez, Marie-Louise-Élisabeth Vigée-Lebrun, Antoine Watteau
- *Regionalism:* Art that expresses the nature of the social and physical environment of a particular region. Artists: Albert Bierstadt, George Caleb Bingham, Thomas Cole, Winslow Homer, Georgia O'Keeffe, Grant Wood
- *Earth Art:* Art that inhabits a landscape, either done outdoors or that brings parts of the outdoors—rocks, soil, plants—inside. It is often temporary and ecologically concerned, symbolizing the relationship of earth and its people. Artists: Andy Goldsworthy, Jeanne-Claude de Guillebon, Michael Heizer, Nancy Holt, "Christo" Javacheff, Anish Kapoor, Richard Long, Alan Sonfist, George Trakas
- *Futurism:* Art that attempts to represent the movement and dynamism of modern life. Artists: Giacomo Balla, Umberto Boccioni, Robert Delaunay, Marcel Dushamp, Gino Severini, Jean Tinguely
- *Modernism:* Art that symbolizes the themes of our times. Artists: Christian Boltanski, David Bomberg, Judy Chicago, Tony Cragg, Marisol Escobar, Audrey Flack, Neil Jenny, Wilfredo Lam, Jacob Lawrence, Wyndham Lewis, R. B. Kitaj, Bruce Naumann, Isamu Noguchi, Georgia O'Keeffe, Pablo Picasso, Faith Ringgold, Fritz Scholder, Cindy Sherman, Bill Viola
- *Pop Art:* Art based on subjects taken from images designed for a mass audience such as comics, TV, and film. It symbolizes the mass-media culture's emphasis on sex, violence, and youth in a witty, gimmicky, or satirical way. Artists: Jim Dine, Richard Hamilton, Robert Indiana, Jasper Johns, Ed Keinholz, Roy Lichtenstein, Claes Oldenburg, Robert Rauschenberg, Larry Rivers, James Rosenquist, George Segal, Andy Warhol
- *Social Realism:* Art that comments on the social condition. Artists: Edward Hopper, Jean-François Millet, José Orozco, Diego Rivera

Formalism

Art that is concerned with the arrangement of the elements
tion following formal rules of structure.

Examples:

- *Abstraction:* Art that is based on real subject matter but which elements. Artists: Jean Arp, Constantin Brancusi, Robert Delaun Jacob Epstein, Lionel Feininger, Helen Frankenthaler, Alberto Giac Hepworth, David Hockney, Marie Laurencin, Fernand Léger, Jacque Louise Nevelson, Ben Nicholson, Giacomo Manzu, John Marin, Ame Modigliani, Henry Moore, Maria Vieira da Silva
- *Classical Greco-Roman:* Art based on the formal principles of beauty lai by the ancient Greeks and Romans. It is characterized by simple, elegant Artists: Phidias, Polyclitus, Praxiteles
- *Conceptual:* Art is seen as an idea that may be represented by a performanc (performance art), a written description, or sketches, for an imagined work. The finished work is only in the mind of the viewer. Artists: Alice Aycock, Jenni Bartlett, Joseph Beuys, Marcel Broodthalers, Alberto Burri, Judy Chicago, Ives Klein, Mario Merz, Mary Miss, Robert Morris, Yoko Ono, Nam June Paik, Lawrence Weiner
- *Constructivism:* Art that is concerned with the process of construction and the physical properties of shapes and forms. It features abstract work, mostly sculptural and very large, that is built of construction materials such as welded metal and wood. Artists: Alexander Calder, Anthony Caro, Naum Gabo, Phillip King, Elaeazer Lissitzky, Liubov Popova, Alexander Rodchenko, Richard Serra, David Smith, Vladimir Tatlin, William Tucker
- *Cubism:* Art that represents three-dimensional objects as if made from geometric shapes and forms. Artists tried to show light as fractured prisms. Artists: Alexander Archipenko, Georges Braque, Paul Cézanne, Le Corbusier, Lyonel Feininger, Juan Gris, Fernand Leger, Pablo Picasso
- *Dadaism:* Art that uses everyday objects in a way that gives them new meaning and elevates them to art. This was the beginning of collage, assemblages, and junk art. Artists: Giacomo Balla, Umberto Boccioni, Marcel Duchamp, Max Ernst, John Hartfield, Hannah Hoch, Francis Picabia, Man Ray, Kurt Schwitters, Joseph Stella
- *Impressionism:* Art based on everyday events and focused on capturing the effect of light and movement. Artists: Mary Cassatt, Edgar Degas, Thomas Eakins, Childe Hassam, Winslow Homer, Edouard Manet, Claude Monet, Berthe Morisot, Camille Pissarro, Auguste Renoir, Alfred Sisley, Henry O. Tanner, Henri Toulouse-Lautrec
- *Minimalism:* Art that uses very few colors and shapes or a minimal amount of preparation; often using industrial materials such as bricks, Styrofoam, neon lights Artists: Josef Albers, Carl André, Dan Flavin, Don Judd, Ellsworth Kelly, Sol LeWitt, Morris Louis, Robert Morris, Louise Nevelson, Ad Reinhardt
- *Nonobjective:* Art based on the arrangement of shapes and forms, having no recognizable subject. Artists: Annie Albers, Willi Baumeister, Stuart Davis, Richard Diebenkorn, Theo Van Doesburg, Hans Hartung, Ellsworth Kelly, Kasimir Malevich, Laszlo Moholy-Nagy, Kenneth Noland, Piet Mondrian, Alexander Rodchenko, Morgan Russell
- *Op Art:* Art based on visual illusions and perceptual tricks. Artists: Bridget Riley, Victor Vasarely

(continues)

purpose to its visual elements, medium, and style. Read about the artist's life and try to find out what reason the artist might give for its creation. What have other people said about the work? Do they agree with the students' ideas about the artwork?

Analyzing the composition. An artwork is made up of many parts. We cannot truly understand it unless we analyze the interrelationship among the art elements, design principles, stylistic quality, and purpose. Introduce composition using the idea of design (see Chapter 12). Explore the relationship among the parts of an artwork by having students re-create the work using a different arrangement of significant features. Compare works that have many similarities or differences in design. Classify works by composition and purpose.

Discovering themes. The theme is the underlying message of the work. In some cases encompassing terms such as *love, hate, power, womanhood,* or *fear* can be used to express the essence of a work. But many works are more specific with themes relating to a particular time, place, and purpose.

All the observations made about the artwork are used to deduce its meaning. The student is the detective and the description contains the clues. Colors, shapes, medium, technique, composition, subject, and purpose all contribute to its message. This is why it is important to study the work in detail before reaching this level of analysis.

Students often have difficulty separating the surface appearance of an artwork from its theme, just as they have difficulty finding themes in literature. Participating in thematic studies and looking at artwork that reflects the general theme is one way to help students see linkages. Another is to tie discussions about themes in a piece of literature to an artwork that shares a similar theme. Students can also generate their own titles for artworks. This along with oral discussion has been found to help students remember artworks better than just describing what they see (Koroscik, 1984).

The fact that there is not always just one correct theme or way to state it can lead to interesting discussions among students. Encourage students to provide support for their views by referring to the work's composition or subject matter. Older students can add relevant historical and social information as well. When students disagree or hold alternative views, foster listening and empathy by having students practice a cooperative strategy such as the line-up, pair and share, or structured webbing (see Chapter 7 for strategy details).

Evaluating artwork. Comparing and classifying require students to make and defend judgments about works of art. They must decide if the works fit a specific set of criteria that determines its style or its

Teaching in Action

Applying Criteria

Help students learn to make judgments about artwork by providing opportunities for them to evaluate artworks against a standard.

Sample Activity: Pictures at the Exhibition

1. Have class create a list of criteria for selecting artworks for an imaginary art exhibition. If desired, the exhibit could have a particular theme.
2. Form students into cooperative groups of four or five and distribute at least twenty postcard-sized reproductions of a wide assortment of artworks to each group. Ask them to imagine they are judges for an art show that only has room for ten pictures.
3. Using the criteria established by the group, select the ten pictures they would display.
4. Have groups share their choices and explain how they used the criteria.
5. Discuss differences among group selections. Were there any works that were selected repeatedly? Were there some that were not selected by any group? Which criteria were the easiest to use? Which were the hardest?

theme. As students become competent at classifying and comparing, help them develop higher evaluation skills. Too often students think that judging an artwork just means deciding if it is good or bad based on whether they like it or not. They need to be taught that the next level of analysis is to compare an artwork to a standard and see how close it comes to the ideal.

Involve upper-level students who have had many opportunities to classify artworks in discussions about standards. Have students think about the following:

- Are there universal standards that apply to all artworks?
- Are some standards applicable to only specific media?
- Can artworks from different cultures or artists be compared to the same standard?
- Should the standards of the time when the work was created be applied?
- Should different styles of art be judged on standards relevant to the style?
- Should a beginner's artwork be judged on the same standards as a professional's?

Help students set reachable standards for their own artwork by having them write individual goals. Technical standards are the easiest for students to understand and accomplish, and they provide a comfortable beginning point. Standards should be specifically related to the

Teaching in Action

Facilitating Research

Intermediate-level students can be expected to carry out research about artworks independently. Facilitate their research by

- Making sure that information is available on their subject.
- Outlining the requirements for the project.
- Delineating the evaluation criteria before they start.
- Showing samples of other student research.
- Creating a resource center in the classroom that contains relevant books, articles, prints, audiotapes, artifacts, etc.
- Modeling expected behaviors, such as using an index, taking notes, etc.
- Enlisting the help of the librarian.

artwork being done. Avoid general goals such as be neat. A primary student might set a personal goal of mixing three different blues to use in a painting. An upper-level student working on a weaving might set a personal standard of having no skipped threads. As students working in the same media develop technical skill, have them work in cooperative groups to set specific standards of workmanship that everyone in the group feels they can accomplish.

Students who have set their own goals are far more aware of the difficulties of setting fair standards and making reliable judgments about artwork. This can lead to discussing the ways artworks are selected for exhibitions or as winners in contests.

Art History

An important way to see deeper into an artwork is to place it in its social and historical context. This involves studying artists' lives, the community they lived and worked in, and the people, ideas, and events that influenced them. It may also mean researching the relevant major events that occurred in the world at large before, after, and during the making of the work. Artworks can be placed on maps and timelines to show these relationships graphically.

Approaches for primary. In the primary grades students need to relate the artwork to their own lives and experiences. This makes places and cultures that are unfamiliar to them more understandable. For example, they can compare a Navajo rug with the appearance and uses of floor coverings they have in their home. Students also benefit from being read stories and picture books that provide background information about art forms of different kinds (see "Books to Share" boxes throughout this book).

"Sketch of Henri de Toulouse-Lautrec." Pencil—Delia, grade 5.

Thinking about Children's Art

This sketch was made to accompany a student report on the artist Toulouse-Lautrec. How does sketching the works of well-known artists help students understand the art better?

Approaches for intermediate. Upper graders who have a wider base of knowledge and better writing skills can research an artwork's background on their own and use what they learn to contribute to class discussions. They can also make displays, games, and learning centers that share this knowledge with peers.

Aesthetics

The simple addition of an *s* turns the adjective *aesthetic* into a noun and enlarges its meaning so as to encompass the study of the nature and value of art. Those who study aesthetics try to answer questions such as, what is art, and does all art have to be beautiful?

Although abstract, classroom discussions of questions and ideas about the nature and meaning of art have been shown to be not only possible but also an excellent way to develop children's reasoning skills (Moore, 1994). Aesthetic questions grow naturally out of discussions focused on selected artworks. For example, a group of second graders studying a piece of sculpture found in a local park and often climbed upon by children could be asked a question such as, "Is this sculpture a work of art or a piece of playground equipment?" Such questions lead students to think about what art is and help them refine their own personal definition of art.

Approaches for primary. Aesthetic questions can take several forms. At the primary level students can be asked to compare artworks to familiar objects and discuss which are art and which are not.

- Are all portraits works of art? What about the photographs taken on school picture day or family snapshots? How do they compare to this portrait we have studied?
- Name something beautiful. Is this work of art beautiful in the same way? Is all art beautiful?
- This clay bowl is in a museum. Our clay snack bowl is not. What is different about the two bowls? Which would you put in an art museum?

Approaches for intermediate. At the intermediate level questions can focus on comparing different works or types of art with which the students are familiar. Pose hypothetical situations that challenge the students' limited views of art.

- Is there a difference between crafts and fine art? Why are some crafts put in museums and others not?
- Which piece of art would you buy? What does a piece of art have to communicate to you to make you want to buy it?
- Is an artwork only understandable in the time, place, and culture in which it was made?

- Is a beautiful natural object a work of art?
- Does art have to be one-of-a-kind or can it be mass produced?
- What if no one could see an artwork. Would it still be art?
- Would you display this work in a museum? In what section would you place it? What would you say about it?

Aesthetic Puzzles

Children's thoughts about art can also be stimulated by asking simple hypothetical questions about art. This kind of art puzzle requires the teacher to challenge the students' thinking. They need to "push and probe the puzzle by pointing out questions that highlight the other side of the issues—or better still, invite open discussion among diverse students to explore it" (Battin, 1995, p. 102). The goal is get students to see the tension in the problem. There is no right answer.

Approaches for primary. Hypothetical situations for primary students should relate to what they know and have experienced in art.

- What if a friend asks to draw your picture. She looks at you and then scribbles all over a sheet of paper. Underneath she writes your name. Would you be happy with the portrait? Would you hang it up? Is it art?
- An artist makes a beautiful clay bowl. Should it be used for eating cereal every day or should it be put in a museum?

Approaches for intermediate. Questions for older students can build on what they have learned about art.

- If the arm broke off an ancient Greek sculpture, should it be fixed? What if it broke into a hundred pieces. Should it be fixed? Does restoring a piece of art change its value or meaning?
- Suppose you learned that your favorite Van Gogh painting was a fake. Would it still be your favorite?
- Max Ernst hung a urinal in an art gallery. Is it art? What if a student in our class did the same thing and turned it in for a grade. Is it art? Why or why not?

Organizing aesthetic ideas. Answering these kinds of questions requires students to organize their thoughts. They need to be able to separate their personal affective response from the physical characteristics of the artwork. They must incorporate what they have learned about the work and other people's ideas about it as well. At a Glance 5.10 provides a graphic framework that can be used to help students think through this process.

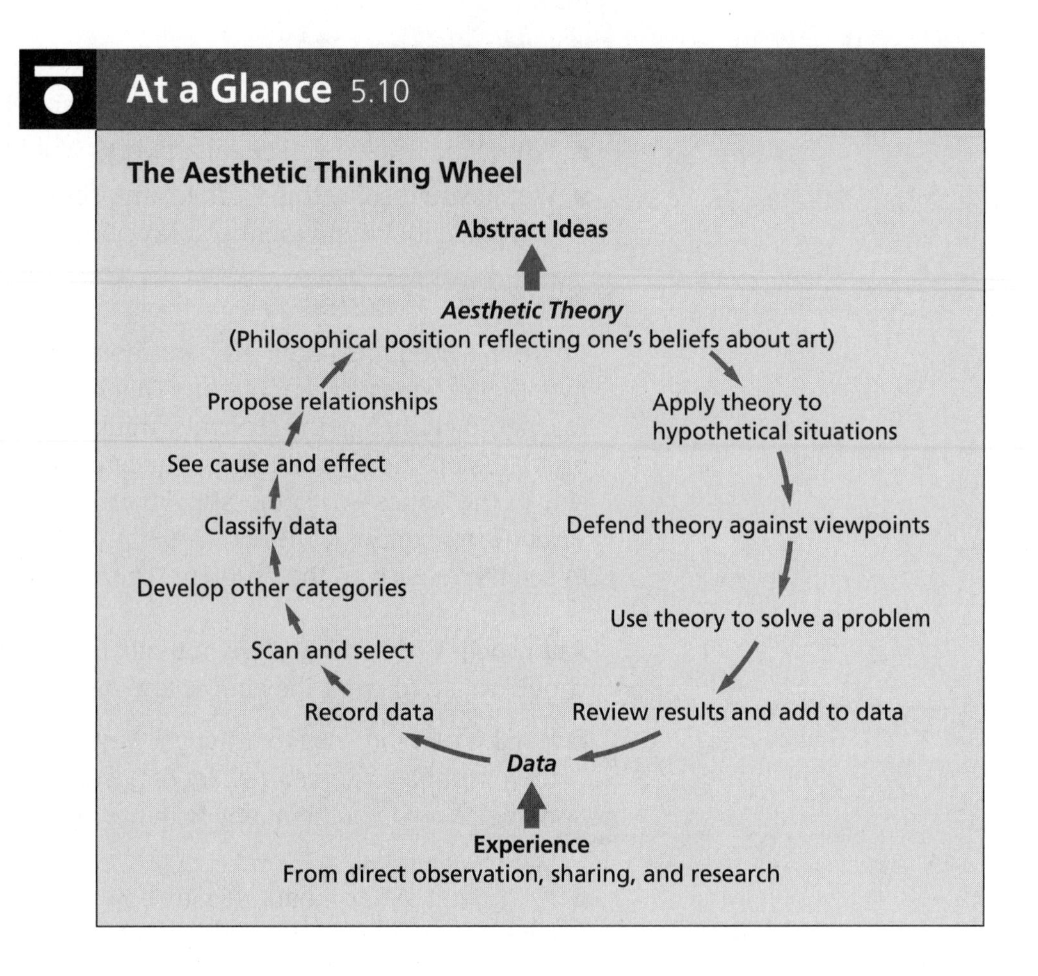

Talking about Art

It is especially important to take time to talk about artworks. There are many reasons to hold discussions as part of art instruction. Discussing art orally allows students to try out ideas in an open forum. They get to hear the ideas of others as they explore their own reactions. Participating successfully in guided art discussions as a student lays the groundwork for being able to confidently discuss art as an adult. Art discussions can be held for all the following reasons:

- To help students look more closely at an artwork
- To share feelings and opinions about an artwork
- To share thinking about an aesthetic question
- To share information about art obtained through research
- To share information about techniques and concepts obtained from creating art
- To talk about a student's artwork and give advice
- To help students improve their behavior or skills
- To make plans for special events
- To summarize what students have learned

Books to Share

Artists and Their Art

More and more books about artists are being written for children. Here is just a sampling:

African Artists

Moore, R. (1994). *Native Artists of Africa.* Santa Fe, NM: John Muir.

African American Artists

Butler, J. (1998). *A Drawing in the Sand: A Story of African American Art.* Middleton, WI: zino Press.
Hacker, C. (1997). *Great African Americans in the Arts.* New York: Crabtree.
Igus, T. (1996). *Going Back Home: An Artist Returns to the South.* Chicago: Children's Book Press.
Lyons, M. (1996). *Painting Dreams: Minnie Evans, Visionary Artist.* New York: Houghton Mifflin.
Sullivan, C. (1991). *Children of Promise.* New York: Abrams.

American Artists

Greenberg, J., & Jordan, S. (1991). *The Painter's Eye: Learning to Look at Contemporary American Art.* New York: Delacorte.
Greenberg, J., & Jordan, S. (1994). *The Sculptor's Eye.* New York: Delacorte.
Greenberg, J., & Jordan, S. (1995). *The American Eye: Eleven Artists of the Twentieth Century.* New York: Delacorte.
Hughes, L. (1995). *The Block.* New York: Metropolitan Museum of Art.
Lowery, L. (1996). *Georgia O'Keeffe.* Minneapolis, MN: Carolrhoda.
Nicolson, N. (1998). *Little Girl in a Red Dress with Cat and Dog.* New York: Viking.
Venezia, M. (1989). *Hopper.* Chicago: Children's Book Press.
Venezia, M. (1990). *Cassat.* Chicago: Children's Book Press.
Venezia, M. (1992). *Pollock.* Chicago: Children's Book Press.
Venezia, M. (1994). *O'Keeffe.* Chicago: Children's Book Press.
Yokoe, L. (1995). *Maya Lin: Architect.* New York: Modern Learning.

Asian Artists

Hamanaka, S. (1999). *In Search of the Spirit: The Living National Treasures of Japan.* New York: Morrow.
Zhensun, Z., Low, A., & Cheng, C. (1991). *Young Painter: Life and Paintings of Wang Yani.* New York: Scholastic.

Mexican Artists

Cruz, B. C. (1998). *José Clemente Orozco.* Berkeley Heights, NJ: Enslow.
Garza, H. *Frida Kahlo.* Broomall, PA: Chelsea House.
Vasquez, S. (1998). *Diego Rivera: An Artist's Life.* Austin, TX: Raintree-Steck Vaughan.
Venezia, M. (1999). *Frida Kahlo.* Chicago: Children's Book Press.
Winters, J. (1991). *Diego.* New York: Random House.

European Artists

Anholt, L. (1994). *Camille and the Sunflowers.* Hauppauge, NY: Barron's.
Anholt, L. (1996). *Degas and the Little Dancer.* Hauppauge, NY: Barron's.
Barnes, R. (1990). *Gauguin.* London: Bracken.
Bjork, C. (1987). *Linnea in Monet's Garden.* New York: Farrar, Straus & Giroux.

(continues)

Books to Share continued

Collins, D. (1990). *Country Artist: A story of Beatrix Potter.* Minneapolis, MN: Carolrhoda.
De Cristofano, C. (1997). *Leonardo's ABC.* Boston: Museum of Science.
Garland, M. (1995). *Dinner at Magritte's.* New York: Dutton.
Harrison, P. (1996). *Art for Young People: Monet.* New York: Sterling.
Harrison, P. (1996). *Art for Young People: Van Gogh.* New York: Sterling.
Hart, T. (1994). *Toulouse-Lautrec.* Hauppauge, NY: Barron's.
Hart, T. (1994). *Michelangelo.* Hauppauge, NY: Barron's.
Johnson, J. (1996). *La Princesa y el Pintor.* Buenos Aires, Argentina: Santillana.
Kinghorn, H., Badman, J., & Lewis-Spice, L. (1991). *Let's Meet Famous Artists.* Minneapolis, MN: Dennison.
Krull, K. (1995). *Lives of the Artists: Masterpieces, Messes and What the Neighbors Thought.* New York: Harcourt Brace.
Le Ford, B. (1995). *A Blue Butterfly: A Story about Claude Monet.* New York: Doubleday.
Malam, J. (1998). *Tell Me About: Claude Monet.* Minneapolis, MN: Carolrhoda.
Moore, R. (1994). *Native Artists of Europe.* Santa Fe, NM: John Muir.
Penguilly, Y. (1994). *Da Vinci: The Painter Who Spoke with Birds.* New York: Chelsea House.
Parillo, T. (1998). *Michelangelo's Surprise.* New York: Farrar, Straus & Giroux.
Richmond, R. (1994). *Animals in Art.* Nashville, TN: Ideals Children's Books.
Rohmer, H. (1997). *Just Like Me: Stories and Self-Portraits by Fourteen Artists.* Emeryville, CA: Children's Book Press.
Schmitt, E. (1997). *Cézanne in Provence.* New York: International Book Imports.
Sweeney, J. (1998). *Bijou, Bonbon and Beau: The Kittens Who Danced for Degas.* San Francisco: Chronicle Books.
Venezia, M. (1989). *Da Vinci.* Chicago: Children's Book Press.
Venezia, M. (1992). *Botticelli.* Chicago: Children's Book Press.
Venezia, M. (1992). *Bruegel.* Chicago: Children's Book Press.
Venezia, M. (1994). *Goya.* Chicago: Children's Book Press.
von Schemm, J. (1997). *Dreaming Pictures.* New York: Prestel.

Native American Artists

Herman, S. (1995). *R. C. Gorman: Navajo Artist.* Broomall, PA: Enslow.
Hoyt-Goldsmith, D. (1990). *Totem Pole.* New York: Holiday House.
Hoyt-Goldsmith, D. (1991). *Pueblo Storyteller.* New York: Holiday House.
Krensky, K. (1991). *Children of Earth and Sky.* New York: Scholastic.
Krensky, K. (1994). *Children of Wind and Water.* New York: Scholastic.
Moore, R. (1994). *Native Artists of North America.* Santa Fe, NM: John Muir.

Discussion Group Size

Whole class discussions allow all students to experience and hear the same ideas and information at the same time. Many art lessons should include a whole class discussion. For example, following a lesson on pattern, the class might discuss ways they have used pattern in their artwork. Whole class discussions, however, require close supervision

"Sacred Lake."
Ceramic—Judy Folwell, 1995.
Montclair Art Museum.

From the Art Museum

This ceramic piece by Santa Clara Pueblo artist Judy Folwell (Native American, 1943–) with its strong visual symbolism and spirituality, represented by familiar waterlife, is an example of the kind of work that can be incorporated into a variety of curricula at different grade levels because it can be looked at from many viewpoints. What discussion questions might be used if it was included in a cross-discipline thematic unit focused on the importance of water, in a scientific study of a local pond's ecology, or as part of research on Native American life and beliefs?

and tight control. Some students may feel intimidated about sharing in a large group.

For these reasons it may be wise to hold small group discussions as well. When there are five to eight students sitting around a table looking at a piece of art, discussions can be more intimate and friendly. This encourages reticent students to participate. Effective art teaching should include many opportunities for students to study and discuss artworks, techniques, and concepts in small groups. Small group discussions can also be used to practice discussion procedures and ideas before meeting as a whole class.

Capturing Their Attention

Discussing, questioning, and responding requires the participation of both students and teacher. There is no reason to expect that students will arrive at the moment of conversation quiet and ready to give their rapt attention and thoughtful responses. Each student brings a wealth of personal concerns and experiences that determine how ready they are to listen and talk. Some students are worried about who they are or are not sitting next to. Others are annoyed because someone bumped them on the way to the rug. Still others are hungry or tired or worried about a sick pet at home. No matter the concern, it is the teacher's job to bring all these diverse minds together for a shared moment and focus them on the wonder of art.

The effective teacher of art wants to reach inside the student, to draw out what is happening there—to truly touch the essence from which the student's art will come. This requires more than the appearance of attention. Using a mix of the following methods can effectively capture student attention at the start of a lesson or discussion:

- *Provide structure.* Capturing attention begins by establishing a structure for listening. From the very first class students should be taught where and how to sit for the lesson, discussions, and conferences. Have students model the correct way to sit. Act out what paying attention looks like: eyes on the speaker, mouth closed. Do not allow students to wander around or converse before the lesson or to slouch or wiggle around while listening to a classmate.
- *Signal.* Establish a signal for coming to attention. One common all-quiet signal is to have students raise an arm and come to attention when they see the teacher's arm raised. Other signals include ringing a bell, counting to a certain number, and echo clapping. (Clap a simple rhythm and have the students imitate it back. Continue changing the rhythm randomly until all students are participating and ready to listen.)
- *Create anticipation.* Give a hint of the wonder to come next: a new artwork to see, a new material to explore.

- *Advertise.* Write a message, puzzle, saying, or cryptic remark on a poster by the door that students can see as they enter, or put one on the instruction easel. Cover an artwork to be studied with a poster advertising a special fact about it, such as "Painting for sale for $53,900,000" (the price for which Van Gogh's *Irises* sold in 1987).
- *Set a mood.* Change the lighting. Play background music or sounds. Make a backdrop. Dress to fit the scene. For example, when presenting Rousseau's jungle scene paintings, close the blinds, turn off the lights, hang up a rain forest backdrop, play a tape of jungle sounds, and wear a safari jacket and a pith helmet.
- *Surprise.* Do something unexpected. Wrap the artwork to be studied in gift wrap and a huge bow. Hold a live animal. Bring a motorcycle into the classroom. Display two apparently unrelated items and challenge students to find the relationship that will lead into the lesson.
- *Draw on current interests.* Stay on top of current fads and trends and choose ones related to the lesson. Hang up an enlarged cartoon or newspaper headline. Sing or play a line or verse from a hit song. In the primary grades use stuffed animals and popular toys.
- *Challenge.* Pose a simple problem that will lead into the discussion topic, such as, "How many colors are in this print? Face forward quietly when you think you know."
- *Go round.* Have students stand in a circle and pass a whispered message or tap a pattern in each other's palm.
- *Enforce.* Have known and predictable consequences for not being ready, and enforce them diligently. Respond immediately to the student who is whispering to a friend, fooling around with a pencil, or creating a distraction.

Holding a Discussion

When students are ready, the discussion can begin. An effective discussion begins with an intriguing question or event and grows as more and more class members participate and become enthusiastic. The following guidelines will help get a discussion started:

- *Think ahead.* Think about the initiating question or event beforehand. Have other questions prepared and ready to use if the conversation bogs down.
- *Set the tone.* Make students comfortable. Let the students know at the beginning that there are no "right" answers nor are they being quizzed.
- *Get excited.* Communicate in a tone of voice that shows wonder, excitement, and a belief in the students' ability to talk about important ideas.

- *Be flexible.* Be open to the flow of the conversation. Allow it to go in interesting directions, but steer it back to the main subject if it strays too far.
- *Summarize.* Act as the students' memory. Every once in a while summarize what they have said, using their names. This tells them you are listening to them closely.
- *Participate.* Enjoy the conversation. Smile. Laugh. Share ideas.
- *Take turns.* Establish a participation policy. Make sure everyone knows how to indicate they wish to speak.
- *Sometimes, withdraw.* When students begin to talk with each other, stay in the background as much as possible. This lets the conversation become theirs and allows them to learn how to discuss independently.
- *Wonder out loud.* Model internal thinking processes by verbalizing thoughts and ideas.
- *Question.* Ask students to clarify their statements when necessary.
- *Awaken.* Draw in students who hang on the edge of the discussion with open-ended questions that have no right answer. Refer to something they have said before or done in their artwork that relates to the discussion, such as "Gary, you used a similar blue in your painting last week. What do you think about the way Cézanne has used it here?"
- *Bring it to a close.* Close the discussion by summarizing what was said, making sure to mention specific ideas contributed. Consider all points of view that have been expressed. Show students how diverse ideas can be accepted and reconciled: "Today, we heard many different ideas about the feeling expressed in this artwork. Some of you felt it showed fear, others anger. Mark made a good point about the sad expression on the face. Harlen noticed the clenched fists. It is a complex artwork that can draw forth such strong reactions in the viewer."
- *Build on it.* Use the conversation. In follow-up lessons return to those ideas discussed and build on them.

Learning How to Discuss

A discussion on any topic requires equal give and take among all members of the group, delivered in an atmosphere of respect. For many students this is difficult in large group settings. Some students are afraid to talk in large groups. Others find it hard to stay focused. Students need to be shown how to participate in a discussion. They need to role play and practice.

Talking about an artwork provides a perfect opportunity to do this. The artwork is in front of them. The whole group can see it, and each student can contribute something. This is different than discussing

Teaching in Action

Taking Turns

Approaches for Primary

At the primary level children often have difficulty controlling themselves when they have something to say. Having them raise their hands helps them contain themselves. When children raise their hands, acknowledge them with a head shake, hand signal, or quiet "You'll be next." When they are acknowledged, they should learn to put their hands down. A group of waving hands can be very distracting to a young speaker.

Approaches for Upper Levels

Discussions in which students must be called on by the teacher lack spontaneity and easily become teacher focused and controlled. This is not a true conversation. Students need to learn how to listen and practice self-control during a discussion. Slowly introduce "no hands" discussions. Establish and enforce discussions in which no interruptions are allowed when one person is talking. Set up a procedure for when two students begin talking at the same time. Let students know that they must listen attentively to know when to enter the discussion. This takes practice by the students under the careful guidance of the teacher. No hands does not mean that the teacher withdraws from the discussion but rather facilitates by asking stimulating questions, drawing in students from the sidelines, and reasserting control if the discussion breaks down.

something they have read or researched and that requires the recall of many facts and ideas. Participating in art discussions is an excellent way to prepare students for discussions in other curriculum areas.

Ideally discussion methods should be introduced in the primary grades so that upper-level students will be well prepared for the higher-level discussions expected of them. In actuality all levels of students may need to be reintroduced to discussion procedures at the beginning of the school term.

The First Discussion

The initial discussion should focus on a nonthreatening question about an artwork, possibly one the students have studied the previous year. During this discussion focus on the mechanics of conversing rather than the content. Do not be afraid to stop the discussion to review the rules or to comment when it goes well. Attention paid to procedures at the beginning will set the stage for exciting discussions throughout the year.

Participating in a discussion is a creative experience. Help students become skillful discussants by reviewing the steps in the creative process and linking them to the discussion format.

Knowledge. Each student brings to the discussion a unique perspective that comes from diverse personal experiences and knowledge. Emphasize that all comments and thoughts are welcomed. If everyone knew and thought exactly the same things, there would be no point to having a discussion.

Skill. During a discussion students must think quickly and logically. They must learn how to offer an opinion, ask for clarification, question, and summarize. If necessary, have students model each of these different response skills.

Motivation. When conducted in an atmosphere of respect and enjoyment, the discussion format motivates students to talk about art. A discussion, as opposed to a question and answer session, allows students to decide when and how they wish to contribute.

Immersion. Students must pay attention and listen closely. They must follow along with what is being said and think about what it means to them personally. Have students practice active rather than passive thinking. First ask them to just sit and think. Then propose a mental problem for them to solve, such as, "Think of three different ways to make gray." Compare how it felt to solve the problem as compared to just thinking aimlessly.

Incubation. As they discuss ideas, students need to try out and reformulate their personal beliefs about art and how to talk about them. Do not rush a discussion. Students do not need to be constantly talking. Teachers should allow about three seconds of silence to pass before jumping into a discussion with another statement or question.

Production. Out of the discussion will come understanding and knowledge about art. Capture these revelations in a graphic format that they can return to later in the year.

Recording the Discussion

Discussions are more meaningful for both students and teachers when the information and ideas are recorded in some way.

Approaches for primary. In the primary grades the teacher can create a simple list or chart that reflects the students' ideas. These charts should be titled, dated, and stored in a big, book-sized class journal. It will then be possible to look back and compare comments about one artwork with another or to mark how students' ability to see details in an artwork have improved.

Teaching in Action

Running a Discussion

The following examples illustrate ways to achieve effective discussions:

1. *Set expectations.* Begin by asking students to define what participation in a discussion looks like, sounds like, and feels like. Record their ideas on a chart. From their comments develop a description of the ideal participant, both as listener and contributor. Rewrite in clear language and post in the discussion area. Refer to it as needed during future discussions.
2. *Model appropriate and inappropriate behaviors.* Using the definition as a guide, have students model the different behaviors they will be expected to demonstrate. For example, ask, "Who can show me how you will sit during the discussion?" or "If you have a good idea, how will you share it?"
3. *Establish consequences for forgetting the rules.* Consequences should be immediate and logical.
   - For small, unintentional interruptions a simple reminder or redirection may suffice. If, for example, a student interrupts someone because of excitement, quietly redirect, perhaps with a head nod or a simple, "Remember to wait your turn."
   - When the discussion becomes animated and several students start arguing privately with each other and not listening to the speaker, say, "Discussion rules, please! If you wish to continue with this discussion, you will have to show you can follow the rules." If several students are involved, and they do not respond to reminders, then it is appropriate to send them to their desks with the assignment to each develop a plan that will make the discussion go more smoothly.
   - If a student makes a comment or behaves in a way that is inappropriate or derogatory, have that student write an apology and/or sit away from the rest in a designated location. For example, a desk in the corner of the room can be the "Stop & Think" place. Students sent to this location might fill out a form explaining why they were sent there and what they should have done instead. Repeated occurrences may result in a private teacher conference to develop a plan to improve behavior.

Approaches for intermediate. Charts and lists can continue to be used at this level. Instead of doing the recording, the teacher can choose a student to be the recorder. It helps if the teacher provides a pre-drawn graphic format for the student, such as a Venn diagram or chart. Students can be expected to record this information, clearly labeled as to topic and date, in their journals for their own future reference. In future discussions remind them to look back in their journals to draw on ideas discussed previously.

Tape recording. There are advantages and disadvantages to taping class discussions. A tape provides the most complete and accurate record of what was said but requires a great deal of time to listen to and transcribe. Tapes of discussions are particularly useful for assessing how well students understand and participate in talking about art and also allow teachers to assess their own performance as facilitators. Chapter 9 delves more deeply into the use of this technology for assessment.

Questions to Ask

Discussions begin with a question. How that question is phrased will make a tremendous difference in student interest and participation.

Types of questions. A discussion is built from a mixture of these four basic types of questions (see At a Glance 5.11):

1. *Comprehension:* These kinds of questions ask who, what, where, and when. They draw upon a student's knowledge, and they usually have only one possible answer.

   In discussions use them sparingly as a string of them tends to become quiz-like. An occasional comprehension question based on previous studies, however, can help students remember past learning and use it in a new context. During a discussion of a new artwork, for example, a teacher might ask students to give the name and title of a work studied previously that might be compared to it.
2. *Application:* These questions require students to think about what they have learned and then use their knowledge to solve a problem, explain an event, or make a prediction. They have a range of possible answers depending on what the student knows and on what the student chooses to focus.

At a Glance 5.11

Questions for Discussion

Comprehension	Application	Opinion	Imaginative
Who painted this picture? What medium did the artist use? When did Seurat begin using small dots of color in his paintings?	If this portrait had been painted by Picasso instead of Renoir, what would be the same? What would be different? Why do you think the potter attached the handle in this way? What would happen if you used the smaller brush instead of the larger one?	Which artwork is more exciting to look at? Do you think this artwork would be more effective if it were larger? Which of these works best represents the stylistic category of surrealism?	What if the Renaissance had never happened? What would our art look like today? How many different ways can a crayon be used? Imagine yourself in this landscape. What would you see? How would you feel? What would you be doing?

Teaching in Action

Fact and Opinion

Students often have difficulty recognizing an opinion, especially when it is embedded in a series of facts. The following activities can be used to help students learn how to support their opinions about artworks:

Activity: Identifying Facts and Opinions

1. Introduce the following statements.
   - Facts are information that can be found by research or by observation.
   - An opinion is what a person thinks based on the facts he or she knows.
2. Looking at an artwork, have students state a fact or opinion about it.

   Example:
   Fact: I see a yellow square.
   Opinion: I like the way the blue line is painted.
3. Divide the class into cooperative groups and give each group a Fact-Opinion die.* Give each group an artwork. In turn have students roll the die and make the appropriate statement. Have one team member record the facts and another record the opinions.
4. When all team members have had at least one turn, share the results with the whole class. How many teams came up with the same facts? How many shared the same opinions?
5. *Imaginative:* Some questions have the power to turn on students' imaginations. These questions are divergent. They have unlimited possible answers. They challenge students to generate many ideas or combine concepts in new ways.

   Imaginative questions can be used to start discussions. They are particularly useful when discussing abstract concepts and ideas. When discussing the effect of Christo's artworks on the public, for example, students might be asked to imagine what might happen if they turned the bridge near the school into an artwork like he did the Pont Neuf in Paris.

*To make the die, put stickers on a regular die and label three sides *Fact* and three sides *Opinion*.

Application questions can be used to add interest to a discussion. They allow students to use what they know as they formulate their ideas. Teachers can ask students to explain how they arrived at an idea or compare one idea to another. For example, in examining one student's weaving, a teacher might ask if anyone has used a similar technique in their work to get a different effect.

3. *Opinion:* Opinion questions have many possible responses and require students to analyze personal feelings, to evaluate, and to judge. They can be answered on two levels. Initial responses to this kind of question draw mainly upon the student's personal response to experiences and concepts. Higher-level responses consist of an opinion and supporting statements and require students to apply their knowledge of art.

At a Glance 5.12

Using the Creative Process in a Discussion

Creative Process	Discussion Components
Knowledge	Contribute what you know
Skill	Use listening and communication skills
Motivation	Become involved
Immersion	Think about what is being said
Incubation	Come up with new ideas
Production	Know more about art

Opinion questions play a very important role in discussions. As students examine a work of art, they experience feelings and make judgments. Asking students to express these is the heart of a discussion. An opinion question makes a good opener for a discussion. It can get students motivated to talk at the same time it provides direction for the discussion.

A discussion that opens with the question, "Do you think this artist was able to capture the feeling of a storm at sea in this painting?" starts the students thinking about their own experiences of stormy weather and how they might express them in the painting medium. It is important to encourage students to provide supporting statements by asking a follow-up question. If, for example, a student states, "It looks stormy to me," ask, "What part of the painting best captures the effect of the storm?"

Responding in Writing

Writing about art in the primary grades. In the primary grades students should be expected to write a simple response to aesthetic questions. Beginning writers can use words and pictures to show what the artwork made them think about. Following the visit to the park sculpture mentioned earlier, for example, students could draw the sculpture showing what they might do about the children climbing on it. Depending on their viewpoint, they might make it easier to climb or fence it off to make it harder.

Writing about art in the intermediate grades. Writing about art allows students to apply and perfect their writing skills. Intermediate students can be expected to write a variety of pieces about an artwork using the writing process. More advanced writers can be asked to support their opinions about art with research.

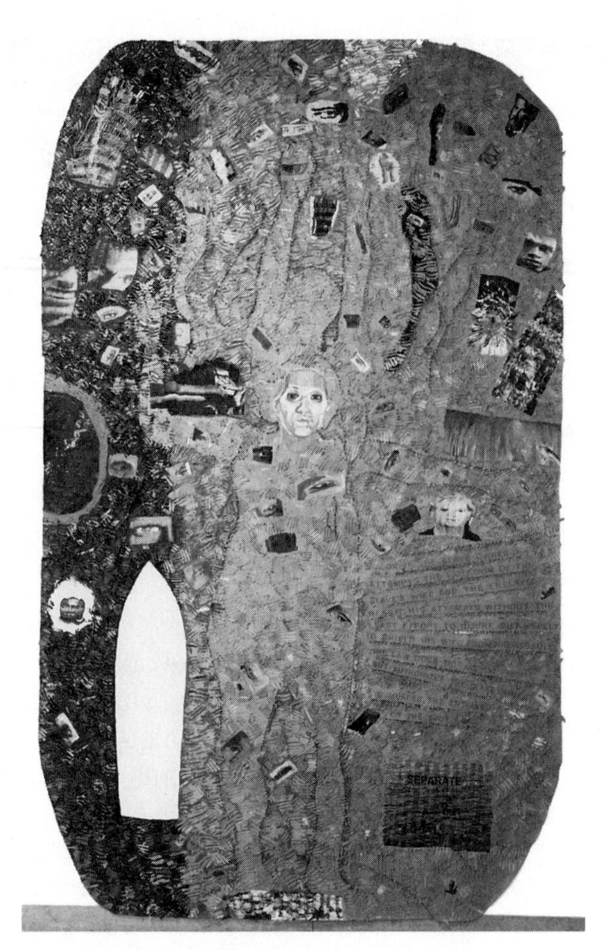

"Autobiography: Water/Ancestors/ Middle Passage/Family Ghosts." Mixed media: acrylic, tempera, oil stick, sewn vinyl tape, cattle tags, and polymer-photo transfer—Howardena Pendell, 1988. The Wadsworth Atheneum. Ella Gallup Summer and Mary Catlin Summer Collection.

From the Art Museum

In selecting artwork for study look for works that have many different levels of meaning. In this self-portrait Howardena Pendell (African American, 1943–) has used an image of herself swimming through words and objects, such as cattle tags, that evoke the legacy of slavery and its effect on her life and the life of all African Americans. In what ways could this powerful work be introduced to students? How would having an understanding of African-American history help students derive more meaning from the work? How could the work be used to motivate students to look deeper into the influences upon their own lives and find ways to communicate about them through their art?

- *Descriptive:* Describe the work using art vocabulary and rich, descriptive language.
- *Comparative:* Compare two different works, two different artists, or an artwork with a poem or piece of literature.
- *Point of view:* Express a supported personal opinion about an artwork.
- *Informative:* Collect information about an artist's life or the creation of an artwork and then write a report.
- *Persuasive:* Write a letter or essay that tries to convince someone to like a particular work or to adopt a particular aesthetic view.

Teaching in Action

Teaching a Painting to Speak

Pamela Gay (1992) suggests that students give an artwork a voice and let it speak through their writing. Have students begin by taking field notes, doing research, and then looking at the work again.

1. View the painting. Look and look again. As Georgia O'Keeffe said, "To see takes time, like to have a friend takes time."
2. Study the painting very carefully. Divide a piece of paper into two columns. On the left side take notes on what you see going from top to bottom or left to right. Be very descriptive. Use vivid adjectives and phrases. "Visit" the painting several times, taking more notes each time.
3. On the right side of the paper write about what the painting and its colors, shapes, and textures make you feel or think. What do you think the artist is saying?
4. Read your notes and make a list of questions you would ask the painting if it could speak.
5. Do research to try and find answers or information that adds meaning to your thoughts. If you cannot find any answers, try inventing some plausible ones of your own.
6. Using your notes and questions, write a conversation between the painting and yourself.

Conclusion

ART FOR THINKING

A picture lives only through him who looks at it.
Pablo Picasso (in Bruner, 1996, p. 22)

The visual images that surround us are not only to be understood by the experts. Those artistic images are messages for all and must be made meaningful through learning activities that teach students how to look at art and express their affective state. Students must learn to describe the work using an art-based vocabulary and use that vocabulary to evaluate the work internally and externally. They must see beyond the surface image and understand that each artwork occupies a unique place in a historical, cultural, or social context. They must stretch their ability to think by participating in discussions that address philosophical questions on the nature of art.

It is the teacher's role to use those teaching strategies and learning experiences that enable all students to think, speak, and write reflectively about art. Teachers must surround students with the wonderfully diverse art of humankind. Students who are prepared in this way are no longer dabblers in art. They have learned to reflect on their beliefs, to listen to other points of view, to present and evaluate opinions based on supporting reasons, and to engage in philosophical inquiry. They have become artistic thinkers comfortable with the language of art.

Teacher Resources

REFERENCES

Battin, M. P. (1995). Cases for kids: Using puzzles to teach aesthetics. In R. Moore (Ed.), *Aesthetics for young people.* Reston, VA: National Art Education Association.

Bruner, J. (1996). *The culture of education.* Cambridge, MA: Harvard University Press.

Davis, J., & Gardner, H. (1993). The arts and early childhood education: A developmental portrait of the young child as an artist. In B. Spodek (Ed.), *Handbook of research on the education of young children* (pp. 191–206). Indianapolis, IN: Macmillan.

Dissanayake, E. (1995). *Homo aestheticus: Where art comes from and why.* Seattle: University of Washington Press.

Feinberg, S. G. (1987). Children's awareness of aspects of competence in drawing. *Visual Arts Research, 14*, 80–93.

Freeman, N. H. (1995). The emergence of a framework theory of pictorial reasoning. In C. Lange-Kuttner & G. Thomas (Eds.), *Drawing and looking: Theoretical approaches* to pictorial representation in children (pp. 135–146). Hertfordshire, England: Harvester Wheatsheaf (Simon & Schuster).

Freeman, N. H., & Brown, N. M. (1993). *The emergence of a theory of picture-production: Intentional net analysis.* Unpublished manuscript, University of Bristol.

Freeman, N. H., & Sanger, D. (1993). Language and belief in critical thinking: Emerging explanations of pictures. *Exceptional Education Canada, 3*, 43–58.

Gardner, H., & Winner, E. (1976). How children learn . . . three stages of understanding art. *Psychology Today, 9*(4), 42–43.

Gay, P. (1992). *Teaching a painting to speak: Using art to teach writing and critical inquiry.* Paper presented at the National Conference on Liberal Arts and the Education of Artists, School of Visual Arts, New York.

Geertz, C. (1976). Art as a culture system. *Modern Language Newsletter, 91*, 1474–1499.

Honigman, J. J., & Bhavnagri, N. P. (1998). Painting with scissors: Art education beyond production. *Childhood Education, 74*(4), 205–212.

Koroscik, J. S. (1984). Cognition in viewing and talking about art. *Theory into Practice, 24*(4), 440–444.

Moore, R. (Ed.) (1994). *Aesthetics for young people.* Reston, VA: National Art Education Association.

Nye, R., Thomas, G., & Robinson, E. (1995). Children's understanding about pictures. In C. Lange-Kuttner & G. V. Thomas (Eds.), *Drawing and looking: Theoretical approaches to pictorial representation in children* (pp. 123–134). Hertfordshire, England: Harvester Wheatsheaf (Simon & Schuster).

Parsons, M. J. (1987). *How we understand art.* New York: Cambridge University Press.

Parsons, M. J. (1994). Can children do aesthetics? A developmental account. *Journal of Aesthetic Education, 28*(1), 33–45.

Reimer, B. (1980). Designing effective arts programs. In J. J. Hausman (Ed.), *Arts and the schools* (pp. 117–156). New York: McGraw-Hill.

Saccardi, M. (1997). *Art in story.* New York: Linnet.

Scott, A., & Stanley, M. (1997). Young children are learning through the arts. *New York State Association for the Education of Young Children Reporter, 24*(1), 1,4.

Stewart, M. (1994). Aesthetics and the art curriculum. In R. Moore (Ed.), *Aesthetics for young people* (pp. 77–88). Reston, VA: National Art Education Association.

Tauton, M. (1980). The influence of age on preferences for subject matter, realism, and spatial depth in painting reproductions. *Studies in Art Education, 21*, 40–52.

Winner, E. (1982). *Invented worlds: The psychology of the arts.* Cambridge, MA: Harvard University Press.

Practical Guides

Battin, M., Fisher, J., Moore, R., & Silvers, A. (1989). *Puzzles about art: An aesthetics casebook.* New York: St. Martin's Press.

Brooks, S. W., & Senatori, S. M. (1988). *See the paintings!* Rosemont, NJ: Modern Learning.

Kohl, M. F., & Solga, K. (1996). *Discovering great artists.* Bellingham, WA: Bright Ring.

Wolf, A. D. (1984). *Mommy, it's a Renoir! Art postcards for art appreciation.* Altoona, PA: Parent Child Press.

Videos

(*Note:* Grade level is in parentheses. See also Chapter 7 "Teacher Resources.")

African American Artist Series (4+), Crizmac

African American Artists Affirmation Today (5+), Facets

Artscape Series (4+), Films for the Humanities

Arts Place Series (1+), Films for the Humanities

Big A Series (2+), GPN

Don't Eat the Art: Sesame Street at the Metropolitan Museum of Art (K–4), Children's Television Workshop

Faith Ringgold: The Last Story Quilt (4+), Crizmac

Lascaux Revisited (5+), Knowledge Unlimited

Life and Art of William H. Johnson (4+), Crizmac

Masterpieces Children's Art Series (Matisse, da Vinci, Cézanne, Michelangelo, Cassatt, Hokusai, Kahlo) (4-8), Crystal

Master Pack (4+), Crizmac

Manabu Mabe Paints a Picture: Japanese Brazilian artist (4+), Facets

Maria Martinez: Pueblo Potter (4+), Crizmac

Marisol (5), Facets

Mountain of the Mind: Chinese painting (5+), Facets

Oriental Art (K-8), Wilton Series Crystal

The Natural Palette: The Hudson River Artist and the Land (4+), Crizmac

Romare Bearden: Visual Jazz (5+), Facets

Understanding Art Series (4–8), Crystal

What Do You See? (1+), Art Institute of Chicago

Wilton Art Appreciation Series (K–8) Crystal

RESOURCES

Prints, Videos, and More

(*Note:* Most of the following publish illustrated catalogs. See also Chapter 7 "Teacher Resources" for even more multicultural materials.)

Art Institute of Chicago
The Museum Shop
Michigan Avenue at Adams Street
Chicago, IL 60603
1-800-621-9337
Posters and postcards from their collection, artifacts from Central America

Crizmac
P.O. Box 65928
Tucson, AZ 85728-5928
1-800-913-8555
Individual and sets of posters, videos, and artifact kits from many cultures, art games

Crystal
Box 2159
Glenville, IL 60025
1-800-255-8629
Poster sets, videos, art timelines, CD-ROMS from many cultures, art games

Dale Seymour Publications
P.O. Box 10888
Palo Alto, CA 94303-0879
1-800-827-1100
Individual and sets of posters of multicultural and math-related art

Davis Publications
50 Portland Street
Worcester, MA 01608
1-800-533-2847
Sets of large laminated reproductions on many topics, including the art elements and multicultural artworks, African artifact kit

Dover Publications
31 E. 2nd Street
Mineola, NY 11501
Postcards and inexpensive books that can be cut apart to use as prints: Native American, African, Asian, Central and South American

Facets Video
1517 W. Fullerton Avenue
Chicago, IL 60614
1-800-331-6197
Videos on art and artists

Films for the Humanities
P.O. Box 2053
Princeton, NJ 08543
www.films.com
Videos on art and artists

GPN
P.O. Box 80669
Lincoln, NE 68501
1-800-228-4630
http://gpn.unl.edu
Videos on art and artists

Knowledge Unlimited
P.O. Box 52
Madison WI 53707-0052
1-800-356-2303
Sets of prints and videos: Native American, African American, women artists, and more

Metropolitan Museum of Art
255 Gracie Station
New York, NY 10028-9998
1-800-468-7386
Prints and postcards of art in their collection

Modern Learning Press
P.O. Box 167
Rosemont, NJ 08556
1-800-627-5867
Shorewood print sets

Museum of Fine Arts, Boston
P.O. Box 244
Avon, MA 02322-0244
Prints and postcards of art in their collection

Museum of Modern Art
11 W. 53rd St.
New York, NY 10019-5401
1-800-447-6665
Prints and postcards from their collection, Chinese brush painting kit

National Gallery of Art
2000B South Club Drive
Landover, MD 20785
Postcards and medium-sized prints of works in their collection

Print Finders
15 Roosevelt Place
Scarsdale, NY 10583
1-914-725-2332
Locates requested prints

Sax Visual Arts Resources
P.O. Box 51710
New Berlin, WI 53151
1-800-558-6696
Print sets and videos featuring African American, African, Native American, and more

University Prints
P.O. Box 485
Winchester, MA 01890
Small, inexpensive, black-and-white and color prints of fine art and architecture

Videodiscs

Videodiscs allow the teacher to show an individual artwork or to put together a customized series of works. The following are available from Crystal Productions:

American Art from the National Gallery

Art of the Western World

Great Artist Series

The National Gallery of Art

CD-ROMs

A Is for Art (K+), Crystal

Adventures in Art (2+), Crystal

Ancient Egyptian Art, Brooklyn Museum

Art Historian, Crystal

Artists at Work (K–6), Wilton Art Appreciation Series, Crystal

Electronic Library of Art, Sony

Escher Interactive: Exploring the Art of the Infinite (3+), Crizmac

Exploring Modern Art, Tate Gallery Microsoft

History through Art, Crystal

Institute of Art, Chicago

Lascaux, Crystal

Le Louvre, Metropolitan Museum of Art

Leonardo da Vinci (5+), Corbis

Look What I See! (K+), Metropolitan Museum of Art

Louvre Museum for Kids (3+), Voyager

Microsoft Art Gallery, Microsoft

Painters Painting, Crystal

Survey of Western Art, Crystal

Telling Images: Stories in Art (2+), Art Institute of Chicago

Van Gogh Starry Night (6+), Crizmac & Crystal

With Open Eyes: Images of the Art Institute of Chicago (3+), Voyager

World of Art, Crystal

Web Sites

The Web is a great place to discover the art of the world both past and present. There are hundreds of web sites focused on art and artists. The following list is just a brief beginning. Visit the major museums listed here. The museum sites usually include sample artworks from their collections. Consult the art link sites to find other museums to visit. Sites also provide links to sources of books, prints, and artifacts.

Museum Sites

American Museum of Folk Art
www.folkartmuse.org

Asian Art Museum of San Francisco
www.asianart.org

Boston Museum of Art
www.mfa.org

California African American Museum
www.caam.ca.gov

Ethnic Art Institute of Micronesia
www.oceanicmuseum.com

Florida Museum of Hispanic and Latin American Art
www.latinoweb.com/museo

Guggenheim Museum
www.guggenheim.org

Institute of Art, Chicago
www.artic.edu

Metropolitan Museum of Art
www.metmuseum.org

Mexican Museum of San Francisco
www.folkart.com/~latitude/museums/m_mexsf.html

Museum of Modern Art
www.moma.org

National Gallery of Art
www.nga.gov

National Museum of American Art
www.nmaa.si.edu

Walker Art Center
www.walkerart.org

Web Museum, Paris
www.oir.ucf.edu/wm

Whitney Museum
www.whitney.org

Art Link Sites

American Society for Aesthetics
Information and publications on the study of aesthetics
www.aesthetics-online.org

Art History Links
http://www.witcombe.sbc.edu/ARTHLinks.html

Arts Links
www.bravotv.com

Dictionary of Art
www.artlex.com

Virtual Library Museums
http://www.icom.org/vlmp

World Wide Arts Resources
http://wwar.com

Part Two

Teaching Art

Chapter 6

The Art of Teaching
Artist and Guide

As teachers we are called upon to be artists. We must remember that the artistry does not come from the quantity of . . . paint, or from the amount of clay . . . but from the organizing vision that shapes these materials.

Lucy McCormick Calkins (1986, p. 9)

ARTISTS AT WORK

First Grade Teachers

Sahreen: Oooh, look at this bluish green I just made!

Teacher: Mmm . . . aqua, beautiful aqua, the color of the sea when it's warm.

Sahreen: Aqua. I made aqua . . . [sings and paints] Aqua blue aqua green aqua sea . . . aqua. See my aqua. There's fish! Fish swim in my aqua. Look!

Gregory: How'd ya do that? Show me.

Sahreen: See. I can teach you. Watch me. Watch! Here's blue. Here's green. Now I whirl them together like this with the brush.

Gregory: Oh, let me try.

Introduction

THE TEACHER

Children's art is influenced by many factors, but none are more important than the artistic role models that they come in contact with throughout their lives. For many children this person will be a teacher. We can all remember teachers who affected us deeply as we were growing up—teachers who helped us discover the miracle of life in a tiny seed or the exhilaration of reading our first book by ourselves. We may not remember their names or what they looked like, but we carry them with us in the way that we see the world. If we want our children to discover the joys of art, then we ourselves must welcome art into our lives. We must show our students that we too are artists.

How can a teacher be an artistic role model? In this chapter we will discover that being an artist is an attitude, not a category. We will look at the myriad ways teachers can bring the excitement of art into the classroom. We will investigate the importance of role models and present ways to model artistic thinking in the classroom.

Setting the Stage

WHO IS AN ARTIST?

Who exactly is an artist? In our culture artists are often identified in very confining ways. In the contemporary art world the successful artist is seen as one who breaks with tradition, flouts the rules of the moment, and establishes a new style. This avant-garde art is often viewed as something mysterious that requires those with special knowledge to interpret, explain, and admire it. This in turn leads to the notion that great artists are solitary individuals, misunderstood and often ignored or vilified by the general public, who are waiting to be discovered by the important, knowledgeable people.

As we will see, defining artists in this way works against the universal need to use the language of art. Many people hold the following misconceptions about artists, which limit their ability to see the artist in themselves:

- *Real artists earn money from their art.* Are artists only those who earn their living creating art? Our commodity-driven society views as artists only those who can sell their artwork. The hobby artist is not considered a real artist. Does the fact that a painting sold for five million dollars make it more beautiful or creative? Many of the world's most beautiful artworks, such as Rembrandt's portraits of his wife, were created as gifts of love. The investment art market should not define artists for us.

? What Do You Think?

Do you have a hobby or sport in which you participate wholeheartedly? How often do you participate in it or even just think about it? How do you feel when you are totally involved in it? What would be your reaction if you could never do it again?

- *Real artists draw well.* Is only someone who draws life-like pictures an artist? A frequent expectation is that those who call themselves artists can draw well. Often people say, "I'm no artist. I can't even draw a straight line." This belief ignores the fact that there are many art forms that are not based on realistic drawing skills, such as working in clay or fiber.
- *Real artists create things to look at, not to use.* The art media people choose to use may also define them as artists. Nonfunctional works are often considered more highly artistic than utilitarian ones. For example, a sculptor of a marble statue is seen as an artist, whereas a potter who makes unique mugs or a weaver of one-of-a-kind shawls is just a craftsperson.

This misconception, according to Jacques Maquet, grows out of the museum experience. Items exhibited in museums are intended to be looked at, not used. Utilitarian objects such as a Thonet bentwood rocking chair or an Egyptian clay bowl only "metamorphose" into art when they are put in a museum setting (1986, pp. 18–22). But art can also be created any time someone manipulates art elements in an aesthetic and meaningful manner, regardless of the end purpose of the object.

Teacher as Artist

Because the term *artist* has been so narrowly defined, and the language of art is not systematically and seriously taught in our schools, most teachers do not recognize when they are functioning as artists. But they are in fact artists. Everyone uses the language of art in their daily lives.

"Artists," writes Elliot Eisner, "are thoughtful people who feel deeply and who are able to transform their thoughts, feelings and images into some public form" (1972, p. 115). Artists work with the elements of visual art—line, shape, color, texture, and dimensional form—to create meaning and order. Choosing the colors, pictures, and arrangements for a class bulletin board, discussing the illustrations in a beloved storybook, or drawing a diagram to illustrate an important concept in science are examples of teachers using art. Students who see certain colors and shapes on the bulletin board

Potlatch Hat. Vegetable fiber, pigment—Haida, Northwest Coast, 1910. Montclair Art Museum. Gift of Mrs. Henry Lang in memory of her mother, Mrs. Jasper R. Rand.

From the Art Museum

This woven hat was originally made to be worn and exchanged during ceremonies of the Haida tribe and served as a marker of status. Today it is exhibited in an art museum. Did the person who created it consider himself or herself an artist? Would we consider the creator of this hat to be an artist? How could comparing this hat to the types of hats they wear help students understand this work better?

learn what is aesthetically pleasing. Students who listen to a teacher talking about the relative size shown in an illustration learn about perspective. Students who see a teacher draw a cylinder using straight lines and an ellipse learn how to represent a cylinder on a flat surface. In these and similar activities teachers, regardless of the subject they are teaching, become artistic role models for their students.

Ways to Model Artistic Confidence

There are many ways that teachers can show children daily what it means to think artistically.

Show enthusiasm. Teachers of art are passionate about their subject. No matter what the subject, teachers who are excited about what they are teaching have students who are enthusiastic about learning. This is particularly important in art. Enthusiastic teachers of art encourage students to think like artists and to use artistic methods in their work, just like enthusiastic teachers of language encourage students to think and write like authors. Teachers who are enthusiastic use words that express excitement and joy as they interact with their students and their art. They respond warmly and positively to students as they take risks using art media or express their opinion about an artwork. "A teacher's love for art," says Bennett Reimer, "should shine through all that is done" (1980, p. 128).

Model self-confidence. Teachers of art believe in themselves. Enthusiasm for art grows out of a sense of competence. Self-confident teachers are not afraid to demonstrate how to use art materials, are willing to share their own artwork with their students, and do not denigrate their own art skills in front of their students.

Too many teachers say, "Don't laugh at my diagram" or "I'm sorry I can only draw stick figures to illustrate my story." Would the same teachers say, "I can't read very well" and then be able to teach their students to become good readers? Is it good teaching practice to tell children "I can't write stories" and then expect them to produce wonderful tales?

When teachers are not confident artists, they need to think about what negative experiences made them believe this. Did a parent tell them they had no talent? Did a past teacher make a thoughtless comment? Did a friend laugh at their labored-over drawing? Often understanding the source of the negative belief can help change one's assessment of artistic potential.

Do art. Teachers of art are not afraid to participate in art activities. In the beginning this may be difficult for some. Many classroom teachers are expected to teach art lessons but have never taken high school

Teaching in Action

Revitalizing the Artist in Yourself

Try the following to awaken your artistic nature:

- Begin with what you know. Follow your interests. Find a painting you love and introduce it to your students. Tell them why you love it.
- Explore your own imagination and creativity. Enroll in an art class. Visit the museum.
- Reach out to colleagues who use art in their classrooms. Share ideas and successful lessons.
- Ask your school or district to offer workshops in integrating art into the curriculum.
- Consult with your school librarian. Find professional books about teaching art.
- Contact parents who have a special interest in art.
- Surf the Internet for ideas, resources, and information on teaching art. (See Teacher Resources for Web sites.)

or college art courses; in many schools required art courses usually end in middle school. When adults have not used the language of art since their early teens, their artwork may regress to early childhood levels (Edwards, 1979).

In order to develop skill in any discipline, we need to be taught and then given situations in which to apply it. School districts regularly provide opportunities that keep the language teaching skills of their faculty up to date. Similarly they should encourage all teachers to regularly participate in drawing courses, attend painting workshops, visit art museums, and read about current art research.

Although participating in these kinds of activities will bolster artistic self-confidence, it is important to remember that students will learn just as much about artistic thinking from a teacher who, although untrained in art, is willing to do art with them. Students whose teachers sit down and enthusiastically explore art materials, or who look closely with them when they are viewing an artwork for the first time, learn how to become artists even more than they would from a highly skilled artist who lacks tolerance for the exploration of beginners.

Take creative risks. Teachers of art are bold. Above all successful teachers of art are willing to take risks: to try new techniques, experiment with unfamiliar media, and creatively incorporate the ideas of others into their own teaching practice. These educators do not rely on canned programs, a single teaching approach, or past lessons. They analyze the needs of their students and create lessons that are designed specifically to increase the skill and knowledge of each

At a Glance 6.1

The Artistic Teacher

The teacher of art should be

- Enthusiastic about teaching art.
- Self-confident in his or her own art abilities.
- Willing to learn about the art of many times, places, and cultures.
- Willing to create art.
- Willing to take creative risks.
- Supportive of the artistic potential of all children.

particular group. These teachers will combine and adapt the teaching methods presented in this book so as to best meet the immediate needs of their students. Although it might be easier to follow the lesson plans in a textbook or copy a pattern from a magazine, they know that kind of teaching will inspire neither them nor their students.

Show support. Teachers of art discover artistic abilities in all their students. Just as they believe that all children will eventually learn to read and write, educators must come to believe that every child can learn to use the language of art to communicate ideas effectively. As we saw in Chapter 4, children of all ages have far more artistic potential than most people believe and that what has been called talent is more the result of definition than birthright. "I think that the very best art teachers are growth-enhancing personalities," writes Judith Rubin, "who nurture the student's sense of self and of competence in a broadly therapeutic way" (1984, p. 293).

Why . . . ?

WHY SHOULD TEACHERS BE ARTISTIC ROLE MODELS?

Howard Gardner (1991; 1999) believes that it is extremely important for children to watch competent peers and adults perform in all the different domains of learning. By watching their teachers, they learn how to use skills and techniques to create meaning. Children need adults who can show them not only how to read and write but also how to draw people in action, and who can explain the meaning of the illustrations in their storybooks. They need to be shown how to diagram the cross-section of a tree trunk and how to select colors and lettering styles to create a dynamic science fair display. They require teachers who can select significant artwork to illustrate concepts

Books to Share

Artistic Role Models

Both positive and negative artistic role models are presented in the following books:

Asch, F. (1981). *Bread and Honey.* New York: Parent's Magazine.
A bear gets conflicting advice on how to improve his painting.

Cohen, M. (1980). *No Good in Art.* New York: Greenwillow.
After a bad experience in kindergarten, a young boy is shown the joy of art by his first grade teacher and his classmates.

dePaola, T. (1989). *The Art Lesson.* New York: Trumpet Club.
In this autobiographical story, the author describes both good and bad experiences with teachers and art.

Polacco, P. (1998). *Thank You, Mr. Faulkner.* New York: Philomel.
A ten-year-old girl with reading difficulties is teased until her teacher discovers her artistic talent and shares it with the class.

Schick, E. (1987). *Art Lessons.* New York: Greenwillow.
A young boy learns how to see like an artist as he accompanies his neighbor on sketching trips.

being taught and who are confident enough to explore all facets of art with their students. Most of all they need teachers, both in the classroom and the art room, who effectively model artistic confidence.

Guiding Ideas

LEARNING BY EMULATION

Although students need plenty of time to explore the possibilities of a medium or technique, teachers should never assume that students will discover all the effective methods of art on their own. Along with ample time to explore, teachers often need to show students what artistic processing and thinking look like. As children move through the grades, they interact with art in a variety of contexts. They learn that the language of art will be used in different ways depending on the approach of the teacher and the concepts being taught. In order to help children reach their artistic potential, we must select teaching methods that reflect our understanding of the different ways children learn.

One of the first ways children learn is by imitating others. From infancy children copy the sounds they hear and the motions they see. Vygotsky (1978) described learning as the process of observing, imitating, and assimilating knowledge from interactions with those who are more knowledgeable in the culture. Adults and older or more knowledgeable peers therefore provide an interactive context in which children build knowledge. The teacher, as the more skilled artist, talks

What the Experts Say

Teacher as Artist

[S]eeing a teacher become ecstatic over a visual work of art is precisely one of the modes of human response that one hopes students will learn to acquire. The teacher as model can provide a vivid image of what such an experience looks like when it is had.
Elliot Eisner (1972, p. 182)

[E]ducation in the visual arts must occur at the hand—and through the eyes—of an individual who can think visually or spatially.
Howard Gardner (1993, p. 142)

A teacher can play an important role in provoking her students intellectually by continually providing occasions that engage and encourage students to be adventurers in learning.
Meryl Goldberg (1997, p. 25)

[T]eachers in the classroom will generally teach or attempt to teach what they believe in, within the constraints of time, space, materials, and their own skill as teachers.
Larry Kantner (1990, p. 100)

Here I am, the teacher turned artist. I have learned to inhabit my images.
To encapsulate emotions, memories, even my subconscious in pictures.
Peter Thacker (1996, p. 47)

about and models the lesson, such as demonstrating how to hold and use a paintbrush to make the different brush strokes.

In order to be successful, however, children must be physically and mentally ready for that specific skill or concept. In order to emulate the teacher's brush strokes, for example, children must have the necessary finger and wrist control. Developmentalists believe that physical, emotional, social, and cognitive growth occurs in sequenced patterns as children mature. Within these sequences each child follows a unique learning curve determined by personality, learning style, and family and cultural background.

Developmentally appropriate practice (DAP) recommends that learning activities should match children's developing abilities (Bredekamp & Copple, 1997). Lev Vygotsky (1978) calls this the zone of proximal development: the point between actual and potential development when children are ready to learn from an adult or more mature peer model. The teacher carefully watches the child to assess the developmental level and then provides those learning experiences that offer the appropriate level of challenge. A child who can skillfully control a paintbrush, for example, will be intrigued by the different ways the teacher used it to apply paint, whereas a child who is still struggling merely to apply paint with a brush will not benefit from being shown the same techniques and may even give up in discouragement.

The art of teaching by showing, therefore, is knowing which strategy to use and when. It is essential to watch each student and constantly assess what that student needs to know at that moment and then select the right approach to show what to do next or to extend the possibilities.

In the Classroom

SHOWING AND TELLING

Modeling artistic skills and decision making is vitally important. In their personal lives many students do not see people creating art nor looking at artworks in a museum. Teachers need to talk out loud about what they are thinking as they demonstrate a technique or look at an artwork. They need to model ways to talk about each other's artworks and provide plenty of opportunities for students to put these ideas and methods into practice. Mini-lessons, conferencing with the teacher and other students, as well as sharing in small and large groups, provide ways for students to role play artistic thinking and practices in the classroom.

When using demonstration and modeling techniques, the teacher's role is to engage the student in learning tasks that are challenging but that the student can do successfully with guidance. The purpose should be clear and the student should feel safe to risk trying the new method. The idea is to stimulate students to form their own concepts or develop their skills. The process begins with the teacher doing most of the thinking and modeling, followed by a period in which the teacher and student work together. If successful, the student will understand what is needed to perform independently.

Demonstrating Skills, Methods, and Artistic Thinking

One way to teach specific skills or methods is for the teacher or a more expert peer to physically demonstrate how to use a particular tool or technique. This has been a traditional method of teaching art for thousands of years. Providing an actual demonstration of how to do something at just the right moment can help students avoid frustration while maintaining their focus on their artistic expression. For example, second graders often try to cut an eye opening for a mask by poking a piece of paper with a scissors. Showing the children how to fold the paper slightly and make a small cut not only frees them to move on to creating the rest of the mask but also shows them a safer way of working.

However, demonstrations can be far richer if they go beyond simply showing the teacher's way of doing something. Students must do more than just watch passively. Effective demonstrations are hands-on for both teacher and student and model artistic decision making. They get the students thinking through carefully worded questions and wonderings. "Engaging student learners is infinitely more successful," writes Kate Johnson, "when those students' teachers are engaged as well" (1995, p. 52).

Show, don't tell. The point of demonstrating is to help students understand the reasoning that underlies what an artist looks like and moves like when using a material or technique. As the process is acted out, so should be the thoughts and questions that the artist might be asking. For example, which of the following would result in students cleaning their brushes more effectively?

- *Telling:* "Wash your brush in water when you are finished."
- *Showing:* After making the above statement, the teacher takes the dirty paintbrush. Dips it in water. Swirls it around. Takes it out and looks at it. Blots it on paper. Sees there is still paint and says, "Oh, it's still dirty. What should I do? Hmm . . . maybe dip it again?" Dips and blots it again and exclaims, "Now it's clean!"

Be conversational. When modeling, think aloud to show the importance of considering and trying various strategies rather than giving prescriptions for behavior. Draw students into the demonstration by asking for their opinion. It is important for students to learn that creating art is a fluid process that often involves trial and error and creative problem solving. This is similar to Maureen Cox's negotiated drawing method described in Chapter 4.

- *Prescriptive:* "Always put a lighter color next to a darker one for contrast."
- *Conversational:* "Hmm, this yellow doesn't show off very well against this gray. Do you think I should try a darker color? What color do you suggest?"

Repeat and vary. It is important to remember that one demonstration may not be enough for a student to acquire competence. Most people need to be shown over and over again, especially if the task seems complicated and has many steps.

- *Repeat:* It is important to watch learners as they try out a new method and to repeat demonstrations as needed. While demonstrations can be given to the whole class in order to introduce everyone to a new material or method, there may be a wide range of needs and abilities in a class, and demonstrations are often most effective when given to one student or a small group who need that skill at that particular moment.

- *Vary:* Because students learn in different ways, it is important to vary the format of the demonstration. Standing in front of the classroom with students sitting at desks is probably one of the least engaging ways to demonstrate effectively. Some students will be too far away to see well or have to watch from a poor angle. Sitting on a rug in front of the demonstrator brings students closer and makes the activity more intimate. Some techniques are better demonstrated to small groups standing around a table or one on one. Consider making an illustrated poster, or an audio or videotape of methods and skills that students can consult when they need that technique.

Involve students. Teachers often feel that as only one person they can never meet everyone's need in a busy active classroom. Research shows that using a more expert peer to help a less expert one is a highly effective way to increase learning in the classroom. Not only does the student being taught improve but the student teaching also makes gains (Azmitia, 1988; Webb, 1989).

- *Student volunteers:* Take a tip from magic shows and invite audience participation. Students can help hold materials, try out a technique, or describe the process as it happens in their own words. For example, in a demonstration of printing techniques invite three students to come forward and roll ink on sample printing plates and then use three different methods of rubbing the print: spoon, hand, and burin. The class could then decide which method would give the effect they want in their prints.
- *Peer "experts":* Use students to demonstrate techniques and encourage them to discuss choices they have made and problems they have solved. Students who have learned a new skill can become future "experts" whom you can call upon to demonstrate the method to a peer.

Alternate and adjust. Gradually release responsibility for the process to the students. It is not enough to tell students what to do or to explain the meaning of an artwork. After observing the teacher or a more expert peer using a technique or describing an artwork, they must have opportunities to practice under the guidance of the teacher as soon as possible and then the space and freedom to use the new learning. For this reason demonstration is often the method of choice for lessons that are followed by an independent work time in which students can try out the technique or concept on their own.

- *Alternate:* After modeling the process several times, allow the students to role play being the teacher or explain what they are doing by "thinking out loud."
- *Adjust*: When students have demonstrated that they grasp the technique or idea, de-emphasize that aspect and focus on those areas that are giving them more difficulty.

Guided Discovery: An Interactive Demonstration

Guided discovery techniques are effective for presenting new art materials or showing how to use special areas of the room. The objectives of guided discovery are to motivate and excite students about the new material or area at the same time as you establish acceptable guidelines. Carefully delivered guided discovery lessons set the stage for well-managed art activities. The three parts are as follows:

1. *The unveiling:* The more enticing the introduction of the supply or area, the more motivated the students will be to try it and follow the guidelines. Wrap small items, such as a box of chalk, in gift wrap; place larger items in a paper bag. Ask a riddle about an art supply or a new area of the room that has been suddenly set up with supplies and eye-catching charts and labels: Guess what the object or area is. Slowly give clues, uncover or unwrap it.
2. *The exploration:* Uncovering the item or area, ask questions that will entice the students to study the material or area closely.
3. *The guidelines for usage:* This is crucial. Draw on students' past experiences, existing classroom rules, and the students' own common sense to elicit the guidelines. At the end summarize the guidelines and, if desired, make a sign or have the students write the guidelines in their own words in their journals.

Modeling Artistic Conversation

Art does not require words. The artist and the viewer need never meet or speak. They communicate through the artwork itself. Art education, on the other hand, requires many forms of communication: showing how to do something, listening to what is to be learned, telling and talking about art.

Much of teaching art is an ongoing conversation with students. It is a conversation that must engage and inspire them. It must draw out the best in them. It is a conversation that has often been ignored in many art programs, in which a lesson consists of reciting a list of directions, and a simplistic "That's nice" or "Good job" suffices in response to a student's work. But effective teaching of young artists demands much more. It requires provocative questions and thoughtful responses.

Listening and Responding

A conversation begins with listening. Teachers must listen to their students in order to engage in a meaningful dialogue. Teachers show they are listening to a student by how they act and by what they do or do not say. Active listeners move closer to the speaker. If they are sitting, they sit side by side, not across. They look at the student's face or the work being discussed. They smile and nod. They do not respond

Teaching in Action

Guided Discovery: An Example

Use the guided discovery format when introducing new materials, techniques, and work spaces in the room.

The Unveiling

Teacher: What do you think I have in this box?
Responses: Something to eat? It's small. It looks like a crayon box shape.
Teacher: I'll pass it around the circle. How does it feel? Does it make any sound when you shake it?
Responses: It doesn't make any noise. It's heavy. It's hard.
Teacher: I'll pull the paper off this end. Can you tell what it is now?
Responses: Oooh. It's a box. I see a box like that over there on the shelf. It's blue and white.
Teacher: (pulls back more of the wrapper) Hmm . . . There seems to be a window here.
Responses: I see it, I see it. It's clay. I have clay like that at home.

The Exploration

Teacher: This is called modeling clay. How much clay do you think is in this box?
Responses: A little bit. Enough to make a dish.
Teacher: Is there anything on the box that tells us about what's inside?
Responses: Oh. It says three colors. I see it says one pound on the end. That's why it was so heavy.
Teacher: Sheryl, will you open the box and take out a piece of clay?
Response: Oh. It's wrapped in plastic.
Teacher: Matt, would you peel off the plastic? Tell us how it feels.
Response: It's sort of hard . . . but soft, too. It makes my hands feel funny.
Teacher: Let's pass the clay around our circle. Each of you tell us how it feels to you. . . . How did the modeling clay feel?
Responses: Sticky. Soft. Like play dough but harder. Greasy. Like plastic stuff.
Teacher: What are some things we could do with this kind of clay?
Responses: Make things . . . like bowls. You could make a car. I think a snake.
Teacher: This clay will now be available for you to use during workshop. I can't wait to see all your sculptures!

Establishing the Guidelines

Teacher: Oh, but where do you think we should use this clay?
Responses: On the tables, like we do the play dough. Near the sink . . . 'cause it makes our hands sticky. And keep it off the floor—it would be yucky to step on.
Teacher: So we should use the modeling clay on the table nearest to the sink and keep it off the floor. How was it wrapped in the box?
Responses: It was wrapped in plastic.
Teacher: Why do you think it was wrapped?
Responses: To keep it clean. So it won't get dirty. It could stick to the other pieces. It could melt all over the box. So it won't get dirty. So it won't dry up.
Teacher: Let's keep our clay in plastic, too. Here are some bags to put it in. Gillian, will you show us how to put the clay in the bag and seal it shut? Put the bag of clay in this box when you're done. . . . Now Sara, will you show us how you will get the clay from the box and take it to the table? . . . Good, now Andrew will you show us how to put it away. Let's write our rules on the box.

(writes):

Use this at the table.

Keep it off the floor.

Put it in bag when done.

Close bag tightly.

A conversation.

Thinking about Children's Art

These second graders are engrossed in constructing a house out of construction paper to be part of a three-dimensional model of a community. Why is it important for the teacher to pay attention to what the group members say to each other? What can be learned from watching their cutting activity? Is this a good moment to say something to them?

instantly and verbally to everything the student says; rather, they wait several seconds or make gentle affirming sounds such as *hmm's* and *oh's.*

The most important part of listening, however, is hearing what the speaker is saying. When students talk about their artwork, they express what is important to them. Teachers must listen closely to discover these threads and then follow up on them in their response.

Paraphrasing. One way to show students you are listening is to paraphrase what they have said. Paraphrasing is restating the students' words or thoughts in a new way. Using a warm, positive tone of voice can turn a simple paraphrase into a compliment.

Student: I placed these green triangles here to balance the picture.

Teacher: Yes, the green shapes do balance your picture!

Summarizing. Although similar to paraphrasing, summarizing is a more complex process. After listening to the student, the teacher combines what was said into a logical, coherent whole.

Student: I was trying to make it look . . . like the beach . . . after the storm. I saw all these colors and stuff in the sky. The ocean was kinda green-blue. I don't know if I mixed that color right. I used the stiff brush to make it look wild.

Teacher: You painted the ocean after a storm using wild brush strokes and many colors.

Staircasing. Listening closely also allows the teacher to build on what the student is saying, adding to and expanding the student's knowledge, vocabulary, or ideas. Because this information directly relates to the student's need or interest of the moment, it is more likely to be remembered.

Student: I made sketches of this old house in my neighborhood. I really liked how the columns in front looked. They remind me of something I saw in a book.

Teacher: Yes, those columns are in the Greek Doric style and tell us the house is Neoclassical in design. Come, let's find a picture of a Greek temple in the picture file and compare it to your sketch.

Ways to Respond

How a teacher responds to a student's artistic thoughts and creations can make a tremendous difference in how students feel about themselves as artistic thinkers. Paraphrasing, summarizing, and staircasing all have positive effects on student motivation and learning. Another method is to use positive feedback.

Giving praise. All teachers want to encourage their students to do their best. Sensitive teachers are often afraid of hurting a student's feelings, particularly when responding to a piece of artwork. These good intentions have led to the practice of unconditional praise, such as "Good work!" and "Super job!" These are fine words, but they do not convey what the student did well. Used over and over, they become meaningless platitudes that leave the student feeling the teacher has paid little real attention to their accomplishments.

"The most powerful pattern of praise behavior," writes M. B. Rowe, "is that which communicates both praise and the reason for the praise" (1987, p. 130). Positive feedback is the alternative to unconditional praise. In positive feedback the teacher focuses on what the student has done well. Instead of saying "Great work!" the teacher describes what the student did: "I see that you used shading to make the house stand away from the background." When delivered with an uplifting tone of voice, such descriptive comments are heard as praise at the same time that they inform. In receiving a uniquely personal comment, students know that the teacher has really looked at their work.

Positive feedback can take several forms.

Describing behavior

- I see that you are using a large brush to paint the background.
- I noticed that you helped Francis put the clay away.

Describing effort

- You spent a great deal of time on your sketches for this project.
- This weaving represents seven days of work at the loom.

Describing artistic decisions

- You discovered a way to attach the leaves to your collage.
- I noticed you chose to use a monochromatic color scheme in this work.

Describing artistic concepts:

- I see that you created a balanced composition.
- The use of perspective in this drawing really adds depth to the picture.

Avoid negative responses. There are other ways of responding that have negative effects:

- *Criticism:* Overly critical comments can demoralize a novice artist.
- *Correction:* Responses aimed at simply fixing an artwork or correcting an idea tell the student the finished work or correct answer is more important than the learning and thinking that occurred in creating it and remove a student's motivation to improve.

Fostering Self-Improvement

When people have worked hard or thought deeply, they do not always accept suggestions for improvement graciously. This is particularly true of student artists. Artists, no matter what their age or skill level, are intimately tied to their work. There is something about using the creative process and transforming a small part of one's universe that gives an individual personal power. A word of criticism or correction takes this feeling away.

How then can students be guided to improve their artwork? The answer is to empower students to make their own criticisms and corrections. This is difficult. Teachers see the work and know what they would do to change it: Just a line here or a splash of color there would turn a mediocre work into a spectacular one. It would be so easy to just tell the student what to do. But it is not the teacher's artwork. Nor will fixing this particular artwork improve the student's next one. Instead students lose their motivation to learn and come to rely on the teacher fixing their work for them.

In order to empower students to make improvements in their artwork and appreciate what they have accomplished, teachers must become superb conversationalists. Conversations and thinking begin with questions. How that question is phrased will make a tremendous difference in how a student responds. Questions are also the backbone of peer and teacher conferences as well as in interacting with individual students and their work.

Questions can help students think about their actions, give direction to their plans, further their understanding of art processes, and assess what they have learned. They also help students develop oral language skills.

Creating a conversational atmosphere. In order to have positive conversations with students, teachers must create a classroom atmosphere in which students feel safe expressing their thoughts and feelings about art.

- *Talk about art daily.* Provide many opportunities to talk about art so that verbalizing about art becomes a normal part of the school day. If students have had experience responding to artwork by others through featured artwork units and through discussing illustrations in books, they will be more comfortable talking about their own work.
- *Pay attention to tone.* Ask questions in a tone of voice that contains enthusiasm and curiosity. Speak gently and make eye contact. When the student responds, practice active listening.
- *Select the right moment.* Students who are deep in thought or production should not be interrupted by questions about what they are doing. Questions are appropriate when students are trying out ideas and want feedback, when they have run into a problem and need direction, or when they think they are finished. Planning time for peer and teacher conferences and whole group sharing builds in ideal moments to ask thoughtful questions.

Questions to Ask about Student Artwork

Each conversation with a student is unique, but having particular goals allows teachers to formulate questions that can help the student develop cognitively. These kinds of questions can help students develop in specific areas:

Oral vocabulary. Ask questions that call for students to describe their ideas or work.

- What textures are you thinking about using in your collage?
- Did you mix any special colors for your painting?

Art concepts. Ask questions about the art elements and principles of design. (See Chapter 12 for specific vocabulary.)

- How have you used pattern in your drawing?
- Did you consider the principle of balance in designing this painting?

Processing. Ask students to review the steps of a process or reconsider decisions.

- How did you make this sculpture stand up this way?
- Did you try other colors before using this one?

Problem solving. Ask students to explore relationships and possible decisions that might help them solve a problem.

- What do you think might be causing that wet paper to curl up like that?
- Why do you think this stone keeps falling off your collage?

Exploring relationships. Art activities can provide an opportunity for students to explore the relationship between actions and objects. Students can be asked to make predictions, connect events, and discover causes.

- What do you think might happen if you wet your paper before painting on it?
- How has the clay changed after being left out in the air overnight?
- What do you think caused these threads to stick out from your weaving?

Integrating subject matter. Questions can be used to relate what is being learned in one subject to another.

- Science: Remember our evaporation experiments in science? Which paint do you think will dry faster, tempera or watercolor?
- Math: What geometric shapes have you used in your house design?
- Language: Which of the authors we have read makes painted paper collages?

Assessing knowledge. Using gentle questioning, teachers can get a feel for what a student knows and understands.

- I see you made a picture of the ocean. Do you remember what we call pictures that have the sea as a subject?
- Can you show me where you used the primary colors in your sketch?

Conferencing

Unfortunately when they are immersed in the hectic activity of an art activity, teachers often find they have little time to talk seriously with individual students and to listen to what they have to say. In order to interact on a one-on-one basis with students, teachers must consciously plan the necessary time.

There are three ways that, when used in combination, effectively allow this type of interaction. The term *mini-conference* is used here to describe the brief conversations that teachers hold with students as they circulate around the classroom. The *teacher/student conference,* on the other hand, is a formal meeting with a definite purpose. The third method of communication is through *response journals.*

Both types of conferences and the response journal can cover a range of concerns. Although most conferences will be involved with

"Sunset at the Lake."
Watercolor—Kevin, grade 4.

Thinking about Children's Art

This fourth grader began by making a pencil sketch and then painting in the bright colors of a sunset. When the paint was dry he added the black silhouettes. Think about what you might say in response to his work? What positive feedback could you give him on his painting method? What artistic decisions did he make? What questions would you ask him?

art production, teachers and students may also talk about artworks they have studied, research they have done, and aesthetic questions they may have. Conferences and journal entries can be used to

- Help a student solve a problem.
- Provide positive support for doing something well.
- Review student research.
- Discuss an artwork or aesthetic question.
- Provide a new direction for research or art creation.

Mini-conferencing. As students work on their art projects or tackle art problems in cooperative groups, teachers need to move about the room, stopping to talk with individual students. These mini-conferences allow the teacher to help students at the moment of need or discuss student progress.

With a practiced eye a teacher can quickly look over a group of students and see who is having difficulty controlling the art medium or coming up with an idea. Responding quickly to these students' needs improves student behavior and artwork by preventing students from becoming frustrated or distracted. Students sitting nearby also benefit as they hear the student and teacher discuss a problem that they may also be having or possibly will have at some later time.

Mini-conferences should take only a minute or two. The teacher might begin by describing what behavior the student is exhibiting and then asking if the student would like help—"I see you have only drawn one sketch so far. Do you need some ideas for your next project?"—and then listening to the student's response to determine how best to help. When the student is back on track, the teacher can move on to others.

One way to help struggling students is to refer to past experiences or instruction. This re-enforces student learning. Students can be directed toward charts or journal entries that might help them. For example, to help a student who expresses difficulty choosing which brush to use, a teacher might say, "Remember when we explored all the different ways to use paintbrushes? Have you looked at the chart we made to see which brush might give you the effect you want?"

Student-teacher conferences. The student-teacher conference is a formalized opportunity for students and teachers to converse with each other. If the teacher has been mini-conferencing throughout the student's creation of an artwork, a final formal conference provides an opportunity to summarize what the student accomplished and then to set the direction for the student's next piece.

Formal conferences should also be scheduled when more in-depth discussion is needed than can be obtained in a mini-conference, such as when a student decides to stop working on an almost completed project. Teachers should also hold a formal conference when a student requests one or when more privacy or space is needed. In a combination writing/art workshop conferences can address both writing and the related artwork (see Chapter 8).

Student-teacher conferences should be scheduled and posted beforehand so that students can be prepared. This type of conference can last five to ten minutes. Determine the number possible in a day or week, leaving time for mini-conferences and small group lessons, and create a conference sign-up sheet with spaces for name, date, and purpose. Actual scheduling can be done by having upper-grade students sign up on a posted form when they are ready. Primary students who wish a conference can do so more informally by taking a clothespin or tag from a bin and putting it by their name.

Students should be expected to bring the required materials to the conference. For example, at a finished work conference a primary student might bring some sketches and the finished artwork. A fourth-grade student might bring a process folio, the artwork, a journal, and some scrap paper and a pencil for note taking.

At the conference. It is important in conferencing to remember that the teacher's role is to help students learn to examine their own artwork. It is not a conversation if all the teacher does is tell the student what to do. Telling the student to use a bigger paintbrush or work on improving technique does not foster problem-solving behavior. Instead, the teacher needs to respond to the work as it is and then ask carefully designed questions that will lead students to discover a workable solution or direction.

Begin by responding to the student's work on a personal level. "Our first job in a conference," writes Lucy Calkins, "is to be a person, not just a teacher. It is to enjoy, to care and to respond. We cry, laugh, nod and sigh" (1986, p. 118). It is a time to show excitement and joy, a celebration of what the student has accomplished so far. This does not mean empty praise but rather words that express what the student has done and how it relates to other works, other studies, or the teacher's personal feelings.

Follow up by asking students to explain what they thought they did well and where they feel they want to improve. Conference questions should match the ability of the student to respond.

Primary Level Conference Questions

- What did you like about making this?
- What could you change?
- What could you add?

Intermediate Level Conference Questions

- What did you learn in making this?
- What was the easiest part?
- What was the hardest part?
- What will you do differently next time?

Recording the conference. Conferencing also provides the teacher with a way to assess student progress. It is important to meet with each student on a regular basis. Establish a system such as a class checklist or have an index card for each student on which is written a brief, dated note about what the student is doing and what was discussed. This will allow you to keep track of who has had conferences. Chapter 9 will expand on how to use such records in evaluating students.

Peer Conferencing (Partnering)

Teachers cannot be everywhere at once. There is a limited amount of time in which to conference with students. One of the best ways to

"At the Circus."
Tempera and colored chalk—Maya, grade 1.

Thinking about Children's Art

In this artwork a young child has tried to capture not only the horseback rider in the ring but also the excitement of the onlooking crowd. In conferencing with this child what might be your first reaction to her work? What questions might you ask her about the way she has represented the crowd?

facilitate conversations about art is through the use of peer conferencing or partnering.

Peer conferences offer many advantages:

- Students are less hesitant to talk to a peer about their work. They are more open to ideas and changes in their work when suggested by a fellow student rather than a teacher.
- They can take place quickly at the moment of need. In a few minutes students can usually find a peer to partner with and share.
- Both students benefit. Both formulate questions about art and use art vocabulary. Both must think about artistic decisions and ideas.
- They make students aware of the individual nature of the audience. Students get to hear one or more person's reactions to their work.

Introducing peer conferencing. If students are prepared properly, peer conferencing can take place with a minimal amount of teacher supervision. This frees the teacher for other activities such as teaching a small group or holding a student-teacher conference.

Begin by holding a class discussion about peer conferencing. Conferencing about art and writing is so similar that the same introductory activities can be used for both:

At a Glance 6.2

Sample Teacher-Student Conference

Teacher: Let's see what you've been working on.
Felicia: I think I'm done with this painting.
Teacher: Do you have the sketches you made?
Felicia: Yep. And here are some color mixing sheets, too.
Teacher: Let's spread them out on the table. (Looks closely at work.) I see many of the grays and blues you mixed over here you ended up using in the sky of your painting.
Felicia: Uh-huh. See, this one's almost exactly the same. I wanted the clouds all the same color, but you know, it's hard to get it exactly alike in each mix. So I swirled them around to like . . . blend in.
Teacher: That was an effective way to approach color mixing, especially in the sky. Will you use that method again?
Felicia: I really like how it looks . . . all swirly-like, like fog coming in. Maybe my next painting could be a foggy morning.
Teacher: Some of these other sketches you did might be a good starting point for the next painting. The idea of fog as a theme would work well in this landscape, I think.
Felicia: Maybe I could try to make it all mysterious-looking . . . like everything's hidden sort of. Like this house could have foggy swirls around it.
Teacher: It looks like you have the start of your next painting here. Now how would you like to present this painting?
Felicia: I thought I could mount it on gray paper and then hang it up in our New Works gallery.
Teacher: Do you have a title?
Felicia: Oh . . . how about *Gray Skies*?
Teacher: Yes, the sky is the main focus of this painting and that title describes it well. Now put your sketches and mixing sheets in your process folio. Okay, now don't forget to go back and write in your journal what you learned about mixing colors and how you'll use it in your foggy morning picture.

- *Role play:* Have students role play how to ask a person to partner, where they may go, how they should sit, and what they should say and do.
- *Set up guidelines:* Create a list of conferencing behaviors and possible questions to ask. For example, when students are ready to conference, they might

  1. Quietly ask someone to be a partner.
  2. Take their sketches and a peer conference form and go to the assigned location.
  3. Talk briefly using a set of questions.
  4. Fill out the form and put it in a designated location.
  5. Return to their activities.

Teaching in Action

Tracking Conferences

It is important to a devise a quick and convenient system of note taking for mini-conferences and teacher-student conferences. There are many approaches. Which will work best will depend on personal preference and individual situations. Over a year a teacher might use several different methods depending on the information desired.

1. *Checklist:* Design a reproducible sheet on which is listed each student's name and descriptive categories that can be quickly checked. If possible try to have all students listed on the front of one sheet. This allows a cursory glance to determine who has been seen and who has not. Staple the sheet to a file folder and carry it during mini-conferences or place it at the conference table. This method works well in situations where time is very limited and students are just learning the artistic process.

   Example **Mini-Conference Checklist**

	Stage of Artistic Process						
Name	**Idea**	**Planning**	**Revising**	**Peer Conf.**	**Prod.**	**Teach Conf.**	**Discussed**
Tom							*using journal for ideas*
Mario							*balancing composition*
Jessica							*using scissors safely*
Carla							*books to consult—Egypt*

2. *Pocket Cards or Stickers:* Make up an index card or large self-stick label for each student. Carry them around when mini-conferencing. During or just after talking with a student jot down the date and what was discussed. Because there is a card or sticker for each student interaction, the teacher can easily file or stick them in the individual student's process folios, creating a detailed record over time. These work well in situations where upper-level students, who are comfortable with the artistic process, are working on major works that take many art periods.

   Example **Conference Note**

   Gabriela Hernandez
   4/3/98
   Working on sketches for backdrop
   Read about rain forest—focus on animals
   Suggested she team up with someone who is doing foliage designs

3. *Taping:* Small hand held tape recorders can quickly capture a conference conversation. If each student has his or her own tape, the recording can become part of the record of the process folio and can be reviewed at the final teacher conference or at parent conferences. Upper-level students can keep their tape in their process folios and have them ready for the teacher when needed. Taping allows teacher and student to revisit their conversation in a way that handwritten notes cannot. This method works particularly well with young children, who find listening to the tapes enjoyable at the same time that they spark memory.
4. *Student Record Keeping:* Ask students to make a notation describing the points of the conference in their journal or on a sheet attached to their process folio. This method helps students revisit and clarify what was discussed as they state it in their own words. It is particularly appropriate for intermediate students who are involved in self-assessment activities.

Peer conferencing.

Thinking about Children's Art

Two first graders have found a place on the rug to share their art/writing journals. What question might they ask each other about their work? What skills are they developing?

- *Practice:* Then have the whole class practice conferencing using a sketch from their journals. As they practice, at first pay attention to process rather than content. When students understand how to conference, the content will become more important.
- *Give responsibility:* As students learn the procedures, give them the responsibility to hold one or more peer conferences about each of their artworks.
- *Monitor:* A sheet to be filled in by both participants and put in the process folio will help keep students on track (see At a Glance 6.3). Occasionally have students turn in these forms to provide a quick check on how the conferences are going.

Group Conferences

Sometimes, because of limited time or the need to work with particular students on conferencing skills, it may be necessary to schedule group conferences. This kind of conference is ideal for helping students learn how to discuss artwork. It should, however, never be the only form of conferencing used. Students need to have one-on-one opportunities with the teacher as often as possible.

Organizing group conferences. Designate a table with seating for four to six as the conference area. When students are ready to talk about their work, they come to the table. Some students may be invited by the teacher, either because they need to practice conferencing skills or because they are at a stage of work where they can easily stop and help others conference.

- *Rotation method:* Students at the table take turns sharing their work and asking questions of each other under the teacher's supervision. Each student shares the work in progress and then stays at the table to ask revision questions of the next student. After participating for a while, the student returns to work and another takes that seat. This rotation method works very well when many students are reaching the revision stage at the same time.
- *Established group method:* Students can take turns serving on a "reviewing board." Two or three students can either sign up or be assigned to meet for ten to fifteen minutes with any students needing revision conferences. This system ensures that all students get an opportunity to practice revision questioning.

Response Journals

There are many different approaches to keeping journals as part of art instruction. Journals can function as sketchbooks and notebooks and can also provide a private place for student-teacher exchanges. In the language arts class response journals are a place for students to write

At a Glance 6.3

Sample Peer Conference Sheets

Primary Format

Artist	**Viewer**
Name	Name
Date	What could be changed or added?
Artwork	

Upper Level Format

Artist	**Viewer**
Name	Name
Date	What questions or ideas did you discuss with the artist?
Subject	
Media	
Purpose/Goal	

the reactions to a piece of literature, sometimes in the form of a letter. Responses may be based on the student's own interests and needs or be in reply to a teacher's question. In art students can write about their own artwork and the problems or thoughts they have about it as it progresses, or they can write about artwork they have looked at closely, asking and answering questions either of their own design or suggested by the teacher.

Response journals can help prepare students to participate in group and class discussions because they allow students to organize their thoughts and questions before hand. They also provide a safe place for students to ask teachers questions they may be too embarrassed to ask out loud.

The teacher's replies to the students' journal entries are as important as the entries themselves. When a teacher writes in the student's

What the Experts Say

[T]he teacher must be dedicated to growth, to her personal growth as well as to the growth of her pupils.
David Elkind (1974, p. 176)

"Talking through" pictorial ideas is the backbone of much classroom practice.
Paul Johnson (1997, p. 22)

Learning is first and foremost a subjective affair in which one's understanding of self and world is transformed, expanded, questioned, deepened, upset.
David Lazear (1994, p. 7)

Through discussions, art problems are stretched beyond their first impressions and ordinary reactions and are built toward extraordinary responses, unusual perceptions and highly imaginative insight.
George Szekely (1988, p. 123)

The guidance and encouragement of an understanding teacher can make a tremendous difference in children's attitudes, interests and development in painting.
Cathy Topal (1992, p. 3)

journal, the student learns that the journal is not just an assignment but also a real place to communicate. Thoughtful, caring written responses by the teacher also encourage student interest in thinking about their art and the art they see around them. Journal replies can

- Share the teacher's personal ideas and feelings.
- Model aesthetic thinking.
- Provide information or direct students to source materials.
- Challenge students to think in a new way.
- Develop students' art vocabulary and ability to write about art.

Teacher Tip

Peer Conferencing Tips

1. Post a list of conferencing questions and strategies near the conferencing area, or copy and laminate conference tips and attach them to clipboards along with conference sheets and a pencil for partners to take with them.
2. Limit conferences to five minutes. Provide inexpensive five-minute egg timers to help students stay on target.
3. Set aside secluded areas for conferencing so that other students are not disturbed.
4. If some students have difficulty with the procedures or controlling their behavior, set up and supervise group conferences so they can have positive conferencing experiences.

At a Glance 6.4

Sample Revision Questions

The following is a sampling of the kind of questions that could be asked at a peer conference. To keep conferences brief limit the number of questions students ask. Use no more than one to three questions at the primary level. The personal level questions work well for young children. Select no more than five questions to use at one time at the upper levels. Construct limited-focus conferences by selecting questions from only one category. A broad conference would have questions drawn from each one.

Purpose

- What is the artist's purpose for creating this artwork?
- Does the sketch relate to this purpose?
- Does the artist have any special goals in creating this artwork?
- Does the sketch relate to the artist's goals?

Design

- What design elements and principles has the artist used?
- Does the design of the sketch carry out the artist's idea?
- Has the artist thought about the medium and technique that will be used?
- What is the focal point of this sketch?
- What is the most interesting part of the sketch?
- Which part is the least interesting?
- Is the artist planning to use any interesting approaches or techniques?

Meaning

- Are the subject and style clear and appropriate?
- Is the meaning of the sketch clear?
- Does the meaning relate to the purpose and goals of the artist?
- Is there anything that is hard to understand?

Personal Reaction

- What I like best is . . .
- If I could change one thing, I would change . . .
- If I could add one thing, I would add . . .
- If I could take away one thing, I would take away . . .

Organizing response journals. Managing an art response journal system can seem daunting at first. There is no way one teacher can write back to every student every day. Instead, responses must be staggered over a length of time. Depending on the class schedule, an individual student might receive a reply once a week or even biweekly. The teacher can collect several journals daily. Teachers need to find the number they can read and respond to comfortably on a daily basis and then form the schedule around that number.

MY ART JOURNAL
Today I made a dinosur fiting.

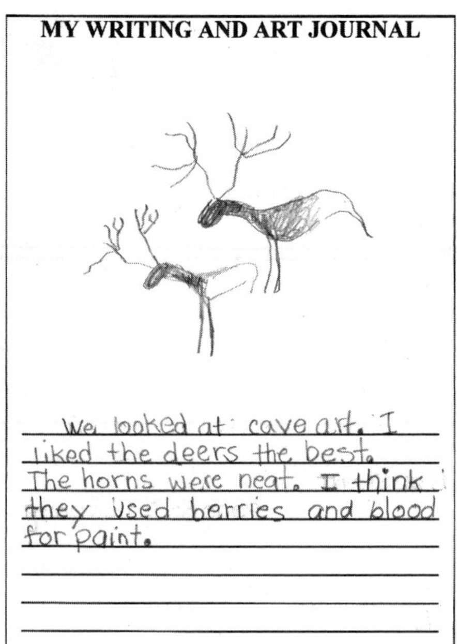

MY WRITING AND ART JOURNAL
We looked at cave art. I liked the deers the best. The horns were neat. I think they used berries and blood for paint.

Journal pages.

Art journal.
Crayon—Frankie, grade 1 (*left*).

Writing/art response journal.
Pencil—Leslie, grade 4 (*right*).

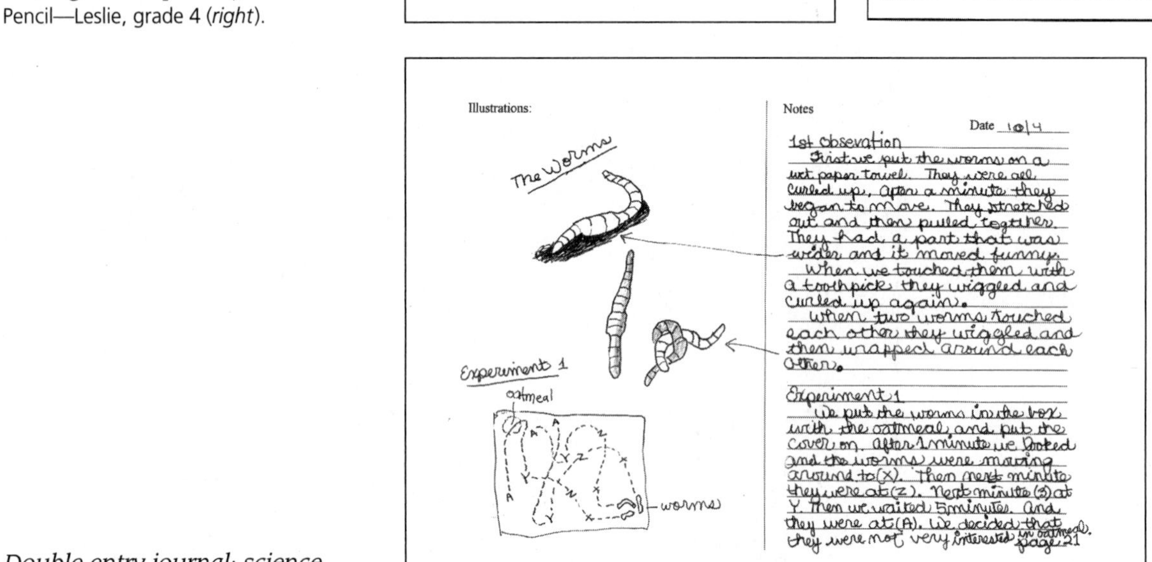

Double entry journal: science.
Pencil and pen—Shawn, grade 5.

Thinking about Children's Art

These journal entries demonstrate some of the different ways art and writing can be combined in student journals. The first grader has recorded a sentence describing what he had painted at the easel that day. The fourth grader has written a response to a featured artwork and the fifth grader has recorded science observations using both graphic images and written descriptions. How do each of these types of journal entries foster the child's artistic development?

Another approach is to use the response format only at certain times of the year, such as when viewing a featured artwork for the first time or when a student completes an artwork. Alternatively, students can combine written and drawn responses into one journal, enriching both subjects.

When a schedule is in place, have students mark the page for which they want a response with a sticky note or special bookmark creatively designed just for this purpose. If there is something in the journal they would prefer the teacher not see, suggest they fold that page over in half. Have a well-marked location where journals are to be turned in.

Growing as Teachers

Teachers, like their students, need to see their own personal growth. They need opportunities to record how and why they chose to do what they do in the classroom. Whether it the first year or twentieth, there is always room to see more deeply into one's approach to teaching. It is especially important to practice the same kind of introspection that we expect of our young artists. Teachers who view themselves as learners will better understand how to teach their students.

The teacher's journal. Keeping a journal of one's thoughts and feelings as a teacher is an enlightening experience, just as it is for students. Looking back over a year's worth of thoughts and responses to the frustrations and joys of teaching makes one appreciate the small things that occur in the daily life of the classroom that are otherwise quickly forgotten. A journal can be a place for comments about students, lessons, and personal experiences that impinge on the teaching process.

It is not hard to find time to keep a journal when students are also required to keep one. Journal time is for the whole class, teacher included. During the time set aside for journal writing teachers should sit beside their students and record their own thoughts in both written and graphic forms. Writing and drawing with concentration and later sharing selected journal entries with the class models successful journaling for the students.

Students who see their teachers keeping journals learn that journal writing is more than a school assignment. It is a model for thinking more deeply about one's life. It is a place for the intrapersonal intelligence to express itself. In writing and sketching, one's thoughts gel, blend, and combine. Through the journal one becomes a deeper thinker and a better student and teacher.

Self-evaluation. The introspective thoughts recorded in one's journal can be supplemented with other tools of self-evaluation to provide more direction to one's teaching. At regular intervals brief responses to questions can provide a measure for personal growth (see At a Glance 6.5).

At a Glance 6.5

Teacher as Artist: A Self-Evaluation

Week of ______________________

How have I modeled artistic confidence?

Have I . . .
- shown enthusiasm? ___
- shown self-confidence? ___
- improved my art skills? ___
- learned more about art? ___
- tried something new? ___
- supported my students' efforts? ___

How have I used art for my students' growth?

Have I provided . . .
- time to draw in their journals? ___
- access to art materials? ___
- a time to share their art? ___
- examples of art by others? ___
- an aesthetic environment? ___
- for their graphic responses as well as written? ___
- integrated art and subject matter? ___

How have I used art for my personal growth?

Have I personally used the language of art . . .
- to respond in my journal? ___
- to learn something new? ___
- for personal relaxation? ___

Keep photographic and written records of class activities and lessons as well. A teaching process folio, like those kept by students, can be used to store and give value to the little bits of teaching—scribbled lesson plans, floor plan sketches, reminders, and abandoned schedules—that otherwise are buried in files or too quickly discarded.

Teacher research. Teachers can also gain insight from the behavior and responses of their students, by conducting research in the classroom. It is helpful to frame a question upon which to base the research, such as, "Do children record more detailed information when they draw first or when they write first?" Teacher researchers use anthropological methods such as interviewing, participant observation, and keeping field notes of conversations (Hubbard & Power, 1993). Checklists of student behavior and work samples can also provide useful data. Teachers can then use the results to improve their teaching methods. But even more importantly, the process of closely observing the students will increase the teacher researcher's understanding of how children think. The work of Katherine Ernest (1994), Ruth Hubbard (1996), and Phyllis Whitin (1996), to name just a few, demonstrate what classroom teachers can learn when they pay close attention to what their students do and say.

Making changes. Each teacher affects thousands of people over a lifetime. Whether in the general classroom or specialized in art, each can give the gift of art to students. Although it is hard to end a year and say good-bye to students moving on, teachers can also see the end as a point of closure and a time to take stock. At the end of each school year take a moment to review the art program. Discard or reformat lessons, materials, techniques, and teaching structures that did not excite the children or that were ineffective. Add something new. Rearrange the furniture and work areas. The new school year will be a chance to begin again. No matter how many years one has taught, change is vital. It keeps the creative process alive and working.

Conclusion

CREATING COMMUNICATION

I was a window, opening for her a world where learning was an adventure to be shared and words were tools to build wondrous castles.
Joan Zatorski (1995, p. 19)

All teachers owe it to their students to discover the artist within themselves. Classroom teachers need to develop artistic confidence and use the language of art in their lessons. Teaching artistically is actively working to create something new in the students' minds whether it is introducing a new way to hold a paintbrush or a new way of looking at a great master's painting. It is a complicated process that takes a lifetime to learn to do well. New teachers watching experienced ones wonder how they know when to tell, when to ask, when to show, when to repeat, and when to listen.

This chapter has tried to break that process down into its components by delineating the way teachers should act and talk in the classroom in order to model artistic thinking and encourage the same thinking in students. Novice teachers are urged to take these pieces, add some students, and from this develop the fluid whole of instruction. Art instruction must be more than just students creating physical objects; it is a time to create communication pathways that go from looking to thinking to speaking to looking again. Art classes should not be silent. Sometimes there should be the low hum of teacher-student interaction, sometimes the animated whispers of students conferencing, and at other times the exuberant voices of students engaged in discussion. In such an environment students will become better thinkers and speakers as they become better artists.

Teacher Resources

REFERENCES

Azmitia, M. (1988). Peer interaction and problem solving: When are two heads better than one? *Child Development:* 59, 87–96.

Bredekamp, S., & Copple, C. (Eds.) (1997). *Developmentally appropriate practice in early childhood programs: Revised.* Washington, DC: National Association for the Education of Young Children.

Calkins, L. M. (1986). *The art of teaching writing.* Portsmouth, NH: Heinemann.

Edwards, B. (1979). *Drawing on the right side of the brain.* Los Angeles: Tarcher.
Eisner, E. (1972). *Educating artistic vision.* Indianapolis, IN: Macmillan.
Elkind, D. (1974). *Children and adolescents.* New York: Oxford University Press.
Ernest, K. (1994). *Picturing learning.* Portsmouth, NH: Heinemann.
Gardner, H. (1991). *The unschooled mind.* New York: Basic Books.
Gardner, H. (1993). *Multiple intelligences.* New York: Basic Books.
Gardner, H. (1999). *The disciplined mind.* New York: Simon & Schuster.
Goldberg, M. (1997). *Arts and learning.* White Plains, NY: Longman.
Hubbard, R. (1996). *Workshop of the possible: Nurturing children's creative development.* York, ME: Stenhouse.
Hubbard, R. S., & Power, B. N. (1993). *The art of classroom inquiry.* Portsmouth, NH: Heinemann.
Johnson, K. (1995). Exploring the world with the private eye. *Educational Leadership, 53*(1), 52–55.
Johnson, P. (1997). *Pictures and words together: Children illustrating and writing their own books.* Portsmouth, NH: Heinemann.
Kantner, L. (1990). Visual arts education and multiple intelligences. In W. J. Moody (Ed.), *Artistic intelligences: Implications for education* (pp. 92–101). New York: Teachers College Press.
Kohn, A. (1993). *Punished by rewards.* Boston: Houghton Mifflin.
Lazear, D. (1994). *Multiple intelligences approaches to assessment.* Tucson, AZ: Zephyr.
Maquet, J. (1986). *The aesthetic experience. An anthropologist looks at the visual arts.* New Haven, CT: Yale University Press.
Reimer, B. (1980). Designing effective art programs. In J. J. Hausman (Ed.), *Arts and the schools* (pp. 117–156). New York: McGraw-Hill.
Routman, R. (1991). *Invitations.* Portsmouth, NH: Heinemann.
Rowe, M. B. (1991). Using wait time to stimulate inquiry. In W. W. Wilhem (Ed.), *Questioning skills for teachers* (pp. 95–106). Washington, DC: National Education Association.
Rubin, J. A. (1984). *Child art therapy: Understanding and helping children grow through art.* New York: Van Nostrand Reinhold.
Szekely, G. (1988). *Encouraging creativity in art lessons.* New York: Teachers College Press.
Thacker, P. (1996). Opening up to art. In R. S. Hubbard & K. Ernst (Eds.), *New entries* (pp. 39–47). Portsmouth, NH: Heinemann.
Topal, C. W. (1992). *Children and painting.* Worchester, CT: Davis.
Vygotsky, L. (1978). *Mind in society.* Cambridge, MA: Harvard University Press.
Webb, N. M. (1989). Peer interaction and learning in small groups. *International Journal of Educational Research, 13,* 21–39.
Whitin, P. (1996). *Sketching stories, stretching minds: Responding visually to literature.* Portsmouth, NH: Heinemann.
Zatorski, J. (1995). I am a mirror, I am a window for a child who needs me. *Young Children, 50*(2), 18–19.

Practical Guides

The following books take you into the lives of teachers who are discovering the artistic power of their students and themselves:

Blecher, S., & Jaffee, K. (1998). *Weaving in the arts: Widening the learning circle.* Portsmouth, NH: Heinemann.
Chancer, J., & Rester-Zodrow, G. (1997). *Moon journals: Writing, art and inquiry through focused nature study.* Portsmouth, NH: Heinemann.
Ernest, K. (1994). *Picturing learning: Artists and writers in the classroom.* Portsmouth, NH: Heinemann.
Hubbard, R. S. (1996). *Workshop for the possible: Nurturing children's creative development.* Portsmouth, NH: Heinemann.
Hubbard, R. S., & Ernest, K. (Eds.) (1996). *New entries: Learning by writing and drawing.* Portsmouth, NH: Heinemann.

Ostrow, J. (1995). *A room with a different view.* York, ME: Stenhouse.
Silberstein-Storfer, M. (1997). *Doing art together.* New York: Abrams.
Szekely, G. (1988). *Encouraging creativity in art lessons.* New York: Teachers College Press.
Szekely, G. (1998). *Art of teaching art.* Needham Heights, MA: Simon & Schuster.

Videos

Art Education in Action Series, Getty, Los Angeles.

Titles: *Aesthetics, Integrating the Disciplines, Making Art, Art History & Criticism, School—Museum Collaboration*

Web Sites

Check out the art lessons on these sites:

Art Teacher on the Web
www.artmuseums.com

Incredible Art Room
www.artswire.org/Ken roar/

Kinderart
www.kinderart.com

Virtual Curriculum
www.dhc.net/~artgeek/index.html

Chapter 7

Artists Together
Cooperation and Consideration

[W]e come together as a group of strangers and through working together become a family of friends.

Muriel Silberstein-Storfer (1997, p. 13)

ARTISTS AT WORK

Group Work

Carolyn: I think this picture would be good.

Sano: Okay, you cut it out.

Gabriela: Look at how many we found already.

Ty: Let me start gluing them down.

Sano: I think we should just put them where they might go and then see if we like it before we glue.

Gabriela: Right, like planning first.

Ty: Okay, give me the pictures and I'll put them on the paper.

Carolyn: Oh, how about we put these small faces in the back and the bigger ones in the front?

Sano: It looks like these are closer then.

Ty: It's looking good.

Sano: What else can we add to show peace? We have all different kinds of people's faces.

Gabriela: I know. How about we trace our hands and put them all around the edge of our mural?

Ty: But we saw that in that Peace Quilt, remember?

Carolyn: But hands are a good symbol for peace . . . like touching and holding hands means you like someone.

Sano: What if we cut out pictures of hands from the magazines? Then we could put them in with the faces . . . overlap them . . . like the people are reaching out, trying to reach each other and make peace.

Gabriela: That's a great idea, Sano. Look, I already found some hands.

Carolyn: Me, too! Our mural is going to be great!

Introduction

THE SOCIAL EVENT

We often view art as an individualistic activity, a way to express one's personal vision. It is true that art can be an intensely satisfying inner experience. At the same time art is also a social communication system. It is a way of sharing our inner thoughts with others. Art that is created in the school setting is almost always a social event. Most art students work side by side with others. There is constant comment and comparison. Students, intentionally or unintentionally, build on one another's ideas and learn from one another. Art classes hum with social activity and conversation. Teachers of art need to take advantage of this natural socializing to help students build effective social skills. In this chapter we will look at ways to foster respect and tolerance in the classroom by creating an atmosphere that accepts and cherishes the differences that make us unique and through art activities that unify student goals and desires.

Setting the Stage

THE SOCIAL SIDE OF ART

Art provides the perfect context in which to introduce social skills:

The art environment is a social one. When taught successfully, creating art can be both motivating and relaxing. In order for the creative process to flourish the instructional environment must be nonthreatening and open to diverse ideas. This is exactly the same setting in which teachers can promote social growth. It should not be surprising that many of the introductory team-building and cooperative activities found in educational literature, such as making a class poster or designing a team logo, are actually group art activities.

Art introduces students to other cultures. Art instruction deals with visual images and culturally based art. The artworks that students study can surround them with and introduce them to the diversity of the world. Art students must address cultural differences as they seek to understand how and why artists from different backgrounds and cultures have created art.

The language of art is open to all. Art is a language that is available to everyone. Students with disabilities can participate fully in art activities. Reading levels, speech disorders, physical handicaps, and language barriers can disappear in a well-designed art program.

Meeting Special Needs

Teachers must address two social issues in the classroom: making the art program accessible to all students, and opening student minds to accepting and welcoming diversity. This means adapting the physical environment and instructional methods to best match each student's

What Do You Think?

Do you think that you treat girls differently than boys? How would you respond if you saw one girl slap another? Would you respond differently if it was two boys or if a boy slapped a girl? Visit a local school and observe how teachers talk to boys and girls. Is there a difference?

needs. It is important to remember that each student is unique. No one solution is perfect for every student with a similar disability or need. Sometimes the teacher will need to create a unique solution for a particular student. For young students each new learning situation may pose a challenge. Older students may already have learned how to integrate themselves into many activities but may still need special assistance at times.

Preparation. Before beginning art instruction try to learn as much as possible about students who have special needs that may require accommodation in art.

- Research and read about the specific disability.
- Acquire any special tools or materials that might be needed.
- Determine what instructional methods are most appropriate.
- Meet the student prior to class and discuss the adaptations. Ask for ideas and suggestions from the student and parent.
- Meet with the special education teacher, if one is involved. Plan instruction together.
- Prepare the classroom. Rearrange furniture, acquire suitable tables and chairs, and locate supplies with the students' needs in mind.

General modifications. Students may exhibit a wide range of special needs. Difficulty controlling large or small muscles may require special art tools, seating, or working space. Visual difficulties may necessitate alternative art materials and approaches to two-dimensional work. Hyperactivity and learning disabilities often call for special ways to present concepts and instructions. At a Glance 7.1 provides specific suggestions for meeting some of these needs.

Meeting special needs is another reason to structure the art program around an art or writing/art workshop in which students can have their own choice of art pursuits. This allows students to work at their own pace and in unique ways. Lockstep art programs, in which all students are given the same assignment and expected to work on it a specified length of time, set many special needs students up for failure.

At a Glance 7.1

Modifications for Special Needs

Special Need	Possible Modification
Visual Difficulties	
Color blind	Place markers and crayons in same color order. Use scented markers and paints. Design lessons that do not rely on specific color combinations.
Limited vision	Use colors student can see. Place screen or textured surface under drawing paper to add texture to drawn lines. Use a fabric marking wheel to create raised lines. Place supplies in same location and label with tactile, identifying symbols.
Unsure of position in space	Provide a rubber mat or low-sided tray for the student to work within. Tell student where materials are located in relation to body and have student touch each one.
Hearing Difficulties	
Has difficulty understanding speech	Make sure student can see speaker. Use hand signals. Physically and visually demonstrate expected behaviors and art skills.
Cannot express self clearly	Learn hand signals. Draw diagrams and pictures. Use visual clues.
Feeling of isolation	Offer many cooperative activities that require all participants' skills.
Physical Difficulties	
Tactilely sensitive	Introduce new materials slowly and in small quantities. If the student is repelled by a material, remove it and offer it again at a later time.
Unsure of position in space	Familiarize student with classroom and location of supplies. Provide a rubber mat or tray for student to work inside. Have student touch supplies and materials they will be using.
Lack of muscle control	Provide sufficient space so that student has room to work. Offer tools that match muscle control, such as large crayons, foam, or stubby brushes and thick paint. Seat student on floor or provide a sloped surface to work on. Tape paper to surface or use a rubber mat. Use hand-over-hand method of showing student how to manipulate art tools.
Limited use of hands and arms	Attach drawing tools and paintbrushes to arm, foot, prosthesis, or helmet. Use cutting wheel instead of scissors.
Weak, fine muscle control	Wrap art tools with foam rubber. Attach tools to a glove with hook and latch tape. Use spring-type scissors (snips).
Learning Difficulties	
Difficulty understanding verbal directions	Give one-step directions. May need direction repeated several times. Physically demonstrate. Give one-on-one attention.
Difficulty understanding basic concepts	Demonstrate using real objects and movements. Repeat information using a variety of modalities.
Difficulty reading/writing	Provide many opportunities for oral and graphic responses. Use alternative assessments.
Emotional Difficulties	
Short attention span	Give brief, specific directions. Use attention-getting transitions. Involve many learning modalities. During discussion and lecture have students respond orally, sing, and move in relation to lesson.
Easily distracted	Limit visuals in instructional areas to essentials. Keep supplies away until ready to use. Allow sufficient room to sit during lesson and to work. Provide "private" but not isolated work spaces.
Lack of self-confidence	Provide activities that are well within capability of student. Offer continuous encouragement. Notice small changes.
Lack of self-control	Provide structure. Make rules clear, but allow options. Do not corner the student. For example, say, "The rule is you must work quietly. Either you can choose to stop talking, or you can choose to work by yourself at another desk."
Insensitive to others	Role play caring behavior. Use team-building methods. Foster caring feelings through cooperative activities.

Alternatively, cooperative group activities and an assortment of small group teaching formats allow special needs students to learn more in a less restrictive and less competitive setting.

Eliminating Bias

From a very young age children are aware of individual differences. By the time they reach elementary school, many children demonstrate intolerance toward those who are different from themselves. Student comments and actions reveal racism, sexism, ethnocentrism, and discrimination against the disabled (Derman-Sparks, 1989).

Because art is a subject in which students interact and converse as they work, the teacher may overhear biased comments. White students and black students accuse each other of name calling and sit separately at the table. Boys call each other sissies and gay. A Jewish student is criticized for not making decorations for the Christmas party. The child with a speech impediment is ignored by the rest of the class and works in isolation.

Art, however, is also a subject in which these issues may be openly addressed. Racist comments can be used as a transition into the study of African-American artists. Sexism can be discussed in the context of studying women artists and their struggles. Cultural differences can be understood and respected through the art of people from different ethnic groups and cultures. Students with special needs can be successfully integrated into the art activities. Activities that help students express their feelings about artwork and differentiate fact and opinion can also be used to improve social relations. Art provides an opportune arena in which to teach students that differences are good but oppressive ideas and actions are not.

Diversity in the Art Class

Elimination of bias cannot be accomplished through a specific curriculum plan nor set of activities. Rather it requires critical thinking and problem solving by both teachers and students. Teachers need to know when to react, what to say, and how to focus attention on unfairness and prejudice. Students need to analyze their feelings and beliefs, control their behaviors, show respect, and build a sense of social fairness.

Teachers begin by establishing respect for diversity in their class. This means that the classroom environment, the lessons presented, and the teachers' verbal responses to students model open acceptance of individual differences.

A bias-free environment. The classroom should model the diversity found in the student population and in our society.

"Rain." Gouache on paper—Jacob Lawrence, 1937. Wadsworth Atheneum. The Ella Gallup Summer and Mary Caitlin Summer Collection Fund.

Thinking about Children's Art

In this work Jacob Lawrence (African American, 1917–) has portrayed a family dealing with a leaking roof in their tenement. The strong solid shapes of their bodies show determination as they cope and endure the downpour. Artworks such as this that create empathy with the viewer by depicting the problems of everyday life are a powerful way to get children thinking about the needs of others. What questions could be asked about this work that would help students from diverse backgrounds identify with the people in the picture?

- *Celebrate the uniqueness of students.* Display photographs of the students, families, and teachers in conjunction with the exhibition of artwork.
- *Mirror a diverse society.* Display images and artworks that reflect the major racial and ethnic groups in the community and in our society.
- *Be fair.* Show a fair balance of images and artworks that depict women, men, diverse family groups, people of different ages and ableness, and from different racial groups in a wide range of non-stereotypic roles and jobs.
- *Avoid tokenism.* Half the images displayed should represent the background of the majority of students. The remainder should reflect the diversity of the community and the society in general (Derman-Sparks, 1989).
- *Avoid stereotypes.* Images should represent actual people, clothing, artwork, and activities of the present. This is particularly true for Native Americans and Africans who are often represented in "tribal" dress of the past or whose artwork is often reduced to simplistic designs that do not reflect the range of styles found across different groups.
- *Be sensitive to skin color.* Offer art supplies that reflect a wide range of skin colors.
- *Combat color discrimination.* Dark colors are often seen as representing bad or evil. Emphasize the positive nature of colors such as black and brown. Relate them, for example, to the forces of nature and the glory of night.
- *Choose books that expand student horizons.* Display and read art books that reflect diverse cultures, beliefs, and artistic heritages.
- *Create a rich picture resource.* Make sure artworks and picture files reflect a wide range of diversity with many contemporary scenes of daily life and art.

Lessons in diversity. Lessons must reflect concern with the fair treatment of all and teach students to value differences.

- *Build a cohesive class.* Spend time at the beginning of every school year on team-building lessons that create a cohesive, respectful group from diverse individual students.
- *Use cooperative structures.* Include many lessons that utilize cooperative activities in which the contributions of each team member are required for the group to be successful.
- *Prohibit put-downs.* Establish and enforce a "no put-downs" rule. Students are often unaware of what words or actions may be perceived as put-downs. Offer several lessons early in the year, and repeat when necessary, in which students role play different

Teaching in Action

Team-building activities help students see both their differences and similarities. This example is an excellent activity for the first class meeting at any level:

Class Puzzle

1. Before class determine the number of students. Take a large sheet of paper and cut it into equal-sized jigsaw-shaped pieces, one for each student and one for the teacher.
2. When students arrive, give them each a puzzle piece and ask them to draw pictures, designs, and symbols that describe themselves and their interests.
3. When students are done, have them sit in a circle and in turn share their piece and tell something about themselves.
4. Place a piece of paper the size of the whole puzzle in the center of the circle. Have students take turns placing their pieces on the paper. Work together to put the pieces together.
5. When all the pieces are matched up, explain that the puzzle represents the class. Each student, like each puzzle piece, is unique and brings special knowledge and skills to the class. The completed puzzle represents the entire class, each individual student joined to the others to form a whole. Ask, "What would the puzzle be like if every piece were exactly the same? What do our differences add to the whole?"
6. End the activity by passing around a glue stick. Have students explain one way they will work to make the class the best ever and then glue down their piece.
7. Display the completed puzzle in a prominent location and draw upon the personal interests shown on it in developing the initial art lessons.

situations that may occur during an art activity in which thoughtless comments and actions can diminish another student.

- *Respect the culture of others.* Avoid lessons that teach about other cultures only in the context of a holiday celebration or that emphasize exotic differences such as unusual customs, foods, and costume. When talking about other cultures present real-life information and explore the culture's variety in depth.
- *Acknowledge limitations.* Teachers should not assume, even if they have done research, that they know everything about a culture different than their own. Even anthropologists who have lived in and studied other cultures intensely do not understand all the nuances of life in another society. Invite parents and members of other ethnic, religious, and cultural groups to share with the class. But be careful of stereotyping one family's lifestyle by making it representative of the whole ethnic group.

Responding without Prejudice

What teachers say and do as they communicate with students provides students with the strongest model of acceptable social behavior.

Teachers need to be aware of their own feelings and prejudices as they interact in the classroom on a daily basis. Some situations may make one uncomfortable or challenge one's deepest feelings. Draw strength from research that shows that students who were given a clear vision by their teachers of the value of working together to create a respectful environment become more socially responsible (Solomon et al., 1988).

- *Address instances of unkind or prejudiced remarks at the moment they occur.* Don't ignore them. Ignoring them will not teach the students to respect one another and allows problems to fester and grow. State matter of factly what was wrong about the comment and ask what the appropriate behavior should be. For example, if a student says, "Mike, you're so stupid. You never remember to clean your brush before putting it back in the paint," the teacher might reply, "Calling someone stupid is a put-down. What should you have said to Mike?"
- *Don't make excuses.* Do not try to explain away a student's hurtful comments or actions to the child who has been hurt or to the class. This teaches that it is all right to make hurtful remarks if you have a reason to do so.
- *Comfort the student who has been put down or discriminated against.* Support the student who has been hurt. Say, "It was unfair for him to call you a name" or "It is wrong to make fun of someone because of who they are or how they look."
- *Model strength.* Teach students to assertively express how they feel or what they do not like about hurtful or biased remarks. Role play situations that might occur having students practice using strong voices and clear words: "I don't like it when you grab the scissors first." "I feel angry and hurt when you call me that."
- *Don't be afraid of making a mistake.* Taking action is far better than doing nothing at all. React to students' comments and actions. This tells students that respect is a serious matter in this class. If necessary, at a later time meet privately with students to investigate an incident further.
- *Find out the real reason for the problem.* Many times unkind comments result when one student offends another unintentionally. In this case a simple reprimand will suffice. If, on the other hand, it is determined that prejudice was the root cause, then offer the victim more support and take further action to deal with the biased student. Immediately make it clear to all students that such behavior is unacceptable in the classroom, and set strict limits on the offending student's behavior. This is essential to prevent other students from joining in attacking the victim. Set up a long-range plan to address the student's bias, involving the parents as well.

What the Experts Say

Dealing with Differences

Instead of striving for more individual activities, we should design learning environments for our children that capitalize on the natural inclination that humans have for social interaction.
David Berliner & Ursula Casanova (1993, p. 66)

Children with disabilities need to see themselves reflected in the world around them, in pictures, in toys, in books, in role models.
Louise Derman-Sparks & the A.B.C. Task Force (1989, p. 39)

Cooperative learning results in more positive social development and social relations among students at all grade levels.
Spender Kagan (1994, p. 32)

[T]he entire school community must be sensitized to acceptance and appreciation of the unique individual participation of students with disabilities.
Lynn Miller-Lachmann & Lorraine S. Taylor (1995, p. 158)

Fostering Acceptance

It takes concerted effort to create a classroom in which diversity is valued. Every student-teacher interaction can expand awareness and foster acceptance. The following are just some ways to eliminate bias in the art class:

- *Celebrate difference.* Do not deny differences in physical ability. Help the students see how they are the same and how they are different.
- *Provide information.* Acknowledge curiosity, anxiety, and fear about people who are different. Then provide factual information and correct terminology. If they agree, have differently abled children show and explain their equipment and special needs.
- *Allow exploration.* Provide items such as eyeglasses with distorting lenses, sound muffling earphones, and adaptive tools for students to try while creating art. But make it clear that it is not acceptable to touch or use a child's personal equipment without special permission.
- *Have the same expectations for everyone.* Encourage all children to work independently and solve their own problems. Research shows that girls and children with special needs are more likely to be given help or to have the work done for them than are boys. Boys are more likely to be shown how to solve a problem (Froschl & Sprung, 1983).
- *Provide opportunities for everyone.* Be sure that all children have an equal opportunity to be called upon and to participate in class activities. Do not allow some students to always call out the

"We are Part of the Earth."
Crayon—Tracie, Sharon and Tessa, grade 4.

Thinking about Children's Art

As part of a unit on ecology students were asked to think of an image that represents our relationship with the earth. Working in a small group these girls have created a picture that represents their idea of the earth and its people. What knowledge have they used to create this image? Are there any stereotypes?

answers. To encourage less verbal students to participate, use a turn-taking system. Waiting at least three seconds for a student to respond in discussion and questioning situations allows quieter students to participate more equally (Welhousen, 1996).

- *Establish a fair way of selecting students.* Make sure boys or more vocal students are not chosen more often than others. Randomly choose students for special jobs, answering questions, and participating in demonstrations and role plays by selecting from shuffled name cards or pulling "choosing sticks" (craft sticks with students' names written at one end) from a can.

Teaching in Action

Empowering Children

Rebecca Ann Janke and Julie Penshorn Peterson believe that children are empowered when they have many opportunities to experience "freedom-within-limits messages" (1995, p. 26). They recommend the following responses in situations where conflicts arise:

"Let's make a decision together."

"Our (work time, reading time, etc.) has been interrupted. What can we do about it?"

"Let's see if we can solve this problem together."

"Remember the guideline we agreed to is . . . "

"Do you need to cool off or are you ready to work this out now?"

"It looks like you want to ________. Let me show you a safe way to do this."

- *Respond equally to everyone's artwork.* Monitor comments about artwork to be sure they describe many aspects of the students' work. Avoid the tendency to focus on girls' neatness, boys' risk taking, and special needs students' technical accomplishments.
- *Facilitate positive interaction among all students.* Make it clear that each student is expected to work with every other. Do not allow students to always self-select their working partners. Regularly assign students to heterogeneous cooperative groups, so that all students get a chance to interact with each other. Consciously pair students so that those with special needs can share in their area of strengths.

Art and Feelings

"Take that, you mean old monster!" declares a first grader, punching a piece of clay. "This is a sad picture because my cat died today," muses a fourth-grade artist. Feelings exist and we must recognize that they affect everything our students do, including the way they manifest their artistic expression. As the brain research cited in Chapter 2 reminds us, the brain cannot separate our emotional state from how we perceive and express our experiences and ideas. The interconnectedness of concepts and emotions, point out the Caines, "should be expected, given the fact that the limbic system mediates both emotion and memory" (1991, p. 57). Emotions color everything we do. We may love to draw and hate to wash dishes. Given a choice, which will we choose to do?

Classrooms are hotbeds of emotions. In addition to dealing with the daily rise and fall of childish loves and hates, likes and dislikes, teachers need to be prepared to deal with the deep feelings that many

"I Love You."
Oil pastel—Nicole, grade 1.

Thinking about Children's Art

Children often endow their artwork with personal meanings of which we may not be aware. Sometimes they are making a picture for someone special to them. What questions could we ask this student in order to find out more about her intentions in making this work?

children bring with them to school. All children suffer loss. Children who are angry or sad or lonely turn inside themselves and are not ready to embrace the differences of others nor cooperate in learning with them. That is why it is important to welcome outwardly expressed feelings into the classroom and show children how to express them in constructive ways. Art can provide a way for children to turn their feelings from inside to outside and learn to appreciate that emotions are common to all people.

- *Share personal feelings.* It is important for children to know that everyone has feelings. Teachers need to share their own personal feelings about stories they love, news stories that make them cry, and artworks that take their breath away. Allow time for children to share not only thoughts but also feelings about what they are learning.
- *Provide models.* Read stories that explore how others have dealt constructively with emotional difficulties.
- *Examine how feelings are expressed artistically.* Provide opportunities to compare two artworks that show different sides of the same subject or theme, such as the feelings of the families pictured in Pablo Picasso's *The Tragedy* and William Glackens' *Family Group*

Evoking Fantasy.

"Dream House."
Colored pencil—Laurel, grade 4.

Thinking about Children's Art

Although much that happens in the classroom is focused on helping children acquire basic knowledge and skills, it is important to encourage the development of fantasy and imagination as well. As an introduction to a thematic unit on shelter, fourth graders were asked to imagine and draw their dream house. How does this type of assignment engage the emotions and allow students to express their feelings about a topic of study? What do we learn about what this student thinks is important to have in a home? What kind of classroom atmosphere is needed to allow students to risk using their imaginations?

(both National Gallery), or the emotions shown on the faces in Edvard Munch's *The Scream* (National Gallery) and Grant Wood's *American Gothic* (Art Institute, Chicago).

- *Provide opportunities to create art daily.* Sometimes it is easier to express emotions in the nonverbal language of art, and one never knows when a child needs that avenue to communicate. Create an atmosphere in which children feel free to turn to art when they are upset.
- *Help refine expression.* Slapping a piece of clay may be cathartic, but it does not help a student examine his or her feelings. As the student works, ask questions that will help young artists clarify ideas and make an organized statement about the feelings expressed. What colors, shapes, or textures will best reflect what they are feeling? What symbols can they use? What details are important to include? There is a difference between expressing hate or anger in art and going out with a gun in one's hand. The difference is that creating an artwork draws on both cognitive

Books to Share

Feelings

Bunting, E. (1996). *Going Home.* New York: HarperCollins.
In this beautifully illustrated book a Mexican-American family is torn between the advantages of the United States and the comfort of family and culture when they pay a bittersweet visit to their village in Mexico.

Cohen, M. (1980). *No Good in Art.* New York: Greenwillow.
A first grader learns to express himself through art.

Hru, D. (1993). *Joshua's Masai Mask.* New York: Lee & Low.
A magic mask helps a young boy see the world through others' eyes and learns it is best to be oneself.

Lorbiecki, M. (1998). *Sister Anne's Hands.* New York: Dial.
A young girl learns about prejudice and love from her black second-grade teacher and uses art to express her feelings.

and emotional reflective powers and in the process of creation allows thoughtful consideration rather than thoughtless action.

- *Welcome fantasy.* Fantasy is natural in the world of art. It is also an important way for people to deal with emotions, worries, and stresses. Imagining an event before it happens can help one be more prepared. Imagining a different reality can help make the real world more bearable. Re-envisioning the past can heal. Imagining the future can provide direction.

Why . . . ?

WHY PROMOTE SOCIAL GROWTH THROUGH ART?

As students share supplies, space, and ideas, they interact on many levels. It is not enough to expect students to get along with one another. Teachers must use these social moments to teach students to respect one another as members of a diverse society and show them how to work together in cooperation as they create and discuss art.

The Benefits of Cooperation

Students do not come to school ready to work together. Studies have shown that when students are given a group task in which they would benefit from cooperation, they compete instead, to the benefit of none (Slavin, 1983; Kagan, 1994). Yet these students will soon be facing employment in a high-tech economy that demands a high level of workplace interaction and cooperative team problem solving. The most common reason people are fired from their first job is a lack of interpersonal skills (Kagan, 1994).

Many students come from homes where they are not exposed to positive family interactions and positive group decision making. Many minority students face discrimination in the community or wider society. Students who have not been exposed to diverse cultures and beliefs may be fearful, insensitive, or antagonistic to those who are different from themselves. Research has found that in classrooms where cooperative learning was practiced, students chose more friends from other races and interacted in a more integrated and positive way. This was true even if the cooperative experiences were only in one subject for a limited time (Slavin, 1983; Stevens & Slavin, 1995).

CELEBRATING DIVERSITY THROUGH ART

Guiding Ideas

Our students live in a society made up of diverse individuals of different ages and genders, representing different regions, religions, ethnicities, social classes, and abilities. Learning to accept, respect, and value these differences is an important part of becoming a contributing member of our increasingly global society. In order to do this teachers must find ways to promote intergroup harmony, positive relationships, and increased self-esteem in all their students. Because art embodies both culture and individuality, looking at and talking about the great art of the world's cultures is a powerful way to teach children to respect and value human differences.

The Culturally Diverse Classroom

Because we live in a pluralistic society, every classroom contains students who have different cultural heritages. In order to teach culturally diverse students, teachers need to be flexible and open. They should recognize differences between home and school cultures and be ready to deal with any potential problems that might arise. They must be knowledgeable about and open to including books, information, and artwork that reflects the native cultures of the students, and they must be ever alert to potential bias and stereotypes in the educational materials and teaching methods that they use.

Lynn Miller-Lachmann and Lorraine S. Taylor (1995) recommend the following teaching approaches for promoting cultural respect in the classroom:

Fairness: Provide a balanced view of all subject matter.

Relevance: Relate teaching content to the cultural backgrounds of the students.

Versatility: No one teaching strategy meets the needs of all students. Styles of behavior, interpersonal relationships, and attitudes toward

"Fever."
Pencil and crayon—Johnny, grade 2.

Thinking about Children's Art

This student has created a visual image to represent how he felt when he was sick with a fever. What skills did this student use in creating this artwork? Why does having a repertoire of artistic skill to draw on help children express their ideas and feelings more effectively?

achievement vary from culture to culture and individual to individual. Teachers must have a large repertoire of teaching strategies and a strong knowledge of the individual needs of each student so that they can effectively match their instruction to the learning styles of their students (Wlodkowski & Ginsburg, 1995).

Cooperation: The use of cooperative learning strategies have been shown to promote intergroup respect and tolerance by enabling students to practice interpersonal skills as they work together toward a common goal. Spencer Kagan (1994) cites the following characteristics that develop in students who participate in cooperative learning tasks:

- Increased social skills.
- More self-direction.
- Higher self-esteem.
- Like class better.
- More empathic to others.
- Learn more.
- Work longer and harder on tasks.
- Minority students do better.

Art and the Holidays

Holiday celebrations and art have long been tied together in our schools. This relationship, unfortunately, often relegates art instruction to a superficial, decorative function. Rows of identical jack-o-lanterns welcome school visitors at Halloween. Green and red paper chains appear at Christmas. Painted eggs line the hall at Easter. These kinds of activities, although pervasive at the primary grades, can be found across all levels. Students follow directions and trace patterns to produce stereotyped images that reflect the beliefs of the majority culture with token recognition of some minority beliefs.

Teachers often justify these activities by stating that they help students learn to follow directions, allow them to practice their cutting and gluing skills, or are done just for fun. But such projects have little relationship to the creative or artistic processes. Nor do they fit in an art program that encourages student choice, respects diversity, and promotes cultural understanding.

Celebrations, on the other hand, enrich all our lives and can be highly motivating for students. Handled with thoughtfulness, holidays and art can be a magnificent combination. In considering how to integrate art instruction and holiday celebration, teachers need to consider several things:

Fairness. Whose holidays should be the focus of art activities? Not everyone celebrates the same holidays. Teachers have several choices:

What the Experts Say

Diversity in the Classroom

Students who experience school as a caring supportive environment in which they actively participate and have opportunities to exercise influence will feel attached to the school community and will, therefore, come to accept its norms and values.
Victor Battistich, Daniel Solomon, Kim Dong-il, Marilyn Watson, & Eric Schaps (1995, p. 648)

[The arts] transcend the limitations placed on the child whose language, culture or life experience is outside the mainstream of American schools.
Karen Gallas (1994, p. 146)

What may elicit frustration, joy or determination may differ across cultures, because cultures differ in their definitions of novelty, hazard, opportunity, and gratification.
Raymond J. Wlodkowski & Margery B. Ginsberg (1995, p. 17)

- Students can study and celebrate the holidays of everyone in the class. They can explore decorations and symbols in the context of how the different students' families observe the holidays. Teachers can invite family members to share cultural traditions and demonstrate how they decorate their homes.
- Students can research holidays, and their decorations and symbols, in the context of learning about another country or culture. If possible, invite people who are from that culture to explain the holiday and its symbols.
- Holidays can be integrated into an instructional unit based on a common theme. For example, incorporate Chanukah, Christmas, winter solstice, and Kwanzaa celebrations into a study of light and its symbolic representation by different cultures and artists.
- No holidays need be celebrated in class, but the class can discuss holidays as part of one's culture and as represented in traditional art forms. During art workshop students can make holiday-focused works of original design whenever they choose.
- The class or school can develop its own celebrations, which reflect thematic studies or student interests, such as holding a Wonderful Water Day to culminate a unit on water.

Artistic intention. Teachers must consider what is the instructional purpose for creating artwork in honor of a holiday. How will students use the creative and artistic processes? Holiday celebrations often are an emotional time for students. They provide the ideal setting in which to involve students in sharing and cooperative planning. Possibilities for creative approaches to holiday art include the following:

Books to Share

Celebrating Humanity through Art

These beautifully illustrated books promote tolerance and respect.

Allen, A. (Ed.) (1997). *We Are All Related: A Celebration of Our Cultural Heritage.* Custer, WA: Polestar.
Mixed media collages by students from Vancouver, Canada, and brief commentary explore their family values (multilingual text).

Bunting, E. (1994). *Smoky Night.* Orlando, FL: Harcourt Brace.
During the 1992 Los Angeles riots, fire drives an African-American boy from his apartment to a shelter where he shares the experience with his Asian-American neighbors. Textured collages frame paintings that capture the chaos and fear of being driven from one's home.

Cheltenham Elementary School Kindergarten (1994). *We Are All Alike . . . We Are All Different.* New York: Scholastic.
Children's drawings illustrate this big book that celebrates how we are all the same and different.

Hamanaka, S. (1994). *All the Colors of the Earth.* New York: Morrow.
Intensely colored paintings compare richly hued skin tones with the wonders of nature.

Kissinger, K. (1994). *All the Colors Are We.* St. Paul, MN: Redleaf.
Beautiful photographs illustrate this book, which explains the color of our skin (bilingual: Spanish).

Lawrence, J., & Myer, W. D. (1993). *The Great Migration: An American Story.* New York: HarperCollins.
Jacob Lawrence's paintings illustrate the story of how African Americans migrated from the rural South to the cities of the North.

Lionni, L. (1963). *Swimmy.* New York: Knopf.
This classic picture book about learning to cooperate with others is illustrated with Lionni's trademark prints.

Pfister, M. (1992). *The Rainbow Fish.* New York: NorthSouth.
The most beautiful fish in the ocean finds friendship and happiness by sharing with others.

Thomas, J. C. (1993). *Brown Honey in Broomwheat Tea.* New York: HarperCollins.
Poems celebrate the black child's beauty.

Walter, M. P. (1995). *Darkness.* New York: Simon & Schuster.
Bold, sweeping paintings by an African-American artist illustrate the beauty of the often ignored deep, rich, dark colors of our world.

- *Share feelings.* Invite students to share their feelings about a special holiday or event in their journals and through drawings, paintings, and collages. Use partner, small group, and whole class sharing time to explore the different perspectives of each student. Create charts that reflect similarities and differences in holiday customs.
- *Do research.* Assign cooperative groups different holidays or aspects of a holiday to research. Have them plan a multimedia presentation about it and then share with the class.

Personal Stories.

"The First Day I Was on Stage."
Crayon—Paige, grade 2.

I was on stage when I was in first grade. It was fun, but I was a little shy. I was excited to be on stage too. I sang with my class. We sang lots of songs. It was fun!

Thinking about Children's Art

Art and writing together provide a powerful way to communicate feelings and experiences. This second grader has created an illustrated story about an experience in her life. How effective would the pictures or stories be on their own?

- *Make a mural.* Have students create a mural reflecting the celebrations of all students in the class or school, which becomes a symbolic statement of the differences and similarities of all.
- *Link personal beliefs.* Discuss the role of art in holiday celebrations. Read books that speak to students at all levels about the importance of celebration in everyone's lives. Explore the link between religious beliefs and art. Then have students write poetry and stories and create artwork that reflect their personal beliefs.
- *Ask aesthetic questions.* Pose and discuss aesthetic questions, such as, Are the holiday decorations sold in stores works of art? Are antique Christmas ornaments that are part of museum collections artworks? Is an African mask used in a harvest celebration and then thrown away a work of art?

Dealing with stereotypes. A major difficulty with holiday art is its reliance on stereotyped images. The prevalence of certain holiday symbols often limit students' ability to create their own. Students become frustrated because they cannot make a Santa or jack-o-lantern,

Books to Share

Celebrations

Angell, C. S. (1996). *Celebrations Around the World: A Multicultural Handbook.* Golden, CA: Fulcrum.
Baylor, B. (1995). *I'm in Charge of Celebrations.* New York: Aladdin.
Chandler, C. (1998). *Harvest Celebrations.* Brookfield, CT: Millbrook.
Chandler, C. (1998). *Carnival.* Brookfield, CT: Millbrook.
Kindersley, B. & A. (1997). *Celebrations.* New York: Dorling Kindersley.
Krasno, R. (1997). *Kneeling Carabao and Dancing Ghosts: Celebrating Filipino Festivals.* Berkeley, CA: Pacific View.
Livingston, M. C. (1996). *Festivals.* New York: Holiday House.
Luenn, N. (1998). *Celebrations of Light: A Year of Holidays Around the World.* New York: Atheneum.
Rosen, M. J. (1992). *Elijah's Angel.* San Diego, CA: Harcourt Brace.
Viesta, L., & Hall, D. (1996). *Celebrate in Southeast Asia.* New York: Lothrop, Lee & Shepard.

for example, that approaches the commercial perfection of the ones sold in stores. It is the teacher's role to face this problem head on and use it as an opportunity to expand student artistic vision, rather than just handing out patterns to copy.

Ways to expand student's artistic imagery include the following:

- *Analyze the purpose of symbols.* Introduce the concept of visual symbols and their various uses, such as comparing signs to control traffic, trademarks to represent businesses, and symbols associated with holidays. Talk about the need for uniformity in symbols that give directions as opposed to those that represent a concept or idea.
- *Investigate the meaning of symbols.* Match symbols to their associated ideas. Are there symbols that are used for more than one holiday? Is there a visual image that has different meanings in different cultures? Have any symbols changed in meaning?
- *Study the role of the symbol in art.* Investigate the role of cultural and holiday symbols in artworks. How have artists incorporated symbols into their artwork? Do holidays play an important role in most artists' work?
- *Research historical change.* Form cooperative groups to research the history of various holiday symbols and to study and share how their representation has changed over time.
- *Display variations.* Create a display that shows many variations of one symbol, such as a collection of hearts of different sizes, shapes, and colors or an exhibit of representations of the American flag done in many media and styles.

"Thanksgiving Dinner."
Crayon—Jessica, grade 1.

"I Like the Pie."
Crayon—Russell, grade 1.

Holiday Art: Thanksgiving.

Thinking about Children's Art

Holidays provide an opportunity to encourage students to move beyond stereotypes and apply their artistic skills. These first graders were asked to draw pictures about what they liked about Thanksgiving. How did this assignment challenge them to represent complex objects while freeing them to create original images? Would copying a turkey pattern or making a hand-traced turkey have accomplished as much?

"I Like Thanksgiving."
Crayon—Drew, grade 1.

- *Experience differences.* Provide multisensory experiences that allow students to see a symbol in more detail. Make forays outside the school to study and sketch items associated with certain holidays, such as the shape and form of pine trees in a nearby park or pumpkins at the local market. Bring in live rabbits to sketch in the spring.

Multicultural Art Displays

It is important to expose children to a wide variety of art forms. One way to introduce art from other times and places is to hang examples in the classrooms and hallways. This introduces children to diverse graphic symbols and the different ways people express

Peruvian Carved Gourd.
Collection of the author.

From the Art Museum

This carved and stained Peruvian gourd can provide a starting point for discussing the art of Peru. How, for example, is it similar to pre-Incan and Incan pottery? What problems did the carver face in creating it? What kind of gourd is it and where might it have been grown? Is it an ancient art form or one created for the tourist market?

themselves through art. Exhibiting works by artists of different ages and genders and from many cultures, especially those that reflect the ethnic and cultural backgrounds of the student body, tells students as well as visitors that the school respects and values everyone's heritage.

Works that are displayed must be carefully selected so as to fairly represent the diversity of the school, society, and world of art. Displayed artworks should do the following:

- *Emphasize similarities among all people.* All human beings have the same needs and emotions. Select works done by artists from different times and places that show similar subjects such as families, children playing games, and pets. Look for works that express basic human feelings such as love, joy, grief, and loneliness.
- *Emphasize cultural distinctness.* At the same time each cultural group has its own way of expressing these human commonalties. Artworks should reflect stylistic differences and the different media preferred in that culture. Be careful to select works that are actually from the culture they represent and reflect the style and approach of that cultural group. Avoid "tourist" works by visitors from another culture, such as a painting of India by a visiting American. These are better used in contexts where the class can discuss and analyze the point of view of the artist.
- *Show human variability.* Works should show a variety of people of different ages, genders, and races involved in a wide range of activities.
- *Represent social realities.* Cultures change over time. Artworks should not just represent the past but also reflect contemporary life as seen through the eyes of currently practicing artists. Works showing Native Americans, for example, should reflect contemporary styles and dress as well as traditional dress from the past.

Curriculum Connections

There are many ways to integrate culturally diverse artworks into the curriculum. A carefully selected artwork or artist that illustrates the unique experience of a culture or group can become the focus of a unit of study. Lessons in history, literature, math, and other subjects can be derived from the artwork. The Florida CHAT program, for example, built a fourth grade unit of study around Faith Ringgold's quilt, *Tar Beach,* which addresses racial prejudice (Wilson in Mitchell, 1994, pp. 56–57). Units built around a unifying theme are also an effective way to incorporate an intensive study of culturally meaningful artworks. A well-chosen theme such as "Who Is an American?" can be enriched by studying how artists from the different ethnic and cultural groups that make up America have represented the country and its people in their art.

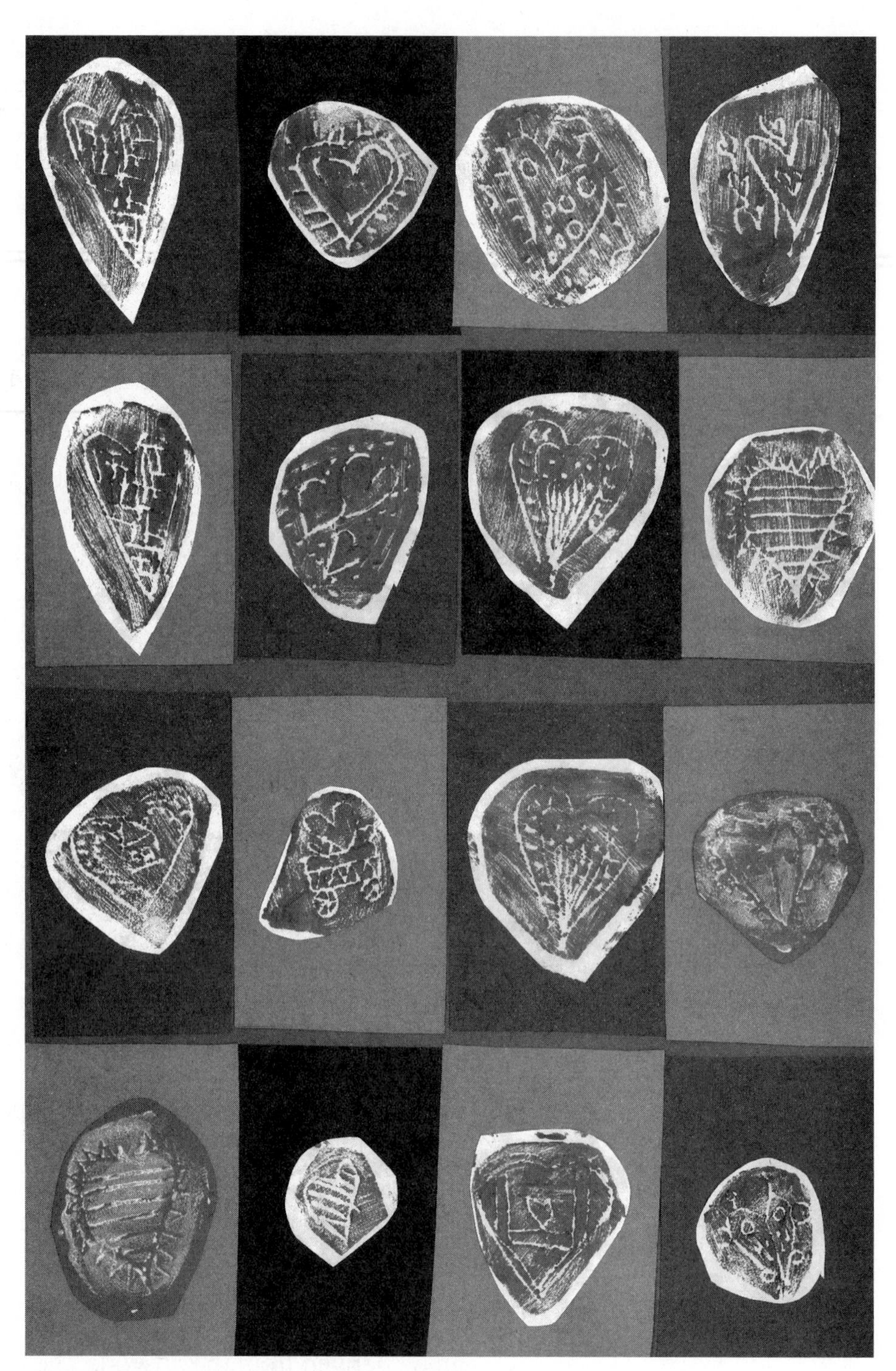

"Hearts."
Styrofoam print mural—grade 2.

Thinking about Children's Art

The heart shape has much symbolic meaning in our culture. Here children have been challenged to see this shape in new ways as each child adds a unique heart image to the pattern of the mural. How is this kind of activity different from having students trace a pattern?

In the Classroom

COOPERATIVE ART ACTIVITIES

Respecting diversity means more than recognizing differences. It also means finding ways that people are similar, establishing common goals, and communicating with one another. Classrooms that are communities build on the strengths of each student to work together to accomplish shared goals. In this approach art becomes a way to bind students and teachers together. Cooperative learning activities provide a powerful way to teach many art concepts and skills. These teaching structures can energize students and motivate them to work harder and more creatively.

Choosing Cooperative Activities

Just working together on a mural or discussing an artwork in a small group, however, is not a cooperative activity. Without proper planning and interpersonal skill training students frequently waste time and learn little. The mural artists end up squabbling over who will paint the foreground. The discussion group loses focus and talks about the upcoming party. When group activities disintegrate in these ways, teachers often give up and return to more teacher-focused lesson designs.

In selecting cooperative tasks for their class, teachers must choose cautiously from many possible cooperative structures. Not all activities labeled cooperative truly are. "The key," writes Alane Starko, "is that cooperative learning tasks . . . should be tasks for which having group participation is a genuine asset for everyone in the group" (1994, p. 279).

Successful cooperative activities should meet the following guidelines:

- Have more than one answer or path to the solution
- Be intrinsically motivating and challenging to all
- Result in a worthwhile product, not points or a grade
- Require the use of many different abilities and skills

Cooperative Strategies for Art

Effective cooperative learning activities are based on formal, interactive structures that can be applied in a wide variety of educational contexts. Each of the structures described here can be used in a variety of ways to present art concepts and skills. At a Glance 7.2 (pp. 278–281) provides guidance in choosing the most appropriate structure for specific art activities.

Pair/team formation structures. Use these structures to quickly form random pairs or teams that will work on a short-term, immediate task

At a Glance 7.2

Cooperative Structures and Art

Cooperative Structure	Setup	When to Use	Examples of Ways to Use It
Circle friends	In circle, standing	Transition into lesson	■ To introduce a lesson on color, have students share their favorite colors. ■ To introduce an artwork, ask: What is your first reaction to this work?
		To refocus group during discussion	■ Following a discussion in which students point out different things in a painting, say: Share one special thing you see in this picture.
Line up partners	Stand in line along classroom wall	Transition into lesson	■ To introduce a lesson on line, have students draw an imaginary line that partner then mirrors back.
		To pair students for an activity	■ With the new partner find a place and share artwork, ideas or try a new technique.
	Double line at door	To conclude a class	■ Turn to partner and share what was accomplished or learned.
Puzzle pals	Students move around room	To create new team	■ Place a matching picture at table where group will be working.
		To transition into team discussion	■ Have group share initial response to picture once it is together.
Corners	Students move to specified locations	To transition into discussion	■ To introduce an aesthetic discussion display four artworks and ask students to stand by the one they think is most beautiful.
		To form mixed teams	■ Take one student from each location to create teams.
Partner/team discussion	At tables	Follow up class discussion	■ Following a lesson on landscape, have students share oral descriptions of a landscape they have seen. Say: Describe a place you have been that would make a good subject for a landscape.
		Precede class discussion	■ Before a lesson on balance, have students share about a time when they lost their balance. Say: Have you ever lost your balance? Describe what it felt like to your partner.
Circle share	Community circle	To transition into topic	■ I am holding a special tool. Turn to your neighbor and tell them how you think it might be used.
		To quickly share ideas	■ I can see many of you have something to say about this painting; turn to your neighbor and tell them your ideas about it.
		To conclude a lesson or discussion	■ Turn to your neighbor and tell them one thing you learned about clay today.
Go 'round	At tables	To brainstorm	■ Pass the paper clockwise around the table. Brainstorm as many different textures as you can.

Cooperative Structure	Setup	When to Use	Examples of Ways to Use It
		To review lesson	■ Pass the paper around the table.See how many ways you can think of to use this new technique in your art.
		To create synergy	■ Pass this paper around the table. When it gets to you draw a line. Your line must be different from and joined to one of the other lines.
Team portraits	At tables	Team building	■ Pass the frame around and write down all the different art media you have used. In the center work together to make a picture that reflects all your experiences.
		To review lesson	■ Pass the frame around and write down characteristics of the Impressionist style. In the center work together to make a picture that reflects this style.
Match up buddies	Students move around room	Follow up lesson	■ On these cards are artworks by the artists we have studied. Find someone with an artwork by the same artist you have and then share your ideas about the works.
		Review vocabulary/ concepts	■ On these cards are written our art words and their definitions. Find the match to your card and be ready to use it in a sentence.
		To form partners/ teams	■ On these cards are a variety of colors. There are 5 color families represented. Match up the color families and then sit with your color team, ready for the painting activity.
Heads together	At tables	Review vocabulary/ concepts	■ Ask a question: Can you name a style of art? Count off five seconds of think time. Roll die: Number one go to board and write your team's answer on the chart.
		Share ideas	■ Ask a question: Is this dish a piece of art? Count off five seconds of think time. Spin spinner. Number twos, in turn, please share your team's ideas.
Webbing	At tables	Share individual knowledge	■ Let's find out what you already know about clay. On your paper slips write down words, ideas, techniques, anything you know about clay. As a team group your slips under headings and put them on your web.
		Increase and organize individual knowledge	■ Each of you have a different Chinese painting. On your slips of paper write down the colors, shapes, forms, textures, subjects, drawing approaches, and other characteristics you see. As a team group your slips under headings and create a web that describes all the Chinese paintings as a whole.

(continues)

At a Glance 7.2 continued

Cooperative Structures and Art

Cooperative Structure	Setup	When to Use	Examples of Ways to Use It
		Review lesson	■ On your slips of paper write down your thoughts about our discussion on beauty and art. As a team group your ideas together to create a web.
		Plan project	■ On your slips of paper jot down things you will need to know or do to complete your project. As a team decide who will do these tasks and in what order. Create a web that shows your project plan.
Sticky notes	At tables	Review vocabulary/ concepts	■ Study the label on your sticky note. As a team decide where it should go on the painting. When I call a number, that team member will come up and place it in the spot.
Experts in action	Various	Teach new skills/ concepts	■ I am giving each team directions for making an origami form. Read the directions and practice making the origami form described. Then we will divide into new teams and each of you will teach your new teammates how to make that origami figure.
Jigsaw	Various	Group projects, such as murals, research projects	■ Each team will be making a mural about the pond. Choose one team member to study the animals, one to study the water, one to study the vegetation, and one to study the rocks. Each will become expert in that area, doing research and making sketches with those from the other teams who are studying the same topic. At the end of the week we will reform into our mural teams to put your ideas together in a work of art.
Describe it	At table	Review vocabulary/ concepts	■ In the envelope is a painting in a style we have studied. Using the vocabulary words on the board, describe the work to your teammates. Your teammates will write down every vocabulary word they hear. When you finish they will try to guess the style and artist.
		Practice talking about art	■ Describe the artwork in front of you so clearly that your teammates can draw an accurate picture of it.
All for one	At table	Group art projects, such as murals and research projects	■ Working together to make a mural means each person must cooperate with the other. Today we will practice sharing supplies. Each of you will have a different color paint. You are to make a painting

Cooperative Structure	Setup	When to Use	Examples of Ways to Use It
			sharing these supplies. Choose topic for the painting off this list. Now who can model for us a way to ask your teammates for a paint brush or a color paint?
Gallery	Start at tables	Increase observation skills. Use vocabulary/ concepts.	■ Look at all the works of art we have created! Move around the room and look at them closely. In journals note down special things you want to remember about each one. Then you will go back to your team and in a team discussion share your thoughts about the question: How have we improved as a class in using the four new media: watercolor, conté crayon, pen and ink, and weaving?
Roving reporters	Start at tables	Increase observation skills. Use vocabulary/ concepts. Practice talking about art. Practice reaching consensus	■ Teammate 1 will be looking for examples of balance. Teammate 2 will look for examples of proportion. Teammate 3 will observe for unity. Teammate 4 will examine these works for movement. Use your journals to record your observations. You will have 3 minutes. At the signal return to your team and together write a description of how these artists used the principle of design to create these compositions.
Memorable work	At tables	Increase observation skills. Use vocabulary/ concepts. Practice talking about art	■ At the signal take the artwork out of the envelope and observe it closely. You will have 10 seconds. Now turn it face down and each of you make a quick sketch on your paper. At my signal pass the paper to your right and add to your teammate's sketch. Continue until you each have your original sketch. Then flip up the original and discuss the results. What was easy to remember? What did everyone forget?

such as discussion of an aesthetic question or exploration of a new medium. (*Note:* For longer, more complex projects such as a mural or a research project carefully select teams for a mix of abilities and maximum cross-race, cross-sex interactions.)

- *Circle friends:* Divide class into two equal groups. Have each group form a circle, one inside the other. Have inside circle turn and face outside circle. Have the student on the inside face the one outside and ask an assigned, open-ended question. Rotate the inside circle and have outside student ask the question. Repeat several times, varying the direction and distance of rotation and alternating who asks the question.

- *Line-up partners:* Have students form a line. Then break line in half and have students move down to form two lines facing each other. Have students ask a question of the one opposite them or do a task with that person.
- *Puzzle pals:* Determine the number of partners or teams needed. Find that number of pictures. (A photocopy of an artwork works well.) Tear each picture into pieces equal to the number of members desired on each team. Shuffle the pieces and distribute one to each student. Students with matching pieces form a team.
- *Corners:* Designate locations in the room as representing an idea, concept, or topic, such as warm colors, cool colors, neutrals, and pastels. Have students take turns stating which location best represents their interest and then moving to that location. That group can then become a working team with a similar interest, or one person can be taken from each location to create a team with contrasting interests.

Sharing structures. These structures are designed to allow students to share ideas and information in a nonthreatening context that fosters close listening. These structures help students learn to talk about themselves and art as they develop empathy for others.

- *Partner/team discussion:* Sit students in pairs or teams of four.* Ask a question or name a topic and allow time for students to think of their responses. Students sitting next to each other share their idea or answer to the question. If they are in teams of four, at a signal from the teacher these students turn and explain what they just shared with the teammate sitting opposite them. If desired, ask the team to create a summary statement or artwork that reflects what everyone said.
- *Circle share:* Students sit in a large circle. They turn to the one sitting next to them and share about the question or topic. That student then turns and shares what was said with the student on the other side.
- *Go 'round:* Give each team one piece of paper and each team member a different color marker or drawing tool. Assign a topic or drawing task. The team passes the paper around in one direction and each team member in turn adds ideas or art to the paper. Teams then share their products with the whole class.
- *Team portraits:* Organize students in teams of four.* Give each team a piece of paper and a pencil. Direct the first student to draw a large rectangle in the center of the paper. Then have the pencil passed

---

*If there is an unbalanced number of students, create one team of five or two teams of three and adjust activities accordingly.

to the next, who draws a line from the corner of the rectangle to the corner of the paper. Continue around the team until a frame is drawn (see At a Glance 7.2). The team members write their names in a section of the frame. Then they take turns passing the paper around and quickly writing their ideas or thoughts on the assigned question or topic in their part of the frame. At a signal the team stops, and they share what they wrote. Then they write a summary statement or create a group drawing or collage in the center rectangle, forming a "team portrait" that reflects the statements they wrote on the frame. (*Note:* Other graphic organizers, such as Venn diagrams, can be used in similar ways.)

- *Heads together:* Assign each team member a number from one to four.* The teacher calls out a question or topic and an amount of time such as thirty seconds. Team members share what they know during that time. At the signal the teacher calls a number at random (numbered sticks or a spinner work well) and that team member shares what the team said with the whole class.
- *Webbing:* In the center of the team place a large sheet of paper with a topic or question written in the center. Give each team member small strips of paper, a different color for each member. Quickly as they can students are to write ideas on the paper strips and place them in web formation around the topic. Any teammate may move a strip or add on to it. When ideas are exhausted, have teams glue down the strips and add connecting lines. Share the completed webs with the class.

Application structures. These structures are designed so that students must use vocabulary, concepts, or skills to accomplish a task.

- *Match-up buddies:* Determine the number of partners or teams needed. Create matching sets of cards such as an art vocabulary term and its definition or an artwork, its style, its artist, and its culture. Shuffle and distribute one card to each student. Students with matching cards form a pair or team.
- *Sticky notes:* Form students into teams of four.* Give each team member a number from one to four. Display artworks around the room. Give each team a sticky note on which is written a vocabulary word or concept. Allow several seconds for the team to discuss the word and decide which artwork displays it. At a signal randomly call a number. Those team members bring up the sticky note and attach it to the artwork and then explain why. Repeat the activity with new notes as desired.
- *Experts in action:* Divide class into teams of four.* Assign each team to learn and practice a specific art technique or concept. These students then become class "experts" in that technique or idea. Have one expert from each team move to another team and teach them

the technique or concept. Repeat until everyone knows all the techniques or concepts.

- *Jigsaw:* This structure, although similar to "experts in action," is more appropriate for longer-term, more complex topics. Divide the class into teams of four.* One member of each team becomes an expert on a topic or technique. The expert groups meet and study their topic or technique together. When they return to the initial team, each expert contributes what he or she knows in creating a team project, artwork, or report. For example, the four members of each team could be assigned to expert groups studying four different printing techniques. When they return to their team, they must work together to use the four methods to create a printed banner.
- *Describe it:* Have students work in pairs or teams of four. Distribute one file folder and an artwork in an envelope or folder so it cannot be seen. Have one student stand up the file folder and place the artwork behind it so the other team members cannot see it. This student then describes the work while teammates try to draw it or identify its characteristics in writing. Many variations on this activity are possible and provide an excellent way to develop vocabulary and art discussion skills.
- *All for one:* In this structure students must work together to create one project. It is particularly useful for teaching roles and the value of cooperating. It makes a good preliminary activity before starting a mural, for example. Divide students into teams of four.* Give each student a specific task such as one student uses the scissors, one the markers, one the glue, and one the paper. Only that student may handle and use that item. Working together, they must create an artwork. Other approaches might include assigning one student the background, one the foreground, one the subject, and one the border. Emphasize the importance of reaching consensus in producing an organized work.

Viewing structures. These structures allow students to look carefully at one another's work done either individually or by a team and give feedback in a positive way.

- *Gallery tour:* Assign students to teams. Students spread their artworks on tables, board, or floor. At a signal all students move about the room to view the works. If desired, the teacher can give specific things for the students to observe. At the signal to return the students reform into teams, and all members share what they saw using the team discussion format.
- *Roving reporters:* Display artworks around the room. These can be individual works, team projects, or artworks being studied. Divide the class into teams of four. Give each member of the team a specific thing to look for or a question to answer. At the signal the "reporters" move about the room studying the works and taking

notes if desired. At the signal to return the students report back to their teams and share what they learned. The team writes a team report or shares orally with the class.

- *Memorable work:* Give each team an artwork to study for five to ten seconds. At a signal from the teacher the team flips the work face down and then either using team discussion or "go 'round," they describe what they saw and then share these descriptions with the class.

Introducing Cooperative Structures

In the beginning developing social awareness and mutual respect is more important than the actual content of the activity. When students are familiar with the roles they must assume and the behavior that is expected, teachers become facilitators rather than disciplinarians and can focus on developing student artistic thinking and problem-solving skills as they work in cooperative groups.

Teachers can improve social function by focusing on a specific skill when needed. The keys to cooperative skill acquisition are plenty of role modeling, positive feedback, and time to reflect on one's performance. For example, if the class is too noisy during teamwork, discuss the importance of using low voices and have students model proper voice level. When students are working, walk over to teams who are quiet, get the attention of the class, and describe in a positive way what the team was doing well. At the end of the activity have the teams reflect on how quietly they worked.

Skills to focus on include positive feedback, reaching consensus, and conflict resolution.

Positive feedback. Have students practice giving one another positive comments that specifically describe what they liked about the other students' ideas or behaviors. (See Chapter 6 for guidance.)

Reaching consensus. Stress the importance of coming to agreement when working with others. Explain that each student's objections must be taken seriously and sometimes it takes creative thinking to come up with a solution that makes everyone comfortable. At the same time emphasize the need for flexibility and putting the group goal ahead of personal goals. Reaching consensus is a creative activity. Show students how it relates to the creative process.

- *Knowledge:* Each team member contributes unique ideas based on personal experience and knowledge.
- *Skill:* Team members must use all their listening and communication skills.
- *Motivation:* The team will not reach consensus and solve the problem unless everyone participates and agrees.

- *Immersion:* Each team member must focus intently on solving the problem, looking for similarities and links in the group's ideas.
- *Incubation:* Team members must be open and flexible, willing to try new approaches. Explore the suggested ideas for all their implications. If some ideas are opposite, try out ones in the middle. If that is not possible, take a new direction and collect new ideas.
- *Production:* When an idea is selected, check that everyone agrees. Acknowledge everyone's contribution and celebrate success.

Conflict resolution. When conflict does arise, students need to have a method in place for resolving it. There are many different approaches to settling differences. Some of these can be summarized as follows:

- *Share:* Share the disputed item or idea. For example, if two students both need to stand in the same location to reach the area they are painting on a mural, they can agree to take turns with one student getting, mixing, and handing the paint to the one who is painting.
- *Compromise:* Take part of both students' ideas or wishes and combine them in a new way. If in making a mural two students disagree on the colors for the background, they can combine the colors in a new way.
- *Get help:* There will be times when students cannot settle problems by themselves. Have in place ways for students to ask for help from peers or from the teacher.

Group Art: Mural Making

Well-designed hands-on art activities provide an excellent way for students to learn to function as a cooperative group. The unpredictability of art media combined with the motivation that comes from seeing a group work progress offer highly stimulating creative problems for teams of students to solve. Although many group art activities are described in this book, mural making is one that is highly motivating and well worth the effort, though often avoided by teachers who are not sure how to organize such a major activity. But mural making does not have to be a fearsome process, especially when the mural is designed to correlate with and illuminate what a class is studying.

Murals can serve many purposes in the classroom. Although the word *mural* is defined in the dictionary as a wall painting, in school parlance it most often refers to any large artwork done by a group of students. Cooperative artworks can forge group bonds, express a group experience, or represent concepts or ideas being studied. Because murals often consist of parts contributed by each member, students must learn to reach consensus in order to be successful. To foster group self-esteem it is important to set a task or problem that is open ended and has many possible solutions.

Starting out. In order for mural making to be a pleasant and rewarding experience, it is important to consider the social aspects foremost. Students will be working in close proximity, and individual behavior can have a great effect on the group; it only takes a few students to destroy the unity of a project. For this reason it is important to select the materials, topics, and group size carefully.

- *Select familiar art materials.* First, it is important in a group project to choose art materials with which everyone has had successful experiences. If students are given a material they have never or rarely used, the mural-making process becomes one of exploration rather than expression of ideas, or if some students are less experienced than others with a material, they often fool around to cover up their lack of expertise.
- *Choose familiar topics.* Rather than springing murals upon students let them grow out of personal experiences or studies. Topics and themes should reflect what students already know something about or have been given time to research. Murals that draw on student self-knowledge—their favorite sports, pets, music—instantly capture attention and unify thinking and can be done at any time. On the other hand, murals that are research based are usually better done toward the end of a unit to summarize the learning in a graphic way.
- *Control group size.* The number of students who can work successfully on a group art project will vary with the nature of the project and the age of the students. In general while students are still getting to know the rules and one another, it is better to start with pairs or threes and provide plenty of modeling of ways to deal with problems that arise. With practice larger groups of four to six can be formed. Whole class group projects work best with smaller working groups and when space, tasks, or time is divided or when students work on individual parts and then come together as a class to complete the final work.

The collection mural. The collection mural is ideal for students making a mural for the first time as it grows directly from their experience and provides an excellent way to model how to reach consensus on placing items on a mural. Have students collect items that relate to a topic or theme being studied. Some simple ideas for collection murals include autumn leaves, pebbles, dried weeds, and other nature items from a walk in the woods, field, or park; candy wrappers and other refuse from the playground or lunchroom; or objects that are all one color, texture, or shape.

To make the mural meaningful take time after the items are collected to have students meet in small groups and discuss why they chose the item(s). Primary children can describe the appearance of the object. Intermediate students might research several facts about it. Students can also sort items and make graphs showing the results.

When small group work is done, have students meet as a class with their items. An ideal setup is to have the students sit on a rug facing a large sheet of paper hung on the wall. In turn have each student briefly present his or her item and then glue it on the paper. As students add their contributions, have them suggest several possible locations and try them out before gluing. When done, display the mural along with photographs of students collecting materials, descriptions or facts about the objects, graphs, and other materials that make the process meaningful.

The quilt mural. Making this kind of mural is much like making a quilt. Each student or small group is given an identical, square piece of paper. On the square the student or group creates an artwork that reflects the topic or theme. When done, students arrange the squares with group discussion and negotiation and then glue them together to form a whole. This kind of mural works well to introduce the idea that the class is made up of individuals who have unique ideas that when brought together form a whole greater than the sum of the parts. It also works well as a way for students to share related research on a topic or to illustrate a sequence of events. Sample topics for quilt murals include the following:

Group building	Research based	Sequences
Self-portraits	Types of animals, birds, flowers, etc.	The school day
My hobbies	Habitats	The seasons
My family or home	Types of vehicles	Metamorphosis of a caterpillar
Sports or music	Nutritious foods	Events in history
My favorite place	Simple machines in use	How something is made

Collage mural. Begin by establishing a theme or topic for the mural and then having students make individual drawings, paintings, or paper figures, or cut pictures from magazines. This kind of mural works particularly well for subjects that contain discrete parts but have an overall relationship. For example, students could go outside and sketch the houses around the school, cut the sketches out, and then glue them on in map-like fashion to the mural, or if they were studying the forest, each student could make a particular tree to create a forest scene.

Be sure students are aware that their contribution will be added to the group mural and must be cut out because the mural paper will form the background. If the mural will show a scene, create a background that contains a large amount of ground and a small amount of sky. This can be done by drawing a horizon line high up on the paper, by gluing on ground- and sky-colored paper, or by having students paint the sky and ground before starting the mural. Sponge-paint backgrounds often work well.

When students have completed their parts for the mural, have them share what they made in a small group. Then have them come together in the same way as for a collection mural to negotiate placement on the background.

The painted mural. There is nothing as vibrant as a brilliantly painted mural done by school children. A mural in which students will be sharing space on the same background paper or wall requires organization and cooperation. Because the process is complex, there is always the grave temptation for the teacher to play an overbearing role in the design of the mural or for one or a few children to assume the major burden of work. This is often seen in the ubiquitous use of black outlining around each child's painting or the use of one child's drawing as the picture that everyone else gets to paint. In order to truly represent the ideas of the whole group the following must be in place:

- *Motivation must be high.* A painted mural should not be tackled just because the teacher wants to try it. Instead, plant and nourish the idea. First, is there an experience or theme that has affected the class deeply? Spend time visualizing images, colors, shapes, and forms that relate to it. If possible, take a field trip to see murals in the community or study the work of Mexican muralist Diego Rivera. What themes and ideas do these murals express? If possible, discuss where the mural will be displayed. Students will be more motivated if they know their work will express important ideas and will be seen in public or even possibly permanently mounted.
- *Decide on the content.* Brainstorm a list of the elements the class feels must be included in the mural. For example, if making a mural about life in the city, students might list the different kinds of buildings, activities people might be doing, vehicles, and other features of city life they want to include.
- *Form small groups.* Students select an area that interests them to work on. Arrange time for students who have chosen to work on similar items to meet and share their ideas, sketches, problems, and discoveries. This small group time is vitally important. It prevents students who are less comfortable in large groups from being left

"Save the Environment!"
Collage mural: cut paper, pencil, and marker—grade 3.

Thinking about Children's Art

This collage mural was created by the combined efforts of four third-grade classes as a culmination activity to a year's study of rainforest, grassland, desert and coastal regions. Because of the limited and unusual shaped space the students were challenged to find places for their contributions. How have students used words and images together? How effectively does it demonstrate what the students have learned?

Protect natural habitats
SAVE THE GRASSLANDS
rotate grazing lands
Grassland Express
rotate crops
Save our food!
Save the crops
snakes
prairie dog
wolf
cheetah
SAVE OUR EARTH
HELP PREVENT FIRE!
SAVE The Animals!
animal life
Save The Rain Forests
Don't start fires
SAVE ME
Only you can

out of the process, and it provides another opportunity for students to share about their art.

- *Gather visual data.* Take time for students to study the visual images that will appear in the mural. Direct observation is the best, but students can also find pictures in books and watch videos. Draw their attention to the colors, values, shapes, textures, patterns, and relative sizes of objects they see.
- *Develop painting skills.* Plan plenty of time for students to explore the paint they will use and make sample sketches and paintings using it.
- *Practice negotiation.* When students complete their sketches, they should meet as a class and agree on how to place them on the mural. It should be the goal to include work by every student while at the same time encouraging the combining and extending of ideas. At this point it may be helpful to cut out the sketches and move them around until the class agrees the composition expresses their ideas.
- *Make a cartoon.* It is important while there is still time to make changes for students to have an idea of how their plan looks. A cartoon is an actual-sized representation of the finished mural. They can do it on a large sheet of brown kraft paper or on small sheets of drawing paper pieced together. Sketching their ideas on the cartoon gives students practice enlarging. (*Note:* This provides a perfect opportunity to learn how to use an enlarging grid; see "Teacher Tip, Math and Art" in this chapter). Hang the cartoon in the class so everyone can look at and discuss it many times before work begins on the final version.
- *Plan the colors.* Using paint swatches, the students can try out colors on the cartoon. Discuss the importance of value and contrast. In a well-planned mural, coloring-book black outlines should not be needed.
- *Organize work teams.* Plan to have small groups working at a time. Start with painting the background. Then have students paint parts that are spaced out so they are not crowded while working.
- *Record the process.* Photograph and videotape the development of the project. Tape record student comments as they discuss their ideas and work.
- *Celebrate.* Take time to celebrate the successful completion of the mural. Hold an unveiling party and invite other students and staff. Display the sketches, cartoon, paint-mixing experiments, photographs, video, and any other materials that will make the process of creating the mural come alive. Make a plaque honoring the students who contributed to the mural.

Teacher Tip

Math and Art

Enlarging a sketch using student-made grids is a fun way to have students apply measuring and spatial skills.

1. Draw a grid of carefully measured squares over the sketch.

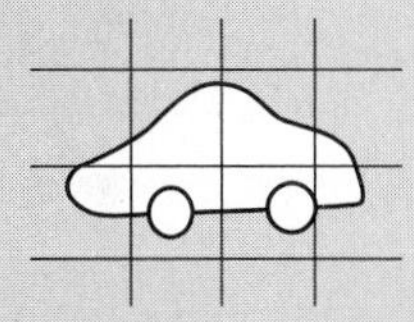

2. Draw a corresponding grid of the same number, but larger-sized, squares on the larger paper. Have students explore different ratios to discover the one that works best for the project.

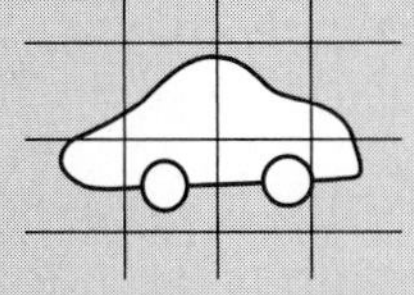

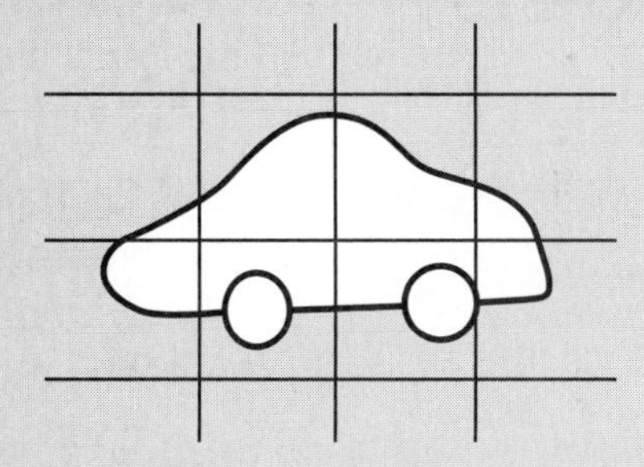

3. Transfer the images that are in each square of the original to the corresponding square on the enlargement.

Beyond the Mural

There are many other group art projects. Just a few are listed here to spark the imagination:

Body shapes. As part of a unit on the human body have students trace each other and cut out a body shape to paint.

Box self-portraits. Have students make shallow boxes from construction paper or tag board. Invite students to fill box with items that express their individuality, and then mount the boxes together on a wall to create a portrait of the class.

Light wall. As part of a unit on light give each student a clear zip-topped plastic bag to fill with transparent and translucent papers and other materials that allow light to pass through in interesting ways. Tape bags together on a glass window to create an amazing wall of light.

Books to Share

Murals

Capek, M. (1996). *Murals: Cave, Cathedral to Street.* Minneapolis, MN: Lerner.
Morrison, T. (1996). *Antonio's Apprenticeship: Painting a Fresco in Renaissance Italy.* New York: Holiday House.
Vazquez, S. (1998). *The School Mural.* Milwaukee, WI: Raintree.
Winter, J. (1991). *Diego.* New York: Random House.

Conclusion

A SOCIETY OF ARTISTS

[T]he real challenge presented to educators and to us all is to become what we teach. The example we set tells children more about how we really feel and think than words do.
Yogesh K. Ghandhi (in Drew, 1987)

Each classroom is a small society. How students interact with one another determines the nature of that society. It is the teacher who determines what kind of interaction will take place by creating an environment that mirrors the diversity of society and nurtures cooperative behaviors. The teacher must personally value and welcome the sharing of feelings. The teacher must model and teach openness and flexibility of thinking, respect and acceptance of diverse ideas. We must acknowledge that social and creative growth is stifled in restrictive, fearful environments where student choices are limited and student exploration of ideas is ridiculed, discouraged, or restricted.

If teachers honor and encourage cooperative, bias-free interrelationships, the classroom will become a place where creativity and artistic thinking can flourish. It will become home for a society of young artists working together to learn the language of art.

Teacher Resources

REFERENCES

Battistich, V., Solomon, D., Dong-il, K., Watson, M., & Schaps, E. (1995). Schools as communities: Poverty levels of student populations and student attitudes, motives and performance: A multi-level analysis. *American Educational Research Journal, 32*(3), 627–658.

Berliner, O., & Casanova, U. (1993). *Putting research to work in your school.* Arlington Heights, IL.: Skylight.

Caine, R. N. & G. (1991). *Making connections: Teaching and the human brain.* Alexandria, VA: Association for Supervision and Curriculum Development.

Derman-Sparks, L., & the A.B.C. Task Force. (1989). *Anti-bias curriculum: Tools for empowering young children.* Washington, D.C.: National Association for the Education of Young Children.

Drew, N. (1987). *Learning the skills of peacemaking.* Rolling Hills, CA: Jalmar.

Froschl, M., & Sprung, B. (1983). Providing an anti-handicapist early childhood environment. *Interracial Books Bulletin, 14*(7), 21–23.

Gallas, K. (1994). *The language of learning.* New York: Teachers College Press.

Janke, R. A., & Peterson, J. P. (1995). *Peacemaker's A,B,Cs for young children.* Marine on St. Croix, MN: Growing Communities for Peace.

Kagan, S. (1994). *Cooperative learning.* San Juan Capistrano, CA: Resources for Teachers.

Miller-Lachmann, L., & Taylor, L. S. (1995). *Schools for all: Educating children in a diverse society.* Albany, NY: Delmar.

Mitchell, R. (Ed.). (1994). *Measuring up to the challenge: What standards and assessments can do for art education.* New York: American Council for the Arts.

Silberstein-Storfer, M. (1997). *Doing art together.* New York: Abrams.

Slavin, R. E. (1983). *Cooperative learning.* White Plains, NY: Longman.

Solomon, D., Watson, M., Delucchi, K. L., Schaps, E., & Battistich, V. (1988). Enhancing children's prosocial behavior in the classroom. *American Educational Research Journal, 25*(4), 527–554.

Starko, A. (1994). *Creativity in the classroom: Schools of curious delight.* White Plains, NY: Longman.

Stevens, R., & Slavin, R. (1995). The cooperative elementary school: Effects on achievement, attitude and social relations. *American Educational Research Journal, 32*(2), 321–351.

Welhousen, K. (1996). Do's and don'ts for eliminating hidden bias. *Childhood Education, 73*(1), 36–39.

Wlodkowski, R. J., & Ginsberg, M. B. (1995). *Diversity and motivation: Culturally responsive teaching.* San Francisco: Jossey-Bass.

Wlodkowski, R. J., & Ginsberg, M. B. (1997). A framework for culturally responsive teaching. *Educational Leadership, 53*(1), 17–24.

Practical Guides

For more information on using cooperative learning in the classroom consult:

Baloche, L. (1997). *Cooperative classroom: Empowering learning.* Englewood Cliffs, NJ: Prentice Hall.

Cohen, D. (1994). *Designing groupwork: Strategies for the heterogeneous classroom.* New York: Teachers College Press.

Ellis, S., & Whalen, S. F. (1990). *Cooperative learning: Getting started.* New York: Scholastic.

Fisher, B. (1995). *Thinking and learning together: Curriculum and community in a primary classroom.* Portsmouth, NH: Heinemann.

Kagan, M., L., & S. (1995). *Classbuilding.* San Juan Capistrano, CA: Resources for Teaching.

Shaw, V. (1992). *Community building in the classroom.* San Juan Capistrano, CA: Resources for Teachers.

To learn more about dealing with children with special needs read:

Society for Developmental Education. (1994). *Creating inclusive classrooms: Education for all children.* Peterborough, NH: Society for Developmental Education.

Dudley-Maring, C. (1990). *When school is a struggle.* New York: Scholastic.

Goodman, G. (1994). *Inclusive classrooms from A to Z: A handbook for educators.* Columbus, OH: Teacher's Publishing.

Putnam, J. W. (1998). *Cooperative learning and strategies for inclusion: Celebrating diversity in the classroom.* Baltimore, MD: Paul H. Brookes.

To prepare for teaching about diversity:

Cahan, S., & Tocur, Z. (Eds.) (1995). *Contemporary art in multicultural education.* New York: Routledge.

Eldrige, D. (1997). *Teacher talk: Multicultural lesson plans for the elementary classroom.* New York: Allyn & Bacon.

To understand children's art:

Levick, M. (1998). *See what I'm saying : What children tell us through their art.* Dubuque, IA: Islewest.

Malchiodi, C. A. (1998). *The art therapy sourcebook.* Los Angeles: Lowell House.

Inclusive Education Resources

The Council for Exceptional Children
1920 Association Drive
Reston, VA 22091-1589

Exceptional Children's Assistance Center
Box 16
Davidson, NC 28036

Inclusion Press International
24 Thomas Crescent, Toronto
Ontario, Canada M6H 2S5
http://inclusion.com

PEAK
6055 Lehman Drive Suite 101
Colorado Springs, CO 80918

Multicultural Resources

Art with Heart
P.O. Box 6367
Syracuse, NY 13217
1-315-474-1132
Contemporary posters and postcards, many featuring Native American and African-American artists

Cherokee Publications
P.O. Box 430
Cherokee, NC 28719
Native American books, posters, kits, videos, and music

Great Alaska Catalog
5750 Glacier Highway
Juneau, AL 99801
1-800-326-2197
Fossilized ivory carvings and scrimshaw by Inuit artists

Mola Lady
8500 Creek Side Drive
Bismarck, ND 58504
1-800-880-6677
Molas made by the Kuna people of Panama

Oxfam America
P.O. Box 821
Lewiston, ME 04240
Handmade items from around the world

Save the Children
P.O. Box 166
Peru, IN 46970
1-800-833-3154
Handmade items from Asia and Africa

Southwest Indian Foundation
P.O. Box 86
Gallup, NM 87302-0001
1-505-863-4037
Native American art and artifacts from the Southwest

UNICEF
P.O. Box 182233
Chattanooga, TN 37422
1-800-553-1200
Contemporary cards featuring multinational artists, artifacts from Africa and Asia

Videos

Many exciting videos, as well as books, programs, and kits, featuring art from diverse cultures are available from the following suppliers. Just a sampling of what is available from each one is listed here. Other multicultural videos and materials are detailed in the "Resource" sections following other chapters.

Cherokee Publications
Box 430
Cherokee, NC 28719
Beyond Tradition (Native American art)

Crystal Productions
Box 2159
Glenview, IL 60025-6159
1-800-255-8629
www.crystalproductions.com
Aboriginal Art (4+)
Chinese Brush Painting (3+)
If Rocks Could Talk (3+)
Latino Art & Culture in the United States (4+ bilingual)
Oriental Art (5+)
World Folk Art (6+)

Crizmac
Box 65928
Tucson, AZ 85728-5928
1-800-913-8555
www.crizmac.com
African American Artist Series (4+)
Anasazi, The Ancient Ones (4+)
Australia Dreamings (4+)
Gente del Sol (Mexico & Guatemala) (3+)
Haitian Visions: A Diverse Cultural Legacy (4+)
Hopi (4+)
Island Worlds: Art and Culture of the Pacific (4+)
Milagros: Symbols of Hope (bilingual: Spanish) (4+)
Navajo (4+)
Oaxaca: Valley of Myth and Magic (4+)
Paths of Life: American Indians of the Southwest (4+)
Tribal Designs (4+)
World Beneath a Canopy: Life and Art in the Amazon (4+)

Facets Video
1517 W. Fullerton Avenue
Chicago, IL 60614
1-800-331-6197
African American Artists Affirmation Today (5+)
Hispanic Folk Art and the Environment (K–12)

GPN
P.O. Box 80669
Lincoln, NE 68501
1-800-228-4630
http://gpn.unl.edu
Reading Rainbow Series

Knowledge Unlimited
Box 52
Madison, WI 53701-0052
1-800-356-2303
Lascaux Revisited (5+)
Hello from Around the World (2–4)
Holidays for Children Series (K–4)

Sax Visual Art Resources
Box 51710
New Berlin, WI 53151
1-800-558-6696
Faith Ringgold: The Last Story Quilt (4+)

Web Sites

Alliance of African American Artists
www.artists4a.com

ArtsACCESS
National Arts and Disability Center
http://www.nadc.edu

Asia for Kids
Multicultural lessons, books, and materials
http://www.afk.com

Celebration Books
Multicultural books and videos
http://celebrationbooks.com

Cooperative Learning Activities
Springfield Public Schools, Springfield, MO
http://204.184.214.251/coop/ecoopmain.html

Centre for Study of Learning and Performance
Concordia University, Montreal, Canada
http://doe.concordia.ca/cslp

Folkart.com
Artworks, posters, and artifacts

Kagan Cooperative Learning Resources
www.kagancooplearn.com

Multicultural Publishing and Education catalog
Multicultural books and materials
http://www.mpec.org

Native Web
Resources for indigenous cultures around the world
www.nativeweb.org

Very Special Artists
Art by people with disabilities
http://www.vsarts.org

Chapter 8

The Artful Classroom
Management and Organization

Art teaching as a creative performance requires the teacher to be an active playful designer of the environment and all the objects and performers in it.

George Szekely (1991, p. 66)

ARTISTS AT WORK

Beginning Art Workshop

Teacher: Please turn to the person sitting next to you in the circle and tell them what you plan to work on today in workshop.

Travis: What are you working on?

Margo: I just began this sketch yesterday . . . it's kind of rough. I was trying to show how beautiful it was at the lake this summer. How about you?

Travis: That's cool. I had a whole bunch of ideas. See, I made all these little sketches. But now I can't decide which to do. You're lucky to have your idea all picked out.

Margo: What's this here?

Travis: Oh, I was making the symbols for all my favorite teams.

Margo: You put the most detail in that sketch, why don't you do that one first? You can always do the others later.

Introduction

AN ENVIRONMENT FOR ART

Anyone who has tried to teach art in a forty-minute art period knows that there is barely enough time to talk about a concept, demonstrate a technique or review what the students should be doing, pass out supplies, work on the art projects, and then clean up. This is not the way artists work. Artists think about what they want to do, perhaps for days. They have studios in which their supplies are always ready. They have no fixed time when they have to stop working. Art instruction needs a better delivery model.

In this chapter we will look at a variety of ways to turn ordinary classrooms into art studios where students have time to think, plan, and do art in a broad spectrum of ways that mirror those of the working artist. We will examine how to coordinate scheduling, room layout, and design in order to surround children by opportunities to use the language of art daily. Where should work tables be located? What kinds of art supplies will be needed? How should they be selected and organized? How can art be scheduled into the day? The answers to these practical questions can determine whether or not children and teachers will be able think and work like artists as they learn about art throughout the school year.

Setting the Stage

HOW CAN WE CREATE A PLACE FOR ART IN THE CLASSROOM?

At the start of each school year teachers walk into freshly cleaned and polished schoolrooms. The walls are bare, the furniture stacked in a corner. Here is a chance to create a uniquely personal environment for teaching, one that matches personal beliefs about how to teach children. If we see our classrooms as studios for learning, we will want to arrange the space so as to facilitate the different ways we want children to learn. As shown in previous chapters, art is far more than playing around with colorful, messy materials. It is a cognitive process that involves thinking, solving problems, looking at artworks, and talking and working with others, equivalent in many ways to learning to read and write. Art should not be separated out for casual, occasional treatment but rather incorporated into the environment that welcomes children each day.

The spaces in which we teach must be more than pretty backgrounds. Thoughtful arrangement of classroom space and attention to aesthetic elements promote student well-being, proper behavior, and artistic sensitivity to the environment. "Classrooms," writes Marjorie Schiller, "need to reflect how we ourselves value art and how it has meaning in our lives" (1995, p. 38).

CREATING AN AESTHETIC ENVIRONMENT

Classrooms must be more than a simple arrangement of well-placed furniture. A classroom where the teacher takes time to carefully consider each element in the room as an artistic one will create an environment that says to all who enter, art is spoken here. Environments that stimulate the senses also energize the brain for learning. "[S]ome of the skill in good teaching lies in the capacity to orchestrate the sensory content of the class," say the Caines (1991, p. 116).

Too many times, however, what ends up in the classroom is the result of haphazard collection and economic frugality. A parent donates a worn rug. A discarded office chair sits in the corner. Outdated, faded maps decorate the walls. New teachers often get the cast-off pieces: unmatched desks and chairs, chipped-top tables, and lopsided shelves. It is hard for teachers, faced with limited funding, to part with items just because they clash with other elements in their

> **? What Do You Think?**
>
> Close your eyes and imagine a beautiful place. What makes it beautiful? What colors, textures, and sensory experiences embody it? Now think about classrooms. Are they beautiful in the same way? Why or why not?

Classroom Meeting Zone.

Thinking about Children's Art

How can classrooms be designed to foster the artistic development of children? What elements has this teacher considered in selecting and arranging the furnishings in this meeting zone? Would children feel comfortable in this space?

rooms. It takes a commitment to surrounding children with beautiful things, a heartfelt belief that nothing should be in our classrooms that does not please the eyes and the senses.

Color and Texture in the Classroom

There are several ways to create such a classroom environment. One of the easiest and most important is to pay attention to the colors in the room. Schoolrooms are naturally full of color: the clothing on the children, the pictures on the walls, the books on the shelves, the art supplies on the counter. The classroom walls, floors, and accessories should not compete with these colors but should provide a restful background. "Our eyes," says Karen Haigh, "should be drawn more to the children and their work than the color of the walls or the background of the bulletin board" (1997, p. 155).

Walls. Walls painted pure white, off-white, pale gray, beige, and the palest tints of blue, pink, and yellow work well as a foil for children's colorful artwork and for displays of art and nature objects. Lighter colors make dark rooms seem bigger and brighter. Warm neutrals such as off-white, beige, and yellow counteract cold fluorescent lighting and make the room feel warmer. Cool neutrals make a sunny room feel cooler. Pink and cool colors such as pastel blue and green have a calming effect.

Floor, furnishings, and accessories. Floor and rug colors should relate to the color of the walls and carry out the neutral color scheme.

The colors of nature—beiges, grays, and browns—wear well underfoot and allow attention to focus on more important elements in the room. Table tops, chairs, and bulletin boards should also be neutral in color.

Remember that the colors of permanent items in the classroom are background colors for the more exciting artwork of the students. Limit the number of colors and patterns found on furniture and accessories. Select one main color such as white, green, or blue and perhaps smaller quantities of a related color. If work tables do not match, paint them or cover them with plastic tablecloths all in the same color. Sew matching color pillows and curtains to cover open storage areas. Buy the same color throw rugs to use for peer conferencing. Cover storage boxes with contact paper or paint them in the selected color. If using patterned fabric or covering, limit it to one all-over design with a small, repeated motif that mirrors the colors in the room.

Bulletin boards. Bulletin boards are essential for displaying children's work and important information. Painting the boards the same color as the walls helps unify the room and draws attention to what is on the board rather than the board itself. Then use a bold splash of color such as bright yellow, red, hot pink, magenta, and orange, all of which are highly stimulating to the senses, in temporary displays designed to attract student attention to something new.

Texture. Even with pleasing colors classrooms can often seem very institutional. Textures can add softness and comfort. Wood furniture and surfaces add warm, natural colors and a rich visual texture. Rugs, bean bags, foam cushions, and pillows add softness and quiet the room. Baskets make ideal storage containers that add to the room's aesthetic effect. Plants soften hard edges and add moisture and oxygen. Aquariums, terrariums, and displays of natural objects such as rocks and shells bring the beauty of nature into the room.

Lighting. Most classrooms have fluorescent lights, which are often cold and harsh and can affect the way students use color in their artwork. Counteract this effect by making the most of any available natural light. Adjust blinds and shades to get the most light from windows. Encourage students to take their work to the window or outdoors to see how it looks in natural light. Set up incandescent table lamps in the library area or in student conference areas to provide cozy, warm spots of light. These are particularly effective on gray winter days.

Sensory Displays

When the background is in place, the stage is set for the small things that will turn a humdrum classroom into an exciting place to which children look forward to coming every day.

Every classroom should be rich in objects and materials that invite children to look, touch, and explore. Placed in various locations around the room with careful attention to aesthetic effect, these sensory materials can relate to different subject areas and topics of study. Clear plastic bottles filled with smooth beach pebbles, shells, seeds, and tiny pinecones can provide manipulatives to sort and group at a math center. A still life of real fruit can accompany books and other materials on nutrition. See At a Glance 8.1 for more ideas.

Classroom as Stage Set

No matter how beautiful a room is, when the classroom environment remains the same day after day, the students no longer look at it with the same curiosity. To ignite interest in a new topic, or renew excitement for a unit that has been dragging on, explore ways to change the environment of the room for a few days. For example, as part of the study of colors at the first-grade level hang rainbow-colored streamers from the ceiling and suspend colored cellophane in front of the windows. During the study of the Sahara desert create a Bedouin "story" tent from striped sheets, and place lambskins and Oriental-style throw rugs within. Gather here to share oral stories and enjoy the effect of the light passing through the "tent" roof. Creative room changes are limited only by one's imagination. Other ideas include the following:

- Darken the room and shine a spotlight on a featured object when discussing shadows, shading, or light effects.
- Create "caves" by covering desks with tablecloths when studying cave art or archaeology.
- Use pieces of artificial turf and real and artificial flowers to create a "garden" when studying plants.
- Use colored tape or white paint to create paths or arrows on the floor when studying lines or mapping.
- Add road signs and have children follow traffic rules as they move about the room.
- Use two colors of carpet squares to create changing patterns to sit on when studying patterns.
- Fill a big, old chest with simple treasures and have a child pull out a surprise each day and make up a story about it as part of a mystery unit.

The extra effort is worth it. Not only will the topic be more memorable for the students but also when the room is put back to normal everyone will see it again with new eyes.

Setting Up Learning Zones

To create a room conducive to the artistic process break up the physical space into distinctive multipurpose areas, each designed to elicit

At a Glance 8.1

Sensory Display Ideas

Subject	Topic	Sensory Display
Math	Adding/subtracting	Clear jars of beads, buttons, glass drops, marbles, mini-plastic figures arranged by color
	Cubic measurement	Graduated jars full of beans or gravel
	Geometry	Three-dimensional geometric forms spot-lighted with a small lamp
	Liquid measurement	Clear plastic liquid measures filled with water colored with food coloring
Science	Plants	An unusual plant such as a cactus, orchid, or bromeliad
	Skeletal structure	Clean, sanitized skull or bones
	Dinosaurs	Large fossil or stratified rock
	Geology	Beautiful rock or crystal
	Ocean/sea life	Large conch or other shells, coral, fish in bowl
	Trees	Tree ring slices, leaves, bark
	Water	Various size and shape clear plastic bottles filled with water to look through
Social Studies	American history	Variations on the U.S. flag—cloth, cloth-ing, pictures
	Native Americans	Still life of native foods: Indian corn, gourds, pumpkins, tomatoes, potatoes
	Prairie pioneers	Still life of rag rug, salt glazed pottery, corn and wheat stalks, grains in clear jars.
	Rain forest	Houseplants (spider plant, bromeliad, orchids), ikat dyed cloth, gum, chocolate, tropical fruits
Language Arts	Any book or poem	Look for an object that plays an impor-tant role in the story or poem

different student behaviors and activities. A classroom that welcomes the language of art has open space that allows students to move boldly in response to an artwork as well as to sit quietly with a partner talking about a work in progress. There must be places for groups of students to work together and private places for thoughtful thinking. Supplies must be convenient and within reach and work surfaces multipurpose and easily cleaned. Materials for learning must be near at hand: art posters, books, audio tapes, manipulatives, and more. There must be accommodation for whole class activities, small group instruction, and individual privacy. We can begin by carefully designing the classroom environment so that we can teach not only art but also all subject areas more easily.

Meeting zone. The hub of the classroom should be a large, open space in which the whole class can sit together for class meetings and whole group instruction. This area can be defined by a rug, dividers, or even a painted or taped boundary line on the floor. An easel, blackboard, whiteboard, or bulletin board should be available for visuals used in whole group instruction or for displaying artwork being discussed. There should be sufficient room for the entire class to sit in a circle. Students can sit on the floor, on carpet pieces, on foam cushions, or on stools or chairs arranged in a circle.

This is where community circle will be held, where books will be read aloud, where featured art will be introduced, and where students will share their artwork with the whole group. It should be comfortable and attractive, but because instruction will be delivered here, have few visual or physical distractions so children can maintain their focus on the speaker and any artwork or other items being displayed or shared.

Movement zone. There needs to be enough open space either in the meeting zone or in contiguous areas so that students can participate in whole class kinesthetic movements and cooperative group activities. If classroom space is limited, take advantage of outdoor areas for organized movement activities. Such movement breaks can stimulate learning by pumping more blood to the brain.

Work zone. This is where the students will produce artwork. The floor should be uncarpeted so spills are quickly wiped up. Large, easily cleaned tables and individual desks should be available for students to work on. In the classroom these can be the students' personal desks, pushed together when they need large surfaces. Some tables may be designated for "wet" work such as painting. Cover these with newspaper or brown kraft paper to make clean-up easier. Reserve others for drawing and other "dry" activities such as journaling and planning. At all levels teachers should provide a few floor or table easels for painting as well.

Adjacent to the tables and ready to use should be the art materials that students need for their work and a sink and supplies for cleaning up. Display exploration results and technical charts on the walls in this area.

Student storage area. Near the work area set up shelves on which to store students' work in progress as well as journals, process folios, and portfolios. All these should be readily accessible at student height.

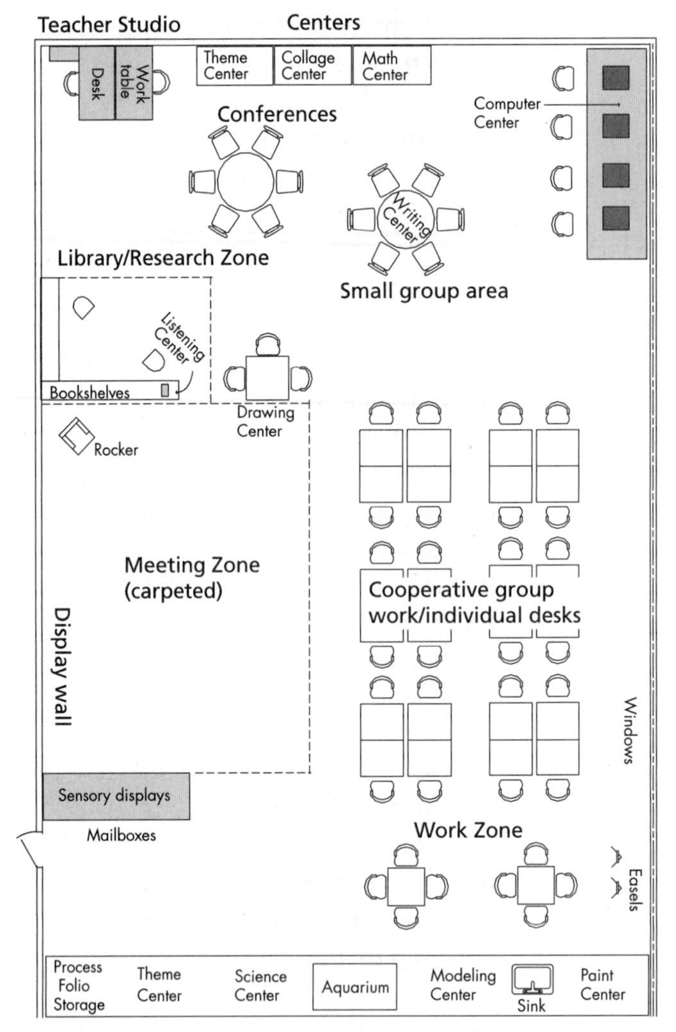

Classroom Layout.

Thinking about Children's Art

This sample classroom layout provides easy access to a variety of learning zones. The carpeted meeting area forms the hub of the room with easy access to the door and the students' desks. The paint and modeling centers are near the sink with work tables and easels close by. A mobile drawing center is centrally located to all areas. The collage center adjoins the math center allowing collected materials to be used in many sorting and graphing activities. What are some of the advantages and disadvantages of this room plan?

Small group/conferencing zone. For small group lessons provide seating for six to eight students around a large table as well as a presentation easel, bulletin board, or blackboard for the teacher. This location also makes an ideal place for teacher conferencing with individual students. The large table and easel or board allows the students' work to be spread out for review.

Partner places. There must be areas that encourage students to sit quietly with one another and conference about their artwork. A pair of chairs set off in a corner, a throw rug for two to sit on in the meeting

Teaching in Action

The Resident Artist

Many wonderful programs exist to bring practicing artists into the schools to work with a few classes for a few days of the year. But teachers are in the school every day and know the children. Who is better able to model the artistic process? Why not set up your own art studio in a corner of the classroom?

zone while the rest are working, a small desk with a table lamp, or even sitting together in the hall are all possible places for two students to talk quietly with each other about their work.

Research center and library. This is where students can find books about art, art prints and artifacts, and picture files. They can also play art games here. Computers and listening stations can be located here as well. This section of the room should be designated the clean-hands area and be located well away from sink and paints. Comfortable chairs, a rug, plastic-covered bean bags, foam cushions, or pillows should entice students to curl up and read or play an art game together.

Display areas. On shelves, counters, and walls display artworks, artifacts, and sensory-stimulating materials for looking and touching.

Teacher's studio. The artist teacher may also wish to designate a small area of the room for personal art production. Depending on the medium of choice this could be a desk, an easel, a work table, or even a loom, set up and ready to use.

In this "mini-studio" keep artworks in progress to work on every day. It does not matter what the art medium is; it can be anything from drawing to weaving as long as it meets safety standards. What is important is that the students see the process of creating artworks on a daily basis. Students will see the teacher preparing, organizing, and cleaning up. Sometimes the work will change dramatically; sometimes the teacher will abandon it to return to it later. Most importantly students will learn that art does not come forth as a finished whole but is a process of growth and change.

This process is fascinating to children. Discussion about what has changed, and thoughts behind the work, will grow naturally from the children's daily observations. There will always be a place for the special visit of an artist in residence. Children need to see different art forms being created by experts. But they also need to see art being created by the people they know well—someone whom they can talk to with ease and who knows them and how to respond to them.

As discussed in Chapter 4, many children who seem to be artistically talented come from homes where they see art being created by the adults around them. Creating one's own art in the school is an ideal way to provide a similar model for all children. It is not enough to be a teacher. What is needed in our schools is the artist teacher: someone who knows what to say to children and how to show them what to do but also someone who is not afraid to model the artistic process.

Planning the Layout

The organization and arrangement of furniture and work areas can either encourage or discourage students from thinking about and creating art. A wonderfully prepared lesson can be ruined by inadequate planning of how the students will utilize the classroom space. The artistic process will not proceed smoothly if students must ask for every material they need for their project or if there is no place to hold a peer conference.

Careful planning of the layout can also eliminate many potential behavior problems. For example, when there are no designated areas for discussing their work, conferencing students may disturb the work of others. In arranging these different learning areas within a classroom, consider student movement and usage.

Consider traffic patterns. How will students move from one area to another? Students carrying cups of paint and containers of water need room to avoid bumping into one another. Can students easily get supplies without blocking access to other areas or to the sink? When students do not have enough passing room for transporting their paper, paints, water, or other supplies, accidents happen.

Provide sufficient work space. Students need to have sufficient and appropriate space in which to work. Is there space for students to work in cooperative groups on a large art project without bumping into one another? Is there enough room for a student to work on a large sheet of drawing paper with supplies and sketches at hand?

Create "private" space. Some children like privacy when they are creating art. Are there places students can work by themselves? Create cozy alcoves or place a desk so that it faces a window view or is partially set off by a low divider. Even a piece of folded cardboard can create a private "studio" at the student's own desk. For safety's sake, however, make sure the teacher always has a clear view of all areas.

Opt for flexibility. How each teacher goes about providing for learning needs will vary widely. There are so many ways to effectively arrange work areas. The key is to keep room design flexible enough to meet the constantly changing needs of the students but at the same

Library/Research Zone.

Thinking about Children's Art

Art activities do not need to be limited to tables. Cozy carpeted areas are ideal for working on drawings, reading an art book or sketching in a journal. Classroom space is often limited, however. What other uses can be made of this kind of area?

time maintain a basic structure so that students can readily find what they need and know how to behave in the room.

Teachers often face less than ideal classrooms. Some are too small. Some have no sink or storage areas. Furnishings may not be suited to art production. Creating a working environment for art instruction may require ingenuity and perseverance.

A combination of large tables and individual desks, for example, is sometimes the best way to provide flexible work areas. The small individual desks found in many elementary classrooms have some advantages. They provide students with personal storage space for basic art supplies and journals, and they can be moved into a wide variety of groupings. For example, they are easily rearranged to make room for a mural or other group project. A disadvantage is that they are often different heights, making an uneven surface for large projects. If possible, adjust groups of desks so that they are all the same height. Large tables, on the other hand, although great for large projects and the sharing of supplies, often take up a lot of floor space, and individual privacy is hard to come by.

Creating Media Centers

Within the classroom art supplies announce the presence of art. They should be well-organized and attractively displayed. Students need to be able to see where the art supplies are and easily obtain what they need for their work. Inviting displays of colorful paints beckon students to the easel. Brilliantly colored markers entice children to draw in their journals. If students do not see certain colors of paper or collections of objects for collages, they are not going to think of using them in their work.

Art supplies do not have to be all in one place or in one art center. In fact, it is better for supplies to be spread around the room in media-focused centers convenient to locations where they are most likely to be used. This creates better traffic patterns and eliminates congestion, mess, and the chance of accidents. Individual media centers can be designed to present the featured medium in an enticing and convenient way that not only makes the room more attractive but also provides information to inspire and to help students work independently. Each media center should display technical charts, a range of artworks in the medium, and books that feature illustrations in the medium as well as the basic supplies.

The following four media centers should be found in every classroom at all levels. As we will see, each medium has its own special needs and best way to be stored. At the beginning of the year start out with just some of the materials and add more complexity as the year goes by and students become comfortable with the offerings. Upper-level centers will naturally become more complex than those intended for primary students as the older students will be more experienced

Teaching in Action

At Home in the Classroom

Jim Greenman (1988) believes that the home is the best model for children's learning spaces. Since the classroom is for most children their home away from home, Greenman recommends that teachers consider all the following elements in planning their classroom environments:

Comfort: We arrange our homes in ways that feel comfortable and restful. There are places to sit and rest as well as move and talk. Both children and adults should feel comfortable working in the classroom. Chairs and seating areas should be sized to the people who will be using them; the room temperature should be moderate and air circulation good.

Order: Rooms in our homes have different purposes, and we behave differently in each. In the classroom different kinds of learning also require unique spaces that have their own structure and behaviors. These need to be slowly introduced and opened up one by one over several weeks' time—while guidelines for use are explained and practiced. Show students how to take and return supplies and how to move safely and quietly from area to area.

Ritual: In our homes we behave in patterned ways; we eat at the same table, sleep on the same side of the bed, and so on. This familiarity and repetition relieve stress and provide comfort. As exciting as we want our classrooms to be, we must remember to always keep some things the same. The meeting area as the hub of the room should remain in the same location over the year so children automatically know where to go at meeting time. Supplies should stay in relatively the same places so children are not wandering in search of scissors or glue.

Softness: We carpet our homes, upholster the chairs, and hang curtains at the windows, but because of the need for cleanliness and fire safety schools tend to have a more office-like appearance. Consider simple ways to provide a homey feeling, such as putting foam cushions or a class-made quilt in the reading area.

Safety and health: At home or school we must protect our children's health. Nothing should be in our classrooms that might accidentally hurt or injure children. However, allowing small risks that are within the children's ability to handle can help children learn to be responsible. First graders can be trusted to hold scissors correctly when passing them to another. Fourth graders can learn to use India ink.

Private and social space: In our homes we arrange living room furniture to ease conversation and put a work desk in a quiet room for privacy. In the classroom we need both private and social space, sometimes at the same time. A large table encourages children working there to socialize and share ideas. An easel off in a corner can provide a quiet moment to experiment with paint.

with a wider variety of materials. (*Note:* More detailed information on each medium can be found in Chapters 11 to 13.)

Drawing center. Although a drawing center may look a lot like a writing center, it is important to have both. Jessica Davis and Howard Gardner emphasize that this shows that drawing is respected as much as writing in the classroom (1993). In the drawing center provide a wide variety of drawing tools including colored pencils, markers, colored chalk, oil pastels, and charcoal as well as an assortment of drawing paper. Pencils, markers, and other drawing materials take up little space. Clear plastic bins on an open shelf or counter can provide ready access to class drawing supplies. Because students will use drawing supplies in so many different contexts, select storage containers that can be easily carried from place to place.

Small stacks of drawing paper in a variety of types, sizes, and colors can be stored on a shelf, counter, or table top. Use a paper-sized box with one end and the top cut off to keep the paper in order. Special cardboard or wood paper files are also available.

Rotate displays of reproductions of drawings by well-known artists, former students, and current students. Hang up class-made charts and artwork that show lines and other effects made with each of the available drawing tools. Keep how-to-draw books in this center as well.

Collage center. A collage center should contain scissors and glue as well as a wide assortment of colored and textured paper, fabric scraps, yarn, and other interesting materials. Arrange these materials by color and texture in low-sided, preferably clear bins, which make the best storage containers for carefully sorted collage materials. Keep them on an open shelf or in a cardboard shoe storage unit so that students can easily make their selections. Label each bin clearly and place in a logical order with the most often used materials in the easiest reached locations. For young children or to accommodate visually impaired students attach a sample of the material to the outside of the bin. A stack of paper plates or small plastic trays should be kept next to the bins so students can easily carry their selections to the work zone. Check, clean out, and refill collage bins regularly. When collage materials are carefully organized and maintained rather than thrown together in an old box, students can appreciate the beauty of the materials and make more meaningful choices.

Complete the center by displaying examples of collages, class-made charts on textures, and natural textured materials.

Modeling center. Nonhardening modeling clay should be precut into softball-sized pieces and stored in clear, self-closing plastic bags or in tightly covered plastic containers on shelf or counter. Store clay tools and plastic work trays next to it.

Rotate displays of topic-related forms such as three-dimensional geometric forms, pottery, and nature objects that have sculptural qualities such as driftwood, unusual rock formations, bones. Show photographs of sculptures by Henry Moore and others.

Painting center. Provide an assortment of brushes, paint in dispenser-type bottles, water cups, mixing trays (or paper plates), newspaper,

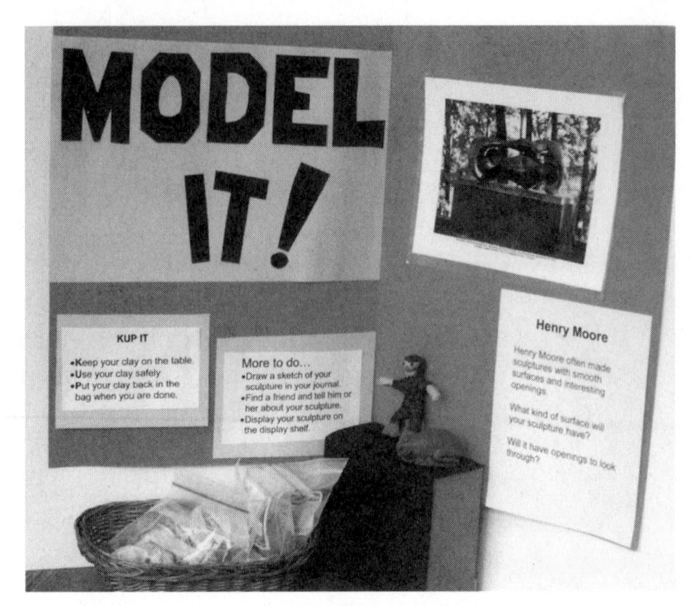

Modeling Center.

Thinking about Children's Art

A basket of modeling clay is accompanied by a display that not only states the rules for using the material but also suggests extension activities and presents the work of the sculptor Henry Moore. A paper-covered cardboard box provides a place for the temporary display of completed sculptures. How does this center encourage children to explore modeling clay?

and paper to paint on. A counter or newspaper-protected table top near the sink makes a good location for painting supplies. Store extra jars of paint on open shelves nearby. Brushes should be stored bristles up in plastic containers that have drainage holes poked in the bottom. Line up water cups next to the sink.

Display a color wheel, value chart, and any charts produced by the class (see Chapter 12). Also include several paintings and/or reproductions that relate to the topics being studied and are changed throughout the year.

SELECTING ART SUPPLIES

Guiding Ideas

In selecting art materials it is important to consider three things: quality, economy, and safety.

Quality and Economy

It is best to purchase the highest quality tools and supplies affordable. Students become frustrated working with dull scissors, watery paint, and flimsy paper. Ideally every classroom should be supplied with every-

What the Experts Say

A Space for Art

We value space because of its power to organize, promote pleasant relationships between people of different ages, create a handsome environment, provide changes, promote choices and activity, and its potential for sparking all kinds of social, affective and cognitive learning.
Lella Gandini (in Edwards et al., 1992, p. 148)

A site for art needs to encompass bold energetic expression and studied, time-consuming precision, solitary work and social kibitzing.
Jim Greenman (1988, p. 162)

An "art period" which is fixed and immovable rarely allows sufficient time for really creative work to develop. A creative act cannot be bound by time.
Charles Silberman (1973, p. 769)

thing needed to teach a high-level art program. Sometimes, however, funding is limited, and teachers must make choices. Always purchase the highest quality tools even if that means buying less expensive consumable supplies at first. Well-made scissors, sturdy brushes, and durable clay tools will provide years of service even under heavy use. During the initial tool-purchasing period it is possible to make do with a minimum supply of purchased paper and paint supplemented by found materials such as corrugated cardboard and grocery bag paper.

When a classroom is well supplied with tools, purchase higher quality paints, paper, and clay. Basic supplies that have a wide range of uses should always be purchased first, followed by the more exciting but often less flexible specialty supplies such as fluorescent paper and precut mounts. At a Glance 8.2 provides a sample listing of basic tools and supplies needed for an elementary classroom of twenty-four.

Safety

It is the teacher who is ultimately responsible for maintaining a secure and safe environment in which students can create. Students who are provided with safe art materials, a hazard-free workspace, and well-defined limits on how they may use tools and materials have the freedom to explore, experiment, and create with confidence. This is a challenging task that requires each teacher to make knowledgeable decisions about how art activities are organized and carried out in the classroom. All teachers must be aware of the risk factors for their students, the content of art materials offered, and the ways to foster safe behavior in the classroom. Children are more at risk from hazardous

At a Glance 8.2

Basic Tools and Supplies for an Effective Art Program for a Class of 24

Art Supply	Quantity
First-Year Purchases: Nonconsumable	
Brayers	
Foam	6
Semi-soft rubber	3
Brushes	
Flat easel brushes (best quality)	12 each—1/2″ and 1″
Round easel brushes (best quality)	12 each size 1, 4, 8
Watercolor rounds	12 each size 4 and 8
Easels	
Primary double-sided easel	At primary at least two
Floor or table easels	At upper levels at least two
Hole punch	
One hole	6 pair
Three hole	1
Needles	
Large eye 3″ plastic	2 doz.
Large eye 6″ plastic	2 doz.
Large sewing needles	2 doz.
Paper cutter	Share one with several classes
Reproductions	
Large prints of major works	At least 10
Scissors	
Round for primary, pointed for upper grades (best quality)	30 pairs
Teachers shears	1 pair
Utility snips	1 pair
Staplers	
Desk stapler	1
Handgrip stapler	4
First-Year Purchases: Consumable	
Basket reed	
Size 2	1 lb.
Size 4	1 lb.
Chalk	
Colored drawing chalk	12 boxes of 24 colors
Charcoal	
12 stick boxes	1 box
Charcoal pencils	30
White charcoal pencils	30
Chenille stems (pipe cleaners)	2 boxes of 1000
Colored pencils	
12 color sets	12 sets (optional)
Crayons	
24 color boxes	24 boxes (optional)
Multicultural sets	12 boxes

Art Supply	Quantity
Clay/modeling compounds	
Nonhardening modeling clay	10 pounds
Glue	
Washable school glue	12 4-oz. bottles
Washable school glue	1 gallon
Markers, waterbase	
12 color sets, wide tip	12 sets (optional)
12 color sets, thin tip	12 sets (optional)
Paint	
Watercolors	12 half-pan sets of 8 colors
Tempera paint	8 quarts—red, yellow, blue, green brown, black, and 2 white
Paper	
White drawing, 12″ by 18″	1 ream
White drawing, 24″ by 36″	1 pkg.
Construction paper, 12″ by 18″	8 pkg. of 100 sheets 1 each—red, blue, green, orange, yellow, violet, black, and brown
Manila paper, 12″ by 18″	1 ream
Tan Kraft roll	36″ by 60′
White tag, 12″ by 18″	1 pkg. of 100 sheets
Newsboard, 12″ by 18″	1 pkg. of 24 sheets
Papier maché paste	
Art paste, 2-oz. box	3 boxes
Pens and ink	
Calligraphy markers, waterbase	10 (optional)
India ink, upper grades	12 bottles (optional)
Calligraphy pen holders	24
Calligraphy C-3 pen points (both upper grade)	1 doz. box
Yarn	
8-oz. cones of assorted fibers	6 cones
Crochet cotton or warp	1 cone

Subsequent Years

- Replace any consumable supplies used.
- Buy refills for watercolors, chalk, and glue bottles.
- Replace any nonconsumables that have been lost or damaged.
- At all levels add: specialty papers (metallic, fluorescent, colored tissue, art mounts, graph paper, charcoal papers); more variety of markers; fluorescent crayons; gold and silver tempera paint, more weaving supplies; craft sticks; dowels; beads, burlap, muslin, texture screens; paper-making supplies; varieties of drawing pencils; stencil and bamboo brushes and any other specialty items desired.
- At the primary levels add: finger paint and paper, bulky yarn
- At the upper levels add washable acrylic paint, oil pastels, regular pastels, plaster, other modeling compounds, drawing and lettering pens, colored inks, safe fabric dyes, and other supplies for particular art forms that relate to the units taught.
- Every year try to purchase several prints and art books, as well as art games, computer graphics programs, and videos.

art materials and activities than are adults because of the following factors:

- *Metabolism:* Children are growing and have a higher rate of metabolism than do adults. This means that toxic materials can be absorbed more quickly into their bodies.
- *Body size:* Because children are smaller than adults, the same amount of a hazardous material will be more concentrated in a child's body.
- *Muscular control:* Children do not have the same muscular coordination or physical strength as do adults. Scissors and cutting tools, for example, may be harder for them to control.
- *Behavior:* The creative explorations of developing artists often put them at risk. Children are more likely to put enticing art materials in their mouth, to chew on paint-smeared fingers, or to sniff harmful odors than are more experienced and wary adults. Children may explore new, unpredictable, and unsafe ways to use tools and materials.
- *Health status:* Each student has a unique health background of which the teacher may or may not be aware. Children who suffer from asthma, for example, may be harmed by dusts created in plaster and clay work. Solvents used in certain art activities may cause epileptic attacks in some children. Other students may be allergic to certain art materials. Children who have had previous exposure to toxins such as lead will be more adversely affected by exposure to the same toxin than will other students.
- *Environment:* How well the classroom environment is maintained will also affect the risk to the students. Dusts and toxins that are allowed to build up on work surfaces over time increase the risk of casual contamination of clothing and skin. Lack of adequate ventilation increases the inhalation of airborne substances. Containers of materials requiring special care in handling need to be clearly labeled and stored in safe locations. Provide rubber gloves, dust filtration masks, and aprons in the location where children will use risky materials.

Choosing Safe Art Materials

Although there are no legally mandated standards or labeling required for art materials, the following guidelines can be used in selecting art supplies for use in the classroom:

Read the label. Many art supply manufacturers participate in the Art and Craft Materials Institute's voluntary labeling program. Products certified to contain insufficient quantities of toxic or injurious ingredients or that are unlikely to cause acute or chronic health problems are given the AP or CP seal. Also look for warning labels such as "Keep out of reach of children," "Flammable: Avoid breathing vapors," "Do not take internally," or "Use in a well-ventilated area." Avoid these products entirely in the elementary classroom.

Teacher Tip

Keeping Children Safe: An Example: Chalk

Identify the problem. Primary students often blow on their chalk pictures to remove the excess pigment. They and others can then inadvertently inhale the airborne dust.

Clearly state the safety rule. When first introducing chalk drawing, instruct students not to blow on their drawings.

Model safe behavior. To ensure safe use demonstrate how to apply the chalk so excessive build-up does not result and how to gently tap off excess pigment into a waste receptacle away from the other students, if it should become necessary.

Reinforce. Commend students when they follow the safety rule.

Correct and repeat. Instantly correct students who use a supply unsafely, and outline and present again the safe procedure.

Model the expected behavior. It is often effective to have students who have not followed the safety instructions physically act out what they should have done or tell or read the safety instructions aloud.

Read the manufacturer's specifications. Most schools are required to have on file the manufacturer's Materials Data Safety Sheet for every product used in the building. This sheet comprehensibly lists the ingredients and health effects for the material. If these sheets are not in the school, consult the school safety officer or write directly to the manufacturer requesting the sheet.

Choose age-appropriate art supplies. Many products are labeled for use by specific ages. When working with mixed age groups select the art materials based on the age of the youngest in the group. Choose art materials designed to be used by school students, not adult artists. Adult art materials often contain more hazardous ingredients.

Avoid old art supplies. It is not unusual to find or be given art supplies that are many years old. What materials are considered dangerous to use has changed as we have learned more about the deleterious effects of different chemicals in our environment. Old powdered paints may contain pigments with heavy metals not found in new products. Old clay may be contaminated with asbestos. It is always wiser to discard any supply that is old or has unknown ingredients even if it looks usable.

Establish safe guidelines for use. Even though an art material may meet all the safety standards, it may not be safe when used in particular ways by the students. It is important to select supplies and tools

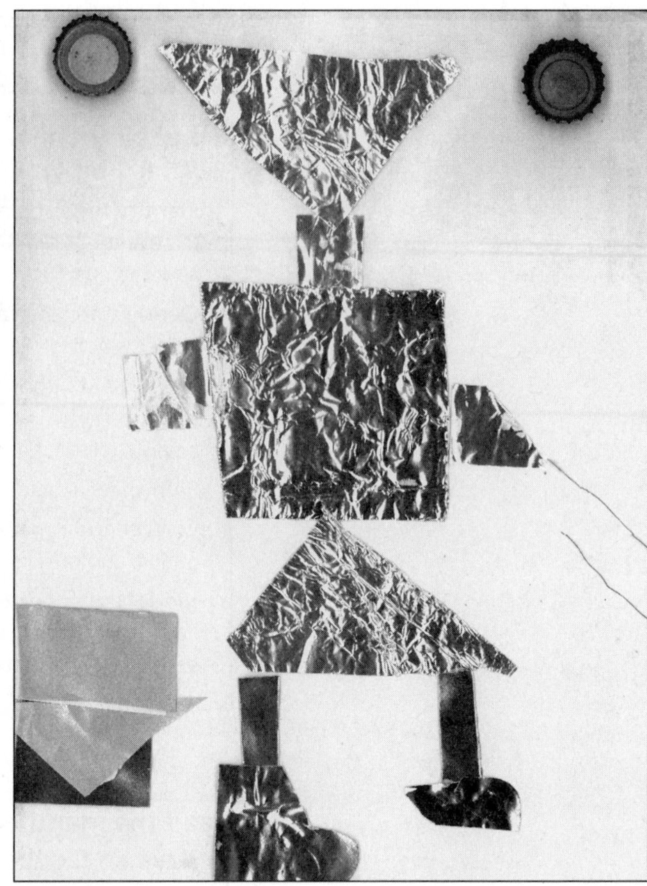

At the Collage Center.

"Animal."
Collage—Kelsey, grade 1 (*left*).

"Alien."
Collage—Robert, grade 1 (*right*).

Thinking about Children's Art

These first graders have chosen cloth, yarn, newspaper, foil, wire, bottle caps, and egg carton pieces from the collage center to use in creating their artwork. Are these appropriate materials for children to use in creating art? How do the materials we offer children influence the art they make? Can you find examples of artists who have used similar found materials in their artworks? How are the art materials offered to children similar to or different from those used by professional artists? Which materials do you think should be available in an elementary classroom?

that match the age and physical development of the students and to then provide detailed instruction on how to use the materials safely. Clearly outline and enforce limits.

Use safe alternatives. Many art materials and techniques used by professional artists are unsafe for school students. There are often alternative art methods or materials that may be safer to use with novice artists. At a Glance 8.3 provides a listing of alternative methods and materials. Other substitutes can be found in the books on art safety listed in "Teacher Resources" at the end of the chapter.

At a Glance 8.3

General Safety Guidelines

Hazardous Materials and Methods	Safer Alternatives
Solvent-Based Products	**Water-Based Products (Washable)**
Oil paint	Watercolors
Varnish	Tempera paint
Paint thinner	Washable acrylics
Turpentine	
Rubber cement	
Rubber cement thinner	White and gel glues
Epoxy	Craft glues ("tacky")
Model airplane glue	
Permanent markers	Water-based markers
Aerosol Sprays	**Nonaerosols**
Charcoal/chalk fixative	Cover chalk drawings with paper and rub off extra dust.
Spray glue	Liquid white and gel glues
Spray paint	Rub paint through screen or sponge paint
Toxic Pigments: Lead and Heavy Metals	
Artist-quality oil, watercolor, and acrylic paints	Student watercolors and water soluble acrylics
Artist-quality pastels	Student pastels
Glazes for firing clay	Lead-free glazes and englobes
Copper enameling	Other jewelry methods
Stained glass	Painting on glass, tissue, and paper
Dusts	
Firing clay	Use only premixed moist clay; wipe down all surfaces and damp mop after each use; or use outside.
Glazes	Wear mask if mixing dry powders, or use liquid glazes.
	Do not allow students to handle unfired glazed pieces unnecessarily.
Plaster	Wear mask and rubber gloves when mixing.
Powdered tempera paint	Wear mask when mixing, or use liquid paint. Do not allow students to use in powdered form.
Fabric dyes	Use only certified nontoxic dyes, natural dyes, and food-quality dyes such as soft drink mixes.
Fumes and Toxic Gases	
Waxes	Melt over hot water, not directly on heat. Never let it get so hot it smokes.
Plastics	Do not melt.
Bacterial Contamination	
Reused food containers (egg cartons, meat trays, etc.)	Rinse containers and their lids in hot soapy water. Soak one minute in a disinfectant solution of $^3/_4$ cup of chlorine bleach per gallon of water. Rinse again to remove the bleach solution.

Why . . . ?

WHY PROMOTE SAFE BEHAVIOR?

No matter how carefully teachers select art materials, children can also behave in ways that compromise their safety. Primary children run with scissors, poke their neighbor with their pencils, and push each other in line. In the upper grades one child may draw on another's paper for spite or throw wads of clay around the room. It is important to establish safe, respectful behavior by firmly establishing guidelines on how students move and work in the classroom. Early class meetings must focus not on learning new art concepts and techniques but on establishing the atmosphere in which art can be created safely.

Establish class rules. It is best if students can participate in creating the rules they will have to follow. Ask the students in what kind of place do they want to create art. Make a list of their ideas. Ask if they have ever been hurt or had something bad happen to them when they were creating art, or tell a story about an accident that happened. Explain why it is important to have guidelines in place so that they can have the kind of place they described in the first list and so that they can work safely. Together develop a simple list of general rules for creating art. Post the rules in a highly visible location and refer to them the instant a student transgresses.

Adjust and adapt the rules. After the class has written the basic rules, show how each individual activity and material fits into these particular rules. As part of the process of instruction, make sure to point out how the students are to use the materials and behave in the context of the class rules. If, for example, one of the rules is to use art materials safely, then as a new art material is introduced it is important to tell the students exactly how to use it safely. If necessary, have the students model safe use or proper behavior. They can, for example, practice holding the scissors safely and walking slowly around the room with them or use the guided discovery method described in Chapter 6.

Repeat and reinforce the rules. When the rules have been established, it is essential to watch students closely and quickly correct unsafe or inappropriate behavior. Do not wait until there is flagrant misbehavior; react to the small misbehaviors of daily classroom life before they become major infractions—the girl playfully poking her friend with the pencil, the boy holding the scissors incorrectly, the group making fun of one another's drawings. Upon observing such behavior, stop the class. Have the student read or say the rule that applies or explain why the behavior was unsafe or inappropriate, and then have the same student demonstrate the proper behavior—using a pencil to draw, holding the scissors with the hand around the closed blades, complimenting one another's drawings.

Establish reasonable consequences. With the class determine what compensatory behavior should follow infractions of the class rules. Emphasize that the consequence should match the behavior. If someone spills something, for example, creating an unsafe condition, the logical consequence should be to clean it up. A student who is bothering others so they cannot listen or work should move to a location away from them.

Respond positively. It is easy to fall into the trap of seeing only the misbehaviors. It is equally important to recognize when students are performing properly. Statements addressed to the whole class rather than to an individual and that specifically describe an observed positive behavior will often instantly improve everyone's behavior. Constantly make affirming descriptive statements such as, "I see many of you carrying the scissors safely," "I noticed you remembered to wash the brushes when you returned them," and "I see that the materials in the collage center have been sorted and put away." These kinds of positive statements repeat and reinforce the expected behaviors far better than a litany of misbehaviors ever can (see At a Glance 8.4).

At a Glance 8.4

Establishing Safe Behavior

Ruth Sidney Charney (1992) suggests the following ways to maintain order and respect in the classroom:

1. Establish a safety signal, such as ringing a bell or holding up one's arm. At the signal everyone must freeze until given permission to "melt." Practice using the signal until compliance is automatic. Use this signal to draw attention to a dangerous situation.
2. Establish a "circling up" procedure. At the signal or command to come to the meeting place students should drop what they are doing and move quickly and quietly to their places on the rug or in the circle. They should practice until they can do this with ease.
3. Reinforce positive behaviors by saying, "I notice that you are . . ." or "I see you have remembered that . . ."
4. Remind students of expected behaviors by saying, "Remind me, what should we do now?" or "Who remembers what we do when . . . ?"
5. Redirect students who are making unwise choices by describing what the better choice might be or by asking the child to make a better choice: "I see you carrying your scissors point up. What is a safer way to carry it? Show me."

In the Classroom

MAKING TIME FOR ART

The room is ready. The carefully selected art supplies are beautifully displayed. Now it is time for art. There are many ways to schedule lessons about art into the school day depending on the needs of the students or the material being studied. The following three approaches, used alone or in combination, are all effective ways to include lessons about the media, methods, and concepts of art into the flow of the school day.

The Mini-Art Lesson

The key word in mini-art lesson is *mini.* Mini-lessons are brief, direct instruction on one specific skill or concept delivered to a whole class, a small group, or an individual child. Too often teachers try to teach too much in one lesson. Students become confused or are unable to use all the ideas at once and so forget most of them. Limiting a mini-lesson to one concept or skill emphasizes to students the importance of what is being taught while providing a clear model for them to follow.

The mini-art lesson is not a formal lesson. Rather it is a brief introduction to or reteaching of a specific skill or technique delivered at the time that students need it. The lesson should last no more than five to ten minutes. It should consist of a brief statement of purpose, a quick student activity for either pairs or cooperative teams, and then a few minutes to practice the task and share it with the group.

The mini-art lesson is an extremely flexible format that builds on the power of teaching students when they are most motivated to learn. Mini-lessons should grow directly out of the students' needs. Many times they will be impromptu as when a teacher notes a specific need. In language arts instruction a teacher might notice that some students have forgotten how to punctuate a direct quotation and would then give a mini-lesson on how to use quotation marks. In art the teacher might notice that some students are having trouble showing people in action in their drawings and would then give a mini-lesson on how the arms and legs bend when people run and jump.

The mini-lesson format should not be used as an introduction to a topic or skill. Rather it should address immediate needs of the students at the time of need. The lesson should be something students can instantly put into practice. The mini-lesson format is the ideal way to accomplish any of the following:

- Demonstrate a specific technique or process, such as how to attach a handle to a clay mug.
- Model safe ways to use a material or tool, such as the correct way to carry a scissors.
- Provide instructions on workshop management, such as role playing what to do when a student is ready to sign up for a teacher conference.

- Model conferencing and sharing techniques, such as how to ask a peer to help with revision.
- Explore or practice using a new medium under close guidance.
- Rehearse problem-solving strategies, such as what to do if too much glue is used.
- Identify a quality in a piece of artwork that is similar to one they have incorporated into their own work.

Mini-art lessons can be taught to the whole class, a small group, or an individual student. They can be carefully planned or given at the spur of the moment. Mini-art lessons could be taught in all the following situations:

Planned/whole class. The teacher wants to relate a particular art medium or method to other studies.

For example, a third grade class has been reading the book *The Chalk Box Kid* by Clyde Bulla (1981, New York: Turtleback). The teacher gives a mini-art lesson introducing safe ways to use chalk and gives students twenty minutes to explore how chalk works on different colors and textures of paper. The class then comes together to share what they have learned.

Planned/small group. The teacher has a small group that is ready for special instructions and/or the teacher wants to use peer teaching to facilitate the use of a medium or technique.

For example, five fourth graders are the first to have finished their Navajo-inspired weavings and are ready to take them off their cardboard looms. The teacher calls these students together and demonstrates how to cut and knot the ends. These students are then designated "knot experts" and will help others in the class as they finish.

Planned/individual. The teacher knows or discovers a special method or technique that will help a particular student and takes time to share it with the student.

For example, a second grader is working on a project about fossils. The teacher shows the student how to make rubbings of the class fossil collection. The student decides to use the technique to create the cover of the report.

Unplanned/whole class. The teacher notices that many or all of the students in the class have the same need or are having the same problem.

For example, in a first-grade class the teacher notices that many children are handling scissors unsafely and need to be retaught. The teacher calls the class to attention and gives a mini-lesson on how to walk with and pass scissors safely, with children modeling the safe behaviors.

Unplanned/small group. The teacher notices that several students have the same need or problem.

For example, in a fifth-grade class the teacher notices that several students are having trouble drawing houses three-dimensionally in their illustrations for books they have written. The teacher gathers the group together and demonstrates several different ways to show buildings in perspective using a box and Cox's negotiated drawing method.

Unplanned/individual. The teacher observes a student with a particular need or problem.

For example, in a fourth-grade class the teacher notices a student who is trying to draw a glass of water as part of a science observation. Stopping by the student, the teacher points out features of the glass and demonstrates how to show the top of the glass and the water using an ellipse rather than a circle.

The Specialized Art Center

Throughout the school year the basic art centers (drawing, painting, modeling, collage) can be supplemented with specialized centers that relate to a thematic unit, featured artwork unit, projects, or a book or topic being studied. The specialized art center can focus on a specific art medium, artwork, or art concept. This kind of center can be set up to be used in combination with learning centers in other subject areas, or it can function as part of an art or writing/art workshop, detailed as follows.

What students do at a center will vary depending on the learning intended.

Exploration center. The purpose of this center is to allow students to discover the potentials of a new medium or method rather than to create a finished work. Invite students to try out a new way of working and record what they have learned on a chart or graph or in their journal. Exploration centers might ask students to experiment, to try out ideas, to make many samples. The key question at such a center is, "How many ways can you . . . ?"

For example, as part of a first-grade study of texture students could experiment with adding a variety of textured substances, such as sand, sawdust, and flour, to paint. In fifth grade, students could explore how many different types of lines they can make using pen and ink. More ideas for exploration centers can be found in Chapters 11 and 12.

Students can share the results of their explorations in many ways. They can place small samples on graphs and charts or glue them into

Teaching in Action

A Mini-Lesson

Lesson begins when teacher approaches a table where several students are painting and notices that the colors the students are mixing are being muddied because the students are not rinsing their brushes properly.

Teacher:	Can each of you point out a color you mixed using just two colors? [*Students each point and name a color.*]
Teacher:	Are you sure you used just two colors? Do you see a way a third color might accidentally get mixed into your paint?
Student:	Sometimes if the brush isn't clean the colors get mixed . . . like here where I smeared some red in my sky.
Teacher:	I suggest you try rinsing your brush like this. [*demonstrates*] Why don't each of you try mixing a color on your newspaper? [*Students each mix a color.*]
Teacher:	Do you see a difference in the color you mixed?
Responses:	It's much brighter. It looks clean. There are no smears.

their journals. Teachers can ask students to explain what they discovered to a small group or to the whole class.

Concept center. The purpose of this center is to help students develop an art vocabulary and to provide practice identifying and using the art elements and principles of design. In an art element center the teacher might ask second graders to find examples of patterns in the classroom and add them to a chart or explore different ways to create patterns using printmaking techniques. A center on the design principle of balance might ask students to look at several examples of balanced artworks and create their own balanced artwork. More ideas for concept centers will be found in Chapter 11.

Concept centers are best when they are part of a featured artwork unit or follow a mini-art lesson on the particular concept. Students can share the work resulting at the center with a peer partner or the whole class.

Responding to art center. The purpose of a responding center is to provide more opportunities for students to look at and respond to artwork. The work featured at such a center should be related to thematic unit, project topic, or featured artwork unit or could review works studied previously. At this center teachers could ask students to look at an artwork and describe it, write a poem about it, analyze it, or try to identify it. This is also a good place for the postcard print sorting activities and art games described in Chapter 5.

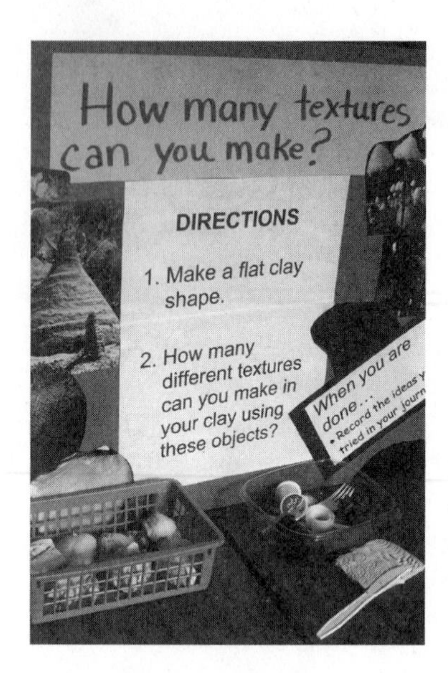

Specialized Art Center: Exploring Texture.

Thinking about Children's Art

At this center students are encouraged to explore making textures by impressing objects into modeling clay shapes. Students are asked to record their ideas in their journals. What other ways could students record and share what they discover at this kind of center? How could the resulting work be tied in with studies in mathematics and science?

Thematic art center. This art center is directly related to the thematic unit being undertaken by a class and may involve using unique art media and techniques. If the theme is "It's a mystery," students might be asked to identify the art materials used in a variety of samples. A class studying "In the news" might create two- and three-dimensional artworks using newspaper. Other media centers can be added in conjunction with the study of a specific topic. When studying the people of Guatemala, students could help set up a weaving center.

Planning specialized art centers. Like basic art centers, specialized art centers should be aesthetically arranged with related books, artwork, photographs, technical information, and related sensory objects as well as the materials to be used and the directions for how to use them. The center itself may be as simple as a folded display board or file folder and supplies arranged in baskets to be taken and, depending on the art activity, used at the work tables, at student desks, or elsewhere in the room. More involved centers may be designed to seat two to four students who work together on the activity right at the center area.

Teachers often use this method when art centers operate in combination with learning centers in other subjects, such as a math center at which students use math manipulates to solve a problem, a social studies center that asks students to research the answer to a question, a writing center that provides materials for writing letters to the newspaper on a topic of concern, a listening center where students can play an audiotape of a book they are reading, a computer center where - students try to solve a computer program game, and a science center where students observe a nature object and record their observation on a chart.

Centers such as these can be adapted for use at all grade levels and can be used instead of or in addition to seat work. Meanwhile the teacher works closely with a group of students, such as when small group reading instruction is in progress. When using this learning center approach, it is helpful to schedule students to visit the different subject centers, as well as the specialized art center, on a rotational basis over the week so that all students get a chance to do every activity.

Art center guidelines. There are many things to consider in designing effective art centers:

- *Make sure it is complete.* Everything the student needs for the activity should be at the center or in the student's desk.
- *Keep activities open ended.* It is important to remember that all centers should encourage creative processing.
- *Avoid busywork.* Classroom time is too valuable to waste. Design center activities to help students grow as artistic thinkers.

Teacher Tip

Constructing Art Centers

An easy way to create an art center is to use an attractively decorated file folder with the directions written on the inside. Stand the file folder up along with the needed supplies and related display materials. When not in use, centers can then be easily folded up and stored in a file cabinet or box.

- *Build in self-checking.* Try to give students the responsibility for tracking what they have done at a center. Have them fill out a self-evaluation form, make a journal entry, or check themselves off a checklist. Provide answer keys to art puzzles and identification activities. Artworks can be added to a student's process folio.

Starting out. "Learning centers," says Greta Rasmussen, "should be staging areas for students to escape from some of the necessary school rigidity into areas of meaningful mental and physical play" (1980, p. 2). Be careful to keep activities open ended. Because students will be working independently, there is a strong tendency to keep the activity very controlled. Having students trace, cut out, and decorate patterns, however, or follow step-by-step directions, is not a creative art activity and should not be used at a center. Instead design the center around a question or problem that has many different answers.

To help students work independently take time to introduce the center and the expected behaviors carefully at the same time that interest and motivation are created. Open the center with great fanfare. Excite the children's curiosity by covering up the center and making a show of slowly uncovering it or store all the materials out of sight in a decorated box or unusual container and together with the students draw out the materials and set up the center. Allow ideas for centers to develop from the children and their interests.

The Art/Writing Workshop Approach

Children need to use the language of art every day, not just once a week. One way to do this is to incorporate art into other class activities through the art/writing workshop approach. This instructional format provides one way to combine the effective teaching methods described in previous chapters with the kind of integrated curriculum approaches presented in Chapter 2. Even more importantly this class structure will also allow the creative and artistic processes to flourish.

This approach is modeled on that of the writing workshop. Language arts teachers face problems in teaching writing that are very similar to those faced in art instruction. Writing, like art, is a creative endeavor. It too requires thought and open-ended time.

Teaching in Action

Sample Specialized Art Centers

Exploratory Centers

Grades: 1–2

Key Question: How many textures can you make?

Supplies: Nonhardening modeling clay, assorted tools and objects to press in the clay (acorns, beads, keys, paper clips, etc.)

Directions:

Make a flat piece of clay.

Use these things to make textures in your clay.

Grades: 3–6

Key Question: What happens when you add different amounts of water to tempera paint?

Supplies: One color of tempera paint, water cups, medium-sized brushes, eye droppers, mixing tray (paper plate), newspaper, white paper to paint on

Directions:

Put a small amount of paint on your plate.

Add a drop of water. What happens?

Try using the paint.

Add more water. Compare the paint/water mixtures.

What did you learn? In your journal record the results of your experiment and list ways you might use the different paint mixtures in your art.

If you have time, use different mixtures of paint and water to make a painting.

Concept Center

Grades: 1–3

Key Question: How many different kinds of lines can you make?

Supplies: Markers, 9″ by 12″ paper on which are ruled squares 3″ by 3″, scissors

Directions:

Fill up each square with only one kind of line.

Cut apart your squares and place them on the class line graph.

Grades 4–6

Key Question: How can you get people to look at a certain part of an artwork?

Supplies: Small pieces of colored paper or paper scraps, scissors, glue, background paper

Directions:

Cut out five different shapes in colors of your choice.

Move them around on the background until you think you have created a focal point.

Show your idea to at least five classmates. Ask them what shape they see first and record their answers in your journal.

Responding to Art Center

Grade 1–3 (Pairs)

Change your arrangement until everyone agrees. Then glue down the shapes.

In your journal write down what you learned about creating a focal point.

Key Question: What do you see in this picture?

Supplies: Several medium-sized reproductions

Directions:

Take turns.

Look closely at one of the paintings.

Give the painting to your partner.

Tell your partner everything you saw.

Check off each painting you do.

Grades 4–6

Key Question: How many styles of art can you identify?

Supplies: A five-minute egg timer; twenty postcard-sized prints with matching cards on which are written the names of different art styles already studied such as Impressionism, Realism, Expressionism, Pointillism

Directions:

Spread the cards face up in front of you.

Turn over the timer.

How many pairs can you make before the time runs out?

Check your pairs. Correct pairs have matching symbols on back.

Select one of the styles and write in your journal what you like about it.

Grade 4–6

Key Question: Can you identify the subject of a painting?

Supplies: A catalog of art reproductions such as the one from the National Gallery

Directions:

Look through the catalog.

In your journal list the landscapes, portraits, and still lifes you find.

Thematic Center

Grade 3

Theme: World of Invention

Key Question: Can you invent a new tool for painting?

Supplies: An assortment of sticks, chenille stems, cloth, cardboard, yarn, foam pieces, etc., masking tape, one color of tempera paint, small pieces of paper

Directions:

Create a new tool for painting.

Try it out.

Draw a diagram and describe your new tool in your journal.

Add your tool to the paint center for others to try.

Teaching in Action

Center Time

Centers are an excellent way to provide time for children to explore and practice using an art medium or method, especially when the center relates to the children's interests or studies. Greta Rasmussen (1980) makes the following suggestions for creating successful centers:

- Enable all students to use the centers. They should not just be for students who have finished their work.
- Schedule every student so that each one has equal time at all centers.
- Choose a length of time for center activities and stick with it. Center time usually ranges from twenty to thirty minutes. Use a kitchen timer to keep everyone on schedule.
- Keep the centers homemade. Avoid the use of purchased worksheets. Teacher-made centers will more accurately reflect what the class is studying.

The workshop approach has been shown to be an effective way to develop children's writing skills. This is because the essential components of the writing workshop are built upon the way children learn. Workshop participants have sufficient time to think and practice new skills. Because it allows students to make choices, they become more motivated to learn. Workshop time also provides many opportunities for students to respond to their learning in a wide variety of ways, while permitting teachers to respond more often and more directly to the students' work.

A workshop approach encompasses all of the following:

- Sensory and kinesthetic experiences
- Cooperative art activities
- Time to explore and use a variety of media
- Time to use the artistic process
- Conferencing and sharing time
- Looking at art
- Thinking, discussing, and writing about art, such as in journals

Instead of being a separate subject requiring extra time in an already full school day, the integrated art/writing workshop helps children express their ideas through both languages. Journals can contain words and pictures. Mini-lessons may focus on grammatical constructions or the use of line in illustrations. An engaging experience may inspire some children to write a response and others to paint one. Classroom teachers who integrate art into their writing programs will find that both programs benefit. Janet Olson (1992),

At a Glance 8.5

The Art/Writing Workshop: A Suggested Cycle

Time: Approximately forty minutes to one hour. This cycle will repeat every five days.

Shared Experience Day 1	Workshop Day 2 to 4	Assessment Day 5
Whole group lesson	Community Circle	Sharing
Team activity or Discussion or Field trip	Independent Work Time Mini-lessons Conferencing	Criteria-based Assignment
Journal Entry	Journal Entry	Self-Assessment

for example, has found that visually oriented students wrote better when they could draw their ideas first, and students who used linguistic approaches created more detailed art when they could write their ideas down and then draw them.

The Art/Writing Workshop in Action

A workshop approach allows all the different parts of the artistic process to be put into practice. The amount of time allotted to workshop will determine how often and in what combination to use the strategies. At a Glance 8.6 shows how to address all the strategies using a five-day cycle of one-and-a-half-hour workshop sessions. Over the five-day cycle students will be looking at art, discussing art, creating art, and evaluating their art at the same time that they are reading and writing. They will also use their developing skills to solve specified artistic problems. The focus of the week's workshop can develop from a thematic unit, a featured artwork unit, or a project approach topic.

- *Whole group lesson:* On Day 1 the group lesson will set the tone for the cycle and may take most of the period. This is the time to present a featured artwork, read a book or poem, or go on a field trip such as a nature walk. Displays in the room should reflect the topic of the experience and related literature and artworks.
- *Community circle:* Following the shared experience, passing a question around the community circle provides a way to refocus the group on following days. The question to ask should be based on the group lesson. It is also beneficial while the students are still in the circle to have students explain their plans for independent

Me
Tap
Tap
2-6
I cen tapdans in
my mom's shos.

Journal Page.
Crayon and pencil—Loren, grade 1.

Thinking about Children's Art

In the primary grades art naturally complements the writing. At this level student journals should be designed so that there is a space for drawing with lines below for writing. In what ways can combined art-writing journals be incorporated into a child's daily learning activities beyond writing workshop?

work time. For example, the opening question might be, "Yesterday we looked at Van Gogh's *Starry Night.* Can you describe a night sky you have seen?" After going around the circle, ask, "What are you working on today?" As the students answer, they can leave the circle and begin work. This creates an orderly transition to independent work time and prevents congestion in the supply areas.

- *Independent work time:* This is when the students will work on reading, writing, and artwork of their choice. If they will be working on an artwork, they will select their art media from one of the four basic media centers or any specialized art center that is available. Also during this time peer and teacher conferences will be held.
- *Mini-lessons:* Mini-lessons delivered on following days will focus on skills and concepts drawn from the initial lesson and the needs of the students. During independent work time the teacher may give short five- to ten-minute reading, writing, or art lessons to individuals, small groups, or the whole class as needed.
- *Journal entry:* Each day students should be given a short, uninterrupted, silent time to write and draw in their journals. They can use this opportunity to describe their plans or what they have accomplished, or respond to the shared experience.

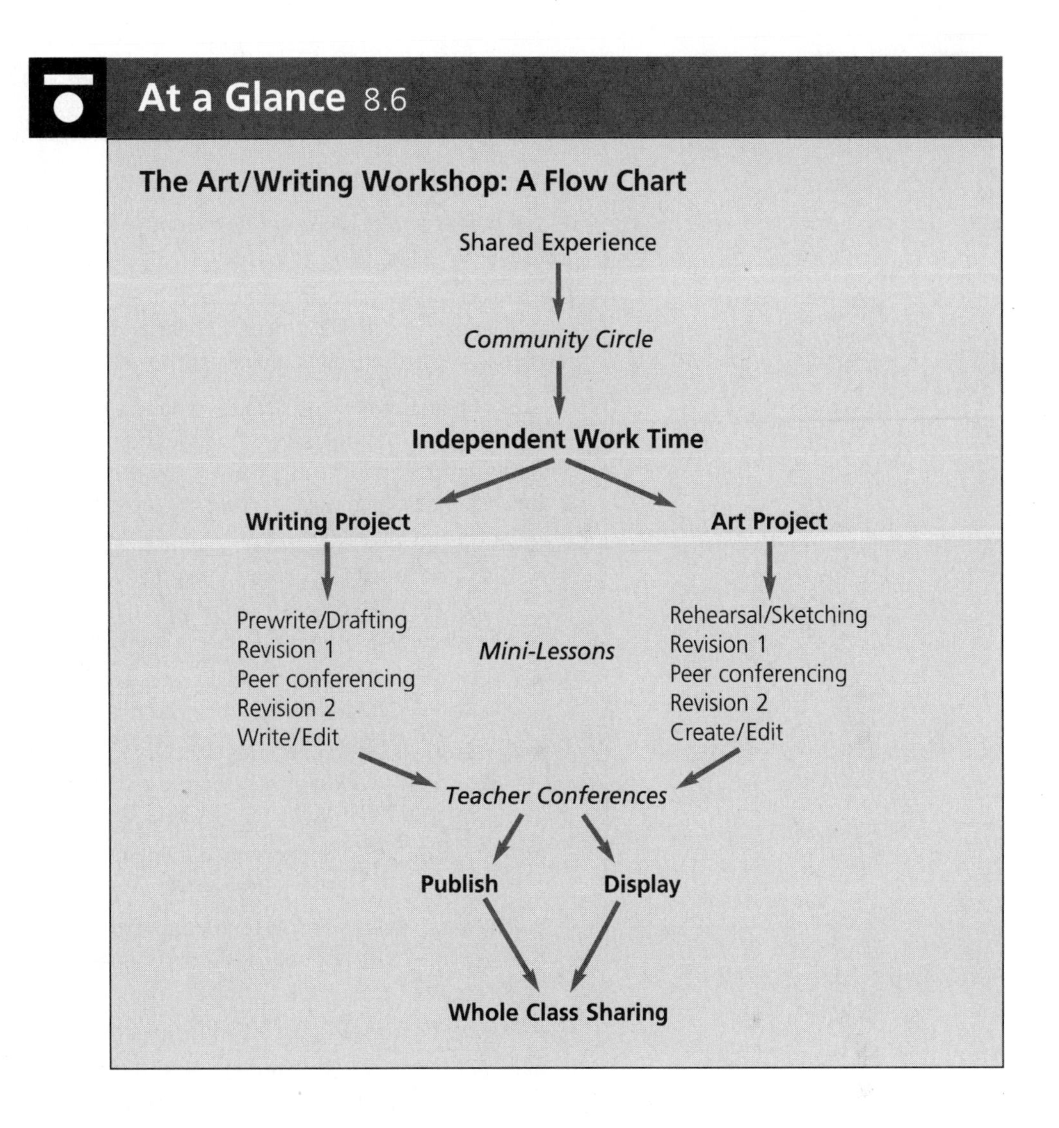

- *Sharing:* On Day 5 of the cycle students will have the opportunity to share what they have done. This can be open to the whole group, or students can take turns depending on the time frame.
- *Criteria-based assignment:* This allows students to solve a problem that is related to the shared experience and community circle activities. A criteria-based assessment for the example about Van Gogh might be to make five or more pictures of a night sky using different media and styles. This might be used as an assessment of skill and concept development and relate to the mini-lessons taught during the cycle as well.
- *Self-assessment:* Self-assessment involves reviewing the work done in the cycle, responding in written or oral form to questions such as, What have I done this cycle? What have I learned? What do I want to work on more?

Teaching in Action

Basic Steps: Art Is a Process

The following activity is one way to introduce the artistic process to students for the first time.

Preparation: Have ready materials for drawing and large signs that name the eight components of the artistic process: rehearsal, sketching, revision 1, peer share, revision 2, production, editing, teacher conference.

1. Explain that all creative activities—writing a story, composing a song, or drawing a picture—go through several changes before they are ready to be shared with others. In art this is called the artistic process. Not everyone thinks through this process in the same way, but everyone goes through the same basic steps.
2. Briefly discuss and demonstrate each step as you hang up the sign.
   - *Rehearsal:* Imagining and planning the work in your mind. (Close your eyes and describe the drawing you will be making. Make sure to include where your idea comes from. *Note:* For primary students you may wish to air draw.)
   - *Sketching:* Making several small pencil sketches that capture your idea in several ways. (Make two or three quick sketches on a small piece of paper.)
   - *Revision 1:* Looking over your sketches and making choices and changes. (Select one of your sketches and resketch it.)
   - *Peer sharing:* Choosing someone to show your sketch. Ask them what they like and what might be changed to improve it. (Select a student and model a peer conference using your sketch.)
   - *Revision 2:* Reconsidering your artwork in light of what your friend mentioned. You may or may not wish to make changes. (Model making a change on your drawing.)
   - *Production:* Creating the artwork. (Enlarge your sketch and add details.)
   - *Editing:* Checking work for neatness and correctable mistakes such as a misplaced line or a fingerprint. (Use an eraser to clean up edges and lines on your drawing.)
   - *Teacher conference:* Sharing your work one-on-one with the teacher. Show students how to sign up for a conference and where it will be held. With the help of a student, model a brief conference. (Have student use your drawing. Ask questions such as, "Where did you get the idea?" "What do you think you did best?" "What will you do differently next time?")
   - *Presentation:* Showing your work to others. (Show students where the mounting area is and how to use it. Discuss display spaces and other ways to share art in the school.)
3. Have students fold a sheet of 12″ by 18″ paper into eight sections. In the first section have them write "The Art Process." In every other box they should write a step and then draw an illustration of it. (Older students may write a description as well.)

Extending the learning: Follow up this lesson with individual classes or mini-lessons that focus on each step. Use role play and modeling to reinforce the steps. Make sure that students know where to carry out the different parts of the process.

Initiating Workshop Time

Workshop time should not start instantly on the first day of school. Rather students should be introduced to the different components slowly over several weeks. Start with shared experiences and community circle (see Chapter 3). Next introduce journaling as a regular class activity. Utilizing the experiences shared in community circle, journals, or questionnaires, students can begin writing their first pieces and planning their first piece of artwork. Some students may decide that artwork created in response to the initial "get-to-know-you" assignments will become the basis for a more complex work. Others may make choices based on personal experiences or curiosity about certain media. The key component of the first project is that students learn that they are responsible for choosing a medium from among those available and must carefully think about the subject of the work and the meaning it will communicate.

During the first few days of workshop the teacher's role is to monitor the students' work, making sure that the students are making effective choices and staying on task. The emphasis should be on students' responsibility in selecting and caring for the art materials and in working diligently on the project they have chosen while following the steps of the artistic process.

This is also the time to establish the sequence of workshop time. Students function better when they have the security of a regular structure. If they know that workshop time always begins with community circle, they will already be mentally prepared to share with the group.

Teaching in Action

Ideas for Art

To get workshop time flowing spend several days at the beginning helping students develop personal resources of ideas for their art. This will provide an invaluable source of art starters for the student.

1. In their journals have students create the following:

   Under the heading FAVORITES create lists of favorite words, colors, art media, artworks, songs, games, animals, places, events, and the like.

   Under the heading THINGS I SEE make lists of what is visible on the wall, inside their desks and lockers, in the school, on the way to school, around their homes, and other places.

   Under the heading FEELINGS make lists of things that make them feel in different ways: things that upset them, things that make them happy, and so on.

2. When students are having trouble deciding on an artwork, have them consult these lists and combine items from several categories.

"The Bridge."
Charcoal—Jennifer, grade 6.

Take my hand,
Hold on tight.
Let's walk together over the
bridge.
Do not watch the water rushing
below.
Look only in my eyes.
We will see beauty together.

Thinking about Children's Art

This elegant sketch was created as part of a study of Chinese landscape paintings. Afterwards the student wrote the accompanying poem. What is the relationship between the art and the writing? How has this student benefited from having the opportunity to create art inspired writing? Why should upper graders participate in writing/art workshop type experiences?

If they know there will always be independent work time, they will not worry if they must leave a work unfinished. When workshop is operating smoothly, it is time to start planning the introduction of new concepts, materials, and skills.

Keeping Students on Track

The driving idea behind the art/workshop approach is for students to move back and forth between art and writing as they express their ideas, choosing the language that best meets their communication needs of the moment with the expectation that they will all do some writing and some art. At the primary level this will come naturally as art and writing feed on each other. At the upper levels there may be some students who seem only to choose art or only to choose writing. If students are avoiding either art or writing because they feel incompetent in one area or the other, then address these issues through teacher conferences, carefully designed mini-lessons, and constant encouragement.

Another way to address this is to require students to use both communication forms in projects that incorporate both, such as creating illustrated books, presentation panels, and advertising campaigns. Another way is to make up individual plans in which students outline how they will combine writing and art in their projects.

Conclusion

DESIGNING A PLACE FOR ART

The environment in which we teach our children matters: it has to be home, resource center, workshop, and gallery all in one, because children are enabled or debilitated by being in it.
Margaret Jackson (1994, p. 9)

How the classroom environment is organized can make a big difference in how our students perceive themselves as artists. When art is a once-a-week lesson, separated from students' daily pursuits, art will be deemed just a pleasant pastime. But if art is taught in ways that integrate it into all the learning going on in the classroom, then students will become confident artists.

Brief mini-lessons that address how to draw a glass as part of a science lesson or how to create an original book cover design can add the power of art to other areas of learning. Art centers can tie art into topics of concern and interest as well as provide safe, controlled access to art materials whenever students have need of them. Teaching art and writing in a unified workshop combined with mini-lessons and specialized art centers fits particularly well into an integrated curriculum and allows a wide range of effective teaching strategies to be used. During workshop time mini-lessons can be delivered at the right moment and to the students who need them. Teacher conferences can be held while the rest of the students work independently, allowing one-on-one interaction. The power of peer conferencing is facilitated. Most importantly, the workshop format provides independent work time for students. During this time they will develop the ability to use the artistic process as they apply the skills they have been taught—skills that involve not just handling materials successfully, but also responding to and deriving meaning from an artwork.

It is the teacher's task to create an environment in which learning can happen. Planning how time and space will be utilized as well as carefully selecting and organizing art materials will allow students to work independently using the artistic process. Establishing safe, respectful behavior will allow the teacher to concentrate on the creative and artistic development of the students. If teachers also design that environment to engage students aesthetically in ways that ignite their senses, the ressult is a potent combination that can empower our students to use the visual/spatial language of art to extend their communication abilities.

Teacher Resources

REFERENCES

Caine, R. N. & G. (1991). *Making connections.* Alexandria, VA: Association for Supervision and Curriculum.

Charney, R. (1992). *Teaching children to care.* Greenfield, MA: Northeast Foundation for Children.

Davis, J., & Gardner, H. (1993). The arts and early childhood education: A cognitive developmental picture of the young child as artist. In B. Spodek (Ed.), *Handbook of research on the education of young children* (pp. 191–206). Indianapolis, IN: Macmillan.

Edwards, C., Gandini, L., & Forman, G. (1992). *The hundred languages of children: The Reggio Emilia approach to early childhood education.* Norwood, NJ: Ablex.

Greenman, J. (1988). *Caring spaces, learning places.* Redmond, WA: Exchange Press.

Haigh, K. (1997). How the Reggio approach has influenced an inner city program. In J. Hendrick (Ed.), *First steps toward teaching the Reggio way* (pp. 152–166). New York: Merrill.

Jackson, M. (1994). *Creative display and environment.* Portsmouth, NH: Heinemann.

Olson, J. L. (1992). *Envisioning writing: Toward an integration of drawing and writing.* Portsmouth, NH: Heinemann.

Rasmussen, G. (1980). *Is it Friday already? Learning centers that work.* Stanwood, WA: Tin Man.

Schiller, M. (1995). An emergent art curriculum that fosters understanding. *Young Children, 50*(3), 33–38.

Silberman, C. E. (Ed.)(1973). *The open classroom reader.* New York: Random House.

Szekely, G. (1991). *From play to art.* Portsmouth, NH: Heinemann.

Practical Guides

To learn more about writing workshops and to get practical management ideas that can be applied to an art workshop consult the following:

Fiderer, A. (1993). *Teaching writing: A workshop approach.* New York: Scholastic.

Jackson, N. R., & Pillow, P. L. (1992). *The reading writing workshop: Getting started.* New York: Scholastic.

For ideas for creating an ideal environment for teaching art read the following:

Adam, E., & Ward, C. (1982). *Art and the built environment.* White Plains, NY: Longman.

Ernest, K. (1994). *Picturing learning.* Portsmouth, NH: Heinemann.

For ideas for learning centers consult the following:

Ingraham, P. B. (1996). *Creating and managing learning centers: A thematic approach.* Peterborough, NH: Crystal Springs.

Isbell, R. (1995). *The complete learning center book.* Beltsville, MD: Gryphon House.

Waynant, L., & Wilson, R. M. (1974). *Learning centers: A guide for effective use.* Paoli, PA: Instructo.

To acquire more specific information on using art materials safely see the following:

McCann, M. (1985). *Health hazards manual for artists.* New York: Nick Lyons.

Spandorfer, M., Curtis, D., & Snyder, J. (1996). *Making art safely.* New York: Van Nostrand Reinhold

Storage Units, Furniture, and Supply Organizers

Calloway House
451 Richardson Drive
Lancaster, PA 17603-4098
1-800-233-0290
Cardboard storage bins, boxes and dividers, display boards, and storage units for centers

Classroom Direct
Box 830677
Birmingham, AL 35283-0677
www.ClassroomDirect.com
Classroom furniture, cubbies and shelves, storage bins

Creative Educational Surplus
1000 Apollo Road
Egan, MN 55121-2240
www.creativesurplus.com
Inexpensive plastic trays, bins, and bottles

J. L. Hammet
Box 9057
Braintree, MA 02184-9057
1-800-333-4600
Classroom furniture and storage items

Lakeshore Learning
2695 E. Dominguez Street
Box 6261
Carson, CA 90749
www.lakeshorelearning.com
Primary furniture, storage bins, foam seating

NASCO
901 Janesville Avenue
Fort Atkinson, WI 53538-0901
1-800-558-9595
Classroom furniture and storage units

Reliable
Box 1502
Ottawa, IL 61350-9914
1-800-735-4000
Office supply storage units and office furniture

Web Sites

Art material safety information can be obtained directly from the manufacturer or try one of these Web sites:

Center for Safety in the Arts
http://artswire.org

Cornell Center for Materials Research
Cornell University
www.msc.cornell.edu

Interactive Learning Paradigms, Incorporated
Material Data Safety Sheet search engine
www.ilpi.com/msds/index.html

National Institute of Occupational Safety and Health
Pocket Guide to Chemical Hazards
www.cdc.gov/niosh

Vermont SIRI MSPS Archive
University of Vermont
http://siri.uvm.edu/msds

Chapter 9

Artistic Assessment
Process and Progress

Students should know what they are supposed to learn and the criteria by which their achievement will be measured.

Carmen Armstrong (1994, p. 169)

ARTISTS AT WORK

Overheard at an exhibit:

"Did you see that painting over there?"

"Which one?"

"That greenish bluish landscape."

"Oh, yeah."

"That's mine."

"It is?"

"Yep."

"Wow, it looks professional. They must have a really great art program here!"

Introduction

EVALUATION

There is an art critic inside everyone. Every time we look at a work of art, we make an assessment. It may be based on personal likes and dislikes. It may be comparative, based on artworks we have seen elsewhere. Sometimes it is based on specific criteria or needs. As teachers we cannot and must not avoid looking at our students and their work with critical eyes. We cannot prevent ourselves from making judgments, nor can we help students grow as artists without assessing their art. Teachers sometimes have a tendency to draw back from assessing student artwork for fear that it will destroy a student's self-confidence as an artist. But evaluation does not have to be a negative process. Rather it can be a powerful way to help students celebrate what they know and can do. Evaluation can also be important in improving our own teaching and designing an effective art program. In this chapter we will look at a variety of ways that teachers can assess the artistic growth of their students, themselves, and their art program.

Setting the Stage

WHAT SHOULD ART ASSESSMENTS BE LIKE?

Whether it is a prepared assessment or a teacher-created one, it is important that the form of assessment used be the best one for the purpose for which it is intended. Assessments for art should fit a number of criteria.

Allow for creativity. There are many assessment methods that are not suited for art and may even inhibit the growth of novice artists. For example, many traditional testing formats, by design, cause competition among students and provide an external reward: the grade. These conditions have been found to undermine creativity and lower the quality of creative products (Starko, 1995).

Assessments that expect all students to produce a similar product or think in the same way do not work well in art, where diversity in ideas is expected and encouraged. Avoid creating an atmosphere of criticism and competition. Students should be compared only to themselves or to a set standard, not to one another. Assessments should be an integrated part of the creative and artistic processes so that students can grow from them, not fear them.

Be useful to students. Assessments should instruct students in how to evaluate their own work and move them in the direction of self-monitoring. Every assessment should provide feedback that students can understand.

What Do You Think?

Has an artwork you created ever been criticized or graded? How did the process make you feel? Did it make you a better artist? Do you think evaluating artwork is useful?

Match the learning task. Art instruction covers a broad range of skills and concepts. Select assessments that best match the learning that is being evaluated. There is no question that memorizing a piece of information such as blue and yellow make green is very different from having to mix the green of fresh spring grass for a landscape. In assessing students' skills and knowledge use tools that provide as much information as possible about the students' ability to think artistically.

Teacher Tip

The Vocabulary of Assessment

Assessment: Making a judgment about a product or a behavior.

Authentic assessment: An assessment that involves a meaningful, real-life, learning activity. Sometimes called alternative assessment.

Criterion: A standard for evaluating or testing something.

Evaluation: A judgment of worth that is based on a set of criteria.

Goal: The expected changes in behavior or learning that the instructional program will produce.

Objective: The expected change in behavior or learning that will occur following a lesson or activity.

Outcomes: Goals written in terms of what students will be able to do.

Performance Assessment: An assessment that requires students to do something to demonstrate their learning.

Portfolio: A collection of materials that show evidence of what a student learned.

Process: How learning was attained or a product produced.

Processfolio: An unsorted collection of materials in various states of completeness that reflect what the student is in process of learning.

Product: The end result of the learning process.

Rubric: A predetermined set of criteria that will be used to evaluate a product or behavior and that establishes a ranking system.

Standard: An outcome that is believed to be obtainable for all students.

Standardized testing: Assessment that is based on a fixed set of standards independent of actual instruction, often normed on a comparative population.

Systematic sampling: Repeated observations taken at regular intervals.

"Self-Portrait."
Marker and crayon—Margaret, grade 2.

Thinking about Children's Art

This portrait was drawn as part of an autobiography assignment. On what basis should it be assessed? What artistic criteria might the teacher provide for student guidance before beginning this kind of assignment?

Be ongoing and process oriented. Effective assessment is totally integrated into the art program; "it does not jump up, like a jack-in-the-box, at the end of a term or a year" (Wolf & Pistone, 1991, p. 8). It is essential to use a variety of carefully selected assessments throughout the instructional period. Each one should be designed to document the process the student went through in learning to think artistically.

Be flexible, fair, and unbiased. Assessment tools should be easy to use and fair to all students. Check for clarity of language and respect for diversity. Evaluate students in ways that best match their learning style and abilities. For example, use observation and oral responses to evaluate a student who is struggling with reading and writing.

Give the desired level of information. It is important to use an assessment tool that will give the feedback desired. A casual observation of a student having difficulty using a calligraphy pen tells the teacher that the student needs individual assistance but not how well the calligraphy lesson was taught. A test that shows that twenty out of twenty students can identify three different styles of art tells the teacher that the lesson on style was highly successful for that class. It does not, however, provide sufficient information to judge the effectiveness of the curriculum in producing artistic thinkers (see At a Glance 9.1).

Encourage and measure higher-level thinking. The main goal of an effective art program is that students become artistic thinkers. Assessments must go beyond determining what facts students know and what art activities they have completed and include a wide variety of evaluation tools that draw from all levels but that emphasize the higher thinking skills. For many years Bloom's taxonomy of cognitive skills (1956) has been used as a model for analyzing the thinking level of learning tasks. This model can also be applied to art assessments (At a Glance 9.2).

WHY ASSESS CHILDREN'S ART?

Why . . . ?

Assessment is a critical component of the art program. It forms the final link in the chain of instruction. Without it there is no way to know whether or not students are learning what the art program is designed to teach. Assessment answers these questions:

- What do students know?
- What can students do?
- How do they know it?
- Is this the best way for them to learn it?

At a Glance 9.1

Assessment Tools and Their Uses

Tool	Level	Uses
Student self-assessment	Individual	Review personal accomplishments and monitor growth.
Journal	Individual	Observe conceptual exploration, evolving insights, patterns of behavior.
Individual observation (Anecdotal notes)	Individual	Record skill level, behavioral patterns and choices, problem-solving methods.
Checklist	Individual/Group	Note patterns of behavior, completion of tasks, skill acquisition, participation.
Process folio	Individual	Note changes in skill level, conceptual understanding, and performance over time.
Content analysis (Conference, portfolio, project)	Individual	Determine quality, completeness, skill level, understanding.
Short answer test/quiz (True/false, Matching, Multiple choice)	Individual/Group	Knowledge of factual learning and vocabulary.
Application sheets Concept maps	Individual/Group	See skill in applying information and concepts.
Essay/oral response	Individual	Discover skill in applying information and concepts.
Criteria-based assignment (Use of rubric)	Individual/Group	Provide information on level of performance in relation to program preset standards.
Performance task (Authentic assessment)	Individual/Group	Reflects ability to apply skills, knowledge, concepts, and organizational tools in relation to preset standards.
Portfolio	Individual	Track artistic growth over time.

Properly designed assessments grow out of the learning standards established for that particular group of students and provide the following information:

Analysis of Individual Student Needs and Knowledge
Informal assessments of student learning can provide immediate feedback in the classroom and help teachers address the progress of individual learners through individualized or small group instruction.

Diagnoses of Class Progress
Teacher-designed assessment tasks allow teachers to evaluate group progress toward curriculum goals. Based on the results, teachers can move ahead or reteach.

Improved Delivery of Instruction
Teacher analysis of the effectiveness of teaching methods and instructional planning can lead to a better matching of art instruction and curriculum goals resulting in improved learning for all students.

At a Glance 9.2

Applying Bloom's Taxonomy to Art Assessments

Knowledge: Asks students to remember, define, or identify information.

Examples:
Who painted the *Mona Lisa?*
Define *repoussé.*
Key words:
Define, identify, recall, recognize, remember.
Who/what was . . . ?

Comprehension: Asks students to describe, compare, or contrast information in their own words.

Examples:
What is the difference between a landscape and a portrait?
Describe the style of art called *surrealism.*
Key words:
Compare, contrast, describe, explain, rephrase.
What is the main idea . . . ?

Application: Asks students to use what they have learned to solve a problem.

Examples:
Use the principles of design to explain the composition of this painting.
Create a clay bowl using the coiling method.
Key words:
Apply, choose, classify, select, solve, use.
Which of these . . . ?

Analysis: Asks students to consider available information, identify causes and effects, and then reach a conclusion or make a generalization.

Examples:
What are the important contributions African art has made to European art?
Based on the review of the work in your process folio, what do you conclude about your progress in art this term?
Key words:
Analyze, conclude, deduce, generalize, infer.
What caused . . . ? What influenced . . . ?

Synthesis: Asks students to apply what they know and can do to a new situation.

Examples:
Based on what you have learned about Egyptian art, create a design for a modern office interior with an Egyptian theme.
Combine features from Egyptian, Greek, Roman, and Chinese architecture in designing an original building.
What would happen if you combined the printing techniques you know with making a collage?
Key words:
Combine, construct, create, design, develop.
What if . . . ?

Evaluation: Asks students to judge the relative value of an idea, solution, or product. Students must form an opinion and provide supporting facts.

Examples:
Which artist has had the most influence on the art of today?
Which of these designs for a teapot would function best?
Key words:
Argue, appraise, assess, criticize, evaluate, judge.
Which/what/who is better, stronger, more important, etc. . . . ?

ASSESSING ARTISTIC GROWTH

Guiding Ideas

The following assessments each have very specific purposes. Some are traditional evaluation methods used in other subject areas, which can also be applied to art. Others, such as process folios and portfolios, are traditional art assessments now being used more widely in other areas. Many are informal methods that will help teachers become better teachers of art. Used correctly and in combination, they will help students learn better and become more self-confident artists.

Process Assessments

Process assessments are those that provide immediate feedback in a classroom. These methods focus on how students are learning rather than what they have learned. They can identify trends and provide substantiation or repudiation of the teacher's personal beliefs about what is happening in the classroom. They are most often used to assess individual and group progress in order to determine what direction instruction should take.

Diagnostic observation. An effective teacher is constantly asking mental questions that assess the progress of each student. From the answers the teacher determines what immediate action to take. Effective diagnostic observation builds over time. The more one observes children creating art, the quicker one can pinpoint the need and determine possible ways to assist. New teachers, however, although lacking in experience, often bring fresh eyes and approaches to the process and see things that slip by a more experienced teacher who may be reacting automatically in the same way to every problem. The key is to maintain the wonder in each individual child's creative thinking while applying past experience customized to each situation.

Diagnostic questions. Depending on the discipline of art being demonstrated, the teacher asks different diagnostic questions about individual students. These same questions can also be applied in checklists and in more formal assessments.

- *Affective:* Do the student's statements reflect a thoughtful personal response? Is the student open to the ideas and feelings of others? Is the student self-directed and motivated to learn about art?
- *Descriptive:* Does the student use art vocabulary? Can he or she define terms and apply them appropriately?
- *Art criticism:* Do statements reflect an understanding of composition design, style, and the ability to make comparisons? Can the student state conclusions about a work and identify purpose and thematic content?

Teacher Tip

Types of Checklists

There are several different ways to manage checklists in the classroom. Each teacher needs to discover through trial and error which format will personally work best in different contexts.

Single-Sheet Class List

A one-sheet checklist with every student's name and a variety of observational categories can allow a teacher to quickly survey an entire class whether involved in creating art or working in cooperative groups. This format makes sure that no student is missed. It is quick and easy to use. It results in a document that the teacher can use in a variety of ways. A disadvantage is that the information will need to be transferred to individual student records in order to be useful in showing patterns of behavior over time. One solution is to design the sheet so it can easily be cut apart and individually filed in the student folders.

Individualized Checklists

Some information is better recorded on individual checklists. These checklists can be filled in during student-teacher conferences or based on interviews and observations. Having students participate in checking themselves off an individual checklist provides self-evaluative feedback. Students can keep their checklists in their process folio, an individual file folder, or a binder. These lists can become an important resource when evaluating a student's progress. They can be shared at conferences and used in writing final reports.

- *Art history:* Do statements reflect a knowledge of names, dates, historical and cultural detail? Can the student apply this information to make generalizations or create something new?
- *Aesthetics:* Do statements express a point of view about the meaning of art with references to the ideas of others? Can the student support an evaluation with relevant observations and data?
- *Production:* Does the student know how to use the media, techniques, and tools? Does the student consider design principles in creating a work? Where is the student in the creative and artistic process? Is a guiding question, demonstration, reminder, or reteaching needed?
- *Performance:* Is the student participating—producing art, asking and answering questions, offering ideas? If not, what is preventing the student from taking part—lack of confidence, knowledge, or focus? What action is needed to change the behavior?

Checklists. In a busy classroom diagnostic observation forms the mainstay of all student assessment. There is a natural tendency, however, to focus on the students with problems. Often teachers miss the quiet or self-directed students . It is important to use other informal assessment methods on a regular basis to ensure that all students receive equal attention. Checklists can meet this need for a fair and accessible informal assessment tool and deserve to be more widely used in the teaching of art. Checklists have many advantages:

- *Systematic and individualized.* A checklist can be designed to meet the individual needs of each teaching situation. If done regularly at a set time, it can represent a systematic sample of the state of the class. If teachers collect information on individual students over time, the checklists can determine patterns of behavior.
- *Broad uses.* Checklists provide an ideal way to record a wide range of art behaviors such as mastery of art techniques, progress on an artwork, social relationships, participation in discussions, level of interest in topics, and much more (see At a Glance 9.3).
- *Quick.* Checklists should be designed so they are quickly filled in. A simple check can indicate the presence or absence of a behavior. A code can be used to indicate a range of behaviors (At a Glance 9.4).
- *Provide student feedback.* Checklists, when recorded objectively, provide an ideal way to give feedback to students and can also be effective management tools. Individual checklists can become part of the student's process folio and be considered in self-evaluations. Posting checklists that show where every student is in the artistic process, for example, lets students see their progress and also provides a place they can check to find someone who could peer conference with them. The same checklist could be used to gather together a small group who are all at the same stage for a mini-lesson.

Anecdotal records. Although checklists can collect a great deal of data on individual students, there are times when more detail is required. At intervals teachers can closely observe students and take brief notes. Formal student-teacher conferences can provide an excellent time to write in detail. Although anecdotal records are very time-consuming to keep, they are rich in data (see At a Glance 9.5).

Anecdotal notes can be helpful in establishing patterns of behavior and for capturing conversation and classroom situations. These data can prove invaluable in customizing instruction for special needs students, in analyzing behavior problems, and for detailing student successes. Detailed notes allow teachers to present a vivid picture of an individual student at conferences. Sometimes the very process of looking intently at a student can help the teacher see that student in a different way.

Anecdotal records can be kept on index cards, self-stick notes, or large adhesive-backed labels that can later be put in a file folder. Notes intended solely for the teacher's use can be recorded in a notebook or the teacher's journal. Keep comments objective. It is important to record only what is actually observed. Notes that contain derogatory or private information lose much of their effectiveness;

At a Glance 9.3

Checklist Designs

Checklists can be designed in an unlimited number of ways. Here are just a few of the possibilities:

Type	Format	Uses
Magnetic Checklist *Advantage*: Provides instant feedback to students and teacher.	Use a magnetic black or white board. Draw the checklist on the board. Make name tags with a strip of magnetic tape on the back. Student or teacher moves the tag to proper category.	■ Keep track of who is using certain books, games, supplies, or tools. ■ See who is at what stage in his or her project. ■ Track who is peer conferencing. ■ Monitor cooperative groups.
Clipboard Checklist *Advantage:* Semiprivate and portable.	Attach checklist to a clipboard.	■ Carry about room and use when mini-conferencing. ■ Use at student-teacher conferences. ■ Use on field trips.
Card Checklist *Advantage:* Portable, individualized, can be filed by student name, activity, or topic.	Make up a card for each student. Attach together on a ring.	■ Carry in pocket and use when mini-conferencing. ■ Use at student-teacher conferences. ■ Use to select students and then note comment.
Sticky Note Chart *Advantage:* Can be small or large, allows room for comments, can become part of child's file.	Make up chart listing student names. Put categories at top. Use sticky notes to mark categories. Can be color coded. Students or teacher writes comments on notes.	■ Use to show tasks completed. ■ Indicate job assignments. ■ Note techniques tried. ■ Track discussion comments.

they cannot be used with students and can be damaging if they fall into the wrong hands.

Audio- and videotaping. It may be difficult for a teacher to make observations when conducting a discussion or working individually with students. One solution is to set up off to one side of the room a tape recorder or camcorder on a tripod and let it run during selected activities. Listening or viewing the tape afterwards can provide a wealth of data about student behaviors, learning situations, and teacher-student interactions. This information is useful for both the teacher and the students. Use a check-off sheet to quickly record this data. Systematic audio- and videotaping can contribute to accurate interpretation of classroom instruction (see At a Glance 9.6).

At a Glance 9.4

Codes for Checklists

Coded checklists provide more information than a simple check-off sheet. It is important, however, to develop a code that is logical and easy to remember. Each teacher needs to do this individually. The following examples are provided as a starting point:

Numerical codes: Codes based on numbers work very well for ranking behavior. Establish a key and keep the number span small.

Example:
0 = Not demonstrated
1 = Beginning to use technique/concept
2 = Practicing technique/concept
3 = Mastered technique/concept

Alphabetic codes: Letters work particularly well when used to stand for a larger word. They can be used to add description to a checklist.

Example:
Pt = Painting
Cl = Clay
Pr = Printmaking
C = Collage

Symbols: Symbols can be used to indicate behaviors and interactions. They can also be used for noting the presence and absence of desired behaviors as well as make simple comparisons.

Example:
+ = On task
– = Off task
* = Working cooperatively
# = Working alone

A coded checklist might look like this:

Student Name	Date	Activity	Technical Level	Task Commitment	Social Interaction
Nathan	10/15	Pt	1	+	+
Janice	10/15	Cl	2	+	+
Sal	10/16	Cl	2	–	–
Kendal	10/16	Co	3	+	+

Key: Cl = clay, Co = book cover, Pt = paint, 1 = low, 2 average, 3 = high, + = positive, – = negative

Journals. Reviewing the ideas students have jotted down in their journals can provide another way to assess what the student has absorbed from the lesson. Set up a system for collecting journals on a regular basis and design a check-off sheet that reflects what is being examined. Journals can give information on student attitudes and affective responses. They can also show the level of thought

At a Glance 9.5

Anecdotal Record Sample

Sample teacher notebook entry for second grader

4/25 *Michael worked on clay sculpture. Doing a head. Asked for help in doing the hair. Told him to try some textures on a scrap of clay. Spent 20 minutes exploring clay textures. Noticed that he shared ideas with others at table.*

Sample index card entry

Angela Mantos Grade 6 Writing/Art Workshop

3/21 *Working on collage, theme of war.*

3/22 *Brought in Life magazine with war pictures.*

3/24 *Talked with me about ideas. She feels very strongly about this topic. Family emigrated because of war.*

3/27 *Worked hard on collage. Wants it to be unbalanced to reflect the disorientation of war.*

At a Glance 9.6

Discussion Participation Checklist

It is often difficult to fill in a list like this while teaching. Consider having a parent, aide, or student assist. An upper grader could help a lower grade level. Alternatively a video camera or tape recorder can be used.

Key

?	Asked question	SUM	Summarized
S	Made statement	SYN	Put ideas together (synthesized)
I	Gave information	=	Compared or evaluated
D	Described artwork or feelings		

Name	Contribution to Discussion	Comment

Teaching in Action

Managing Journals

Whether exclusively dedicated to art or combined with writing, journals are a valuable resource for capturing and assessing student learning. Journals need to be available at all times in class. There is always the danger, however, that students will lose or forget their journals if allowed to take them home. At the same time it is important for students to learn to keep a journal outside of school as well.

One solution is for students to have two journals: a response journal, kept in class, in which they sketch and record art ideas; and a second journal, or sketchbook, which the student uses outside of class.

Set up a system for collecting and sharing the out-of-class sketchbooks at regular intervals so that students do not just let them gather dust. An up-to-date out-of-class journal can provide a good measure of student interest and attitude.

the student is applying in different situations such as in answering a written follow-up discussion question.

Self-evaluations. One of the main purposes of assessment is to teach students how to evaluate their own work. Self-assessment is an integral part of the artistic process and learning to think artistically. In art production students are introduced to self-assessment as part of the revision process. This can be expanded upon by providing time for students to write self-evaluations not just on their art production but also on their growing understanding of art analysis. These thoughts can be recorded in their journals or on teacher-designed evaluation forms geared to specific activities (At a Glance 9.7).

Task Assessments

Task assessments are brief activities or puzzles that challenge students to apply what they have learned. When carefully designed, task assessments can provide invaluable information about what students know and can do. Use short answer formats cautiously, however. In creating a short-answer evaluation consider the following:

What is being evaluated? Task assessments can provide information on factual knowledge, such as identifying artists, defining art vocabulary, differentiating between fact, opinion, and falsehood, and matching cause and effect. Some can require students to use the creative process.

Is this the best format to obtain this information? Often teachers can obtain the same student knowledge in the process of doing other kinds of assessments, such as conferences, essays, projects, and class discussion.

At a Glance 9.7

Self-Evaluation Formats

Journal prompt:

Examples

Primary: Draw yourself making your painting. Show how you felt about it.
Write one thing you learned about the painting we looked at.

Intermediate: Compare this artwork to others you have made.
Describe a problem you solved in making this work.
Write one thing you learned from our art talk today.
What influenced you most in creating this work?
Describe the most important thing you did to make your cooperative team art project successful.
Describe one way you contributed to our discussion about Surrealism.

Evaluation Form
Example: Project

Name: ____________________ Date: __________

Review your performance on this project.	**Needs to Improve**	**Fair**	**Good**	**Excellent**
1. The project met my stated goal.	1	2	3	4
2. I completed all parts of the project.	1	2	3	4
3. I used the artistic process	1	2	3	4
4. I worked cooperatively.	1	2	3	4

Example: Discussion

Name: ____________________ Date: __________

Review your participation in today's discussion.

Discussion topic: ____________________

1. I offered a comment.	Yes	No
2. I asked a question.	Yes	No
3. I listened closely to others.	Yes	No

The discussion made me think about: ____________________

Teaching in Action

Integrating Self-Evaluation

Institute self-evaluation as a regular procedure that students come to expect and prepare for mentally. Some of the following methods are simple enough for primary classes but can be used equally well at higher levels.

Examples

Closing circle: End the art workshop by having students form a standing circle. Give a self-evaluation prompt suitable for the age level and activity being done, such as, "In one sentence share something you learned about art today." Pass around a special object used just at this time such as a giant paintbrush or a beautiful stone. Have each student hold the item as they share.

Shared summary: This is a good format to use if time is very limited. If students are in their seats, have them turn to their partner. If they are standing in line, have them turn to the student behind them. Give the self-evaluation prompt and have students take turns sharing.

Work ticket: Have prepared preprinted self-evaluation tickets (see example). Three minutes before the end of the work time remind students to fill out a ticket and have a friend witness it. Collect the tickets as they leave the room. Vary the prompt to match grade level and activities.

Artwork Ticket

Name: ______________________ Date: ________

What did you learn about art today?

____

____

____

____

Witness: ______________

Journal entry: Close each workshop with five minutes of silent writing time. Ask students to think about what they accomplished, what satisfied them, and what they plan on doing in the next workshop.

Is this task fair to everyone? Does the task require reading or writing skills that may be beyond some students' capabilities? Can special needs students do the same task as everyone else or are modifications needed?

How will the results be used? These kinds of assessments are best used to help students see what they already know and what they still need to learn or to provide group data. When results are used to compare individual students or determine competitive grades, they destroy students' motivation to do art.

Ways to use task assessments in an art class. The key to using short answer formats is to not use them as tests that will produce a grade. Instead think of them as surveys, data collection devices, think sheets, and puzzles. Task assessments can be effective in the following ways:

- *To provide baseline data.* A "topic preview" given before the start of a study can provide information on what factual and basic information students already know about the topic. A review at the end can demonstrate how the group has improved in these areas. These assessments should not be individually graded. Share results with students in ways that show the group's performance, such as through graphs and basic statistics. Students who are used to being graded may need extra reassurance in order to relax during the administration of a preview. Make sure not to use the word *test* and emphasize it will not be graded or recorded under their name in any way. Since only group data is desired, do not have students put names on the task sheet.
- *To assess mastery of important facts and vocabulary.* In designing short answer assessments, do not rely exclusively on reading and writing tasks. Art is a visual-tactile language. Provide plenty of graphic images and manipulatives. Art puzzles, sorting card activities, matching games, completion exercises, diagramming, and time lines can provide review of facts and vocabulary related to art studies as well as information about what students have remembered (see At a Glance 9.8). Consider using these as self-assessment tools rather than whole class assignments.

It is important to remember that these kinds of assessments, although useful, show only a limited view of a student's capabilities. A student may be able to create beautiful pieces of pottery and yet not be able to do a crossword puzzle using clay vocabulary words. That is why it is important to use a mix of assessments in an art program.

Performance Assessments

How students apply what they have learned is far more important than simple memorization of facts and vocabulary. Performance assessments allow students to demonstrate how they approach and carry out meaningful art tasks. Performance assessments focus on how students apply their knowledge and skills to solve problems. They allow students to use the creative and artistic processes and so provide the best match with the goals of art education.

At a Glance 9.8

Art Short-Answer Task Assessments

Concept maps
Students are presented with a blank web or chart on which they must place information. This challenges students to show the interrelationships among ideas or concepts or to demonstrate a knowledge of cause and effects.

Example
Put these words on the web: bisque, coil, cone, fired, glaze, kiln, leather-hard, moist clay, slab, thrown.

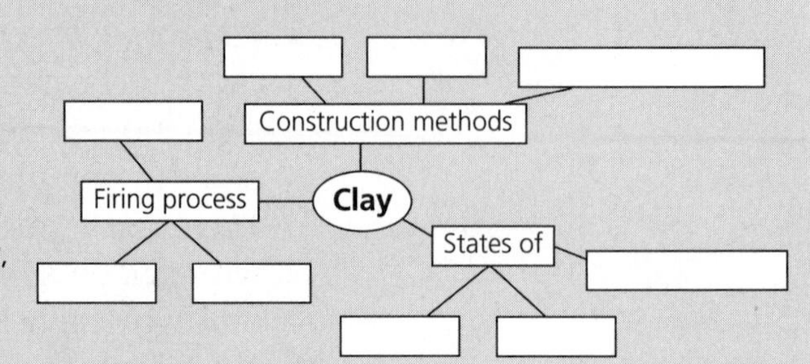

Crossword puzzles
Students must read a definition and recall a vocabulary word. The crossword format encourages correct spelling. Higher-level thinking can result when instead of a definition a fill-in-the-blank format or an example or application is given.

Example

Across
2 Use to join two pieces of clay
3 We use a __________ to tell how hot the kiln is.
4 Clay is baked in a __________ .

Down
1 We __________ clay to make it hard and durable.
3 Extremely fine soil is called __________ .

Diagrams
Students either label a teacher-prepared diagram or create an original diagram that illustrates an idea or concept.

Example
Label this color wheel. (Alternative: Draw and label a color wheel.)

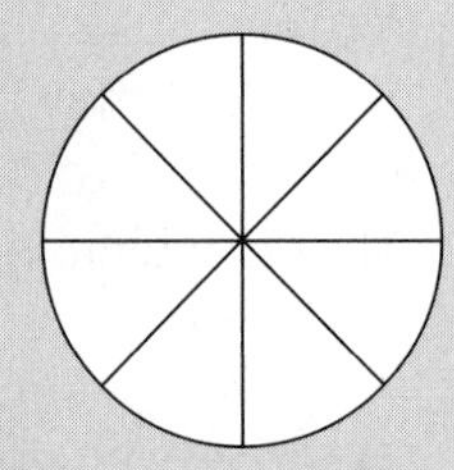

Completion exercises
Student places a term in a sentence so that it makes sense. Completing the sentence should require more than simply knowing a definition; it should make the student apply the meaning of the word. *Note:* Make sure the word to be filled in matches the sentence grammatically.

Example

1. This painting is a good example of the style of ______________ .
2. A kiln is used to make clay ______________ .

Matching

Give students items to put into pairs. These can be vocabulary words and their definitions, concepts and examples, or better yet, mini-prints of artworks and related descriptions.

Example:

Match the artwork and its culture.

Nine-patch quilt	Ghana
Sumi-e	Java
Adrinka cloth	Amish
Mola	Japan

Sorting

Give students items to put in groups. Items can include miniprints, vocabulary and concept words, or art tools.

Example:

Sort these cards by style

Place these words under the proper category on the chart.

Group these tools by media.

Time lines

Give students items to place on a time line. Items can include artists, artworks, styles, media, and so on.

Example:

Place these media on the time line indicating when they first appeared in human history:

Basketry, cave painting, metal sculptures, pottery, weaving

Paleolithic	Neolithic	Bronze Age	Iron Age

Examples of performance assessment tasks include the following:

- Writing and presenting a research project on a type of art
- Analyzing one or more artworks orally and/or in writing
- Creating a unified series of artworks that meet specific criteria
- Keeping an art journal/sketchbook over a set period of time
- Creating and presenting a portfolio
- Creating a dramatization based on an artist's life

Performance assessments, according to Douglas Reeves, director for the Center for Performance Assessment (1998), have become popular for the following reasons:

- Teachers feel they are fair to students and offer valuable information about what students know and can do.

Teaching in Action

Task Assessment: A Self-Assessment Activity

Directions: Before beginning your clay project, please fill in a questionnaire about clay. Put the completed questionnaire in your process folio. When you have finished your clay project, do a second questionnaire. Compare your answers to the first one. What did you learn more about?

What I Know about Clay

What I Know About Clay

Name: ____________________ Date: ____________

1. Clay comes from ____________________.
2. To join clay pieces together I must use ____________________.
3. Clay is leather-hard when it is ____________________.
4. Clay is baked in a ____________________.
5. Clay that has been fired once is called ____________________.
6. Clay is coated with ____________________ to make it shiny.
7. The baking temperature is measured with a ____________________.
8. Another word for *firing* is ____________________.

- Parents and business people feel that they are rigorous because those who perform cannot just guess the right answer but must demonstrate their research or solution.
- Administrators like them because there is evidence that they help diagnose learning needs, help students learn better, and improve performance on standardized tests.

Designing performance assessments. A well-designed performance task requires students to perform, create, solve a problem, or make a discovery. In doing so students must tap into higher-level thinking skills and invent solutions that have real-world application. When designing performance tasks, teachers need to ask the following questions:

- Is this task meaningful for the students? Will it result in something that will be valued by the students?
- Is the task in line with grade-level objectives and curriculum standards?
- Does it allow students to make choices and solve problems?

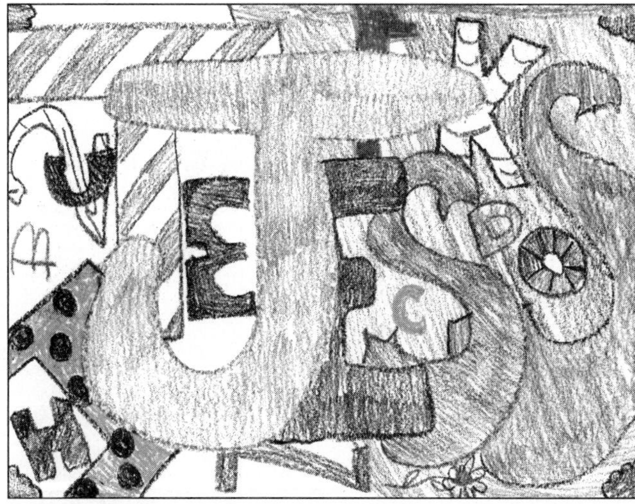

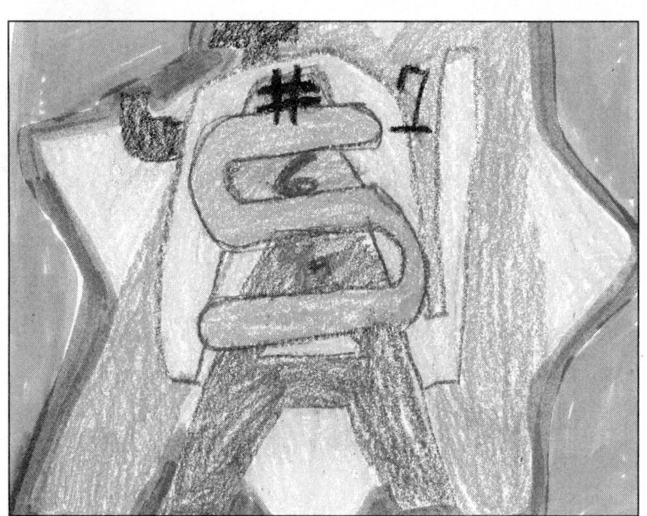

"Our Names."
Crayon and marker—Marissa (*top, left*), Jesssie (*top, right*), Danielle (*bottom, left*), and Jason (*bottom, right*), grade 5.

Thinking about Children's Art

For this get-to-know-you assignment these fifth graders were asked to create a design using the letters of their names arranged so that the whole paper was used and the name was difficult to decipher. Which students successfully met this criteria? Do criteria such as these help students produce more successful artwork? What other criteria might have been given for this assignment?

- What skills does the student need? Will the task require a wide variety of skills drawn from the different multiple intelligences that utilize the strengths of different learners?
- How will students demonstrate these skills?
- What criteria will be used to evaluate their skills?

Using performance assessments. In the classroom a performance task will often look no different than regular assignments. The difference is in the preparation of carefully constructed criteria for evaluation.

"Products of the Grasslands."
Crayon, pencil and marker—
Daniel and Nicholas, grade 3.

Thinking about Children's Art

This poster was created in response to a social studies assignment during a unit on the grasslands of the United States. How have the students combined visual images and words to demonstrate what they have learned about agriculture in this region? What drawing skills have they demonstrated? Could this assignment be considered a performance assessment for both social studies and art?

These criteria grow out of the teacher's objectives for the class and the general standards or goals that students are expected to attain. The National Standards for Visual Arts (At a Glance 1.4), state standards, and local art curricula can provide guidance in developing specific criteria against which to compare student performance.

Developing criteria for a rubric. To use any of these general or local standards as an assessment tool for performance tasks, they must be converted into specific evaluation criteria. This set of criteria or rubric establishes the specific skills and level of quality expected. The teacher determines this level based upon the grade-level objectives and the amount of progress the teacher expects students to make toward the general standards in the instructional time frame and through the activities being evaluated (At a Glance 9.9).

Using rubrics. A rubric provides a predetermined rating scale or scoring guideline against which to measure each student's art performance. This method of assessment is invaluable in assessing the

At a Glance 9.9

Developing Assessment Criteria from a General Standard

1. Choose a general standard.
Example: National Standard: K–4: Know the differences among materials, techniques, and processes.

2. Write a standard for school/district art program.
Example: Local Standard: By the end of fourth grade, students should be able to identify eight different media categories and give examples of each, explain the steps needed to use them successfully, and use these media to create a work of art.

3. Write specific objectives for each grade level that will produce students who can do what the standard describes. Note these should be more specific and often include aspects of other standards.

Example: Grade-level objectives

By the End of Grade 1:
a. Students will match student-created artworks with the media used (drawing, painting, collage, clay).
b. Students will use the four media to create artworks.
c. Students will describe how media was used to create their artworks.

By the End of Grade 2:
a. Students will match student-created artworks and reproductions with the media used and compare and contrast differences in how the media was used (drawing, painting, collage, clay, printmaking).
b. Students will use several different forms of and techniques for each of the media to create artworks.
c. Students will describe orally the steps they used to create their artworks.

By the End of Grade 3:
a. Students will identify the media and technique used to create sample artworks from different times and places as well as their own (drawing, painting, collage, clay, printmaking, fiber).
b. Students will use a variety of techniques and processes in creating artworks in the six media.
c. Students will write descriptions of how to use these media to create artworks.

By the End of Grade 4:
a. Students will write descriptions of artworks from selected times and cultures that refer to the media, techniques, and processes used (drawing, painting, collage, clay, printmaking, fiber, sculpture, pen and ink).
b. Students will produce and present a portfolio of work that shows a range of media, technique, and processes.
c. Students will write an essay describing the process they went through in creating each work in their portfolio and comparing their work with that of other times and cultures in terms of media use.

4. Write a set of criteria (rubric) for judging the success of each student in achieving each objective.

Example

Rubric for Grade 1, Objective a:
4 Student matches all examples correctly and provides added description (Challenge).
3 Student matches all examples correctly (Mastery).
2 Student matches most examples correctly.
1 Student matches few or none of the samples correctly.

Rubric for Grade 4, Objective c:
4 The essay is well organized with the comparisons to other works fully integrated into the flow of the text. Descriptions are highly detailed and organized (Challenge).
3 The essay tells how each work was done in clear language and in proper sequence. For each media there is a comparison to a work from another culture or era. These works are clearly identified and described (Mastery).
2 The essay describes how the student produced each work. Comparisons to other works are incomplete and/or lacking in detail.
1 The essay describes how the student did some of the works. Comparisons to other works are incomplete or missing.

process of thinking about and creating art. Using a rubric allows teachers to fairly evaluate performance tasks, such as creating a portfolio of artwork or doing an art research project, against a measure of quality. Each student is compared to the criteria set forth for the task rather than to other students in the class (see At a Glance 9.10).

The rubric or assessment criteria must be designed prior to the students beginning work on the assigned task. Knowing what is expected of them provides students with a guide for success and enables them to make more effective choices as they work and learn. Having the assessment in hand allows the teacher to monitor progress toward the objective more efficiently and helps keep the students on task. As students work on artworks, research projects, or prepare portfolio presentations, the rubric provides the standard for which to aim. Teacher Meg Keller-Cogan finds that "whenever students are provided with criteria, they meet or exceed them. It's important to eliminate the mystique surrounding evaluation. Students should not have to guess as they prepare an assignment" (Allan et al., 1993, p. 68).

In order to make a rubric reliable and consistent in use follow these guidelines:

- *Be specific.* Describe observable behaviors for each level. Avoid general rankings such as *poor, average, good,* or *excellent.* These terms are open to interpretation. For example, instead of saying the student must make a good collage, describe the specific things that must be included in the collage, such as the student will use a variety of papers, colors, and shapes to create a collage that is unified and has a focal point.
- *Provide examples.* When presenting the rubric to the students, provide actual samples, preferably student-done, that demonstrate the different levels of response. Keep these samples on display while students are working, and use them comparatively when making the final evaluations. This helps keep evaluation consistent over the class and from term to term.
- *Use sorting.* When possible, sort completed works by one criterion at a time. This combats the "halo effect" in which a general, overall impression may affect the evaluation.
- *Collaborate.* Work with colleagues to define common rubric frameworks so that scores mean the same thing in different subjects and classes. Work together to decide how many levels there should be in all rubrics and use the same terminology. It is confusing to students if a 3 means progressing on one teacher's seven-point rubric and proficient on another teacher's four-point scale.

Written Responses

An effective art program wants students to become capable of writing about art. Written responses require students to communicate their artistic thinking using the tools of language arts. This is a key component of

At a Glance 9.10

Writing a Task Rubric

1. Determine the number of descriptive rankings. Rubrics can have two or more. Most have five or six.
2. Begin by writing the description of an acceptable performance. Then write a description of an unacceptable performance. Next complete the descriptors for the levels in between.

Example

General Six-Part Rubric Format

6	Narrative description of an exemplary performance
5	Narrative description of an acceptable performance
4	Narrative description of a performance that is acceptable but not as good as a 5
3	Narrative description of a performance that is a little better than a 2
2	Narrative description of an unacceptable performance that shows effort but demonstrates major misunderstandings
1	Narrative description of an unacceptable performance that showed little effort
0	No performance

art instruction, but it also adds an entirely different dimension to art assessment and calls upon teachers of art and teachers of writing to work together.

Writing in the art area can be approached in several ways:

- A writing/art workshop, managed by a classroom teacher or by an art specialist and grade-level teacher working together, provides the ideal setting in which to combine art learning and writing skill development. Students can write and sketch in their journals and discuss art with classmates. From these experiences students develop ideas for written responses on art topics. Art ideas can be addressed at the same time students develop their writing skills.
- Art specialists and language arts teachers can collaborate. Students can discuss art ideas in art class and write about them in English class. The art teacher evaluates the work for artistic ideas, the English teacher looks at the writing quality.
- Art specialists can assign and evaluate writing tasks in consultation with the language arts teachers and in coordination with the school's writing program. This means the art specialists become familiar with grade-level standards in writing, spelling, and grammar. They analyze individual capabilities of the students, which allows the art specialist to evaluate both ideas and writing.

Designing evaluative writing tasks. Writing intended for assessment purposes begins with a rubric that provides guidance for student

Teaching in Action

Using a Rubric in the Classroom

- Rubrics can be used at all levels. The key is to use easy-to-understand language and make sure students understand the criteria. Instead of using the word *rubric,* for example, use *scoring guide* or *project rating scale.*
- Introduce the performance task. If the task has several components, list each component separately on a chart. At the primary level keep performance tasks simple with no more than two components.

Example:
First Grade Portfolio Project

TASK: Choose one piece of art you did during workshop.

- Mount it.
- Write your name on the front.

Example:
Fourth Grade Portfolio Project

TASK: You will be collecting examples of the artwork you did during workshop time. The purpose is to create an organized and beautiful display of what you have accomplished by the end of the year. To do this you will:

- Look through your process folio and select at least six works that represent the different media, techniques, and ideas you used.
- Mount each work on an appropriate background.
- Use the computer to make a title/artist/medium/date label for the front.
- Provide the criteria for each component. Show examples as you explain each level.

Example:
Scoring Guide Fourth Grade Portfolio Project

5 More than six works have been chosen. Each work represents a different media or approach. All works are mounted in way that enhances the quality of the artwork. Labels are accurate and designed to complement the artwork.

4 Six works have been chosen. Each work represents a different media, technique, or idea. All works are mounted on colors and shapes that relate to the artworks. They are accurately labeled.

3 Six works have been chosen. Each work represents a different media. Works are mounted and labeled.

2 Less than six works are chosen and/or different media, techniques, and ideas are not represented. Several works are mounted and labeled.

1 Less than six works are chosen and/or different media, techniques, and ideas are not represented. Few works are mounted and/or completely labeled.

0 Not done.

- Give students a check-off sheet to help them keep track of what they have accomplished. On the sheet have upper-level students write the criteria for each component in their own words. Ask primary students to explain the criteria to a partner. Check for misunderstandings.
- On due date have students use the criteria to evaluate their own work. Then collect for teacher evaluation.

response and assessment. The rubric spells out the format for the piece, the kinds of information and ideas required, and the writing standards that will apply.

Writing tasks can elicit a wide range of artistic thinking, from listing steps of a process to arguing whether or not an object is a work of art. Students can be asked to

- Describe feelings, ideas, or artworks.
- Compare two works of art.
- Explain causes and effects.
- State art concepts in their own words.
- Tell how to do something.
- State a position and defend it.
- Provide examples of an idea.

Approaches for primary. At this level ask children to use a combination of words and pictures. Many may still be using invented spelling in their writing. To help children with ideas and spelling have them brainstorm a few words they may wish to use in their writing and write them on a chart where everyone can see it. Writing ideas for primary include the following:

- Drawing a response to an artwork and then writing a sentence describing it. For example, after looking at a Jackson Pollack painting, a child draws a picture of herself with colors and lines all around. Below she writes, "I see colors and lines."
- Drawing a numbered set of pictures showing how to do something and writing simple labels for each one.
- Looking at a piece of art and then writing an imaginary story about it.
- Writing sentences with an illustrative picture in a journal.
- Discussing whether or not an object is art and then drawing a picture of where it should be put, such as in a museum or on a breakfast table, with a simple sentence describing the place.

Approaches for intermediate. Most students at this level are able to write one or more descriptive paragraphs, compose a short story, and produce illustrated research reports of several pages. They should be able to edit their work for basic spelling and grammar. Post a chart and provide vocabulary lists to help them with spelling the words needed for the writing task. Suggested writing tasks at this level include the following:

- Describing a piece of art or a reaction to a work using specific art vocabulary words
- Responding to journal prompts

Teaching in Action

Sample Writing Task Assessments

Grade 1 Task

Draw picture and write a sentence below it that shows how this painting makes you feel.

Art Concept Rubric

Picture shows feeling; expands meaning of words	4
Picture shows feeling; words relate to it	3
Picture shows feeling; words do not relate to it	2
Picture shows feeling; no words written	1
No picture, no words	0

Grade 4 Task

Write a letter to the artist explaining why you like or do not like her artwork. Describe the work so the artist will know which one you have selected.

Art Concept Rubric

6 Artwork is described using many vocabulary words and descriptive adjectives; the opinion is well supported with at least four facts or observations.

5 Artwork is described using at least five vocabulary words; opinion is supported by three or more facts or observations.

4 Artwork is described using at least three vocabulary words; opinion is supported by two facts or observations.

3 Artwork is described; opinion is supported by a fact or observation.

2 Artwork is described; opinion is unsupported.

1 Artwork is not described and/or no opinion is given.

0 Not done.

Grade 6 Task

Write down your plans for creating your next artwork. Be specific. Include all the steps you will go through in its production. Refer to the artistic process and any influences or inspirations that will affect your work. Read the criteria for assessment carefully before you begin.

Art Concept Rubric

5 The artistic process guides the plan; inspiration is clearly described and referenced.

4 Plan lists steps in order based on artistic process; reference is made to artwork, literature, or other influences.

3 Plan lists steps in order; reference is made to the artistic process.

2 Plan lists steps in order; no further detail is given.

1 Plan lists some of the steps or steps are not in order.

0 Not done.

- Writing an imaginary story or poem inspired by viewing an artwork
- Writing sequenced directions for using a specific medium, technique, or art concept
- Writing a simple biography of an artist
- Composing and sending a letter to a favorite artist or illustrator
- Researching and writing an illustrated report of one to three pages on an artwork, an art style, or the art of a culture
- Writing an essay arguing that an object is or is not a piece of art

Evaluating written tasks. Writing, like art, is a creative process and should not be given a simple grade. Before students turn in their writing, encourage self-evaluation using the art/writing rubric for the piece. Make sure there is enough time for writing tasks to be shared with a partner or in cooperative groups. Students will do a better job if they know peers will be reading their work. Students who feel successful in writing about art are more willing to do so in the future.

Portfolios

Portfolios and art go together. Creating a portfolio should be the most important performance task a student does each term. Too often, especially at the lower grades, students take home their artwork as soon as they complete it. When it is gone, it is forgotten, and a wonderful learning and assessment opportunity has been lost. It is not surprising that in such a situation many children have no idea how they are progressing in artistic skills nor that they have few personal artistic goals. Portfolio creation has long been a major focus at the high school and college levels of art instruction. It should be equally important at the elementary school level.

Portfolios allow students to display not only their production skills but also critical and aesthetic skills as they analyze their works and make and defend their choices. Students also assess their own progress as they review and organize what they have accomplished over a period of instruction.

Process folios. Student portfolios cannot be produced unless the system for creating them is in place from the very first day of art instruction. Teachers should inform students of the portfolio project and the criteria against which it will be assessed at the very start of instruction. Then they should supply students with a storage system, such as a process folio, for collecting their work over a period of time; from that process folio students will select works for their final portfolio.

During the school year process folios should be constantly in use. Here is where students store works-in-progress, sketches of future ideas, media explorations, photographs of three-dimensional and large group projects, self-evaluations, graded essays, and work that has been on display and is now being saved for possible inclusion in the portfolio. It is a messy, disorganized conglomeration of artistic progress.

It is helpful to have upper-level students keep a contents list on the front of the folder. As they add materials, they should briefly note the date and the item. This will allow the work to be ordered chronologically later to see growth and development. If works are on display or taken home, this should also be noted. They may later be desired for inclusion in the culminating portfolio. Encourage younger students to put a date on or attach artwork tickets to the items they put in their process folios.

Keeping a process folio has many benefits. Besides providing a storage place for ultimate portfolio creation, process folios can be used in these ways:

- *Planning instruction:* Regularly look through the process folios to gain an idea about what students seem to know and where they are having difficulties.
- *Self-evaluation and peer review:* At regular intervals hold a "process review" and have students look through their process folios and order the materials. In revisiting past work, they may make some exciting discoveries about how they have improved or changed direction. On occasion have them select something from the process folio and share it with a peer.
- *Teacher conferences:* The process folio provides background when discussing a finished work. Look through it with the student and write down comments you both make about what went well and what was difficult.
- *Storage of ideas and art experiments:* Help students to see that a process folio is more than a place to dump stuff. It can be an amazing resource. There may be a sketch that they started earlier and now have the technical skill to work into an artwork. Forgotten paint mixing experiments can now be used in a current collage. A fun way to do this is to have a process folio scavenger hunt. Give students a list of possible items they might be able to find in their process folios and a set amount of time. Then have students share some of their discoveries in cooperative teams or with the class.
- *Monitoring progress:* Are many students starting works and not finishing them? Do they do enough planning and sketching before beginning a final work? Is there a growth in skills and knowledge? Are there noticeable patterns of behavior?
- *Portfolio selection:* At set intervals meet with the students to select work to go into the portfolio.

Teacher Tip

Storage Systems for Process Folios and Portfolios

Some suggestions:

- **Paper or tagboard folder:** Put two sheets together, then bind on three sides using folded over paper. Folder can be reinforced with clear package sealing tape.
- **Expanding wallet folders:** Available from office supply houses.
- **Literature organizers:** Use as an open cubby system for bulky items, in coordination with a folder for storing and protecting flat artworks.
- **Magazine cases:** Intended for magazines these narrow open topped cardboard boxes are durable and easy to store on a counter or shelf. Larger works can be rolled for storage.
- **Large flat boxes with lids:** Although these are the most durable they also take up the most space and are relatively expensive. They work well when portfolios are passed on from grade to grade.
- **Corrugated cardboard folders** (poster size): Available from teacher supply catalogs these are very durable and can be passed on from year to year. Students can also make their own from large cardboard cartons.

Process folio and portfolio storage systems. In selecting a storage system ask the following questions:

- *What is the size and nature of the work?* The larger and bulkier, the bigger the storage container must be.
- *How long will it be in use?* The longer it is used, the sturdier it must be. A folder used for one month can be made from construction paper, but one used for an entire year is better made from tag or poster board.
- *What is the age of the children?* Primary students need a system that is at their height and color coded for quick access. Upper-level students can use more complex closures and filing systems.
- *Where will they be stored?* Shelving systems, file cabinets, boxes, or crates all require different designs for individual portfolios.
- *How and when will children get access to the folios?* If all the folios are stored in one place or box, only one student can get a folio at a time. Consider grouping folios by table or cooperative team or keeping them in desks or on a counter.

Defining the portfolio. A portfolio is a collection of selected works that demonstrate both process and product and that represent a designated period of time and specified work. The contents of a portfolio

At a Glance 9.11

Process Folio Contents: A Sampler

Process folios can take many forms depending on the age of the students, the method of instruction being used, and the topics being taught. At various times a process folio might contain any or all of the following:

Anecdotal records
Audiotape of child talking about work
Bits and pieces left from making something
Checklists
Comments, written or oral, made by child
Finished work
Journals
Letters sent and received
Notes taken by child or teacher
Photographs of child working
Raw data collected by child
Research materials; brochures, postcards, magazine articles
Parent comments
Practice pages
Samples
Self-evaluations
Sketches
Teacher assessments
Tests
Tools in use
Videocassette of child working
Works-in-progress
Worksheets

will vary depending on its ultimate use in student assessment and its ultimate destination. Portfolios can cover a range of time periods:

- The work produced in one marking period, one semester, or one school year
- The work produced in a combined writing/art workshop
- The work produced as part of a long-term project
- The work produced over a school career

The audience. A portfolio is an important communication tool. It shows the teacher the student's individual accomplishments. It allows parents to enjoy the efforts of their children. It lets next year's teacher know what the student learned and accomplished. Most importantly it speaks to the student, who can use it to see personal growth. Over time it can show increasing fine motor control and artistic growth in all areas.

Students can share their portfolios with other students as well. Arrange for a Portfolio Day. Pairs of students or cooperative teams can look through each other's folders and write comments about the works. Or schedule an exhibit entitled "From Our Portfolios." Hang works that have been selected for the portfolios and invite friends and families.

"The Neighborhood."
Pencil—Jim, grade 5.

Thinking about Children's Art

A great deal can be learned from looking closely at a student's artwork. What can be learned about this boy's drawing development and technical skill? How well does he understand perspective? Does the piece show inventiveness and creative risk taking? Does it provoke a response in the viewer? Would this be a good work to include in this student's portfolio?

Portfolio contents. Portfolios will vary based on what is selected for inclusion. A portfolio is not just a folder kept to show people what the class is doing or what the teacher is teaching. Rather it should be a record of what the individual child is learning, how the child has grown in understanding and skill. Sheila Valencia (1990) suggests that portfolio collections should reflect what learning is valued. This means that the contents of each portfolio cannot be dictated as to a precise number of pieces nor should each contain exactly the same pieces all done on the same day with the purpose of going into the portfolio. Some works should be selected by the teacher. For example, teachers might identify particular growth areas to document and then look for examples that illustrate the child's progress. To document increasing drawing skill in second graders a teacher might look for instances where students have used overlap in their drawings.

In specifying what students should include in their portfolios, it is important to phrase the contents in general, open-ended terms rather than as specific pieces so that the portfolio is truly a personalized picture of an individual student's progress. Specifying that every portfolio have a collage, a drawing, and a painting not only limits student choice but also dictates a superficial level of selection. Instead describe selection criteria that require students to use analytical and evaluation skills. A requirement that the portfolio contain at least six works in at least four different media forces students to consider the media used in each work as one of several elements upon which to base their selections (see At a Glance 9.12).

Labeling the work. Attaching descriptive notes, or in K. Jervis's terminology (1996) an "entry slip," to each piece put into a portfolio helps an outside audience understand the context of the work and why the student selected it. Slips can include the student's name, the date, and the reason for selection. In addition it is helpful to include the specific learning objectives to which the piece relates. If the piece was done as part of an assignment, the directions for the assignment should be included as well.

Portfolio evaluation. Completed portfolios should be evaluated against the criteria established at the beginning. Students can be asked to do a self-evaluation first. If desired, a partner or a peer review board can check the portfolio, then give it back to the student with suggestions for improvements. The teacher can then conference with the student, and together they can carefully look over the portfolio. "[L]earning to look at a child's work in relation to the child," writes Jervis, "is a compelling reason for collecting the work in the first place" (1996, p. 20).

At the conference the portfolio itself will suggest directions for discussion. The focus should be on what the student has accomplished as demonstrated by the selected works and related materials. This is the time to celebrate accomplishment and to suggest future directions, not to offer criticisms. It should be a beginning rather than an ending. Students should be proud to take their portfolios home to share with family and friends.

Sharing the portfolio. Looking through a student's portfolio, no matter whether it is a first grader's or a sixth grader's, is a wonderful experience. It is a summary of that student as an artist at that particular moment in time. Together with the student look for the presence of the following qualities:

- *Developmental level:* Look for growth in the use of visual symbols to create meaning. Have fine motor skills become more refined? Is there increasing detail, accuracy in proportion, and the use of overlap, varying points of view, and perspective?
- *Technical skill*: Look for examples that show skillful and appropriate use of the tools and media.

At a Glance 9.12

Creating Portfolios

The following examples provide just a small sampling of possible art portfolio contents. (*Note:* A complex portfolio may have several purposes.)

Purpose: To show artistic growth over a period of time.

Contents:

- Examples of work done at different times, ordered sequentially
- Sketches done for these works
- Self-evaluations from different times
- Anecdotal records over time
- Conference reports
- Videotape showing student doing same activity at different times
- Written description of what student thinks was learned

Purpose: To show understanding of art concepts.

Contents:

- Examples of works that display specific concepts
- Sketches for these works
- Performance tasks showing application of these concepts
- Self-evaluations on use of concepts
- Anecdotal records, videotape showing concepts being applied
- Piece of writing that explains or uses the concepts

Purpose: To demonstrate competence in using the creative/artistic process.

Contents:

- Works that were created using the artistic process
- Sketches, revisions, and related materials that were part of creating these works
- Records of peer and teacher conferences
- Checklists showing progress on works
- Self-evaluations on using processes
- Anecdotal records, videotape showing student involved in processes, such as a sharing session
- Written record of steps taken in creating the works

Purpose: To show next year's teacher what the student can do.

Contents:

- Sampling of artwork showing range of ability and skills
- Example showing how the artistic process was used
- Checklist showing patterns of behavior
- Self-evaluations of progress, skill level, and knowledge
- Written description of what student believes was learned

Purpose: To show development of an idea or how a problem was solved.

Contents:

- The finished work or project with documentation (photos, videos, sketches, notes) that show how it was done
- Self-evaluations of thinking, planning, and solution
- Written description by student of what was learned, difficulties faced, and future directions

- *Understanding:* Find pieces that show what the student has absorbed and then applied from the lessons taught. If, for example, several periods of instruction focused on using symmetry, look for examples of symmetry in the student's work.
- *Inventiveness:* Search for those pieces that show risk taking even if the result was unsuccessful. Has the student experimented with materials, ideas, and techniques?
- *Commitment:* Look for multiple drafts and revisions leading to a final piece. Do the works show time and effort?
- *Expression:* Are there pieces that reflect the student's personal interests, feelings, and desires?
- *Communication:* Does the student have works that provoke a response from others?
- *Cultural awareness:* Are any pieces reflective of or created in reaction to art from other cultures that were studied during the semester or year?

Passing it on. Depending on the final destination of the portfolio, different culminating activities may be appropriate:

- If portfolios will be sent on to the next year's teacher, students could write a letter to the teacher explaining why they chose the pieces they did. The teacher can also include a synopsis of the portfolio conference and perhaps a brief outline of what they covered in class.
- If the portfolio is going home, students can prepare a similar letter for their parents.
- In some cases teachers may ask students to make a second selection from the work in the year's portfolio to be included in a multiyear portfolio that will travel with them throughout their school careers. Usually they will select only two or three pieces from each year that meet specific criteria.

Multimedia Presentations

Teachers can also ask students to create multimedia presentations that combine a variety of tasks that can be assessed. Depending on the students' grade level and art experiences, presentations can range from those that focus on a particular concept to those that summarize everything the student has learned in a unit or year. Creatively designed presentation tasks are highly motivating for students, challenging their thinking and setting the creative process in motion.

Well-designed multimedia presentations have several interrelated parts, each utilizing different approaches to the material. Ideas are limited only by the teacher's or students' imagination. Tasks can include

Teaching in Action

Introducing Portfolios

1. Early in the semester or school year introduce students to the requirement that they create a portfolio representative of the artwork they accomplish during the course of instruction. Show several examples of portfolios at that grade level.
2. If creating an art portfolio is new to the group, ask students to brainstorm ways that a collection of their artwork might be useful to themselves and others.

   Example:

   WHY MAKE A PORTFOLIO?

   Show improvement

   See what we know

   Show our effort

   Help plan what to do

   See things we could change

   Share at conferences

   Share our ideas and feelings
3. Provide students with a list of the portfolio contents and evaluation criteria. In the lower grades write the contents list on a chart and post it in the process folio storage area.
4. Explain that throughout the semester or year they will be expected to collect examples of their work in a folder called a process folio. At specified intervals, such as every month or marking period, they will select examples from their process folio, mount and label them, and put them in the portfolio.
5. Have the students either make a folder to be used as their process folio or distribute the containers that will be used. Encourage them to personalize it with artwork.
6. When students finish, show them where their process folios will be stored and have students put them away.

researching, writing, creating art, incorporating music, using technology, and performing scientific experiments. They are an ideal way to combine learning in several subject areas. For each subject area a separate rubric can be designed allowing the presentation to provide assessments in several disciplines.

Project Boards

Project boards have much in common with portfolios. Boards, like portfolios, represent a selection of work done over a specific time period. The difference is in the preparation and presentation of the selected work. Project boards allow students to graphically share with parents and the public the process they went through in accomplishing a piece of work. They are particularly useful for cooperative projects that are hard to include in a portfolio.

Teaching in Action

Multimedia Presentation Ideas

1. Create an advertising campaign for your favorite ______________ (color/art element/art media/artwork/artist/art style, etc.).

   Sample tasks:

   Design a billboard.

   Write a brochure.

   Compose a jingle.

   Plan and hold a kick-off celebration for your ad campaign.

   Videotape a TV ad.

   Tape a radio ad.

2. Plan and hold a birthday party for ______________ (favorite artist/person in a portrait/character in a storybook).

   Sample tasks:

   Write and illustrate an invitation.

   Make a guest list.

   Select gifts that each guest might bring and design appropriate gift wrapping.

   Make party favors.

   Choose food to serve.

   Invent games to play.

3. Plan your future career.

   Sample tasks:

   Research and select a possible career.

   Design a place of business: Draw blueprints and build a scale model.

   Design a sign for outside the business.

   Create letterhead and associated stationery.

   Design an ad campaign.

   Plan a wardrobe for your job.

4. Plan and design a special exhibit for an art museum.

   Sample tasks:

   Select a type of art for your exhibit and research it.

   Select the works to be displayed.

   Choose wall colors, lighting, background music, etc.

   Plan the display and build a scale model.

   Write commentary for each work.

   Write a catalog for your exhibit.

   Make a poster advertising your exhibit.

   Videotape a TV interview about the exhibit.

   Hold an opening for your exhibit.

Creating a Project Board.

Thinking about Children's Art

Project boards are one way students can present what they have learned over a period of time. What decisions does this student face as she arranges photographs, artwork, and descriptions of the process she went through into a unified presentation? How does this process help students assess their own work?

Panels can include plans, sketches, revisions, photographs of the work in process, and student writing about the project. The students arrange these materials on a piece of heavy cardboard or a folded piece of poster board in an informative, attractive, and eye-catching way. Assessment criteria can focus on the success of the presentation.

Panels can be created in place of a portfolio or in addition to one. One individual work can be featured or several related works can be displayed together.

In the Classroom

USING ART ASSESSMENTS

Teachers should plan all assessments before instruction begins. Pre-planning also ensures the use of many different kinds of assessments. Ruth Mitchell emphasizes that looking at a whole art unit and designing assessments that attend to all the learning expected helps teachers "become aware that imitation, allusion and variation are also part of artistic work. They cannot fall back simple-mindedly on the metrics of invention and spontaneity they have long prized in children's drawings and paintings" (1994, p. 65). Assessments that give several types of information, that allow for individual differences, or that teach as well as assess, result in a richer, more rounded view of student progress.

The following Florida Institute for Art Education assessments for its CHAT (Comprehensive Holistic Assessment Task) art unit based on the study of Faith Ringgold's *Tar Beach* demonstrate how assessment can be embedded in instruction (Mitchell, 1994, p. 56–57):

- *Initial journal entry:* Written reaction to first viewing of artwork and analyzed for understanding using a rubric.
- *Anecdotal records:* Teacher comments about class activities and individual student performance.
- *Initial drawing:* Drawn following first viewing of the artwork and analyzed for understanding using a rubric.
- *Responses:* Student-responsive written piece or artwork following each lesson and discussion about the artist, the historical influences, and the interpretation of symbols.
- *Self-assessments:* Made following each response.
- *Cooperative art project:* Paper collage quilt.
- *Reinterpretation piece:* Written and artistic reaction to how ideas have changed following study of the artist, historical influences, and interpretation of symbols.
- *Analysis piece:* Written explanation of how their artwork relates to the featured work.
- *Process folio:* Collection of work from unit: including written pieces, drawings, quilt sketches, quilt blocks, teacher-completed rubrics for all assessments.

This example shows how art instruction can be made richer by the assessments that accompany it. The assessments themselves are teaching tools. They make sure that lessons touch all the ways the language of art can be used: to interpret others' art, to express ideas and apply methods, to invent new meanings, and to communicate about art. They help students focus on what they need to be learning and set the benchmarks for successful artistic growth (see At a Glance 9.13).

Reporting to Parents

The purpose of art assessment is to create a description of each student as an artist that will be useful in improving the student's performance. A report, no matter how authentic the assessments upon which it is based, is no more than a snapshot of a continual process of change and growth. For this reason reports to parents should be as detailed as possible and focus on the process of learning, not the products. A single grade in art tells little about what students know and can do in all

At a Glance 9.13

Example Assessment Plan

Yearly Assessment Plan

General Grade-Level Standard	Assessment Type	Specific Task	Frequency
Affective			
Students can . . .			
Express orally and in writing how an artwork makes them react personally.	Checklist Writing task	Discussion Participation sheet Artwork response sheet	At every discussion After viewing selected works
Production			
Students can . . .			
Identify specified media, materials, techniques, processes.	Portfolio	Select and label works for portfolio	End of marking period
Create artwork using various media, tools, techniques, processes.	Checklist Portfolio	Artistic process chart Art media selection Exploration sheet	Daily Daily After media mini-lessons
Use tools and materials safely.	Checklist	Behavior chart	Daily
Description			
Students can . . .			
Express orally and in writing the effects created by different media and methods.	Journal Writing task	Artwork descriptions Artwork response	Check weekly After viewing selected works
Use specified art terms, art elements, and design principles orally and in writing to describe artworks.	Writing task Multimedia	Artwork response Museum plan	After viewing selected works Due end of first marking period
Criticism			
Students can . . .			
Classify and compare artworks. Task assessment orally and in writing based on design, technique, media, purpose, theme, style, and history.	Task assessment Multimedia	Venn diagram Webs Museum plan	After study of selected work Due end of first marking period
Analyze orally and in writing the relationships among an artist's life, cultural background, and the art created.	Multimedia	Artist's life playlet	Due end of second marking period
Art History			
Students can . . .			
Identify artworks from specified cultures, times, and places.	Assessment task	Card sort	4 times a year
Place artworks on a time line and explain historical influences.	Assessment task	Chart to fill in	4 times a year
Aesthetics			
Students can . . .			
Express a supported opinion orally and in writing about the nature of art.	Checklist Multimedia	Discussion participation Museum plan	After small discussion Due end of first marking period.

(continues)

At a Glance 9.13 continued

Example Assessment Plan

Yearly Assessment Plan

General Grade-Level Standard	Assessment Type	Specific Task	Frequency
Performance			
Students can . . .			
Use the artistic process.	Checklist	Artistic process chart	Daily
Ask and answer questions about art.		Discussion participation	At every discussion
Work with others to create and talk about art.	Checklist	Coop behavior chart	During team activities

the different skill areas. One student may be strong in clay work yet weak in analyzing works in relation to their history. Other students can talk about art but struggle to produce it. Teachers who recognize the complexity of art should strive to give parents assessment profiles, portfolios, and narrative summaries (see At a Glance 9.14). These kinds of reports celebrate students' art accomplishments even as they inform about student needs.

Creating an assessment profile. A profile is a prepared form that contains the rubrics and evaluations from all the different assessments the student has completed as well as summaries of checklist data and anecdotal notes. These individual profiles provide a wealth of information that can

- *Improve instruction.* The teacher can use these data to see individual strengths and weaknesses, discover patterns of behavior, and from this customize teaching for that student.
- *Inspire students.* Profiles help students see what they have mastered and give them the basis to set future goals. For example, a student may see that the only printing technique not yet attempted is silk-screening. This is then used as a starting point for the student's next series of artworks.
- *Inform parents.* Sharing profiles with parents is far more helpful than giving a single grade. It allows parents to see exactly what their child did or did not accomplish. In cases where a single grade is required because of school policy, consider sending home the profile as a much-needed supplement, while at the same time advocating a change in reporting methods.

At a Glance 9.14

Sample Narrative Report

Report for Third Marking Period

NAME: *Amy* SECTION: Grade 3

Affective: Student can express orally and in writing how an artwork makes her feel.

Amy wrote a very detailed description of how she felt looking at Degas' Woman with Chrysanthemums. She often shares her feelings about art during circle time.

Art Production: Student can safely and responsibly use four basic art media with a variety of techniques and the artistic process, to creatively communicate ideas, experiences, and stories.

Amy successfully used crayon, paint, printed paper, and collage in the creation of her "Class Flower Sale" poster.

Art Description: Student can orally and in writing use grade-level art vocabulary to describe works of art.

Amy uses the terms for the art elements in her descriptions of artwork.

Art Criticism: Student can orally and in writing compare two artworks and explain how the elements of art have been used to communicate ideas, purpose, or theme.

Amy was able to compare Monet's Water Lilies and Van Gogh's Irises in a written essay.

Art History: Student can identify grade-level-specific artworks by culture, time, and place of origin and use this information to compare the works to her own art.

Amy can identify the works of the major Impressionists and can define the style of Impressionism.

Aesthetics: Student can state an opinion about an artwork and provide two or more supporting facts or observations.

Amy is able to support her opinions about artworks using the facts we have learned in class.

Performance: Student participates in discussions by asking and answering questions, shows effort by performing the steps of the artistic process, maintains a process folio/portfolio, and completes assigned writing tasks such as journal entries and artwork responses.

Amy's journal reflects her thoughts about the artwork studied and her plans and ideas for her own work. She has added three pieces to her portfolio this marking period: a chalk drawing of the pond done on site, a painting of the pond, and a pencil study of frogs.

Portfolios and parents. Portfolios provide an excellent picture of the process of learning. If possible, send home portfolios at regular intervals. Before sending them home have students write a letter to their parents telling them what they want them to notice the most. Include a form on which parents can respond (At a Glance 9.15).

Parent-teacher conferences. When meeting with individual parents, it is not enough to show the finished works. Be ready to share information about their child's artistic process. Process folios, journals, photographs, and anecdotal records should form the basis of discussion.

When talking to parents about their child, remember to

- *Be organized.* Have everything to be shared at the conference neatly ordered and readily available.
- *Be discreet.* Keep other students' work out of sight. Do not discuss other students by name.
- *Be positive.* Emphasize what the student can do. Phrase the student's needs in terms of skills that need work. Provide specific ways that these needs will be addressed.
- *Be resourceful.* Parent conferences are the ideal time to ask for volunteers or for contributions for the art program.
- *End upbeat.* Close the conference on a positive note. Share an especially interesting artwork or tell a positive anecdote about the student.

Conclusion

MAKING THE GRADE

Assessment is the glue that binds together instruction, students, and goals. Without assessment there is no art program, only a series of unrelated art activities. How we choose to assess students' artistic growth takes us back to the questions and answers that began this book: What do we believe art is and why do we teach art to our children?

If art is a communication tool—a language—then we will assess how well students can use the materials and techniques of art to express their ideas and learning regardless of the subject matter. If art has syntax—a set of culturally determined rules—then we will assess how well students understand and use those rules to make meaning in their own works and that of others. If art is an expression of one's culture that changes over time, then we will assess how well students comprehend the art of their culture now and in the past and their ability to compare it to the works of other times and peoples. If art is a creative pursuit, then we will look for that spark of invention brought into being through the artistic process.

At a Glance 9.15

Portfolio Response Sheets

Primary Format

Student response

Dear Family,

This portfolio contains the most important work I did in art this marking period.

I am especially proud of ______________________________.

Something that I will work more on is ______________________.

Your child,

Parent response

To my child,

I am especially proud of the way you ______________________.

____

Love,

Upper-Level Format

Student response

Write a letter to your family about your portfolio.

1. Tell them which work makes you most proud.
2. Tell them something that you learned.
3. Tell them something you will be working on improving.

Parent response

After looking at your child's portfolio please respond on this form.

The thing that impressed me most about this portfolio was:

____

____

____

____

Teacher Resources

REFERENCES

Allan, K., Keller-Cogan, M., & Sugarman, J. (1993). Make authentic assessment work for you. *Instructor, 105*(1), 66–68.

Armstrong, C. (1994). *Designing assessment in art.* Reston, VA: National Art Education Association.

Bloom, B. B. (Ed.) (1956). *Taxonomy of educational objectives.* New York: McKay.

Jervis, K. (1996). *Eyes on the child: Three portfolio stories.* New York: Teachers College Press.

Mitchell, R. (Ed.) (1994). *Measuring up to the challenge: What standards and assessments can do for arts education.* New York: American Council for the Arts.

Reeves, D. (1998). Practical performance assessment for busy teachers. *Learning, 26*(4)58–60.

Starko, A. J. (1995). *Creativity in the classroom: Schools of curious delight.* White Plains, NY: Longman.

Valencia, S. (1990). A portfolio approach to classroom reading assessment: The whys, whats and hows. *The Reading Teacher, 43,* 338–340.

Wolf, D. P., & Pistone, N. (1991). *Taking full measure: Rethinking assessment in the arts.* New York: American Council for the Arts.

Practical Guides

Batzle, J. (1993). *Portfolio assessments and evaluation: Developing and using portfolios in the K–6 classroom.* New York: Creative Teaching.

Clemmons, J., Laase, L., Cooper, D., Areglado, N., & Dill, M. (1993). *Portfolios in the classroom: A teacher's sourcebook.* New York: Scholastic.

Graves, D., & Sustein, B. (Eds.) (1992). *Portfolio portraits.* Portsmouth, NH: Heinemann.

Helm, J. H., Beneke, S., & Steinheimer, K. (1998). *Windows on learning.* New York: Teachers College Press.

Videos

Rethinking Assessment Grant Wiggins
Center on Learning Assessment
Tom Snyder Productions
1-800-32-0236

Process Folio/Portfolio Supplies

BrownCor
Box 14770
Milwaukee, WI 53214
1-800-327-2278
Plain boxes in all sizes and shapes, including lift-lid boxes (literature mailers), cardboard folders (variable depth mailers), and corrugated stacking bins

Calloway House
451 Richardson Drive
Lancaster, PA 17603-4098
Boxes for storing portfolios

Reliable
Box 1502
Ottawa, IL 61350
1-800-735-4000
Folders of all kinds, including plastic file folders, expandable and box bottom; also inexpensive literature organizers and lift-lid boxes

Chapter 10

Art Beyond the Classroom

School and Community

The private act of making art needs to be balanced by the public event, including the exchanges between artist and audience, as well as the celebrations that provide additional insight.

George Szekely (1988, p. 154)

ARTISTS AT WORK

First-grade conversation at the museum:

Oh, it's so big! Hey, Maurice. Did you think it would be so big?

It's real bumpy, too.

Don't touch it! Remember we can only touch with our eyes like Mrs. Garcia said.

Yeah. I can feel the bumps with my eyes.

So can I.

How do you think the artist made it so big? I couldn't even reach the top.

Must be a giant size artist . . . as big as my Uncle Bob maybe?

Wouldn't it be fun to have a sculpture like this for our very own?

I wouldn't want it in my house. It's too big. There wouldn't be room for my family.

No, I meant like at school, in the playground.

We could see it every day.

It could be a huge space ship ready to take off. Zoom . . .

Let's build a big sculpture when we get back . . . maybe we could use the blocks.

Or boxes . . .

Introduction

REACHING OUT

It is not enough for students to participate in a well-supplied, carefully planned art program. They also need many opportunities to see that art is not just something children do in the classroom, but rather it is a vital part of many people's lives. In this chapter we will look at a number of ways to provide such broadening art experiences by reaching out into the community that surrounds every classroom.

Setting the Stage

WHAT ENCOMPASSES COMMUNITY?

The classroom community is just a small part of a much wider community through which art experiences can be developed. Wise teachers do not rely only on themselves to be a sufficient artistic model for their students. They go out of their way to utilize the many artistic offerings available in the community as a resource.

Other classes. Every classroom is surrounded by other classrooms where art may also be happening. Consider pairing up with a class at the same grade level for a joint art project, to share finished work, or to attend a special art program together. Team older students with younger ones for student-taught art lessons, peer conferencing, and to help with displays.

Other teachers. Every school has teachers who are highly interested in art. Find out who has taken art courses, has an artistic hobby, or loves to attend museums and galleries. Invite them to share their knowledge and experience with your class. If you cannot get a substitute, switch classes for the sharing time.

Parents. Similarly survey parents to find out who has participated in artistic pursuits, has a special art interest, or has traveled and experienced works of art in other places. Invite them to share with your class.

Libraries. Libraries often sponsor exhibitions of artwork or may be able to put teachers in contact with arts groups in the community.

Community groups. People who share similar interests often form groups that sponsor educational activities of all kinds. Most areas usually have local groups of painters, photographers, quilters, weavers, potters, and more. Check museums, newspapers, and libraries to find out how to get in touch. These groups may have or know of special art programs that relate to what your class is learning in art.

What Do You Think?

Do you know where to see art and sculpture in your community? Start making a list of community art resources for future reference.

Local artists. Look in the newspaper or consult with community arts groups to discover local artists who might be willing to visit your class and share some of their expertise. Perhaps your school district is part of a network of districts that support arts-in-education programs that help fund artists' visits.

Museums and galleries. Explore the museums and galleries in your community. Arrange field trips to exhibits that relate to what is being studied. If you cannot go to the museum, find out if the museum will bring an exhibit or educational program to your school.

Local businesses. Hospitals, offices, state and county buildings, universities, and banks often sponsor art exhibits or have permanent collections of art and sculpture. The best way to discover these is to visit those that are within travel distance of the school. Check to see if they will allow student groups to visit.

Parks and playgrounds. Visit county and state parks and playgrounds in your area to see if there are any sculptures on display. These are often ideal locations for an art field trip combined with a picnic and sketching.

Why . . . ?

WHY EXPAND ART BEYOND THE CLASSROOM?

Teachers who make the extra effort to go beyond the classroom door enrich the lives of their students tenfold. Students who have been to museums become museum goers. Students who have met and talked to artists see art as a viable life pursuit. Students who have gone to parks, farms, zoos, city streets, and other interesting locations to get ideas for their art learn that ideas for art come from everywhere. In addition:

- *Students come in contact with expert role models.* Working with students from other classes and grade levels allows students to come in contact with a wider range of diverse ideas than they will just in the classroom. Older students are role models for the

What the Experts Say

Americans Support the Arts

Nine out of ten respondents (91%) believe that it is important for children to be exposed to theater, music, dance, exhibitions of paintings and sculpture, and other cultural events.

Ninety percent of parents with school-age children want their children to have more experience with the arts than they had when young.

Percent of Americans who attended an art museum at least once in the past year:

1974	48%	1984	58%
1975	43%	1987	55%
1980	60%	1992	53%

Source: Louis Harris (1992)

younger ones. The younger ones reinforce the idea that art skills develop and improve with experience. Seeing experienced artists provides much-needed adult role models for young artists. They can see an expert thinking and exploring ideas through art.

- *Students become better artists.* Teaching other students helps the teaching student to formulate and apply art concepts. Seeing expert artists at work shows students how artists handle art media with skill and thought.
- *Students become relaxed patrons of the arts.* Visiting a gallery or museum exhibit takes away the strangeness of these institutions and allows students, many of whom may have never or rarely visited museums and galleries, to practice viewing behaviors that will make them more interested and effective museum goers.
- *Students discover that art surrounds them.* Seeing art displayed in locations around the community helps students understand how art is a valued part of the environment in which they live and will someday work.
- *Students perceive the beauty that exists in their world.* Field trips for creating art help students see the world around them with new eyes.

Making Contact

Teachers must work to create ties with local museums, arts groups, ethnic cultural groups, and other community organizations that offer special programs to schools in their area. At a Glance 10.1 provides examples of ways local groups and organizations can help school

At a Glance 10.1

Community Resources

This list provides just some ways to link school and community. Explore your local area to discover more.

Organization	Provides
Art galleries	Catalogs Exhibits Links to local artists
Arts organizations	Contests Exhibits Lists of local artists Support for school programs Visiting artists
Art stores	Brochures on art supplies Demonstrations of new supplies and techniques
College/university art department	Art exhibits Information on art careers Outdoor sculptures Student guest artists
Craft fairs	Place to purchase art for school Direct contact with local artists Information on techniques Place for students to sketch/interview
Craft guilds (quilting, sewing, spinning, weaving, etc.)	Guest demonstrators Exhibits Fairs Research resource
Cultural centers	Ethnic heritage information Festivals Links to ethnic artists Research resource
Dramatic groups	Backstage tours Costume design Lighting/design Set design
Library	Links to local artists Exhibits Place to exhibit student works Research resource
Museums	Behind scenes display creation tour Exploration kits Guided tours of exhibits In-school programs On-line sites Outdoor sculptures Research resource

(continues)

At a Glance 10.1 continued

Community Resources

Organization	Provides
Parks	Outdoor sculptures Places to sketch
Zoo	Animals to study and sketch In-school programs

art programs. Most organizations are anxious to link up with schools. They see the students as future members and supporters of their programs.

Guiding Ideas

LINKING WITH THE WIDER COMMUNITY

Students need to know that art plays a vital role in their own school. One of the first to turn to for help is the art specialist if there is one in the school.

The Role of the Art Specialist

The addition of an art specialist who is trained in a wide range of art processes and techniques and who can model expertise in the visual arts is essential to the classroom art program. Unfortunately not all schools provide an art teacher at the elementary level. In 1982 58% of small elementary schools and 61.3% of large elementary schools had such a specialist (Leonhard, 1992).

When an art specialist is provided, it is important to see the art program not as an alternative to art in the classroom but as an expansion of it. The art room is where children will go to learn more advanced methods of working, to see artistic thought processes modeled, and to find a place where the language of art is honored.

The Reggio Emilia schools of northern Italy, for example, value the language of art so highly that they include one art specialist and a well-stocked art studio for every four classrooms. Individual or small groups of children move to the studio when they wish to express their learning in a visual form or when they need to learn specific techniques. The art teacher or *atelierista* meets regularly with the classroom teachers to offer insight into the children's thinking and to participate in the design of student-generated theme studies (Edwards, Gandini, & Forman, 1993).

This is where the art specialist belongs—working with classroom teachers, not apart from them. The art teacher brings to the school community special expertise and a different approach to learning, which should be highly valued. In the field of visual art the art teacher is the master, fellow teachers and students the apprentices. Art specialists can share their knowledge with students and parents in the following ways:

- Instruct students in specialized art skills and concepts
- Foster the creation of art journals by all students
- Publish newsletters about art events in the school and the community
- Equip, maintain, and facilitate use of a school art studio
- Model the process of art creation by creating personal artworks in the school setting
- Instruct parents and the community in the importance and meaning of art creation for their children

Collaboration. Too often the art specialist, when provided by a school district, has been used to provide the classroom teacher needed preparation time. This has led to overworked art specialists meeting class after class with little time to consult with fellow teachers or do their own artwork. At the same time the classroom teacher, believing that art instruction is taken care of, does not provide meaningful art experiences in the classroom.

It does not have to be this way. Delivery of art instruction can change when the art specialist collaborates with the classroom teacher. There are many creative ways to deliver art instruction when the goal becomes effective, integrated teaching rather than lockstep instruction in separate subject areas.

Ways that art specialists can collaborate with classroom teachers include the following:

- Provide instruction and workshops for classroom teachers so as to increase the artistic confidence of all who work with the students
- Participate in the design of instructional materials, classroom environments, and curriculum units so that visual art becomes an integral part of all subject areas and help teachers select curriculum-expanding artworks, books, games, and art activities
- Maintain a resource of art prints, games, and activities to share with teachers
- Work together on the creation of process folios, portfolios, and displays that show students' learning across the curriculum
- Collaborate with classroom teachers in the direct instruction of students
- Provide time and space for students to work on curriculum-related art projects
- Meet regularly with classroom teachers to discuss individual student progress

Learning about the Other Side of Art.

Thinking about Children's Art

A professional watercolorist shows students how he carefully mounts and frames his paintings. What are these students learning about how artists value and care for their artwork that would not be learned from studying reproductions?

School Visitors

Students need to see adult artists at work. These encounters provide the models upon which they will base their definition of an artist. The two formats for an artist visit are artist-in-residence and guest artist.

Artist-in-residence. Artist-in-residence programs place an artist in a school for a period of several days to several weeks. This allows students to develop rapport and become involved in the artist's work. This type of program is often funded by local arts or educational groups. The artist-in-residence can interact with students and parents in many ways:

- Give lectures to students and parents about their art
- Hold student and parent workshops to explore their art form
- Demonstrate their art form to classes
- Serve as a role model by working on their own art in the school
- Work closely with a small group of selected children
- Organize and carry out a special art project, such as creating a mural or building a raku kiln, with the students.

Guest artist. The guest artist visits for perhaps forty minutes to an hour. Such a brief visit must be carefully planned in advance in order to be beneficial for the students. It will be up to the classroom teacher and art specialist to prepare the students ahead of time. They need to make sure the students know the vocabulary the artist will use, have some idea of the art medium to be shown, have prepared questions, and understand acceptable behaviors. The guests also need to know what to expect. At a Glance 10.2 provides a sample letter to visitors to help them prepare for the visit.

Short visits by guest artists can contribute to the art program in the following ways:

- Give an expert demonstration of a technique that is beyond the skill of the teacher
- Answer questions about problems students may be having using the artist's medium
- Show examples of their artwork
- Tell students how they became artists
- Discuss their own art with individual students or a small group.

Remembering the visit. Before the visit students should make a list of questions for the guest. At the primary level the teacher might record the class's questions on a large sheet of chart paper. Older students can write their questions in their journals.

Students should be expected to record what they learn during the artist's visit. Encourage primary students to make sketches of artists and their work. Remind older students to write down answers to their questions.

After the visit gather the class together and on chart paper record what they observed and learned. Have them use this chart to write a thank-you note to the artist. Students can also use the chart to write a summary of the visit in their journal or for their art portfolio.

Collections

In addition to artists, teachers can also arrange visits from parents and community members who have interesting collections of originals collected while traveling. Experiencing real artworks can flesh out the limited sensation of seeing reproductions. Classroom teachers and art specialists should search the community for hidden treasures such as African masks, Pueblo pottery, Navajo rugs, Chinese painted silks, and more. Other types of collections may represent a special interest, not necessarily art-related, but which can be built on as part of an integrated unit. For a study of insects a butterfly collector might show part of a personal collection and allow students to make sketches.

At a Glance 10.2

Guest Artist Guidelines

When planning an artist's visit, do not rely on a phone call alone. It is easy to forget important details. Help guests prepare by sending a letter with the information they will need for an effective presentation.

Sample letter

Dear Ms. Garcia,

Thank you for offering to visit our class on Friday, June 6th. We will expect you at 1:30 p.m. in Room 23. Please stop in the office when you arrive. They will tell you how to reach the room. You may also ask for a custodian to help carry your artwork.

The students are very excited about your visit. They have been making clay sculptures and pots using slabs and coils. They cannot wait to see your pottery and ask you questions about working with clay. I will have the students seated on the rug when you arrive.

In order to make the visit go smoothly, I have attached a list of guidelines that have proved helpful to other visitors.

Sincerely,

General Guidelines for Guest Artists

- Please let me know several days before the visit what you will need for your presentation. There are large tables, easels, and a sink in the classroom. There is also a projector screen and a mounted TV/VCR.
- Our class periods are 40 minutes. Plan your presentation to last 25 minutes. This will allow time to set up and to answer questions at the end.
- Students are curious about how people decide to be artists. Be ready to talk about how you became an artist and why you chose the medium you did.
- Students are more attentive to demonstrations and hands-on activities. Be prepared to show how you work. Bring supplies, an unfinished artwork to work on, and samples of your artwork at various stages. If possible, have something the students can touch or do.
- Young people are more sensitive to toxic materials than adults. Do not bring any solvents, permanent markers, solvent-based glues, oil paints, varnishes, sprays, or dusty materials.
- You may wish to write a brief information sheet about your art or directions for a special technique that the students might want to try. It can be copied for the students here at school.

Collectors can present these works in several ways:

- Talk to the class about how and where they obtained the item and any pertinent information they know about it. Some may wish to show pictures or slides of where the art originated.
- Explain why they chose these particular pieces. What were their criteria of selection?
- Set up their display in a corner of the classroom. Have small groups visit and ask the guest questions while the rest are involved in another activity. This format works particularly well for primary students.

Student activities. Before the collector shares the artworks, have the students predict what they might be, based on simple clues such as country of origin or art medium. During the sharing have students take notes and make sketches. After the collection is gone, have students record what they remember individually and as a group. Try to find similar examples in books and art prints. Compare the art seen to those familiar to the students.

School Gallery

Another way to bring art into the school is to provide a rotating gallery space in a prominent location in the building, such as the entry, the main office, or the library. Artists are always looking for places to exhibit their work, and schools can provide a safe, public location for local artists. Collections can also be exhibited. Organizing and scheduling these exhibits should be the responsibility of one person who can make sure the exhibits reflect the studies of the majority of students in the school.

Consider holding an opening of the exhibit for the students to attend and meet the artist or collector during the school day. Then hold a more formal opening for adults at night.

Working with Parents

Parents can be ardent supporters of art in the school. They can provide information about students, donate needed supplies, and help with major art events. By sharing children's learning visually through their art parents can better understand what their child is learning in school.

Communicating with parents is not as easy as it is with students. Parents may work long hours and be unable to come to school regularly. Some, newly immigrated, may not know the system or the language. Others may suffer from illness or family problems. Art, like music, can reach out to these parents in ways that other school subjects cannot.

Art exhibits and displays. Parents like to see their children's work on display. Send home a brief note to let parents know when their child's work is hanging in the school. Make sure the note is in the parents' native language. Check that all artwork hung in public places is clearly and correctly labeled with the child's name so parents can find it easily.

Newsletters. Send home a short weekly, biweekly, or monthly newsletter that describes what is happening in the classroom. Keep the tone light and joyful. Make it interesting for the whole family. Include art puzzles, mystery artists, art Web sites, news about local art events and shows, and other items that will get family members involved with art. Use the newsletter to ask for donations of otherwise discarded supplies such as Styrofoam trays and cloth scraps for the art program.

Art kits. Create interactive learning kits about art that children can sign out and take home to enjoy with their families. At the primary level include a picture book about art, directions for a simple, related art activity that can be done with supplies found in the home, and a stuffed animal or toy. At the intermediate level kits can consist of an art game or puzzle or a reproduction of an artwork and a story about the artist. All levels enjoy mystery boxes that contain an unusual artwork or artifact and a set of clues to challenge the family to discover all they can about the work. Draw on upper graders' greater knowledge about art by having them make up games and kits for students in the lower grades.

Kits can also contain questionnaires about art. For example, students can interview family members about their favorite artists. At school the data collected can be converted into class- or even schoolwide graphs that provide useful information about the school community.

Workshops. Schedule parent-child art workshops where parents and their children can work together on cooperative art projects such as murals and sculptures. The collection murals described in Chapter 7 are ideal for mixed aged groups.

Volunteers. Parents can provide extra hands when needed. Setting up art displays in the school is an ideal way parents can help overworked teachers. Have parents give out supplies or supervise cleanup for large projects such as murals. Invite them to come on art field trips.

When working with parent volunteers, it is important to make them feel appreciated and competent. Do not expect them to know what to do without your guidance. To make the experience go smoothly remember to

- Send home formal written requests for volunteering that spell out the job, including place and time, even if you have already asked informally. This provides a physical reminder to the parent and lets them know specifically what they will doing.
- Send a note the day before to remind parents of their participation.
- Provide on-the-job, detailed instructions and a demonstration of what is to be done. For example, if the parent will be taping up artwork, specify exactly where, how far apart, and in what way to use the tape. If the parent will be helping students organize their process folios, work together on the first one or two.
- Make sure all the supplies the parent will need are ready and waiting.
- Try to thank parents verbally before they leave, but also send home a written thank-you.

Field Trips

Nothing can compare to the lasting impressions that field trips make. Field trips replace the humdrum of the school day with new sights and sensations. They substitute new vistas for familiar walls. These kinds of experiences broaden classroom instruction and motivate students to apply their understanding of art.

Where to go. There are many places to take students to experience art. Some lie just outside the school. Others require forays into the larger community. Choose places that relate to what students are currently learning. A trip to look at Egyptian antiquities will be far more meaningful for students who are immersed in a study of ancient civilizations. Consider distance and cost. Field trips do not have to be elaborate. Sometimes the best field trips are spur of the moment forays into the streets around a school to make quick sketches. At a Glance 10.3 offers many suggestions for places to go.

Planning the trip. Near or far a field trip will be only as effective as it is planned to be. Careful preliminary planning can make the day of the trip a pleasurable learning experience. Lack of planning, on the other hand, can not only diminish learning but perhaps lead to disaster. Before the trip make sure to do the following:

- *Visit.* Visit the location and take notes. Make or acquire a map. Note the location of bathrooms, food, and child-attracting hazards.
- *Explain.* Along with the permission slip, send home an explanatory letter that tells parents the purpose of the trip and what the children will be learning. Ask for parent chaperons.
- *Delegate.* Meet with parent volunteers and explain their responsibilities. Provide them with maps and other needed materials such as a bag for carrying student journals.

"Fir Tree." Jordan, grade 5.

Thinking about Children's Art

There are many ways to increase students' ability to represent meaningful ideas with visually rich images. One of the most important is to provide many opportunities to sketch from nature. Often it not necessary to go very far from the school. This drawing is a sketch of a small tree growing on school property. What has this fifth grader learned about the way evergreen branches grow?

- *Pre-teach.* Before the trip involve students in studies that prepare them for what they will see. If primary students will be seeing a large sculpture, for example, introduce the word *sculpture* and the concept of three dimensions, present a photograph of the sculpture, talk about the sculptor's life and anything else that will provide a basis for understanding. Excite interest with questions that can only be answered by the trip.
- *Document.* Decide how the students will record their impressions. Will they take their journals for sketching and note taking? Will they make a special booklet for the trip in which their questions are already recorded? How will they carry pencils or pens safely? Will they take photographs?
- *Make rules.* Hold a class meeting to review class rules and set up standards of behavior for the trip.
- *Organize.* On the day of the trip group students and provide a map and itinerary. Assign a parent supervisor to each group. Younger students can make special symbols to wear that indicate to what group they belong.
- *Oversee.* During the trip circulate among groups, supervising behavior, and make sure that no one misses the high points of the visit.

At a Glance 10.3

Ideas for Field Trips with an Art Focus

Places to view and learn about artwork:

Art exhibit
Art gallery
Art museum
Art show
Artist's studio
Bookstore
Children's "discovery" museum
Craft show
Colleges and universities
Framing store
Homes of local collectors
Local banks and libraries
Other schools

Places to sketch or get ideas outside of school:

Apartment house
Aquarium
Bakery
Beach
Bicycle shop
Bookstore
Botanical garden
Building site
Car dealership
Carnival
Circus
City street
Creek
Country road
Drugstore
Ethnic festivals
Factory
Fair
Farm
Field
Florist
Forest
Garden, private
Greenhouse
Hiking trail
Historical reconstructions
Lake
Lumberyard
Marina
Native American powwows
Neighborhood
Newspaper press
Quarry
Parade
Park
Playground
Pet store
Pond
Printing shop
River
Scenic overviews
Sports complex
Supermarket
Zoo

Places to sketch or get ideas at school:

Art room
Art storeroom
Cafeteria
Classroom
Computer lab
Inside bookbag
Inside desk
Inside locker
Inside pocket or purse
Hallway
Library
Music room
Outside school
School bus
School entrance
Stage
Stairway
Parking lot
Playground
Science room

Books to Share

Visiting the Museum

The following books can be used to prepare students for a trip to a museum:

Primary

Cohen, M. (1979). *Lost in the museum.* New York: Greenwillow.
The message of this book, "stay together," is important for any class going on a field trip.

Freeman, D. (1966). *Norman the doorman.* New York: Viking.
A little mouse living in a suit of armor gives tours of the museum to his friends.

Lionni, L. (1995). *Matthew's dream.* New York: Knopf.
A visit to a museum inspires a young mouse to become a painter.

Walsh, V. (1997). *Going to the Getty.* Los Angeles: Getty Museum.
A simple text details a visit to the museum.

Intermediate

Armstrong, C. (1994). *My art museum: A sticker book of paintings.* New York: Philomel.
Follow clues to match stickers to the proper gallery. To make the sticker reusable glue them on tag board and laminate. Use hook and loop tape to attach them to their places.

Belloli, A. (1994). *Make your own museum.* Malibu, CA: Ticknor & Fields.
A three-dimensional model of a museum to put together.

Clayton, E. (1996). *Ella's trip to the museum.* New York: Crown.
A young girl imagines she is inside the paintings.

Finn, D.(1985). *How to visit a museum.* New York: Abrams.
How to look and act in a museum.

Konisberg, E. L. (1987). *From the mixed-up files of Mrs. Basil E. Frankweiler.* New York: Aladdin.
This novel about two children who run away and hide out in the Metropolitan Art Museum has long been a favorite with fourth graders.

Papajani, J. (1983). *Museums.* Emeryville, CA: Children's Book Press.
This nonfiction book explains different kinds of museums and what goes on in them.

Wyse, L. (1998). *You can't take a balloon into the Metropolitan Museum.* New York: Dial.
In this wordless book a guard chases a balloon through galleries of art.

- *Review.* After the trip provide time for the students to share their feelings about the experience and review what they learned.

In the Classroom

CREATING EFFECTIVE DISPLAYS AND ART EVENTS

It is easy to look at the products of children's art activities as objects that can fill up an empty bulletin board or add a touch of color to a hallway. But as we have seen, children's artwork is so much more. First and foremost it is a powerful form of communication and as such has the potential to inform and educate those who take the time to look at it and "read" what it says about growing minds. It can be an important way to link the young artists in a classroom with the wider community that surrounds them.

There are many wonderful ways to display children's artwork so that not only is it admired, but it also educates.

Classroom Displays

Work displayed in the classroom should have a direct relationship to what the students are studying and what they need to know. Artwork in the classroom must be more than just a colorful background. Rather classroom displays should be informative, drawing students to look at them again and again. Consider displaying art in the following ways:

- *Art display:* To charts and graphs attach samples created by students as the result of their explorations with media and methods. Display these samples in the art centers. For example, samples showing brush strokes made with different brushes could be put on a chart and hung in the painting center to help students select the brush that best meets their needs.
- *Science display:* Display science diagrams and nature sketches alongside the actual objects or experiments, or reduce them in size and use them to illustrate worksheets and handouts.
- *Math display:* Hang up artworks that reflect numerical concepts, geometry, or patterns. Have students make up math problems to accompany the works.
- *Social studies display:* Display artworks that reflect what is being studied along with a student-researched fact or description. For example, a picture of a desert could have a caption reading, "A desert is a place that gets less than two inches of rain a year."
- *Language arts:* In the reading area display student-written and illustrated books, posters advertising the students' favorite books, and illustrated poems.
- *Inventor's corner:* Create a special display area in the classroom for creative works such as diagrams of inventions and fantasy pictures. Hang up work done both in school and at home, accompanied by the student's written description. Change these pictures often to encourage students to think creatively.
- *Artist of the week:* Set aside a small area in which to display personal information and works by a featured student each week. Include photographs, a list of the child's favorite colors, hobbies, and pets, vital statistics or a biography, positive comments by classmates, and artwork selected by the student. On the first day of the week have the student tell something about the artwork he or she has selected.

Public Displays

Displays that are intended for a wider audience need to be more encompassing than those intended only for the class. Here is a wonderful opportunity to share what the students have learned with other students,

Presentation Panel: "Trees Around Our School," grade 3.

Thinking about Children's Art

Presentation panels are more than a decorative display of student work. What does this presentation panel tell us about the tree study done by this third-grade class? How many subject areas are represented? What role did art play in the children's learning?

teachers, parents, and school visitors. Since the public display will be seen by people who have not participated directly in the artistic process with the students, it is not enough to just display the finished work. Doing so diminishes the process the students went through to create it and is a missed opportunity to educate others about what the class is studying.

To begin decide what the purpose of the display will be. If the sole purpose is to boost the ego of the students or the teacher, the focus is on the finished product rather than the process. Teachers often become fearful to display work that they consider less than high quality because parents or administrators might see it and judge them to be poor teachers. This leads to showing only those children's work that is adult-pleasing and rejecting work that looks out of control or messy. Other teachers want to be fair and show everyone's work but do not want some children to feel bad if their work is not as well done as others. This leads to having children do cookie-cutter-type projects so everyone's will look similar.

If, instead, teachers view the purpose of the display as a way to teach outside viewers what the children think and feel about a topic of study, they are promoting a totally different approach to art. To begin teachers need to think not of a bulletin board waiting to be filled but of presentation panels created with the class in order to summarize, celebrate, and present to a wider audience what the class has accomplished and learned.

Creating a Presentation Panel

Creating a presentation panel is more than tacking up some work. It is a learning process that allows students to exercise choice, cooperation, and creativity, and to apply evaluation skills.

Formats for panels. The term *presentation panel* is used here to refer to any large-scale public display of student work that is educational in nature. The actual display could be as simple as work mounted on a bulletin board or a wall in the hallway, and this will probably be the most common format in schools. However, if possible, consider mounting the work on a series of panels—sheets of large construction paper (24″ by 36″), poster board, painted or paper-covered corrugated cardboard, or foam core boards. This method has many advantages:

- The panels can be prepared in the classroom and then hung outside.
- Teams of students can be assigned to work on separate panels.
- Individual work is less likely to fall off and be damaged or lost.
- The display can be moved to a different location such as sharing it with another class if necessary.
- Stiff panels can be stood up accordion-fold fashion on a table on which artifacts are also displayed.
- The presentation can be saved and used later in the year to review what was learned or bound into a giant book to be shared with future classes.

Components of a presentation panel. The presentation panel should consist of both a visual display and a written narrative that addresses two different audiences: one for the students and one for the parents and other adults in the community.

- *Visual elements:* The visual display should include much more than the students' artwork. The goal should be to provide a picture of all the thought and activity that went into the creation of the final works. Display photographs, charts, graphs, webs, maps, actual artifacts, art reproductions, and any other visual materials that help to explain the process.

- *Student narratives:* The student narrative should explain in their own words what they thought about, did, and learned individually and as a class. This can be presented as student-written captions to the work displayed, writing pieces that were done as part of the project, and direct quotes from the students as recorded by the teacher during the study, taken from anecdotal records and audio- and videotapes. Since this writing is directed toward other students, it should usually be written in large letters using the basic alphabet or cursive style being taught in the school unless a special effect is desired.
- *Adult narrative:* The teacher writes this narrative to explain the purposes, goals, and learning discoveries of the class. It can have brief headings that attract the viewer's attention and then a more detailed description underneath. This can be done using hand lettering but is more easily accomplished with a computer and a large-sized font.

Getting started. Students should know at the very beginning of a study that there will be a visual-narrative presentation of their work. This helps them think more about how they will record and express what they are learning as they become involved in the unit. The process folio is an invaluable tool in making sure students have a place to put those items that they think will help them remember what they have done. As students work, the teacher needs to make sure to remind them to save the bits and pieces of their learning and to take the time to record direct quotes either in anecdotal records or by taping.

They should save all class-created charts, graphs, and so on as well. Many will probably be hung in the classroom during the study, but if there are a great number, consider putting them together in temporary book form by using a stiff cardboard backing and loose-leaf rings. That way they can be taken apart for later display.

Presentation day. Set aside a block of time for planning the display with the class. The teacher can give the class more or less control over what will be included in the presentation depending on the students' age and experience. The following is one way to organize and create presentation panels as a class:

- *Plan.* Together create a chart highlighting those things that the students think would be the most important parts to share with other classes, parents, and school visitors.
- *Sketch.* Sketch a plan of how these items will be spaced out on the presentation panel. Which ideas need a lot of space? Which are the most important? Should the panel be laid as a sequence of events,

Teacher Tip

Mounting Center

It is a good idea when creating presentation panels and portfolios to set up a mounting center on one of the work tables for students to use in mounting their artwork. In the center place the following supplies:

Construction paper and/or tag board in a range of colors for mounts
Stapler and/or white glue
Scissors, including ones that cut fancy edges
Ruler
Self-stick labels for names and titles (or make pre-printed name tags on the computer)
Rubber stamps and stamp pads to create borders (optional)
Examples of different kinds of mounts

as a web, or as a flow chart? If there are a certain number of major ideas, perhaps the presentation could be divided into equal parts.

- *Brainstorm.* Then brainstorm what visual elements could be used to illustrate these ideas.
- *Set criteria.* Develop a list of criteria for selection. What kind of work do the students want others to see? This is an excellent way for students to apply evaluation processes.
- *Select visuals.* Have students examine the contents of their process folios, the class charts, and the other visuals—photos, maps, and so on—for things to include. At the primary level or when creating panels for the first time at the upper levels, this process may be combined with a student-teacher conference. Later this might be a good peer partnering activity.
- *Create new visuals.* The students may discover that they cannot represent the entire process with existing work. Some students may want to create additional work to unify the presentation.
- *Mount visuals.* As a class decide how to mount the work to present a unified appearance. Use color, shape, and size to make the presentation more uniform. For example, students may decide to use blue paper with wavy edges to mount work for a presentation panel on their ocean research. Create a mounting center where students can get the chosen materials for framing their work.
- *Make a title sign.* Make a large sign describing the presentation. With the class decide on the title of the presentation, identify the class, and add the date, if desired. Create eye-catching visuals. This can be the task of an individual, a team of students, or the teacher and can involve drawing, cut paper, paint, or even a

"School Bus."
Cut paper—Lindsey, grade 2.

Thinking about Children's Art

A mounting center allows students to think about different ways to frame their art. How has this second grader expanded the meaning of her work by adding an arrow pattern to her paper mount? What kinds of activities would help students think more deeply about how their work is presented?

computer poster-type software program (see "Teacher Resources" at the end of the chapter).

- *Write student narratives.* Students, even at the primary level, can write captions, explanations, labels, and headings for the selected visuals. This process helps them remember, rethink, and reinvent their work. Emphasize that they use their best writing and spelling. Use peer editing to double check the work. At the primary level using lined sentence strips (available from many school suppliers in a variety of colors) provides needed guidelines and ensures the lettering is large enough. Upper-level students can place lined grids beneath white paper to provide a guide or use their measuring skills to draw guidelines.
- *Write adult narratives.* Although teachers can do this on their own, the students will benefit from discussing the purpose of the project and what they think they learned. Teachers can then incorporate this information into their adult narrative.
- *Put it together.* If the work will be hung on an existing bulletin board or wall, roll out a sheet of brown kraft paper on the classroom floor

Teaching in Action

Ways to Mount Two-Dimensional Artwork

Method 1: Single Mount

- Select a piece of construction paper or tag board slightly larger than the artwork. Standard paper sizes can be mounted on the next size up (8½″ by 11″ on 9″ by 12″, 12″ by 18″ on 18″ by 24″, 18″ by 24″ on 24″ by 36″).
- If necessary, trim the artwork slightly, but never cut off any major part of a work or change its original shape, such as turning a rectangle into a circle or animal shape.
- Center the artwork. The bottom margin can be slightly larger than the top.
- Staple or glue the work to the mount. If gluing, place a tiny amount of glue in a thin line around the outer edge. Do not put glue in the center of the work as that will wrinkle and sometimes discolor it.
- Attach name and title to mount using a self-stick label.

Method 2: Double Mount*

- Cut a piece of white or black paper so that it is about one inch longer and wider than the artwork on all four sides.
- Center the work on this paper and glue down lightly.
- Place work in center of a larger piece of colored construction paper and glue or staple.

Other Methods

- *Student-made mats:* Cut openings in construction paper by folding it in half and cutting on the fold or by drawing the opening and then cutting it out.
- *Commercial mats:* Pre-cut mats, designed to fit standard-sized art paper, are available from most art suppliers. They give work a very finished appearance and are reusable many times.
- *Strip mounts:* Glue a strip of corrugated cardboard or a wooden dowel to the top back edge of an artwork. Punch holes in the ends of the cardboard and attach a piece of yarn for hanging. This works well on cloth and fiber projects.

**Note:* Double-mounted artwork is easier to remove from presentation panels, an important consideration if students will eventually take work home.

and have students place the work in its possible location. Alternatively, hang the paper on a classroom wall and have students tape the work in place. As a class discuss the overall effect and make any agreed-upon adjustments. Make a sketch to work from and then collect the work and hang it in the final location as planned. If individual panels are being made, use the same method, or give teams of students each responsibility for putting together one panel. When the work is arranged on the panels, put them side by side as they will be displayed and discuss the effect with the class. If the arrangement is agreeable, glue down the pieces with white glue and let dry. Then hang completed panels.

Teacher Tip

Teacher's Display Tool Kit

The following items are indispensable when putting up displays. Transport them to the location of the display in a carry tote or tool box.

Calligraphy pens, markers, and steel brushes. These can be invaluable for hand lettering signs and posters.

Fine nylon thread. Use to suspend items from ceiling.

Fine wire. Use to suspend and support items and to affix objects on to cardboard panels.

Masking tape. Use on most surfaces for temporary displays.

Mason's chalk line. Use this to mark a straight edge when mounting work on a wall.

Ruler. Use to measure distances between works and to trim mounts.

Shears. Use to trim mounts and cut thread.

Small tacking stapler. Use for attaching items to cork boards and cork strips.

Staples and staple remover.

Straight pins. Use for attaching thick work to cork boards, cork strips, and some kinds of ceiling tile. (*Note:* Use with care around young children.)

T-square. Use to make perpendicular lines and edges.

In addition a paper cutter should be available for teacher use in a teacher's room or at the office. For safety's sake avoid having a cutter in a classroom or allowing student use.

Creating Aesthetic Displays

Presentation panels will, by their very nature, contain a wide range of disparate materials (see At a Glance 10.4). The challenge is to arrange these items in an attractive and attention-getting way.

The following guidelines can help teachers focus on the basic aesthetic design of the display:

Keep it simple. "The human mind," writes Margaret Jackson, "longs for simplicity and goes to great lengths to assimilate information from the world around it in an understandable form" (1993, p. 71). With so many pieces involved in making a presentation panel, it is not necessary to add extraneous decoration. Include only works and narrative that help explain the learning process. Avoid commercially made bulletin board cutouts and stereotyped symbols.

Make it representative. Make sure that every child is represented by one special work, but do not try to include every work done by every child or every single class chart and graph.

Displaying Three-Dimensional Work.

Thinking about Children's Art

Paper-covered coffee cans and strips of tag board have been used to create an attractive showcase display of children's clay work. What other information could have been provided to make the display more informative for parents and community?

Use color to unify. Choose a neutral tone for the panel background such as white, off-white, beige, gray, or black. Then select one basic color for the mounts. In selecting the basic mount color, consider the colors that are in the works to be mounted.

- Delicate and neutral-tone work should be mounted on colors that are only slightly deeper or lighter in value. A very pale work mounted on a black background will look even paler. A very dark work mounted on a very light background will look darker.
- Strongly colored works look best on neutral backgrounds, especially white and black.
- The mount color will bring out its complement in an artwork. For example, a red mount will emphasize greens, an orange mount will emphasize blues (see Chapter 13 for more details on combining colors).
- If in doubt about the mounting color or if there is a wide variation in the works, it is always safest to double mount all the works on black or all on white.

Allow sufficient space. All works need some space around them. "Busy" works need more space than quiet works.

Keep it perpendicular. Make sure that all horizontals and verticals are in line. Use a ruler, T-square, or chalk line.

Stagger the placement. Avoid hanging work in even rows. It is very hard to get each work exactly in line. Instead stagger the pieces, mixing together different sizes, while striving for balance. Place larger pieces centrally with smaller ones around them or place the large ones to one side and have the smaller ones trail off to the other side.

Teacher Tip

Health and Safety Regulations

Before planning any display, be sure to check on the school's fire code and safety guidelines. There are usually restrictions on how close to doorways and fire exits displays may be set up. There may also be restrictions on how much of a wall may be covered with paper, how close to the ceiling it can reach, and whether or not items can be suspended from the ceiling.

Always make sure that there are no sharp edges or corners that could hurt children, and be sure that the display does not block walkways.

At a Glance 10.4

Trees: A Sample Presentation Panel

Presentation panels can contain a wide variety of work. For example, a first-grade presentation panel for a class of twenty-six children* showing what they learned during a month-long study of trees might include the following:

- Three memory sketches of trees done at the very beginning of the study
- Quotes about what each child thinks is special about trees
- Six observational tree drawings done while looking at a tree in the school yard
- Five rubbings of tree bark and actual pieces of bark
- Two paintings done with sticks with captions telling what it felt like to paint with a stick
- Actual tree branches
- Three leaf prints with labels identifying the tree they are from
- Pressed leaves
- One tree ring drawing and an actual cross-section of a tree
- Tree trunk measurements
- A chart listing uses for wood
- A class collage mural of things made from wood
- Handmade recycled paper quilt made by the whole class
- A class-made web about trees
- A class-made map of trees growing around the school
- Photographs of children drawing the trees, making paper, and painting with sticks
- Two three-dimensional tree house designs
- Four tree house stories

Note: Each child has one individually created artwork on display.

Consider eye-level. There is a tendency to hang artwork up high so that it is not touched or damaged. Doing so, however, makes it difficult for other students to enjoy and learn from the display. Teachers can foster appreciation of class displays by taking their classes on viewing tours of the school and modeling ways to look at and enjoy the displays without touching.

Respecting Children's Work

No matter where the artwork is displayed, it is important to show respect for the individual artist by making sure the work is shown to its best advantage. Take care to do the following:

- *Label it.* Clearly label all displayed work with the child's name so that parents and friends can readily find it. Do not, however, write

Teaching in Action

Displaying Three-Dimensional Work

Three-dimensional work can be very challenging to display. It is best to display it at slightly different levels so that each individual work can be enjoyed.

- Attach small pieces to a cardboard or foam core panel using nylon thread or wire passed discreetly around the pieces and then pushed through the board and tied or twisted in the back.
- Suspend light works from the ceiling by pins and thread. There are also special hooks to use on suspended ceilings.
- Arrange work on a table in front of the presentation panels.
- Paint the inside or outside of various-sized boxes to serve as sculpture stands for large pieces. Stack the boxes so work can be displayed both inside the box and on top of it.
- Cover large institutional-sized food cans with colored paper and place colored pieces of stiff cardboard on top to make smaller display stands that work well in showcases.

names or captions directly on the child's artwork as the work belongs to the child. Use a separate piece of paper or write on the mount.

- *Care for it.* Work should not be folded, wrinkled, or soiled.
- *Value it.* Do not cut large pieces off or use a mat to change the shape of the work without consulting the child.
- *Accept it.* Do not draw on, outline, or change an artwork in any way to make it look "better." This insults the children's ability to express themselves and reflects a lack of self-confidence on the part of the educator.

Art Events

Another way to share children's learning with family and friends is by staging an art event. Such events allow students to interact with their audience and can take many different forms and serve a variety of purposes.

Parent-child workshops. Art provides a wonderful way to bring parents together with their children for a learning experience. Many of the group art activities in described in Chapter 7 are ideal for mixed-age groups. Collection murals, quilt murals, and cut paper murals all allow a range of contributions. Parents also enjoy painting and using clay alongside their children. Watching the interaction among family members can also be a rewarding experience for teachers, who may gain special insights into parental expectations and concerns.

Teacher Tip

Displaying Children's Art at Home

Parents are often bewildered by what to do with the artwork that their child brings home from school. It is helpful to send home a note that provides some guidance.

Dear Family,

This year your child will be making many artworks for different purposes. Each artwork is unique and represents your child's thoughts and feelings. Please take a moment to enjoy the work with your child. Ask your child to tell you what he or she was thinking about when creating the work. What did he or she learn when making this work? Is there a special story to go with it or was it inspired by something being studied in class?

There are many ways to display your child's art. Many families hang each new piece on the refrigerator door with magnets, but that is not the only way. Some children like to have a special place in their bedroom to hang their work.

You can buy an inexpensive frame that fits school-sized paper. Choose a special work to be displayed and replace it at intervals. Usually the frame will allow stacking several works on top of each other behind the one on display so it will also provide a safe storage place over the years. Someday your child will enjoy looking at his or her art and remembering that special moment.

Sincerely,

Your Child's Teacher

Art shows. Putting on an art show is an excellent way to link young artists with an audience. The process of looking through their portfolios, selecting work that represents their most important efforts, mounting it, and preparing written materials to go with it allows students to see their artwork in a new way. "Artworks that are 'completed' by being placed in a folder," points out George Szekely, "are not finished in the artist's mind until they are presented to and studied by an audience" (1988, p. 154).

There are many ways and locations in which to organize such a show:

Teaching in Action

A Gallery of My Own

Artist/teacher George Szekely assigns each student a personal gallery space in the school. This space could be in the hallways, gymnasium, or cafeteria, or students could even a create a personal show inside a large box. He gives students the responsibility for planning a schedule for the display of their own work, found objects, or the work of a guest artist. Students produce written press releases, brochures, and catalogs to accompany their show. Other students are asked to pose as newspaper reporters, art critics, art collectors, and even museum guards.

"Through the Gallery Owners' program," says Szekely, "students take over exhibition responsibilities usually held by the teacher. While they are learning about the exhibition process and their own art, students also discover audiences—how to involve, interest, and effectively communicate with a public" (1988, p. 156).

- A class could hang artworks around the classroom and then write invitations to another class or two to come to a gala opening. Celebrate by passing out a student-created catalog and serving a small snack.
- Hang the artworks outside the classroom and write up a brochure to distribute to each class asking them to enjoy the show when they pass by.
- Join together with several classes or the whole school and hold a large exhibit in the halls, cafeteria, or gymnasium. Advertise the show by sending invitations home to families, hanging up posters, and making brochures and catalogs. Have students work in teams to create a decor and hang the work in attractive ways.
- Contact local businesses to see if anyone would be willing to display the children's artwork. Many small businesses are happy to link with schools in their neighborhood. Students will work harder if they know their work will be seen by a wider audience.

The Celebration

Thematic units, projects, literature-based units, and featured art units all lend themselves to grand finales. Art will play a major role in all of these, whether it is creating a rain forest in the classroom for a "Rain Forest Safari" or putting on a dramatization of *Charlotte's Web.*

As At a Glance 10.5 shows, celebrations and festivals rely heavily on visual and spatial elements, often combined with written work, in order to change the environment and bring learning alive. Successful celebrations share what the children have learned in a highly interactive way and are much like presentation panels brought to life.

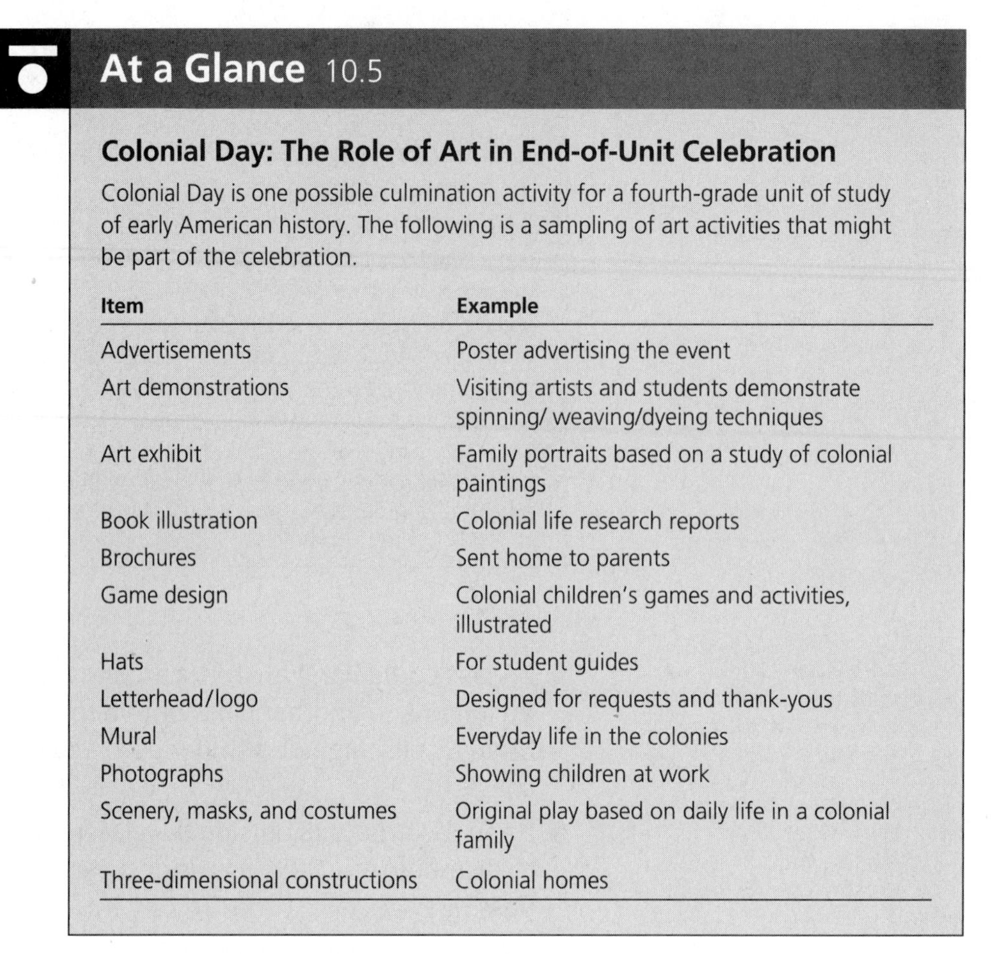

At a Glance 10.5

Colonial Day: The Role of Art in End-of-Unit Celebration

Colonial Day is one possible culmination activity for a fourth-grade unit of study of early American history. The following is a sampling of art activities that might be part of the celebration.

Item	Example
Advertisements	Poster advertising the event
Art demonstrations	Visiting artists and students demonstrate spinning/ weaving/dyeing techniques
Art exhibit	Family portraits based on a study of colonial paintings
Book illustration	Colonial life research reports
Brochures	Sent home to parents
Game design	Colonial children's games and activities, illustrated
Hats	For student guides
Letterhead/logo	Designed for requests and thank-yous
Mural	Everyday life in the colonies
Photographs	Showing children at work
Scenery, masks, and costumes	Original play based on daily life in a colonial family
Three-dimensional constructions	Colonial homes

A celebration can be a small event held in a classroom, to which parents are invited, or it can be a major school happening that involves the efforts of many classes in the school. It takes a tremendous amount of work on the part of students and teachers, but is always worth the effort. Celebrations bring closure to a unit of study in which students have expended a great deal of time and energy. Celebrations provide an excellent performance assessment tool that allows students to share what they learned independently. They also provide an important link with the wider school community and the students' parents, informing them of the learning that has been happening in the class. Most importantly celebrations are events that students will remember all their lives.

Putting a Celebration Together

Planning for a celebration begins not at the end of the unit but, like presentation panels, at the beginning. Students should know what they are working toward. Will they be expected to put on a play, mount an art exhibit, create a hands-on museum? To whom and where will they be presenting?

- *Brainstorm.* Create a list of possible activities that might take place at the end of the unit. Would the students want to put on a play, create a hands-on museum, mount an exhibit, invite other classes to a teach-in, and so on? (See At a Glance 10.6.)
- *Make a choice.* Choose one or two possible events and set a date even though setting a date may seem scary early in a unit. In reality doing so can provide a direction to the study unit that makes the learning more focused and meaningful. Students who are studying the water cycle, for example, will pay more attention if they know they will be dramatizing it for their parents.
- *Start making contacts.* Contact visiting artists, reserve exhibition space, and make special items such as costumes. Make sure parents are informed well in advance of the date so they can arrange to attend.
- *Collaborate with others.* Invite other teachers to help with the event. Celebratory events provide the ideal occasion to coordinate teaching with reading, special education, speech, physical education, music, and art teachers.
- *Arrange supervision.* Start early to enlist help from parents in planning the event. Parents can help obtain special supplies and refreshments, make scenery and costumes, assist with rehearsals, murals, and other special projects, such as decorate T-shirts to wear during the event.

At a Glance 10.6

Ideas for Celebratory Events

Each of these ideas can be used individually or combined in many creative ways:

- *Carnival:* Put together carnival-type games that relate to the theme and utilize information the students have learned so parents must rely on their children for help in winning. Hold the carnival outdoors and invite performance artists to perform.
- *Demonstration:* Have students demonstrate what they have learned. They can do science experiments, oral readings, art activities, and more.
- *Dance or dramatization:* Bring to life a book, folktale, historical event, life of a famous person, or scientific concept such as the growth of a seed or the metamorphosis of a butterfly.
- *Exhibit:* Create a beautiful display of work done during the unit and have students act as guides.
- *Mystery search or safari:* Create a treasure hunt or puzzle for visitors to solve from clues revealed in the students' work and/or by interviewing the students.
- *Video:* Produce a video that illustrates the students' learning, and have a premier showing for family and friends.

- Create promotional literature. As the date grows closer and plans are finalized, begin creating literature and artwork to advertise the coming event. This provides the ideal time to introduce poster and brochure design (see Chapter 12) and have students work in teams to create a publicity campaign.

Design the visual elements of the event. Starting about a week before, have students begin to make the visual elements that will define the space of the event: the scenery for the play, the artwork that will turn the room into a special environment such as a forest, space capsule, or treasure hunt, depending on the theme of the celebration.

Conclusion

OPENING THE CLASSROOM DOOR

The language of art is more than a means of learning. It is a vital component of life in our communities. It provides employment, entertainment, and beauty. Our students must see art in its living context. We begin by displaying art in our classrooms and hallways while teaching our students how to be both artists and audience. We must introduce our students to role models from the community—people who are not only expert in their field but also passionate about the role of art in their lives. We must share with them the artistic wealth that is stored in the museums, parks, and buildings that surround our school. Most importantly we must include parents in these artistic experiences so that they can learn and grow not only in understanding their children's art but also in valuing the role of art in our community.

For our society's sake we must open the classroom door and bring in audiences, experts, and events that make art a meaningful part of both students' and their families' lives.

Teacher Resources

REFERENCES

Edwards, C. P., Gandini, L., & Forman, G. (1993). *The hundred languages of children: The Reggio Emilia approach to early childhood education.* Norwood, NJ: Ablex.

Harris, L. (1992). *Americans and the arts IV. Schools, communities and the arts: A research compendium.* New York: American Council for the Arts.

Jackson, M. (1993). *Creative display and environment.* Portsmouth, NH: Heinemann.

Leonhard, C. (1992). *The status of arts education in American public schools. Schools, communities and the arts: A research compendium.* New York: American Council for the Arts.

Szekely, G. (1988). *Encouraging creativity in art lessons.* New York: Teachers College Press.

Teacher Guides

For ideas for creating presentation panels see:

Helm, J. H., Beneke, S., & Steinheimer, K. (1998). *Windows on learning.* New York: Teachers College Press.

Hodgson, N. (1991). *Improving classroom display.* Norfolk, England: Tarquin.

Horn, G .F. (1973). *Visual communication: Bulletin boards, exhibits, visual aids.* Worchester, MA: Davis.

For guidance in hand lettering see:

Solo, D. X. (Ed.) (1995). *100 ornamental alphabets.* Garden City: Dover.

Solo, D. X. (Ed.) (1997). *100 calligraphic alphabets.* Garden City: Dover.

For more ideas for field trips consult:

Redleaf, R. (1997). *Open the door: Let's explore more: Neighborhood field trips for young children.* St. Paul, MN: Redleaf.

Software

The following software can be used by students for creating captions, signs, posters, and banners:

Print Artist (Knowledge Adventure)
Print Shop Deluxe (Broderbund)
SuperPrint (Scholastic)

Videos

Don't Eat the Pictures: Sesame Street at the Metropolitan Museum, Crystal Publications

How to Visit an Art Museum, Art Institute of Chicago

School-Museum Collaboration, Getty Education Institute

Web Sites

Lincoln Center Institute
www.lincolncenter.org

National Assembly of State Arts Agencies
http://www.nasaa-arts.org

Our Stories, Grade 1

Art and writing naturally go together. Children need many opportunities to create art to illustrate their stories and to write stories to accompany their art.

"I like caterpillars."
Marker and pencil—Megan, grade 1.

"What it feels like to be sick."
Marker and crayon—Laurel, grade 1.

"Dinosaurs are fighting. They are big. The end."
Tempera paint—Michael, grade 1.

A World of Colors

What We Learned Thematic units allow students to explore concepts from multiple perspectives. In art we explored mixing the secondary and tertiary colors. In science we learned about the spectrum and the reflection of light. We learned that paint pigments mix differently than colored light does.

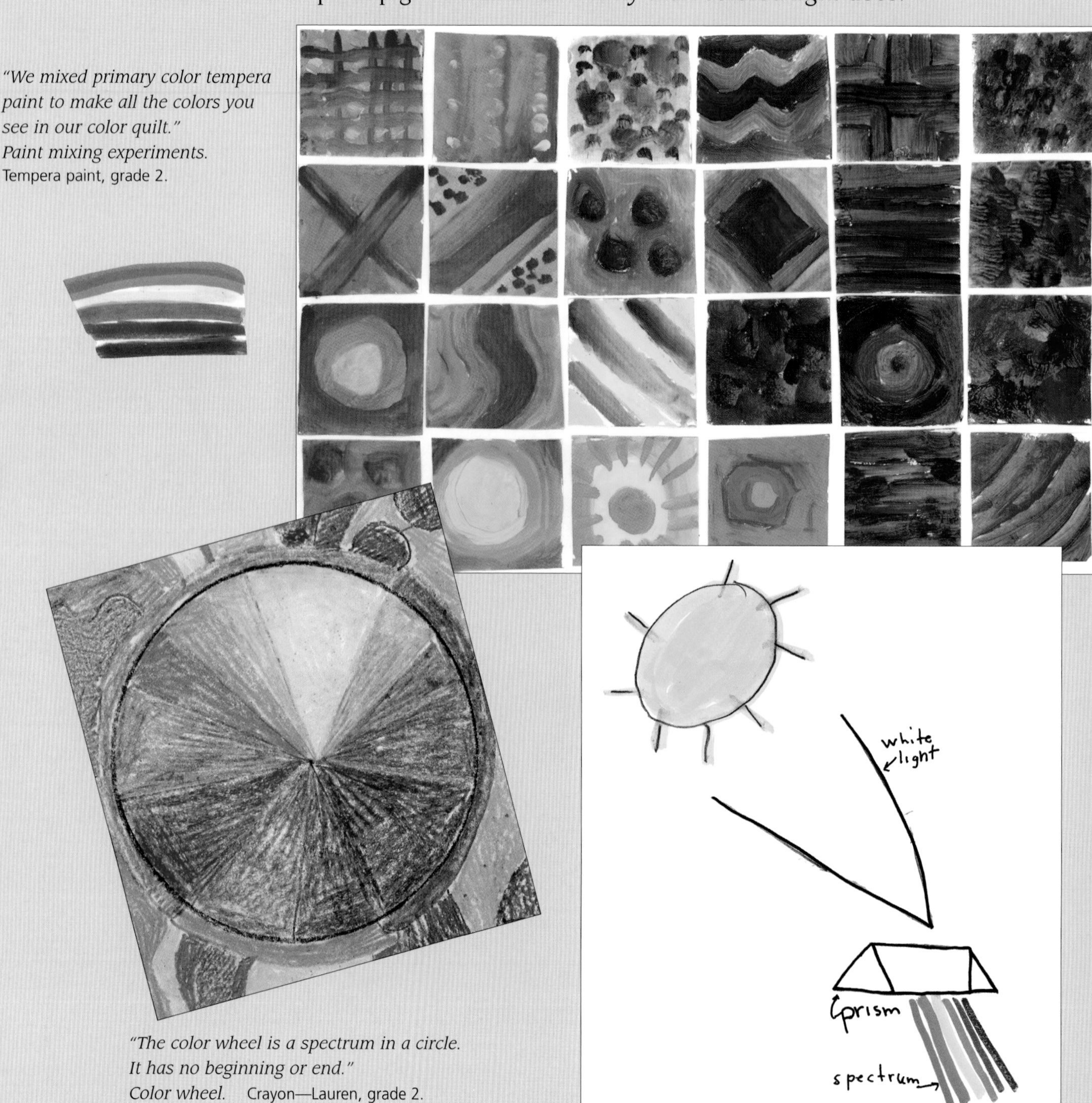

"We mixed primary color tempera paint to make all the colors you see in our color quilt."
Paint mixing experiments.
Tempera paint, grade 2.

"The color wheel is a spectrum in a circle. It has no beginning or end."
Color wheel. Crayon—Lauren, grade 2.

"Prisms are cool. They make white into rainbow colors."
Science Notes. Marker—Marissa, grade 2.

A Thematic Unit, Grade 2

What We Did In language arts we read poetry about colors, and then we wrote our own. We mixed colors and then made paintings inspired by our poems.

"Mixing colors is lots of fun. You can make a lot of colors from just a few."
Blue face. Tempera paint, cloth, and paper—Tracy, grade 2.

"Blue Man."
Color poem by Tracy.

Blue

Sometimes blue is
happy.
Sometimes blue is sad.
What would you
do if your face
was blue?
Would you feel
Happy and sad too?

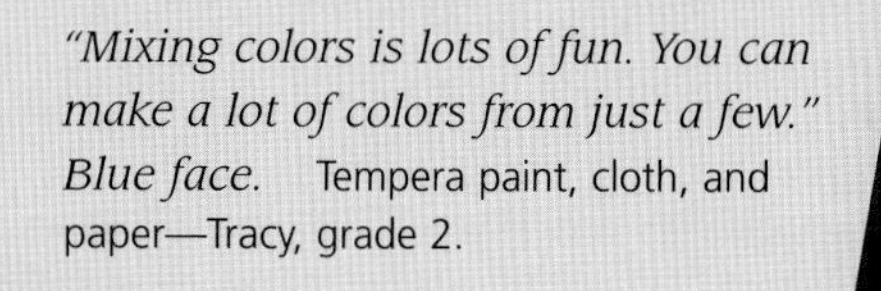

"Green Jungle."
Color poem by Brittany.

Dark green
Light green
Yellow green
Leaf green
There's lots of green in the
jungle.

Green to hide in
So the lions can't find you.
Nice safe green.

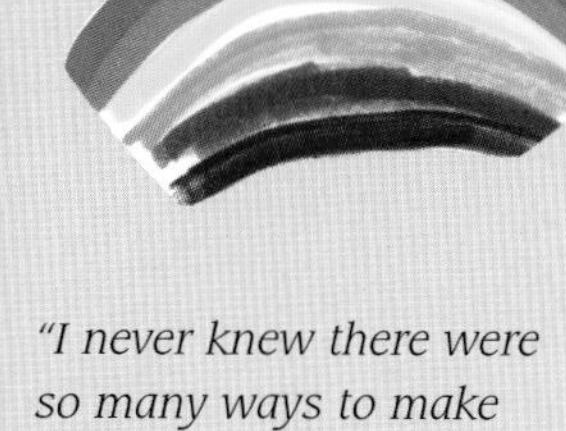

"I never knew there were so many ways to make greens."
Lions in the jungle.
Tempera paint—Brittany, grade 2.

Learning about Ourselves

Art provides a way for children to share information about themselves. It allows them to discover what we share in common and what are our differences. To learn about each other, we made graphs to show our hobbies. We looked at portraits done by other artists and then drew our self-portraits. We made pictures of the people who are important to us.

"My mom gets all dressed up for work."
Oil pastels—Loren, grade 3.

"My dad lifts weights. He is very strong. I want to be strong like him."
Colored chalk—Brian, grade 3.

"My mom and dad are the best in the world."
Marker and watercolor—Kristy, grade 3.

And Creating Community, Grade 3

We are a community of learners. Each of us looks different and likes to do different things. But we all have the same needs. We want to be safe, respected, and treated kindly. This is who we are.

Class quilt. Crayon and marker—grade 3.

Name poem by Mariah.

"My Favorites." Marker—Marie, grade 3.

From Loom to Computer

Other cultures come alive as students manipulate yarns to create art inspired by traditional art forms.

"We studied the yarn designs of the Huichol people of Mexico. It inspired me to try to create areas of color and pattern using yarn."
"Blue Bird." Yarn and wool collage—Francis, grade 4.

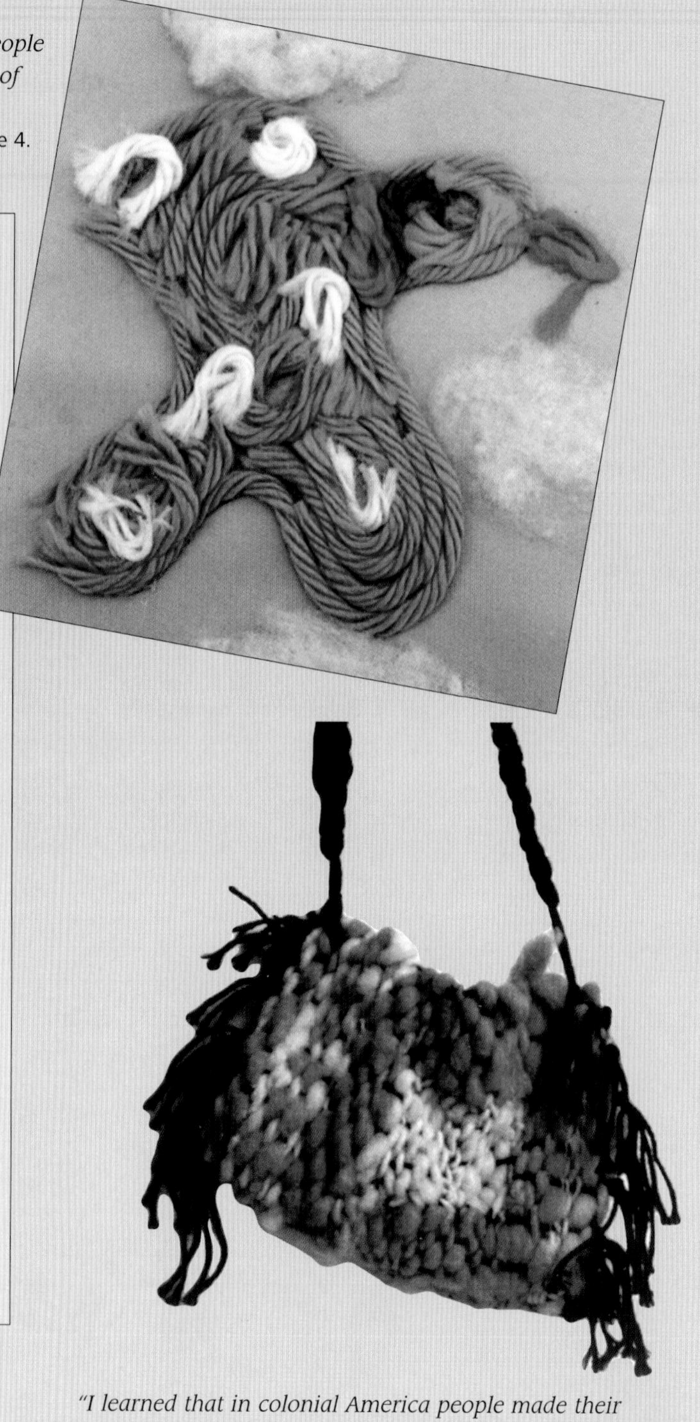

"The Navajos weave beautiful rugs based on geometric-shaped designs. In my tapestry I created a picture of a pine tree by weaving a triangle shape."
"Pine Tree." Tapestry weaving—Kevin, grade 4.

"I learned that in colonial America people made their own cloth. I spun the wool into yarn with a spindle and then dyed it with onion skins. It took a long time. If I lived back then, I probably wouldn't have many clothes."
Woven bag. Hand-spun, hand-dyed wool—Lauren, grade 4.

A Study in Patterns, Grade 4

Old and new come together in the creation of patterns and the discovery and application of mathematical concepts.

"The computer makes it easy to draw symmetical shapes."
"Duckie." Computer graphic—Connie, grade 4.

"We were exploring how to make geometric shapes on the computer, and I made this bird."
"Aurora." Computer graphic—Carolyn, grade 4.

"We designed motifs on the computer and used them to create patterned paper for our neighborhood mural."
"The Neighborhood." Collage mural, grade 4.

Exploring Form and Design, Grade 5

Each attempt to create a three-dimensional object challenges students to see in new ways and to solve new problems while building on past experiences.

"You have to make the stem much thicker than it would be in glass so it can support the weight of the clay."
Goblet. Painted modeling dough—Gayle, grade 5.

"When you carve the clay, you create shadows."
Mask. Carved clay—Edward, grade 5.

"I learned that you have to make sure that the coils are joined together, if you don't want your pot to fall apart or leak."
Coiled pot. Glazed, fired clay—Nick, grade 5.

Part Three

Producing Art

Chapter 11

Building Artistry
Process and Production

Deep knowledge often comes from learning things through the hands as well as the mind.

Muriel Silberstein-Storfer (1996, p. 15)

ARTISTS AT WORK

Artists Conferencing

Brent: Look at how these two colors mixed together. I didn't think they would do that. Maybe I could use this color in this painting I want to do of my house.

Shanelle: Let me see your sketch. Where would you use that color?

Brent: I was thinking it would be just right for the roof. The shingles are kind of old and this looks like an old gray shingle color.

Shanelle: What other paint samples do you have?

Brent: I have these other grays and over here are my samples for the sides of the house. It's green.

Shanelle: You made lots of grays. How about using several of these different grays for your roof?

Brent: I hadn't thought of that. Yeah, that's a good idea. I could make it look kind of 3-D that way. Maybe I should go make some more samples—this time using several grays.

Introduction

PRODUCING ART

The word *art* probably derives from the Renaissance term *arte* meaning craftsmanship. Today the word still carries much of this connotation. Artists are expected to know the nature of the art media they are using and to handle it with skill. We also expect that people knowledgeable about art will be able to use art terms meaningfully in discussing works of art—both their own and others'.

This chapter introduces the vocabulary, definitions, and basic art media that are used in most classrooms. Rather than presenting novel, ready-made art activities, we provide information that will allow both the novice and experienced educator to look at ordinary paper, paint, and modeling materials as tools for thinking and learning as students experience the artistic process firsthand.

Setting the Stage

WHAT DO ARTISTS DO?

Artists create visual and physical forms that imaginatively convey ideas, experiences, and feelings. Across the span of history art has been created for a wide variety of purposes. Before students can begin to create an artwork, they need to have a sense of purpose, to know why they are pursuing this particular activity. Because art materials are intrinsically appealing to the senses and invite exploration, it is easy to think that is sufficient motivation for students to create art. Unfortunately when exploration forms the sole basis for art creation, students are left with the feeling that although fun, art is relatively unimportant compared to the other school subjects, which prepare them for life.

Every art lesson, every discussion of a work of art must address the question of purpose. See At a Glance 11.1 for reasons why people create art. Whether working on an individual project or discussing a work as a class, the following questions, based on the range of purposes for which art has been created, can elicit thought and discussion of a work's purpose:

- What can be learned from this artwork?
- Does this artwork add value to an everyday object, or can it change the everyday surroundings?
- Does this artwork express the artist's feelings or ideas about the topic?
- Does this artwork attract and fascinate the eyes and hold the attention of the viewer?
- What story does this artwork tell? Is it imaginary or true?

At a Glance 11.1

Reasons for Creating Art

Communicative: Art can convey information.

Decorative: Art can be used to make objects of daily life special and more valued.

Expressive: Art can be used to show a personal vision or an emotional response to an experience.

Illusionary: Art can be used to trick the viewer's eye.

Illustrative: Art can be used to convert information in another field, such as literature or physical science, into a visual or physical form.

Narrative: Art can tell a story or record historical events.

Persuasive: Art can change the viewer's ideas about a concept or belief.

Religious: Art can express religious beliefs or be used to create objects that have a ceremonial role or serve as a symbol of belief.

- Does this artwork challenge or change what one believes about an idea or concept?
- What does this work of art say about the time and culture in which it was made?
- Does this artwork represent the artist's or culture's religious beliefs?

The Basic Media

The nature of an artwork is intimately tied to the medium and methods that the artist chooses. Each medium requires different skills and knowledge and may be valued in different ways by different cultures. Certain methods may go in and out of style. New techniques are invented; hard-to-find or less effective materials are abandoned.

Contemporary media can be divided into two general areas. *Graphic media* produce works that exist in a relatively flat plane such as drawing, painting, and collage. *Sculptural works* exist in three dimensions and can be seen from many viewpoints.

Many media, of course, cannot be defined in one strict way. The boundaries blur and blend with the creativity of the artist. Crafts, for example, is an all-encompassing term for those art forms, both two- and three-dimensional, that are useful, that grow out of the creation of useful objects, or that utilize materials or techniques traditional to the creation of everyday objects. Crafts cover a wide range of both two- and three-dimensional media and methods including pottery, basketry, weaving, and jewelry. For most of the world these works are the most important art forms, the ones that decorate and enliven people's daily lives.

Students need to tap into the historical and ethnic heritage of their cultures through studying about and using these art forms. These involve learning specific techniques and helping students appreciate the value of handcrafted objects.

Media for the Elementary School

From the wide range of media available to artists some have become traditional in school art programs. They have persisted because they are cheap, safe, or readily available. Some of these media, such as play dough and crayons, are used only by children. Others, like markers, tempera, and construction paper, are used more heavily by students than adult artists. This is also true of many art techniques, such as crayon scraffitto. To save costs children are often asked to be creative with the discards of a consumer society—cereal boxes, egg cartons, and paper towel tubes.

In general teachers should strive to give their students real art materials. Although some common adult art materials such as oil paint and stained glass are not safe for students to use, many fine art materials such as charcoal and watercolor can be used by children of all ages. Students need high-quality brushes, artist's drawing pencils, and strong sturdy paper if they are to be expected to work at a high level. Paintbrushes that lose their hair, paints that crack, and glues that do not hold can frustrate young artists. Parents who see what appears to be trash glued on a paper are likely to discard the work.

The following art media should form the basis of elementary art programs. Each will be examined in detail in this and the next two chapters.

Clay. The flexible, forgiving nature of basic modeling compounds such as play dough and modeling clay allows students to explore three-dimensional forms in a way not possible with any other medium. All children need to have many opportunities to work with modeling materials. This improves visual perception and lays the groundwork for increased skill in all the other areas of art, especially drawing. Working with modeling materials also requires students to plan ahead mentally and use a step-by-step approach in order to be successful.

Drawing. Drawing media consist of any tool that leaves a relatively dry mark or line on the picture surface such as pencil, chalk, and pen and ink. Often used in art instruction because they are cheap and easily maintained and stored, drawing media and techniques form the backbone of instruction. It is through drawing that students can quickly express their ideas in any subject. It is through sketching and planning that students can set a course for using or enhancing other

Teacher Tip

An Artist's Vocabulary

Craftsmanship: Skill in handling materials and tools.

Design: The arrangement of all the visual elements into an artwork that accomplishes its intended purpose.

Graphic arts: Artworks that are two-dimensional.

Landscape: Art that represents natural inland or coastal scenery.

Media: The materials and tools used to create a work of art.

Portrait: A likeness of a face.

Seascape: Artwork that shows a view of the sea.

Still life: Representations of inanimate objects.

Style: A particular combination of media, technique, and ideas that produces artwork with a distinctive appearance.

Subject matter: Something represented in a work of art.

Technique: Specialized procedures and methods used to create a work of art.

Theme: A unifying idea or concept.

art media. Drawing is found in the illustration of books, the sketches for a painting or a mural, and the design on a pottery vase.

Computer graphics. This new and growing art medium employs technology to allow artists to create and magnify effects based on repetition, exaggeration, and multiple dimensions that were tedious or too difficult to accomplish through existing media.

In this time of rapid change more people are likely to have a computer in their homes than art supplies and there is an increasing desire to produce beautifully designed graphics. A lack of instruction in computer design and artistic self-doubt, however, have led to a reliance on clip art and canned graphic programs. Being able to use the computer artistically empowers the artist in us all. Studying and creating computer images also prepares students for understanding and appreciating the visual effects that already permeate our culture and sets the stage for new art forms of the future.

Fiber. A fiber is any thin, flexible material that can be woven or interlaced. Fibers of plants and animals have been used from earliest times to create both useful and decorative objects. Learning to create baskets and textiles, studying their historical roots, and relating the design of these art forms to cultural and artistic trends ties the present to the heritage of the past.

Books to Share

Purpose

The following books can be used to introduce the different purposes of art to students:

For the Primary

Angelou, M. (1994). *My painted house. My friendly chicken.* New York: Clarkson-Potter.
A young boy shares the artwork of his culture: the painted houses of the Ndebele of Africa.

Florian, D. (1993). *The painter.* New York: Greenwillow.
This book uses simple text to explain what a painter does and feels.

For the Intermediate

Kesselman, W. (1980). *Emma.* New York: Doubleday.
An elderly woman takes up painting as a way to surround herself with the joyful memories of her life.

Locker, T. (1994). *Miranda's smile.* New York: Dial.
An artist tries to paint his daughter's special smile.

Schick, E. (1987). *Art lessons.* New York: Greenwillow.
An eight-year-old boy takes drawing lessons from a neighbor and learns to see as an artist.

Paper. Artists have worked on many surfaces, from the stone wall of caves to the wet plaster of the frescos, but in our culture paper and art go together. We can draw and paint on paper. We can cut and glue it into collages. We can even turn it into three-dimensional forms and sculptures. In the school setting paper usually forms a mainstay of an art program.

Paint. There is nothing more sensorial than applying a wet fluid medium to a surface. Paint has been an important art medium since the cave art of the Paleolithic and links the child at the easel with painters across the centuries. Varying in color, intensity, and thickness, it allows a wide range of expression. Learning to control the nuances of painting helps students develop confidence as artists. Paint allows students to expand upon their drawings and to explore what happens when colors are mixed and combined.

Photography. Our environment is full of photographic images. We spend hours watching television and videos. Like the computer, the camera is commonly found in most homes. But although it is often not seen as such in the general culture, photography is an art form. It is the creation of graphic images that can be manipulated and used for all the same purposes as a drawing or painting. Students need to learn to analyze and evaluate photographic images. They need to be taught how to use their cameras and camcorders to capture their lives artistically.

Printmaking. Making a copy of an image is a powerful experience. Printmaking allows children to see art as going beyond the one-time experience. It provides a wonderful introduction to the world of publishing. At the same time each handmade print is unique, requiring the students to turn images around in their minds and visualize how the process itself will affect the end result. Students can use a wide range of printing techniques. Some are appropriate for creating decorative papers, others for enhancing drawings and paintings or producing effects not possible in other ways.

Sculpture. Sculptural activities allow students to work with space. They must think about forms from more than one viewpoint and manipulate the relationships among them. Sculptures can be made from a wide range of materials including paper, clay, cardboard, blocks, wood, metal, and stone.

Media and Instruction

Experiencing an art medium directly allows a student to better understand the kinds of decisions an artist must make. For this reason it is important to expose students to a range of media and techniques. At the same time briefly sampling hundreds of art materials and methods does not allow them to develop the level of skill needed to feel confident as artists and to express ideas meaningfully. Teachers must strike a balance between breadth and depth.

Regardless of which media the teacher selects for a grade level, each should be the major focus of study for a sufficient length of time so that students can gain confidence and skill. This medium should form the basis of instruction, and the teacher should encourage students to practice and master it to the highest level. This requires a sufficient length of time for students to learn about the medium. One forty-minute period spent making a small weaving or doing a crayon scraffito project will not suffice.

The components for mastery of a medium include the following:

- *Role of medium:* Introduce students to the way the medium is used by other artists. Discussion should focus on how the medium influenced the appearance and form of the artwork. Why did the artist choose the particular techniques used? How did the medium determine the resulting form?
- *Examples:* Give students the opportunity to look at actual samples and reproductions of artworks done in that medium. Discuss and analyze these works in terms of the relationship of the medium to the form of the work.

- *Exploration:* Next the students need to try out the medium to determine its possibilities and limitations for themselves. During this period no finished product is expected; instead students should collect information about what can and cannot be done and then discuss what they have learned with their classmates. For example, if the medium is tempera paint, students could try applying it with different brushes to different surfaces. Older students can take notes on their discoveries and then use these in planning future artworks.
- *Practice:* When a medium is introduced or a technique taught and explored, students need a period of time to try using it in a meaningful way. They can design original works that incorporate the medium or they can be challenged to use it in class projects of different kinds ranging from creating charts and examples to working on a class mural or presentation. In addition students should be enabled to use the medium across the curriculum when appropriate.
- *Availability:* The medium should not disappear after its introduction and practice but join a growing selection of materials from which students can choose in designing their artworks. It should remain easily available for students to use and incorporate into their later artwork.

Building a Base

In the primary years students should not be overwhelmed with a wide variety of media and methods. A few basic materials carefully introduced and well practiced will actually allow novice artists more freedom in their work as they can be more concerned with ideas than with simply exploring the material on a sensory basis.

For the primary grades drawing should form the mainstay of the art program. First graders can be introduced to all of the basic drawing materials—pencil, marker, crayon, and chalk—and then use them across the subject areas. In addition first and second graders can begin to use tempera paint and watercolor. They can also make paper collages, produce simple prints, and learn introductory modeling techniques.

In the intermediate years students begin to study more about the cultures of the world. This is a good time to introduce fiber art, printmaking, sculpture, and more advanced pottery methods using some of the wonderful artworks of Africa, Asia, and South America as inspiring examples.

At a Glance 11.2 suggests one possible way to introduce art media. The order represented is based on the need to build a firm base in general technique and broad-based media before learning specific skills. However, each teaching situation is unique, and teachers should select media first and foremost based on the particular needs of a given school population. Students who lack basic skills in the general media should work for mastery in these before learning more specialized techniques.

At a Glance 11.2

One Way to Introduce Paper Collage

In the following example a second-grade class is studying the five senses.

Exploration

Day 1
Introducing the collage center. Community Circle: Place an assortment of different kinds of paper in a colorfully decorated box. Pass the box around the circle. Each student draws out a paper and describes it. Place empty labeled collage center containers in the center of the circle. Have students in turn put their paper in the one in which they think their piece belongs. Discuss the choices students make. When done, put the paper containers in the area that will be the collage center for the year.

Day 2
Exploring paper. Form students into teams. Pass out a variety of papers. Have students come up with at least three different ways to group them. Then have them tear them into shapes and glue them onto a piece of paper. Discuss how it felt to tear the paper. Describe the torn edges. At the end have teams put scraps in proper collage bins.

Day 3
Introducing scissors. Use guided discovery to introduce scissors and to set up guidelines for safe use. With the class make a chart to hang in the collage center.

Day 4
Exploring scissors. Have students select paper from the collage center and then use the scissors to make as many different kinds of cuts as possible. Meet as a group to share results and create a chart. Have students record scissors guidelines and ways to cut in their journals.

Day 5
Exploring adhesives. Form students into teams. Give out paper, scissors, and a variety of adhesives—white glue, school glue, mucilage, paste, glue sticks, etc. Have groups try them and note the good and bad features of each. Meet as a class to share results. Make up a chart to hang in the collage center. Discuss ways to control application of the glue.

Developing Control (practicing making collages)

(The following activities can be done as a group, in teams, or individually at the collage center.)

Day 6
Using paper, scissors, and glue. Sense of hearing: Play various pieces of music and have students cut out shapes that reflect the sound and glue them to a background. Meet as group to discuss their choices.

Day 7
Using paper, scissors, and glue. Sense of taste: Students taste several familiar foods and then select paper that reflects that taste and make a collage. Meet as a group to discuss their choices.

Day 8
Using paper, scissors, and glue. Sense of sight: Place a variety of interestingly shaped objects on the students' desks. Challenge students to select one object and without drawing it try to cut its shape out of paper. Suggest that they move their eyes along the edge of the object as they try to cut it. Have them cut out the same object several times in different colors and sizes. Use the cut-out shapes as well as the shaped holes that were left over to create a collage.

Day 9

Using paper, scissors, and glue. Sense of smell: Put safe, pleasant scents, such as shampoo, detergent, cinnamon, on cotton balls and place inside tightly capped plastic cups, such as yogurt or margarine containers. Poke holes in the top. Students sniff one of the "mystery" smells and then make a collage that expresses a memory that smell evokes. When done, have a partner try to match the collage with the smell.

Day 10

Using paper and other materials, scissors, and glue. Sense of touch: Have students bring in objects with different textures. Put them in a touch box and have students try to describe them. Introduce some unusually textured materials to the collage center, such as metallic and velour paper, aluminum foil, sandpaper, yarn, and cloth. Invite students to select papers and other materials that feel different and make them into a collage. Encourage them to explore ways to change the texture by folding, crumpling, tearing, and poking holes. Then pair with a partner who with eyes closed tries to identify the papers in the collage just by touch.

Day 11

Using paper and other materials, scissors, and glue. Have students get all their collages from the past week from their process folios and put them together into a book. Include student writing such as poetry or science notes about the senses. Make a collage cover for the book that reflects all the senses and bind it together.

Developing Concepts (using texture)

Day 12

Rehearsal and sketch making. Read the book *Lucy's Picture,* by Nicole Moon (1994, New York: Dial). Ask students to imagine what it would be like to be unable to see. What kind of art would they be able to perceive? What senses would they use? Introduce the word *texture.* Brainstorm a list of papers and materials from the collage area that have different textures. Ask students to close their ideas and imagine a collage that could be seen with the fingers. What would they picture in their collage? How would these papers feel? Have students cut out shapes from papers of their choice and arrange them on a background without gluing them down.

Day 13

Peer partnering. Ask students to meet with a partner. Take turns closing eyes and gently touching the potential collage. Help each other decide if the textured shapes can be sensed with the fingers. Ask, Is this exciting to touch? Do I feel anything surprising or pleasant? When I open my eyes, does it look the way it feels?

Responsive (creating a collage that can be "seen" with fingers)

Days 14–16

Production. Students work on their collages in art workshop setting. As needed, the teacher mini-conferences with students.

Days 17–18

Teacher conference. Hold conferences with students as they finish their work. Discuss the decisions they made in making the collage.

Days 19–20

Sharing. Have students share their work in small or large groups. Create presentation panels showing the students working on their collages and explaining that these are collages to touch.

If a particular medium relates to topics being studied in other areas or to a theme unit, it will certainly be more meaningful if it is introduced in conjunction with it.

Developing Skill in Art

In order to produce art, students need a foundation of skills, techniques, and concepts. Just as in reading, writing, or mathematics teachers must accept that a range of art skills will be found in every class. The successful teacher provides for these variations by designing appropriate instruction that best meets each student's individual needs.

Exploration. All art production begins with exploration. This is the time during which artists learn the nature and potential of an art medium or technique. For the very youngest of children this may involve scribbling with markers, mashing play dough with a fist, and splashing paint across the easel and may represent the bulk of their work. But older children also need time to freely explore before producing a finished work. Questions such as, "Does this brand of blue and yellow tempera mix the color green I want?" or "How wet is the clay today?" must be answered before they can plan an artwork.

Ways Teachers Can Facilitate Exploration

- Provide easy access to art supplies.
- Make sure an ample amount of art materials is available.
- Provide plenty of open-ended work time. Younger or less experienced children will require more time than older students, who can apply knowledge from previous explorations.
- Encourage students to explore with a partner or in a cooperative group. As students make new discoveries and share their results, learning is maximized.
- Share individual explorations with the whole group by making charts and graphs showing the results of explorations, such as a chart of samples showing the effect of using different-sized brushes or a graph of how long clay wrapped in different materials takes to dry out. This also allows many art explorations to be integrated with the application of math and science skills.

Developing control. When the artist has explored the media or technique, the next requirement is to develop control over it. Students will need opportunities to practice using that medium or that technique. How much practice students need will vary. The goal should be to practice until the skill is automatic. If artists have to think about the mechanics of working, then they cannot concentrate on meaning and purpose. It is essential that students be introduced to new media and techniques slowly, have time to utilize them in a variety of ways, and once mastered be able to return to them as needed.

Teaching in Action

Place Logical Limits on Exploration

Students are not creating when they are exploring, although the knowledge they gain will contribute to the culminating creative process. They are learning the working qualities of a material or the potential uses of a tool. Do not be afraid to set limits to the range of exploratory behaviors. Throwing clay at the wall will not help a child learn that wetter clay is less rigid. Banging markers so hard that the tips are driven inside does not help the child to discover the range of lines markers can make.

Sample Guidelines for Exploration

- Keep the material in the designated workspace.
- Use the material in a safe and respectful way.
- Put the material away properly when done.

Ways Teachers Can Help Students Gain Mastery

- Begin by offering one new material or technique at a time.
- Once introduced, make sure that the material is available for students to use regularly.
- Provide plenty of time for practice activities.
- Encourage students to make quick sketches in their journals showing different ways they could use the material or technique.
- Have partners or cooperative groups brainstorm different ways to use the material or technique.
- Show that practice activities are valued by incorporating them into process folios and displaying them with completed works.
- Incorporate that material or technique into criteria-based assignments, art centers, and other areas of learning. For example, after introducing and exploring pastels, and as part of a weather unit, take the class outside in different weather and have them make a series of pastel sketches of the sky.

Developing concepts. Having obtained a level of confidence with an art medium or technique, the artist is ready to use it to obtain knowledge of art concepts. This is a period of vocabulary building and challenging students to think about the decisions they are making as they use the material. It is the beginning of seeing the communicative potential of the medium.

Ways Teachers Can Foster Concept Development

- Introduce art vocabulary and concepts and have students use them in a variety of ways such as in art games (Chapter 5) and cooperative team activities (Chapter 7).

- Provide time for students to look at examples and discuss them.
- Hold peer and teacher conferences to discuss student ideas, sketches, and sample projects.

Developing responsive artwork. Shapes, colors, and words alone do not make a meaningful artwork. Combining these to communicate a feeling or idea to others is what changes a piece of art from a simple statement of "this is what I can do" to a thought-provoking visual encounter with the artist's mind. As children develop skill in using art materials, they need to have something meaningful to communicate. Responsive artwork can grow out of personal experiences or illustrate poetry and stories. It might reflect thematic studies and research or it may show the artist's deep-seated concerns about the world and others. Now is the time for students to experience the creative process as they attempt to combine all that they know to make a meaningful work using the language of art.

Ways to Guide Students to Create Responsive Artwork

- Provide instruction on the elements of art and the principles of design.
- Encourage students to try out a variety of techniques, materials, and compositions to discover the most effective combination.
- Use writing to initiate art and art to initiate writing.
- Encourage students to create artworks that reflect personal experiences and beliefs.
- Integrate ideas through cross-disciplinary studies, thematic teaching, or the project approach.
- Provide time for sharing student artwork with peers.
- Conference regularly with students and discuss their ideas for their artwork.
- Look at selected artworks and discuss the artist's meaning.

Structuring Instruction for Skill Acquisition

In the classroom teachers must expect to see individual variation in the process of skill acquisition. Although at the lower grades, for example, most children will require a period of time for exploration, there will always be some students who because of previous encounters with art media move quickly to concept formation and creating responsive artworks. At the upper grades students usually take less time freely exploring. Yet there will always be those who, because of a lack of art background, need longer.

When students do not receive sufficient time to move through the process of skill acquisition, frustration and failure result. This is why lockstep instruction, in which everyone is expected to complete the same project in the same amount of time, is ineffective. Independent workshops, small group instruction, and open-ended lesson designs have been shown to be effective ways to meet the needs of diverse learners in other subject areas and can be used in art as well.

Why . . . ?

WHY HANDS-ON ART?

Art activities can seem daunting to the classroom teacher. There are supplies to organize and distribute. It is time consuming. Creating original art takes longer than filling in a worksheet, and of course there is the resulting mess to clean up. Still it is vital that students create their own art as well as look at the art of others. Hands-on art production helps students grow in the following ways:

Deeper understanding. Students remember better when information is multisensory and made concrete through their own actions. "We never stop learning through movement, touch and imagery" (Berliner, 1984, p. 106).

Hand-eye coordination. Creating art provides needed opportunity for children to develop physical control over large and small muscle movements and to control visual tracking.

Sequencing. Creating a work of art requires students to plan ahead as they select the materials they need and decide in what order they will proceed.

Self-confidence. Learning that they can control artistic media and use it to effectively communicate ideas is a powerful boost to student self-confidence. As they grow in artistic skill, they will see themselves as more competent artists who are willing to take risks as learners.

What the Experts Say

Building Artistry

It is important for children to feel in control of the media they are using.
Laura Chapman (1978, p. 149)

Whether it be modeling in clay, building with blocks, or wielding a brush, a pencil, or a magic marker, the child must first spend many months coming to know the medium.
Howard Gardner (1980, p. 58)

Continued experience leads to greater skills and a broader repertoire of means of expression. When children have learned to use some tools easily, they can quickly learn to use other similar tools, particularly when the teacher encourages them to see and feel the relationship.
June King McFee (1961, p. 139)

Appreciation of the art of others. In creating their own art, students learn how artists think in the context of reflecting and analyzing their own artistic productions.

Guiding Ideas

THE ARTISTIC PROCESS

The actual process of creating an artwork can be viewed as complementary to that of writing (At a Glance 11.3). When the art program is designed to allow students to use the artistic process, artwork becomes more creative, thoughtful, and innovative.

Rehearsal

Before any piece of artwork can come into existence, it must first exist within the mind of the artist. Rehearsal is the process of visualizing the planned artwork in one's mind and deciding how one will proceed. Very young children do not separate the acts of thought and creation. Their art is an instantaneous, explorative combination of their level of cognitive understanding and a kinesthetic response to the art materials. For older novice artists this process is more complex. Although they will always need to explore new art materials before using them in responsive ways, students who have participated in a rich art program will develop a good sense of the possibilities of an art material. They can mentally predict what kinds of lines a crayon will make or the way tempera paint will flow on to the paper. They can manipulate this knowledge in their minds and imagine what a drawing or painting they are planning might look like before crayon or brush touches paper. Rehearsal provides the time for students to begin to incubate their ideas.

Introducing rehearsal methods. Beginning in the primary grades teachers can introduce children to the idea of rehearsal. It is important to start with a kinesthetic link that ties their past exploration experiences to the task at hand. Young students can be asked to make an "air" drawing, using their finger as a drawing tool as they imagine sketching their idea in the air in front of them. Students can pretend they are making different brush strokes, shaping clay pots, or "weaving" a thread in and out as they kinesthetically rehearse their idea. Many students, especially those with a strongly developed bodily-kinesthetic intelligence, find this method very satisfying and may continue to use it as a preferred way of planning an artwork even after they develop the ability to visualize their work in their minds.

At the next level students can be asked to picture the artwork they will be doing in their minds. The teacher can help guide novice students by offering descriptive statements, such as, "Imagine starting your painting. What is the first color you choose? Where do you put it on the paper? How will your brush move?" Students should be encouraged to develop their own way of using this skill. Some students find that closing their eyes helps. Others need to find a particular

At a Glance 11.3

The Writing and Art Process: A Comparison

Writing/Art Process	Description
Prewriting/Rehearsal	Students visualize and plan what they will create.
Drafting/Sketching	Students quickly capture ideas in written or graphic format.
Revision Stage 1	Students review draft/sketches using self-assessment techniques.
Peer Share	Students show drafts/sketches to partner, small group, or whole group and receive feedback.
Revision Stage 2	Students respond to feedback by making changes.
Production	A written piece or artwork is created.
Editing	Work is reviewed by peer or teacher for correctable mistakes.
Teacher Conference	Students meet with teacher to discuss work and make plans for sharing it.
Publishing/Presentation	Work is shared with others in some special way.

sitting position or location that helps them feel relaxed. Quiet background music can be played for a group just starting out, or individual students can listen to music of their choice using a tape recorder and a headset at a listening or "imagining" center. Visualizing one's plans mentally requires strong spatial skills.

Students with well-developed language skills can be asked to write and talk about their plans for their artwork. Students can jot down notes or tell a partner the supplies they think they will need, the colors and shapes they will use, and the idea or mood they plan to express. Some students benefit from writing a story or poem before beginning the work. Others find it helpful to make a list of related words or list the steps they will be following.

Developing rehearsal skills. In the beginning students will need to be taught and then practice using all these different approaches. Over time individual student preferences will become apparent. For some students one method may work better for one media than another. For example, some students find it easy to mentally visualize a drawing but prefer to "air" paint before putting brush on paper. Teachers should encourage advanced students to use the method that best meets their needs.

Throughout the instruction in rehearsal methods teachers should emphasize that rehearsal is important for preparing oneself to create. It is equivalent to warm-up exercises done before an athletic event or preparing an outline before writing a report. Rehearsal activities,

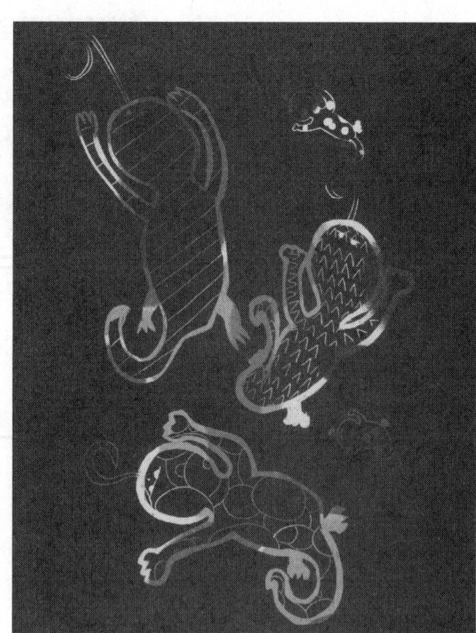

Revision in Action.

Salamander Sketch.
Marker (*left*).

"Salamanders."
Crayon scraffito—Kyle, grade 5 (*right*).

Thinking about Children's Art

Compare the sketch and the finished work. What changes has this student made in the design of the images and the composition of the work? How did making sketches help this student think through his ideas? What questions might a peer have asked him about his sketches that would have given him the direction he needed to finish the work?

however, do not produce a rigid plan that must be followed to the letter, any more than warm-up exercises determine the resulting athletic performance or the outline dictates the completed piece of writing. It is only a beginning—a guide—that gives direction but does not determine the final destination.

Sketching

Sketching is a powerful tool for students to learn to use. Sketching is visual thinking. It is a way of making sense of one's thoughts, playing with meaning using visual elements, and exploring ideas on paper. The ability to quickly capture ideas graphically is one that will be useful throughout one's life. From making a quick sketch of where the movers should put the furniture to drawing a view of one's new home to describe it to a friend, being able to sketch is a competency that everyone can use.

These sketches will give direction to the planned creative work. They provide an opportunity for the student to try out several versions of an idea before beginning the larger work. Sketches can be any size and done in any medium. Although pencil is the most common, crayon, oil pastel, or paint can sometimes provide a better way to try out ideas for color combinations. Torn and cut paper shapes can be rearranged again and again to try out relationships among size, shape, and color. Corrugated cardboard can be folded and taped or stapled to make quick models for three-dimensional ideas. Nonhardening modeling clay can be used to try out sculptural forms that will later be produced from firing clay.

In addition to planning sketches teachers should encourage students to make quick sketches in their journals, logs, or notebooks following shared experiences and lessons in all subjects. Small pieces of paper should always be available to capture a fleeting idea. When students are looking for ideas for their artwork, these experience-based sketches will provide an invaluable resource. For this reason students should collect their sketches and practice pieces, not discard them. When the study is complete, the sketches can be reviewed and even mounted to accompany the finished work in order to record the process of its creation.

Revision

Revision is the process of reviewing and re-examining one's work in preparation for taking the concept to another level. It is a process that is essential for development as an artist, and yet it is often the least practiced of skills. Even young children, however, can be taught how to look at what they have done and plan what they should do next.

Lucy Calkins describes the purpose of revision as being "not to correct but to discover" (1986, p. 88). It is the process of clarifying one's ideas and finding a new direction. It is looking at the work with new eyes—re-"visioning." The revision process may sometimes lead to a change in the work itself, but often it may suggest a totally new direction to take in one's work as a whole.

Revision methods. Revision may mean examining each sketch and deciding which ones to pursue further:

- It may mean studying a sketch and deciding which colors or techniques will best express the mood desired.
- It may mean looking at the way objects in the work balance each other and then deciding to add something to change the effect.
- It may involve listening to the responses of others and deciding that those responses do not truly reflect the intended meaning. This may lead to a change in the work itself or perhaps the creation of another piece.

Teaching how to revise. The steps in revising a work need to be taught in small, focused bits that relate to the developmental level and experience of the students. In the primary grades revision can be as simple as asking oneself or a peer a question about the work. The teacher can model the process by thinking out loud during a demonstration, such as saying, "Well, this green doesn't seem to show up very well against this blue. I think I'll change it to a lighter green."

Henri Matisse,
Beasts of the Sea, 1950.
National Gallery of Art, Alis Mellon Bruce Fund.

From the Museum

Henri Matisse's cut paper collages were created when the aging artist was ill and bedridden. He would cut out paper shapes and then direct an assistant to place them where he desired on large sheets of paper tacked to the wall. How do you think having an intermediary between the plan and the physical production of a work affects the artistic process? Which part of the artistic process is most important? Why is it important for children to be given the opportunity to experience all parts of the process?

During partnering sessions and when peer conferencing, students should be encouraged to talk about the changes they make and why. At the intermediate level revision can become a complex process involving oral responses, written comments, filling in checklists, drawing graphic images, and answering questions asked by peers or the teacher.

Creating an atmosphere that encourages revision. Often there is a fear on the part of novice artists that artwork cannot be changed. Revision can only happen in educational contexts where students feel that they have many opportunities to try out ideas. This requires ample independent work time and a teacher who encourages students to take risks by providing ample supplies. The teacher must create an atmosphere that emphasizes the importance of the process of creating a meaningful body of work over the appearance of one particular final product. In such an environment sketches and alternative versions produced become a valued part of the student's process folio rather than mistakes to be thrown away.

Peer Sharing

It is only by seeing their work through the eyes of others that students can know what their art has communicated. At the primary level sharing can begin with one student showing a piece of artwork and then talking about it to the whole group, a small group, or just the teacher. Classmates can be asked to respond to the work on a variety of levels depending on their experience. Student responses can range from emotional reactions to analyzing how the medium relates to the message. Responses can be in many forms including oral discussion, written comments, a sketch, or completion of a checklist.

Production

The production of the work should be the culmination of thoughtful reflection on the original idea, done with the most skill and knowledge that the students at that level can obtain. This is the high moment of creativity when knowledge, skill, and meaning-making come together. It is also a very important part in teaching students to appreciate the art of others. It is only when the hands-on production follows planning, revision, and sharing that students begin to understand how an artist tries out ideas, discarding some, elaborating others, and incorporating knowledge—all for the purpose of creating meaning.

Students who are expected to produce an attractive finished artwork that meets the teacher's criteria in the twenty minutes following the presentation of a lesson will not understand why art is created. Students who cannot produce within such constraints come to believe they are not capable in art. Instead of appreciating the thought and reflection behind art creation, students subjected to this kind of art instruction will always believe that artworks are instantly and magically created by gifted artists. It is only through experiencing the creative and artistic process that students truly come to understand and appreciate their own art and the art of others.

Editing

Editing in art is different than in writing. In writing we look for spelling and grammatical mistakes no matter what type of writing it is. In an artwork the nature of the medium will determine what we examine. In a drawing we might analyze the contrast between drawn objects in the foreground and the background. We might examine the shape and thickness of a clay mug. We check a weaving closely for loose stitches. Each medium has its own standards and structure. It is not enough to ask students if they did their work carefully and neatly. Students need to be taught the specific qualities for which they must check or edit the work.

Teacher Conference

As was delineated in Chapter 6, the purpose of this conference is to help students focus on what they have accomplished, to see the direction they have chosen to go, to look back at paths not selected, and then to guide students in finalizing the form and direction of the artwork.

Presentation

Completed work should be afforded the attention it deserves. When a work is completed during an art period, the teacher should immediately respond positively to the student. The work should be mounted. This can be facilitated by having a presentation station set up in the room complete with paper for framing and examples of the various types of mounts possible (described in Chapter 10 in more detail). With the student decide how and where to best display this particular artwork. It is these thoughtfully created and presented artworks that should appear on the bulletin boards and in the hallways of our schools.

Introducing the Artistic Process

Students need a gradual introduction to the artistic process. A first grader who is still exploring and developing basic skill with a medium is not ready to go through several steps of revision and conferencing. Even at this level, however, children will benefit from sharing their work and hearing the response of other children to what they have created. This will set the stage for using revision in the higher grades and also give children practice talking about artwork. At a Glance 11.4 shows how to gradually introduce the artistic process over the primary years. This approach can also be used to introduce the artistic process to older students who have never experienced this kind of art program.

At a Glance 11.4

Introducing the Artistic Process

Component	Level 1	Level 2	Level 3
Rehearsal	Students move arms as they imagine making the artwork.	Students close eyes and visualize the artwork under guidance.	Students visualize stages of creation with guidance.
Sketching	Students draw in journals. These are called sketches.	Students must make a sketch before starting an artwork.	Students must make several sketches before starting an artwork.
Revision 1	Teacher asks, "Is there anything you want to add or change?"	Student asks self, "Is there anything I want to add or change?" Checklist may be used.	Student reviews sketches, chooses one, revises, if needed.
Peer Share	Student shows sketches to others.	Student shows and explains sketches to others. Listens to comments.	Student shows and explains sketches to others. Asks questions and responds to comments.
Revision 2	Not applied yet.	Makes changes if desired.	Studies comments and addresses them in work or in other versions.
Production	Student creates work. One medium offered.	Student creates work. Several media offered.	Student creates work. Many media offered.
Editing	Student checks work for one characteristic.	Student checks work for several characteristics.	Student checks others' work for several characteristics.
Teacher Conference	Student shows work to teacher. Teacher responds.	Student shows and tells teacher about work. Teacher responds.	Teacher and student discuss decisions made and plan for future.

In the Classroom

PAPER AND PAINT

What would children's artwork be like without paper and paint—paper to draw on, cut, fold, and glue, and paint to swirl and mix and splatter? These two media more than any other form the core of what we think of as elementary school art. In this section we will look at the many creative and thoughtful ways students can use these two materials to create art.

Paper

The highly flexible nature of paper and the wide range of thickness, textures, colors, and sizes that it comes in allow it to be used for an extraordinary range of activities. It is not surprising that so many art activities for children rely on the use of paper. There are thick papers and smooth papers, textured papers, tissue papers, and many more. All of them beckon to the artist in us to create something wonderful. At a Glance 11.5 explains the vocabulary of paper, and At a Glance 11.6 describes the different kinds of paper.

At a Glance 11.5

The Vocabulary of Paper

Crease: Folding the paper and running a finger or straight edge along the fold.

Grain: All machine-made paper has a grain. Paper, especially in the heavier weights, bends and tears more easily along the grain.

Indent: Using a blunt instrument to press a line into the paper. The paper is then folded along the impression.

Pound (lb.): Paper is measured in pounds per ream or per 1,000 sheets. The higher the poundage, the heavier the paper.

Ream: A ream of paper is equal to 500 sheets.

Score: Using a sharp knife to cut about two-thirds of the way through the paper. Then fold on the cut.

Making Paper

Making hand-formed paper is an excellent way to help children appreciate how paper is made and to make them think carefully about how they use it. It can also be used to correlate with studies relating to recycling. The goal in introducing students to papermaking is to give them the skills needed to create paper on their own. This then allows them to choose to make their own paper to fulfill special needs they may have in designing a piece of artwork. For example, a nature collage may be enhanced by the addition of paper made with impressed flowers in it.

Introducing papermaking. Children are always fascinated by learning how familiar materials are made. Paper is no exception. Introduce papermaking by having students tear a piece of soft, absorbent paper such as a napkin or tissue and then closely examine the torn edge with a magnifying glass. Try to identify individual fibers. If possible, compare these fibers with slides showing plant cells. Explain that the fibers come from the plant cell walls. Plant fibers are held together with a cement-like substance that must be broken down before paper can be made.

Brainstorm a list of ways the fibers could be broken down. If desired, research methods that have been used in the past and compare them to those used today, or read sections from the book *Paper by Kids* (Grummer, 1980) or *From Tree to Paper* (Davis, 1995) (see "Teacher Resources").

Making paper. This simple method can be introduced to primary students and used with increasingly complex variations by students

At a Glance 11.6

Types of Paper

Acid-free paper. Paper from which all the acid has been removed to prevent it from becoming yellow and brittle over time.

Bond paper. Paper that has been sized or sealed with a gluey mixture to make it less absorbent.

Coated paper. Sometimes marketed as fadeless paper, this paper is colored by printing a layer of ink on one or both sides. At 50 lb. it is thinner than construction paper but more resistant to light. Color may be coated on one side only or it may be a different color on the other side. An ideal paper for fine collages.

Another coated paper is finger-paint paper, which has a glossy, smooth coating on one or both sides and high wet strength.

Construction paper. This is a 70 to 80 lb. slightly absorbent paper that cuts, tears, and glues well. It comes in a wide range of colors including skin-toned assortments. Colors often fade when exposed to light.

Drawing paper. A wide range of papers are marketed for drawing. They usually have a dull, slightly textured finish and are heavier and more absorbent than regular bond paper.

- *Manila paper* is an inexpensive cream-colored drawing paper often used in schools.
- *Charcoal/pastel paper* is a strong paper with a textured surface. It comes in a range of soft colors.
- *Newsprint* is a thin, off-white, inexpensive paper for quick sketching and papier mâché work. It yellows and becomes brittle in just a few years.
- *White drawing paper* comes in a wide variety of weights and sizes. It can range from a very smooth surface to one with a slight tooth.

Rag paper. Paper that has a high percentage of cotton or linen fibers in it. This is high-quality paper that is very durable and has a high wet strength. It will not yellow or become brittle for many years. Many watercolor and printing papers have a high rag content.

Specialty paper. There are myriad other types of paper. Here are a few that students love:

- *Foils:* Metallic paper and holographic papers can be used to add sparkle to collages.
- *Printed papers:* Paper such as wallpaper and commercial art papers that come in animal skin and textile prints can be combined with handmade decorative papers.
- *Velour paper:* This has a simulated velvet finish that adds texture to collages. It also takes pastels well.
- *Transparent and translucent papers:* Cellophane, art tissue, tracing paper, and rice paper can be used to add another dimension to collages.

Tagboard. Tag is a lightweight, flexible, nonabsorbent board available in 100 to 200 lb. weights that works well for sculptural projects. Oak tag is a cream-colored version. Showcard is a colored version.

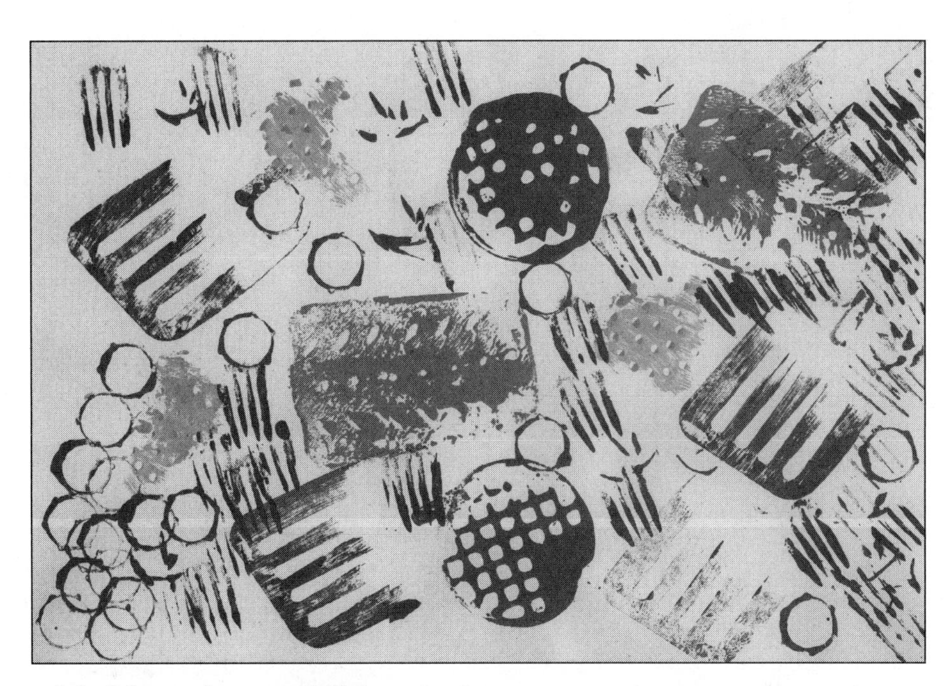

"Kitchen Drawer Print."
Monoprint—Shane, grade 1.

Thinking about Children's Art

This print was made by dipping various kitchen utensils in tempera paint and stamping them onto the paper. What has the child learned about the shapes and forms of these objects? What makes this activity different from using ready-made rubber stamps?

through the grades. It is ideal in that it requires no special equipment (see At a Glance 11.7).

Decorated and Printed Papers

Decorative papers are papers that have an overall design. Handmade decorative papers provide an exciting alternative to plain, colored commercial papers for use in students' artworks.

Students can produce far more varied and interesting papers to use in their collages and books than can be found in any store. Producing decorative papers also allows students to explore new techniques and to develop skill in handing a variety of materials. It allows students to design just the right colored or patterned paper to use in a particular artwork.

Students should collect the decorative papers they make in their process folios for use in later projects. Encourage them to share papers with other students. Keep a special bin in the collage area for their contributions.

The following ways to make decorative papers just skim the surface of possibilities. After introducing the concept through several lessons, such as the ones that follow, set up an art center where students can

At a Glance 11.7

Making Paper Step by Step

This simple method can be introduced to primary students and with increasingly complex variations used by students through the grades. It is ideal in that it requires no special equipment.

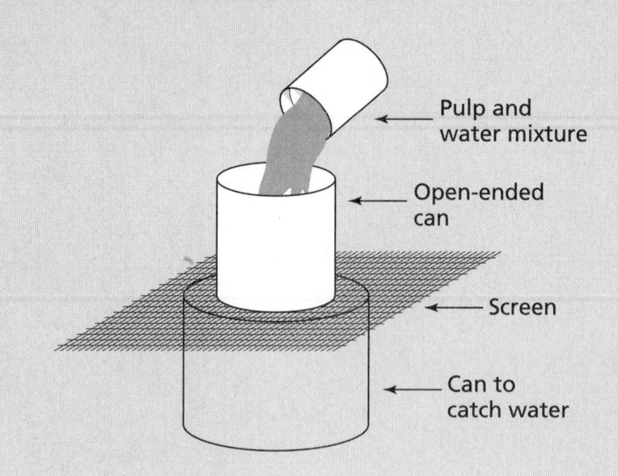

Materials

- Inexpensive napkins or tissue paper
- Small yogurt or other plastic containers with tight-fitting lids
- A large can with the lid cut off
- A smaller can with both top and bottom cut off
- Two pieces of screening
- Newspapers

Method

1. Tear napkin into tiny bits.
2. Place in yogurt container. Fill halfway with water. Put on lid and shake for about five minutes until paper is dissolved.
3. Place one piece of screen over the top of the larger can.
4. Place the smaller can on top and pour dissolved paper fibers into it. (*Note:* It may take some practice to get the screen covered evenly. If necessary, the pulp can be collected off the screen, put back in water, and redone.)
5. When water has drained through, remove the top can, place the second screen on top, and squeeze out the excess water.
6. Continue blotting the screen and pulp sandwich between sheets of newspapers until it is only minimally damp.
7. Slowly lift up top screen. If it is sufficiently blotted, it will not stick.
8. Starting at an edge roll the newly created paper off the bottom screen and place flat to dry.
9. The round paper that is produced is rather thick and absorbent. Students can experiment with drawing on it, cutting it, and gluing it.

Color Variations

With practice students can make paper on their own. They can make more colorful papers by adding any of the following:

- Food coloring
- Tempera paint
- Bits of colored tissue or construction paper
- Glitter or bits of cellophane and foil papers

Texture Variations

The texture or tooth of the paper can be changed by using screening with a different mesh size or by using another material in place of the top screen, such as a piece of felt or a plastic tray. Natural materials can also be added. Grass, flowers, or seeds can be dropped into the pulp after it is poured.

Sizing the Paper

Handmade paper tends to be very absorbent. Commercial paper is usually sized. Students can size their paper using liquid starch. Dip the paper in the starch and let dry, or brush the starch over the paper until it is damp and iron it dry.

invent their own techniques. Encourage students to use their decorative papers in collages and handmade books. Make a chart of samples of student-created papers labeled with a description of how each was made along with a list of possible uses.

Introduction to decorative paper design. One way to introduce students to the wonderful ways decorative papers can be used is to share the many books that feature collages, such as books by Eric Carle, Lois Ehlert, and Leo Lionni (see Books to Share in this chapter). Try some of these activities:

- Have students look through the books and tally how many different kinds of papers the artists used.
- Have students select one of the papers they found and brainstorm a way it might have been made.
- Create a graph showing how often certain papers are used in the illustrations.
- Try to duplicate the effect of some of the papers used in the books.

Batiked paper. Batik is a method of dying cloth using a wax resist to block out areas from receiving the dye. It was traditionally used in Indonesia to create richly patterned fabric. A similar effect can be obtained on paper.

Show the students samples of batiked cloth and point out the small cracks in the wax. Explain that these are created when the fabric is folded and placed in the dye bath and the waxed areas crack. Color a design using heavy crayon on a sheet of strong but light paper such as white drawing paper. Gently crumple up the crayoned paper, cracking the crayoned surface. Then brush the paper with a dark-colored tempera paint or in the upper grades with India ink. Wipe the excess paint or ink off the surface of the crayon with a paper towel or sponge.

Dyed paper. Very absorbent papers, such as paper toweling, paper placemats and handmade papers, can be dyed using thinned tempera paint, food coloring, or safe, purchased paper dyes.

To begin fold the paper into rectangles, triangles, or accordion folds. Dip the folded corners or edges into different colored dyes or thinned tempera paint. Keep the paper in the dye until it is absorbed to the point desired. Place other corners in the same or different colored dyes. When dyeing is judged sufficient, open the paper up carefully. Remember paper is very weak when wet.

Place the paper open flat on newspaper to dry. Paper may be ironed when dry to remove wrinkles and folds.

Grained paper. Grained papers are papers that can resemble wood or striated stone but can also be fanciful in design. Begin by showing students examples of wood with a distinctive grain. Cut notches along one edge of a hand-sized piece of cardboard. Use the cardboard to either apply the paint by pulling it across the paper to resemble wood grain or to drag across a still wet painted paper so that the color or paper underneath shows through. Experiment with different placements of the notches, explore other ways to move the cardboard, and try mixing several colors of paint on the paper before spreading them.

Marbled paper. Marbled paper traditionally was made with oil paint and turpentine. This is very unsafe for children to do. The following method provides a better alternative:

1. Fill tray half full of liquid starch.
2. Thin nontoxic acrylic paint with water until it runs off a spoon.
3. Drop different colors of paint onto the surface of the starch. Gently swirl the colors around with a spoon.
4. Slowly lay a sheet of paper flat on the surface of the starch so that it floats. Do not let it slide under the surface.
5. Carefully remove paper and place face up on the newspaper to dry.

Monoprints. A decorative paper monoprint is created by stamping an overall design on a piece of paper. There are a multitude of ways to create these one-of-a-kind prints. Set up an art center with basic printing materials: low-sided trays and thick tempera paint or water-based printing ink or stamp pads. Put out a variety of objects and let students be inventive. The following list of objects to try provides only a starting point: berry baskets, blocks of wood, bottle caps, cardboard tubes, cardboard pieces, erasers, forks, leaves, potato mashers, rubber stamps, seashells, sponges, spools, stones, and so on.

Painted papers. Students love the freedom to experiment with blending colors of paint. These explorations make excellent decorative paper for collages. Watercolor on wet paper, experiments with different brush strokes, or using different tools to apply paint can all result in eye-catching papers.

For example, yarn dipped in paint can be placed on one side of a piece of paper with one end extending beyond the edge. Fold paper over it. Place hand gently on top of folded paper and pull out the yarn with a back and forth motion. Tempera-dipped yarn can also be snapped across the paper.

Interesting visual effects can be created by pressing or rubbing paper with the following materials dipped in tempera paint: batting, bubble wrap, cloth, cotton balls, felt, and more.

Spread drops of thinned tempera paint by tipping the paper in different directions or by blowing out through a straw. (SAFETY NOTE: Prevent students from inhaling paint by cutting a small slit in the straw, and avoid the occurrence of hyperventilation by having students count to thirty between blows.)

Place thin paint mixed with a small amount of detergent in a shallow tray and blow bubbles with a straw. Drop a piece of paper face up on the surface to capture a bubble print.

Roller prints. Glue yarn, corrugated cardboard, and/or cloth shapes to a cardboard tube. Let dry and then dip in tempera paint and then roll it over a surface.

Relief prints. A relief print is produced by raising areas of a design slightly above the surface, rolling water-based printing ink or tempera paint across the raised surface using a brayer or rubber roller, and then placing paper on top and rubbing the raised parts. There are a variety of ways to produce the "plate" for printing.

- *Cardboard:* Glue cardboard shapes to a piece of similar cardboard.
- *Styrofoam:* Sticky-back Styrofoam is available from art suppliers. Cut out shapes and stick to a cardboard backing.
- *Textured:* Glue materials having a slightly raised texture to a cardboard backing. Try sandpaper, cloth, corrugated paper, and gravel.

Incised prints. An incised print results when a line or shape is pushed into or cut out of a surface. The background remains raised so it is that area that prints the color. The lines or shapes remain the color of the paper. A single picture can be produced or it can be printed over and over to create an overall pattern.

Sanitized Styrofoam food trays or Styrofoam plates are an ideal material for children to use. They can easily draw detailed pictures and designs on the soft surface with a pencil or ball-point pen. For variety try cutting the Styrofoam into an interesting shape before incising the drawing.

Modeling clay. Nonhardening or firing clay can be used in the same way. Create a shape with a flat surface and then use a pencil or tool to incise lines or press in shapes using various small objects such as paper clips and bottle caps.

Using Decorative Papers

It is important to remember that the making of decorative paper is not an end in itself. Decorative papers are not finished works of art. They are a material from which to make wonderful collages, books, and sculptures.

When the techniques have been introduced, students must be guided in discovering ways to use their papers, such as through the following exercises:

Books to Share

Papermaking

Share the following books to introduce students to making paper:

Davis, G. W. (1995). *From tree to paper.* New York: Scholastic.
Gibbons, G. (1983). *Paper, paper everywhere.* New York: Harcourt Brace Jovanovich.
Rumford, J. (1996). *The cloudmakers.* Boston: Houghton Mifflin.
Wilkinson, B. (1997). *Papermaking for kids.* Layton, UT: Gibbs Smith.

The following books introduce students to how paper is made:

Flemming, D. (1991). *In the tall tall grass.* New York: Scholastic.
———. (1992). *Lunch.* New York: Scholastic.
———. (1992). *Count.* New York: Scholastic.
Flemming's three books are illustrated with handmade paper collages and can be used to inspire students to create colorful handmade paper collages.

1. Cut up a variety of decorative papers. Have each student select one. Ask them to study the paper and name three different ways it could be used in an artwork.
2. Have students create individual or class books of decorative papers they have made. Glue in samples, a description of how it was made, and suggested uses. They can also include artwork using the papers.

Cut Paper

Cutting paper is a skill that develops with practice. In the primary grades children make rapid progress in their ability to cut a wide variety of papers ranging from tissue to cardboard when given sufficient opportunities to apply their skills. Children who continue to have difficulty handling scissors or cutting specific materials may need special attention (see Teacher Tip: Solving Cutting Problems in this chapter). In the upper grades most students should be able to cut with precision through single and multiple folded papers of all kinds.

The following lessons can be taught at different levels depending on the experience and skill level of the students. The goal is to introduce students to safe scissors handling, show them the different kinds of cuts they can make, and present several art forms from other cultures that show how paper cutting can be used to create meaningful artworks. (See At a Glance 11.8 for a description of cutting tools.)

Introduction to scissors. Students need to be introduced to scissors and how to use them at every level. This type of lesson should be repeated whenever necessary to re-establish safe behavior. It makes an

Teacher Tip

Solving Cutting Problems

When a child has trouble cutting:

- *The scissors may be held incorrectly.* Check that the scissors is being held vertically and the child can open and close it easily. Use training scissors with double handle holes to guide the cutting and help the child learn how it feels to hold the scissors correctly.
- *The material being cut may be too heavy or too light for the scissors being used.* Substitute a sharper scissors or try a pair of snips. Alternatively substitute a material that is easier to cut. Primary students often have difficulty cutting some fabrics and yarns with the small scissors they need to use. Always have some precut materials available for them to use as well.
- *The child may not have sufficient hand strength.* Make sure scissors are lightweight and not too large for the child's hand. Look for scissors that have a large enough lower grip that the child can use several fingers. If there are still difficulties, try squeeze scissors or a rotary cutter.

ideal guided discovery lesson. (*Note*: See Chapter 6 for a detailed discussion of designing and using guided discovery lessons.)

Begin by allowing students to observe scissors and how they are used very closely. One way is to have them record their observations, both drawn and written, in their journals or notebooks. Another way is to have them orally share their ideas with a partner. Based on their observations, help them generate a list of safety rules. Keep these posted for reference throughout the year.

Expand on the basic lesson by having them make posters showing the safe way to use scissors or have selected students demonstrate following these rules. Primary students should practice handing scissors—handle first, blades held closed—back and forth to each other.

Cutting out shapes. There are two basic ways to cut. One is to draw a shape first and then cut it out. The other is to visualize a shape and then cut it out freehand. Teachers should give students the opportunity to use both methods.

- *Method 1: Pre-drawing.* Start by asking children to draw any shape on their paper and then cut it out. When finished, have them describe how they went about cutting it. Where did they start? How did they turn the paper? Did they cut off the scrap in one piece or many pieces? Which parts were easy to cut? Where did the scissors change direction? What difficulties did they have? Follow up by having them draw a second shape and, based on the discussion, try a different way to cut it out. Novice cutters often feel they must follow the contours of a shape and run into difficulties when faced

At a Glance 11.8

Cutting Tools

All-purpose snips. Snips have spring-apart blades and a locking mechanism. They are invaluable for cutting items such as heavy cardboard, carpet, wire, branches, and other heavy materials. Small snips are available for students who lack sufficient muscle control to operate regular scissors.

Rotary hand cutter. A rotary cutter is a cutting wheel similar to those used in quilting. It is useful for special needs students who cannot use regular scissors and for students who want to cut graceful curves and straight edges. Look for one that has a covered blade. It should always be used on a cutting mat.

Stencil knife. Sixth-grade students who are working on detailed cutouts can learn to use a stencil knife with supervision. Stencil knives must be used with a cutting mat underneath. Teach students to press lightly and to cut away from their other hand. It is helpful to tape the paper to be cut onto the cutting surface. Change blades often. A dull knife is more dangerous than a sharp one.

Student scissors. Scissors for student use should be sharp enough to cut the materials being offered to them. They should open and close easily and be strong but lightweight. Make sure the same scissors can be used by both right- and left-handers. Primary students should use blunt-ended scissors. Older students need scissors with points so they can cut holes into the center of paper. Scissors that make zigzag and curved cuts are now available and are fun to use in making collages.

with intricate zigs and zags. Show students how to cut away the excess and then cut into the notches.

- *Method 2: Freehand.* Students can develop eye–hand coordination and perceptual growth by looking at an object and then trying to cut it out from a piece of paper. Start at the primary level with simple, familiar items that are fairly two-dimensional, such as a dish or a spoon. Offer upper graders more complex shapes, such as vase or even a still life or posed figure. (*Note:* An interesting variation on this lesson is to have students tear out the shape rather than cut it.)

Folding and cutting. Very early on give primary students the opportunity to investigate what happens when they cut a folded piece of paper. Being able to make two or more duplicate shapes or a symmetrical shape increases the student's ability to use paper expressively. Although some may discover this technique on their own, most students benefit from a brief mini-lesson in which the teacher demonstrates folding and cutting and then allows ample opportunity for them to practice.

Cutting symmetrical shapes. Children take great delight in the wondrous symmetrical shapes they can create using just a scissors and paper. Line symmetry can be introduced in the primary grades. These are shapes in which one half is a mirror image of the other.

Symmetrical shapes can be cut from a folded piece of paper. In demonstrating how to cut out symmetrical shapes, emphasize that the cut needs to start and end on the folded edge. Older students can try point symmetry using paper folded into quarters, eighths, or more.

This activity makes an ideal addition to math lessons on symmetry as well. Expand the lesson by having students look through books and magazines to find examples of symmetrical shapes or take a walk to find symmetry in nature and in local architecture.

Students can also be introduced to examples of *Wycinanki,* traditional cut paper designs from Poland, and *Amate* images from Mexico as well as those of other cultural groups such as the Chinese, who also have a long tradition of paper cutting as a folk art. These intricately designed art forms will expand the students' view of what it is possible to do with just a scissors and a plain piece of paper.

Fastening Methods

There are a multitude of adhesives, fasteners, and tapes on the market that can be used in collage and paper sculpture. The following list provides a sampling. Always check the safety of an item before using it with students (see Chapter 8 for guidelines).

- *Adhesives:* Look for water-based glues that do not release dangerous fumes. Gel glues, quick drying white craft tacky glues, and the traditional white glues can be used to glue most papers, fabrics, and light objects to collages. Colored white glues are also available and can be used to add raised lines to an artwork.

- *Fasteners:* Glue should be the first choice for paper sculptures. If the glue is too slow drying, try using removable masking tape, paper clips, or clothespins to hold the work while it is drying. When paper sculpture requires more holding power than glue alone can provide, use staples and paper fasteners. A bookbinder's long-reach stapler is handy for reaching inside large sculptures. A hand-grip stapler is often easier to use on odd-shaped works. Another way to securely attach heavy tag and cardboard together is to poke holes with an awl and use wire or chenille stems.

- *Tapes:* In general students should avoid tape in finished artworks. It is not permanent and cannot be painted over. A light masking tape can be useful in holding glued work together as it dries or for trying out temporary arrangements. An exception is colored self-stick tape, which can add an artistic component to collages as well as serve to attach items.

Collage

Collage is a mainstay of most art programs particularly in the elementary school. It requires only scissors, paste, and inexpensive or discarded materials and is easy to clean up after. These are not the

"Rainforest Animals."
Collage—Ashleigh, Carl, Ada, Lauren, Shaheeda, and Jimmy, grade 2.

Thinking about Children's Art

These second graders have each researched and then created an individual animal to add to their small group mural about the rainforest. What kind of negotiations might have taken place as the children decided where to place their animals in the limited space of the paper? Why does the medium of collage lend itself to cooperative group work?

reasons, however, for having children create collages. Collage is invaluable because it allows students to play with shapes, colors, pattern, and textures as they apply principles of design, and it allows them to see everyday objects—bits and piece of scrap paper, cloth, and more—as artistic elements.

Introduction to collage. All students need easy access to collage materials as they create art. Classrooms should have a carefully arranged collage center where containers of collage materials are

Teacher Tip

Paper for Collages

Always be on the lookout for interesting and unusual collage papers. Expand the textures and colors of paper available for collage work by offering any of the following:

Advertising brochures, candy wrappers, doilies, napkins, paper place mats, paper towels, shelf paper, blotter paper, coffee filters, gift wrap, magazine pages, napkins, newspaper, photographs, rice paper, sandpaper, tissue, typing paper, wallpaper, and waxed paper.

kept (see Chapter 8 for suggestions). Art lessons should focus on selection of materials and creating alternative arrangements before gluing.

Learning how to select collage materials. Often students select materials for their collages based on whether they like them or not, or just because the object is novel. One way to help students think about their choices is to have them draw a material out of a bag and tell one way each item could be used in an collage. This is a good warm-up during community circle or a good cooperative team activity.

Expand this exercise for older students by having them think about the meaning of objects in collages. As they look at their own work or the work of others, have them list their ideas under the following categories:

- *Real*: Item is used as it really is, such as when wallpaper is used on a wall in a picture of a room.
- *Representation:* Item is used as a representation of something else because of some shared characteristics, such as using a piece of grained paper for a tree trunk.
- *Symbol:* Item stands for a real item, such as using cut-out flowers from a piece of wallpaper as wheels for a car.
- *Design element:* Item provides contrast, balance, texture, or color to the collage but does not represent any real object.

Build on this activity by looking at collages by Picasso, Braque, and others and collage illustrations in children's books and classifying how the different materials are used. Then have students prepare charts of potential collage materials and list different ways the papers and objects could be used. Later when conferencing with students about their collages, ask them to describe and classify how they used the different materials in their work.

Teacher Tip

Collecting Collage Materials

Students can find many collage materials around the home. At the beginning of the year send home a letter such as the one below asking for contributions. Adjust the list to reflect your class's personal needs.

Dear Family,

The collage center is an important part of our art program. Please help us by sending in any of the following materials: beads from old costume jewelry, carpet scraps, fabric scraps, felt scraps, lace, ribbon, shells, thread, yarn, wallpaper scraps.

All contributions will be greatly appreciated. The students' creativity in using these supplies will just amaze you.

Sincerely,

Your Child's Teacher

Collage sketches. Encourage students to try out several arrangements of their selected collage materials before gluing them down. The following activity is just one of the many ways to foster this approach:

Give each student a background sheet and the same assortment of paper shapes. The shapes should be various sizes, colors, and textures. For primary students limit the shapes to just three or four. Older students can use more. Challenge them to make as many different arrangements as possible in a given amount of time. They should make a pencil sketch of each arrangement they design. A paper folded into sixteenths makes a good place to record the sketches.

Discuss the results of the exercise and record how many different arrangements each student made. Upper graders may wish to cut up the sketches, sort them, and tabulate the total of number of variations. Sketches can also be categorized by, for example, symmetrical vs. asymmetrical and related to mathematical concepts and the principles of design.

More than paper collages. Paper is not the only material used in collages. Natural objects such as stones, twigs, and leaves can be

Teacher Tip

Texture Collages

The tactile nature of collages make them an ideal art form for children with limited vision. Share the book *Lucy's Picture* by Nicola Moon (1994). In this simple story a young child makes a special collage for her blind grandfather. Describe the different textures of collage objects as students work with them.

Make collage storage areas accessible to all children. Attach samples of the materials to the outside of storage containers so children can select their own materials.

collected on nature walks and added to collages. Aluminum foil, beads, bottle caps, cotton balls, fabric, ribbon, and other materials can also be used. Challenge students to find items that will extend the meaning of their artwork, such as using a bit of old lace to evoke the feeling of age in a collage portrait of a grandmother or adding real seashells and sand to a collage of the ocean.

Paper Sculpture

Except for the ubiquitous fans and paper airplanes of childhood, students rarely explore the dimensionality of paper unless they are introduced to its possibilities. There are many techniques for turning flat sheets of paper into three-dimensional forms.

Folding paper. Folding paper is a skill that is developed in many contexts in the classroom. From early on teachers can ask students to fold their paper in half or quarters for classwork guidelines. Build on this beginning with the following integrated lessons.

In mathematically related lessons challenge them to divide paper into various numbers of sections. Ask them to try folding the paper into various fractional parts, or into equal triangles, squares, or other geometric shapes. Create patterns and designs by coloring the various shapes created. Start with different sized and proportioned rectangles. Fold them the same way. How are the created shapes different? Does it make a difference in the resulting shapes if the first fold is vertical or horizontal? Show students how to create clean folds by running a pencil or other tool along the crease.

Challenge students to invent new ways to use folded papers by making a cooperative group sculpture. Give each student a piece of sturdy paper or tag to fold. Glue and staple the finished pieces together.

Paper folding techniques. When students are able to fold paper with clean, straight folds, introduce them to the various three-dimensional forms that can be made by bending, cutting, folding,

Teacher Tip

Paper Scoring

Scoring or lightly cutting into the surface of paper or cardboard makes it easier to fold. Show primary students how to score by pressing hard with their pencil point when drawing a fold line. Older students can use the tip of a pointed scissors. Allow students time to practice until they can apply just the right pressure. At that point introduce scoring as a way to add dimension to paper. Curved score lines can be reverse-folded to create unusual effects.

- Try scoring different weights of paper and tagboards. Have students compare the results.
- Have each student create a scored and folded paper design.
- Make a wall of the different effects that can be created with paper scoring.

gluing, and notching. After students have practiced these forms, have them think of different ways to use them in artwork.

- *Models:* Relate paper forms to those found in the environment. For example, take primary students to the playground. Compare the forms of the playground equipment with paper forms they can make. Have students work together to create a three-dimensional model of the playground. Amusement parks, circuses, and buildings also provide fertile sources for model building.
- *Boxes:* Take apart boxes of different designs. Trace the opened-up forms. Have students create their own paper container design and think of the different contents it could hold. Study the art of Japanese package wrapping.
- *Stabiles:* Look at contemporary sculptures that are based on simple geometric forms such as the stabiles of Alexander Calder and the work of Tony Smith.
- *Mobiles*: Explore Calder's mobiles and then suspend paper shapes and forms so that they move in the air currents. Tie in science and math by finding balancing points and relating them to the weight of the forms. Or take the project further and study paper airplanes and then design original flying paper objects.
- *Puppetry:* Three-dimensional paper techniques can also be used to create original puppets to dramatize a story or play. For example, join paper cylinders with pipe cleaners to create simple marionettes. Attach forms to paper lunch bags to produce hand puppets.
- *Dioramas:* Construct flat rectangular boxes or use cereal boxes with one large side cut out to make mini-stage sets or dioramas. Use folded paper forms to create dimensionality.

Teaching in Action

Paper Direction

Introduce students to the terms *landscape* for paper held with the long side horizontal and *portrait* for paper held with the long side vertical. These are the terms that are used in most computer word processing programs. They provide a simple way to differentiate the paper position. Display a labeled painting of a landscape and of a portrait in the room for reference.

Papier mâché. The ability to turn discarded newspapers into large, sturdy forms has always made papier mâché attractive to teachers faced with limited art budgets. Unfortunately the wonderful possibilities for three-dimensional sculpture are often lost in the resulting mess of torn-up newspaper and sticky paste. Fortunately the availability of new art pastes has made papier mâché less messy. These cellulose-based pastes that disappear from surfaces and clothing when dry and can be stored in covered containers replace the formerly common flour paste.

Papier mâché lends itself particularly well to cooperative projects. A large class sculpture of a dinosaur set up in the back of the room, which groups of students work on in turn, or a model community, in which pairs of students work together to create papier mâché buildings, are examples of some common ways to develop skill in using papier mâché. Students can also make life-sized sculptures of animals they are studying and masks for a play. Papier mâché also ties into the study of sculptural forms from many cultures.

Other Paper Techniques

The versatility of paper lends itself to a wide range of other uses. The following brief descriptions introduce these art forms. Obtain further directions from the sources listed at the end of this section.

Paper beads and jewelry. Long, skinny triangles of paper rolled up on a straw for primary students or a toothpick for intermediate students can form lightweight beads for stringing into original necklaces and bracelets. Coat one side with white glue before rolling. Decorative, patterned, and metallic papers can be used. Pieces of cardboard with miniature collages, and papier mâché can be used for pendants and earrings.

Origami. This Japanese form of paper sculpture is based on a series of basic folds. There are projects suited to all levels of students. Because it is best learned by imitating a more skilled practitioner, it makes an

Teaching in Action

Introduction to Papier Mâché

Regardless of the age of the students, if they have never used papier mâché, they need to be introduced to the medium on a small scale in a controlled context such as a guided discovery lesson. This provides the opportunity to lay the foundation for effective and safe working methods. For most students this can be done effectively by showing them how to cover a simple, sturdy cardboard form such as a cereal box with papier mâché.

- Begin by having students examine the form. Note the number of sides. Explain that papier mâché is covering a sturdy base with layers of pasted newspaper in order to create a strong, paintable sculptural form.
- Demonstrate how to tear the newspaper on the grain to form strips. Have each student tear several sheets of paper.
- Brush paste on each side of the strip and place it on the box. A long-handled, wide, stiff-bristle brush works well. Emphasize that students work over the newspaper-covered table, and provide a paper towel for wiping sticky fingers. Avoid getting paste on the floor. It is extremely slippery.
- Cover all sides of the box. Strips should run in the same direction. Students may need to be prompted to turn the box over.
- Repeat with a second layer going in the opposite direction. (*Note:* It may be helpful to use plain newsprint for alternating layers so students can see where they have missed.)
- Continue layering the pasted strips. Three to five layers make a sturdy surface for this beginning project. The last layer should be plain newsprint or white paper toweling. This provides an easy-to-cover surface for later painting.
- When done, place project on a sheet of plastic near a heater or in the sun. Turn daily so all sides dry.
- When dry, students may glue on additions and paint their boxes. Some possible ideas for the boxes include cutting the wide side to create a lift lid box for storing school supplies, cutting the narrow side off and inserting the hand to make a hand puppet, adding doors and windows to create a building.

ideal peer-taught mini-lesson. After teaching several groups each a different project, have these "experts" then teach members from the other groups.

Quilling. The art of rolling thin paper strips into curvaceous abstract and figurative forms has gone in and out of style since the fifteenth century. A toothpick can be used to roll the strips. The strips can then be glued to each other or to a background. Quilling provides another way to texture paper for sculptural projects.

Connections: Paper

Paper can be connected to so many areas of the curriculum. The following give just a brief idea of the wide possibilities:

Teacher Tip

Other Bases for Papier Mâché

Many other items can serve as a base for papier mâché work:

- *Cardboard:* Cardboard cartons can be used for large pieces. Cut cardboard pieces and cardboard tubing can be taped together to form a wide range of sculptures including robots, vehicles, and more. Upper graders can make more elaborate forms from wired-together chicken wire.
- *Removable molds:* Masks can be formed on Styrofoam tray bases. (See Chapter 7 for sanitizing methods.) Plastic spread containers and balloons can be used to form rounded shapes. Papier mâché does not stick to plastic, Styrofoam, or balloons, making removal of the base form easy.
- *Clay:* Nonhardening clay can be used to create finely detailed molds suitable for puppet heads and jewelry pieces. It can also be used to build up features for a mask on a Styrofoam tray base. Use small, torn bits of newspaper instead of strips to avoid wrinkles.

Language arts

- Collage provides a graphic way to introduce children to the use of metaphor. For example, David Dias in Eve Bunting's book *Smoky Night* (1994) used carefully selected papers and objects to frame his painted illustrations and reflect the meaning of the story. Ask students to look at the materials surrounding each page and describe how the shape of the papers and the choice of objects represent visually the meaning of the author's words.
- Use paper sculpture to create three-dimensional scenes showing the setting of books being read.
- Make papier mâché puppets to dramatize students' own writing. Put on puppet shows for children in other grades or classes.

Math

- Because collage involves the collection and organization of a wide variety of materials, it also provides many opportunities for children to practice sorting and grouping. Primary students can sort unsorted materials by several characteristics and then place them in storage bins. Older students can design their own classification systems for the collage area.
- Mathematical concepts such as symmetry and the qualities of geometric shapes can be investigated as students make cut paper collages.
- Challenge students to name the geometric forms used in their paper sculptures. Create a table showing which forms are used most frequently.

- Create graphs showing how long it takes for various thicknesses of papier mâché or pulp to dry. Weigh projects when wet and when dry and calculate how much water was lost to evaporation.

Science

- Examine paper fibers under a microscope. Test the strength of various papers when wet.
- When making paper, experiment with different mixtures and methods. Compare the paper produced.
- Explore how paper can be folded to increase its strength. Challenge teams of students to build a structure from four sheets of paper that will support a book.

Social Studies

- Have students research the history of paper making.
- Find out more about traditional folk arts based on paper cutting as found in China, Mexico, Poland, and many other places.
- Study the development of collage and the political climate of Vienna at the time of the Dadaists.
- Research the shadow puppets of China and Indonesia. Use paper fasteners and stiff tagboard to make jointed puppets for an original shadow play.

Dance

- Have students imagine they are a piece of paper. Ask them to make themselves smooth, folded, wrinkled, and crumpled into a ball.
- Invite students to invent a series of movements showing how a piece of paper blows in the wind or is made into something, such as a paper airplane or a puppet.

Dramatics

- Mime how paper is made starting with felling the tree until it is put in the wastebasket.
- Dramatize one of Eric Carle's, John Keats', or Leo Lionni's stories using stick or papier mâché puppets and creating handmade decorative papers for the scenery.

Music

- Challenge students to invent ways to make different sounds using paper, such as singing through a paper tube or tearing newspaper. Use the resulting "instruments" to create rhythms.
- Listen to selected pieces of music. Create patterns using cut paper shapes paper that reflect the rhythm of the music.

Books to Share

Paper

Ancona, G. (1994). *The piñata maker/El pintero*. Orlando, FL: Harcourt Brace.
Vivid photos show how an elderly Mexican piñata, puppet, and mask maker carries out his craft.

Baker, J. (1987). *Where the forest meets the sea*. New York: Greenwillow.
———. (1991). *Windows*. New York: Greenwillow.
These books show how natural materials can be used together with paint and paper to create evocative collages.

Bunting, E. (1994). *Smokey night*. Orlando, FL: Harcourt Brace.
Illustrator David Dias uses carefully selected papers and objects to frame his painted illustrations and reflect the meaning of this story about a young child's fears during the Los Angeles riots.

Carle, E. (1984). *The mixed-up chameleon.* New York: Crowell.
———. (1987). *The tiny seed.* Natich, MA: Picture Book Studio.
———. (1987). *A house for Hermit Crab*. New York: Scholastic.
These are just a few of Carle's many books. A video is available that shows how he creates his art using tissue paper (see "Teacher Resources").

Czernecki, S., & Rhodes, T. (1992). *Pancho's piñata*. New York: Hyperion.
This book tells the story of the first piñata and posadas customs. Collage illustrations mirror Mexican art.

Davol, M. (1997). *Paper dragon*. New York: Atheneum.
This Chinese folktale tells about a clever artist who saves his village from a dragon by inventing ways for paper to hold fire, wind and love.

Ehlert, L. (1991). *Red leaf. Yellow leaf*. Orlando, FL: Harcourt Brace.
———. (1995). *Snowballs*. Orlando, FL: Harcourt Brace.
A wide variety of collage items are used to illustrate these two sprightly picture books.
———. (1997). *Cuckoo cucu*. New York: Scholastic.
A simple bilingual Spanish/English text is illustrated with collages based on Mexican cut paper designs.

Hughes, L., & Bearden, R. (1995). *The block*. New York: Metropolitan Museum of Art.
Langston Hughes' poems about life in New York City are illustrated with the collages of Romare Bearden.

Lee, H. V. (1994). *At the beach*. New York: Henry Holt.
Delicate pastel cut paper collages illustrate a story about children learning to write Chinese characters in the sand.

Lionni, L. (1967). *Frederick*. New York: Scholastic.
———. (1969). *Alexander and the wind-up mouse*. New York: Scholastic.
These books feature a variety of decorative papers used with other types of paper in collages.

Small, D. (1987). *Paper John*. New York: Farrar, Straus & Giroux.
John lives in a paper house in a paper town. When the town blows out to sea, John saves the day by turning his house into a boat.

Painting

It is colorful, wet, and unpredictable. It is the beloved medium of early childhood and the rich tool of the master. From the first wild strokes of the preschooler to the thoughtful brush movements of the adolescent, painting provides a unique way to visually communicate ideas.

When children pick up a paintbrush and paint, they are carrying on a long tradition that links them with the triptych painter of the Middle Ages, the Chinese landscape artist, the Renaissance portrait painter, the Mexican muralist, and Jackson Pollock and his action painting. The struggle is the same. How can one use paint and tool to communicate to others what one feels and knows?

Painting has always played an important role in early childhood education. Easels and paint are a regular fixture in preschools and kindergartens, and young children are encouraged to paint daily. But something happens when children enter the elementary grades. The easels disappear. Painting becomes something done occasionally for a special project, perhaps a class mural or a diorama. In the art room painting is just one of many media offered every few weeks in a cycle of collage, drawing, and assorted crafts.

We cannot expect our students to become confident painters when painting is so peripheral to their artistic experience. No wonder students expect brushes to work like pencils and become frustrated when they do not. Painting is not drawing. Painting allows children to directly experience color and texture in a way drawing does not. Because children spend most of their school day manipulating pens and pencils, wielding a paintbrush requires a new level of concentration. Because painting involves controlling a sometimes unpredictable medium, it challenges children's creativity. Children need many experiences with paint in order to confidently paint their ideas and thoughts. See At a Glance 11.9 and 11.10 for descriptions of paint and brushes.

Finger Paint

Although often thought of as a messy activity for preschoolers, finger paint is an excellent way to introduce students at all levels to color mixing and texture, using the artist's most sensitive tool—the fingers.

Initial experiences with finger paint should focus on controlling the medium and discovering different ways to apply the paint. After students have become proficient at handling finger paint, this versatile medium can be used to effectively teach introductory color mixing.

Applying finger paint. The key to turning finger painting from sloppy smearing to thoughtful learning is in the method of distributing the paint. Instead of plopping the paint directly on the student's paper, place fingerprints in a carefully selected palette of colors on a disposable tray, paper plate, or even a sheet of paper. Provide damp sponges or wet paper towels for them to wipe their fingers. Students of all ages love the tactile

At a Glance 11.9

Types of Paint

Paint selected for student use must first of all contain safe ingredients. It should also come in a full range of colors and offer unique textural qualities. For the lower grades it is important that paint be washable and the colors not stain hands, furnishings, or clothing. The following paints meet these requirements:

Finger paint. Thick, paste-like, washable finger paint comes in a full range of colors, including neons and glitters. Sold in both bottles and tubes, it provides an inexpensive way to introduce even primary students to paint as a textural medium.

Tempera paint. Tempera paint is the mainstay of school art programs. Water-based and brilliantly colored, it flows on to paper with ease. Washable formulas are designed to wash out of clothing. It is marketed in liquid form, dry cakes, and powder in a full range of colors including metallics, fluorescents, glosses, and glitters.

- *Liquid:* Look for a liquid paint that is thick and creamy. This minimizes spills. Gallon jugs of paint can be fitted with special paint pumps to make distribution easier. The addition of a small amount of liquid detergent will help it spread and wash up more easily.
- *Dry cakes:* The dry cakes come in plastic trays and are a neat way to store and distribute paint. Unfortunately students do not usually wet the cakes enough to get the same strong rich colors of the liquid form. The results tend to look more like watercolors. Mixing colors is also more difficult. Show students how to dampen the cakes before beginning their work and then rub the surface to get a good depth of color.
- *Powder paint:* Avoid powder paint if possible. Although less expensive and easy to store, mixing the paint releases pigment into the air that is unsafe to breathe (see Chapter 8). When mixing powder paint, make sure to do so away from children. Slowly add water to the paint until it is thick and creamy in consistency.

Watercolor. Watercolor comes in quarter and half pan sizes and tubes. Younger children do better with the larger pan size. Look for brands that wash out of clothing. Older students can use sets with smaller pans and more colors. Select sets with sturdy plastic boxes that can be refilled. Certain colors, such as yellow and blue, are used up more quickly than others, and refilling the sets makes economic sense. Upper elementary students can explore tube watercolors, which provide richer, deeper tones in a full range of colors.

sensation of dipping their fingers in the colors of their choice and then applying the paint to their paper.

Art center activities

- *Exploring finger paint.* Begin with one color of finger paint and small two- or three-inch squares of paper. Challenge students to invent as many ways as possible to apply the paint using just one finger, making a sample on each square. When dry, have students explain their application techniques.

At a Glance 11.10

Types of Brushes

There are so many different types of brushes available at such a wide range of prices that teachers often have difficulty selecting the best ones for children. In general it is wise to buy the most expensive brushes possible. A well-made, cared-for brush will last through years of constant use by children. Inexpensive brushes quickly lose their hair or the ferules become separated from the handles. It is better to start with a small selection of good brushes in small and medium sizes and then slowly add variety over time, rather than buying sets or grosses of poor quality ones.

The following descriptions will help in deciding brush purchases.

Bamboo: The traditional brush of Chinese calligraphy and painting makes an excellent detail watercolor brush. The bamboo handle of these inexpensive brushes is lightweight and the brush comes to a fine point. They last a long time if they are not allowed to stand in water. Provide students with inexpensive plastic or home-made cardboard brush holders.

Bristle brushes: Bristle brushes have stiff natural or synthetic hairs. They are very durable and work well with thick paints, on textured surfaces, or in instances in which the brush will be used roughly.

Easel brushes: These are long-handled brushes intended for use at an easel or when standing up. They work well for primary students as they differ significantly in length from pencils and allow a more flexible grip and increased arm and wrist action. They come in a variety of shapes and hair types.

Flats: This term is used to describe a brush that is flatter than it is wide. They are sold by the inch. A three-quarters to one-inch size makes a good general purpose background brush.

Foam: Inexpensive foam brushes can be used to create interesting effects and for painting wide areas on larger works.

Nylons: Nylon brushes are stiffer and less absorbent than hair brushes. They work well with acrylics as they wash up cleaner and the stiffness increases the textural possibilities. They come in all shapes including flat and round.

Rounds: These brushes have a round shape starting at the ferule. They may be pointed or have a stubby end. They come in a range of sizes. A size 2 is extremely fine. A size 7 or 8 makes a good medium detail brush for tempera and watercolor work.

Wash: Wash brushes have thick, absorbent, natural hairs and are designed to hold large quantities of thin, watery paint. Size 10 or larger are good sizes for wash brushes.

Watercolor brushes: These brushes have a short handle and absorbent natural hairs. They come in a wide variety of shapes including flats and rounds. They are good for both watercolor and tempera painting.

- *Exploring surfaces.* Traditional finger paint paper provides a smooth, white painting surface, but try other papers as well: brown kraft paper, white drawing paper, and colored construction paper. Divide the students into small groups and give each group a different type of paper. Challenge them to apply the paint in different ways and then compare the results. Note which papers curl up or wrinkle when dry.
- *Exploring color mixing.* It is easier for novice painters to control the amount of paint applied when using fingers than when using a brush. Use finger paint to introduce color mixing to primary students. Start with adding white and then black to one color. Then introduce mixing two primary colors to make a secondary.
- *Exploring texture.* When students are adept at color mixing, have them use finger paint to capture textures. Put out examples of textured material such as tree bark, rocks, and fabrics. Ask students to replicate these textures using finger paint. Explore different application methods including scratching through to the surface using fingernails and simple tools such as notched pieces of cardboard.

Group activities

- Sort and group finger paint sample squares and make a chart or graph. Squares can also be effectively combined into a finger quilt.
- Create a class book or wall chart of the resulting samples.
- Students can also cut up their texture studies and place them in the collage center for later use in their artwork.

Tempera Paint

Careful planning will help students learn to use paint as a medium of communication. Although tempera paint is one of the most widely used art media in schools, students do not often receive sufficient instruction and time to develop independent painting skills. Children who do not get enough time to explore color mixing and other painting techniques cannot use paint to thoughtfully express themselves. The paint controls them instead of them controlling the paint. Students should be given opportunities to explore painting at a paint center, as part of cooperative group activities and during independent workshop time.

Paint Center Supplies

A successful painting center should allow students to get their own paint and brushes without waste or mess. How this is designed will vary depending on the age, experience, and number of children who will be using paint daily. A well-organized center will contain palettes on which students will place their paint; bottles of paint that allow

"Sunset."
Tempera—Jiaying, grade 3.

Thinking about Children's Art

This third grader has used one color of tempera paint plus white to create her picture. How does limiting the colors of paint a student uses help develop painting skill? How could this kind of challenging art skill lesson be tied into studies of light and shadow in science or be used to inspire poems about a favorite color?

easy distribution; clean, dry brushes sorted by size; and newspapers for covering tables or desks. It is better to keep paper on which to paint in a separate location. This keeps it clean and acknowledges that paper has many uses besides painting.

Paint palettes. A palette holds an artist's paint while painting. There are many different palettes on the market for tempera painting. Each has advantages and disadvantages.

- *Disposable cups*: Small, low-sided paper or plastic cups can be placed on small trays with sides. These work well for younger students who need a larger paint container or when the paint is runny. They are also useful when using nontraditional brushes such as sponge brushes or when dipping in sponges and other objects for decorative paper techniques. Wrapped in plastic bags, paint-filled cups can be stored several days. Because paint is in individual cups, a mixed-up paint color can easily be replaced with a new cup. On the other hand, the cups are easier to spill or drop when carried.
- *Disposable palettes:* Paper, Styrofoam, and plastic plates work well as temporary palettes when paint is fairly thick, such as finger paint or tube acrylics. Paper plates can be used only once. Styrofoam and plastic can be saved and even washed and reused several times. Although cheap and readily available, plates have the disadvantage that the paint colors mix together more easily on the flat surface. Plates work well for upper-level students and for mural work at all

levels. They also allow large nontraditional objects to be used for painting.

- *Egg cartons:* Sanitized Styrofoam egg cartons combine the advantages of the first two palettes. They allow paint to be separated into compartments but form a solid one-piece unit. With the increasing problem of bacterial contamination it is imperative that egg cartons be sanitized before use or purchased new. To sanitize, soak the cartons in a mixture of three-quarter cups chlorine bleach to one gallon water for one minute. Wrap egg cartons in plastic bags for wet storage.
- *Reusable cups*: Nonspill paint cups have a specially designed top that prevents paint from spilling if the jar tips over. A separate, tight-fitting lid keeps paint from drying out. These work well at the primary level. Holders are available to make it easier to carry and use up to six colors at a time.
- *Reusable palettes:* Plastic paint palettes come in a wide variety of styles. Look for ones with fairly large, deep paint wells. Six wells work well at the elementary level. Multiple section trays work well for more advanced upper graders. Trays of wet paint, like egg cartons, can be wrapped in plastic bags for storage. Although plastic palettes will inexpensively provide years of use, their major disadvantage is that they must be washed when paint colors are mixed up or no longer needed. For this reason they work best with older students who can handle this task on their own with a minimum of mess. Soaking them in a bucket of water before washing makes the task simpler, especially if paint has dried.
- *Covered trays:* Covered paint palettes are also available. Airtight lids keep paint in use from drying out and allow students to quickly return to a work in progress. Some contain disposable paper liners and a sponge to dampen, which work well with thick tube paints. A well-designed system can keep paints usable for as long as four weeks and are well worth the investment for older students who will be working on a painting over a period of time.

Water cups. Water is an essential part of the painting process. Having an adequate supply of clean water allows students to effectively clean their brush and mix fresh colors. Water cups need to be large enough to hold sufficient water so students are not consistently interrupted in their work to get clean water. If several students are sharing water, cups need to be larger than if used by an individual. Cups should have a wide base and be filled only halfway to keep the center of gravity low and minimize tipping. A variety of containers can be used. Coffee cans are a good size for sharing. Putting the plastic lid on the bottom of a coffee can will prevent rust stains on counters. Empty icing containers make a good individual or pair size.

Teacher Tip

Paint and Clothing

Teachers often have to deal with upset children and parents angered by paint stains on clothing. There is less likely to be a problem, however, if teachers notify parents beforehand about the importance of painting in learning and advise on clothing considerations. Parents can be informed in many ways:

- Send home a letter at the beginning of the year explaining why the children will be painting and describe the different paints used in the class. If washable paint is being used, make sure parents know this. Parents who remember paint stains from their childhood may not know that new formulas are available. Detail the kind of clothing students should wear, such as sleeves that easily push up over the elbow. Include washing instructions for removing paint. This is also a good time to ask them to send smocks in to school.
- Hold a parent-child painting workshop in which parents paint alongside their child.
- Keep copies of the washing out paint instructions, and give them to students who accidentally do get paint on their clothing. Example:

WASHING OUT PAINT INSTRUCTIONS

- Scratch off any dried paint that is on the surface.
- Rub detergent or stain remover into the stain.
- Wash by hand or in machine.
- Check that paint is gone. If not, scrub again.
- When spot is gone, line dry garment.
- Do not put garment in dryer until stain is gone. Heat may set the stain.

Keep plenty of containers available at all times so that students can have two containers when using watercolor and mixing washes. Keeping an extra supply of filled containers of clean water in the paint center allows students to quickly replace water when in the middle of painting. One student can be assigned to the task of emptying and filling the water jars on a rotating basis.

Distributing paint. One of the reasons paint is often not offered regularly is because distribution can be a hassle. The goal should be to teach students how to get their own paint with a minimum of mess and bother.

Teacher Tip

Brush Storage

Between uses always store brushes hair end up. Buy special brush holders or use a plastic container with holes poked in the bottom. This allows water to escape and preserves the handles.

- *Start simply.* Primary students need to be provided with a few colors and a limited variety of brushes at the start. As they master getting these supplies, add more colors and brush types. In the beginning two or three colors of paint should already be in the selected cups or palettes. This allows students to concentrate on carrying the paint carefully to and from their work area.
- *Use dispenser bottles.* When students are successfully handling the paint palettes, introduce small refillable squeeze bottles of paint with screw-on lids or bottles with paint pumps. Show students how much paint to take and then closely supervise in the beginning as they take one supplementary color. With time more color choices can be made available. (*Note:* It is important to keep the spouts clear of dried-up paint. Check tops daily. Cover paint pumps with plastic bags at the end of the day to prevent drying out.)
- *Plan ahead.* If a large number of students will be painting daily, such as when creating a mural, it is time efficient to have the basic paint colors already placed on palettes. Have students volunteer to do this task before classes begin or the day before. Filled palettes can be wrapped in a sealed plastic bag, where they will keep for several days. When ready to paint, students can then independently add any extra colors they need. At the end of the day students who are not finished can wrap their palettes in a plastic bag and store it till the next day. This cuts down on distribution time in following days.
- *Provide personal palettes.* Having their own personal palette for which they are responsible encourages students to take better care of their paints. Provide upper-level students with sturdy palettes with tight-fitting lids or a zip-lock bag for storage labeled with their name. Each student should be responsible not just for filling but also cleaning and drying their palette as needed. When teaching a mini-lesson, make up the paint palettes with the selected colors for the lesson in advance, so students can concentrate on the lesson rather than getting supplies.

Teaching in Action

Mixing Colors

Mixing colors is one of the most exciting parts of painting, but it should not be left to chance. Teaching children how to mix colors successfully expands their ability to use paint expressively. Never tell children not to mix their colors, but show them how to do so with control. Here is one way to teach this:

Demonstrate how to dip brush into lighter color first and place a drop of color on the newspaper. Then wash brush, blot on newspaper, and dip into second color. Mix it into the drop of the first color. Ask, "What would happen if I added two drops of a color to the other? What if I started with the darker color first?" Next challenge students to see how many different versions of the two colors they can create, painting one mixture on each paper square. Allow students to experiment as a group or at a paint center. Provide extra paint or paper as needed.

Have students share results with a partner. Did they both mix the same versions of the colors or are they different?

Art center activities

- Exploring the brush. First demonstrate how to dip the brush into the paint and paint a line. Then challenge students to paint as many different kinds of lines as possible, such as thick, thin, wavy, until their papers are full of lines. When students have filled up their paper, have them share their results.
- Compare similarities and differences in the lines each student made in their paintings and how they were made.
- Adding texture. Provide sand, flour, oatmeal, and salt for students to add to their paint. Explore what happens.

Group activities

- Look at other children's paintings or reproductions of artwork and try to guess how the colors were mixed or what kind of brush was used.
- At community circle have each student share a way to paint a line.
- Make a chart showing the different versions of each combination placed in order of lightest to darkest, brightest to dullest, etc.
- Have students label their paint samples and store them in their journal or process folio for reference. Encourage them to look at these when planning a painting.
- Start a paint riddle activity. Put up a sample of one student's mixed color in the painting center. Challenge students to make a match.
- Make a labeled wall chart of mixed color samples.

Teacher Tip

Paint Smocks

Students need ways to protect their clothing while painting. An unfortunate spill can quickly turn a child's joyful painting experience into one to avoid. Primary students, especially, need protection as they work with paint.

- A man's shirt with the sleeves trimmed short and worn backwards makes a convenient smock for primary children. A clothespin can be used to clip it closed in the back, making it easier for young children to help each other to put it on and off.
- Personalized T-shirts, decorated with the student's name, and artwork using fabric paint or crayons, make an easy-on, easy-off alternative that appeals to middle elementary students.
- Older students reject wearing these kinds of smocks. Offer plastic aprons instead.

In addition, always remind students to

- Wear old clothes on days they know they are painting.
- Roll their sleeves up above their elbows.
- Never paint directly on the smock. The paint will go through it and on to clothing.

- Use samples to create a class mural (see Chapter 7).
- At community circle place the mixed color paint samples in the center. Have students pick a sample and brainstorm a name for the color. Names can reflect mixing, such as reddish brown, or can reflect uses for the color, such as wet rock gray, rainy bark brown, and spring grass green.

Watercolor painting. Unlike tempera paint, watercolor sets are easily portable and always ready to use. This makes a tray of watercolor sets an important addition to any painting center. They are ideal for quick sketching, adding color to a drawing, or working outdoors on nature sketches. They are not, however, a substitute for tempera paint. Watercolors use different brush skills, color mixes, and working approaches.

Introducing watercolors. To help children develop control over the paint, provide two water containers and label one "Mixing" and the other "Cleaning." Demonstrate how to place a brush full of clean water from the "Mixing" jar on every pan of color in the set to soften the paint. Show how to gently rub the brush on a color of choice and then paint a line on a sheet of white paper. When done, blot brush on newspaper and use the "Cleaning" jar to wash it clean. Together with children, make a chart showing the steps. Add pictures, if necessary.

Books to Share

Painting

Bulla, C. R. (1998). *The paint brush kid.* New York: Random House.
de Paola, T. (1988). *The legend of the Indian paintbrush.* New York: Putnam.
Calders, P. (1990). *Brush.* New York: Kane/Miller.
Clements, A. (1988). *Big Al.* New York: Scholastic.
Cooney, B. (1990). *Hattie and the wild waves.* New York: Penguin.
Rylant, S. (1988). *All I see.* New York: Orchard.

Art center activities

- Have students try to make a gradation of lines of one color from weakest to strongest. At upper levels introduce terms most *transparent* to most *opaque.*
- Before painting, wet paper using a damp sponge. Explore what happens when paint is applied.
- Challenge students to wet their entire papers, fill paper with colors, and then blot up areas with a tissue or paper towel to create special effects such as clouds or textures. At the paint center explore other materials for blotting, such as sponge pieces, cotton, fabric, and so on. Is the effect similar or different?
- Provide two-inch squares of paper and challenge students to mix as many versions of a selected color using just different amounts of paint and water. Then they should try mixing pairs of colors in differing amounts of water. Upper graders can use a pencil to label their mixtures, such as two drops blue, one drop yellow, one large brush full of water, before painting them on the square.
- Challenge students to combine wax, in the form of candles or crayons, and watercolors to create a variety of special effects.
- Try painting over chalk, marker, pencil, or charcoal. What happens when you draw over wet or dry paint? Try the same methods with tempera paint. What is the result?

Group activities

- Have students think of uses for some of the watercolor effects, such as a sunset for a blending of orange and yellow, or fireworks for a spread-out dot.
- Look at watercolor paintings and identify areas where paint was used on dry paper and places where paper was wet.
- Write descriptions of the wet-on-wet effects in journals or on a class experience chart.

- Sort and group completed squares from center activities. Did everyone get the same color using the same combinations? Why or why not?
- Have groups agree on color formulas and then try to mix them and each get the same results.

Connections: Paint

Paint is another tool for learning. Applying painting skills in other curriculum areas helps students as they make connections across disciplines. Mixing and matching paint colors might be a good way to accurately record the colors seen in a science observation. Planning and painting a mural of a revolutionary battle may make the facts more memorable. Painted illustrations make original stories come alive.

Language arts

- Use paintings to illustrate or inspire stories and poems.
- Use the color samples created at paint centers as inspiration for composing poems about color or for writing detailed descriptions of the colors.

Math

Use eye droppers to measure out different quantities of two colors of paint. Order the resulting mixtures and write an equation for each (e.g., 2 red + 3 blue = 5 purple).

Science

- Integrate finger painting with the study of fingerprints or the sense of touch. Use the wrinkling and curling of painted paper and cardboard to introduce the study of absorbency.
- Use the scientific method to investigate color mixing. Write a question, hypothesis, procedure, results, and conclusion to accompany paint-mixing experiments.
- Compare the color wheel to the spectrum. Investigate how mixing pigmented color is different from mixing colored light.
- Use watercolor paints to test the absorbency of different materials. Paint on each material and time how far the paint spreads and how long it takes to dry.

Social studies

- Study the cave paintings of France and Spain and rock art of the southwest United States and Africa. Research the pigments and tools used by the first artists. Have students make their own pigments using ground charcoal, white chalk, and soil mixed with various binders such as milk, cooking or mineral oil, and glue. Invent new brush designs by taping cloth, cotton, paper, cardboard, etc. to sticks. Try out the invented paints and brushes on flat rocks.

- Research the history and composition of different paints and how the use of these paints has changed over time. Compare paints and brushes used across cultures.

Dance

- Have students imagine they are paintbrushes. Ask them to move like the different brush strokes.
- Invite students to invent and then mime a series of movements showing a painting being made. At the same time have the other students try to paint the painting that is being mimed.
- Form students into small groups. Assign each group a paint color. Have them create a movement to express that color. Then have groups mix and blend their color movements together to make new ones.

Dramatics

- Have groups of students create skits demonstrating different painting methods or ways to solve a problem associated with painting, such as how to clean up a paint spill.
- Form older students into small groups. Have each group research and then dramatize the creation of a famous painting, such as Michelangelo's ceiling frescos in the Sistine Chapel or Jackson Pollock's action painting *One.*

Music

- Listen to selected pieces of music with distinctive rhythms or read the book *I See the Rhythm* by Michele Wood and Toyomi Igus (1998, Emeryville, CA: Children's Book Press). Paint lines or shapes that reflect the rhythm and mood of the music.
- Match musical chords to different colors on the color wheel and create a musical color wheel.

Conclusion

THE ART OF DOING ART

With each new medium a new invention must occur.
Elliot Eisner (Arnheim, 1989, p. 4)

It is easy to watch children exploring art materials and methods and to forget that a great deal of mental processing is going on at the same time. Introducing students to the artistic process is one way to make the mental processing of the artist more visible and valued, just as using the writing process helps students understand what a writer does. It is important to remember, however, that these are processes, not step-by-step directions. The goal is to help students internalize the process so that they not only think like artists but are artists.

Teacher Resources

REFERENCES

Arnheim, R. (1989) *Thoughts on art education.* Los Angeles: Getty Center for the Arts.

Berliner, D. (1984). The half-full glass: A review of research on teaching. In P. L. Hosford (Ed.), *Using what we know about teaching.* Alexandria, VA: Association for Supervision and Curriculum Development.

Calkins, L. (1986). *The art of teaching writing.* Portsmouth, NH: Heinemann.

Chapman, L. (1978). *Approaches to art in education.* Orlando, FL: Harcourt Brace.

Gardner, H. (1980). *Artful scribbles.* New York: Basic.

McFee, J. K. (1961). *Preparation for art.* Belmont, CA: Wadsworth.

Silberstein-Storfer, M. (1996). *Doing art together.* New York: Abrams.

To Learn More about Paper

Ayture-Scheele, Z. (1987). *The great origami book.* New York: Sterling.

Brommer, G. F. (1994). *Collage techniques.* Worcester, MA: Davis.

Grummer, A. (1980). *Paper by kids.* Minneapolis: Dillon.

Jackson, P. (1991). *The encyclopedia of origami & papercraft techniques.* Philadelphia: Running Press.

Roukes, N. (1993). *Sculpture in paper.* Worcester, MA: Davis.

Sivin, C. (1986). *Maskmaking.* Worcester, MA: Davis.

Tejada, I. (1993). *Brown bag ideas from many cultures.* Worcester, MA: Davis.

Toale, B. (1983). *The art of papermaking.* Worcester, MA: Davis.

To Learn More about Painting

Silberstein-Storfer, M. (1996). *Doing art together.* New York: Abrams.

Topal, C. W. (1992). *Children and painting.* Worcester, MA: Davis.

RESOURCES

Videos

Art is . . . Video Series, Crystal
- Paper, Scissors and Glue
- Tearing and Cutting

Basic Paper Sculpture Techniques, GPN

Three-Dimensional Forms in Paper, GPN

Creative Young Child Series, GPN
- Fingerpainting
- Painting

Handmade Paper, Crystal

The Paper Crane Reading Rainbow Series, GPN

Web Sites

Students can display their art on the following Web sites.

Art Soup
yahooligans.com

Bravotv
bravotv.com

Global Show-n-Tell
telenaut.com/gst

KidLit
mgfx.com/kidlit

Chapter 12

Art and Design

Form and Function

For me all is in the conception—I must have a clear vision of the whole composition from the very beginning.

Henri Matisse (1946, p. 410)

ARTISTS AT WORK

Designers Thinking

Tom: What is your piece of cloth from?

Paulo: It's from an old pair of jeans.

Tom: Mine's from my dad's favorite flannel shirt. It was worn out.

Teacher: Please make a large circle. Now who would like to be the first to place their quilt piece? Okay, Jenny, will you please put your piece in the middle? Now who has a piece that will look wonderful next to Jenny's?

Tom: I think mine will. Look, it has the same kind of red in it.

Teacher: Let's try it. . . . What do you think?

Jenny: Tom's right. It does have the same red in it.

Teacher: Which of our pieces of cloth should come next?

Loretta: Mine has a plaid like Tom's, but I don't think we should put two plaids together. That's boring.

Frank: If you put it on the other side of Jenny's, it kind of makes a pattern.

Teacher: That's a very interesting way to think about what we're doing. Are we trying to make a pattern?

Shaun: Yeah, that's what we should do.

Jenny: But I don't think there are enough plaid pieces to make every other one a plaid. Do you?

Shaun: Oh, maybe we should just spread out all the pieces and see whether or not some kind of pattern is possible.

Teacher: Shall we do that?

Others: Yes.

Introduction

MAKING DECISIONS

Is this too colorful? Is that too large for the space? Does this match? Does that look good together with this? We spend our lives making decisions based on our knowledge of the elements of art and the principles of design. A knowledge of design is essential for understanding the fashions we wear and the advertisements we see, for planning the interiors of our homes, and for choosing the shapes and forms of the products we buy. Every well-planned art lesson is a lesson in design. In this chapter we will introduce the vocabulary of design and present ways of incorporating design principles in a wide range of classroom activities.

Setting the Stage

WHAT IS DESIGN?

Design refers to the arrangement of the visual and spatial qualities that can be found in two- and three-dimensional images and objects. It is a set of organizing principles around which a work of art can be built or analyzed. These elements and principles of design are flexible building blocks that can be rearranged in a multitude of creative ways depending on what the artist wishes to communicate. Artists must choose and use the elements and principles that best express their intended meaning, carefully considering the relationships among the parts of the work and studying how each will affect the quality and form of the whole. Design also gives us the vocabulary to describe what we see when we look at a work of art (see At a Glance 12.1).

The Elements of Art

The tools of the designer are the visual elements—line, shape, color, texture, form, and space—that are found not only in all art but also in almost everything we look at and use. Being able to find these elements in our environment and in human creations provides a basis for talking about and analyzing the objects that surround us. Teaching design begins with providing students with a strong grounding in the identification, conceptualization, and application of these elements.

? *What Do You Think?*

Think of some ordinary thing you use every day such as a pen, a chair, or a cooking pot. Why do you think it is shaped the way it is? How does it feel when you use it? Is there anything you would change about its design? Who do you think decided it should be that size, shape, and color?

At a Glance 12.1

A Vocabulary of Design

Actual texture: The surface quality of real materials.

Art elements: The basic visual and tactile qualities of an artwork: line, color, shape, value, texture, form, and space.

Asymmetrical balance: The visual elements are placed in varying positions in the work in order to create a sense of balance, rather than being placed on either side of a central axis.

Balance: A state of equilibrium in the composition of an artwork.

Boundary: The edge of a shape or pictorial surface.

Color: The surface quality of an object or substance as revealed by the light that reflects on it and seen as a hue in the spectrum.

Color wheel: An arrangement of colors based on the three primaries and the colors that result when two neighboring pairs are mixed together. The order mirrors that of the spectrum.

Composition: The arrangement of the art elements into a unified whole.

Contour: The outer edge of a shape or form.

Design: The organization that makes the parts of something work together to create a whole.

Design principles: The structures used to arrange the elements of art into a unified whole: order, repetition, variety, emphasis, movement, balance, and unity.

Diagonal: A line or direction that is neither perpendicular to nor parallel with either the base or side of an artwork.

Dominance: The position held by those elements or that part of an artwork that receives the most emphasis and importance.

Emphasis: The creation of focal points or areas that draw and hold the eye.

Focus (focal point/area): The most important part of an image or artwork.

Form: Form has two meanings: It can refer to the whole of a work of art; and it can refer to the three-dimensional equivalent of shape that has the qualities of mass and volume.

Geometric shapes (forms): Mathematically defined shapes (forms).

Horizontal: A line or direction parallel to the base of an artwork.

Hue: A color, e.g., red, yellow, and so on.

Intensity: The brightness or dullness of a color.

Intensity chart: A chart on which color samples are arranged from brightest to dullest.

Invented texture: A surface treatment that produces a tactile experience created by the artist.

Line: A mark left on a surface by a moving point.

Motif: The dominant design feature in a pattern, artwork, or building style.

Movement: A change in position or direction.

Negative space: The areas of a work in which all form or material is absent. In a sculpture it is a hole or empty space. In a two-dimensional work it is those empty shapes left after the positive shapes are placed.

Order: The organized placement of art elements.

Organic shapes (forms): Amorphic shapes (forms) that have the characteristics of natural organisms such as plants and animals.

Organic unity: An artwork in which every part is so integrated into the whole that the work is like a living organism.

Pattern: A repeated, recognizable combination of art elements.

Placement: The locating of art elements in particular locations in the artwork.

Positive space: The space occupied by the images and art elements that make up a work.

Primary colors: The three basic colors from which all other colors are derived and which cannot be mixed from the other colors. In painting these are red, yellow, and blue. In colored light they are magenta, cyan, and yellow.

Proportion: Size and spatial relationships.

Radial balance: A state of equilibrium or balance produced by locating the art elements evenly around a central point.

Repetition: Repeating the same art element or images within an artwork in order to create stability or rhythmic movement.

Rhythm: A sense of movement in a work of art created by the repetition of imagery or art elements.

Secondary colors: The colors created by mixing two of the primaries together.

Shape: A two-dimensional area or image that has defined edges or borders.

Simulated texture: An illusion of a textured surface created by the artist.

Shade: A color darkened by the addition of black.

Space: An open or empty area in an artwork.

Symmetry: Equilibrium or balance created by placing art elements equally on both side of a central axis.

Tactile: Pertaining to how something feels to the touch.

Texture: The tactile or visual surface quality of an object or artwork.

Tint: A color lightened by the addition of white.

Three-dimensional: Having height, width, and depth.

Tone: The relative lightness or darkness of a color.

Two-dimensional: Having height and width.

Unity: The interrelationship of every part of a work to every other part.

Value: The range of lights and darks of the colors.

Variety: The amount of differences seen.

Vertical: A line or direction that is perpendicular to the base and parallel to the sides.

"Wall of Lines."
Pen and ink—grade 6.

Thinking about Children's Art

This mural was created from line samples drawn at an exploration center for pen and ink. The assignment was to completely fill a square with an arrangement of unique lines. How well have students accomplished this goal? How will this activity increase their skill using the medium of pen and ink?

The art element activities that follow are intended to provide a small sampling of ways to increase student perception of the visual and tactile components of art. They are not intended as stand-alone lessons but should be carefully integrated into units of study such as those centered around a featured artwork that incorporates those particular elements. For example, a study of a sculpture by Henry Moore would relate well to a discussion of form, while Joan Miró's paintings lend themselves to the study of lines and shapes. They can also be part of community circle, art centers, and cooperative group tasks as well as forming transitions between activities.

Begin by focusing on the characteristics of one element at a time before using them in combination. This allows students to gain confidence in their ability to see and use it. As students gain perceptual awareness and vocabulary, add more complex tasks. Challenge them to apply their knowledge of the elements in the discussion of a wider variety of artworks and in the creation of artworks in different art media.

Line

A line is the path of a moving point—the mark made by a tool drawn along a surface. It can be seen as an edge or contour separating an area of space from the background, or it can be used for surface enrichment. Lines have length and width. They come in different types such as wavy, straight, zigzag, and curved. Lines can divide or unify, show position and direction. They can be horizontal, vertical, or diagonal. Drawn closely together, lines can create the illusion of textures and values. Lines can also be expressive. They can reflect movement and feeling.

Awareness activities

- *Line walk.* Head out to the playground or take a walk around the school. Have students point out examples of lines that they see. At the primary level have students touch the lines directly or have them trace them in the air with their fingers. At community circle have the students describe the most interesting line they saw.
- *Line collection.* Upper-level students can take their journals and capture the lines they see in sketches and written descriptions. Back in the classroom ask students to compare their ideas and sketches. Develop a class chart of suggested ways to use line to show such natural objects as grass, clouds, leaves, bark, etc. As students create their own artwork, encourage them to use the ideas from their journals and on the chart.

Art center activities

- *Exploring line.* Have students fold a piece of paper into sixteen sections or give them small precut squares of paper. Provide students with simple drawing materials such as crayons or markers. Challenge them to invent as many different ways to draw lines as they can.
- *Linear words.* Challenge students to letter a word of their choice in as many different ways as possible using different types of lines, such as dotted lines, thick and thin lines, double lines, swirly lines, and so on. Have them draw each word design on a separate paper so they can be used in group sorting activities.

Group activities

- *Line sort.* Have students work in pairs or cooperative groups to sort and group the line samples completed at either of the centers. Ask students to identify different qualities such as thick, thin, curved, zigzag, etc., and create a class graph, chart, or quilt-type mural. Display the resulting work and refer to it often in future discussions about the use of line in artworks.
- *Line exchange.* Have students, working in pairs, draw a line on a piece of paper. Then have them exchange papers and use their imagination to create a picture that incorporates their partner's line. Share the resulting artworks and discuss how they used each initiating line. Did it become part of a contour or edge? Was it used

Books to Share

Line

Barrett, P., & Barrett, S. (1972). *The line Sophie drew.* New York: Scroll Press.
Blair, M. (1996). *The red string.* Joshua Tree, CA: Children's Library.
Christiana, D. (1990). *Drawer in a drawer.* New York: Farrar, Straus & Giroux.
Drescher, H. (1983). *Simon's book.* New York: Scholastic.
Schaefa, C. L. (1996). *The squiggle.* New York: Crown.

to define an area or shape or to decorate something in the picture? Which was the most common use?

- *Line chart.* Give each team a selected artwork. Have them make a chart detailing the different uses of line in the work. Have teams share their results and create a class summary chart. As they study other artworks, add observations to the chart. From the chart determine whether certain types of artwork or works from particular cultures more frequently use line in a particular way. Have more experienced students compare how lines are used in the works of different artists such as in Pieter Bruegel the Elder's drawing *Landscape with the Penitence of St. Jerome* and Edvard Munch's *The Scream*.

Shape

Next to line, shape is one of the easiest elements for students to find and describe in artworks. A shape can be described most simply as an area that stands out from its surroundings because of a defined boundary or a difference in visual appearance. It may have an outline around it or be a different texture, color, or value. Shapes are the building blocks of an artwork. They are formed the minute an artist joins the ends of a line together or blots paint on a paper.

Shapes can be two- or three-dimensional. Geometric shapes are based on mathematical principles. Organic shapes resemble the irregular and curved shapes found in nature. Because learning the names of the basic geometric shapes is one of the important activities of early childhood education, most students enter the primary grades being able to recognize circles, squares, triangles, and rectangles. Shapes that have names and defined characteristics are easier for young students to discover in the environment and in artworks.

Awareness activities

- *Discovering shapes.* Start by having students point to geometric shapes they see in the classroom. Then play the traditional game Hot and Cold with a focus on shape. Choose a shape in the room and have students try to find it. Use degrees of hot or cold to let them know when they are getting close.

- *Shapes around us.* As a class create a chart of shapes found in the environment and in artworks. List everyday objects next to the geometric shape that is most similar to it, such as table top—rectangle; garbage can lid—circle. Point out when students use these shapes in their artwork to represent similar objects. When students are comfortable with the basic shapes, add the less common ones such as parallelograms and trapezoids. As students gain competence, add organic and symmetrical shapes.
- *Organic shape search.* Talk about organic shapes and find examples in the classroom and outdoors. Follow up by reading books that look at the relationship between shapes and natural objects (see Books to Share: Shape).
- *Cloud shapes.* Take students outside to study and sketch the shape of clouds. Use white chalk on blue paper. Identify the different kinds of clouds. Follow up by sharing a book about clouds (see Books to Share: Shape). Then write captions for the cloud sketches.

Art center activities

- *Symmetrical shape find.* Find examples of symmetrical shapes in magazines and use them to create a photomontage.
- *Creating symmetry.* Show students techniques for creating symmetrical shapes such as drawing one side of the object in chalk and then folding on the center line and rubbing. Another method is to fold a paper in half and make a cut starting and ending on the folded edge. Set up a center where students can explore making symmetrical shapes and using them in original artworks.

Cooperative group activities

- *Organic shape chart.* Have primary students work in cooperative groups to cut out pictures of nature objects with similar shapes, such as flowers or leaves. Assign each group a different item and ask them to glue them on a sheet of paper. Join the papers together to create a wall of organic shapes that students can refer to when doing their artwork.
- *Shape sort.* Ask teams or pairs of students to sort geometric and organic shapes by their symmetrical qualities. Ask, "Which geometric and organic shapes are symmetrical?"
- *Shape combine.* Give pairs or teams of students precut shapes, or at the upper levels a list of shapes, and challenge them to combine them to create something new. Follow up by looking at artworks, such as the work of Marc Chagall and André Derain, to see how

Books to Share

Shape

Brown, M. (1979). *Listen to a shape.* New York: Franklin Watts.
Burns, M. (1994). *The greedy triangle.* New York: Scholastic.
Carle, E. (1972). *The secret birthday message.* New York: Harper Trophy.
Carle, E. (1984). *The mixed-up chameleon.* New York: Crowell.
Carle, E. (1996). *Little cloud.* New York: Philomel.
Dillon, L. & D. (1994). *What am I? Looking through shapes at apples and grapes.* New York: Blue Sky.
Dodds, D. A. (1996). *The shape of things.* Cambridge, MA: Candlewick.
MacDonald, S. (1994). *Sea shapes.* Orlando, FL: Harcourt Brace.
Morgan, S. (1995). *Spirals.* New York: Thompson.
Morgan, S. (1995). *Triangles and pyramids.* New York: Thompson.
Shaw, S. (1947). *It looked like spilled milk.* New York: Harper & Row.

other artists have combined shapes to create meaningful images. (This can also be used as an art center.)

- *Shape deconstruction.* Give pairs or teams of students a complex shape and have them discover as many of the simple shapes within it as possible. (This can also be used as an art center.)
- *Mystery shape puzzle.* Pair up students and stand a file folder up between them. One student draws a picture made up of several shapes or arranges a group of precut paper shapes and then describes it to the other student, who tries to draw it based solely on the artist's description and without looking at the original. This is an excellent activity for developing listening and visual description skills. Repeat it often. To make it more challenging add or substitute other art elements.

Value

Value refers to the lightness and darkness of an area. Value is created by the way light is reflected off a surface. It is one way objects can be differentiated from one another. Value can show dimensionality through the creation of shadows and shading. Graduated values slowly change from dark to light tones.

Value is what allows us to see the form of the objects around us. Without contrast and shadow, such as on a moonless night, objects literally disappear before our eyes. In artwork this is even more true. Students need to develop their ability to see and apply the contrasts in value that separate shapes and lines from their surroundings and to perceive gradual changes from light to dark that can be used to create three-dimensionally on a flat surface.

Awareness activities

- *Value sort.* Have students classify objects by lightness and darkness. Give students actual objects, pictures cut out of magazines, or paint samples in a range of values and have them create a graduated sequence.
- *Out of focus.* Take slides of common objects and artworks that have a wide range of values including some strong darks and lights. Have students ready with paper and charcoal. Project a slide completely out of focus. Ask students to color in the dark areas. Improve the focus slightly and have students add the new values that appear. Continue in stages until the work is completely in focus and students have shown a range of values.
- *Pressure value.* In the primary grades or with novice students, work on having them vary the pressure they use in making lines with crayon, pencil, charcoal, and chalk. Point out differences in value that are created by pressing harder or lighter.
- *Show examples.* When looking at artworks, point out the ways artists use contrasting values to make the important parts of their work stand out, such as in the work of Rembrandt and Georges de la Tour. Look at pencil drawings such as M. C. Escher's, which show graduated values.
- *Value still life.* Shine a strong light on an arrangement of three-dimensional objects that have all been painted white. Move the light to different positions and study the shadows and highlights that are formed. Do the same with a student's face.

Art center activities

- *Contrasting values.* Have students explore what happens when different color markers and crayons are used on white, gray, and black paper. Which colors show up best? Which are hard to see? Measure and graph the distance at which it becomes hard to see a line of each basic color on the three background colors. Encourage students to consider the value of the background color and the distance the viewer will be in selecting the color of their drawing tool.
- *Mixing values.* Have students mix various values of gray using black and white paint on small squares of paper. Primary students can mix two or three grays, intermediate students can be expected to create a wide range of values. Have students work in groups to create a graduated sequence. These can then be made into a class chart or in the upper grades students can cut the squares into smaller pieces and use them to create a chart in their journals.
- *Create the illusion of texture.* Challenge upper-level students to make a flat piece of paper look bumpy or textured just by varying the values.

Books to Share

Value

Allsburg, C. (1995). *Jumangi.* Boston: Houghton Mifflin.
Lionni, L. (1961). *On my beach there are many pebbles.* New York: Mulberry Books.

Group activities

- *Create value studies.* When students can control the pressure they apply, challenge them to create a range of dark to light values. Have students work in groups to create a graduated value scale, each group using a different drawing medium such as different hardnesses of pencil, charcoal pencils (white and black), stick charcoal, crayon, and pastel.

Texture

Texture refers to the way something feels when it is touched. It can refer to the surface quality of the materials used or created in an artwork—the flow of the paint, the tooth of the paper, the wetness of the clay. Experiencing texture activates two sensory processes. In daily life we experience many textures through contact with our skin. In creating art, fingers feel the smoothness of the paper, the waxiness of crayon, the stickiness of glue. These tactile sensations are part of what makes creating art so pleasurable.

Completed artworks, on the other hand, are usually not experienced by touching but through eyes alone. Light and shadow fall differently on objects with shiny surfaces than they do on rough and bumpy ones. The perception of surface texture and its representation in artwork is intricately tied to skill in seeing and creating value.

Artists can include actual textures in their work by affixing real materials that have unique tactile qualities, such as when gluing cloth to a collage. They can simulate textures by creating the visual illusion of a tactile quality using a variety of art techniques including shading and pattern, or they can design an invented texture by applying materials to the surface such as by building up heavy layers of paint. Like line and color, texture can be used to differentiate areas of an artwork.

Awareness activities

- *Touch box.* Increase sensitivity to texture by eliminating visual input so the student can focus entirely on the tactile sensations. Make a touch box by cutting a hand-sized hole in a small box and covering the hole with a piece of cloth. Place unusual textured objects (avoid sharp edges) in the box and invite children to reach in and describe what they feel.

- *Texture envelope.* Glue a piece of flat, textured material, such as cloth, sandpaper, or corrugated paper, to a piece of stiff paper. Place the paper in a brown envelope. Give one to each student and ask them to close their eyes, reach inside, and feel the material. Then ask them to either describe the sensation orally, in writing, or by drawing a picture of something of which it reminds them.
- *Texture talk.* Fill a bag with small pieces of cloth with different textures. Have the class sit in a circle and pass the bag around. In turn each student should reach inside without looking and select a piece of cloth and then describe what the cloth feels like. Upper-level students can build on this experience by writing a description or story about a character who might wear clothing made from this kind of cloth.
- *Texture treasures.* Create a collection of textured materials for students to use in their artworks. Hold a texture hunt and collect natural materials from the vicinity of the school yard. Have students bring in otherwise discarded textured materials from home (see At a Glance 12.2). When sufficient items have been collected, place an assortment in the center of a community circle and have students in turn select one of the materials and give an example of how it could be used in an artwork. Create a chart of their ideas. Decide how the materials should be sorted and store in clear containers in the collage area.
- *Texture match-up.* Study the way artists have represented texture in their drawings and paintings. Compare objects in the works to actual objects such as a velvet dress to a piece of velvet or a still life of fruit to the actual fruit.

Art center activities

- *Create an illusion.* Challenge upper graders to make a flat piece of paper look textured just using values created with one color of drawing material.
- *Invent a texture.* Have students explore ways they can create unusual textured surfaces by gluing combinations of materials such as sawdust, sand, gravel, wrinkled paper, and so on to paper or cardboard or by adding similar materials to paint.
- *Rubbings.* Put out flat, textured objects such as the sides of plastic berry baskets or plastic texture screens (available from art suppliers). Have students explore different effects they can create by placing paper over the texture and rubbing it with the side of a crayon.
- *Paper texture.* Provide small pieces of paper in one color and have students explore different ways to change the texture of a piece of paper, such as wrinkling it, folding it, poking holes in it, and so on. Use the textured papers for cooperative group sorting, to make a class texture chart, and/or to create a group artwork.

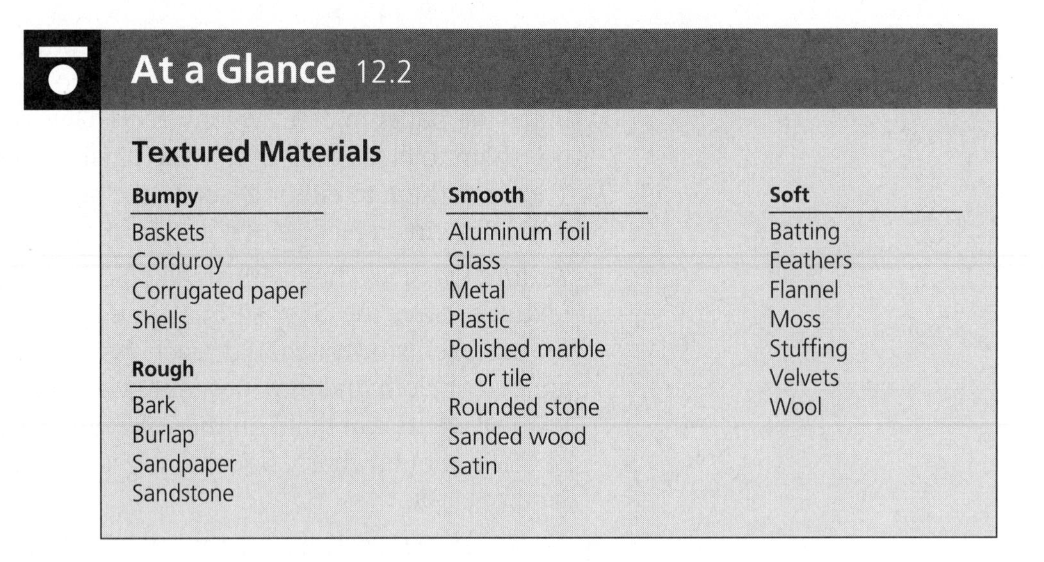

At a Glance 12.2

Textured Materials

Bumpy
- Baskets
- Corduroy
- Corrugated paper
- Shells

Rough
- Bark
- Burlap
- Sandpaper
- Sandstone

Smooth
- Aluminum foil
- Glass
- Metal
- Plastic
- Polished marble or tile
- Rounded stone
- Sanded wood
- Satin

Soft
- Batting
- Feathers
- Flannel
- Moss
- Stuffing
- Velvets
- Wool

Group activities

- *Texture windows.* Have students clip a picture from a magazine that contains an interesting texture. Cut the clipping to fit inside an envelope and then cut a small window in the envelope so only the texture shows. Have students exchange envelopes and try to describe and then guess what the texture is.
- *Texture samples.* Brainstorm and list as many different textures as possible. Distribute small squares of paper. Have students work in groups to create as many different textural effects as they can. Younger students can use pencil or crayon. Challenge upper graders with charcoal, pastel, or paint. Use the resulting squares to make a texture chart. Group similar textures together, and next to each group have students list possible objects that might be represented with that texture.
- *Texture mural.* Expand this activity by having each student select one of these textures and create a large sample of it. As a class plan how these could be put together into a class mural. They could be used as is to create a texture quilt, cut into geometric shapes and arranged into a nonobjective work, or cut into nature shapes to create a landscape or forest scene.

Color

Color attracts the eye. It awakens our interest and heightens our emotions. In the hands of the skilled artist color can establish a mood, create a focal point, or convey a message. The way surfaces reflect the different wavelength of lights determines the color we see. *Hue* is the term used for the common name of a color as determined by its place on the spectrum. Intensity describes how bright or dull the color is.

Books to Share

Texture

Baker, J. (1987). *Where the forest meets the sea.* New York: Greenwillow.
Baker, J. (1991). *Window.* New York: Puffin.
Day, N. R. (1995). *The lion's whiskers: An Ethiopian folktale.* New York: Scholastic.
Desimini, L. (1994). *My house.* New York: Henry Holt.
Ehlert, L. (1991). *Red leaf yellow leaf.* Orlando, FL: Harcourt Brace.
Ehlert, L. (1994). *Mole's hill.* Orlando, FL: Harcourt Brace.
Ehlert, L. (1995). *Snowballs.* Orlando, FL: Harcourt Brace.
Fox, M. (1989). *Shoes from grandpa.* New York: Orchard.
Heide, F. P. (1970). *Sound of sunshine, sound of rain.* New York: Parent's Magazine.
Hughes, L., & Beardon, R. (1995). *The block.* New York: Metropolitan Museum of Art.
O'Neil, M. (1969). *Fingers are always bringing me news.* New York: Doubleday.

Colors can also have value. This refers to how dark or light the color is. A neutral color reflects most or none of the light, creating the effect of white, black, and gray. Colors can be changed by mixing them together, placing them next to each other, and changing the color of the light source. A color wheel and intensity chart show the relationship of various colors.

Awareness activities. The following activities help children discover the nuances of color:

- *Developing color vocabulary.* At the primary level many children have a limited vocabulary for thinking about and describing colors. Provide students with paint chip samples and have them sort them into related groups. Discuss the different ways to classify colors. What words can describe these groups? Then have students try to match the chips to items in the room, outside, and in artworks. Which colors are used more than others? Which are best for natural objects?
- *Naming colors.* Share some of the paint color names. Do they relate to where the color is found or how it is used? For example, does the color soft rose resemble the flower color? Have students mix a color using paint, give it a name, and invent ways the color could be used.
- *Read about color.* Read books that describe or show the importance of color. Barbara Brenner's *Color Wizard* (1989) tells a story about a wizard who changes a gray world to a colorful one. *Color Sampler* by Kate Westray (1993) introduces primary students to color concepts.

- *Introduce the color wheel.* The color wheel is a tool for mixing and combining colors. Primary students should be introduced to a simple wheel or six-point star that shows the three primary colors and three secondary colors. Upper-level students should be familiar with color wheels that show the tertiaries as well. Pass out the color wheels. Have students relate what they know to the wheel. Primary students can use the rainbow as a guide. Read a book about color mixing such as *Mouse Paint* by Ellen Stoll Walsh (1989).
- *Teach the spectrum.* Older students can tie in with learning the spectrum in science. Introduce them to color concepts using books such as Ruth Heller's *Color Color Color* (1995) or *Colors: A First Discovery Book* (1989), which use color acetates to show how colors mix. Ask, "How are the spectrum and a color wheel alike?" Explore the difference between mixing pigments and mixing color light using color paddles (available from art suppliers) or used theater gels.
- *Learn the color groupings.* Teach students the names of the primary, secondary, and, for third grade and up, tertiary colors. Use chants, songs, and games to help students remember the order of colors. For example, dress up as a character named Mr. or Mrs. ROY G. BIV (red, orange, yellow, green, blue, indigo, and violet) who wears rainbow-colored clothing.
- *Provide color wheels.* Provide students with small color wheels to use when mixing colors. Upper graders can make their own color wheels. If possible, let them keep the wheels in their journals or process folios. If they must be shared, laminate them and put them in a container at the paint center.
- *Color and feelings.* Psychological investigations of color have shown that color can affect people's feelings and actions. It is a powerful tool for conveying a message or feeling. At the primary level students should learn about the power of color. Have students brainstorm feeling words that different colors invoke in them. Be open to all kinds of responses. Read poems about color such as Mary O'Neil's *Hailstones and Halibut Bones* (1961). Have students write individual and class poems about color.
- *Color and meaning.* When students share their artwork, ask them why they chose the colors they did. Do any colors have special meaning for them?
- *Warm, cool, and moody.* As students become more skilled in controlling color choices and mixing paint colors, have them analyze their color choices in more depth. Do all bright colors make people feel happy? Do dark, drab colors make everyone feel sad? Which colors are considered warm, which cool? Why? How does the color of a room affect one's emotional state? Which color combinations are pleasing? Which colors clash? What is the role of current fashion

in people's view of pleasing color combinations? How does the fashion industry control what colors are popular?

- *Color in artworks.* Have students look at the colors in artworks and share their responses. Study artworks such as Henri Matisse's *Dinner Table (Harmony in Red).* How would changing the colors in the work affect the mood of the picture? How has color use changed in artworks? What has been the effect on the art and advertising of today now that fluorescent and neon color art supplies are available?

Art center activities

- *Painting color wheels.* Explain that the purpose of the wheel is to help in mixing colors and in selecting related colors for color schemes. Students should select two primary colors. Then they should mix these colors in different quantities and use them to completely cover four-inch paper squares. Share the completed painted squares and have students find the colors on the color wheel. (See At a Glance 12.3.) Use the completed squares in any of the following ways:
  1. Group completed squares into a large, vibrant color wheel.
  2. Have students brainstorm possible uses for the colors they mixed, such as using yellow greens to paint leaves on a spring tree.
  3. Create a large wall chart for future reference.
  4. Create a class mural using the squares, combining related color squares into groupings such as greens used in grass and trees, blues used in the sky, and so on.
  5. In cooperative groups try to match the painted color samples to colors in artworks.
  6. Invent names for the colors that are mixed.
- *Complements and intensity.* Have students look at color wheels, select a color, and then name the color opposite it. Introduce the term *complements* for this pairing. Ask students to select one primary and its complement. Challenge them to make as many mixtures as possible using these two colors. (*Note:* Students will need to mix a secondary color for the complement before beginning.) Paint each mixture on a three-inch square. Have students compare completed squares. What happened to the colors? Did different pairings produce the same color mixtures? Order squares from bright to dull. Use the samples to create an intensity chart or in activities as listed previously for the color wheel. Pursue the study of intensity further with follow-up discussions such as these:
  1. Name and identify uses for bright and dull colors.
  2. Look at the environment and artwork and identify bright and dull colors.
  3. Create artworks that use only bright or only dull colors.

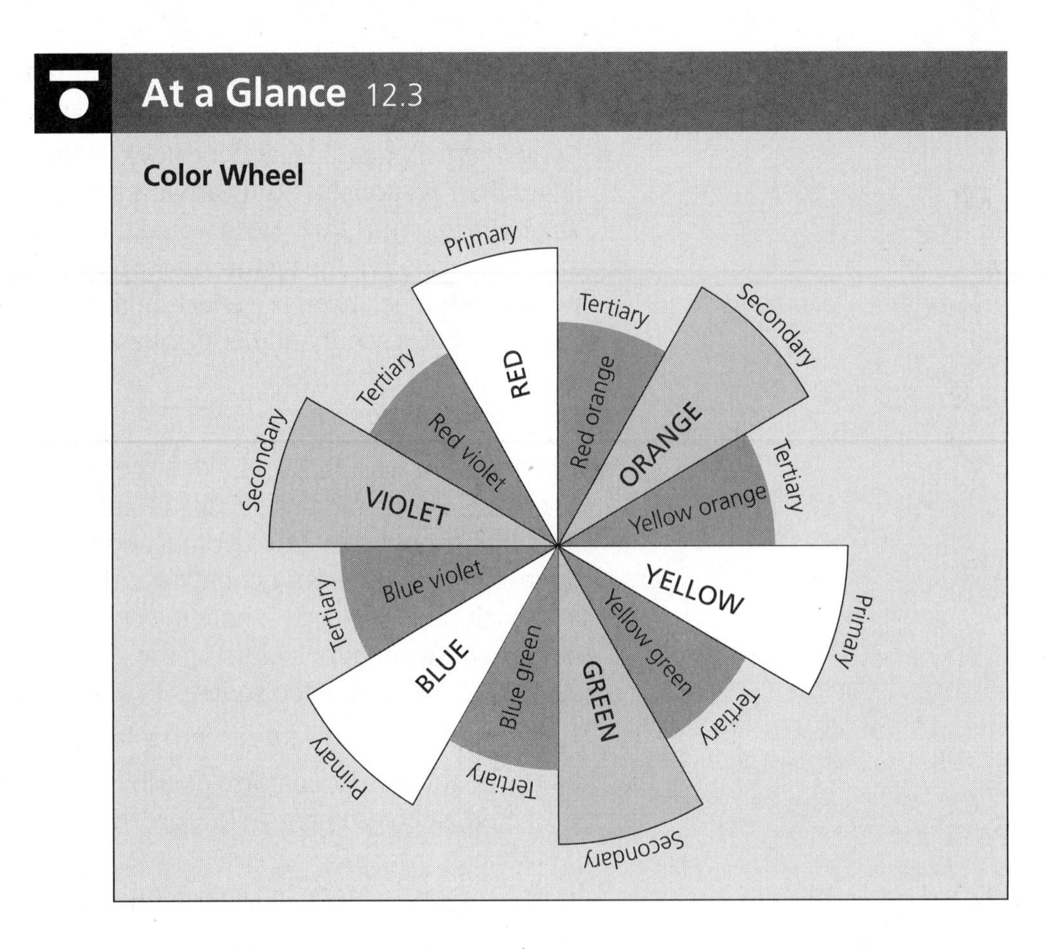

4. Have advanced students try mixing together complements and tertiaries.
5. Try to mix colors to match those found in nature and artworks.
6. Identify colors that could be called neutral. What is their relationship to the color wheel?

- *Color and light.* Colors change under different colored lights. To introduce this idea to students create colored light boxes in which they can view their artworks. Paint the inside of large boxes black and stand on their sides. Insert a different colored light bulb through a hole at the top of each box. Begin by using strongly colored bulbs such as red, yellow, and black light. Have students place one of their artworks in each box in turn. How does the color of the light change the appearance of the work? When students understand the concept, compare "white" light bulbs of different wattage and types such as soft, normal, high intensity, and full spectrum. Ask, "Should artists think about the lighting in which their work will be seen? Should artworks created before the invention of electricity be lit differently than those created after it? How should museums be lit?"
- *Color shadows.* Provide students with empty self-stick slide frames, cellophane, or theater gel scraps and two pieces of clear acetate cut

At a Glance 12.4

A Vocabulary of Color

Hue: The common name of the color

Primary Colors: These are the colors that cannot be mixed.

- Yellow
- Blue
- Red

Secondary Colors: These colors are made by mixing the three primary colors.

- Red + Yellow = Orange
- Blue + Yellow = Green
- Blue + Red = Violet

Tertiary Colors: These colors are made by mixing the secondary colors with the adjacent primary colors.

- Orange + Yellow = Yellow Orange
- Orange + Red = Red Orange
- Green + Blue = Blue Green
- Green + Yellow = Yellow Green
- Violet + Blue = Blue Violet
- Violet + Red = Red Violet

Tint: This is created by adding white to a color

Shade: This is created by adding black to a color

to fit the slide frames. Have them create a design from the transparent materials and sandwich it between the two acetate pieces, and then insert it in the slide frame. Project the slides as large as possible on a white background. Have students stand or move between the projector and the screen and study the color of the shadows created. This activity ties in beautifully with music, movement, and dance activities. Have students select music to accompany their slides and put on a color shadow show.

Group activities

- *Scavenger color hunt.* Introduce students to the variations within a color grouping by having a color scavenger hunt. Have them work in groups or pairs to collect as many art materials as possible that are all one "color." Assign a different color to each group and make sure there are plenty of different color papers, markers, pastels, and so on available about the room. When the groups are finished, ask them to compare the colors of the items they collected. Are they exactly the same or are there variations? Ask, "What is a true red or green? How do we know when we see it? What affects our perception of color?" Encourage students to create artworks using colors from just one color family.

Books to Share

Color

Brenner, B. (1989). *Color wizard.* Orlando, FL: Harcourt Brace.
Cole, A. (1993). *Color.* New York: Dorling Kingsley.
Ehlert, L. (1989). *Color zoo.* New York: HarperCollins.
Heller, R. (1995). *Color, color, color.* New York: Putnam.
Jonas, A. (1989). *Color dance.* New York: Greenwillow.
Lionni, I. (1959). *Little blue. Little yellow.* New York: Mulberry Books.
Marcos, S. (1999). *The story of colors/La historia de los colores.* El Paso, TX: Cinco Pintos.
O'Neil, M. (1989). *Hailstones and halibut bones.* New York: Doubleday.
Shalom, V. (1995).*The color of things.* New York: Rizzoli International.
Walsh, E. S. (1989). *Mouse paint.* New York: Trumpet.
Westray, K. (1993). *Color sampler.* Boston: Houghton Mifflin.
Yamaka, S. (1995). *Gift of Drescoll Lepscomb.* New York: Simon & Schuster.

- *Effect of background.* Color perception is also affected by the color of the surroundings. As they work in cooperative groups, challenge students to make two colors look like three or three colors look like two just by changing the background color. Provide a wide range of colored paper cut in small squares and a similar color range of larger paper for the background. Ask questions such as, "Which combinations of colors make the small square look lighter or darker? Is there any combination that makes the color look more yellow or blue or red? Does the location of the squares on the background paper make a difference?" Explore the role that background color plays in different artworks. What would happen if the background was changed? What should artists think about when selecting colors for their work? See At a Glance 12.4 for a vocabulary of color.

Space

Space is the perception of distance or openness on a surface or in the environment. It is also the area an object or artwork occupies. Because space is not seen directly but exists by assumption, there is a strong visual tendency to focus on the color, shape, and texture of an object rather than the space it takes up. Unlike the other elements, space is not manipulated directly but by moving or changing other elements. A heightened awareness of the space that an object occupies and that surrounds it is what differentiates an artist's vision from that of others.

Two-dimensional space occupies the height and depth of a flat surface. The picture plane is the surface space on which two-dimensional works are created. Three-dimensional space has height, width, and depth and can be real as in sculpture or illusionary as in a realistic painting of a still life. Size, placement, shading, and overlap can create the appearance of three-dimensional space on a flat surface. Positive space is space occupied by an object or shape. Negative space is empty area in or surrounding an artwork.

Awareness activities

- *Point of view.* Because objects occupy space, they can change shape when viewed in different ways. For young children this is often confusing. A cylinder looks rectangular from the side and circular from the top. In the primary grades introduce the concept of point of view. Hold up a real object and have students describe what it might look like from the top or the back. Then examine the object from that perspective. When students have been successful with real objects, introduce photographs and drawings of objects and scenes that show different views. Have students identify the viewpoint. A picture from the top might be called a bird's eye view, one from below a worm's eye view.
- *Taking a different view.* Encourage students to consider their viewpoint when creating a work of art. When they create sketches, ask them to explore their subject from different views before settling on one perspective. Look at artworks with unusual points of view such as Georgia O'Keeffe's close-ups of flowers.
- *Overlap.* Understanding that an object continues to occupy space even when it is hidden behind another is a concept that develops in the primary years. To expand students' perception of space have them start by moving three-dimensional objects so parts are partially hidden. Cut out shapes and explore overlapping them in different ways. Study the new shapes and different effects that are created. Find examples of overlap in artworks. Ask students to imagine or sketch what the rest of a partially hidden shape or object in the work might look like.
- *Seeing spaces.* Be alert to opportunities to help children begin to see the difference between positive or occupied space and negative or empty space. For example, when children are cutting out shapes from paper, make sure to point out the holes that are created. Encourage children to look through the holes and place the holes over different colored papers. Suggest that they try to fit their cut-out shapes back into the holes and explore using the holes in their artwork. Ask them to describe what is the same and different between the hole and the cut-out shape. Also point out negative spaces in three-dimensional objects and artworks, such as the opening in a teacup handle or the negative spaces in the sculptures of Henry Moore. Read books that utilize cut-out openings, such as

Lois Ehlert's *Color Zoo*, Ed Emberly's *Go Away Big Green Monster* (see the following Books to Share), and Leo and Diane Dillon's *What Am I?: Looking through Shapes at Apples and Grapes* (see Books to Share earlier in this chapter).

- *Isolate negative areas.* In sketches have students outline or darken in negative areas so they can see their importance to the work.
- *Draw negative shapes.* When they are drawing from life, have students air draw negative shapes before drawing on the paper or have them try drawing only the negative shapes. Objects such as chairs and trees are particularly suited to this exercise.
- *Cut out the background.* Require students to make one of the sketches for an artwork by using only cutouts of its negative shapes.

Art center activities

- *Sketch three-dimensional pieces.* Have students sketch the negative shapes in their own three-dimensional works and in the work of other artists.

Group activities

- *Using overlap to create the illusion of space.* Students can use overlapping shapes to create the illusion of space and distance in their work. Working in teams, explore how size and placement can be used to show spatial relationships. Ask, "How can overlap show an object in front or behind another? How can the objects be shown farther apart or closer together?" Suggest that before drawing or painting students play with cut paper shapes to find the best position for overlapping shapes in order to create the feeling of depth in their work. These exercises can be tied into perspective studies.
- *Mobiles and stabiles.* Study the use of space in Alexander Calder's mobiles and stabiles. Work in cooperative teams to create mobiles and spatial environments using cardboard pieces and paper folding techniques.

Form (Mass and Volume)

Used in the context of the elements of art, form refers to objects that occupy three dimensions either in reality or in an illusion. Because our eyes are separated, each eye sees a slightly different view of an object. The brain overlaps these two images to create a stereoscopic or three-dimensional view of the world that allows us to perceive depth. It is this perceived dimensionality or form that is manipulated by artists in creating artworks. Geometric forms include spheres, cubes, rectangular and triangular solids, pyramids, cones, and cylinders. Organic forms are those found in nature: the spiraled shell, the ovaloid egg, the bell-shaped flower.

Books to Share

Space

Ehlert, L. (1989). *Color zoo.* New York: HarperCollins.
Emberly, E. (1992). *Go away big green monster.* New York: Little, Brown.
Jonas, A. (1984). *Holes and peeks.* New York: Greenwillow.

Awareness activities

- *Seeing form.* Introduce children to the names of the basic geometric forms as they play with blocks and manipulate everyday objects. Although it is easier for teachers to say *box* and *tube,* children will not learn terms like *cube* and *cylinder* unless teachers use them regularly. As with shape use games and songs to help younger children visualize forms.
- *Form building.* Have children sit in a circle. In the center place a variety of blocks. In turn ask each to choose a block, name the form, and then add it to a cooperative block structure.
- *Name it.* Select one child to call out the name of a geometric form. As quickly as possible have pairs or teams list as many objects having that form as possible. Check and consolidate lists and create a form chart.
- *Find a form.* Take a walk in the neighborhood and point out examples of forms used in buildings.

Art center activities. (*Note:* Three-dimensional activities are an important part of developing artistic thinking. Too often art programs emphasize two-dimensional activities over those that involve manipulating forms in space. It is important to remember that knowledge about how actual forms interrelate in space is essential for representing form in two dimensions. There should be at least one three-dimensional art center, such as the ones that follow, available regularly at all levels.)

- *Blocks.* Building with blocks is not just for preschool and kindergarten. It is an important activity for all students. Physically manipulating solid forms helps students develop their spatial abilities. At the primary level provide large wooden blocks in the basic geometric shapes. At third and fourth grade introduce smaller wooden geometric blocks and interlocking centimeter cubes. At the fifth grade level and up provide architectural wooden blocks. These are available in sets that include Egyptian, Greek, Roman, Middle Eastern, and medieval architectural forms. There are also wooden block puzzles for building arches, pyramids, and more. At upper levels set out blocks in a center or game area that includes challenging questions

Books to Share

Form

Baker, A. (1994). *Brown rabbit's shape book.* New York: Larousse Kingfisher.
Felix, M. (1993). *House.* Mankato, MN: Creative Editions.
Stevenson, R. (1992) *Block city.* New York: Puffin.

and suggestions, such as, "Can you build a bridge to support a weight of at least 500 grams?" Encourage students to "save" structures by sketching them from varying viewpoints. Point out how shadows can be used to show solidity and dimension.

- *Clay.* Equally important is to provide easy access to clay. Students need to be able to actually shape the forms and create new ones in developing their understanding. As explained in Chapter 8, non-hardening modeling clay stored in plastic self-seal bags or covered plastic containers should be available at all times in a modeling center. For variety offer other modeling compounds such as play dough at the primary, salt-flour clay, and the new super doughs periodically. Again encourage students to save their work by sketching the forms that they create.

Group activities

- *Make paper forms.* Have students invent a three-dimensional paper form based on paper folding techniques. Look at the forms from different viewpoints and count the sides. Have students combine forms to create a cooperative group sculpture.
- *Combining forms.* Have teams work together to construct sculptures or buildings using small uniform forms such as Legos, stones, pop-sticks, Styrofoam pieces joined with toothpicks, and so on.

Why . . . ?

WHY TEACH DESIGN?

Design plays an important role in our lives. We buy a product because of the enticing design of its wrapper. We prefer to sit on a well-designed chair that fits the form of our body rather than a poorly designed one that cramps and tires us. We get angry when a tool does not function in the way it was designed to work. How things are designed entertains us, comforts us, and challenges us every day. An understanding of design can help students function better in many ways.

Students who have an understanding of design can do the following:

Perceive more deeply. The study of design allows students' natural perception of the shapes, colors, values, textures, and forms found in

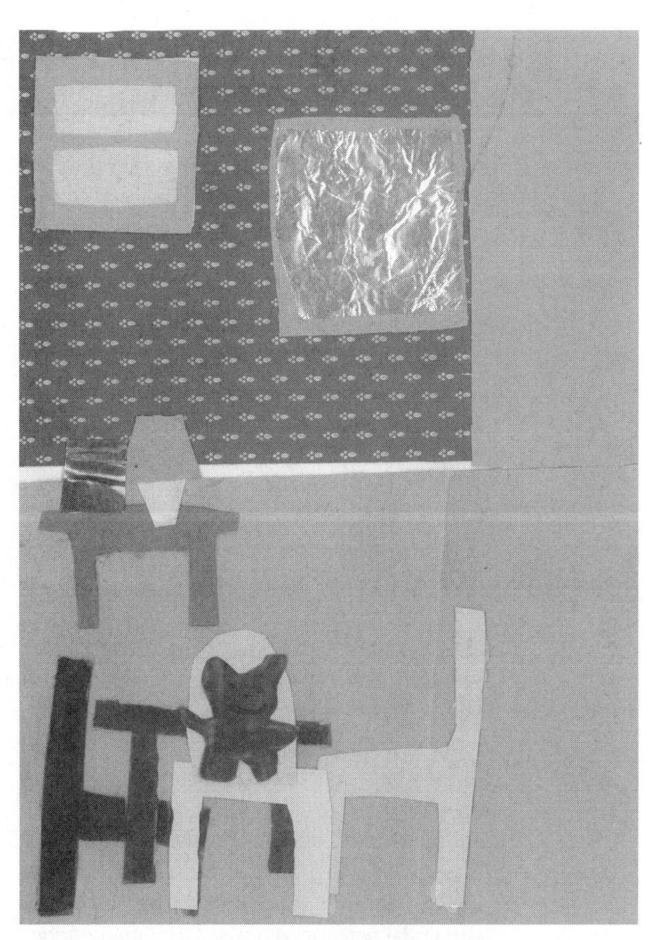

"My Teddy Bear Tea Party."
Collage—Amy, grade 2.

Thinking about Children's Art

After observing shapes in Van Gogh's painting, *Bedroom at Arles*, this second grader has created an illusion of depth by overlapping shapes and placing them at different heights in creating a picture of her room. How does thinking about the arrangement and meaning of shapes on a flat surface help children communicate ideas better?

nature and used in artworks to become more finely tuned and focused on the differences, similarities, and relationships among them.

Think more deeply about relationships. Finding patterns and understanding the way that the parts of a particular thing are put together to make the whole work is the basis of how the brain learns. Studying design builds on the natural direction of learning and provides students with a better knowledge of visual and spatial relationships that form the framework for the way we interact with our environment. It also provides an experiential grounding in geometrical concepts.

Make better artistic decisions. Separating out particular design principles and seeing how other artists have used them helps young artists think about the arrangements in their own work. They learn that it

Teacher Tip

Differences in Perceptual Awareness

Some students have difficulties perceiving relationships among shapes, colors, textures, and forms. Color-blind students, for example, will have difficulty with many of the color exercises discussed in this chapter. Students who are blind or have limited vision may be far more perceptive of textures. Many young children can see the whole of a real object but cannot break it into constituent shapes or parts.

Other students may have trouble differentiating between similar shapes, seeing negative spaces, or separating the figure from the ground. Often, but not always, students with problems differentiating shapes may have trouble in reading or math. This may be a clue that the child has a learning disability. Consult with the school nurse and special education staff when such difficulties are noted during art activities.

When a student is having difficulty with design activities, do not instantly assume that the student just needs to work harder or needs more repetition of the directions. Instead, find the students' area of strength. Make sure that design activities allow students to use these strengths. Color-blind students, for example, should work with the colors they can see. A student who finds it easier to arrange real objects on a paper can do design activities using pictures clipped from a magazine rather than cut paper shapes.

The key to successfully meeting the needs of diverse learners is to avoid closed design exercises that limit choices, such as a lesson in which everyone must mix red and green to explore making different browns. Such a lesson would be useless for a student with red-green color blindness. Similarly requiring everyone to create the effect of distance using three shapes in three sizes may prove difficult for a child with visual perceptual difficulties. Open-ended lesson designs allow learners with diverse needs to be successful while also allowing creativity to flourish.

is not the art media that controls what happens in an artwork but the decisions of the artist.

Discuss art more fluently. Learning to understand and use the principles of design empowers students as artists and audience because students derive a common vocabulary that they can use in thinking about, responding to, and talking about art.

Express their ideas more clearly. By manipulating the art elements in their own work and analyzing the varied effects they can create, young artists learn how to use these principles to convey meaning to others.

Become wiser consumers. Learning how to evaluate design will help students make better decisions about the objects with which they choose to surround themselves in their lives.

DESIGN AND FUNCTION

Guiding Ideas

There are many different ways to look at design and to classify the basic principles. Artists, architects, and designers all look at design in slightly different but basically similar ways. The artist attempts to organize the art elements into a composition that best expresses the intended message. The architect must incorporate the existing environmental conditions, relevant governmental restrictions, and human needs and desires into the design of a building. Designers must decide how to interrelate the visual, spatial, and tactile effect they wish to create with the function of the article they are designing. For each, design is the search for the right balance among the various parts to meet their particular needs and goals (see At a Glance 12.5).

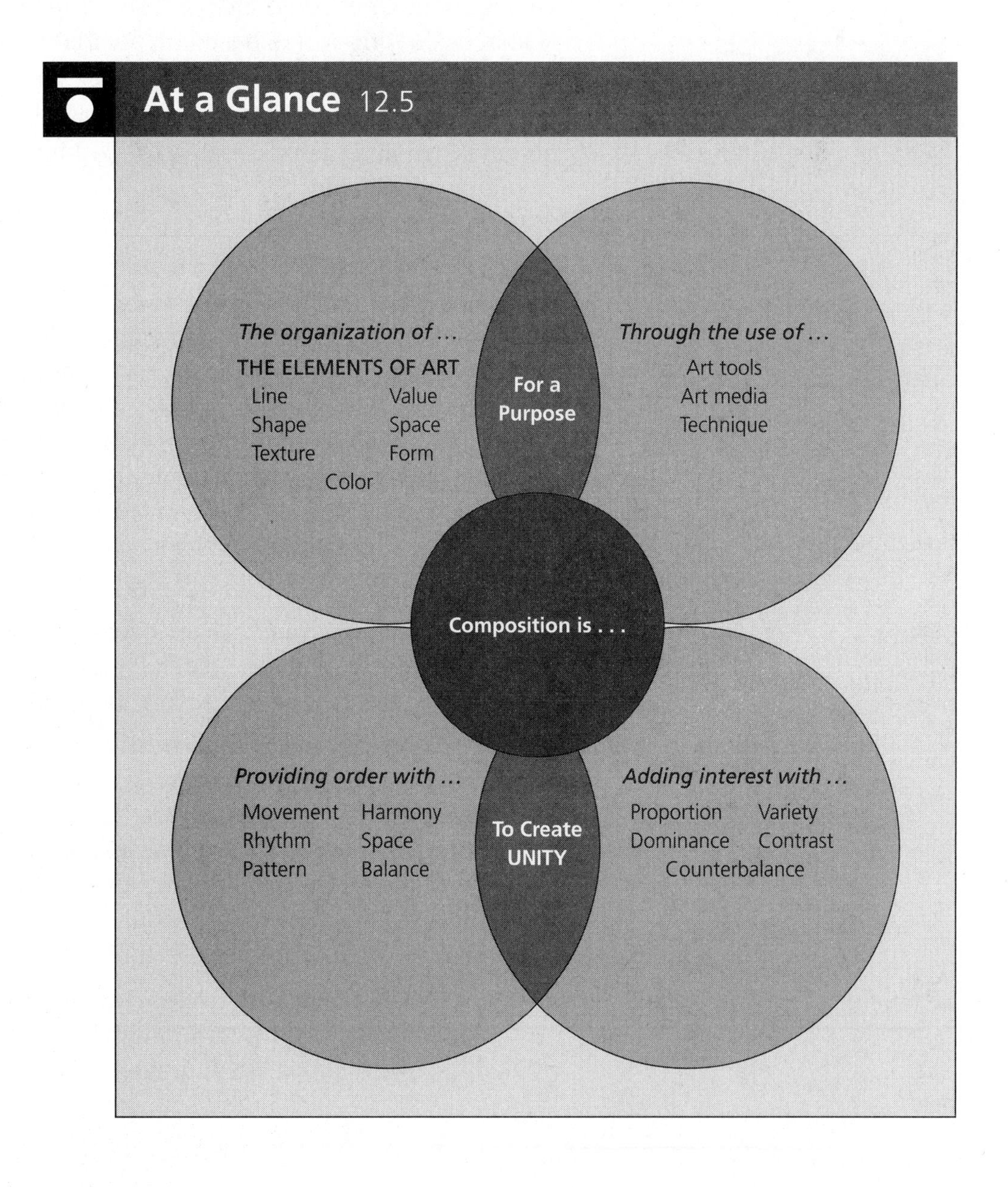

It is also important to remember that the design principles described here provide directions, not prescriptions. There is no one correct way to use them in an artwork. An artwork with a great deal of variety, for example, is not necessarily better than one with very little. Rather, how design concepts are used depends on purpose and choice. Knowing how to apply design concepts will help students take control of their own work and the artistic decisions they make.

There should be three objectives in teaching about design:

- Students must become visually aware and learn to identify the art elements and design principles used in their own art and that of others, as well as in the objects they use every day and in the environment that surrounds them.
- Students should have opportunities to assess their own beliefs and values about what constitutes a well-designed work and to develop skill in evaluating works based on a variety of design concepts.
- Students should participate in activities that allow them to create art for a wide variety of purposes while applying what they know about design and then assessing the result.

Design Awareness

Developing sensitivity to design means learning to appreciate the influence of one element on another. Much of how we see objects in our environment is the result of how our mind interprets visual input. Donald Hoffman (1998) hypothesizes that there are innate visual processing rules that allow us to construct and therefore see a three-dimensional world. These visual constructs cause us to perceive the relationships among visual elements in distinct ways. June King McFee and Rogena Degge (1977) have summarized the visual constructs that seem to influence how we perceive relationships among elements as follows:

1. *We look for variety in order.* When everything is the same, we become bored. Our eyes constantly search for that small difference—the spot on the white piece of paper, the one broken tile in the floor. An artwork can be made more interesting by adding something different.
2. *We see order when things are similar and variety when they differ.* A brick wall looks very regular and organized; a stone wall built from irregular stone of different sizes and shapes appears irregular. Artwork that contains similar shapes arranged in very orderly ways will appear calmer and more restful than a work that has many dissimilar colors, shapes, and textures.
3. *Every element in an artwork influences the others.* Things look bigger or smaller depending on what is next to them. A color will look darker or brighter depending on the colors that surround it.

4. *Things that are closer together look more alike than things that are farther apart.* When objects are placed close together they seem more related to each other than to objects that are farther away. The eye creates a pattern and sees the group as a kind of whole.
5. *Our eye completes what is only suggested.* We see dots placed in a row as a line. A face can be indicated with a circle, two dots, and a line. An artist can create order and movement by placing elements in a row.
6. *We see order in dissimilar things when the spacing is equal and variety when the spacing is unequal.* When we need to make different elements in a work more orderly, we can move them so the spacing is more equal between them.
7. *When confronted with several visual constructs, we will perceive some as more dominant than others.* A work of art may be quite complex with many relationships. The eye will be drawn to those with the most variety or that take up the most space or are the most perplexing. Complex works require careful study by the viewer.
8. *Strong contrasts, extended distances between similar things, and acute angles create strong kinesthetic feelings.* Our eyes are drawn to bright colors and strong contrasts. When these are located in different places in a work, our eye moves from one to the other. Similarly when objects are widely spaced, our vision jumps back and forth, creating a sensory dynamic. Because we live with gravity, we expect objects to behave in certain ways. Leaning poles fall. Objects that are smaller and thinner at the bottom tip over. Acute angles and diagonals therefore create visual tension in a work.

The Principles of Design

These visual constructs form the basis for the principles of design:

Order and variety. Understanding order and variety begins with being able to differentiate between them. Order refers to how the art elements in a work are organized. Artists can determine how much order the eye perceives by the way they arrange chosen art elements. They can build on the idea that when looking at an artwork the eye searches for and tries to create order. The eye will group together things that are similar in color or shape. A highly ordered composition, for example, contains elements with many similarities arranged in a strongly organized way. The artist creates order by using similar colors, putting similar shapes and textures close to each other, balancing elements in the work, and using repetition and pattern.

Variety, on the other hand, refers to the differences found in a work. Things that are very different from each other make the eye

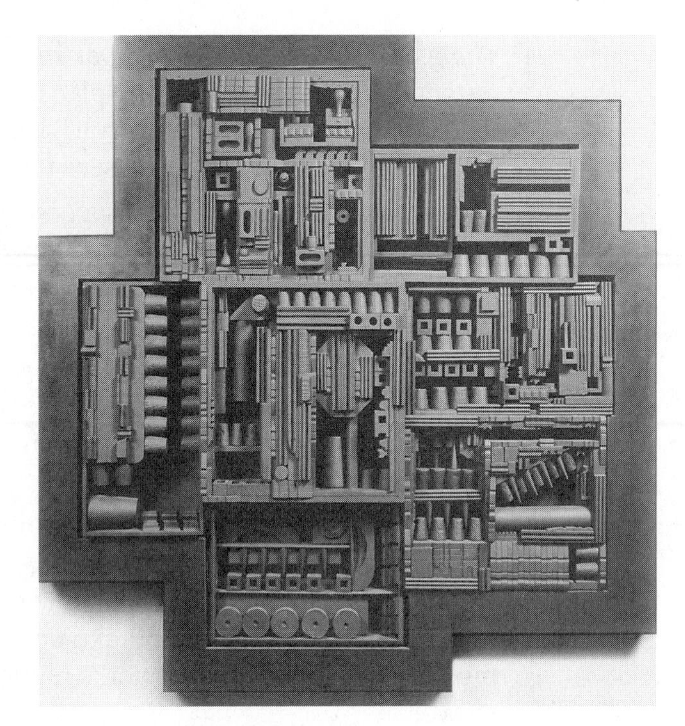

Louise Nevelson, Black Zag A, 1968.
Montclair Art Museum. Purchase made possible through a special gift from Florence F. Schuman, 1987.

From the Museum

There is both order and variety in this work by Louise Nevelson, which features wooden objects painted black and arranged in various groupings and patterns. It is a good example of a work that can be used effectively to increase the design awareness of students at all levels. What are some questions that you could ask that would help students discover the relationships among the elements in this work? What mathematical concepts can be found in the work?

move from one to the other. A work that is all one color with no other differentiation is no different than a plain piece of paper. It is dull to view. A work that is full of variety with many colors, shapes, textures, and lines, on the other hand, may be exciting to look at. Excessive variety, however, can make a work highly complex and difficult to understand (see At a Glance 12.6). If there are no places for the eye to rest, the viewer may quickly tire of looking at it or may even feel dizzy.

The balance between variety and order found in an artwork will depend on the artist's purpose. For example, some artists, such as Bridget Riley, who uses optical illusions in her work, want viewers to feel disoriented when looking at their work. The highly ordered, symmetrical landscapes of an artist such as pre-Expressionist Fernand Hodler, on the other hand, create a deep sense of calm.

Introducing order and variety. At the primary level develop a sense of order and variety by providing many opportunities for students to explore similarities and differences in artworks and visual images.

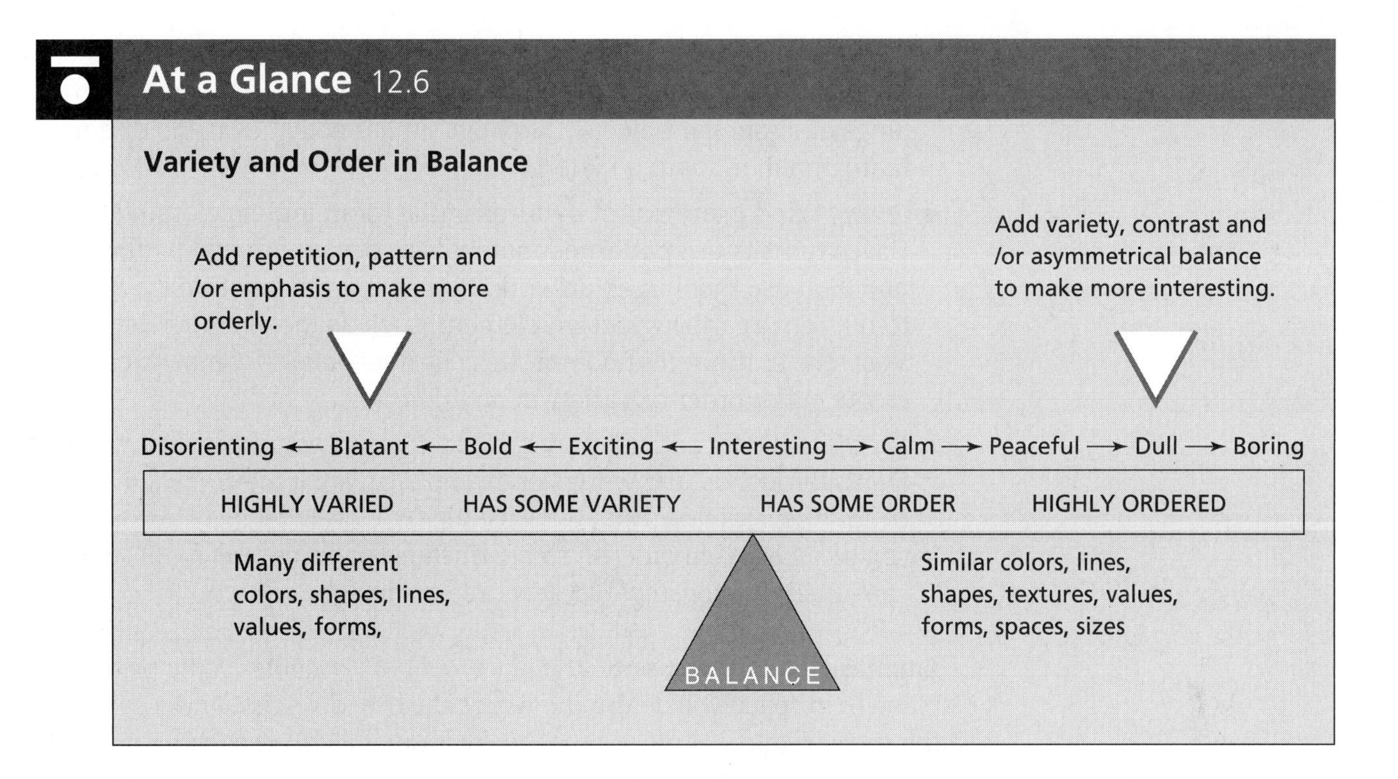

- *Develop a vocabulary.* At every opportunity have students describe similarities and differences in size, shape, color, and position. Give students shapes to sort and colors and textures to compare and order in different ways.
- *During sharing.* Have students, when sharing, identify the different shapes, colors, textures, and lines that they have used in their art. Ask them to point out ones that are similar or that are arranged in a regular pattern.
- *When looking at artworks.* Compare the effect created in artworks that have a great deal of variety and those that have only a little. For example, an Amish nine-patch quilt could be compared to Faith Ringgold's *Tar Beach.* Even though both artworks are quilts made from fabric, how is order and variety reflected in the design?

Applying order and variety. When students can easily describe differences in art elements and recognize order and variety in artworks, emphasize application of these principles.

- *Sorting for effect.* Introduce upper-level students to the role of variety by having them sort small mini-prints by the amount of variety they find and then discussing the visual effect.
- *Sketching for effect.* When students are sketching ideas for artworks, remind them to consider the effect they wish to create and the amount of order or variety they need to use.

- *Creating order.* Working in teams, have students use color, shape, texture, and/or line to create a sense of order from magazine clippings of dissimilar objects. Carry out similar activities using dissimilar textured or colored materials.
- *Pattern.* Find examples of patterns in the room and on clothing. Have students use patterned materials or design original patterns and then use them in an artwork. Compare works that utilize pattern as an organizing design element, such as the work of Victor Vasarely, to those that do not. Discuss how pattern can be used to create either order or variety in an artwork.
- *Repetition.* Order and unity are created in an artwork by repeating elements throughout the work. For example, an artist may repeat a shape or color several times in a work. Groups of closely related elements can be repeated in order to create rhythms, patterns, and motifs that can visually tie together different areas or images in a work.

Emphasis and movement. The placement of elements on the picture plane or in space will determine where the eye looks first and also what the eye will ignore. Emphasis is the creation of focal areas or points that attract the eye of the viewer to a location in the work and hold it there. In an artwork such areas can be given dominance through the use of color, contrast, and line direction. The placement of the focal point determines how the viewer will be drawn into viewing a work and establishes communication.

Movement, on the other hand, is the way the eye travels over the surface of the artwork. The direction and boundary of two-dimensional work surfaces create different eye movements. Art elements placed inside a rectangle move differently than those placed within a triangle or circle. Three-dimensional artwork must be viewed by moving not only the eye but the body as well, creating an exploratory "dance."

Emphasis and movement work in tandem. Interesting artworks attract the eye to the focal point and then draw it outward to other parts of the work. Use the following activities to help young artists discover the role of emphasis in artworks:

- *Identifying foreground and background.* The ability to see what is in front and what is behind develops before children can apply the concept to their own work. Introduce the terms *foreground* and *background* starting at the first grade level when discussing artworks. Provide plenty of opportunities for children to describe what they see in photographs and in a variety of different types of artwork. Ask, "What is happening in the foreground of this picture? What colors, shapes, or objects do you see in the background?"
- *Background sort.* Give partners or groups mini-prints of artworks and have them sort them by similarities in the background.

- *Focal point.* The focal point or area is that part of a work to which the eye is drawn first. It may be the most meaningful part of a picture or the most colorful or the most disturbing. Novice artists are often so involved in creating the parts of their work that the main focus of the work is lost. Help students by creating a chart listing ways to draw attention to the main interest of a work, such as using more detail, applying more intense colors, creating a strong contrast in value, or framing the focal point. At sharing and conferencing refer to the chart when discussing a student's work. Challenge more experienced students to draw several sketches for a planned artwork, using the same concepts and elements but changing the location of the focal point in each one.
- *Discovering the main focus.* Select artworks that have a main focus that clearly stands out from the background, such as Rembrandt's *Portrait of the Artist's Son*, Renoir's *Girl with Watering Can*, Diego Rivera's *Girl with Lilies*, and John Audubon's *American Flamingo*. Have students identify the main focus of the work. Compare these works to those that have an overall pattern, such as Mark Tobey's *White Journey*, Alma Thomas' *Red Rose Cantata*, or Andy Warhol's *Soup Cans*.
- *Movement.* Cut out several similarly sized squares, circles, and triangles from different colors of paper. Lightly tape them close together in the center of a large sheet of paper. Slowly move one of the shapes away from the group. Ask students to raise their hands when it no longer looks like part of the group. Tape it down in the new position. Ask, "Why does it no longer go with the others?" Draw a black dot on each shape. Ask, "Do they look like a group again? How does it make your eyes move? How many groups are there now?" Add another shape next to the one standing alone. "How many groups are there now? How do your eyes move?"
- *Contrast.* Cut out several squares in the same size but in different colors, textures, and patterns. Hang up several large sheets of paper in a similar range of surface finishes. Hold up the squares and have students suggest which one would stand out most from each background. Discuss the role of contrast in creating emphasis. Brainstorm ways to create contrast, then form cooperative groups and have each use a different method to make a shape stand out from the background. Compare their efforts to the way contrast is used in works of art.
- *Moving around.* On a large sheet of kraft paper display a large sculpture, such as a group box sculpture or another three-dimensional object, in the center of the room. Have students model looking at the sculpture from all sides. Have one student move around the piece,

call out, "Freeze!" and have another student trace around the feet, creating a record of the student's sculptural dance. Repeat until all students have had a turn.

Unity. Unity is organizing the individual art elements that make up a work of art so that it is seen as a whole. Unity refers to the interrelationship among all the elements of an artwork. It is what results when all parts are balanced with the purpose of the piece. When all parts work in harmony, unity results. There is a balance and rhythm to the work that carries the eye into it and holds the attention of the viewer. There is enough variety to maintain interest, but the artist restrains and organizes this variety to avoid confusion and disunity.

Planning a Unified Composition

Planning a composition is an integral part of the artistic process. It is essential to the creation of any artwork. Most novice artists, however, tend to focus on developing parts of a work in sequence rather than seeing the whole throughout the creation. They may begin by drawing the main interest and then add the background components. In sculpture they work on one side and then turn it to the other. Artistic thinkers, on the other hand, can visualize the interrelationships among the parts as they work. They move back and forth from foreground to background. They constantly turn their sculpture as they work. They visualize the whole composition as they manipulate the parts.

This skill does not necessarily develop on its own. Students need to see successful compositions, talk about how artworks are designed, and learn how to plan and make adjustments to the composition of their own work. However, it is not necessary to have a separate unit focusing just on designing a composition. The teacher can introduce design principles as part of the artistic process. Students can be asked to think about them when making their sketches. The teacher can point out examples in the students' own work or refer to an example in a familiar or featured artwork. Decisions about design can be discussed during peer and teacher conferences.

They can also be the focus of sensory awareness activities, class discussions, art centers, mini-lessons, and group activities such as are suggested in the sample activities that follow and those found in the books recommended in Teacher Resources at the end of this chapter.

Introducing composition. Planning is integral to creating a unified composition. Even the very youngest students who still need to work directly will benefit from being taught to take several quiet minutes to think about their work and rehearse what they will be doing before beginning to use the art materials. Share Bruce McMillan's wonderful book *The Picture That Mom Drew*. This rhythmic cumulative text introduces the elements of art and the idea of how parts combine into a whole as an artist draws a pencil sketch of her two children at the beach.

Questions to ask. Asking questions that elicit design decisions and encouraging children to act on their ideas is also beneficial. Asking the child what color paints will be needed for a painting before beginning and then giving only those colors fosters a consideration of overall design in a way that allowing random choice or providing teacher-selected colors does not. Questions for young students can address many areas of design:

What will be the most important part of your picture?

Where will you place the most interesting part of the picture?

What will be the biggest thing in your picture?

Will your picture have something in the middle or things on each side?

How will you make the background different from the foreground?

What textures, patterns, or kinds of lines will you use?

Developing Composition Skills

Ask more experienced students to think about the different relationships that are represented in the design of an artwork. A discussion of the compositional decisions made by an artist is an important part of studying a featured artwork and should lay the framework for analyzing the student's own work. They can also explore changing the relationships within a composition to see how the parts related to each other and the whole.

Balance. Balance—the creation of visual equilibrium—is one way to create unity and order in an artwork. How elements are arranged in a picture can produce a restful feeling or visual tension. Artistic elements can be seen to have force or weight as if they were operating under gravity. Symmetrical balance is when the elements are exactly balanced on each side of the vertical or horizontal axis of an artwork. Radial balance arranges the elements around a central point. Asymmetrically balanced works use contrasting elements to create a feeling of equilibrium. Have students classify artworks based on how they seem to be balanced. Encourage students to try balancing their own work in unusual ways.

Proportion. Proportion refers to the relationship among size, number, and placement of the elements in a work. Proportion can be used to create the illusion of depth or texture on a flat surface, or it can be used to create exaggeration and distortion. The use of proportion is most clearly seen in two-dimensional works that utilize perspective and in sculptures that have been designed to be viewed from particular angles.

Explore proportion by having students enlarge or shrink a sketch, or by having them convert one of their own artworks or that of another to fit inside a different shape background. Share Pat Hutchin's book *Shrinking Mouse* (1997, New York: Greenwillow) to introduce the idea of drawing objects smaller to make them look further away.

Cropping. How does the movement, emphasis, and proportion of the work change when parts are removed? Discuss the role of cropping as a way to revise artworks. Make photocopies of the students' own work or of featured artworks and ask students to explore what happens if they crop off parts of the picture.

Placement. What happens when the elements of an artwork are moved to different places in the work? Have students cut out images and elements from copies of their own art or from the artworks of others and rearrange them. Discuss how changing the position of elements in the work affects the focus and proportion. Challenge students to redraw their own work or famous artworks with elements moved, changed in size, or distorted.

Analyzing compositions. Overlay artworks with clear acetate or blank overhead transparency sheets and use a marker to highlight points as they are made during group discussions of design. Alternatively, direct an overhead projector at a poster-sized print and highlight elements using a marker on a blank transparency.

Language Arts and Design

Design principles can also be applied across the curriculum. Combining words and visuals, for example, is a common classroom activity. From book illustrations to posters students are constantly being asked to consider the relationship between words and images.

- *Look at the design of book illustrations.* Introduce children to the design principles by discussing the way illustrations in books being read are designed. Look for patterns, rhythms, focal points, variety, and order. Ask, "How has the artist designed this illustration to reflect the meaning of the words?"
- *Apply design principles.* Continue to refer to design principles whenever students create works that combine art and writing, such as invitations, cards, posters, and advertisements.
- *Design lettering styles.* Have students design a lettering style that matches the meaning of a word, saying, or poem. How, for example, would a design for the word *running* be different from one for *sleeping?* Ask, "Does this word or poem require more order or variety to best express its meaning?"

- *Use the design vocabulary.* Studying the art elements can build a vocabulary of descriptive language. Have students brainstorm words that describe different colors, shapes, or textures. Then have students use these words to write a descriptive paragraph or poem describing a special object or place.
- *Tell design stories.* Make up "oral design stories" illustrated by using a flannel, Velcro, or magnetic board.

Math and Design

The interrelationship between design and math is powerful. Developing a concept of shape and space are important in both art and mathematics. Proportion, pattern, and balance are design concepts that overlap both math and art. Measuring skills are of utmost importance in the design of many objects.

- *Geometry.* Combine the study of shape and three-dimensional forms with units in geometry. Use student artwork to illustrate mathematical concepts such as symmetry and the qualities of geometric shapes and forms. For example, relate the study of symmetry to mask-making activities.
- *Proportion.* Explore size and shape relationships by using visual constructs combined with application of mathematical measurement skills. What happens to the dimensions of a work when it is squeezed or expanded? Challenge students to re-create one of their own works or a featured artwork on a larger or smaller background paper. How must the elements of the work be changed to keep the original balance and focus of the work?
- *Explore patterns.* Find examples of patterns in the room and on clothing. Compare works that utilize pattern as an organizing design element to those that do not. Discuss how pattern can be used to create either order or variety in an artwork. Have them design original patterns, perhaps using a graphic art software program, and then use them in an artwork. Compare these patterns to those found in math. Explore and color code a hundreds table or multiplication table at the upper levels. Challenge students to convert visual patterns into numerical ones.
- *Play with balance.* Compare the use of a balance scale to seeing balance in an artwork. Observers of child art have pointed out that young children tend to make symmetrically balanced compositions (Edwards, 1979). It is very common for primary students to begin their works in the center of the paper and add supporting elements on either side, such as in drawing the typical house framed by two trees. However, they are not aware that they do this. It is important to point out examples of balance in their work and the art of others. As children work, during sharing and when conferencing, describe

how elements balance each other. One way to introduce the concept of balance to young children is to run a ribbon down the center of a symmetrical or balanced artwork. Set up a balance scale and attach cut-out representations of the elements in the work to equal size weights. Have students describe an element and which side of the ribbon it is on. Then have a student come up and put the representation on the matching side of the scale. Compare the balance in an artwork with balance in a number sentence or algebra statement. This activity can be developed into a learning center or cooperative group activity.

Science and Design

Balance, symmetry, and pattern are also found in the scientific study of nature.

- *Balance.* When students are aware of the concept of balance and can describe it in their own work, have them compare works that are symmetrical to those that are balanced in other ways. Many works feature more complex forms of balance. Introduce upper-level students to works that have radial symmetry and those that are asymmetrical. Create a model of asymmetrical balance using a board on a fulcrum. Show how a larger object can be balanced by a pile of smaller ones or one a distance away. Discuss why artists might want to draw the eye away from the center of a work. As students become more sophisticated in seeing balance, try the same activity as above but use different size weights that relate to the size and strength of the objects in the work.
- *Symmetry.* Explore balance further by looking for examples of symmetry in natural forms. Ask students to consider in what way the natural symmetry of our body has influenced the art we create. How is the role of symmetry similar or different from that in nature?
- *Pattern.* Explore the role of pattern in camouflaged animals. Have students use patterned materials such as cloth, wallpaper, and patterned pieces cut out of magazines to create artwork in which pattern is used to define or hide shapes and images.

Social Studies and Design

There is no universally accepted definition of good design. Over time and in different cultures artwork has been created that reflects different approaches to these organizing principles. Fashions change. Combinations that are meaningful in one context may be mysterious in another. Cultural styles and current standards of beauty often dictate design relationships. At one point in time artists may value line quality over color effects. At another time textural qualities may be more important than three-dimensionality.

Designing is deciding. Because at different times and in different places artists have made different decisions about which combination of elements best meets their needs, it is important in teaching design to use examples from many cultures and art periods so students are exposed to a wide range of approaches to design, rather than to just the artistic taste of the day. Creativity in art requires a broad understanding of the interrelationship of function, design, and social standards. Students need to grapple with artworks that make them question accepted concepts and have a foundation from which to risk trying something new.

- *The effect of design on social behavior.* Have students research studies on the effect of design on behavior and its use in advertising. Why are cereal boxes the color they are? What are the most common colors of candy? Why? What kind of product containers have orderly designs? Which have a great deal of variety?
- *Cultural variation in design.* Examine artworks from other cultures that utilize art elements in different ways. For example, how is the repetition of art elements used in Australian Aboriginal art and Mexican folk arts compared to the paintings of Grant Wood? Have teams create group artworks based on the repetition of a particular color, shape, or line. Combine into a mural or wall hanging.
- *Explore cultural perspectives.* Find examples where artists "break the rules" or examine works from cultures with different design traditions. Challenge older students to explore the cultural perspective of design such as demonstrated in the following questions:
  1. How radical can artists within a culture be before their work is rejected?
  2. How do our beliefs about design affect how we see and judge the art of other cultures? Why, for example, was the art of the Maya called grotesque and primitive by Europeans when it was first discovered but is now highly admired?
  3. How can we understand why the Egyptians showed the pharaoh larger than the servants in their art, but it still looks "wrong"?

Music and Design

Compare and contrast the musical design elements with those of art (At a Glance 12.7). Rhythm, for example, performs the same role in art as it does in music. It unifies a work by drawing the different elements together. Rhythm in both art and music is built from repetition and pattern. Although in art this is created by repeating colors, shapes, lines, and patterns throughout the work, in music the rhythm is built from repeated beats.

- *Design to music.* The sensory activity of painting or drawing to music with different rhythms unifies art and music kinesthetically and helps students discover the role of rhythm in both. (See At a Glance 12.8.)

At a Glance 12.7

The Design Elements of Music

Dynamics: The relative change in volume of a sound

Form: The structure of a piece of music

Harmony: The blending of sounds simultaneously

Melody: A series of sounds or notes that form a pattern

Rhythm: The movement of sounds through time

Texture: The combination of sounds to create a certain quality

Timbre: The unique quality of a sound, also called tone color

- *Create a visual rhythm.* Another activity is to assign each member of a cooperative group a different color and shape. Have the students invent a rhythm and then working together have the group combine their colors and shapes into a unified composition that visually represents their rhythm. This can also be done with familiar songs. Explore ways to represent the song line and musical form.
- *Musically represent a picture.* Vice versa, start with an artwork and represent the work through the creation of an original piece of music perhaps with student-made instruments. What sounds would the lines, shapes, colors, and patterns make? Is the work harmonious or dissonant, loud or soft?
- *Make musical shapes.* Play snatches from different kinds of music while students draw the lines or shapes that the music evokes.
- *Compare artistic and musical elements.* Relate the elements of line, color, texture, and space to the corresponding elements in music.
- *Compare color and melody.* In teams match melodies to different colors and in a darkened room use a slide projector or overhead to project that color on a wall while the melody is played. Combine this with related dance movements to create a multimedia presentation.
- *Compare tone and value.* Discuss tone color in music and compare it to color and value in an artwork.
- *Express musical feelings in artwork.* Play a piece of music and have students create lines, shapes, or colors that reflect how the music makes them feel.
- *Express artistic elements through music.* Have students create sounds and rhythms to go with different kinds of lines or shapes.
- *Represent a song or instrument in an artwork.* Read Eric Carle's *I See a Song* (see Books to Share: Music), in which the music of a violinist comes to life. Invite students to create artwork that

At a Glance 12.8

Inspirational Music

The following pieces provide a range of rhythms and melodies that will inspire the artwork of young artists:

Artist	Title
Various	*African Fete 3*
Benedictine Monks of Santo Domingo de Silos	*Chants*
Hamza El Din	*The Water Wheel*
Claude Débussy	*The Snow Is Dancing, Play of the Waves*
Glatunji	*Drums of Passion*
Ferde Grofé	*Grand Canyon Suite*
Gustave Holst	*The Planets*
Tokeya Imajin	*Dream Catcher*
Wolfgang Amadeus Mozart	*Eine kleine Nachtmusik*
Northsong	*Song of Amazonia*
Michael Oldfield	*Tubular Bells 1 and 2*
Putumayo	*Latino! Latino!*
Rumilajita	*Wiracocha*
Camille Saint-Saëns	*The Swan*
Frédéric Chopin	*Piano Concerto No. 2 in F Minor*
Igor Stravinsky	*Petruska*
Andrew Vasquez	*Wind River*
Bill Wheelen	*Riverdance*
World Meditation	*Chants from around the World*

illustrates a particular song or musical instrument. What colors, lines, shapes, and textures relate to the music? How can musical rhythm and harmony be expressed?

- *Represent rhythms visually.* Play short selections of musical pieces with different rhythms. Have students draw or paint lines and shapes and use colors that relate to the rhythm they hear.
- *Discover rhythms in artworks.* Have students find repeated shapes, colors, lines, and so on, in artworks such as in Alma Woodsey Thomas' *The Eclipse* and William H. Johnson's *Going to Church.* Then have students create a tapped rhythm that expresses the visual rhythm in the work.

Design and Purpose

How a designer uses these principles is strongly influenced by the artist's purpose and how the finished work will be viewed or used in its intended setting. An artist commissioned to create an artwork to

Books to Share

Music

Carle, E. (1973). *I see a song.* New York: Crowell.
Wood, M., & Igus, T. (1998). *I see the rhythm.* Children's Book Press.

be hung on a wall in a home, for example, must take into account not only the dynamic of the image that he or she desires to create but also the distance from which it will be viewed, the color of the walls, and the furnishings that will surround it. In the same way a potter must consider the comfort and balance of a cup handle as well as its visual form. The design of a work can be judged by how well the artist met the intended purpose by combining visual constructs with functionality.

Determining the purpose of an artwork is one of the first steps in developing its design. In some cases the purpose of a work may be simple and straightforward. But in other situations artworks have several layers of purposes, each of which influences the design choices the artist makes. For example, students may start out with the assignment of drawing a detailed picture of a leaf in their science journals. The basic purpose of the drawing is communicative—to visually explain what a leaf looks like. This purpose will cause students to try to draw as realistically as possible. However, the leaf drawing is also functional. In making the drawing the student will gain a better understanding of the structure of a leaf. Adding labels and a caption will help increase the function of the drawing. It is also decorative in the sense that it makes the journal more special to look at—much more interesting than if it just contained verbal description. Many students will choose to use colors, values, or varied thicknesses of line, or even add a background, to increase the decorative aspects of the drawing. The drawing may also be expressive. If the student thinks the leaf is beautiful or ugly, the artwork may reflect this through the way the colors and lines are combined. Some students may use shading to create the illusion of dimension.

Having students identify their purpose before creating a work of art is an important part of the design process. It takes only a small amount of time at the beginning of an assignment but is extremely helpful in focusing students' attention on the design decisions they need to make. Often when students make artwork that does not match the needs of the assignment, it is because the teacher has not made clear the purpose of the work.

For young children considering purpose can be as simple as the teacher asking, "What will you do with this work when it is finished?"

Teaching in Action

Design Stories

Capture young students' attention by making up simple stories to accompany design discussions. For example, the story that follows could be used to illustrate the concept of using placement to show distance.

Materials: Five paper shapes about the same size and a large sheet of background paper, tape. (*Note:* A flannel, Velcro, or magnetic board could also be used.)

The Story

Once there were five friends, So Square, Tippy Triangle, Rex Rectangle, Cira Circle, and Olive Oval. [Show each shape as the name is said].

Every day at school they liked to play on the playground. First they had to line up at the door. [Tape shapes in line on background paper.]

Ask, "Who is the closest? The farthest away?"

When everyone was in line they could go out to play. [Tape shapes randomly to background.]

Ask, "Who is closer? Who is farther away?" Accept all responses.

They liked to play with each other. Sometimes So played with Tippy. [Move the lower shape up and next to the higher shape.]

Ask, "Who is closer? Who is farther away?" Discuss any changes in responses.

Sometimes Rex played with Cira. Move shape down next to other one.

Ask, "Who is closer? Who is farther away?" Discuss any changes in responses. Have children suggest other playmates to match up. Discuss who is closer and who is farther after each move.

When they were done playing, they lined up to go back into school. [Line up the shapes.]

The Concept: Summarize the concept discussed in the story: Things higher on a paper look farther away than things lower. Things in a straight line look the same distance away. Show students examples of this concept in artworks, photographs, and book illustrations. If students notice a relationship with size, discuss that as well.

Follow up this story by having students make a class mural of the playground showing themselves playing with their friends.

Older students can be asked to consider purpose in more depth, such as considering what message or idea they are trying to convey and then thinking about what design elements will best convey their ideas.

For some types of artwork specific functions are an integral part of the work and can be strictly defined. Clay cups should not leak. Posters should be easily readable. Providing opportunities to design useful objects allows students to apply their ideas about design and explore the range of creative possibilities that exist within a set of functional limitations. See At a Glance 12.9 and 12.10 for specific design-related activities.

At a Glance 12.9

Multidisciplinary Design Activities

The following multidisciplinary studies provide the ideal context in which to teach students the relationship between design and function:

Architectural Design

Subjects:	Art, history, math
Sample activities:	Design a dream home.
	Draw elevations of an original design for a building.
	Build a scale model of an original design for a building.

Advertising Design

Subjects:	Art, English, social studies
Sample activities:	Design an advertisement to sell a product.
	Design a poster to advertise an event or support a cause.
	Put together a multimedia ad campaign including advertisements for newspapers, flyers, brochures, website, billboard, and other promotional materials.

Calligraphy

Subjects:	Art, English, history
Sample activities:	Design a lettering style to fit a word, phrase, or poem.
	Hand letter a famous quote.
	Design an initial letter for a chapter in a novel.

Fashion Design

Subjects:	Art, history
Sample activities:	Design a contemporary garment based on a historical one.
	Design a garment for a specific career or occupation.

Graphic Design

Subjects:	Art, English, math
Sample activities:	Arrange articles, captions, and artwork and select typefaces for a page in a newspaper or magazine.
	Design cards for special occasions.

Industrial Design

Subjects:	Art, math, social studies
Sample activities:	Draw to scale designs for a new vehicle or piece of furniture.
	Redesign a common, everyday item to fit a specific situation or use, such as a bed for use in gravity-free outer space.

At a Glance 12.10

Dancing and Dramatizing Design

Dance

Have students create movements that relate to the different art elements and design principles.

Line: Have the class line up and then move in different ways such as straight, curved, and zigzag.

Shape: Give students lengths of yarn and have them work in groups to form different shapes.

Color: Have students select a color and invent a movement to represent it. Then have students blend their movement with a partner to form a new "color."

Texture: Ask students to imagine they are walking barefoot on different kinds of textured surfaces.

Value: Invite students to invent a body position to represent dark and another to represent light. Play a piece of music that slowly gets louder, such as "Sunrise" from Grofé's *Grand Canyon Suite.* Keeping with the music, have students gradually change their position from dark to light.

Space: Have pairs or groups of students join hands to create open spaces for others to pass through.

Variety and order: Demonstrate order by having students stand in rows and move in unison. Introduce variety by having students change their movement when signaled or touched. Demonstrate different degrees of order and variety such as having all the students in outer rows, diagonal rows, or at random move differently from those inside.

Repetition: Have students create dance patterns of repeated steps and motions.

Balance: Have students, first individually and later in pairs and teams, demonstrate different kinds of balance with their bodies.

Unity: Go to a ballet or watch a video dance performance. Have students look for the ways line, shape, and space are used. Discuss how color, texture, and value are used in composing a dance.

Dramatics

- Create skits about a color, line, shape, or texture.
- Dramatize a story about the mixing of two colors, such as Ellen Walsh's *Mouse Paint* (1989) or Leo Lionni's *Little Blue. Little Yellow* (1959) (see Books to Share: Color).
- Do choral readings of poems about color, wearing original hats or masks in that color.
- Have students work in small groups to create skits showing how an artist planned and carried out a featured artwork. What did the artist do first?
- Demonstrate design principles by having students take the role of various art elements, such as a red square, a zigzag line, and so on. Then have "director" artists take turns arranging the "elements" into different compositions.

Teaching in Action

Looking at Design: Two Lessons

My Favorite Toy: Primary

When introducing the practice of sharing things from home at the beginning of the school year, encourage students not only to tell what the item is and where they got it but also to comment on the design of the object. This will provide them with a way of a making a more meaningful presentation.

Create a chart with the following sentence starters:

- This toy is fun to play with because . . .
- I like the way it looks because . . .
- If I could change it, I would . . .

Follow up by having children draw pictures of their toy in the place they keep it at home and discuss how it does or does not fit with other things in their rooms or their homes. Challenge them to redesign the toy to make it even more fun to play with.

Buying Spree: Fourth Grade and Above

Have students look through a catalog and select an item they wish they could own. Have them answer the following questions about it and then draw a picture of the object in the place they would put it in their home.

- For what will I use this?
- Where and when will I use it?
- Is its durability important to me?
- Does its design make its use and meaning clear?
- Is it designed to be useable?
- Does it have enough variety to be interesting to look at or touch?
- Does it relate to the rest of my surroundings and belongings?
- Does it fit my personal way of working?
- Does it make me feel important, tell about who I am, or make my life better?

More to Do

Have students ask design questions about groups of objects that interrelate, such as a set of clothing, matching stationery, or furnishings for a room. Also challenge them to redesign commercial objects to make them more functional or better able to fit in a chosen environment.

Evaluating Design

Although design is an integral part of every human-made object, the quality of the design varies widely. Every time a person selects or buys an object to use or to decorate the environment, that person is making a design decision. Students who have learned to consider the relationship between an object's design and its function will be better able to create a personally satisfying environment in which to live.

Books to Share

Design

These books can expand students' understanding of design:

Blosfeldt, K. (1986). *Art forms in the plant world.* New York: Dover.
Brommer, G. (1985). *Art in your world.* Worcester, MA: Davis.
Fiehl, C. & P. (1998). *1000 chairs.* New York: Taschen.
Gordon, L. (1996). *ABC of design.* San Francisco: Chronicle Books.
Haechel, E. (1998). *Art forms in nature.* New York: International Book Imports.
McMillan, B. (1997). *The picture that mom drew.* Chicago: Walker.
Moss, M. (1991). *Fashion designer.* Meriden, CT: Crestwood.

Those who are aware of the importance of design will think about their choice and ask themselves questions as they make their decisions. Teachers need to provide opportunities for students to practice asking and answering these kinds of questions, such as by asking students to consider familiar and popular objects in relation to their design. Design can be evaluated on several levels:

- *Use:* Is the object useable?

  Example: Is the chair designed so someone can actually sit on it?
- *Function:* Do the materials and form of the object relate to its function?

  Example: Is the chair designed to fit the human body and provide comfort?
- *Meaning:* Does the object have meaning to its audience, to its culture, to humankind?

  Example: Is the design of the chair mundane and ordinary, unique and innovative, cheap or costly?
- *Visual quality:* Do the art elements work together with the object's use, function, and meaning?

  Example: Does the color and style of the chair fit the living environment?
- *Information:* What does the object say about the culture and its history?

  Example: Does the design of the chair reflect current technology, the influence of past styles, or cultural beliefs about what a chair should be?

Designing for Function

The designer's problem is to create objects that are composed of the right balance of visual elements for the way that they will be used. There is no one correct solution to this problem as can be seen in the wide range of functional designs of so many simple objects, ranging from teacups to pencils.

Before they begin an artwork, help students develop a set of criteria or rubric against which they can compare their finished works. (At the primary level this can be done as a whole group. This works particularly well for cross-discipline projects that have defined purposes such as making a poster about saving endangered animals or designing book covers for original stories. At the upper levels students can work in cooperative groups or on their own to develop their own set of criteria for each of their artworks.

An evaluation tool should include the following considerations:

- How will it be used?
- Where will it be used?
- Who will use it?
- What value or status will it give the user?
- Does the material/media used fit its form and use?
- Do the arrangement of elements used enhance its use and appearance?

In the Classroom

BOOKS, SCULPTURE, AND FIBER

In the classroom there are many opportunities for students to apply the principles of design. In this section we will examine a broad range of art activities that by their very nature require consideration of design in order to fulfill their function.

Making Books

Nowhere are artistic design and words more closely tied together than in the art form of bookmaking. Handmade books are one-of-a-kind creations that provide a place to capture one's thoughts and stories within a carefully designed container. Making their own words into a book provides children with the opportunity to make design decisions such as the following, which will allow their writing to be more meaningful:

- What kind of paper should be used?
- What shape should the book be?
- How should the book be put together?

Answering these questions requires the bookmaker to analyze ideas to be communicated through the visual elements that surround and enfold the words. Children can design blank books for journaling, create bound folders for portfolios, and bind handwritten or computer-composed stories, poems, and essays into elegant book forms.

At a Glance 12.11

Parts of a Book

Cover: A sheet of paper or board that protects the pages of the book

Endpapers: Paper, often decorated, that is glued to the inside cover of the book

Signatures: Groups of folded sheets of paper that are bound together into the book

Spine: The back edge of the book where it is bound together

This section presents several book forms ranging from simple softcovers to books with sewn bindings. Although the simpler forms are most commonly used by primary students, older students will also find these quickly made designs appropriate for many of their writing activities. The more elaborate forms can also provide an ideal way for an older, experienced student to work together with a younger one to bind a special piece of writing. Or a small, cooperative group can work together to bind class writing collections.

Introducing bookmaking. The following activities can be used to introduce students to the book as an art form. It would be appropriate to offer these lessons to students who are at the stage of preparing a final copy of a piece of writing.

Begin by introducing students to the wonderful variation in the design of books. Explore what students think a book is. What do they think makes a book similar to or different from a computer or a video? Why is art important in books?

- *Book sort.* Have students sort books into groups based on size, shape, the way they open, cover material. Make a list or graph showing the results.
- *Book parts.* Have students examine an assortment of different kinds of books and try to determine how they are constructed. They can list cover materials, stitching, or gluing techniques, paper type used for pages, etc. Compare commercially bound books to handmade ones. How are they similar? How are they different? (See At a Glance 12.11.)
- *Book illustration and layout.* Have students each select a book and record number of illustrations, location in book and on page, size, etc. Have students determine the difference between a book that is a picture book and one that is not.
- *Illustration and establishing mood.* Have students compare color and style of illustrations to the genre of the book. Which kind of books have pastel illustrations, brightly colored ones, dark, deep colored

At a Glance 12.12

The Tools of Bookmaking

Awl: This is the essential tool for bookbinding. Use it to prepunch holes through the pages and covers of the books. An awl can go through thicker and heavier materials than can a hole punch. The amount of pressure applied will determine the size of the holes made. Place a pad of newspapers or a Styrofoam tray underneath the paper to be punched to provide ease in making the holes.

Covers: A variety of materials can be used for book covers. Construction paper, poster board, and tagboard are often used for softcover books. Covers can be made more durable by covering them with clear self-adhesive paper. The cardboard backing of hardcover books can be covered with drawing paper, construction paper, gift wrap, wallpaper, or fabric.

Cover backing: Hardback books require two pieces of mat board, chip board, light cardboard, or corrugated cardboard cut slightly larger than the pages to be bound. Empty cereal boxes and packing boxes can provide a free source of cardboard for cover backings.

Glue: Use only white glue or craft glue in very small amounts. Glue can cause cardboard to warp. If necessary, weigh down freshly glued covers with books, bricks, or heavy boards until dry.

Needles: Because the holes will be prepunched into the paper, students can use a blunt needle. This makes the sewing process safer for the younger students. Look for large-eye tapestry or safety needles that will fit the thread or yarn selected.

Paper cutter: A paper cutter, for the teacher's use only, will help immensely in obtaining straight, evenly cut pages for bookmaking. Pages should be trimmed before binding and then carefully clipped together using paper clips or clothespins.

Tapes: Cloth, plastic book tape, and clear packing tape can be used to reinforce spines and bindings.

Thread: Some binding techniques require sewing. Interior sewing should be done with a heavy quilting thread or medium-weight crochet cotton. Visible stitching can be done in any decorative yarn, string, ribbon, or raffia.

ones, bold graphic images, realistic detail, fantasy elements, and the like? Create a graph of the results.

- *Illustration and personal style.* Find examples of the same story, such as "Little Red Riding Hood," illustrated by different artists. Have students compare and contrast the illustrations. What did the artists see differently? What did they do the same? Did they choose the same parts of the story to illustrate? Why or why not? Did they use different art media? Does it change the mood of the story?
- *Words as art.* Have students compare and contrast the way the words are placed on the page in several books. What is the effect of a page full of words and one with wide margins? How does the size of the letters affect the meaning of the words? What are some

Teacher Tip

Paper for Bookmaking

- All kinds of paper can be used for the pages of blank books. Plain paper such as typing or duplicating paper should be used for journals and sketchbooks as it provides a good, inexpensive surface for both writing and drawing. If the book will be used for watercolor or charcoal sketches, drawing or watercolor paper will provide a more absorbent, textured surface. For more elaborate books a wide variety of beautiful fine-quality papers with imprinted designs and borders, now being marketed for laser printers, can also be used in bookmaking.
- Lined paper such as composition and loose-leaf paper can be used, although the lines may hinder the freedom to sketch in journals. Primary students, who must have guidelines for writing, can instead use paper with a blank top and several lines on the bottom of each sheet.
- Scrapbooks, photo albums, and other books in which materials will be pasted can have heavier pages made from construction paper or charcoal paper.
- Finished pieces of writing and artwork can also be bound into books. When binding pieces of completed writing, make sure that there is an ample margin on the left-hand side to allow room for the sewing or stapling. If necessary, widen this edge by gluing on a paper strip. Depending on the size of the book, this margin should extend at least a half inch from the fastening of the binding. This allows for the folding of the pages that occurs after binding.

unusual ways that words can be used as part of images? How are titles and headings differentiated from the body of text?

- *Laying out text.* Photocopy pages from a variety of books in which the text has been laid out in different ways such as in columns, around pictures, etc. Have students color in the text as a block of color. Discuss the visual effect created. Cut out the text and try rearranging it in other ways. How many different ways can blocks of text be placed on a page? Which ones look balanced? Try different sizes and shapes of paper and compare results.
- *Revising page layouts.* Photocopy several pages of each student's writing and artwork in several sizes (use enlarging and minimizing function on copier or scanner). Encourage the students to cut out the words and pictures and try arranging them in different ways on several different sizes of paper. If a computer and scanner are available, import the art into the writing and explore various layouts.
- *Book cover design.* Place an assortment of books on display. Have each student choose one of the books based on the cover alone. Have the students explain what features about the cover attracted them. Analyze the covers in terms of colors, style, placement of words, and how accurately they reflect the contents of the book.

Softcover books. This is the simplest and most versatile book form. It can be used for a short-term journal, report, or story and can be made in many sizes and shapes. A softcover book consists of the following:

- *The cover:* Select a paper or piece of tagboard twice as long and equal in height to the pages of the book. The paper may be folded or cut into a separate front and back. The cover may be decorated before binding.
- *The pages:* If the book is to be written before it is bound, allow at least one and one-half inches of blank space along the bound edge for the pages to fold back without hiding the writing.
- *The binding:* Place the pages inside the folded piece of paper and bind using one of the following methods:
    1. *Stapled.* Fasten the pages together about one inch from the edge to be bound using a row of staples. The stapled edge can be covered with cloth or plastic tape for a more finished effect.
    2. *Tied.* Punch a pair of holes using an awl or heavy hole punch. Then thread through yarn or heavy cord and tie in a bow.
    3. *Sewn.* Use spring-type clothespins to hold the cover and pages together. Place the clipped-together pages and cover on a cushion of newspaper or a Styrofoam tray. Using an awl, punch a line of small, evenly spaced holes one inch in from the edge. The number and spacing of the holes will be determined by the stitching that will be used. Using a tapestry needle and heavy crochet cotton or cotton rug, warp sew the edge using a decorative stitch, such as the ones illustrated in At a Glance 12.13. (See also At a Glance 12.12 for suggested tools.)

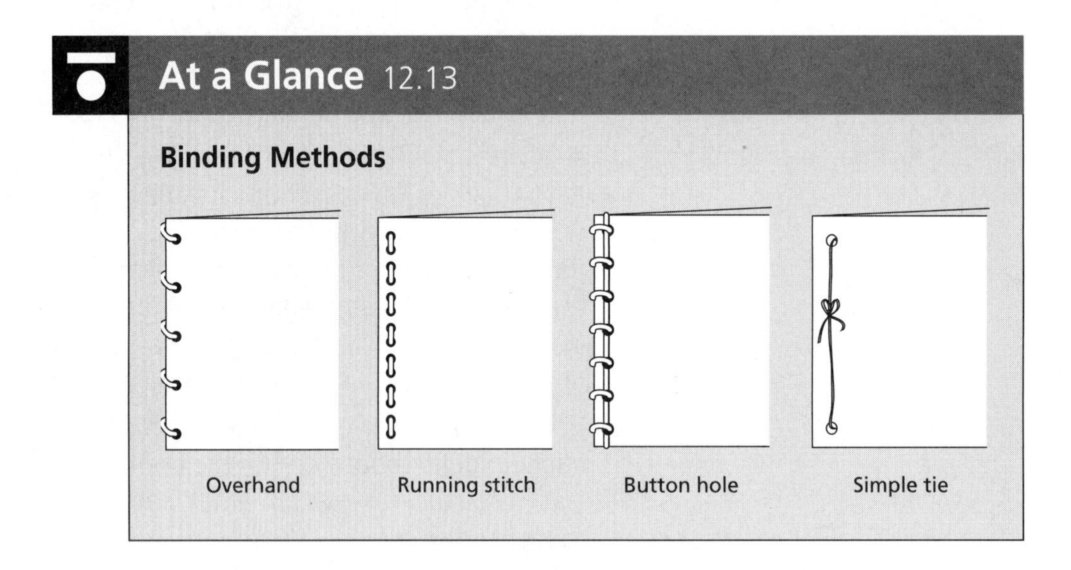

At a Glance 12.13

Binding Methods

Teaching in Action

Making a Class Big Book

1. *Start with an idea.* Primary students who have been exposed to oversized books as part of their reading program enjoy making their own versions. A class big book can be a community effort with pairs of students working on each page. Older students will also enjoy creating big books to accompany oral presentations or to display finished artwork, maps, or science illustrations. There are many places to get ideas for a class book.
   - Use cumulative and repetitive books as a model with children substituting their own words into the pattern.
   - Children can offer their own personal definitions of a word, such as "Cooperation is when . . . "
   - Children can remember a class experience or trip by writing down their descriptions.
   - They can record the steps in a science experiment.
   - Each child's poem or story can be a page in the book.
2. *Record each idea or sentence.* Locate the writing at the top or bottom of a sheet of large paper, using only one side. Either 12″ × 18″ or 18″ × 24″ works well.
3. *Select an art medium.* With the class, talk about what would be the best way to make the illustrations for the book. Decide whether to make the illustrations directly on the page or on separate paper and glued on.
4. *Distribute the pages.* Have children work alone or in groups, depending on the number of pages to complete the illustrations. Do not forget to make a title page and front and back covers.
5. *Bind the pages together.* Using one of the binding methods for sewing a soft-cover book, put the book together.

The portfolio. Making a handmade portfolio is an ideal activity to begin the school year. As students learn how to make a hardcover, they also take ownership of their portfolio. Ask them to select colors and designs that reflect characteristics about themselves and that will make their portfolio unique and easy to find. Have them predict what might be in the portfolio by the end of the term or year and record their ideas in their journals.

An advantage of the hardcover design is that it allows the portfolios to be stored upright so they are much easier to use than flimsy paper ones. Decorate one or two cardboard boxes, large enough to hold all the students' portfolios, with a class collage of drawings and magazine clippings that reflect the interests and experiences of the students. This activity can be used to get to know the students better as they share information about themselves. To establish ownership make sure students add their own unique decoration to the inside and outside of the portfolio. (See At a Glance 12.14.)

At a Glance 12.14

Making a Portfolio

There are many different ways to construct portfolios. The following traditional style portfolio can easily be made by upper-level elementary students and provides safe storage for their work. Finished portfolios are sturdy enough to be stored upright in a box or plastic crate.

Materials needed

2 pieces of corrugated cardboard (A) cut to the desired size of the finished portfolio.

2 sheets of paper (B) at least 2 inches larger in both directions than the cardboard (or one equivalent piece).

2 sheets of paper (C) the same size as the cardboard. These may be decorated with an all-over pattern.

2 pieces of fabric (D) 4 inches wide and the length of the folding edge of the portfolio.

6 lengths of ribbon (E), about 12 inches each.

White glue and scissors

Directions

Step 1: Glue sheets of paper together, if necessary. Place cardboard pieces (A) side by side on top. Leave an even amount of paper projecting, on all sides. Leave a space between boards in center.

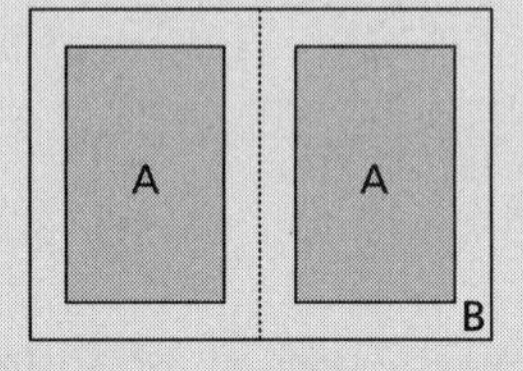

Step 2: Cut off corners of paper (A) as illustrated.

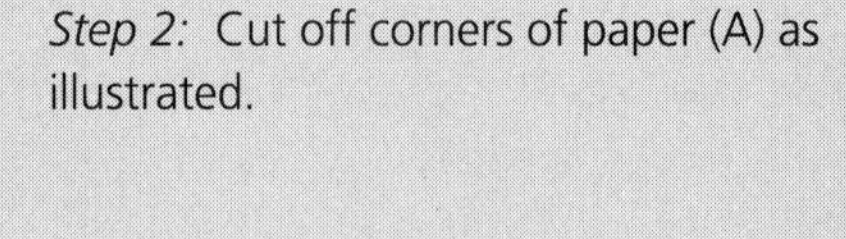

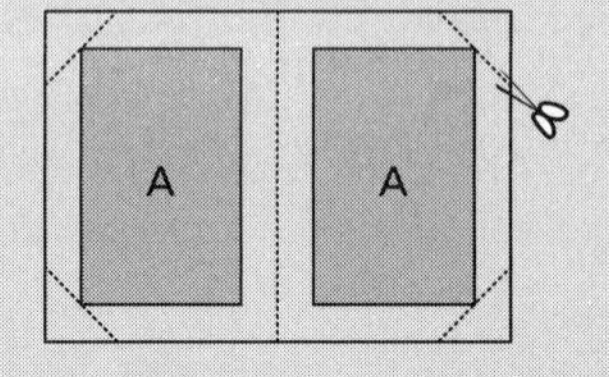

Step 3: Fold flaps over and glue down.

Step 4: Attach ribbons as shown.

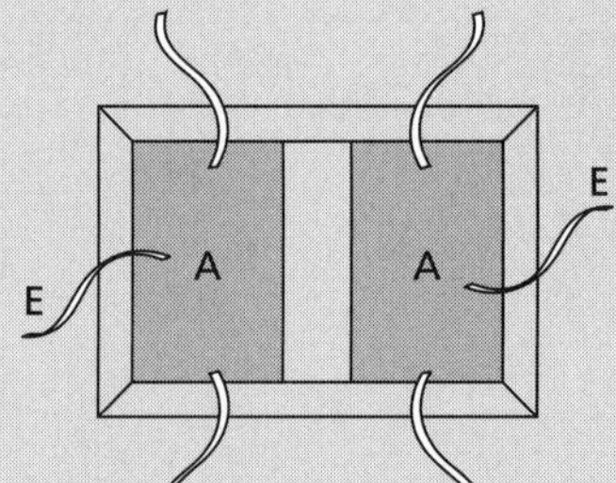

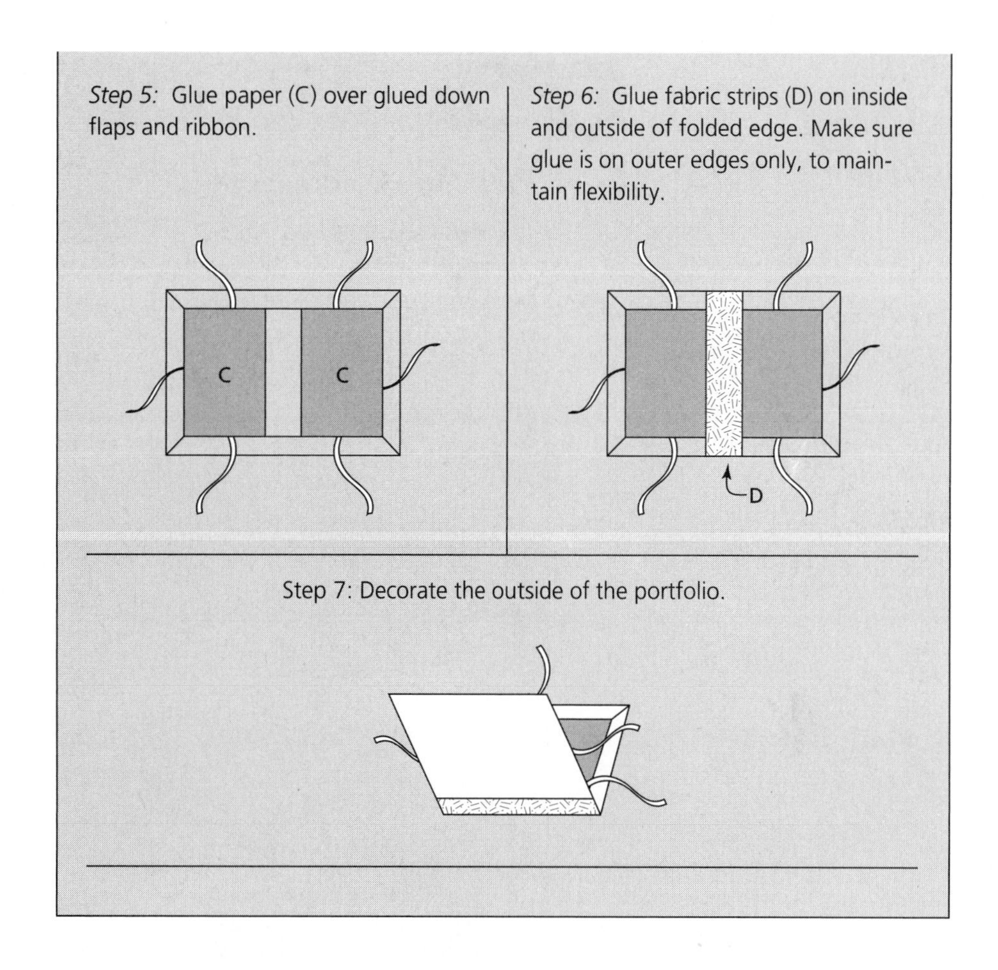

Step 5: Glue paper (C) over glued down flaps and ribbon.
C
C
Step 6: Glue fabric strips (D) on inside and outside of folded edge. Make sure glue is on outer edges only, to maintain flexibility.
D
Step 7: Decorate the outside of the portfolio.

Hardcover books. When students are comfortable with making hardcovers, introduce them to sewn books. These books are put together by sewing the pages to the end paper or a cloth backing, which is then glued to the cover. This method is particularly suited to books that will be read often.

Sewing a book together is an excellent way to introduce children to sewing techniques. For first-time sewers paper is easier to handle than cloth. It does not wrinkle and pull the way cloth does. The holes are already prepunched, providing an easy-to-follow guide and making mistakes easy to pull out. Thread and needles are larger so students can easily see their work, and only a fairly short piece of thread is needed, eliminating frustrating tangles. See At a Glance 12.15 for step-by-step directions.

Folded books. There are a variety of ways to make booklets by folding paper. Traditional Chinese and Japanese books used an accordion fold format. This is a useful form for beginning writers as it allows them to see the whole sequence of the story at once. It is also easy

At a Glance 12.15

Making a Hardcover Book

Folded-Paper Method

- Prepare cover as described in the portfolio section, but do not glue on the end paper.

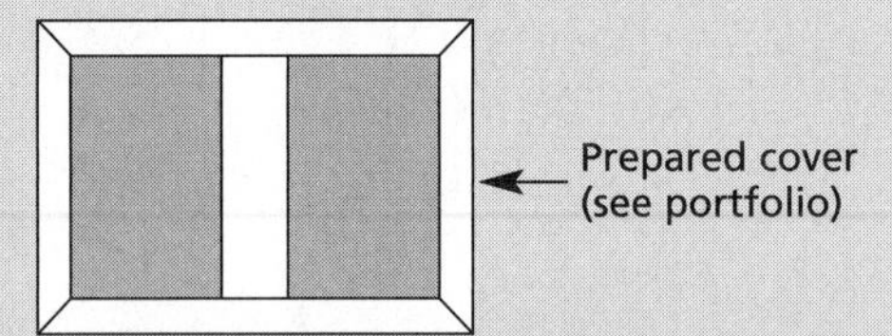

- Fold paper for pages in half so that they fit neatly inside the folded cover.
- Fold the end paper over the pages so that the right side is facing the pages.

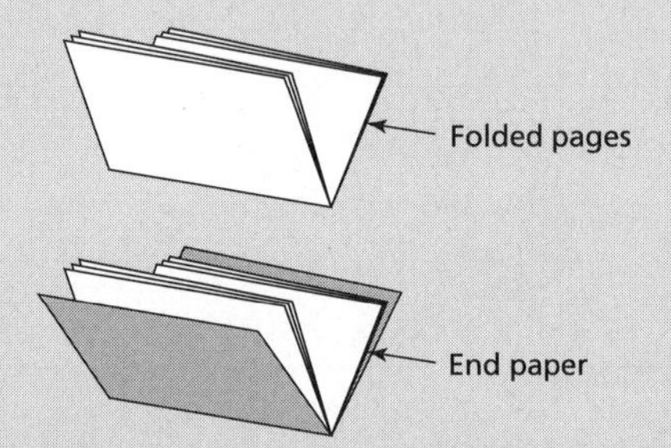

- Clip pages together and open to center fold. Using an awl, make a line of evenly spaced holes.

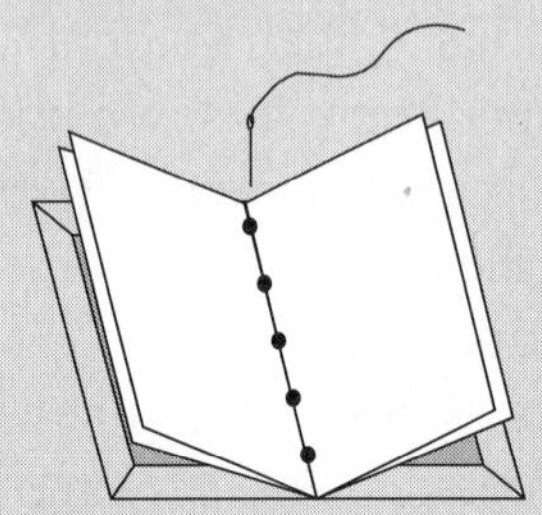

- With needle and thread use a backstitch to sew the pages and end paper together.
- Place a thin line of glue around the back edge of the end paper, being careful not to get glue one inch on either side of the spine. Then glue it and the pages to the inside cover of the book.

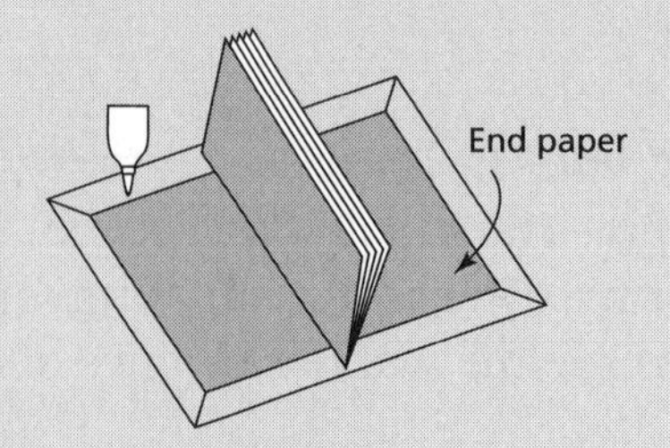

- Wipe off excess glue and then press the book under boards or heavy books so it dries flat.

Dealing with Separate Pages
In cases where pages are separate such as when printed out on a computer, join them before sewing.

- Carefully arrange the pages in the order desired. There must be an even number. Add a blank page at end if necessary.
- Take the top page and the back page and glue them to a one-inch strip of muslin. The top page should face down and the back page face up. Leave about one-quarter inch between the pages. Repeat for each front and back pair of pages in order.
- Place the joined pages face up on top of the right side of the end paper. Then follow directions for the sewn method starting at Step 4.

to display the finished books. Clever folding creates a simple origami book that is useful for teaching sequencing skills and writing short stories. (See At a Glance 12.16.)

Shaped books. Book covers and pages can be made in shapes other than rectangular. Encourage students to be inventive in designing their books. Do not use commercially sold patterns for shaped books. Students at all levels are quite capable of making designs that will better represent their own concept. Not every page in a book needs to have the same shape. Students can design their books in shapes that reflect their writing. For example, a book about a trip to New York City could have the top edge of each page cut to resemble a silhouette of one building so that when all the pages are together the full skyline is seen.

The goal is for students to see the design of the book as an integral part of the message. Students should ask themselves how the shape of the book can enhance or detract from their writing. Not every book should be shaped. A mini-lesson on shaped-book design could begin by studying exceptional shaped books such as *The Very Grouchy Ladybug* by Eric Carle (1977, New York: Harper & Row) and *Color Zoo* by Lois Ehlert (1989, New York: HarperCollins).

When students have decided that a shaped design will best display their writing, they can experiment with designs by making mini-mock-ups of possible shapes. Peer and teacher conferences can help the student choose the final shape. Construction of books that have shaped covers is similar to that of the softcover side-sewn ones. Use softcover materials and any of the side-sewn methods to join the pages. If only the pages are shaped, any binding method can be used (see At a Glance 12.13).

At a Glance 12.16

Making a Folded Book

Accordion Fold Method

- Cut a long strip of paper and fold it back and forth into accordion-style pleats. Glue on another piece if a longer book is desired.
- Cut a front and back cover from construction paper or poster board and glue to the front and back of the book.

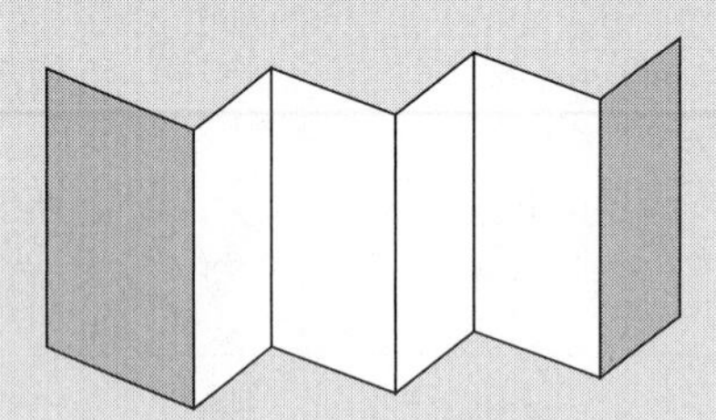

Accordian fold method

Origami Book

- Fold paper into eight sections as shown.
- Cut where indicated.

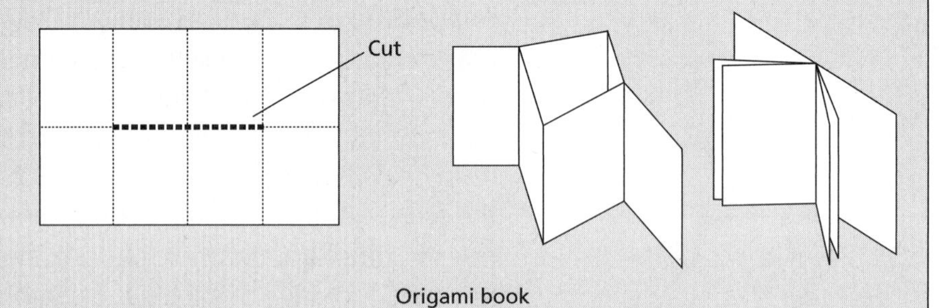

Origami book

Interlocked Pages

- Fold several sheets of paper in half.
- Take all but one sheet and on the folded edge cut as shown.
- Insert the uncut folded page to lock them all together.

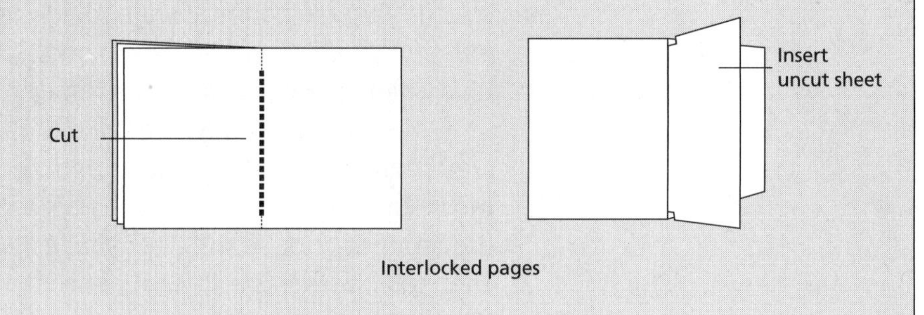

Interlocked pages

Teaching in Action

Inspire student bookmaking by displaying winners of the Caldecott Award given to outstandingly illustrated children's books, such as:

Aardema, V. (1976). *Why mosquitoes buzz in people's ears.* NY: Dial.
Brown, M. (1979). *Shadow.* NY: Macmillan.
Bunting, E. (1994). *Smoky night.* NY: Harcourt.
Hall, D. (1980). *The ox-cart man.* NY: Viking.
Macauly, D. (1991). *Black and white.* New York: Houghton Mifflin.
McCully, E. (1993). *Mirette on the high wire.* New York: Clarion
Rathmann, P. (1996). *Officer Buckle and Gloria.* New York: Putnam
Say, A. (1994). *Grandfather's journey.* New York: Houghton Mifflin
Sendak, M. (1964). *Where the wild things are.* NY: Harper & Row.
Weisner, D. (1992). *Tuesday.* New York: Clarion.
Wisnieski, D. (1997). *Golem.* New York: Clarion.
Yolen, J. (1988). *Owl moon.* NY: Philomel.
Young, E. (1990). *Lon Po Po: A Riding Hood story from China.* New York: Philomel.
Zelinsky, P.O. (1998). *Rapunzel.* New York: Dutton.

Making connections. Bookmaking also offers many opportunities to unite art and other disciplines.

- *Cross-discipline journals.* Handmade journals, logs, and books can reflect work in all subject areas.
- *Research presentations.* Students skilled in binding and layout techniques can present the results of their research in well-prepared, thoughtful ways, instead of as a simple stack of papers. Teachers in all areas will find students more interested and creative when they are given control over the final appearance of their research.
- *Portfolios.* Handmade portfolios can be used for both art, writing, and work from other disciplines.

Books to Share

Bookmaking

Aliki. (1988). *How a book is made.* New York: Harper Trophy.
Kehoe, M. (1993). *A book takes root: Making a picture book.* Minneapolis, MN: Carolrhoda.
Oxlade, C. (1995). *Writing and printing.* New York: Franklin Watts.
Stephens, J. (1995). *From picture to words.* New York: Holiday House.
Stowell, C. (1994). *Making books.* New York: Kingfisher.
Swain, G. (1995). *Bookworks: Making books by hand.* Minneapolis, MN: Carolrhoda.

Building

Our bodies have been designed to function in a three-dimensional world. Since people first began to create art, they have had the urge to pick up a piece of wood or a lump of clay and form it into something that can be turned over and over and experienced from all sides.

When we work with sculptural forms, we react as we would to any object. We experience them both visually and spatially, as well as tactilely and intellectually. Sculpture takes art off the flat surface and adds dimension. It challenges students to imagine objects from more than one point of view and draws upon their designing skills in a way that two-dimensional artwork does not.

Learning about sculpture begins in the primary years with the introduction of simple three-dimensional materials that allow children to build works with a minimum of technical requirements such as clay, cardboard, wire, and blocks, and then should proceed to more advanced media requiring more technical control, such as carving and firing clay, in the later years. At a Glance 12.17 introduces the vocabulary of sculpture.

Nonhardening clays. Clay and children just naturally go together. Many students by the time they have entered elementary school have used play dough of various kinds and are ready for a material that allows more definition of form. Nonhardening clay compounds answer this need.

Nonhardening modeling clay provides an excellent medium for primary students or novices of any level to make the transition into the more traditional firing clays of the artist. Using modeling clay, students face many of the same design decisions and learn many basic skills they will need later when using firing clay. Using modeling clay, students can learn to make a ball, roll out coils, and attach two pieces without a seam. Unlike firing clay, however, nonhardening modeling clay can be safely used in the classroom.

Consider giving each student his or her own personal piece of modeling clay, stored in a plastic bag in desk or clay center, to be used as needed for exploration or when planning ideas. This means students will have many more opportunities to sculpt and design in three dimensions than if they are limited solely to firing clays that must be used outdoors or in a specialized clay workshop. At a Glance 12.18 shows various techniques for working with both modeling and firing clay.

- *First explorations.* Show children how to break their clay into pieces and knead it to warm and soften it. Start by letting students explore the possibilities of the clay without providing models. After the exploration have children share some of their

At a Glance 12.17

Words of the Sculptor

Additive sculpture: Sculpture in which parts are added on in order to create dimension

Bas-relief: An artwork in which three-dimensional forms rise up slightly from a flat surface

Carving: Removal of material in order to create dimension

Construction: An artwork that is built from component parts often using industrial materials

Mobile: A delicately balanced arrangement of objects suspended in air

Modeling: Creating three-dimensional forms from a malleable material that can be pushed, pulled, or patted into place

Stabile: A term coined by Alexander Calder to refer to abstract sculptures formed of flat elements arranged dimensionally and attached to a fixed base

Subtractive sculpture: Sculpture in which parts are removed or carved away to create dimension

Three-dimensional: Anything having height, width, and depth

discoveries. Ask them to demonstrate how they made the clay into different shapes. Make a class chart or big book of their ideas. If possible, take photographs of the children with their first creations for them to look back on later after they have mastered more skills.

- *Developing skills.* As children continue to work on their own with their clay at the modeling center or art workshop time, comment on the forms they make. Describe how they moved their hands and attached pieces together. If necessary, demonstrate ways to roll a coil or attach two pieces together without a joint showing.
- *Developing concepts.* Encourage them to turn their work around and view it from all angles. Have students compare their sculptures to forms found in the environment and in other artworks. Introduce words that describe dimension, such as *height, width, depth,* as well as the names of the three-dimensional geometric forms.
- *Developing responsiveness.* Provide many opportunities for students to use their clay. For example, use it to create figures for dioramas or to re-enact stories read in class. Use it to build scientific models such as of an insect or a flower. Set up a small rotating area where completed works can be displayed for a day or two. Older students can write a brief description to accompany the piece and make sketches of it in their journals. Younger students can provide an oral description of it.

At a Glance 12.18

Clay Techniques

The following methods can be used with both modeling and firing clay:

Pinch Pots

Many young children enjoy making "nests" out of clay. The idea of making a container to hold something is a powerful one. For this reason pinch pots are a good introduction to pottery techniques. Making a pinch pot teaches students how to control the pressure of their fingers to create an even thickness of clay.

- Start with a ball of clay. Tap it lightly on the table to make a flattened base.
- Insert thumb into center of ball.
- Place remaining fingers on outside of ball and gently press walls of pot between fingers and thumb until the wall is an even thickness all the way around.
- In the beginning emphasize obtaining as even a thickness as possible rather than being concerned about the resulting shape of the pot.
- As students develop skill, they can explore combining several pinch pots together, making lids and handles, adding decorative incising and impressed textures.

Functional design questions to ask:

Are the sides even in thickness?
Is the top edge smooth and free from cracks?
Does the piece sit well on its base or does it roll or tip?
Are added-on pieces, such as handles, securely attached with no joints showing?
Are handles and knobs sturdy enough to support the weight of the finished piece?

Slab Structures

Flat pieces of clay can be used to build square and rectangular containers and forms.

- Flatten a ball of clay with the palms and then use a rolling pin to roll out an even thickness of clay about half a centimeter thick.
- Cut out the bottom and sides of the container. (*Note:* It is helpful for students to make a paper or tagboard actual-sized model first. They can then use the paper pieces as a guide to trace around.)
- Join edges together so no joints show.
- Clay slabs can also be used to make tiles that can be decorated with a slightly raised picture made of clay or stamped with textures. Firing clay makes beautiful-sounding wind chimes if the clay slabs are not too thick and are fired in a kiln.

Functional design questions to ask:

Are the slabs securely attached, with no joints showing?
Are the slabs even in thickness?
Are the edges smooth and without cracks?
Is the piece stable?

Coiling

Coiling is an advanced pottery technique most suitable for students who have demonstrated they can join pieces of clay together securely.

- Trace around a circular lid to create a base.

- Roll clay between palms to create long coils about the thickness of the thumb. If it is easier for the students, they may also be rolled on a covered table top.
- Attach coil to base (use water to dampen firing clay) and spiral around. Smooth joint on the inside so there are no cracks or gaps. The outside can be smoothed or left with the coils showing.
- Continue building on by adding more coils, smoothing the inside each time. Coils placed on the inside edge of the previous coil make the pot go in. Coils placed on the outer edge make it flare out.
- Try using other shapes for the base. What happens when using a square or triangle? Or combine coiling with a pinch pot or slab structure.

Functional design questions to ask:
Is the inside smooth without cracks, spaces, or holes?
Are the coils lined up so that they make a transition smoothly into curves?
Is the top rim smooth and free of cracks?
Does the piece sit securely on its base?

Firing clay. Creating something that will last beyond one's lifetime is an empowering act. Firing clay provides just such an opportunity for students and is well worth all the extra preparation that is required to use it safely.

Firing clay is a special kind of earth that is formed by the decomposition of rocks through weathering. It consists of extremely fine particles that have collected together, usually by being carried by water and deposited where the water slows down. For this reason clay deposits are usually found on the sides of slow-moving creeks and rivers.

Clay is found everywhere, but impurities that are picked up in the course of its travels make each local clay unique. An excellent introduction to clay work is to take students on a trip to a clay deposit for the purpose of collecting and preparing samples of local clays. Such a trip ties in well with studies of earth science and erosion. In addition, because clay has been used by people the world over, clay work can also be related to the marvelous pottery of the past and present. Studies of the clay work of the Neolithic period, Mesopotamia, Egypt, Greece, the civilizations of the Aztecs, Incas, and Chinese, as well as the art of the Native American people, all take on more meaning when students have experienced clay themselves.

Although exploring and experimenting with local clays is always an exciting learning experience, it is often wiser to purchase premixed moist clay for beginning potters to use. The uniform consistency of prepared clay makes it easier for them to control it. Commercially available clay comes in a variety of colors and textures and children can try the different kinds and even combine them in interesting ways. Because clay is a complex medium to work in, requiring specialized

Clay Horse.
Modeling clay—Stephanie, grade 5.

Thinking about Children's Art

Working in three-dimensions challenges students to think about design in different ways. What design problems did this student have to solve in order to create this self-supporting sculpture of a rearing horse?

equipment, teachers thinking of using firing clay with their class should consider taking a pottery course as well as consult the references at the end of this chapter. At a Glance 12.19 provides a vocabulary for firing clay.

Constructions. Being able to create something substantial that occupies space and vision is an immensely important experience for young artists. Three-dimensional constructions provide this opportunity.

Constructed sculptures are three-dimensional artworks built from parts. These parts can be drawn from a wide variety of materials ranging from paper to metal and can be created in any size. Sometimes they are tiny enough to fit in the palm of the hand, or they can be large enough for students to crawl inside. As with clay, constructed sculptures provide students with tactile and spatial experiences that improve their understanding of how three-dimensional objects function in space.

The main consideration in selecting materials for constructed sculptures is the students' ability to join them together easily and securely. Trying to attach objects together in three-dimensional space is a challenge for all students. At a Glance 12.20 provides some suggested methods.

Construction materials. A multitude of materials can be used to create three-dimensional sculptures, either alone or in combination. Many are available free or are relatively inexpensive. Offer these to students on a regular basis, perhaps in a construction center that can be used whenever a student needs to design a model (see At a Glance 12.21). Construction activities integrate well with studies of homes, inventions, and simple machines. In science students can be challenged to build models of bridges that hold a specified weight, towers of a certain height, or houses that collect solar energy. They can bring to life architectural achievements of the past by incorporating elements into the design of original structures.

Books to Share

Clay

Bahti, M. (1997). *Pueblo stories and storytellers.* New York: Treasure Chest.
Baylor, B. (1987). *When clay sings.* New York: Atheneum.
Dixon, A. (1990). *Clay.* New York: Garrett.
Hawkinson, J. (1974). *A ball of clay.* Chicago: Alfred Whitman.
Hughes, L. (1994). *The sweet and sour animal book.* New York: Oxford.
James, B. (1994). *The mud family.* New York: Putnam.
McLerran, A. (1991). *Roxaboxen.* New York: Lothrop, Lee & Shepard.
Roussel, M. (1990). *Clay.* Vero Beach, FL: Rourke.
Winter, J. (1996). *Josephina.* Orlando, FL: Harcourt Brace.

At a Glance 12.19

A Vocabulary for Firing Clay

Firing clay: Fine, decomposed rock that is malleable when damp. For safety, use only clays that are certified talc-free. Clay that contains talc may also contain asbestos.

White earthenware: A smooth, gray clay that fires white.

Indian red: A reddish clay that fires brownish red.

Terra-cotta: A reddish clay with grog added to reduce shrinkage.

Glaze: Finely ground minerals that are applied to clay and then fired to a glassy surface coating in the kiln. For safety's sake use only lead-free liquid glaze.

Kiln: A furnace made of firebrick for heating clay pieces to temperatures of 1000° Fahrenheit or more.

Modeling tools: Any object that can be used to cut, mold, or shape the clay. Objects can be as simple as craft sticks and plastic knives. Also on the market are plastic, wood, and wire-tipped tools.

Slip: A thick, semi-liquid mixture of clay and water used to join to two pieces of clay together.

At a Glance 12.20

Fasteners for Constructions

Craft glue: Water-based white craft glues offer a faster drying time at a higher cost. For certain materials, such as irregular natural objects, using a craft glue can lessen a student's frustration while working. It does not, however, hold objects much more securely than the less expensive white glues.

Fasteners: A variety of fasteners exist, the most popular being the paper fastener, which allows movement as well as a stable bond. Other fastening methods include chenille stems and wire, which can be used to create strong joints and hinges.

Staples: Students love to staple things together. Stapling forms a quick, secure bond in relatively thin materials such as paper and cardboard. Handgrip-style staplers, rather than desk staplers, function better for sculptural work; they are lighter and can reach into narrow forms. Stapling requires a certain measure of hand strength, and students need to be instructed in how to use staplers safely.

Tape: The first fastener students usually reach for is cellophane or masking tape. It is also the least aesthetic and effective of all the joining methods. Students need to be taught that tape is a temporary adhesive to be used when trying out an idea that might be changed or to hold work together in conjunction with slow-drying glues.

White glue: In most instances white glue is the adhesive of choice. It is both inexpensive and safe for students to use, and it is available in washable formulas. Unfortunately it is also slow in drying, and primary students in particular are often easily frustrated when they cannot attach things together as quickly as they would like. It is essential to show students how to use masking tape to hold objects in place while glue is drying.

At a Glance 12.21

Materials for Constructed Sculptures

Cardboard: Chipboard, corrugated cardboard, mat board, illustration board, tagboards, cereal boxes, cartons, paper towel tubes

Chenille stems

Craft sticks

Paper

Styrofoam: Sanitized trays, egg cartons, plates, cups, packing beads, and sheets used for insulation

Toothpicks

Wood

Connections: Clay and Constructions

Creating sculptures to express learning in other curriculum areas allows students to bring their spatial and bodily-kinesthetic domains into play in a way not possible through two-dimensional graphic symbols. There is a reality to making a model of a pyramid that transcends a written description or drawing. Three-dimensional media should be a major part of a student's studies as in the examples that follow:

Language arts

- To help develop richer descriptions of characters and setting in student writing assignments have them create three-dimensional clay models of the whole figure or character's face or build a model of the setting and have the clay figures act in it.
- Make word pots designed to hold a particular word, such as a "surprise" pot or a "smile" pot. What shape would it be? Then write a poem inspired by the piece.
- Write a play and then construct hand puppets using firing clay or modeling clay for the heads, or create wooden marionettes.

Math

- At the primary level students can use small clay sculptures to practice computation. For example, have students make small balls or other shapes from two different colors of nonhardening clay. Have them join several from each color together to make a sculpture. Then have them write the algorithm represented in the final sculpture, such as $-3 + 4 = 7$.
- Bring word problems to life through the creation of nonhardening clay sculptures that represent the items in the problem.

Teacher Tip

Using Clay Safely

Firing clay deposits a fine dust on hands, tools, and work surfaces. This dust can cause a variety of problems if not controlled.

The Workspace

Clay is dirt from the ground. It can contain molds and other contaminants. Do not use clay in an area that is also used for eating or other general uses, such as a classroom. Firing clay is best used in a room set up exclusively for art activities or best of all—outdoors.

Working Guidelines

Strictly enforce safe working guidelines. Clay dust easily becomes airborne and inhaled, causing respiratory problems, especially for those with allergies or asthma.

- All students need to learn to keep their hands away from their faces while working and to dampen them often with a small amount of water.
- Do not allow students to clap or rub their hands together, raising dust.
- Make sure students keep their clay on newspaper or another removable work surface covering.
- Students with allergies may need to use other modeling compounds that do not create dust and to work in a different location.

Clean Up

- After students are finished working, gently fold and throw away any newspaper used to cover work areas so that a minimum of dust is spread.
- Wipe all surfaces regularly after clay use.
- Wash all tools and anything else that came in contact with the clay.
- Damp mop the floor.

- Clay also provides an excellent tool not only for teaching the different geometric forms but also for assessing student understanding. Asking students to make a cone of clay requires them to have a good understanding of a cone's basic characteristics.
- Build three-dimensional models of geometric forms and calculate the volume of each. Then join them into a sculpture and calculate the total volume.
- Calculate the perimeter and area of model buildings.
- Construct scale models from originally designed plans.

Science

- Measure the strength of bridges and towers built from different materials and using different geometric forms.
- Conduct experiments to determine which kind of adhesive works the best with which material.

- Conduct experiments to determine which modeling compounds are the most flexible, strong, durable, and so on.
- Look for structural elements in nature, such as shells, plant, and beehives, as inspiration for sculptures.

Social studies

- Study the sculptures of ancient and modern cultures. Discuss how the design of the work reflects the available materials, cultural beliefs, and social needs.
- Compare pottery techniques from several different cultures. Which ones are similar? Which ones are unique?
- Study the use of sculpture as monuments for important historical and social events.

Dance

- Study a sculpture or building and then try to express its form through movement and body position.
- Create a dance that reflects how a clay pot or sculpture is formed.

Dramatics

- Dramatize the life of a famous sculptor or potter.
- Create skits that show the construction of a house.

Music

- Match musical pieces with sculptural forms and structures.
- Construct sculptures that create musical sounds or design musical instruments.

The Fiber Arts

There is nothing so functional as making a piece of cloth. Since earliest times people have created cloth to provide warmth and comfort for the body and the home. Introducing students to the process of designing cloth helps them appreciate the relationship between design and function. This is particularly true if the fiber art activity is closely related to work being done in other areas of the curriculum. For example, at the primary level fiber activities can form part of a thematic unit such as "Living with the Weather" or a project-approach topic centered on clothing. At the upper levels fiber activities can be related to science studies such as in weaving cotton and linen and exploring natural plant dyes to accompany a study of plants, in processing wool to accompany a study of mammals, and in relating silk processing to the study of butterflies and moths. Or fiber processing can be related to the study of peoples and cultures in which fiber art has played major

Books to Share

Architecture

D'Alelio, J. (1989). *I know that building.* Washington, DC: Preservation Press.
Glenn, P. B. (1993). *Under every roof.* Washington, DC: Preservation Press.
Malone, M. (1995). *Maya Lin: Architect and artist.* Berkely Heights, NJ: Enslow.
Munro, R. (1986). *Architects make zigzags.* Washington, DC: Preservation Press.
Nicholson, J. (1994). *Homemade houses: Traditional homes from many lands.* Sydney, Australia: Allen & Unwin.
Robbins, K. (1984). *Building a house.* New York: Four Winds.
Wilson, F. (1988). *What it feels like to be a building.* Washington, DC: Preservation Press.

roles, such as in Guatemala, Iran, or among the Navajo. Fiber processing can also relate to studies of lives in the past such as colonial period studies. Comparing how people around the world have designed very different-looking fabrics for similar purposes is an ideal way for students to discover the creative aspects of design.

Fiber awareness. Begin any study of fiber art with activities that develop students' awareness of the role fabric plays in their lives.

- *Fiber and function.* Inventory and graph the different fabrics and their uses in their homes and/or in their clothing. Research and collect samples of different fibers and fabrics and create wall charts to display in the classroom.
- *Explore fiber scientifically.* Set up a fiber center where students can examine and test different fibers using magnifying lenses, microscopes, scales, water, and so on. Explore questions such as, Which fibers break easily? Which stretch? Is there a difference if they are wet or dry?
- *Process fibers.* How do fibers get turned into cloth? Explore fiber processing by inviting a spinner to visit the class, visiting a sheep farm, if possible, and/or having the students create their own yarn. Wool is the easiest fiber to process by hand. Explore washing it, picking out the dirt particles, carding it with hand cards or a dog brush. Unwinding silkworm cocoons is another exciting way to explore raw fiber.

Spin it. Watching wool turn into yarn seems miraculous. Spinning requires just the fingers or a simple spindle. Before beginning explore commercial yarn, untwisting it to see how it is made. If possible, have a spinner demonstrate for the class. Then introduce the students to spinning. Spinning makes a wonderful cooperative activity for children of all

Teaching in Action

Washing Wool

If possible, obtain a raw fleece from a sheep farmer or from a weaving supplier.

1. Fill three dishpans half full of warm water.*
2. Add one-quarter cup detergent to the first two pans.
3. Add a capful of water softener to the last pan.
4. Place the pans in a row on a table or low counter.
5. Have each student take a handful of fleece and move from pan to pan down the row, immersing the wool in each pan in turn.
6. In the first two pans pull the wool apart and move gently in the water to release the dirt.
7. Rinse the wool in the last pan.
8. Place it near a heater or in the sun to dry.
9. When dry, fluff lightly by pulling the fibers apart. Use the clean wool in a collage or for dyeing and spinning.

* For large classes set up several sets of pans to speed the process.

ages or even parent–child pairs such as at a workshop. Because spinning involves using each hand in a different way, beginners are often more successful if they divide the separate hand motions between two people. They can also help each other remember the movement pattern.

Dyeing fibers and yarn. Students often have no idea how yarn and fabric obtain their colors. While many dyeing activities are not safe for children, the following methods are easily and safely accomplished using a Crock-Pot or slow cooker and allow children to experience the wonder of color change. Dyeing also provides many opportunities for children to apply measuring and timing skills. Make up charts and graphs showing what happens during the dyeing process.

(*Note:* In any dyeing activity no matter how safe the materials being used, always model safety practices. For example, wear rubber gloves and a protective apron when handling the hot dyestuffs.)

- *Drink mix dyeing.* Many packaged dry drink mixes contain acid-based dyes, which can be used to brilliantly color washed wool, silk, and wool and silk yarns. To dye: Either stir one kind of mix into a Crock-Pot half full of hot water, add yarn or fiber, and then simmer until the depth of color desired is obtained, or for a multicolor effect place the fiber or yarn in the water first, sprinkle several different flavors on top in different locations, and simmer until color depth is obtained. Then rinse in fresh water. The various colored fibers dyed in this way are often very exciting to spin into yarn or to use in collages.

Teaching in Action

Spinning Wool

The Spindle

Make a spindle from a twelve-inch length of a quarter-inch-diameter dowel. Screw a cup hook into one end. Stick a potato or apple (a traditional practice) or nonhardening modeling clay on the other end as a weight.

To Attach Wool to Spindle

1. Stretch: Stretch out carded wool so that it is very long and skinny.
2. Twist: Demonstrate how to twist wool into yarn with the fingers.
3. Wrap: Attach the twisted end to the spindle by wrapping it several times around the hook.

To Spin Yarn

1. Pinch. With thumb and index finger pinch the wool about one inch above the hook.
2. Spin. With other hand give the spindle a spin while bottom rests on the table. It should turn about five turns.
3. Stop. Stop the spindle and hold it still.
4. Slide and pinch. The fingers of the other hand slide up the wool another inch. Pinch the wool again and then repeat the above steps.

Hint

This process is an excellent way to teach cooperation. Assign two students to work together as partners. One student is the spinner, the other the pincher. The spinner does Steps 1 and 4. The pincher does Steps 2 and 3. It usually takes five to ten minutes for the pair to learn the pattern. It helps if as the children work, they chant "Pinch, spin, stop, slide."

To Lengthen the Yarn

When the piece of spun yarn is too long to hold comfortably, untwist the end from the spindle hook and wind the yarn on to the spindle. Rewrap the new end to the hook and add on a new piece of stretched-out carded wool by pinching the raw wool and the yarn end between thumb and index finger and spinning the spindle.

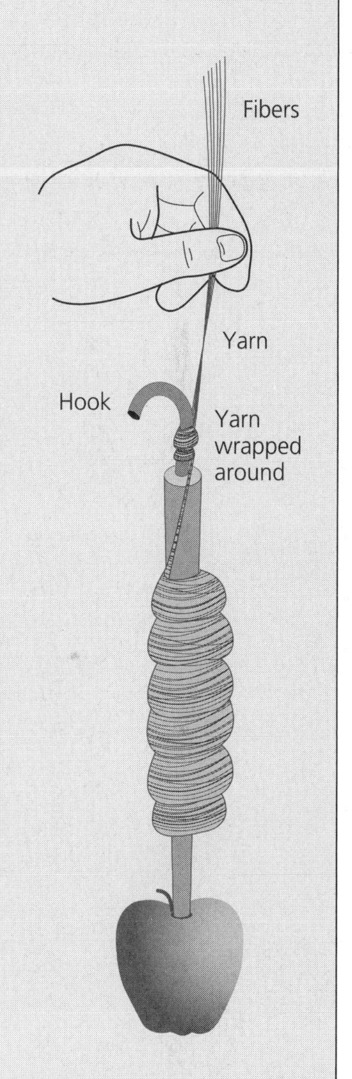

- *Natural dyeing.* One of the most important uses of plants in the past was as a source of fabric dye. Natural dyeing just naturally fits into any study of plants and their uses. At a Glance 12.22 suggests safe sources of natural dyes. To dye: Place a quantity of the plant material in a Crock-Pot half full of water. Simmer until the water takes on a deep color. Strain out the dyestuff and place the fiber or yarn

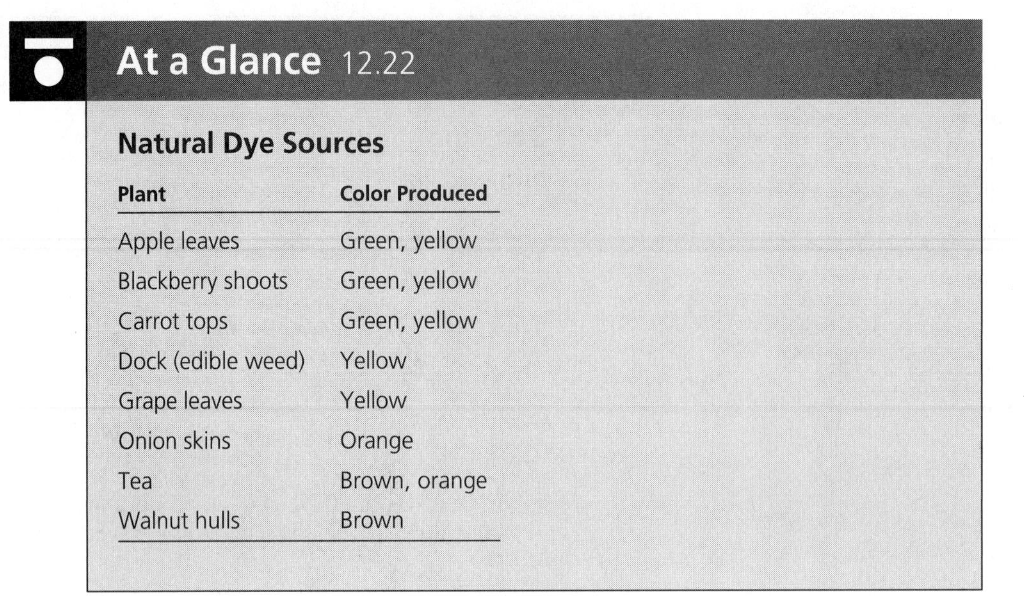

At a Glance 12.22

Natural Dye Sources

Plant	Color Produced
Apple leaves	Green, yellow
Blackberry shoots	Green, yellow
Carrot tops	Green, yellow
Dock (edible weed)	Yellow
Grape leaves	Yellow
Onion skins	Orange
Tea	Brown, orange
Walnut hulls	Brown

in the pot. Simmer until desired color is reached. Then rinse in fresh water. Natural dyes work on fibers of all kinds. The addition of alum to the dye pot will make the color slightly stronger or a different tone. Explore using different amounts and kinds of dyestuff. Does it make a difference if the plants are fresh or dry? What happens if the plant material is left in the pot with the fiber or yarn? Natural dyes are not colorfast. Explore what happens when dye materials are placed in the sun over a period of time.

Books to Share

Fiber

Blood, C. L., & Link, M. (1980). *The goat in the rug.* New York: Four Winds.
A personable goat explains how her mohair is converted into a blanket.

dePaolo, T. (1973). *Charlie needs a cloak.* Englewood Cliff, NJ: Prentice Hall.
Frolicking sheep explain how wool is converted into cloth.

Hong, L. T. (1995). *The empress and the silkworm.* Morton Grove, IL: Albert Whitman.
This book retells the tale of how silk was discovered.

Parenteau, S. (1978). *Blue hands, blue cloth.* Chicago: Children's Press.
The story of an indigo dyer in Africa.

Williams, S. A. (1992). *Working cotton.* Orlando, FL: Harcourt Brace.
This book presents the daily life of a migrant family who picks cotton in California.

Ziefert, H. (1986). *A new coat for Anna.* New York: Knopf.
During World War II a mother trades a watch for wool and with the cooperation of many others makes a coat from scratch.

Designing yarn. All yarn is not the same even when made from the same fiber. Have students work in cooperative groups using a Venn diagram to compare and contrast a sampling of different yarns in terms of thickness, flexibility, and ply (the number of individual yarns that are twisted together to form one thicker yarn). Decide which yarns would be useful for making different types of fabrics. Which would make a good rug, baby jacket, or socks?

The tactile and visual qualities of a fabric result from how the yarns are designed. At a center or working in pairs have students design unique yarns by twisting together short lengths of yarn in a combination of different colors, thicknesses, and textures. These short designer yarns can later be used in weaving activities, as described later in this section.

Weaving. Weaving is based on a series of repeated motions, which students of all levels can learn.

- *Learning the technique.* In the primary grades students can be taught the in-and-out motions of weaving by weaving together paper strips. Next they can transfer this skill to thick yarn stretched on a notched piece of cardboard (see At a Glance 12.23). They can also explore weaving on simple table looms and rigid heddle looms.
- *Exploring weaves and patterns.* Upper graders can use cardboard looms to explore different weaves and patterns, such as twill and plaid, and to learn various tapestry techniques. They also can apply what they know about simple machines in analyzing the mechanisms of a four-harness table or floor loom.
- *Weaving and computers.* Although a unit on weaving fits very well with the study of colonial life or Native American cultures, the relationship between the ancient technology of weaving and computers is surprisingly close. An interesting study is to investigate how Jacquard looms work. These early predecessors of the computer operate using a punched card system. Have students work in a team to come up with a ten- to twenty-card design. On each card the students should indicate which yarns are lifted and which are not. Then, using a cardboard or frame loom, have the team try to weave their pattern with some team members individually lifting the indicated yarns and others passing through the shuttle, beating the yarn in place and moving the cloth forward. There are also computer programs that can be used to design weaving patterns. Try to arrange an opportunity for students to see a professional weaver use a computer-linked handloom.

Stitchery. Decorative embroidery and stitchery is found worldwide. It is a way to draw with thread and yarn that expands the potential for pictorial design using fabric. It is often found on ethnic costumes and

At a Glance 12.23

Basic Weaving Methods

The following provides a very brief overview of weaving techniques that can be effectively taught in the classroom. For more detailed instructions consult the books recommended at the end of this chapter.

Paper weaving. Give each student a full sheet of construction paper and several precut strips of paper. Show them how to fold the paper in half and starting on the folded edge cut a series of slits going toward the open edge but stopping at least an inch from the actual edge. This is a good time to have students apply measuring skills by drawing a "warning line" one inch from the open edge.

Primary students should be given inch-wide strips and shown the weaving pattern and taught to say "over-under" or "up-down" as they work. This is called plain weave. Compare this pattern to other on-off/up-down patterns such as light switches and raising one's hands in class. Find examples of woven cloth that the children are wearing.

Upper graders who have had weaving experiences can use thinner strips and try more complex weaves. For an interesting effect try weaving patterned wallpapers or magazine pictures.

Stripes, plaids, and other special effects. Stripes can be created by changing the color of yarn after weaving several rows. Plaids are created by winding on alternating colors during warping the loom. Have students explore the different effects they can create simply by varying color before trying more complex weaves. They can make interesting checked patterns by weaving alternating rows of two different colors. Washed, dyed unspun wool can be inlaid to create interesting textures. Knotted pile inlays can be created using rug-making techniques, as described further on in this section.

Knotted rugs. Persian carpets are created from rows of knots held in place by plain weave inserted at intervals. After several rows of knots are made, the resulting pile is trimmed to the desired height. The process is quite time-consuming, so have students explore making miniature rugs on 6″ × 9″ cardboard looms, or have a cooperative team work together on a larger one.

Rag rugs. Using old clothes for rugs and quilts is an early American tradition that ties in well with teaching about recycling. Have students bring in cloth scraps and cut them into skinny strips. Weave them together on a cotton, wool, or synthetic warp, using a cardboard or more complex loom. Have students consider how the patterns and colors of the fabric enrich the design of the cloth.

Tapestry. Weaving shapes and pictures is a more complex technique but one that is very satisfying for many upper level students. Many people have woven tapestries as a way to record events and cultural images. Before beginning study tapestries from across cultures, such as those of the Incas and the Middle Ages, to see how a woven picture differs from a drawn and painted one. A separate shuttle or bobbin is needed for each color used in one row. The interlock technique and the slit method are shown here.

Teacher Tip

Making a Cardboard Loom

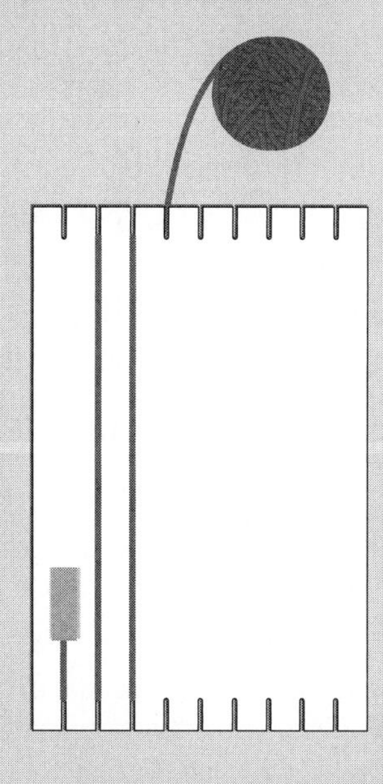

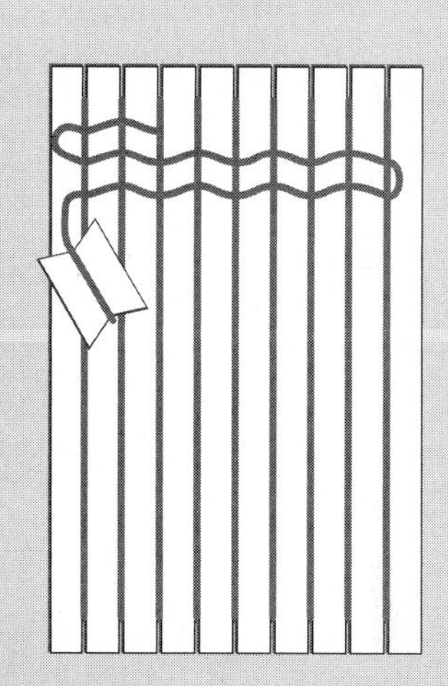

1. Use rectangular pieces of chipboard or corrugated cardboard either 6″ × 9″ or 9″ × 12″ in size.
2. Cut notches either one-half inch (primary) or one-quarter inch (upper) apart on the two short ends of the rectangle. Again have students use a ruler and apply their measuring skills.
3. Hook the end of a ball or cone of yarn into the first notch on one end and tape in place.
4. Wind yarn around loom, hooking it in opposing notches each time. Pull taut but not so hard that the cardboard bends. When the other end is reached, cut and tape down the end. (This is called warping the loom.)
5. Using a cardboard shuttle, weave in and out of the stretched yarns (warp).
6. To end a color or to start a new shuttle, take the end and weave it back into the row.
7. To remove finished weaving from the loom, cut across the back creating a long fringe and then tie groups of fringe together at the edge of the weaving using overhand knots to keep the weaving from unraveling.

home furnishings. Compare, for example, how different cultures have used embroidery to decorate traditional dress.

Students can be taught several simple stitches using large needles, yarn, and burlap as a background. It helps if they draw their picture in chalk before beginning.

Appliqué. Appliqué is the creation of visual images using cloth and stitchery techniques. Sometimes holes are cut in the cloth so that

Teaching in Action

The Human Loom

The following activity makes a wonderful and exciting cooperative team activity at the same time that it teaches the basics of weaving. It also works well with mixed age groups such as at parent–child workshops. Those who have participated in this activity usually have little difficulty understanding how a loom works.

1. Divide students into teams of four or more.
2. Have students decide who will be the shuttle. This is the person who will pass the yarn through the weaving. Next select the caller, who will call out which yarns to lift. The rest will be weavers in charge of lifting the yarns. (*Note:* They may rotate these jobs at set intervals.)
3. Give each team's weaver two lengths of yarn at least six feet long. Tie the team's yarn together at one end using an overhand knot.
4. Have the caller hold tight to the knotted end and direct the weavers to take their yarn ends in each hand and pull taut.
5. The "shuttle" operator holds a full stick shuttle of yarn.
6. At the agreed signal from the caller the weavers lift their right hands and lower their left hands and the shuttle passes the yarn through the resulting space (shed). Then the caller signals them to reverse the position of the hands, and the shuttle is passed back.
7. Continue with the alternate lifting and lowering of the hands until the shuttle can go no further. Knot weavers' ends together and compare the weavings accomplished by each team. Ask, "Are they all the same? If not, what factors might have affected the way it was woven?"

colors from underneath show through, such as in the *molas* created by the Kuna people of San Blas, Panama. For young children colorful felt is easy to cut and provides an ideal material for early appliqué works in which the pieces are glued together. It also makes an ideal material for older students who are including simple stitchery as well.

Quilting. Quilting is an ancient practice that allows students to work together to make a whole from their unique parts. Emphasize the co-operative nature of the process on the final form of the quilt by having them sit in a circle and each in turn place his or her piece on the floor in a possible location. Use this as an opportunity to discuss the role of variety, emphasis, and rhythm in making the quilt work as a unit. Third graders and up can learn to use a sewing machine and sew the quilt together or enlist the aid of parents in the process. To carry the idea of working together to accomplish a goal even further consider donating the quilt to one of the many organizations that help children in need.

Ideas for quilts include the following:

Mola. Kuna people of San Blas Islands, Panama. Collection of the author.

From the Museum

Because most fiber art is made to serve a functional purpose, it provides an ideal context in which to ask aesthetic questions. For example, this appliqué piece, originally made to be part of a Kuna woman's traditional blouse, can be studied on many different levels. Who made it and why? Can we describe the way art elements are arranged into a composition? How does its design represent the culture of the Kuna artist who believes that all things, including the mola she makes, contain a spirit? How does this piece of cloth function in a garment? Should it have been separated from the blouse and its matching back panel for sale to tourists? Is it a piece of art?

- *The family quilt.* Have each student bring from home a piece of cloth about nine inches square that comes from a piece of old clothing. Have the students write about the cloth and what it means to them. A good story to read in conjunction with this activity is *The Patchwork Quilt* by V. Flournoy (see the following Books to Share).
- *The crayon quilt.* Using regular crayons and white muslin squares, have students create a quilt square that illustrates a topic or an idea being studied, such as the ABCs, math problems, animals in their habitat, ways to save water, the constellations, and so on. The possibilities are limitless. Remind students to leave a seam allowance around the edge where they do not write or draw. When they are done, iron the squares to make them permanent.
- *The appliqué quilt.* Apply iron-on adhesive backing to cloth. Have children use this to cut out the parts of their picture and then arrange them on a muslin backing. Iron the pieces down and sew into a quilt.

Books to Share

Weaving

Ahiagble, G., & Meyer, L. (1998). *Master weaver from Ghana.* Seattle, WA: Open Hand.
Story of how the weaving of *kente* cloth ties together a community.

Allen, C. (1991). *The rug makers.* Austin, TX: Steck-Vaughn.
In this photo essay a young boy from India explains how Oriental carpets are made in his village.

Angelou, M. (1996). *Kafi and his magic.* New York: Crown.
The story of *kente* cloth.

Castaneda, O. S. (1993). *Abuela's weave.* New York: Lee & Low.
A Guatemalan girl and her grandmother grow closer as they weave cloth to take to market.

Heyer, M. (1986). *Weaving of a dream.* New York: Puffin.
A Chinese folktale about a brocade weaver whose tapestry is stolen.

Miles, M. (1979). *Annie and the old one.* New York: Little, Brown.
A Navajo girl learns how to weave.

Mitchell, R. (1997). *The talking cloth.* New York: Orchard.
The story of the *adrinka* cloth of the Ashanti of Ghana.

Roussel, M. (1995). *Songs from the loom.* Minneapolis, MN: Lerner.
A photo essay shares the Navajo weaving tradition as a young girl learns from her mother.

Solo, M. (1997). *Angela weaves a dream: A story of a young Maya artist.* New York: Hyperion.
A photo essay describes the technical, social, and religious context in which a young Maya girl weaves.

Tuyet, T. (1987). *The little weaver of Thai-yen village.* Emeryville, CA: Children's Book Press.
A Vietnamese girl maintains her ethnic identify as she adjusts to life in the United States.

Conclusion

THE DESIGNING TEACHER

But the artist is born to pick, and choose, and group with science, these elements, that the result may be beautiful—as the musician gathers his notes, forms his chords, until he brings forth from chaos glorious harmony.
James McNeill Whistler (1945)

All of us live in a constantly changing stream of visual forms, shapes, and images that affect what we do and how we live. Educators who appreciate the intricacies of design can give their students the tools they need to become more responsive to this visual wonderland and can empower them to modify and change their environment to best meet their own personal needs and values.

We begin by awakening our students to the art elements that make up the visual images in our environment. We make our students aware of the process of design by making them sensitive to the relationships

Books to Share

Quilting, Appliqué, Stitchery

Cha, D. (1998). *Dia's story cloth.* New York: Lee & Low.
Laotian refugees tell of their emigration from Laos through a traditional story cloth.

Coerr, E. (1986). *The Josephina story quilt.* New York: Harper Trophy.
A young girl makes a quilt about her journey west.

Duvall, J. D. (1997). *Ms. Moja makes beautiful clothes.* Emeryville, CA: Children's Book Press.
An African-American woman makes wearable art for actors, performers, and costumers in museums.

Flournoy, V. (1985). *The patchwork quilt.* New York: Dutton.
An African-American family is bound together in completing the quilt started by an ailing grandmother.

Heal, G. (1997). *Grandpa bear's fantastic scarf.* New York: Beyond Words.
Grandpa bear knits a wonderful scarf.

Howard, E. (1997). *The log cabin quilt.* New York: Holiday House.
Pioneer family chinks the cabin walls with precious cloth scraps.

Johnson, T. & dePaola, T. (1985). *The quilt story.* New York: Putnam.
A treasured quilt comforts two little girls from different times.

Kurtz, S. (1991). *The boy and the quilt.* Intercourse, PA: Good Books.
A little boy learns to make a quilt.

Kusken, K. (1994). *The patchwork island.* New York: HarperCollins.
A mother makes an "island" quilt for her son.

Mills, L. (1991). *The rag coat.* New York: Scholastic.
Struggling in poverty, a mother makes her daughter a patchwork quilt coat to keep her warm.

Paul, A. W. (1991). *Eight hands round: A patchwork alphabet.* New York: HarperCollins.
A delightful history of traditional quilt designs.

Polacco, P. (19988). *The keeping quilt.* New York: Simon & Schuster.
A quilt links generations of a Jewish family together.

Presilla, M., & Soto, G. (1996). *Life around the lake.* New York: Henry Holt.
Tarascan women record their village's history in embroideries.

Ringgold, F. (1991). *Tar beach.* New York: Random House.
An autobiographical story of growing up incorporates many African-American traditions.

Shea, P. S. (1996*). The whispering cloth: A refugee's story.* Honesdale, PA: Boyd's Mill.

Willard, N. (1997). *Mountains of quilt.* Orlando, FL: Harcourt Brace.
A piece of quilt becomes a magic carpet.

Xiong, B. (1989). *Nine-in-one Grr! Grr!* Emeryville, CA: Children's Book Press.
A Hmong folktale is illustrated with pictures based on Hmong story cloths.

between form and function. When we teach writing, we call students' attention to the form of their pieces. Does it have a beginning, middle, and end? Does each paragraph have a topic sentence and do all the sentences relate to that topic? Does the entire piece hold together as a unit with purposeful focus? In the same way students need to analyze the composition of artworks they see and create.

The end result of this increased sensitivity is the opening of our eyes to the richness and diversity of design in both nature and in art across time and culture. It empowers us to choose in a meaningful way the objects that surround us.

Teacher Resources

REFERENCES

Edwards, B. (1979). *Drawing on the right side of the brain.* Los Angeles: Tarcher.

Hoffman, D. (1998). *Visual intelligence: How we create what we see.* New York: Norton.

Matisse, H. (1945). Notes of a painter. In R. Goldwater & M. Treves (Eds.), *Artists on art* (pp. 409–413). New York: Pantheon. (Original work published 1908.)

McFee, J. J., & Degge, R. M. (1977). *Art, culture and environment.* Dubuque, IA: Kendall/Hunt.

Whistler, J. A. M. (1945). The ten o'clock. In R. Goldwater & M. Treves (Eds.), *Artists on art* (pp. 349–350). New York: Pantheon. (Original work published 1885.)

To Learn More about Design

The following books discuss design in much more depth or provide information on a specific area of design. Consult these when planning design activities.

Blosfeldt, K. (1986). *Art forms in the plant world.* New York: Dover.

Brommer, G. (1985). *Art in your world.* Worcester, MA: Davis.

Gatto, J. A., Porter, A. W., & Selleck, J. (1986). *Exploring visual design.* Worcester, MA: Davis.

Gordon, L. (1996). *The ABC of design.* San Francisco, CA: Chronicle Books.

Haechel, E. (1998). *Art forms in nature.* New York: International Book Import Service.

Itten, J. (1970). *The elements of color.* New York: Van Nostrand Reinhold.

To Relate Art, Music, and Movement

Britsch, B. M., & Dennison-Fansey, A. (1995). *One voice: Music and stories in the classroom.* Englewood, CO: Teacher Idea Press.

Herman, G. N., & Hollingsworth, P. (1992). *Kinetic kaleidoscope: Exploring movement and energy in the visual arts.* Tucson, AZ: Zephyr.

Page, N. (1995). *Music as a way of knowing.* York, ME: Stenhouse.

The following sets of posters provide an example of how each element and design principle is used in artworks:

Seven Elements of Design

Seven Principles of Design (both Art Chart Poster Series, Crystal)

To Learn More about Clay and Sculpture

Petersen, S. (1996). *The craft and art of clay.* New York: Prentice Hall.

Sapiro, M. (1983). *Hand building.* Worcester, MA: Davis.

Silberstein-Storfer, M. (1997). *Doing art together.* New York: Abrams.

Similansky, S. (1989). *Clay in the classroom.* New York: Teachers College Press.

Topal, C. W. (1998). *Children, clay and sculpture.* Worcester, MA: Davis.

To Learn More about Fiber Art

Appliqué and Stitchery

Beaney, J. & Littlejohn, J. (1997). *A complete guide to creative embroidery: Designs, textures, stitches.* London: B. T. Botsford.

Caraway. C. (1981). *The mola design book.* Owings Mills, MD: Stemmer House.
Chan, A. (1990). *Hmong textile designs.* Owings Mills, MD: Stemmer House.
Soltys, K. (1998). *Appliqué made easy.* New York: St. Martin's.

Quilting

Kiracafe, R. (1993). *The American quilt: A history of cloth and comfort 1750–1950.* New York: Clarkson Potter.
Lyons, M. E. (1993). *Stitching stars: The story quilts of Harriet Powers.* New York: Scribner.
Mazloomi, C. (1998). *Spirits of the cloth: Contemporary African American quilts.* New York: Clarkson Potter.
Saunders, D. (1991). *Amish quilt designs.* New York : Dover.

Spinning and Dyeing

Kroll, C. (1981). *The whole craft of spinning from the raw material to the finished yarn.* New York: Dover.
Svinick, E. (1974). *Step-by-step spinning and dyeing.* Racine, WI: Western.
Wigginton, E. (Ed.). (1973). *Foxfire 2.* New York: Doubleday.

Weaving

Alland, M. (1963). *Rugmaking.* New York: Chilton.
Brown, R. (1983). *The weaving, spinning and dyeing book.* New York: Knopf.
Held, S. E. (1998). *Weaving: A handbook of the fiber arts.* Orlando, FL: Harcourt Brace.

RESOURCES

Videos

Design

Art is . . . Video Series, Crystal

Elements of Design

Principles of Design

Bookmaking

Reading Rainbow Series, GPN Video

Simon's Book shows how the author wrote and drew the book and then visits the printing plant to see the book being made.

Sculpture

3 2 1 Contact Series, Crystal

Architecture

American Craft Museum Still Video Series, Crystal

Clay Figures, Animals and Landscapes

Clayworks

Functional Pottery

Arts-a-Bound Series, GPN Videos

Architecture

Sculptor

Forming and Constructing

Elementary Art Skills Series, Crystal

Modeling and Construction K–3 and 4–8

Maria (presents work of noted Pueblo potter Maria Martinez), Crismac

Potters of Oaxaca, Crystal

Public Sculpture: America's Legacy, Video and Learning Kit, Crystal

Reading Rainbow Series, GPN Videos

Galimoto. Visit with a wire sculptor.

The Wonderful Towers of Watts. Shares the sculptural work of an Italian immigrant.

Sculpture and the Creative Process, Crystal

Fiber

Reading Rainbow Series, GPN Videos

The Carousel. A quiltmaker explains how to make a quilt.

The Purple Coat. A visit to the Fashion Institute of Technology shows how garments are designed.

The Patchwork Quilt. Children at the Boston Museum make quilts.

Tar Beach. Based on Faith Ringgold's quilt.

Faith Ringgold: The Last Story Quilt, Crizmac

CD-ROMS

Wilton Art Appreciation Series, Crystal
Color
Elements of Art
How Artists See
Sculpture

Web Sites

These sites will link you to many others:

American Architectural Foundation
www.amerarchfoundation.com

Association of Clay and Glass Artists of California
www.acga.net

International Sculpture Center
www.sculpture.org

Minnesota Center for the Bookarts
www.mnbookarts.org

Quilt Channel
www.quiltchannel.com

Weaving Museum and Research center
www.weavingartmuseum.org

Chapter 13

Art and Technology
Change and Conformity

[N]o one has ever existed in a state unmodified by the customs of his own time and place.

Clifford Geertz (1976, p. 36)

ARTISTS AT WORK

At the Computer

"Look, I can make my house look like it's brick."

"How did you do that?"

"Look down here at all the different fill patterns. Put the mouse on the one you want and click. Then click where you want to fill."

"Oh, I'm going to put this stripe pattern on mine. Hey, it looks like shingles."

"Hey, what would a polka-dot house look like?"

"Let's try it!"

Introduction

FACING CHANGE

Today's students have a new way of talking about art. Click, mouse, and fill are said as easily as line, brush, and pattern. Art, like society, is not static but constantly acquiring new media and approaches. Educators must recognize that art instruction also needs to keep pace or risk being considered irrelevant by the ultimate consumer—the student.

Up to this point this book has concerned itself with what most art educators would consider to be the nuts and bolts of instruction in a well-balanced art program. In this chapter we will closely examine the role of art instruction in the context of a technological society and challenge teachers of art to think about art in new ways. As part of this discussion many questions will be raised. Should art instruction incorporate the new and unproved? Should it cater to the desires of technologically sophisticated students? Do they still need to know how to look at and make traditional art forms? Should students learn to make advertisements and videos as part of the art program?

Setting the Stage

WHAT IS THE TECHNOLOGICAL SOCIETY?

The rapid changes taking place in contemporary society are fueled by technological advances and the corresponding social responses. As with all changes some of these new art forms are promising and some are bewildering. Which will stand the test of time and which are fads? What criteria does a technological-based art form need

to meet to become a focus of art instruction in the elementary and middle school?

One result of the technological revolution has been that traditional art forms that were created to meet direct personal needs have been replaced with mass-produced objects designed to be sold quickly and cheaply as a way of satisfying artificially created desires. Traditional designs, techniques, and tastes handed down over generations have been supplanted by fads in hairstyles, clothing designs, and "hot" color schemes that sweep through communities for just weeks or months. Aesthetic beliefs are no longer absorbed just from one's ethnic background and community but are disseminated across global airways.

Technology makes it easier to copy others' ideas and has put into the hands of the many the ability to produce items that were once the domain of the specialist. A copy machine rather than a zinc plate produces multiple copies of a drawing. A photograph takes the place of a painted portrait. A computer allows us to design personal stationery at a moment's notice. The video camera makes everyone a filmmaker; the computer turns novice draftspeople into animators; the digital camera replaces the darkroom; and personal web pages allow all to try their hand at advertising layouts to be viewed worldwide. The old master, whose teaching was based on wisdom developed from years of experience working with a medium, has been superseded by students who are often more comfortable with new technologies than are their teachers.

It is essential to start teaching these new technologies in the art program in the earliest grades. This is the world of art in which the child lives when outside of school. As discussed in Chapter 3, instruction must build on the experience of our students in order to be effective. There is a copy machine at the local supermarket. Cameras, computers, and video cameras are in so many homes. They are fast becoming the most common way that individuals create visual images to meet daily needs: a card to send a friend, a sign for the door, a poster announcing a local event.

If we expect our students to make effective aesthetic choices, understand the visual images that surround them, and be able to create art that is personally meaningful, then we must address the technological arts that surround them.

Why . . . ?

WHY TEACH MEDIA LITERACY?

It is not only the techniques for making photographs, incorporating reproduced images, and creating video that we must teach. Students must also learn to evaluate the visual images that result and that pervade the mass media of our culture. It is the rare student who enters school and has not been exposed to such images. Magazines heavily

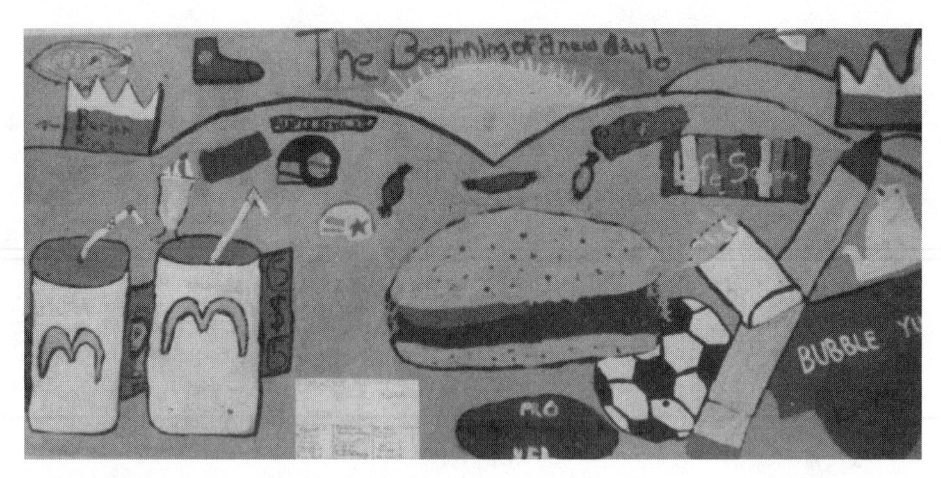

"The Beginning of a New Day."
Tempera—grade 6.

Thinking about Children's Art

As part of a unit on Pop Art these sixth graders have created a mural depicting a landscape littered with symbols of our mass culture. Based on the way the images are represented do you think they view these cultural icons positively, negatively or both? What questions could the students be asked to help them reflect on their work and derive its different levels of meaning?

illustrated with photographs are more common in students' homes than original artworks. Television and VCRs bring animation and film experiences to the preschooler.

By kindergarten age most children have spent the equivalent of four years of college classes watching television. Students age eight to fourteen spend approximately 20% of their waking hours in front of the television. The average eight-year-old watches for two and a half

What the Experts Say

Art and Technology

The computer can be seen as another concrete material that can be explored.
Jane Ilene Davidson (1989, p. 10)

While art experience, particularly in the visual arts, has been thought of as an individual process, the new technology tends to open the potential for collaborative techniques by groups and individuals.
Robert Loveless (1980, p. 242)

If computers were ever the enemies of art, this is not so anymore. . . . Now, from the moment we turn on the machine, we are in a world of imagery.
Jonathan C. Matthews (1997)

Of all the uses of technology in the classroom, video is a wedge that opens the chasm between what is and what could be.
Kathleen Tyner (1994, p. 25)

hours daily. By adolescence that amount has increased to four hours daily (Davies, 1996). The influence of this exposure is tremendous.

Even at the primary level teachers face students who have seen thousands of visual images, and the images they have seen are not necessarily the ones teachers might choose for their students. Comic page superheroes are better known than N. C. Wyeth's book illustrations. The art on the back of the cornflake box is more familiar than that in the museum. Violent images, cartoon characters, and commercial symbols derived from the media often appear in children's drawings.

The teacher faces the Herculean task of expanding the visual experiences of students while at the same time making them more aware of the quantity, purpose, and quality of the mass culture visual images that bombard them daily.

Guiding Ideas

MEDIA LITERACY

The mass media consist of the print media—newspapers and magazines—and the electronic media—radio, recordings, television, film, video, and the Internet. Advertising supports and promotes the messages of each. Visual images form the core means of expression for these embedded ideas, and artists offer their talents as advertising and product designers.

Exposure, however, is not equivalent to knowledge. Students must be made aware of the influence of the taken-for-granted mass media in their lives and the way art is incorporated into every waking moment. Instruction in the persuasive power of mass media and the role of art begins with media literacy. John Davies defines media literacy as the ability to identify the functions of mass communication, the conscious selection and usage of these media, and the acquiring of the level of understanding needed to consider the impact these media have on one's life and on society in general. Students need to be taught that "the media are symbolic (or sign) systems which need to be actively read, and not unproblematic, self-explanatory reflections of external reality" (Davies, 1996, p. 3).

Analyzing Mass Media

Personal communication is direct. The message is intended for an individual or small group. It is often interactive, requiring participation by both sender and receiver as in a conversation or through a letter. Mass media speaks to the wider audience. It is noninteractive. The audience is acted upon by the producer who tries to create needs and desires in the consumer.

The purpose of mass media mirrors that of art. It can inform, persuade, and entertain. It can tell a story or promote a belief and, like art,

Teaching in Action

Making Students Aware of Visual Images

Media literacy begins with awareness. Teachers must begin by making students knowledgeable about the visual images that surround them, identify the purposes of the images, and analyze how they personally are affected by them.

Count. Have students tally the number of visual images in their classroom that come from cartoons, films, and TV shows. Look at such things as notebooks and pencils. Are they surprised by the number they find? Did they buy the item because of the images on it? Do these images help them learn better or make the product better? Should those images be there?

Classify. Build awareness of the nature of the visual images by having students work in teams to sort advertisements from newspapers and magazines into categories based on art elements and design principles. Primary students can sort by subject or by the art elements they find. Older students can sort by composition layout, lettering style, or color scheme. Have teams present the results of their categorizing and then create a class grouping. Discuss what characteristics seem most common and why that might be. Also look for what is not common. Are there many pastel colors, for example?

Link art and mass media. Use every opportunity to make students aware of the link between commercial media and art. Pursue questions about television and commercial products whenever they occur. Topics for discussion often arise as part of art discussions. For example:

- The *Mona Lisa* and Grant Wood's *American Gothic* are often featured in television commercials. Discuss why these particular works are commercialized and others are not. How does the message of the original work change when it is made part of another message?
- The work of Andy Warhol and other pop artists, in which commercial images are incorporated into their art, provide another lead into discussing the influence of commercial images.
- Who are commercial artists? What do they do? How is their training different from that of a noncommercial artist? How is their work different from an artist who is not employed to produce art for a particular purpose? Both Andy Warhol and Georgia O'Keeffe began as commercial artists. What influence did their commercial training have on their artwork?

Preferences. Have primary students bring in a picture of a favorite cartoon or TV character. Older students can bring in an advertisement for a favorite product or music group. Create a class graph based on these images. Discuss how they learned about this character, product, or group. Why do they like them so much? Do boys and girls have different preferences? Why? What creates popularity?

Reconfigure. Have students change parts of a commercial image—cartoons, product symbols, or advertisements—and recombine them to produce a message that is the opposite of the original one, for example, turn a violent superhero into a gentle one or an ad to buy a car into one to give a car away.

it transmits culture. Art instruction provides the perfect arena in which to introduce students to the analysis of the visual images that permeate our society. Applying the vocabulary and mind-set of the artist to the analysis of commercial products empowers students to become wiser consumers and better able to create technology-based art forms. The same questions apply whether the work being studied is a portrait by Goya or a cereal box, a Dürer print or computer clip art.

- Who created this object?
- What was the creator's purpose?
- What is its message?
- Does its design match its purpose?
- Does it belong in a museum?

Commercial Art

Art that serves the social, political, and commercial interests of society has long existed and has been valued in different ways over time. Analyzing commercial works helps students see how art forms can be used to persuade. Rather than forming a separate unit, the study of commercial art design is best integrated into studies in language arts, social studies, and science. Students reading Chris van Allsberg's *Jumangi* (1995, Boston: Houghton Mifflin), for example, could compare the illustrations to advertisements for the movie and video. Students studying life during the early 1900s could investigate how products were advertised at that time and discuss whether or not these ads would be persuasive today. In a science unit on nutrition students could analyze the nutritive value of various cereals and then look for commonalties and differences in the box designs. Is there a relationship between persuasiveness and nutritional value? These kinds of activities can provide the perfect platform for collaborative teaching by classroom teachers and art specialists.

Discovering the impact of graphics. In forming opinions about commercial works, students should first look at examples and then define the basic persuasive components by asking questions about the artist's design decisions. These kinds of questions help students separate the often overpowering effect of the total advertisement from the discrete elements that come together to create the overall message.

- Why were these particular shapes, lines, textures, and/or colors chosen?
- Why was this style of lettering used?
- Why was this particular feature emphasized?
- Why was this particular art media or art technique selected?

This analysis can then be followed up with hands-on activities that allow students to manipulate and change these characteristics. This enables them to visually try out their ideas. They could, for example, redesign a cereal box using different colors, lettering, or art technique.

Matching the message. In creating commercial works, students must also consider the nature of the persuasive message. When should it be portrayed subtly; when should it hit the viewer over the head? How can advertising artists reach a select audience; how can they reach a diverse one? Have students compare advertisements that are directed to different personal interests, economic levels, or age groups. Compare, for example, ads for teen magazines and those for high fashion, car, and gardening magazines. Discussion of commercial art messages can include the following topics:

- *The role of art elements.* How do the shapes, colors, patterns, and textures reflect the meaning of the message? Are some colors, for example, more exciting, elegant, or happy than others?
- *Popularity.* Do commercial images mirror what is popular, or do they create popularity? In what messages are popular ideas reused; in which ones is the artist innovative?
- *Status.* How is status indicated by the artist's selection of colors, shapes, and textures and the way the work is designed?
- *Appeal.* How does the artwork make the consumer feel about the product? How should consumers "read" commercial art?

Creating persuasive works. Students can then be asked to apply what they have discovered by analyzing commercial art in producing persuasive works of their own. It is important that these works should be real, that is, they should have a clearly identified purpose that engages the students in persuading a real audience. Students can design posters for school events or create advertisements to sell their own hand-crafted artworks at a craft fair or to solicit funds for a needy cause.

If possible, there should also be a measurable way for the novice commercial artists to judge their success. For example, primary students can track which books are the most read in their class or school. Then they can design advertisements for their favorite book or author, display them, and collect data to see if more students than before choose that book. See At a Glance 13.1 for suggested activities.

Toys, Comics, and Games

Toys, cartoons, and games are the stuff of childhood. These are the things that occupy children's minds and distract them from the serious work of school. They are a pathway into a child's imagination carrying strong cultural messages. Toys and other childhood pursuits

At a Glance 13.1

Commercial Art Activities

The following is just a brief sampling of possible cross-disciplinary activities that can be used to teach media literacy. Most can be adapted to use at any grade level.

Possible Formats

- *Advertisements:* Create an advertisement for the class, school, or community newspaper.
- *Billboards:* Make a billboard (group mural) to display in the hall or lobby of the school or in a community gathering place such as a local library, store, or bank.
- *Bookmarks and buttons:* Create bookmarks or buttons and distribute them to fellow students.
- *Bumper sticker:* Design a bumper sticker and distribute it to parents and community members.
- *Cartoons:* Make a cartoon for a class, school, or community newsletter or newspaper.
- *Posters:* Make a poster to display in the classroom, hall, library, or community gathering place.

Specific Suggestions by Subject

Language arts. Promote a favorite book, book character, author, television show, film, or video, or encourage reading.

Math. Advertise math events occurring in the school, programs featuring math on television, and community math-related events. Promote math awareness in daily life.

Music. Advertise an upcoming musical event in the school, community, on radio, or on television, or promote a favorite musician, music group, type of music, or musical composition.

Science. Conduct studies related to media understanding, such as testing which color people see most quickly and clearly or what size letter can be seen from different distances, and advertise the results. Advertise school and community events related to science, science-related television programs, and new scientific discoveries. Promote healthy living and the proper care of pets.

Social studies. Promote a school or community event, encourage participation in a good cause, or increase awareness of social services available. Advertise cultural programs and ethnic foods, music, art, and celebrations. Create awareness of current political and social happenings in the world. Promote good behavior and citizenship.

are important in forming a child's view of the world. Some are educational, making the child think and solve problems. Others such as toy guns and villainous action figures mirror the violence of our world. Children form a major portion of the mass audience addressed by toy advertising. Millions of dollars are spent by the toy industry to convince children that they cannot live without the latest movie-generated toy figure or game.

"Smile America."
Oil pastel and collage—Matt, grade 4.

Thinking about Children's Art

This fourth grader has combined words and images in an attempt to persuade the onlooker. Would this poster convince you to brush your teeth? What is the relationship between this work and the commercial images to which the child has been exposed through the mass media?

In the classroom toys, games, and cartoons provide an ideal way to draw upon student interests and pull them into discussions about art and cultural influences as they talk about how the design of these items affects their use and meaning.

Toys in the classroom. There are many ways to incorporate toys into the study of art. Toys can be used to spark the imagination and get students motivated to create art. They can be used as examples of three-dimensional objects and as cultural artifacts.

- *Toys as models.* Toys can function as a source of three-dimensional objects that are intriguing to students. Teachers can keep a collection of small toy cars, plastic figures, and stuffed animals, for example, for them to draw. Occasionally set up a still life of toys, grouping them thematically. Try still lifes with old-fashioned toys or all stuffed animals. Children can also bring in a favorite toy and, after sharing what is special about it, draw it.
- *Toys and aesthetics.* Toys can provide a forum for discussing aesthetic questions. How do the shapes, colors, patterns, and textures used enhance the function or attraction of the toy? Are some colors, for example, more commonly used for some kinds of toys? How is the size of a toy related to its attraction to children? Is there a difference in how toys for different age children are designed? How do the materials the toy is made from and the mechanics of its manufacture determine its end form? Are toys art? Do they belong in a museum?
- *Toys and imagination.* Toys naturally draw children into fantasy worlds. Spark imaginative artwork by having students fantasize their toys coming alive. What would they do? Where would they live? What adventures would they have? Ask students to combine two or three toys together to invent a new one or imagine and design a totally new one. Relate the creation of fantasy toys to the study of surrealistic artworks. Extend the experience by having students sketch and then model their designs three-dimensionally in clay, cardboard, or wood. They could sew stuffed toys. They could describe how children can play with the toy they have designed and then create an advertising campaign to accompany it.
- *Toys as sculpture.* Most toys are three-dimensional, designed by anonymous artists. Look at toys as pieces of sculpture and ask questions about their design and form. Redesign toys as sculptural works. Make them larger and out of different materials. Use broken toys to construct sculptures. Look at artworks that incorporate toys or parts of toys into their design. How does the incorporation of toys in an artwork affect its meaning?
- *Toys as cultural artifacts.* Toys can be used to initiate discussions about art history. Look at portraits of children and their toys from

the past, such as Claude Monet's *Jean on a Wooden Horse* or Pierre Auguste Renoir's *Mother with Children* and compare the toys to those of today. Ask students to create self-portraits including their favorite toys.

- *Toys as history and culture.* Trace the changes in toys over time. If possible, collect examples such as Barbie dolls that show how a toy has been adapted to changing societal views. Predict what toys might be like sometime in the future. For example, if archaeologists of the distant future found a collection of toys from today, what might they think of our society? Compare the toys of today with those of other times and places. Are toys as important in other cultures? How are the clay marbles and dice of Neolithic children similar to those of today?

Cartooning. Cartoons are a ubiquitous art form of our society and cannot be ignored by the teacher of art. For many children raised on hours of Saturday morning cartoon viewing, cartoon images provide the most important drawn models for their artwork.

A cartoon approach to art is found not only at home; it permeates the school environment as well. The simplified stereotypic shapes of the cartoon are found in the commercial wall decorations of the classroom and the illustrations on student worksheets as well as among the clip-art choices on the word processor. Students need to become aware that cartooning is but one of many ways artists can approach the creation of visual images, one that can serve some purposes well but that is not the only choice. They need to be able to examine cartoon images with the critical eye of the artist. To do this students must be made aware of cartoons as art and visual symbol.

- *Cartoons as models.* As Brent and Marjorie Wilson (1977) have pointed out, cartoon images form one of the basic sources of imagery in children's and adolescents' drawings. Children need to become aware of this influence and be shown that there are other sources of imagery. That is why it is important to display and study many different styles of art and to avoid plastering the classroom with comic-like images. At the same time this does not mean that teachers should denigrate students' interest in drawing from cartoons. There is much they can learn from studying how objects and actions are represented on the comic book page. It is much easier for students to visually understand simplified two-dimensional comic figures than to convert the nuances of a real three-dimensional object on to a flat sheet of paper. Provide many opportunities for students to see a variety of approaches to the creation of visual images. One way to do this is to collect an example of a specific cartoon image such as a bowl of food, and place it in conjunction with a real bowl of food as well as artworks that show the same subject. Have students compare these visual images. If a computer with a scanner

"Bad Day for the Woodcutter."
Marker—Justin, grade 5.

Thinking about Children's Art

In this cartoon a rural student uses the format and symbolism of contemporary cartooning to humorously illustrate one of his basic fears about cutting wood. What elements in the drawing are direct borrowings from the cartoon genera? How could this cartoon be used to inspire a story?

is available, scan the cartoon image and a photograph of the object into a graphic arts program. Encourage students to superimpose them and manipulate them.

- *Cartoons as art.* Cartoons can be studied as a unique style of art and compared to other styles. Discussions can focus on the artist's intent and the relationship of cartooning to book illustration. Look for similarities and differences within the cartoon form itself. Compare the work of different cartoonists. Look for the influence of cartooning on advertising and fine art such as the work of pop artists. Students can be introduced to digital cameras, photo-editing software, and graphic arts programs as a way to convert real images into cartoon-like ones. Study what happens to the object as it undergoes the transformation. What is lost and what is gained?
- *Comic page symbols.* Understanding cartoons requires a learned vocabulary of visual symbols. For example, solid line balloons represent spoken words; broken line ones indicate thoughts. Have students explore comic pages for examples of these visual symbols and create a class chart. Invite students to use these symbols to compose an original story or to retell a familiar one. Then challenge them to invent their own versions of the symbols and to rewrite their stories using their new forms. Is the result understandable to other students?

How do people learn to read these kinds of symbols? Pursue the idea of visual symbols across cultures. Can people in other cultures understand our symbols? Can we understand theirs? How are they similar to written language? Compare them to the pictographs of early languages such as those of Egypt, China, and Mesopotamia.

- *Cartoons as stories.* Tie the study of cartoons in with literature and language studies. Converting the plot of a story into a sequence of cartoon frames helps students organize their ideas. Compare comic book versions of famous literary pieces to the actual writing. What has changed? How do the visual images enhance or detract from the meaning of the story?

Games to play. Board games and card games can also tie student interest and art together. Students can look at existing games as artworks. How were they designed? Why were particular colors, shapes, patterns, and forms chosen? Try redesigning playing pieces and boards for classic games such as checkers and chess or create new games that are designed to be artworks as well as amusements.

To reinforce ideas and concepts encourage students to design games with an art focus. Students can create games that introduce the art elements, such as identifying shapes, colors, or three-dimensional forms.

The Electronic Arts

Art forms that require electricity for dissemination—radio, television, CD-ROM, film, and video—are considered the electronic arts. All these art forms, except radio, create a visual reality constructed by the sender. How images are selected, framed, and superimposed encapsulates the message. Students need to ask these questions:

- Is this reality or a construct?
- Is this truth or fiction?
- Is this trying to persuade or entertain?
- Is it broad-minded or one-sided?

Then follow up with a critical analysis of the end result:

- Is the message visually clear?
- Do the images flow together into a unified whole?
- Does every frame contribute to the total piece?
- Have colors, sound, and point of view been used to enhance the message of the piece?

In addition to watching and analyzing films and videos students will become more astute viewers and users of these media when they have the opportunity to create their own productions. The world looks very different through the lens of a camera.

Of the electronic arts, video production, with its close relationship to photography and the ready availability of camcorders, is most easily incorporated into the art curriculum. When joined with a computer, animated videos and claymation can be produced even by elementary school students.

Computer graphics. Although plugged into the wall, computers are different from the other electronic media. Computers are active rather than passive. Unlike film and television, with computers the viewer can interact and change the visual images. There is a freedom and playfulness associated with the computer that relates to the seeming impermanence of the image—if the image is unpleasant, it can be changed or deleted.

Not surprisingly computer graphics software has changed the way much art is made. Computers eliminate the tedium of creating precise duplicate images. They allow the artist to invent a form and then manipulate it in space while applying varying viewpoints. Computers allow the artist to take a drawn image or photograph and create different versions of it, placing it in different color schemes and compositional arrangements. More and more the computer is found beside the other media of the artist.

On the other hand, computer graphics can be used just as easily in inartistic ways. Poorly chosen and placed clip art and a limited array of copyright-free images that come bundled on every computer flood our vision with the most banal and least meaningful of visual forms. Without instruction in computer graphics and critical analysis of the images produced, students will never be able to effectively use the powerful capabilities of their computers to create art. Students need to analyze the effectiveness of different fonts, clip-art selections, and canned layouts and become comfortable creating their own.

In the Classroom

COMPUTERS AND CAMERAS

Technological art involves making artistic decisions about the arrangement of art elements to create a composition while using a machine. In doing so, not only do students develop more technical skill with computers and cameras, but they also become more critical of the mass media that surrounds them.

Teachers should explore the potentials of these media with their students as a way of increasing media literacy as well as expanding their artistic repertoire. The introductory activities described here may inspire further study of these media. Computer graphics, photography, and video production are technically complex art forms. This section is designed as a basic introduction to these fields; it offers ways to begin to utilize them in the classroom with a special emphasis on integrating them across the curriculum.

For more specific details and advanced techniques consult the references at the end of the section or take hands-on workshops locally. Teachers who are already using these media in the classroom can also serve as an important resource.

Technology as Art

It does not matter what tool an artist uses. If an artist makes effective artistic decisions and communicates ideas, then that person is creating art. In the early days of photography critics were quick to warn that the camera would replace the eye of the artist. Instead, photography has forced artists to look more closely—to hone their vision to see what the camera does not. It has freed artists rather than destroying them.

In the same way the computer has released artists from the tedium of drawing the same shape over and over to create a pattern. It allows animators to concentrate on form, action, and special effects rather than coloring segment after segment. Shapes can be cut and pasted, flipped and duplicated, manipulated and viewed from varying viewpoints. The artist can try out ideas quickly without losing the original one. There is a freedom to play without worry. And for the novice student there is no incriminating paper trail of error or rejects.

The third technological art form presented here, video production, is relatively new to the classroom and yet it is the perfect way for students to capture action and interaction. Planning a video and creating a production take away the mystery of television and film and empower students to look at the electronic arts critically through artist's eyes.

All three media are linked together not only in requiring sophisticated knowledge and technical skill but also in the ability to use one to enhance the others. Computers can be used to edit photographs and video. Photographs and video can be imported into a computer graphic. Together they can be combined in the creation of a Web page. At a Glance 13.2 offers a working vocabulary of technical terms.

Computer Graphics

The computer provides students with another way to draw and paint. Instead of paper there is a computer screen. A mouse, graphic tablet, or light pen replaces pencil and brush. Pigments are pixels of colored light. But although the tools are different, the same artistic questions must be asked and decisions must be made. Is this line long enough and dark enough? Do these colors enhance each other? Should this shape overlap that one? Students can be expected to use and develop the same artistic critical thinking skills as might be expected in any area of art.

At the same time the computer is also different from drawing and painting. There is a transient nature to the computer–artist interface. A drawn image can disappear or be changed in an instant. There is no

At a Glance 13.2

Talking Technology

Computers

Animation: Giving motion to a visual image.

Desktop publishing: The creation of the layout of a document on the computer screen complete with type and graphics.

Desktop video: The creation of an animated video or the editing of video footage using a computer.

Digital: Information in a form that can be processed by a computer.

Icon: A visual symbol used to mark a command button.

Import: To transfer clip art, photographs, or video images into a computer artwork or word-processing document.

Palette: The range of colors available in the graphics program.

Web page: A site on the Internet where an individual, business, or educational concern displays computer graphic images that may contain information, photographs, video clips, artwork, and links to other Web pages; also known as Web sites.

Workstation: The arrangement of one computer and its equipment such as a printer, scanner, and touch tablet.

Photography

Definition: The clarity of detail an observer sees in a photograph.

Depth of field: The distance range in which objects in a photograph look sharp and clear; adjusting the focus sets the camera to the proper depth of field.

Developing: The process of chemically converting light-exposed film to a negative image.

Double exposure: Two pictures taken on the same piece of film.

Focal length: The distance between the center of the lens and the film. The longer the focal length, the larger the image will be on the film.

Printing: The process by which timed light of measured intensity passes through a negative on to light-sensitive paper to create a positive image.

Video Production

Animation: Moving images created by filming small changes in artwork.

Claymation: Animation created by changing the position of objects and photographing the changes frame by frame.

Location: The place where the video is being made.

Scene: The action taking place at the same location and time.

Script: A set of written directions for a video production.

Sequence: A series of shots that relate to each other.

Shot: One run of the camera.

paper trail of rough erasers and muddied paint. For many students this can be a liberating experience. There is more willingness to take risks, to try new combinations, and to dive into projects that on paper might seem daunting. In many ways practicing art composition on the computer is more like practicing a musical instrument. The image, like a musical note, exists for a brief moment and then it is gone. At the same time there is the choice to make the work permanent. The image, like a musical performance, can be recorded to immortalize the event.

Art on the Computer

Designing art lessons for the computer is no different than planning those using more traditional media. Lessons should grow out of student interests and meet student needs. Computers, however, should not be used merely as a replacement for more traditional media. Teachers need to ask themselves if the computer is the best tool for accomplishing their objectives. Lessons should be designed to take advantage of the student's ability to use the computer to make changes instantly, to create multiple copies of an image, and to combine photographic, animated, and video images in the same work. The ability to save stages in the process of creation can be important when work is being assessed in specific ways. The ability to transfer artistic elements from one work to another can be used in developing related works or for group projects.

The goal for using the computer as an art medium should be to enable students to enhance their ability to make effective, thoughtful art. The computer should be one of many choices available when they are trying to solve an artistic problem. Students should be able to decide when it is better to use the computer rather than hand letter a sign or draw an object freehand. They should know how to look critically at an artwork created on the computer and give reasons why using the computer enhanced or detracted from the idea or message of the work.

The following activities are designed to be an introduction to the computer and can be used at many grade levels. The goal is to show how to integrate the computer into the art offerings rather than to provide a computer-focused set of lessons.

Introducing the Computer

Many students are more comfortable with using computers than are their teachers. Learning the basics of how to turn the computer on, how to insert disks and CD-ROMs, and how to manipulate the mouse or paint tablet usually takes only a few minutes. This can be done through a guided discovery lesson in which the teacher establishes guidelines for use, emphasizing safe and careful handling. It is important to post the guidelines at the computer workstation to remind students of the accepted procedures.

"Street Scene."
Computer graphics—Clark, Shannon, Bert, and Denise, grade 3.

Thinking about Children's Art

Using a simple drawing program these third graders have created buildings using computer drawn rectangles. Is this a good use for the computer's capabilities? How does being able to make perfect rectangles affect the appearance of the children's artwork? Did they use the computer creatively?

Instruction in using the software can be done either as a whole group lesson or by using cooperative group techniques. For whole group lessons a projection screen or hookup to a television monitor is essential. With one of these in place the teacher can demonstrate the different menu selections in plain view of the class and then invite students to come up and model what they have learned.

If neither of these methods is possible, then it is better to use the "expert in action" technique as described in Chapter 8. Begin by instructing a group of four or five students in the application of the program. Then have each of these "experts" teach another group of four students until the whole class has received instruction and become expert.

Selecting Software

It is important to select software that best matches the tasks the students will be doing. In many cases it is better to invest in software that is specifically designed for a particular purpose rather than trying to get one program that does it all. Focused software is often more direct and easier to use. Programs that perform many functions may require more intensive instruction and also run the risk of students accidentally or on purpose getting into sections that do not apply to what they are doing, thereby wasting precious working time on what are often limited-access computers.

Software offerings change rapidly, so rather than specifying specific programs this section provides general guidelines that will help in selecting the best software for specific purposes. For more specific recommendations consult Teacher Resources at the end of the chapter. At a Glance 13.3 provides a computer vocabulary.

Drawing or paint software. There are a variety of software programs available that will serve young artists well. At the primary level and for introducing older students to computer art for the first time a simple program with limited choices is often the best. Sometimes the drawing or paint program that comes bundled with a machine or as part of a multifunction word-processing program will prove sufficient. These programs usually allow the student to use the mouse to draw various size lines, make basic shapes, and fill in with colors and patterns. Drawing programs designed for younger children are also available.

In selecting a program make sure that it allows free drawing on a blank screen. Sometimes the words *art* or *drawing* appear in the title of programs that are no more than coloring books in which predrawn characters and objects are placed into prepared settings. It is therefore wise to preview software before purchasing it.

Illustration software. As students gain experience and control over creating images with the computer, offer them more complex art-specific software. These programs allow more manipulation of the drawn objects and may provide the ability to tilt, rotate, and stretch a drawn object and convert a drawing to three dimensions.

Word-processing or print studio software. Although not art programs per se, these kinds of programs can be used to provide lettering in different fonts and sizes for a wide variety of projects such as collages, posters, and artwork labels.

Photo-editing software. Students who are accomplished at freehand drawing and manipulating images on the computer can be introduced to photo importation and editing using digital cameras or scanned images.

Animation software. This software may be packaged with photo-editing or drawing software and allows drawn or imported images to be animated.

Video-editing software. This software allows the user to hook a camcorder to the computer and feed in video images, where they can be edited. Computer-created artwork and graphics can also be added to the video.

At a Glance 13.3

Computer Talk

CAD (Computer-Aided Design): Software designed for mechanical or architectural drawing that allows the artist to precisely manipulate forms.

CD-ROM: A read-only laser-encoded optical storage disk that cannot be altered.

Floppy disk: A three-and-a-half-inch magnetic disk in a plastic case used to store writing, artwork, or photographs, allowing the information to be transferred to another computer. It also provides a backup in the event a computer's hard drive is damaged. It is good practice to copy irreplaceable pieces on to disks.

Graphics tablet: An electronic pad that can be drawn on with the image then appearing on the computer screen; also known as a drawing tablet, touch pad, or digitizer table.

Hard drive: The memory and storage area of the computer, which can be used to store software programs and work in progress.

Image-editing program: Software that allows the user to edit photographs and clip art.

Light pen: An electronic tool that allows the user to draw directly on the computer screen.

Mouse pad: A cushioned surface used under the mouse. A larger-sized pad than normally used makes it easier for beginning computer artists to move the mouse as they draw.

Pixel: Locations on the computer screen that can be described mathematically and that define a single point of color. The more pixels one can view on the screen, the more precise an image one can draw. Some programs show the identifying number of the pixel as one works, making it possible to return to the exact location.

Printer: Select either an ink jet or laser printer to print out graphic art in both black and white and color.

Projection screen: A device that hooks up to the computer and projects an enlarged version of the image on a computer screen for whole class viewing.

Scanner: A device that turns a visual image, such as a drawing or photograph, into a digital form readable by the computer.

Planning Computer Access

Because computers and all their related equipment involve a great deal of expense, what is available for classroom use may vary greatly from school to school. There may be a stand-alone or networked workstation of one or more computers in the classroom or there may be a computer lab in which there are enough computers for every student to have one but only on a scheduled basis. Depending on the set-up, the computer can be used in different ways.

One computer and a printer in the classroom. The advantage to having a computer in the classroom is that it is always available.

Teacher Tip

Making Do

It is possible to introduce students to computer art without a lot of fancy, up-to-date equipment. While new computers may be faster and more versatile, an older computer can often be used for many introductory computer activities. An Apple II GS or an Apple 2e with a Koala pad and used with a simple drawing program can function well at the elementary grades.

In some school districts these kinds of computers are in the process of being discarded, and with luck it may be possible to find one that can be used exclusively for art activities in the classroom.

Unfortunately access is limited by the fact that only one to three students can use the computer at a time. If only one computer is available, then it is vitally important to make use of computer graphics' most unique features in a way that allows all the students access to the machine.

Multiple computers in the classroom. If there is a bank of three or four computers sharing a printer, computer access can more easily flow into the activities of an art/writing workshop. One computer can be designated for quick projects such as typing in a word and printing it out for use in a poster or label. The students can then use the others on an as-needed basis for more complex works.

Computer lab. The advantage to having a computer lab is that there is a computer for every student. The disadvantage is that using the lab on a whole class basis means that all students must use the computer for their artwork at the same time whether the computer is the best choice for their idea or not.

One way to take advantage of the computer lab is to use its facilities when introducing new programs. This is the time whole group instruction is most effective. Following instruction several lab sessions can be devoted to exploring the parameters of the software. Students can try out different features, print out samples, and create a personal or class computer art notebook to provide a guide for future decisions about artworks. Back in the art/writing workshop students familiar with what is available at the lab can then plan how they will use the computer and can go to the lab as needed.

(*Note:* For most of the following activities a printer is essential. However, it does not need to be a color printer. If necessary, students can add color to their work using other art media such as markers and crayons.)

One-Computer Activities

A single computer set up in the corner with a drawing program on which some students doodle when they are done with their other work, or on which students take occasional turns in some sort of rotation, wastes the resource. Instead, the computer should be integrated into the program so that it is used to meet specific instructional and artistic needs.

Rather than tying up the single machine with a line of students each trying to make a complete artwork, have individual students use the single computer to create unique parts to add into works being done in other media. For example:

- *Wonderful words.* Have students type in a poem or series of words on a topic using a font and style that best reflects the meaning of the words. Print out the words, cut them apart, and use them in a collage, poster, illustration, or other work.
- *Unique papers.* Using the stamping or duplicating part of a software program, students can create an original pattern or overall design, which can then be printed out, colored if desired, and incorporated into a collage.
- *Duplicate images.* Use the computer to create a quick composition of lines and open shapes. Print out two or three copies and then color them in different ways using traditional art media.
- *Different versions.* Students can use the computer to create alternative sketches for works that will be completed in other media.

Multiple-Computer Activities

The following activities are suitable when there are sufficient computers for every student to frequently spend an entire period at the computer. Such activities, in addition to those listed for the one-computer classroom, fit well into a writing/art workshop basis as not every student will need access to the computer at the same time. In an established art workshop normally some will be sketching, some writing, some conferencing, and some using other art media. If more students need the computer than there are computers available, those students who are waiting a turn can participate in peer conferences rather than waiting in line.

Computer as tool. Students should sketch out their ideas for an artwork and be able to justify why the computer would be the best tool to use to create it. For example, a student who has planned a composition that involves overlapping circles of different sizes might feel that the circle tool on the computer would be the best way to create this composition. After a brief conference with the teacher during which it would also be decided if the computer was the best way to add color to the work, this student would then be allowed to create the piece using the computer.

Computer as resource. Vice versa, the teacher, in conferencing with a student about plans for a work, might suggest that the student use the computer to accomplish all or part of the work if it seems the most appropriate way to do so. For example, if a student is unsure about the relative position of various shapes in the work, the teacher could suggest that the student use the computer to try out several versions.

Computer as creative processor. Special features of the computer can be used to create works that cannot be done in any other way. Students who are experienced with these features can plan them into their artworks. These features can include incorporating scanned images and photographs into a work, creating a series of works based on manipulating an original image, and incorporating art and words into a unified layout.

Computer Lab Exercises

When students are familiar with the menu and can manipulate the various elements of the program, the following exercises will develop skill using the computer as an artistic tool. The works resulting from these exercises can be used to illustrate student-created booklets, charts, or journal entries that students can refer back to in planning future works.

Investigating line. Have students use only the line command to investigate the effect of different thicknesses and directions of lines. Students can explore what happens when lines intersect and can be challenged to create the feeling of depth. Using the invert color feature, they can see how the line design would look if the lines were white on a dark background.

Because this activity forces students to explore just one facet of the menu, it is a good one for students just starting out using the computer and relates well to design studies. It also develops control using the mouse or touch pad effectively. Similar exercises can be designed that focus on other menu choices such as the rectangle and circle tools or the spray paint tool.

Playing with pattern. Next introduce students to the computer's potential to create pattern. Using the free-draw elements, students should create a motif and then explore different ways to create a pattern. This gives them the opportunity to learn how to use the cut and paste or stamping tools. The resulting patterns should be printed out and saved in a pattern reference book. Extra copies can be used as part of collages.

Containing color. Color on the computer does not work quite the same way as it does in painting. Students need many opportunities to use the color tools including fill and spray paint to develop a sense of what colors are available on the particular software and how they look on the screen as compared to when they are printed.

Novice students, particularly in the elementary grades, need to learn to look carefully at their outlines to be sure they are complete so that filled color areas do not leak into others. They also need to learn how to precisely control the color tools so that color goes exactly where they want it. Have students investigate ways to change the colors. Some software programs also allow artists to create their own mix of colors. The zoom tool or pixel tool can be used to change the color of individual pixels and create new color effects.

Manipulating imported images. When students have developed basic computer art skills, teach them how to scan or import digitized images into their graphics art program. This may be done using software specifically designed for this use (see Teacher Resources).

Advanced activities. For many students the basic activities listed in this section will prove sufficient challenge. But as students become more technologically sophisticated, more powerful programs can be used. While it goes beyond the scope of this book to provide details on the more complex uses of the computer, the following list will provide direction for those looking for more to do with their students:

- Create a "slide" show of works by one or more students using the slide show option available on many drawing programs.
- Add sounds or music to an artwork.
- Convert two-dimensional drawings to three-dimensional ones using a high-level drawing program.
- Animate drawings to create a cartoon using special software.
- Create a personal Web page design using special software.

Photography

Photography has come a long way since it first appeared over 150 years ago. Lightweight, inexpensive, and often disposable, cameras have made photography the art form of the masses. Today homes are more likely to have cameras than artist's paints.

The use of photographic visual images to sell products and spread information around the world has helped create a global culture. Photographs illustrate newspapers, magazines, books, and Web sites and provide the visual images that people have come to think of as real.

Learning how photographs are taken and produced helps students become more critical of these pervasive and often subversive images

Books to Share

Computers

Introductory

Burkhart, C. (1998). *Surf Sammy's new computer.* Redwood City, CA: Roof Publishing.
Claybourne, A. (1996). *Usbourne computer dictionary for beginners.* Tulsa, OK: EDC Publishing.
Cromwell, S. (1997). *My first book about the Internet.* New York: Troll.
Jortberb, C. (1997). *The first computer.* Edina, MN: Abdo and Daughters.
Kazunas, T. & C. (1997). *Personal computers.* New York: Children's Press.
Kazunas, T. & C. (1997). *The Internet for kids.* New York: Children's Press.
Sabbeth, C. (1995). *Kids' computer creations.* Charlotte, VT: Williamson Publishing.
Sabbeth, C. (1998). *Crayons and computers: Computer art activities for kids ages 4 to 8.* Chicago: Chicago Review Press.
Steinhauser, P. (1997). *Mousetracks.* Berkeley, CA: Tricycle Press.

Advanced

Baker, C. (1997). *Let there be life: Animating with the computer.* New York: Walker.
Grotta, S. W. (1994). *Digital imagining for graphic artists.* New York: McGraw-Hill.
Hall, K. (1998). *The color printer guidebook.* San Francisco: No Starch Press.

that influence how they view themselves and their culture. Through consciously creating and assessing their own photographs and how effectively they communicate their ideas, children learn how photography can be manipulated to create an illusion of reality. At a Glance 13.4 describes photographer's tools.

Photographic awareness. Photographic awareness starts in the earliest grades with exercises designed to teach children that the eye can look at things from many different perspectives. Later, similar exercises can be repeated at upper grade levels to reinforce these ideas when introducing photographic techniques.

- *Viewfinders.* Cardboard tubes or index cards with small holes in the center can be used as "viewfinders" to help children isolate bits of visual images from their surroundings, such as finding details in the classroom. These kinds of activities should play a regular role in classroom lessons and should be integrated across the disciplines. Have students decorate a personal viewfinder to keep in their desks and use it to find details in an artwork as part of an art lesson, on a printed chart as part of a grammar lesson, on a graph during a math lesson, or outside on a science nature hike.

At a Glance 13.4

Tools of the Photographer

Camera: A light-proof box with an opening that allows light to be focused on a light-sensitive material such as film

Film: A light-sensitive material that records an image

Filter: A tinted piece of glass that adjusts the color of light entering the camera

Lens: A curved glass that brings light rays to a focal point on the film

Light meter: A device that measures the amount of light reflecting off a surface

Photogram: A picture made without a camera using light-sensitive materials

- *Point of view.* These same viewfinders can be used to introduce the concept of point of view to young students. After students have had many opportunities to use the viewfinders to isolate details, encourage them to move their bodies to a new position so they are looking at the same image or object from a different position. Have them describe how the image changes. Encourage students to sketch what they see from these different positions. Next find examples of artwork and photographs that show unusual points of view. Have students try to identify where the artist or photographer was in making the picture. Do the same thing with book illustrations and photographs in newspapers.
- *Vocabulary.* Viewfinder activities can be designed to introduce students to the following terms:

  Blowup: A photograph that is larger than the actual object

  Close-up: A photograph taken from closer than normal viewing distance

  Long shot: A photograph taken from far away

  Medium shot: A photograph taken from normal viewing distance

  Panorama: A view wider than 90 degrees similar to or greater than that covered by our binocular vision
- *Looking closely.* Close-ups in particular can play an important role in getting students to examine objects more attentively across the curriculum. Use hand lenses to examine the details of a small object such as a coin or insect. Select one small detail such as the insect's leg and draw it large enough to fill the paper. Discuss how a close-up can help an artist or scientist see more intently. Play a visual perception game with the class. Show photographs or slides of an object starting with an extreme close-up of a detail and working out to a long-distance view. Have students raise their hands when they think they know what it is. Follow up by sharing a book such as Tana Hoban's picture book *Look Closer* (1971, Macmillan) or Dillon

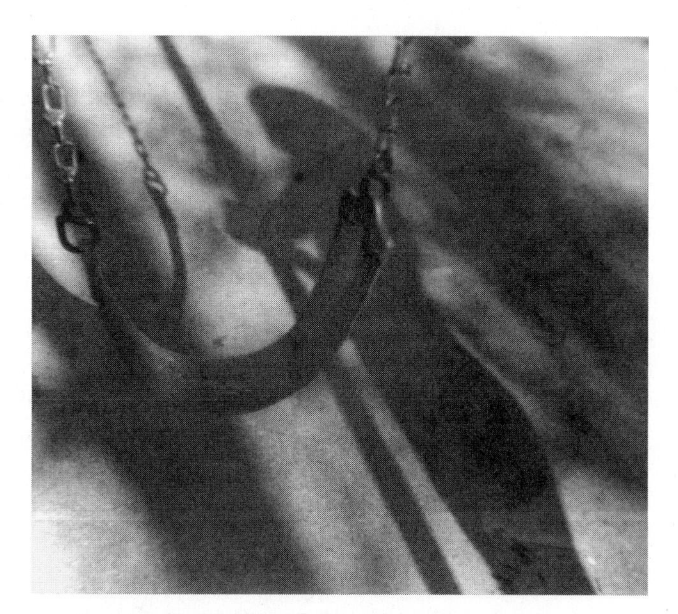

"The Swing."
Photograph—Corey, grade 4.

Thinking about Children's Art

Photography helps children see everyday things in new ways. This fourth grader has captured a subtle arrangement of light and shadow. From what point of view was this photo taken? Would a child have selected the same view for making a drawing or a painting? How could this photograph be used to inspire a poem or piece of writing?

and Dillon's *What Am I? Looking Through Shapes at Apples and Grapes* (1994, Blue Sky), which use differently shaped windows to focus on interesting parts of photographs. In the upper grades use these books to inspire students to create eye-catching books using their own photographs or photographs clipped from magazines.

- *Enlargement.* Display the same photograph or artwork reproduction in two very different sizes. A postcard and a poster make a good comparison. Have students identify what is the same and different about the two pictures. Ask them which image seems more real and why. Then have students individually or in teams draw their own enlargements from a small sketch, photograph, cartoon, or print using a grid system (see Chapter 7).
- *Analyzing purpose.* Collect photographs designed to sell various products that depict families, homes, vacations, and so on. In addition ask students to bring in family photographs. Working in teams, sort the photographs by subject matter. Then sort these groups by photographer's purpose. How does the purpose of the photograph change the way the photograph is taken? What is the difference between a snapshot, an action shot, and a posed picture? Do people take photographs differently when they are shooting a once-in-a-lifetime event? Conclude by making a bulletin board of the photographs grouped by purpose to refer to as students continue their study of photography.

Composing the picture. Composing a photographic image is a little different from composing art elements in an artwork. Although in both cases the artist selects a visual image to capture, in artwork the elements can be moved around until they are in the relationship the artist desires. In a photograph the artist must move the camera's lens around to select a part of a larger reality. This selection process is the heart of creating a meaningful photograph. It is what makes photography an art form.

Students often lose sight of the composition process when they are looking through the camera. Like most untrained photographers they become more interested in the subject matter than in the way that subject matter is presented. They want to take a picture of their friend rather than create a composition that shows how their friend is feeling. It is the teacher's job to help students learn how to combine their desire to capture a particular subject with the principles of design that will make the photograph more meaningful.

- *Applying the principles of design.* Photography is an ideal medium to use as part of lessons on design. Begin by collecting photographs taken by students and from magazines. Have teams of students look for examples that illustrate the principles of design that are being studied and create charts or booklets that show the selected photograph next to a description of the principle.
- *Developing a selective eye.* Cropping is a technique often used to improve finished photographs. It is also a good method for helping students learn to see and compose better photographs before using the cameras so film is not wasted. Begin the activity by showing several poster-sized photographs to the class or small group. Have students come up and move precut paper frames around until they think they have framed a good composition that has a definite center of interest. The following questions are useful in guiding students in their selection process:
  1. Does the most important part of the subject—the center of interest—fill the frame?
  2. Does the background add or distract from the subject?
  3. Is the horizon line placed so that it emphasizes the subject? If the center of interest is on the ground, is it higher than the center? If the center of interest is in the sky, is it below the center of the picture?
  4. Is the size of the objects in the photograph apparent?
  5. Is there something in the foreground or are there receding lines to add dimension to long views?

Photography in the Classroom

Having cameras available in every classroom allows teachers to incorporate photography across the curriculum. Teachers and students

Teaching in Action

How to Crop a Photograph

1. Have each student clip a large photograph from a magazine or calendar.
2. Using a viewfinder—an index card with a rectangular opening cut out of it—students should select a part of their photo that they think makes a good composition.
3. Using the ruler, students should draw a rectangle around the selected part and cut it out and mount it on tagboard.
4. On the back of their cropped pictures the students should write their center of interest.
5. Next have them exchange cards with a partner and discuss the composition using the previously listed questions.

Lesson Follow-Up

- On the board write *close-up, medium shot, long shot,* and have students come up and place their card under the heading they think it belongs. Ask, "Does the distance from the object change how the photograph is composed?"
- Use the completed cards to illustrate principles of design or add them to journals or a picture file.

are more likely to take photographs of classroom activities when the camera is at hand, and instruction in photography most naturally fits where students are interested in capturing events important in their daily lives. Photographs can be used to do the following:

- Illustrate student writing and reports
- Record stages in a science experiment
- Capture a role play or dramatic performance
- Record a field trip or special class celebration
- Preserve the process of creating an artwork or social studies project

The camera. If students have little experience using cameras, they will need time to learn how to handle them carefully and effectively before they can use them independently. The following activities can be used as whole class or small group lessons. Some can also be set up as independent learning centers.

For teaching purposes simple cameras with a minimum of special features work best. These can be found quite inexpensively so that every classroom can have one or two cameras available to students on a regular basis to use in recording their projects. In addition there should be a student set of cameras in the school to be used when teaching a whole class specific camera techniques. The addition of several instant or digital cameras and more complex automatic cameras for teacher and advanced student use expands the photographic possibilities for students.

Introducing the camera. There are many different types of camera on the market. Most students will be familiar with automatic cameras that require no special settings, but photography will become more meaningful if they understand how a camera works. If possible, collect a variety of different cameras that students in small groups or at a learning center can handle and examine. Give students a sheet with descriptions of different parts and challenge them to locate the parts on each camera. Have students create labeled sketches of a camera in their journals.

Students should be able to find, identify, and explain the function of the following parts:

- *Aperture:* The size of the lens opening through which light can pass.
- *Film advance:* A knob or lever that moves the film forward to the next frame. Advanced cameras do this automatically.
- *Focus:* A mechanism that adjusts the distance setting of the lens.
- *Flash:* A light that operates when there is not enough natural light for the film.
- *Light meter:* A light-sensitive instrument that measures the amount of light striking the film or paper.
- *Rewind mechanism:* A button or knob that causes the film to roll back into the canister. Advanced cameras do this automatically upon reaching the end of the film.
- *Shutter:* A curtain that opens and closes, allowing light to reach the film. The shutter release is the button that opens and closes the shutter. Shutter speed is the amount of time the shutter is open. If possible, students should open the camera back and watch the shutter open and close.

Taking good photographs. Developing technical control over the camera takes a lot of practice. This can end up being very expensive when there are hundreds of students to teach. It is essential for students to learn basic photographic skills and techniques before they are given film.

Begin by having students examine and sort photographs that exhibit technical problems such as blurred images and not enough light. Have students look through photographic articles and manuals to try and identify the cause of the defects and then create a class chart. Follow up with hands-on practice activities such as those that follow here:

- *Stabilizing the camera.* One of the biggest problems novice photographers, especially at the primary level, have is holding the camera still. Either they shake the camera when operating the shutter release or they take the photograph when the camera is still moving into position. The following activity helps students learn to stabilize their camera:

Teacher Tip

Cost-Effective Photography

There are a number of ways to lower the expense of teaching photography to large numbers of students.

- If students can afford it, ask them to bring in their own roll of film and then have them develop it on their own.
- Purchase black-and-white film in bulk rolls and roll it into canisters using a lightproof bag or darkroom.
- Enlist the help of a high school or college photography club to help develop students' black-and-white film.
- Use a digital camera and photo-editing software.

1. Working in pairs, one student can be the photographer while the other strikes a series of poses.
2. After placing a small, plastic bottle of water on top of the camera, the photographer tries to shoot imaginary pictures of each pose without knocking the bottle off and while making sure the water is still before "clicking."
3. Students should alternate roles, with each series of poses changing faster and faster.

- *Keeping the lens clear.* Another problem of novices is keeping fingers away from the lens. One method is to have students work in pairs with empty cameras. As one student "takes pictures," the other one poses while keeping an eye on where the partner's fingers are and offering a reminder if necessary. Another method that can be used with young children is to attach a textured paper spot to the location where fingers should be placed.

Photograms

Many situations may preclude students from actually developing and printing their own photographs. Creating a photogram is a good way for students to see the process of developing in action.

1. Prepare lightproof envelopes using black construction paper with folded-over, stapled edges.
2. In a low light area place a sheet of light-sensitive photogram paper (available from many art and science companies) in each envelope.
3. Have students select their objects from small items such as bottle caps, keys, and leaves, and explore possible arrangements on a plain sheet of white paper the same size as the photogram paper.

4. When their composition is planned to their satisfaction, students should take an envelope, their objects, and a flat tray of water outside.
5. There they remove the paper from the envelope and quickly place their objects as planned.
6. When they think the paper has darkened sufficiently, they must place it face down in the pan of water to stop the action of the light.
7. Place completed photograms on a flat surface face up to dry.

Lesson extensions

- Try making photograms while moving some of the objects.
- Make a photogram collage of old black-and-white negatives. Tape the negatives to the paper in low light and then expose them briefly to the sun.
- Cut up photogram images and use them in collages or scan them into a computer graphics program.
- Discuss whether or not a photogram is a photograph. Does a photograph require a camera? Study the photograms of Man Ray. How do photograms fit the ideas espoused by the Dadaists?
- Create a chart showing how the process of making a photogram is similar to making a photograph.

Video Production

Moving visual images swirl around our students daily in a world dominated by television and its companion, the VCR. Students passively receive the messages that others send them. The camcorder, incorporated into the classroom curriculum, can enable students to better understand how these images manipulate what they think and give students a powerful tool for recording messages of their own.

Camcorders in the Classroom

Photography is a way of capturing a moment in time. Video production is an extension of photography, capable of capturing the passage of time. It is the ideal medium for recording the activity of students as they explore learning. Videos can be created that do the following:

- Record puppet shows, dramatic productions, and role plays
- Show how to do something such as use a camera or make a painting
- Capture the changing nature of a piece of artwork
- Demonstrate changes that occur during a science experiment
- Tell stories or send messages

Books to Share

Photography

Conford, E. (1994). *Get the picture, Jenny Archer?* Boston: Little, Brown.
Gibbons, G. (1997). *Click!: A book about cameras and taking pictures.* Boston: Little, Brown.
Graham, I. (1995). *How it works: Cameras.* Roslyn Heights, New York: Shooting Star.
Morgan, T. (1991). *Photography: Take your best shot.* Minneapolis: Lerner.
Oxlade, C. (1997). *Cameras.* Chicago: Lorenz.
Price, S., & Stephens, T. (1997). *Click: Fun with photography.* New York: Sterling.
Welch, C. A. (1997). *Margaret Bourke White.* Minneapolis, MN: Carolrhoda.

Dissecting a Video

Videos are an ideal tool for helping students develop a critical view of television and film productions. Because the video can easily be started and stopped and put into fast or slow motion it is easy to work through a video with a class, taking time to analyze how it was made.

Introduce video analysis by showing students a short five- to ten-minute video on a topic related to studies in one of the curriculum areas. After showing it, pass out storyboard worksheets and have students try to remember the key points of the production by filling in a scene on each section of the board. Then reshow the video and ask students to make additions and corrections. Not only does this activity develop understanding of how the video was put together, it also will help students understand the content of the video better.

Next discuss or review point of view (see photography section). Then introduce the following cinematic terms, which relate to point of view in video production:

- *Flashback:* A scene or sequence inserted in a video to re-establish an earlier event
- *Panning:* Moving the camera in a steady arc either along the line of the horizon or to follow a moving object
- *Slow motion:* Action that is shown slower than the speed at which it actually happened
- *Time-lapse:* Action that in reality takes hours or days, speeded up and shown occurring in only a few minutes
- *Zoom shot:* A photograph taken while the angle of view was being changed

Now reshow the video a third time. This time ask students to note the camera operator's point of view on their storyboards. Follow up with a discussion focused on the relationship between the point of view and the subject matter of the scene, such as, at what points are close-ups or zoom shots used?

Preparing for viewing. As videos are shown as part of the curricula studies of the class, always take a few moments to discuss the introductory title scene. Compare it to the cover of a book. Does it get you interested in watching? What information does it tell you? Can you tell if the video will be fiction or nonfiction from the introduction? Also point out the use of titles anywhere else in the video and take the time to look at the information contained in the credits. What does it tell you about the making of the video?

Developing a critical eye. Invite students to compare educational videos seen in school to the television shows they watch at home.

Comparing production techniques. Ask students to create storyboards for a favorite TV program, including notations on point of view and camera angles, as a homework assignment. Create a graph showing different categories of programs and the occurrence of selected filming techniques such as panning in car chase scenes or close-ups to show emotion on a person's face.

Ongoing Video Studies

Over time as other videos are shown to the class, ask students to point out particularly noticeable examples of the use of a certain viewpoint to express or clarify an idea. Questions to ask that focus on video design as an art form include the following:

- Does the sequence of images in the video seem realistic and logical?
- Does the camera angle enhance the appearance of the images on the screen?
- Are alternating points of view used to emphasize certain information or events?

Producing a Video

When students can dissect the videos they watch, they can begin to plan their own productions. At a Glance 13.5 describes video production tools. One way to begin, especially at the lower levels, is to plan a whole class production. In making a video it is easier to shoot it as one unified piece rather than trying to shoot bits that will have to be edited together at the end, so initial planning is essential.

For a class video select a subject that relates to current lessons. Good beginning video ideas include re-enacting a historical event, role playing proper behavior such as getting on and riding the school bus, or taking a tour of the school.

On a large, wall-sized storyboard plan the different scenes of the production and discuss the point of view to be used. Also create a list of the various jobs that will need to be done and select the students who will perform them. A job list might include some of the following:

- *Actors:* Learn lines and carry out roles.
- *Camera operators:* Operate camera. Select one operator for each scene.
- *Costumers/Make-up artists:* Prepare actors for the filming.
- *Credits:* Design and create the credits on a sheet of 12″ × 18″ paper.
- *Cue cards:* Design, create, and display cue cards.
- *Electricians:* Plug in equipment and charge batteries.
- *Lighting:* Check and arrange light sources.
- *Props:* Obtain and set up props.
- *Scenery:* Design, create, and set up scenery.
- *Sound engineers:* Coordinate musical backgrounds and microphones.
- *Special effects:* Create unusual sounds and visual happenings.
- *Writers:* Write the script for the production.
- *Titles:* Design, create, and display titles for beginning of scenes on 12″ × 18″ paper.

Practice makes perfect. Before actually filming the production, have all the participants run through their assignments. Since videotape can be rerecorded, practice filming scenes to get just the right view.

This is also the time to adjust the lighting. Most camcorders can film in limited light and adjust well to changes in lighting, but avoid filming against a lit background such as a window.

Filming. When everything is planned and all the needed items are created, filming can begin. Start by reminding all the students that they have to be absolutely silent during filming, especially if they are not using a separate directional microphone. It is good to establish a signal such as holding up an ON THE AIR sign or a raised arm whenever the camera is running. Moving chairs and desks can create annoying noises. If possible, seat the audience on a rug. Also remember to put a sign on the door or station a student there to avoid unfortunate interruptions.

- *Camera setup.* For a beginning production avoid moving the camera. Set the camera up on a tripod so that it covers the entire scene.
- *Introduction to the video.* Start by filming the title scene card for about two minutes. This creates a long trailer into the production. If music will accompany it, have the sound technicians operate the

At a Glance 13.5

Video Production Tools

Camcorder: A camera that records action on videotape. A full-sized camcorder takes a VHS tape that fits in a VCR. Palm-sized cameras are easier to handle but require an attachment to the VCR to play the tapes.

Credits: A listing of personnel who worked on the video as well as the location of the shoot and acknowledgment for music used in the production.

Cue cards: Large signs that tell actors what they are to do or say.

Directional microphone: A separate microphone that picks up sound from one source and is used to replace the multidirectional built-in one in cases where background noise is a problem.

Storyboard: A sheet on which are printed a series of boxes used to plan the major events in the video.

Titles: Sign or scene that introduces a video production or video sequence.

Tripod: A stand for holding the camcorder essential for most video work.

Videotape: Magnetic tape used to capture video images. These are available in two formats: VHS and 8mm. VHS is more commonly found in schools and can more easily be used in school VCRs for playback purposes.

tape recorder, fading the music out at the end. Stop the camera and set up the initial scene.

- *Capturing the action.* Use the zoom lens found on most cameras to vary the point of view. The camera can also be panned and the angle adjusted using the tripod mechanisms. Keep all changes slow to avoid making viewers dizzy. It helps to mark the area covered by the camera by placing tape on the floor so young actors stay within the frame of the camera.

Claymation

Claymation is another fun way to introduce video production, especially to younger children, who are avid viewers of commercial claymation films. Children can work in small groups to write their script, draw their storyboards, and create their clay actors.

Preparing for filming

- Create claymation actors using nonhardening modeling clays.
- Make a backdrop by folding an 18″ × 24″ sheet of paper in half and creating a floor/ground on one side and a background on the other. Prop it up on a desk pushed against a wall or board.
- Blocks and toys can function as walls and furnishings.

Teacher Tip

Musical Rights

Most recorded music is copyrighted and cannot be used for public viewing without permission of the copyright holder. Videos made just for classroom use can use any music but cannot be shown outside the classroom. Consider having students create their own original music to accompany their video productions.

- Use artificial or real plants for outdoor scenery or film outdoors if desired.
- Title and credit signs.

Procedure

1. Set the camcorder on the tripod, focus it on the scene, and lock it into place. It must not move at all during the filming.
2. Have the camera operator film the title card for two minutes. Include music if desired. Stop filming.
3. Place clay actors and props in desired position. Run camera for one to two seconds. (*Note:* If children are too young or inexperienced to use the camera this way, invite an older student or parent to help. You may also wish to have students experiment first to find the right length of time for your camera and to learn what that length of time feels like.)
4. Have students move their clay figures very slightly and film again for one to two seconds.
5. Repeat the process, capturing the action as planned on the storyboard.
6. If dialogue accompanies the story, try to use a directional mike that the speaker can talk into directly. Alternatively sound can be dubbed in later using a tape recorder.
7. End by filming the credit sign accompanied by music.

Explore special effects. Children often believe that many special effects they see on television are real. Creating their own special effects helps them understand the difference between reality and fiction. Explore some of these ideas or invite students to invent their own.

- Fine nylon thread attached to objects will make them appear to fly.
- Filming an object and then carefully keeping the camera in the exact position after the object is removed can make it look like the object disappeared.

Books to Share

Video

Krauss, R. (1997). *Take a look, it's in a book: How television is made at Reading Rainbow*. New York: Walker.
Oxlade, C., & Rowe, J. (1997). *Movies*. Portsmouth, NH: Heinemann.

- Moving the background behind a stationary object can make the object look like it is moving or create the effect of an earthquake.
- Tilting the camera can make it look like the characters are going up or down a hill.
- Filming a small object next to a big one can make the smaller one look farther away.

Animation

Animated videos can be made similarly to claymation. Students can make a series of drawings showing small changes and then videotape them for one or two seconds each. This process is made easier by using a photocopier to make multiple copies of the part of the picture that does not change, or by using a computer drawing program to repeatedly duplicate the picture. Specialized animation software programs can also be used to add special effects.

Making Connections

Language arts

- Combine computer graphics with original poetry and stories.
- Use photography to illustrate reports and personal stories.

Math

- Graph the different purposes for which photographs are used in a particular magazine.
- Use computer graphics to create eye-catching pictographs and games.

Science

- Photograph stages in the growth of a seed or plant.
- Videotape the transformation of a chrysalis to a butterfly.
- Videotape the results of an experiment so it can be reviewed to check for accuracy in observations.
- Create a time-lapse sequence showing the growth of leaves in the spring or the turning of colors in the fall.

Social studies

- Videotape interviews with people who are knowledgeable about the topics students are studying. For example, when studying local history, interview older people about the younger days in their lives.
- Create a claymation or dramatized video re-enactment of a famous event from history or from current events.

Dance and dramatics

- Use photography and video to record student-performed dances.
- Videotape student-presented puppet shows, role plays, and playlets.

Music

- Compose original music to accompany videotapes and have students play it on instruments of their own design.
- Use musical instruments to create a sound effects tape to use in video productions.

Multiple Images

No discussion of technology and art would be complete without addressing the use of the copy machine. Here is a tool found in every school that offers unlimited possibilities for art. Especially where computer access is limited, a copy machine can perform many similar functions. Images can be duplicated to create multiple copies. They can be enlarged or shrunk, reversed, or printed darker or lighter. Multiple copies of sketches can be made and then colored in different color schemes or cut apart and rearranged. Artworks can be photocopied at different stages to record the process of creation. What the copy machine lacks is the instant reaction of the computer as well as the ability to deal with a large volume of work. In the long run it is best used to meet the needs of individual students as they work rather than trying to copy whole classes of work on a regular basis.

Updating the Art Program

There is no question that these newer art forms are more complex and require more technical knowledge and more expensive equipment. A computer and a floor loom cost about the same. It would be best to have both, but a loom is less likely to be found in our students' homes. It is wiser to invest first in the computer, the video camcorder, and the cameras that directly meet the needs of the students and will motivate them to create art. Later purchase the loom. It can even be hooked up to the computer to create a powerful marriage of old and new.

Conclusion

ON-LINE ARTISTS

[M]edia education aims to foster not simply critical intelligence, but critical autonomy . . . i.e., the ability to think independently based on evidence, inquiry and reflection.
Len Masterman (1970, p. 71)

Art is a flexible language; the tools used, although important in determining the final visual form, do not formulate the message. The artist does. The question is not what something is made from but what aesthetic decisions did the artist make in creating it. The technological arts belong in the classroom because they are an increasingly important way that people in our society communicate ideas and beliefs. Instruction needs to give students the technical and critical skills necessary to address the art forms that will be most readily available to them in the future. It behooves teachers to become comfortable with these media and to welcome them for their ability to motivate and excite their students.

In conjunction with learning how to use these media to create art, students also need the opportunity to learn how to read and understand it. They should develop a discerning eye that is not convinced by splashy, poorly designed graphics or stereotyped comic book images but that searches and values rich, meaningful images that communicate on multiple levels.

Teacher Resources

REFERENCES

Davidson, J. I. (1989). Children and computers together in the early childhood classroom. Albany, NY: Delmar.

Davies, J. (1996). *Educating students in a media-saturated culture.* Lancaster, PA: Technomic.

Geertz, C. (1976). Art as a culture system. *Modern Language Newsletter*, pp. 1473–1499.

Loveless, R. L. (1980). Excerpts from opinion papers. In J. J. Hausman (Ed.), *Arts and the schools*, p. 242. New York: McGraw-Hill.

Matthews, J. C. (1997). *Computers and art education.* www.ed.gov.databases/ERIC_Digests/ed410180.html

Masterman, L. (1970). *Teaching the media.* London: Routledge.

Tyner, K. (1994). Video in the classroom. *Arts Education Policy Review, 96*(1), 18–26.

Wilson, B. & M. (1977). An iconoclastic view of imagery sources in the drawings of young people. *Art Education, 30*, 4–12.

Practical Guides

The following books provide detailed information on the technical and aesthetic aspects of computer graphics, photography, and video production:

Curchy, C. (1998). *Educator's survival guide to TV production equipment and setup.* Englewood, CO: Libraries Unlimited.

Greh, D. (1990). *Computers in the art room.* Worcester, MA: Davis.

Holtzman, S. R. (1997). *Digital mosaics: The aesthetics of cyberspace.* New York: Simon & Schuster.

Jacobsen, L. (Ed.). (1992). *Cyberarts: Exploring art and technology.* San Francisco: Miller Freeman.

Kyker, K., & Curchy, C. (1995). *Video projects for elementary and middle school.* Englewood, CO: Libraries Unlimited.

Lovejoy, M. (1996). *Postmodern circuits: Art and the artist in the age of electronic media.* Englewood, NJ: Prentice Hall.

Pedersen, T., & Moss, F. (1998). *Make your own web page.* New York: Scholastic.

Penny, S. (Ed.). (1995). *Critical issues in electronic media.* Albany, NY: State University of New York.

Spatter, A. M. (1998). *The computer in the visual arts.* Reading, MA: Addison Wesley.

Videos

Arts-a-Bound Series, GPN Videos
Photographer

Brooks Institute of Photography
Photography Video Series

Computer Animation Festivals Series, Crystal

Films for the Humanities and Sciences
Images: 150 years of Photography

Media Educational Foundation
Masters of Animation

Advertising and the End of the World
NECA

Reading Rainbow Series, GPN Videos
Liang and the Magic Paintbrush
Visit to a computer graphics studio
The Sign Painters Dream
Visit to a sign-making plant
The Brush Visit with three-dimensional animation artists

CD-ROMs

Better Photography: Learning to See Creatively, Crystal

Software

Note: Some of these programs contain coloring-book type activities. These are not creative art. Use only the free-draw sections that allow students to start with a blank screen and draw their own lines and shapes.

Drawing/Paint Programs

Beginners:

Art Dabbler by MetaCreations

Art Explorer by Adobe (MAC)

Brushstrokes by Claris (MAC)

Creating Computer Art (MAC/WIN)

Dabbler by Fractal Design (MAC/WIN)

Flying Colors by Davidson (MAC/WIN)

Kai's Supergoo by MetaCreations (MAC/WIN)

Kid Pix by Broderbund (MAC/WIN)

Advanced:

Illustrator by Adobe (MAC/WIN)

Painter 6 by MetaCreations (MAC/WIN)

Photo-Editing Programs

PhotoDeluxe by Adobe (MAC/WIN)

Print Shop Deluxe by Broderbund (MAC/WIN)

Animation Programs

Bryce 4 by MetaCreations(MAC/WIN)

Canoma by MetaCreations (MAC/WIN)

Ray Dream Studio by MetaCreations

Video-Editing Programs

After Effects by Adobe (MAC/WIN)
Bytes of Learning by MP Express (MAC/WIN)
Premier by Adobe (MAC/WIN)

Accessories

Electronic pen performs mouse functions by directly touching the screen
- kidpoint by KB Gear Interactive

Pressure-sensitive drawing tablet
- Pablo kidboard by KB Gear Interactive
- KidDraw & SkidDoodle by KB Gear Interactive

Glossary

Abstract Art that focuses on the design and arrangement of shapes, colors, and forms. The subject matter may or may not be recognizable.

ACMI The Art and Craft Materials Institute. This organization certifies the safety of art materials.

Acrylic A polymer-based paint.

Aesthetic response A heightened sensory awareness that draws one's complete attention to something that is beautiful or surprising.

Aesthetics The philosophical study of the nature and value of art.

Affective Relating to the emotions, senses, and feelings.

Anti-bias teaching Creation of a community of learners in which prejudice and discrimination are directly addressed.

Appliqué An artwork created by sewing together layers and pieces of different fabrics.

Apprenticeship To work for an expert practitioner in a selected field in order to learn the skills and practices needed for that pursuit.

Art center An organized area containing carefully selected art supplies and activities for students to work on independently.

Art criticism The study of similarities and differences in artworks in order to build an understanding of the works as well as an evaluative base.

Art elements The basic visual and tactile components of what we see or experience through our senses; they are found in the environment and in artworks: color, shape, line, form, pattern, texture, and space.

Art history The study of the social and cultural context in which an artwork is created and exists.

Artifact A handmade object intended for daily or ritual use that represents the ethnic heritage or life style of a group of people.

Art production The creation of a work of art.

Art therapy The use of art to release and express deeply felt experiences and emotions, done with the assistance of a trained therapist.

Art/writing workshop A block of time during which students work on related writing and art projects of their choice.

Assemblage A three-dimensional artwork that is composed of objects that were originally intended for other purposes.

Assessment The gathering of all information, including tests and grades, that describes student performance and that bears directly on decisions that will be made about the students and how they will be taught.

Background The part of an artwork that surrounds the main subject or focus areas.

Balance The arrangement of elements in an artwork so that a visual equilibrium is created.

Bas-relief Artwork in which some parts project from the background to form raised areas.

Batik A process in which parts of a fabric or paper are covered with a substance or material that prevents dye or coloring from reaching those areas.

Bisque Unglazed clay that has been fired one time in a low firing of the kiln.

Brain-based learning The selection of teaching strategies based on current knowledge of how the brain processes information.

Brainstorming A teaching strategy in which participants generate ideas on a topic or solutions to a problem in an open and accepting environment.

Brayer A rubber roller used to apply ink in printmaking.

Calligraphy The art of hand lettering.

Cartoon A drawing symbolizing or characterizing some action, person, or event. Also the preliminary full-size drawing for a mural.

Center of interest The main area of an artwork on which the eye focuses.

Ceramic An object made from clay that has been fired in a kiln.

Charcoal A soft black drawing material made from baked wood.

Cityscape An artwork having a whole or partial view of a city as its subject.

Claymation An animated video made by slowly moving clay figures.

Cognition The process of knowing.

Coil Long, rolled-out clay ropes used in forming pottery.

Collage An artwork created by gluing together an arrangement of paper, fabrics, and other objects.

Color The element of art that is based on the perception of different wavelengths of light by the eye's sensors.

Color scheme The combination of colors found in an artwork.

Color wheel A graphic diagram that shows the relationship among colors.

Commercial art Art that is designed for business purposes.

Community circle The gathering of a class in a circle with the purpose of having everyone share information, respond to a prompt, or answer a question.

Composition The arrangement of the elements of art into a unified whole through the use of organizational principles. The term is used interchangeably with artwork.

Computer graphics Visual images created with the use of a computer.

Conflict resolution Settling differences using a set of techniques designed to defuse anger and allow rational decision making.

Construction An artwork created from pieces of other materials and objects such as pieces of wood or parts of broken toys. An assemblage is a form of construction.

Contour The edge of an object or the line representing it.

Contrast The use of different colors, values, textures, and other elements to create emphasis and interest in an artwork.

Cooperative learning Using a learning structure that promotes positive group interaction and decision making.

Crafts Art forms designed to serve a useful purpose, such as a ceramic bowl or a woven shawl.

Creative process The mental processes and skills used to produce something that is unique.

Criteria-based Based on a set of requirements.

Decorative Used as an embellishment or ornament.

Depth The real or apparent distance created in an artwork.

Design The selection and arrangement of elements in an artwork.

Detail A small part of an artwork.

Developmentally appropriate (DAP) Activities, content, or techniques that are selected as being suitable for the age, experience, and physical and mental growth of the child.

Discipline-based art education (DBAE) A philosophy of art education in which art is seen to be equal to other academic subjects, and in which the critical, historical, and aesthetic components of art are given equal weight with hands-on production.

Divergent thinking The ability to come up with many different ideas.

Domain The discipline or craft of an intelligence.

Dominant The most important or powerful part of an artwork.

Dyeing The absorption of color into a material such as cloth, yarn, fiber, or paper.

Elaboration The ability to expand and build on ideas.

Element of art A visual or sensory part of an artwork used to create the composition. The elements of art include: line, shape, color, value, texture, space, and form.

Embedded art unit Lessons that teach art skills and concepts in relationship to what is being studied in other curriculum areas.

Emergent problem A problem that arises in the process of trying to do something.

Emphasis A principle of design in which art elements are arranged to draw attention to certain areas of the work.

Emulation Modelling or copying the behavior of another.

Engraving The carving of lines into a surface to create an image or to create a surface to be printed.

Expert Someone who has mastered the skills required in a domain so as to perform at the highest level.

Exploratory learning Gaining knowledge through the use of one's senses.

Favoritism The first stage of Michael Parson's levels of aesthetic development in which one reacts to an artwork based on whether one likes it or not.

Figure-ground differentiation The ability of the eye to separate an object from its background.

First-order representation A symbol form created directly from an experience.

Focal point The main part of an artwork to which one's eye is attracted.

Folk art Traditional art forms made by people using techniques and cultural symbols passed down over generations and meaningful to themselves and their community.

Foreground That part of an artwork that appears closest to the viewer.

Form A three-dimensional object. The term can also refer to the style or composition of a work.

Free expression The unhindered manifestation of feelings and emotions through one's artwork.

Gallery A space devoted to the display of artwork.

Generic imagery Generalized symbolic representations that convey culturally meaningful information as represented in logos, diagrams, cartoons, and clip art.

Gestalts Symbols that must be viewed as a whole rather than analyzed in parts.

Glaze A thin coating of silica and other minerals that melts to form a glass coating on clay when fired in a kiln.

Guided discovery A teaching strategy for introducing art materials and art centers for the first time.

Horizontal Parallel to the horizon.

Hue The name of a color, such as red.

Illustrate To create artwork that represents the ideas and subjects contained in a piece of writing.

Image The likeness or representation of an object.

Immersion The stage in the creative process in which one is so totally consumed by the problem that one becomes unaware of the passage of time or other distractions.

Incubation The period of time during the creative and artistic process during which the creator thinks both consciously and unconsciously about solutions to the problem.

Individualized imagery Unique (one-of-a-kind) graphic representations presented in the distinctive artwork of individual artists.

Initial imagery Simple graphic symbols drawn by young children that are culturally and socially understandable and acceptable.

Intelligence The biophysical potential for interacting with the environment in a certain way.

Intensity The strength or brightness of a color.

Kinesthetics The awareness of bodily movement and sensory input.

Landscape A work of art that features a view of the natural environment.

Learning center An area in the classroom at which are set out information, directions, and supplies and that students can use independently.

Learning style A preferred way of learning that is used by the student to approach all tasks.

Learning zones Areas of the classroom set up for particular learning experiences, such as a meeting area or a reading area.

Line A continuous stroke made with a tool. It can also be a boundary between or around shapes.

Literature-based instruction The organization of lessons and activities around the topics, concepts, and themes found in a carefully selected shared piece of literature.

Loom A device upon which cloth is woven.

Materials safety data sheet (MSDS) Information prepared by manufacturers that details the ingredients and safety procedures for a material.

Media literacy The ability to understand and critically analyze the messages contained in television, cinema, advertising, and other commercial and public media.

Medium (plural: media) The material used to create an artwork.

Middle ground That part of an artwork that seems to be between the foreground and the background.

Mobile An artwork with moving parts.

Model An object that represents something. A person who poses for an artwork. To shape and form something from a pliable material such as clay.

Mood The feeling created by an artwork.

Mosaic An artwork made from tiny bits of material such as glass, tile, or stones.

Motif The repeated graphic image or images found in a pattern.

Motivation A person's inner desire to accomplish some task.

Movement The arrangement of art elements so as to make the eye move to different parts of the work.

MDS Materials data safety sheet issued by the manufacturer of a product detailing the ingredients and health hazards.

Multimedia Using a combination of visual, auditory, and/or tactile approaches.

Multiple intelligences A theory of intelligence proposed by Howard Gardner in which intelligence is seen as multifaceted. The biological and psychological potentials within each individual are seen as being divided among distinct, interlocking capacities to solve problems; these include linguistic, logical-mathematical, spatial, musical, bodily-kinesthetic, interpersonal, intrapersonal, and naturalistic abilities. Gardner postulates that there may be more.

Mural A painting on a wall or any large artwork designed to attach to the wall.

Museum A building or place where works of art are displayed.

Negative shape The area, space, or background around an object.

Negotiated drawing A strategy for teaching drawing in which the teacher elicits artistic decisions from the students and represents them in a drawing.

Nonobjective art Art that has no recognizable subject.

Opaque Not allowing light to pass through.

Open-ended Not having a predefined solution or ending.

Overlap To cover or extend over part or all of an object.

Palette A surface or container for holding and mixing paint.

Pastel A high-quality colored chalk.

Pastels Colors to which white has been added.

Pattern A design in which art elements are repeated in a regular or irregular way.

Perceptual Obtaining information by means of the senses and the mind.

Peer conferencing Pairs or small groups of students discuss one student's work and give their responses and offer suggestions.

Performance assessments A test or project that allows students to demonstrate what they have learned by applying the information in a practical way.

Pictorial imagery Young children's first recognizable drawings.

Portfolio A carefully selected grouping of work that meets a set of criteria. It may represent a set period of time or work on a specified topic, or may document a particular area of growth.

Portrait An image of a face.

Positive feedback A response to students that describes what they have done well.

Positive space The area that makes up an object not including the background or surrounding space.

Primary colors The three colors—red, yellow and blue—from which the other colors can be mixed.

Principles of design The organizational concepts that artists used in creating a composition. These include: emphasis, balance, proportion, rhythm, variety, movement, and repetition.

Prints Multiple images made from an original.

Problem-finding The ability to discover problems to be solved in the process of working on a task.

Process A series of steps directed toward a goal.

Process folio A collection of on-going work including roughed out ideas, successful and unsuccessful explorations, and other related materials.

Product The finished work of art or outcome of an activity.

Production In discipline-based art education, the creation of a physical work of art.

Profile The outline of an object, such as the human face, viewed from the side.

Project approach An approach to curriculum design in which topics based on children's interests form the basis of independent research and activities.

Proportion The size relationship among objects.

Purpose The reason why an artwork is created.

Realistic The representation of objects as they appear in life.

Relief print A print made from an original in which parts have been removed or cut away, such as a carving in wood.

Repetition The duplication of a shape, color, motif, or image over and over.

Representation The expression of ideas or knowledge in a symbolic form such as an artwork, piece of writing, dramatic performance, chart, or graph.

Representational Artwork in which the subject is recognizable.

Reproduction A copy of an original.

Resist A process in which a material is used to block or prevent another material from adhering or being absorbed.

Rhythm Movement in an artwork created by the use of repetition.

Rubbing An imprint of a textured surface made by placing paper on the object and rubbing the surface with a soft drawing material such as a pencil or crayon.

Rubric A set of criteria against which something can be evaluated.

Schema A recognizable graphic image.

Scrimshaw A carved or engraved object, often made from whale bone.

Sculpture A three-dimensional work of art.

Seascape A work of art that shows a view of the sea.

Secondary colors The colors produced by mixing the adjacent primary colors.

Second-order representation A symbolic form developed from a first-order representation.

Self-expression The free representation of personal feelings and ideas in an artwork.

Self-portrait A image of oneself by oneself.

Shade A color made darker by the addition of black.

Shape A two-dimensional enclosed area.

Silhouette A representation of an object's shape using a black or dark, shadow-like shape showing no detail.

Sketch A quickly done drawing that records an idea or impression.

Slab A flattened piece of clay of even thickness.

Slip A wet, fluid mixture of clay and water used to join together two pieces of firing clay.

Space Open areas in an artwork or sculpture. Also refers to the illusion of depth in a two-dimensional work.

Spatial Dealing with the relationships among shapes, objects, and space.

Spatial memory Long-term memories that are placed on a mental map of relationships.

Spinning The twisting of fibers into yarn.

Spectrum The full range of visible light.

Stabile A rigid, stationary nonobjective sculpture.

Staircasing The building of instruction based on student knowledge and ideas.

Stencil A hole cut in paper or some other material through which paint or some other medium can be applied in order to create a copy of that shape.

Stereotype A simplified, standardized representation of an object or person that is lacking in detail and originality.

Still life An artwork that shows an arrangement of inanimate objects.

Stipple Using the tip of a paint brush to create small dots.

Studio An artist's workspace.

Style The distinctive characteristics of an artwork.

Symbol A graphic image that has a meaning beyond its outwardly visible form.

Symmetrical Having the exact same elements on one side of a line or point as on the other.

Synthesis The combination of discrete parts into a fluid whole.

Tactile Having to do with the sense of touch.

Taxon memory Long-term memories built up through repetition.

Technique The physical manipulation of materials to produce a desired effect.

Tempera A water-based opaque paint.

Texture The tactile quality of a surface.

Theme A unifying idea or concept.

Thematic teaching A curriculum design in which learning activities are organized around a common theme.

Three-dimensional Having height, width, and depth.

Tint A lighter version of a color made by adding white.

Toxic Harmful or poisonous.

Translucent Light can pass through, but it cannot be seen through.

Transparent Can be seen through.

Unity The organization of elements in a work to create a harmonious whole.

Value The lightness or darkness of a color.

Variation Differences between elements and objects.

Variety Having a range of differences that create interest in an artwork.

Vertical Perpendicular to the horizon; going up and down.

Viewfinder An opening or frame used to look through in order to isolate a part of an object or scene.

Visualize To create a mental picture.

Visual literacy The ability to comprehend graphic images.

Visual memory The ability to remember graphic images.

Visual texture The tactile appearance of a surface.

Warp The yarn placed on the loom in preparation for weaving.

Wash A thin, transparent layer of paint.

Watercolor A paint that uses water as a medium.

Weaving Interlacing yarn in a pattern to create cloth.

Web A graphic chart made by linking words and ideas together.

Weft The yarn that is woven into the warp to create cloth.

Writing process The steps used in creating a piece of writing, including but not limited to rehearsal, drafting, revision, editing, and publishing.

Zone of proximal development The point between actual and potential development at which the child is ready to learn from an adult or more expert peer.

References

Art History and Appreciation

Batterbury, A. (1975). *The Pantheon story of art for young children*. New York: Pantheon.

Blizzard, G. (1992). *Come look with me: Exploring landscape with children.* Charlottesville, VA: Thomasson-Grant.

Bloom, J., & Blair, S. S. (1997). *Islamic arts*. London: Phaidon.

Clarke, D. (1998). *African art*. New York: Knickerbocker.

Cummings, P. (1992). *Talking with artists*. New York: Bradbury.

D'Alleva, A. (1993). *Native American arts and cultures*. Worcester, MA: Davis.

Davidson, M. B. (1984). *A history of art*. New York: Random House.

Epstein, V. S. (1978). *History of women artists for children*. Denver, CO: VSE Publisher.

Fane, D. (Ed.). (1996). *Converging cultures: Art and identity in Spanish America.* Berkeley, CA: University of California.

Finely, C. (1999). *Aboriginal art of Australia*. Minneapolis, MN: Lerner.

Highwater, J. (1978). *Many smokes, many moons: A chronology of American Indian history through American Indian art.* New York: Lippincott.

Isaacson, P. M. (1993). *A short walk around the pyramids and through the world of art*. New York: Knopf.

Janson, H. W., & Janson, A. F. (1987). *The history of art for young people.* New York: Abrams.

Krystal, B. (1999). *100 artists who shaped world history*. San Mateo, CA: Bluewood.

Lewis, S., & Coleman, F. (1994). *African American art and artists*. Berkeley, CA: University of California.

Paine, R. T. (1992). *Art and architecture of Japan*. New Haven, CT: Yale University.

Schuman, J. M. (1981). *Art from many hands*. Worcester, MA: Davis.

Sickman, C. S. (1992). *Art and architecture of China*. New Haven, CT: Yale University.

Sullivan, M. (1996). *Art and artists of twentieth-century China*. Berkeley, CA: University of California.

The Art Book. (1994). London: Phaidon.

The Twentieth-Century Art Book. (1996). London, Phaidon.

Willet, F. (1993). *African art: An introduction.* London: Thames & Hudson.

Dance

Bennett, J. (1995). *Rhythmic activities and dance.* Champaign, IL: Human Kinetics.

Ebensen, B. (1995). *Dance with me.* New York: HarperCollins.

Weiwsan, J. (1993). *Kids in motion: A creative movement and song book.* Milwaukee, WI: Hal Leonard.

Literature

Hearne, B. G. (1990). *Choosing books for children: A commonsense guide.* New York: Delacorte.

Ivy, B. (1995). *Children's books about art.* Palo Alto, CA: Dale Seymour.

Jensen, J., & Roser, N. L. (1993). *Adventuring with books: A booklist for pre-K–grade 6.* Urbana, IL: National Council of Teachers of English.

Lima, C. W. (1993). *A to zoo: Subject access to children's picture books*, 4th ed. New York: Bowker.

Ross, E. (1994). *Using children's literature across the curriculum.* Bloomington, IN: Phi Delta Kappa.

Music

Anderson, W., & Lawrence, J. (1991). *Integrating music into the classroom*, 2nd ed. Belmont, CA: Wadsworth.

Fiarotta, N. (1995). *Music crafts for kids: The how-to book of music discovery.* New York: Sterling.

Hart, A. (1993). *Kids make music! Clapping & tapping from Bach to rock.* Charlotte, VT: Williamson.

Palmer, H. (1990). *Homemade band: Songs to sing: Instruments to make.* New York: Crown.

Web Sites for Teachers

Art and Culture
www.artandculture.com
Links to information on all the arts.

Artful Project
http://humanities.uchicago.edu/homes/SMART/SMART.form.html
Artwork search engine.

Art Teacher on the Net
www.artmuseums.com
Links to art organizations and musuems, lesson ideas.

Educational Resources Information Center (ERIC)
www.askeric.org
Source of information on teaching and educational research.

Library-in-the-Sky
www.nwrel.org/sky/teacher.html
Links to education sites by subject.

Teachers Net
www.teachers.net
Lesson bank, research resources.

Index

Italicized page numbers represent occurrences in boxes.